Roots Remembered

ROOTS
REMEMBERED

The Moudys, Talleys, Apples, Smiths
&
My Life

To Gene —
Hope you enjoy some of our
family's history!

Roark V. Moudy
Roark V. Moudy

Published by

Creative Continuum, Inc.
1045 N. Armando St., Ste. G
Anaheim, CA 92806
866-799-2738
www.creativecontinuum.com

Contents

Preface

For more than ten years, I have had an insatiable appetite and desire to learn about my family's origins. This subject became more pronounced for me the older I got. My intensity was greatly impacted when my mother passed away. I realized that I knew very little about my ancestors and my heritage beyond my immediate family. I realized that I wanted to pass along my family's background and heritage to my children and grandchildren before the sun sets on my life's horizons.

My interest in family history filled me with the desire and impetus to research through fact finding, interaction of us who remain, reading printed materials and then to write about my family and its early beginnings as well as its' effect in shaping my life. This effort took me back far beyond those individuals whom I knew personally and with whom I cherished first hand relationships. It has taken me back to the early roots of the caldron of people we know as America.

Most Americans had their beginnings at the docks of various ports of entry as they fled from tyranny and sought religious freedom. Obviously, if the search continued, a vast majority of us would find that our forefathers, who landed on the eastern shores, were Europeans and later others came from Africa, Asia, and other countries throughout the world. My ancestral ties include a Native American Indian tribe, the Cherokees, some of the original Americans.

My effort to correlate and tie together the many facets of this sometimes extensive and abundant information has been an exciting, yet often difficult, adventure for me. This journey has allowed me to look into the past and realize the ever widening paths and branches of family identity and the significant role that my ancestry has made and the imprint that it has left on my life. This aspect and the impact on one's life is not always considered to be significant. This 'patch work' of a family quilt has shown me otherwise.

I think that family history is important for some people. In conversations I have had on this subject, I have found that one's heritage is very important, particularly to an eastern or southern family. Those geographical areas were the cradle of American liberties and ideals. The Mormons treat ancestry with importance and dignity compelling believers to explore and research their forefathers as far back into antiquity as possible or for at least five generations. However, for a southern boy, family history is important from a family standpoint simply for the sake of carrying on the family name and its heritage. For me, I am the last link on the end of a branch of my family's tree. That sounds as if there is finality to it. In reality, it isn't because every person belongs to a family as a child, mother or father forever. I suppose that is in essence destiny when the end of that family tree branch is concluded regardless of its importance to male egos from a name continuation standpoint. At least one can never forget or disregard his family's facts of origin. As life continues, there will be others appointed in some way to carry on the family name, traditions, and history of ancestral roots into the new millenniums.

My family's heritage is rich with personal experiences. Outsiders and certainly most of my relatives would never consider themselves rich by most contemporary standards of bank accounts, real estate, and the number of 'toys' one owns. These were not what made my family so important and endearing to me. From the earliest, those pioneering family generations had a great love and compassion for one another; they set high standards for conduct, ethics and respect for life; they always believed in God, the great Creator of the universe and His Omnipotence and Omnipresence as their protector of life on earth. They held steadfastly to the conviction that there was One Living God who gave them Eternal life by simply believing in His Son, Jesus Christ. This foundational belief, through faith, brought them through many rough periods of life.

Mortal man is never given the chance to relive any part of life over again. Perhaps everyone has had specific experiences or periods of their lives when they would, if given the chance, change things that are now part of history and do things quite differently. We have all probably heard people say that sort of thing at one time or another. Very few say that if given the chance, nothing would be changed. As for me, I'm somewhere in between. That is, I don't have a lot of things that I wish I could change but there are a few. In a general sense, I feel that I have lived a good life. I know that I have had an easier life than my parents. I believe that my parents had a better life than did their parents. That is first hand knowledge. Beyond those generations, one can only surmise that the same applied to my ancestors and the many preceding generations. Even though this is a simplistic statement, it is logical. With each generation, there have been new frontiers to conquer that in turn improved life and living standards.

I marvel and revel at how many of my ancestors survived the difficult times, circumstances and situations that they encountered in early America. In reality, it is a miracle. Undoubtedly, it was only through the grace of God Almighty that they were able to overcome the many hardships. Indians massacred a few. Indians took at least one into captivity. Some became ministers for the cause of Christ Jesus. Some of them moved with the great expansionist movement from the East and tracked with the development of the West. As the frontier moved, so they moved too.

This continued, in some instances multiple times, until they found their place to settle. Perhaps more realistically, they became tired of moving and could no longer gather the strength to start over again from scratch. My ancestors withstood and endured the horrors and destruction of the greatest civil war that has ever occurred in this country and perhaps in the entire world. My early relatives had values, convictions, and ties which spread across both the South and the North. So strong were their ideologies, they fought each other in some battles of the Civil War. These tragic battles were fought without the members of the families even realizing that they were fighting each other until after the war ended. Perhaps with the exception of not having lost their land, my relatives, for the most part, had to reconstruct their lives after the Civil War. An undying spirit, strength and a belief in God carried them through the War, the expansion of the frontier westward, and the forced march of the souls who were cold and hungry on the Trail of Tears.

Some of them fought in the early battles for our liberty from England in the Revolutionary War. Still others served our country in the Indian Wars, the Spanish-American War, and all of the global conflicts beginning with World War I and those thereafter.

My ancestors entered this country in eastern ports of entry when America was in its early formative stages. They participated in all the wars of this country, both great and small, to protect the freedoms we strongly cherish. They traveled to new frontiers as they participated in the great expansion from the Atlantic to the Pacific Oceans. It took a couple of centuries, but from Philadelphia, Pennsylvania to Los Angeles, California and all points in between, my greater extended family was there participating in the democratic processes of this great land!

The ancestral broadness of my family at large is similar to overloading a funnel as I have attempted to bring a collage and tapestry of life over many generations down to a few focal points. It is like an artist working with a variety of woods who is trying to make each piece of inlay fit perfectly together. So it is with seeking the facts relating to history. Some segments can be unclear or missing; the connecting string breaks at one point but is picked up again later; records are lost or destroyed; stories are handed down which leaves one to wonder how true it is after all of its embellishments.

To connect with the past, I have used stories told directly to me, stories from third parties, pictures, tombstones in cemeteries, records both official and unofficial, published and unpublished writings, books, the Internet, written letters, collected obituaries and any other source which provided me with information or insights regarding family history. Recently, I found a poem by Thelma Green Reagan that was most appropriate to one's efforts to finding the facts relating to ancestral history. I have chosen to include it here.

The Recording of a Cemetery

Today, we walked where others walked
On a lonely, windswept hill;
Today we talked where others cried
For loved ones whose lives were stilled.

Today our hearts were touched
By graves of tiny babes;
Snatched from the arms of loving kin,
In the heartbreak of the ages.

Today we saw where grandparents lay
In the last sleep of their time;
Lying under trees and clouds —
Their beds kissed by the sun and wind.

Today we wondered about an unmarked spot;
Who lies beneath this hollowed ground?
Was it a babe, child, young or old?
No indication could be found.

Today we saw where Mom and Dad lay.
We had been here once before
On a day we'd all like to forget,
But will remember forever more.

Today we recorded for kith and kin
The graves of ancestors past:
To be preserved for generations hence,
A record we hope will last.

Cherish it, my friend; preserve it my friend,
For stones sometimes crumble to dust

And generations of folks yet to come
Will be grateful for your trust.

Reproduced from the USGenWeb Tombstone Transcription Project, www.rootsweb.com, November 4, 2003.

Tracing and identifying the many branches and limbs of the family tree is not easy. However, I have been fortunate in that several of my relatives have had a similar interest and I have been able to share information as it was discovered. The generations come and go, each contributing to the growth of the ever-spreading concentric rings of new descendant relatives and relations. For each person, a specific segment of the past has more importance or relevance to his or her interests. I have concentrated mostly on the direct descendants rather than on the numerous elongated branches and arms that spread out in a spatial sort of way making them nearly too numerous to document. I took special interest in the Moudys, Talleys, Apples, Smiths, and Roarks.

An all-inclusive writing, I have learned, makes the task virtually overwhelming. I have, therefore, chosen to pen the details of the events, family history or developments mostly within our country, which have been outstanding or seemingly important to me from my perspective.

I have written this material for the benefit of my children, my grandchildren, their future offspring and interested relatives. Hopefully, they will have an ongoing interest for family history. Although my interest and enthusiasm has reached a fever pitch, I am not sure the interest of my children has even become lukewarm. I constantly remind myself that I only decided that family history was important after I reached the age of fifty-five. Then it came on rather slowly. My mother enjoyed talking about the days of her youth and childhood, and I found myself indulged when she would take a notion to discuss her life. I began to take notes on scraps of paper. To my good fortune, I was able to gather information for about the last ten years of her life. Those were invaluable times for me. My only regrets were that I hadn't started sooner so I could have discussed other points of interest that I later came to realize that I had missed out on. I'm sure there are many others who have found themselves in the same predicament.

In our young years, the ancestral past is like an old dust covered trunk. We know it's there but often don't take time to explore what is in it. We are living our lives to the best of our ability. We're busy looking ahead and not much attention is paid to the past. At a young age, the future is the most important issue at hand. The past is over; we can't change anything about it. The past, however, can help us understand ourselves better.

Being that my family is the end of a branch on my ancestral tree in terms of passing on the family name, I am compelled to write about my life not so much for my children but especially for my grandchildren. The age in which they live is void of similar struggles for survival, which I encountered. Yet, in a pure literal sense they have their own problems as they see their kaleidoscope of life. I relish the effort to accomplish this writing so they will have a strong appreciation of their connection to the past. I am also doing it for my own benefit; to organize, present and understand the many aspects of my family's fascinating history. Such an effort could become a lifetime commitment because the family never ends. I think Shakespeare said it best, 'Life is but a stage!" That is, people come and go in a continuous process.

In reading and understanding history, my family probably isn't too much different from many other Americanized families of immigrants. It is not so unique as to set apart any special individuals whom became renown for contributions to society in political, military, inventive or commercial sorts of way. To my knowledge, it just didn't happen.

My efforts include an intertwining of my own life…a sort of autobiography. I felt ancestral history of my family was an integral part of understanding the way life has worked out for me. Without the family background and history, the portrayal would be incomplete in my opinion.

It is with deep love, my appreciation for my wife and family, and convictions about life that I want to recognize, through this writing and compilation, my two daughters, Leslie Ann (Moudy) Collins and Jacquelyn Denise (Moudy) Aufhammer. They have been two of the mainstays of my life. In addition, my six grandchildren (Collin Littlepage Aufhammer, Claire Hamilton Aufhammer, William Roark Aufhammer, Donovan Roark Collins, Kiley Elisabeth Collins and Mackenzie Nicole Collins) are the new generation who will be challenged by the new frontiers. It is my hope that this presentation will be important historically to each of them in terms of their family's heritage as well as being a bit entertaining. Beverly, my wife, has been my life's partner who God gave me. Without her, most of my adult life would have been very different. She has been a stalwart support in my life.

Even though this book has its end, life continues on for each succeeding generation. The family goes on just as well. History continues its path of highlights and pitfalls intermixed with daily living as an integral part of life. There may be that one relative, possibly yet unborn, who will feel the desire to carry on the story of this family's history. Maybe they will fill in the blanks of yet to be generated data and information for the benefit of others who come behind them as I have tried to do.

Hopefully, this book will be handed down to several generations of my descendants. Maybe they will find some measure of inspiration from it to help them in their time of struggle or discontentment. At least they can know from whence they came.

I pray for God's blessing on each and every individual relative, those living and those who will come at their appointed time. I pray, as well, for Christ's return which would leave all of this effort as a simple moot point. Glory to God!

Dedication

This book is dedicated to my dear mother, Hestella (Talley) Moudy. She was always in my corner and wanted the very best for me.

My mother was my foremost encourager throughout my life. She believed in me. She had faith in me. She was my primary mentor. She was my stalwart supporter. She was also a strict disciplinarian. I knew the sting of her switch or the toughness of her hand on my behind when I disobeyed.

The best and most important thing she ever did for me was to teach me the way to Eternal life through a personal belief in Jesus Christ. In that regard, she had a lot of personal help and assistance from my dear Aunt Bessie (Moudy) Barrick. Aunt Bessie, who was a minister of the Gospel and a pastor in the local Belleville Assembly of God Church, had an important role in teaching me about Jesus in her church. I still have some of the Vacation Bible School work that I did at the age of five.

My father, William Lewis Moudy, did not accept Christ until later in his life. Then he became a dedicated zealot. However, he taught and instilled in me a strong work ethic. He was a hard worker. He probably didn't have a choice since he had a very limited education. Often, he worked at two jobs on successive work shifts with two different employers to earn enough to pay the bills.

I have had a deep love and appreciation for my parents my entire life. Even as a youngster, I knew the conditions and circumstances of our family. That understanding kept me motivated to achieve a better life and always with a focus on God's love for me.

Success wasn't handed to me on a silver platter. I know what it is like to live 'on the other side of the tracks'. Such living conditions can cause one to be driven and put forth the extra effort to seek a better life. So we did. That was the primary reason for leaving Arkansas and moving to California. I cannot imagine what my life would have been like had we not made the move. In California, there was promise for a new life. As my dad said more than once, 'California is the land of milk and honey.' My parents gave me the opportunity to find out for myself. Regardless, I know it was all part of God's plan for my life!

Hestella (Tally) Moudy
1905 - 1989

Statement of Appreciation

It would have been impossible for me to collect the many pictures and family tree information without the invaluable help and assistance of my dear cousin, Anne Moore. She has been a tireless contributor of material, traveling during ill health to court houses, searching for documents and copying documents. She obtained family pictures for me as well and kindly aggravated some of my relatives by urging them to make sure to provide me with information and family pictures in their possession. For many years she has been a writer for the *Yell County Record*, which included many articles relating to Talley Family history.

I was only acquainted with my immediate Moudy family; but I wanted to better understand the 'clan' and relate to the extended family and its history. One of the very best treasure troves for me, and the event that propelled me headlong into this project was meeting Ellen Bouton Moudy Capehart. She is a very dear lady from my home area of Danville, Arkansas. I met her when I was on vacation in Arkansas in fall of 2001. Through my cousin, Doyle Barrick, I learned that she had a virtually completed project of the Moudy family roots, including pictures. He arranged for us to meet during which time she so generously shared and allowed me to copy all of her work. She widely opened the doors of information on the Moudy family for me in terms of specifics. I owe her a great debt of gratitude and want to express my deepest appreciation for her work and generosity.

I also thank Doyle for his many wonderful stories about relatives who have lived in the Yell County area. He has a wonderful memory. He should be given an honorarium of recognition for his extensive knowledge of the families of Yell County, especially those who once lived on Riley Creek, in

Belleville and Danville Areas.

Another cousin, Sharon Threatt, helped me by using her computer and typing skills to forward information to me over the Internet. Inputting family trees on endless hours is not fun but Sharon did it. She also secured documents for me from some historical societies and surfed the Internet to inform me of data and information that I could use.

My cousin, Mabel (Shott) Barrick has written several books relating to branches of my family including the Moudys and the Apples. She is a very talented weekly writer for the *Yell County Record* newspaper. She granted permission for me to use some of her work, which I certainly used and appreciated.

Finally, I say to my family and friends, whom I seemingly abandoned for so long and could only talk about my project's progress when we met, thanks for your patience! It's over!

Roark V. Moudy

CHAPTER ONE
Family Roots Remembered

Before delving into details of family history, it is worthwhile to examine briefly what made our country a magnet for down trodden immigrants of the Old World seeking basic freedoms in the New World. For the most part, my early ancestors were part of the incoming group of New World settlers from Europe. They wanted freedom from oppression, the right to choose religious beliefs and an opportunity to join the economic struggle. America represented and offered that opportunity to become independent individuals. America was a new and expanding country. Many issues are intertwined within the written verbiage. In some instances, these matters are the underlying strengths relating to struggle and success. Most of the historical data relating to my heritage begins in the late 1700s or early 1800s, mostly after the Revolutionary War.

In reality, many of my ancestors began their American journey just before or shortly after America had become a nation. Most of the earliest relatives discussed herein were alive and certainly knew of George Washington, our very first President. Many of my ancestors relocated from the eastern shores and moved inland to settle frontier lands west of the Appalachian Mountains in the first half of the 1800s. Relocation to the west was not without danger and severe hardships.

The Native Americans were still roaming the land somewhat freely as they tried to resist the 'euro-settler' invasion. The Indians were still very protective of 'their lands and hunting grounds'. As a result, many white settlers, including entire families, died at the hands of Indians, including the Cherokees, Shawnees and numerous other tribes. Families were attacked in their homes, while working the fields on their farms or on the dirt roads traveled by the settlers. The attackers usually killed the white settlers; however, a few were taken prisoner and removed to Indian camps and tribal communities. This was particularly true in southwest Virginia in the late 1700s and through the turn of the century. Many stories are recorded substantiating and corroborating these horrible events. Under these circumstances, there is little doubt why the white population would fear, resist and develop hatred for American Natives. On the other hand, the Indians were to experience the breaking of numerous treaties made between them and the white people.

By 1850, the country had seen twelve Presidents come and go from office. These Presidents were stalwarts in leading this young and energetic nation and included such individuals as Adams, Jefferson, Madison, Monroe, Jackson, Van Buren, Harrison, Tyler and Polk. The number of states that had joined the Union totaled thirty-one in 1850, with California being the most recent to join the Union.

The major event after the Revolutionary War was the Civil War, which was devastating in terms of people killed, use of national resources to support the effort, and economic impact. The physical and psychological impacts were catastrophic and horrific and took a toll on all citizens regardless of where sympathies may have lain. A substantial portion of the generations of the time, particularly in the South, never fully recovered during their lifetimes. It was a horrible time in our country's history! It's amazing that under these circumstances, three states joined the Union during the Civil War. They were Kansas, West Virginia, and Nevada. Abraham Lincoln was our 'Civil War President.' Andrew Johnson, who was succeeded by Ulysses S. Grant, followed Lincoln in office. By the time President Grant completed his tenure in office in 1877, thirty-eight states had joined the Union. States that would later join the Union were all located west of the Mississippi River.

The United States government wielded more power as the country grew. Laws were being promulgated that would have everlasting influence nationally and internationally on our political and judicial system. People continued to press forward and westward seeking new opportunities and inexpensive land. Generally, our leaders provided one direction for all citizens. The government protected and maintained our freedoms, gave citizens an opportunity to attain some measure of success in their lives provided each person was willing to work for their expectations, and tried to instill a sense of pride and unity.

How did people, specifically my ancestors, make their way to Arkansas from the eastern shores? At one time, Arkansas was known as the "land of opportunity". There are those who believe that the movement to the area began because of the Louisiana Purchase on April 30, 1803, which opened up a new frontier to the early would be settlers. As news of land with plenty of timber for building log cabins, fertile plains and valleys, woods filled with wild game and an ample water supply from springs and creeks fell on the ears of young adventurous men and women of the Carolina's, Georgia, Virginia and Kentucky, the movement started. Whether our ancestors knew precisely where their final destination would be at the time of their departure is unknown. Probably not, since this would be worked out with the land management agents located at the Arkansas Post and Fort Smith.

They did know that their homes would be in the Arkansas district or Territory of Missouri since, at the time, Arkansas was not a state. It joined in 1836. The area lacked schools, churches, doctors, and trading posts. The settlers would have to literally make everything that they did not bring with them, including furniture, soap, bullets, and even whisky. Being self-sufficient was paramount to survival. Most of the settlers were European including Irish, English, German, and Polish descendants. This included the Talleys, Moudys, Smiths, Apples, Roarks, and Riders from whom I have directly descended.

Although land ownership was the magnet drawing them westward, not all of them secured the plots of ground made available to settlers through the acts of congress, beginning with the Act of 'Sale of Public Lands' on April 24, 1820. As would be expected, many of them did, in fact, receive land grants and land patents. The applications were often made for multiple tracts of land varying in size from about 40 to 160 acres. Most often the recipient did not obtain all the tracts for which he had applied. On my mother's side of the family, my grandfather, great grandfather and great

great grandfather obtained land through this system. Some members of my father's extended family were also successful in this regard.

Land patents were received by my ancestors whereby they obtained more than 2,200 acres of pristine forested land with the certificates of ownership being issued by eleven U.S. Presidents including Chester A. Arthur, James Buchanan, Grover Cleveland, Ulysses S. Grant, Warren G. Harding, Rutherford B. Hayes, Abraham Lincoln, William McKinley, Theodore Roosevelt, William H. Taft, and Woodrow Wilson.

For many years, family to me meant solely the Talleys and Moudys. As a child, I wasn't really exposed to any knowledge or recognition that a far greater extended family existed. Occasionally tidbits of additional information would surface, but nothing seemingly of major proportions or significance. In my later years after I developed a strong interest in the family history, I begin to learn about my ancestors. Having taken the 'bait' so to speak, I greatly indulged myself in trying to learn as much as I could about any and all of my family, its history, and roots.

The various branches of my family, for the most part, eventually settled in several communities of Yell County. These communities were in close proximity to one another and included Riley Creek, Dutch Creek, Spring Creek, Havana, Belleville, Harkey's Valley, Dardanelle, Chickalah, and Danville, which became the county seat.

The area was originally occupied by several tribes of Native Americans but primarily by the Cherokee Indians. Indian cemeteries existing in the area attest to this fact. History is replete with information relating to their trials and tribulations as well as their treatment by the euro-settlers. White man's history in what is now Yell County begins in the early 1800s. Many of those arriving early were farmers. They were impacted over several decades by periods of great success and other times by major disasters.

Information presented here is intended to provide a history and flavor of this area in Arkansas from its earliest beginnings. The area attracted numbers of brave, adventuresome people. Even though it was called the 'Land of Opportunity', it wasn't much of an opportunity for many who came and did not always live up to their expectations over the many generations. In many ways, development was quick in terms of the stream of people choosing to relocate to the area. Yet it was slow to develop and use modern methods of roads, electricity, municipal water, telephones, and sewer systems. Following is a list of some of the events or developments in Yell County over the years.[1]

- Cherokee Indians settled the area after 1790 through land granted to them by treaty.
- In 1819, Arkansas was still a territory. Arkansas was the twenty-fifth state admitted into the Union in 1836.
- The community of Chickalah was chartered in 1838.
- The boundaries of area to be known as Yell County were established in 1840.
- The county was named after a well-known Governor, Archibald Yell.
- The original mail service to this area was delivered by horseback once a week to Monrovia, a community between what is now the Wilson Church and the Petit Jean River.
- After a survey, Danville was selected as the county seat due to its central location.
- Captain J. B. Howell named the town of Danville after a steamboat he had arrived on while being transported up the Petit Jean River in 1840.
- Before coming to Yell County, Captain Howell had operated a steamboat on the White River in northern Arkansas.
- Captain Howell owned 3,000 to 4,000 acres of land on and near the Petit Jean River near Danville.
- Captain Howell saw the town develop from a wilderness area into a community.
- The Baptist Church in Dardanelle was chartered in 1840. The denomination became active in Danville in the fall of 1854.
- The Methodists began a movement in the area in 1860.
- In 1861, there were 82 slaves in the area between the ages of five to sixty.
- In 1865, a young man preached on the courthouse lawn wearing

a Confederate coat and Union pants.

- A post office was established in Danville on June 7, 1869.
- Freight and luxurious steamboats from St. Louis, Cincinnati, Memphis and New Orleans beginning in the 1850's plied the Arkansas River.
- Many skirmishes were fought during the Civil War near Dardanelle. The Baptist Church was badly damaged. Both armies in the conflict used it. Restitution was made by the government after the War.
- Captain Howell owned and operated a ferry crossing the Petit Jean River at Danville for a fee until 1875. Sometime there after, no fees were charged.
- Captain Howell lived in the area until he died and is buried in the Old Danville Cemetery.
- In 1875 news came that a railroad would be coming through Ola, Danville, Belleville, Havana and on to Booneville. Over 1,000 laborers were hired to lay the tracks and build the bridges and depots. Workers who cut crossties were paid twenty-five cents for each crosstie delivered to the construction site. Trees were felled and cut accordingly within two miles of the work areas along the route. One man spent his time arranging for food for the workers. The camp had one Holstein cow that supplied milk and butter. Supposedly the cow produced eight gallons of milk daily and was kept standing and securely tied to a feeding tub. Two or three animals were purchased daily to supply the meat.
- Alexander Graham Bell invented the telephone in 1876, but it was not available in this area until many years later.
- By 1890, Danville's population was 2,000.
- A pontoon bridge was built across the Arkansas River at Dardanelle connecting with Russellville across the river in 1891. Previously, there had been ferry operations at times.
- Grace Baptist Church was chartered in 1891.
- Belleville was larger than Danville in 1892. Belleville consisted of two banks, sawmills, cotton gins, fine stores, and hardware and

farming supply stores in 1892.

- The railroad was completed and the first passenger train arrived in Danville on December 10, 1899. A great celebration occurred as people came from far and near to see the train. It was a carnival atmosphere. It has been said that when the train appeared it was BIG and Loud and the people were truly frightened. Thereafter, people would stroll on the tracks on a Sunday afternoon date.
- The town of Danville was incorporated in 1899.
- In 1900, a ground meat patty was placed between two pieces of bread in New Haven, Connecticut to create the first hamburger.
- Death was a frequent visitor in these times. As of 1900, life expectancy for women was 43 years and for men, 47 years. One child in ten died before age two.
- The bridge over the Petit Jean River near Danville was built in 1901. It was twelve feet wide. It didn't take long before it became a favorite place to pose and take pictures.
- This area of Arkansas had a very cold winter in 1905. It stayed so cold for so many days that the Arkansas River froze over. Wagons were said to have driven across the river often with teenagers hanging on for a free ride. Many wore holes in their shoes from dragging them on the ice.
- In 1905 the electric iron was invented but it did not come to Yell County until several years later. The women continued to use smoothing irons heated on wood stoves or on the fireplace hearth.
- In 1915 refrigerators were invented but Danville still did not have a dependable source of electricity.
- Sidewalks were put in place between 1920 -1925. The streets remained dirt.
- There was a great flood in 1927 that left over 140,000 people homeless.
- On September 29, 1927, Charles A. Lindberg flew the 'Spirit of St. Louis' from Tulsa, Oklahoma to Little Rock, Arkansas. It was

a widely publicized event with people stationed along the way to spot his airplane as it flew over. In Belleville, the Belleville Booster Day group watched for the plane, which was to arrive after it had flown over the Rural Record Shop and Mt. Magazine between noon and one o'clock on its way to Little Rock. Many people from the area traveled by train to Little Rock to get a glimpse of Mr. Lindberg. The cost of the ticket for a little girl, her sister, and her mother was $13.00 round trip on the 'Doodle Bug.'

- In 1929 was the Great Stock Market Crash and many businesses went into bankruptcy. That was followed in 1930, and lasting for four years, by a great drought. It became known as the 'Dust Bowl' and many people in Yell County began a new migration to the 'Land of Milk and Honey.'
- Another disaster struck in 1930, a major flooding of the Petit Jean River. The flood level reached 26 feet on the Arkansas River. In Yell County, crop losses were estimated to exceed $100,000.00.
- In 1935, the U.S. Forrest Service announced plans to build a lake out of Belleville. It was named Spring Lake.
- In 1939, there were 49 telephones in Danville, 11 in Belleville, 34 in Ola, and 29 in Plainview for a total of 123.

These are a few of the facts and events that were important in the development of these communities and the tough encounters with Mother Nature, which resulted in very difficult financial conditions for most families.

———

[1]   *History of First Baptist Church, Danville, Arkansas, May 25, 1900-2000.* Winchell Sides and Wndell W. Sides, Co-published.

CHAPTER TWO
My Mother's Ancestors

The Talley Name

The name Talley,[1] or Tally, is said to have been derived, according to some authorities, from the French word Tallie. Others believe that the name was taken from an ancient French word 'taillis' meaning 'a copse or grove' simply because of the geographic location and residence of the first bearers of the name. The English family of Tallis took its name based on its location. This surname eventually became Americanized as 'Talley'. Among the many early forms of the name were Taillis, Talles, Tallis, Tallys, Tolly, Tallie, Tollye, Tailley, Talleye, Taulley, Tolley, Tally, and Talley. There are other forms extending the spelling and pronunciation, but the latter two are the most common in use and generally accepted in America today.

Record of the English family of Tallis was to be found in the year 1273 of one Richard Taillis of Coventry Cornwall; in the early sixteenth century of Thomas Tallis or Tallys, a noted composer of cathedral music, who is believed to have been born about the year 1514 and to have died about 1585; and about 1698, of one Aaron Tallis of London.

It is not definitely known whether the American families of the name Talley were of English or French descent. It seems probable that all of the families of the name were of common origin at a remote period. They probably were originally French and later went to England and even later to America.

The first of the name in America are believed to have been Elizabeth Talley of Henrico County, Virginia in 1636; Lias Talley of Charles City County, Virginia in 1637; Eliza Talley of James City County, Virginia in

1638. Unfortunately, no definite records have been found concerning their families or descendants.

One Thomas Talley, or Tolley, is said to have made his home at Boston, Massachusetts in the latter half of the seventeenth century and is said to have had issue by his wife, Mary, including John (who died young), Hannah, Jane, and John.

Richard Talley, or Tally, of Dorchester, Massachusetts, who is recorded in records in the latter half of the nineteenth century, is generally believed to have been a brother of the above-mentioned emigrant Thomas of Boston. Richard first married Sarah Blake, by whom he was the father of several children. In 1677, he took Elizabeth Grossa as his second wife and with whom he left no issue.

One authority claims that an emigrant by the name of Tallie came from France to Wilmington, Delaware in 1672 and became the ancestor of most of the families in that vacinity and in the South, but no definite records are given and little reliance can be placed in the family 'tradition', which is the only reference cited.

William Talley, who came to America shortly before 1686 and entered at Philadelphia, Pennsylvania, may possibly have been the founder of the above mentioned 'tradition' but that, too, is not probable. He married the widow, Elinor Janson or Johnson, and was probably the father, by her, of Thomas and Mary. Thomas was the father of William, David, Mary, Hannah, Susanna and Samuel.

Of the sons of Thomas (the son of the emigrant William), William is said to have first married Hannah Grubb about 1735 and to have been the father by her of Sarah, Charity, Thomas, and William. He had further issue by his second wife, Catherine: Susanna, Martha, Priscilla, Elizabeth, George, and David; Thomas' son Samuel married Margaretta Cloud, by whom he was the father of Thomas, Joseph, John, Samuel, Phebe, Susanna, Hannah, Elizabeth and Margaret.

Among the many later records of the family were those of Ruben Talley of Virginia who married Martha Dyer in 1773; William Talley of Cumberland County, Virginia, about the same time, married Fanny Daniel and was the father by her of at least one son named William; William Talley, who married Lyda Cole in 1791; and George and Michael Talley, who married Sally and Barbara Cole, respectively of Virginia in 1793.

The descendants of these and possibly of other branches of the family in America have spread to practically every state of the union and have aided as much in the growth of the country as their ancestors aided in the founding of the nation. They have been noted for their energy, industry, integrity, ambition, piety, perseverance, patience, loyalty and courage.

Among the Talleys who fought in the battles of the Revolution War were Anthony, Charles, Billy, Henry, John, John Jr., Nathan, Thomas Grief, Robert, and William of Virginia; Isaac, William and Farrell of Pennsylvania; and numerous others from the various New England and southern colonies.

The Talley Family

The Talleys, related to my family, immigrated from England to the United States and settled in Virginia. Details are not available as to whom these original émigrés might have been. Historical information establishes the initial identity of the Talley family with which I am related and begins with Willis Hill Talley. He was born in the United States and may have been the first born to possibly the original immigrant family in this country. Willis Hill Talley[2] was born about 1797 in Halifax County, Virginia and was reared in this location. When he was about twenty-five years old, he married a relatively older lady, for that day and age, Nicey Paralee Carver on September 16, 1822 in Person County, North Carolina, which was her birthplace. She was twenty-two years of age having been born in 1800. Nicey's parents were Robert Carver and Prudence Hamlin.

Down through the generations of Talleys, they were business oriented people as well as farmers. Many records and receipts bear the signature of James Pleasant Talley and Joel A. Talley, who apparently assisted him in his varied activities of being a businessman, farmer and public servant. Little information is known about other members of the Talley family and additional research is needed. We know that they were astute traders, both in real estate and in personal property, in addition to being excellent craftsmen, building their homes, furnishings, and cabinets oftentimes. They were a thrifty people, believing strongly in 'an honest day's work and an honest day's pay'. In those early days, hard currency was very scarce and hard to obtain. Trading often evolved around both parties to a transaction being of good character and honesty. There were no credit bureaus, thus a net worth had to be built by each individual.[3] Obtaining credit at the time of need was in reality a promise to pay at a later time usually associated with the harvesting and sale of their crops. Livestock was often valued and traded in the settlement of obligations. The personal promissory note was widely used in place of currency, especially on directly negotiated transactions, recorded in court records and cleared, when payments were made. It was a long hard trip to the County Courthouse, so the local Justice of the Peace was in many cases the court recorder, judge and jury. Such a person was James Pleasant Talley. He was also the First Group of Commissioner to serve old James County when it was formed by the State of Tennessee General Assembly. He was Postmaster of Thatcher, Tennessee and operated a general merchandise store at this location five miles south of Birchwood and two miles south of Salem. He lived in a two-story clapboard covered log cabin.

In 1832 the family moved to and settled in the Salem community, Hamilton County, near Birchwood, Tennessee. This area is on the main road from Blyth's Ferry, Birchwood, Harrison to Chattanooga, which is known as 'Thatchers.' It is also close to the Bald Hill Cemetery. Here a post office was located in a General Merchandise Store near to the Thatcher land, which was located two miles west on the Tennessee River. This was a thriving business location and was considered 'somewhat' as the gathering place for the local citizens to socialize with one another. At the time, it is believed that they had three sons: the first-born was Joel A. Talley, born about 1823 in Virginia. Prior to the second son's, Jesse Robert Talley, birth the family moved to Person County, North Carolina and probably close to Nicey's parents. Jesse was born on April 22, 1826. William Compton Talley, the third son, was also born in Person County, North Carolina on February 28, 1828. Both Jesse and William were to become doctors. The family remained in this area until 1832 when they moved to Hamilton County,

Tennessee. During the ensuing thirty-five years, more children were born into the family, which reached a total of fourteen children. It was while living in Tennessee that Nicey Paralee (Carver) Talley died in 1854.

Some two years later, in 1856, Willis Hill Talley remarried. His second marriage was to Martha (Cates) Rector who had four children from a prior marriage. They continued to live in Hamilton County until 1864 when they moved to Allen County, Kentucky. Willis and Martha had four children through their union, two of which were born while they were living in Tennessee. Martha died in 1875, probably in Kentucky. Willis Hill Talley died in 1880, also in Kentucky. However, his eldest son, Joel A. Talley, had died in Arkansas about ten years prior.

Willis Talley and Nicey Carver had the following children.

Name	Date Born	Location	Date Died	Location
Joel A. Talley	abt. 1823	Halifax Co., VA.	1870	Arkansas
Jesse Robert Talley	4/22/1826	Person Co., N.C.	5/12/1904	Unk
William Compton Talley	2/28/1828	Person Co., N.C.	10/7/1898	Unk
Mary Talley	abt. 1835	Hamilton Co., TN	Unk	Unk
Nancy A. Talley	abt. 1837	Hamilton Co., TN	Unk	Unk
Charles L. Talley	8/27/1840	Hamilton Co., TN	2/18/1918	Unk.
Barton Wilson Talley	3/16/1842	Hamilton Co., TN	6/14/1932	Unk
Sarah Talley	Unk	Hamilton Co., TN	Unk	Unk
James Talley	Unk	Hamilton Co., TN	Unk	Unk
Nicey Talley	Unk	Hamilton Co., TN	Unk	Unk
Moses Talley	Unk	Hamilton Co., TN	Unk	Unk
Joseph Talley	Unk	Hamilton Co., TN	Unk	Unk

Following are the Children of Willis Talley and Martha (Cates) Rector:

David Ellington Talley	8/13/1857	Hamilton Co., TN	Unk	Unk
Greenberry Kates Talley	10/16/1858	Hamilton Co., TN	Unk	Unk
Willis Edward Talley	3/27/1866	Scottsville Co., KY	Unk	Unk
Martha Lucinda Talley	abt 1869	Scottsville Co., KY	Unk	Unk

One has to wonder why Willis and Martha chose to move to Kentucky

13

in 1864 through areas which must have been under close scrutiny and surveillance by the military, since the Civil War was still being fought. It had to be a very dangerous trip. Even though they moved on to a new life in Kentucky, the seeds of life had already been planted in East Tennessee for a large successor lineage of the Talley clan.

The beginnings of the Talleys, as we know the history, began here with the lineage down through my grandfather, Andrew Jackson Talley. Willis Hill Talley is my great great grandfather through Joel A. Talley. The second generation Talleys brought about a relationship to the Joseph Roark family with the Talley family. The Roark family had lived in East Tennessee for most of the 19th century. The Talleys resided in Hamilton County in East Tennessee beginning and during most of the mid-quartile years of the 1800s.

The Talley family was to become intricately connected and identified with the Roark family. My mother's paternal grandparents came from these two families. Both families were settled in East Tennessee. The Roarks and Talleys resided in Hamilton County near Chattanooga, in nearby communities.

"In the early fall of 1846,[4] Juda and Joseph (Roark) received one of those shocks that come only to parents and the magnitude of which can only be understood by parents. Their second daughter, Sarah Elizabeth or 'Liz' as she was known to her family and friends, told her parents that she intended to marry within the next few days. Elizabeth was eleven at the time and would not celebrate her twelfth birthday until New Years Eve! Her husband to be was Joel A. Talley, 23, son of William H. Talley and Nicey Paralee (Carver) Talley, who had married in Rhea County on August 29, 1821 before Justice of the Peace, Jesse Thompson. Joel had been the first of twelve children. The thoughts and concerns of Joseph and Juda at the time can only be imagined. Nevertheless, a wedding was held in the home of the bride's parents, and Elizabeth and Joel A. Talley were pronounced man and wife. Whether or not neighbor William Killian, his son Henry, who was Elizabeth's age, or others of the Killian family attended the wedding is unknown."

It was in Hamilton County, Tennessee where Joel Talley met Sarah

Elizabeth Roark. Perhaps, their contact with each other was initiated at the General Store owned by James Pleasant Talley since Joel was known to have assisted him in his business activities. Times were difficult on the new frontier. Children seemed to leave home and get out on their own at an early age (probably no more than twenty years for a male and fifteen or sixteen for a female). Joel was on the older side of the age group when he met Sarah, who was on the younger side. It had to have been a major upset for Sarah's parents, Joseph and Juda Ann (Carr) Roark. Perhaps they viewed the marriage as a child marrying a man far too old for her. There isn't any way of knowing if an effort was made to try to talk them out of their decision.

Such a marriage today would not be allowed. Elizabeth, no doubt, had learned a lot from her experiences on the frontier since every girl was taught to cook large meals on a hearth or wood burning stove at best, sew, make soap, mend everything, help with the farm animals, canning and preserving food, caring for children from babies to their own age, and dispensing home remedies to sick family members and neighbors. The body of knowledge seems endless, particularly, for a twelve-year-old girl! Could Elizabeth accomplish all that was expected of her as a wife? Perhaps she was 'older' for her age. It could have been that she knew that her family was nearby to help her and Joel if needed. She was a brave young lady at her age.

As was to become the custom for the Roark family,[5] "Following the marriage of Elizabeth to Joel, Joseph gave the young couple eighty acres and provided them a house to live in just south of Joseph's home place. This was a practice that Joseph was to follow with each of his children as they married and were ready to start their family. A unique feature of Joseph's land gift was that in no instance was a deed of record placed in the county courthouse. Doubtless a deed or similar instrument was given to each of the children when the gift was made, but no deed was ever recorded. Elizabeth and Joel, along with each of the other children when a gift of land was made, took the deed provided by Joseph to the county tax office to establish ownership in their name and their responsibility for taxes. The eighty-acre tract provided to the Talley's consisted of the two forty-acre grants, which Joseph had received through the Ocoee District, Grant Nos.

2131 and 3176. The farm was in Section 21 and was located adjacent to and west of the land grant of M. H. Conner."

It would appear, from available information, the Roarks were a more affluent family compared to the Talleys. This isn't merely a supposition. Based upon known subsequent events, Joel Talley had financial set backs and his father-in-law had to bail him out of his difficulties. There isn't any known record of Joel's father lending a financial helping hand. Perhaps these issues and problems contributed to Joel's decision later to attempt to relocate his family to Arkansas.

There were also the acute problems of reconstruction in the South after the War Between the States. Animosities continued to exist between the sympathizers of the North and the South subsequent to the War even though they lived in the same or nearby communities. Another prominent element, which could have been a factor, was the availability of settlement lands in Arkansas where Joel could start afresh and leave all of the issues of family and war behind.

"The year following her marriage,[6] Elizabeth Talley gave birth to her first child whom they named Amanda. The mother was thirteen. Juda and Joseph were grandparents at age thirty-four." Amanda died at the age of sixteen.

The children of Joel A. Talley and Sarah Elizabeth Roark were:

Name	Date Born	Location	Date Died	Location
Amanda Talley	1847	Hamilton Co., TN	1863	Hamilton Co., TN
Elizabeth Talley	1850	Hamilton Co., TN	Unk	Hamilton Co., TN
Mary C. Talley	1852	Hamilton Co., TN	1932	Yell Co., AR
Joseph W. Talley	1856	Hamilton Co., TN	1872	Yell Co., AR
Benjamin Franklin Talley	4/9/1859	Hamilton Co., TN	3/29/1931	Seymour, TX
Andrew Jackson Talley	10/11/1861	Hamilton Co., TN	4/30/1948	Riley Creek, AR
Margaret Ellen Talley	12/24/1865	Hamilton Co., TN	12/27/1935	Bradley Co., TN
James William Talley	2/17/1867	Hamilton Co., TN	5/18/1955	Hamilton Co., TN

The family grew steadily after Sarah and Joel married. Almost every two or three years a new addition was born. The land given to the family was on the south side of the Tennessee River. The Cherokee Indians formerly claimed these lands. Joseph Roark was one of the early settlers in the area. Being close to the Tennessee River, it was good farming land, having been enriched over the years by silt deposits from occasional flooding.

As the political climate changed during the ten to fifteen years following their marriage, the life of Joel and Elizabeth also changed drastically. Andrew Jackson was not yet four months old when "Joel A. Talley enlisted in the Union Army on March 1, 1862 at the age of 39 at Ooltewah.[7] He was mustered into Company G of the 5th East Tennessee Infantry Regiment, on May 21, 1862, at Camp Pine Knot in Kentucky." Why his sympathies were with the Union rather than the Confederacy is unclear, particularly since his parents were from Virginia and North Carolina and many of his neighbors sided with the South. Nevertheless, East Tennessee was seriously divided on the issues which led to the Civil War and many local young men chose the North as well as the South.

"Records of the 5th East Tennessee Regiment indicate that Joel was court-martialed in February, 1863, for being absent without leave and was 'sentenced to hard labor 30 days and one month's pay deducted'.[8] The reason for Joel's absence can only be a guess, but with the death of his daughter, Amanda, one can safely surmise that he might have returned home to East Tennessee because of that event. He was absent from duty again in November and December in 1863 and was officially charged in August, 1864, with desertion on December 28, 1863." He was not apprehended and probably was at home in 1864 when his daughter, Margaret Ellen, was born. After the War was over, it can be assumed that he remained at home until his youngest son, James William was as born on February 17, 1867. One can only imagine the problems Joel encountered in crossing the lines between the Union and Confederate armies when they were at War and, particularly after Hamilton County was occupied by Union forces in December, 1863, how, as a fugitive, he could not have traveled with any great freedom."

During 1864, Joel's father, Willis Hill, and the remnants of his family left Hamilton County, Tennessee and relocated to Scottsville, Kentucky. Did Joel in some way try to assist his relatives in this move? Did the move contribute to Joel's decision to desert the Union Army? Is it possible the pressure of having a son sympathetic to the Union might have caused Willis Hill Talley to make the decision to move? No one will ever know but it does leave one to ponder.

After the Civil War ended, rebuilding homes and farms was no easy task. In some instances, the marching armies had burned homes. Animals, including cows, pigs, chickens, oxen, and horses had been confiscated by the soldiers. Both armies tried to give certificates of debt as payment on occasion but such debt instruments were only as good as the government backing the debt. The difficulties of trying to begin again may not have offered the opportunity that Joel was trying to find. Maybe the sentiments remaining after the war ended continued to plague Joel. For example, within the family, Joel's brothers-in-law enlisted in the Calvary and fought for the Confederate States. Perhaps the political persuasions of having served on opposite sides of the conflict caused ill feelings within the family. For whatever reason, almost four years after the end of the Civil War, Joel left home again. Some information indicates the reason for leaving was that Joel and Sarah had possibly separated.

It is believed that Joel set out in late March or April 1870 for Arkansas. His son-in-law, William M. Smith, had convinced Joel that Arkansas land was cheap and offered plenty of opportunity to start over. On this excursion, he took his three oldest sons, Joseph, Benjamin, and Andrew, and traveled with his newly married daughter, Mary C. (Talley) Smith and her husband. William M. Smith already had relatives living in the area of Yell County, Arkansas. The locale of the Dardanelle Township near the Arkansas River became their destination.

Joel appeared to be successful in his efforts to find a new way of life in Arkansas. In fact, later that year, Sarah Elizabeth was planning to make the move with the remainder of the family to Arkansas when she learned of the deaths of Joel and their oldest son, Joseph. Family stories relate that Joel and his eldest son, Joseph, died in Arkansas later in 1872 from having eaten 'green corn' and were buried there by the two younger brothers, Benjamin and Andrew. Although the location of their burial is unknown, it is believed that the location is in the vacinity of Chickalah, which is near Dardanelle, Arkansas. Other information indicates that the two died from pneumonia. According to census records, taken September 6, 1870 in Yell County, Arkansas, Benjamin and Jack were eleven and nine years of age respectively. In order to pay for the expenses of the burials, the two boys sold all of their belongings, including a wagon and team of mules or horses. Their older sister, Mary C., and brother-in-law, William M. Smith, helped them bury their father, Joel, and their brother, Joseph.

They then began working their way back home to Tennessee. The trip took several weeks. They traveled by foot, and en route they worked along their way for 'bed and food.' They completed the journey successfully, although they encountered many difficulties and hardships along the way. They both returned home to Hamilton County, Tennessee probably sometime in 1872. They were living with their mother in 1880 when they were included in the local census of June 12, 1880.

An interesting observation about the deaths of Joel and Joseph is if the two had taken ill after having eaten some 'green corn', were Ben and Jack with them? It is not known if this was a direct factor in their deaths. It seems logical that the other two sons would have eaten the same corn and yet they did not die or did they eat it? I find it interesting that the two younger boys, who would have been by the side of their father and older brother most of the time, didn't die from the same problem. How did they avoid eating the green corn? Maybe it was some other malady, such as pneumonia, that caused their deaths?

Census records of 1870 for Dardanelle, Arkansas indicates that Joel A. Talley (46 - born in North Carolina), Joseph (W) M. Talley (13 - born in Tennessee), Benjamin Talley (11 - born in Tennessee), and Andrew J. Talley (9 - born in Tennessee) were all counted and included in the census. It was also noted that all three boys could read and write but their father could not. No doubt they had gone to school as well as being taught by their mother. Joel and the oldest son, Joseph were listed as 'farm workers.'

During Joel's absence, Elizabeth, turned to her father for help. It appears from available records that Joseph Roark, prior to Talley's leaving his home for good, several times interceded financially for Joel Talley in legal matters. In 1851, Joseph assisted Talley in settling a judgement against him by John Wilson; in 1855, Joseph paid a judgement against Talley by Binyon and O'Conner; and as late as 1871, Joseph purchased a note against Talley to settle a judgement in favor of A. Mangrum. Joseph paid the real estate taxes on land owned by Joel and Elizabeth from 1866 through 1870 and, in 1870 apparently filed suit and secured a forced sale of the Talley tract to pay debts accumulated by Talley. While not totally clear, it appears that Joseph had given title to the Talley tract to Elizabeth and Joel at an earlier date.

When Joel left "in 1870, Elizabeth lived near her father in Hamilton County with her youngest two children, Margaret Ellen and James William, ages six and three. Living with her was Margaret Smith, a twenty-eight year old domestic servant. The 1870 Census listed the value of her real estate as $333.00 which was one-tenth that of her father's probably indicating a small farm or a mere homestead."[9] Joel was to never return to Tennessee.

In 1883, Elizabeth saw her children mature and begin to leave home. Benjamin and Andrew left home in June 1883, and according to family tradition relocated to Texas to do extremely well in business. On August 28, 1883, Elizabeth's mother died at the homestead and was buried beside her father in the Bald Hill Cemetery.[10]

Having had an enriching and exciting adventure with their father earlier may have planted the seeds of continued adventure in Benjamin and Andrew. They had apparently liked what they saw in Arkansas. Within several months, they to decided to return. Whether Benjamin and Andrew ever made it to Texas together is unknown. They supposedly had that destination in their plans when they left home. The available information indicates that both Benjamin and Andrew together returned to Yell County, Arkansas when they left home for the last and final time. I have wondered if, on their return to Arkansas, they visited with their aunt Mary Ann Scott who was living with her family near Van Buren, Arkansas. Benjamin made his way to Texas at some point in time by way of Arkansas.

Benjamin married Mary A. (unknown) in 1885, possibly in Arkansas. The exact date of the marriage is unknown. (Mary A. Talley was supposedly born in Arkansas in February 1879. This is obviously in error since she would not have been getting married at age six or seven or the marriage date is incorrect). She and Benjamin had a son a year later. By recordation in the 1900 Census of Delta County, Texas, the son was born in September 1886 in Texas. This Census also confirms the age of Mary then being twenty-one and Benjamin, forty-one. They were the only Talley's recorded in that census. If Benjamin did marry in Arkansas, he left for Texas soon thereafter. It is also possible that he moved on to Texas and then got married. For certain, his first-born son arrived while the family was in Texas about a year after he married.

Andrew's sister, Mary Ellen Talley,[11] married Thomas Palmer Chambers, and moved to Arkansas. They initially settled in Logan County but later relocated to Chickalah, in Yell County.

There are also family recited stories that Andrew Jackson Talley was told by a doctor to move to Arkansas for health reasons. Also for health reasons, Andrew was told by this same doctor in Tennessee to chew tobacco!

Supposedly, the three boys' and their father's original excursion west included Texas in their itinerary. Thus the previous reference attributed to the two boys going to Texas to do well in business may have been their original planned destination when they left home. Nevertheless, they went to Yell County, Arkansas, where they lost their father and older brother. Andrew settled down while Benjamin ultimately moved on to Texas.

It was during the time the Smiths were living on Dutch Creek that Rebecca Adeline Smith and Andrew Jackson Talley first met. He would travel from Chickalah, where he lived with his sister, Mary Ellen (Talley) Chambers, to Dutch Creek to spend time with Rebecca as they courted and fell in love. The distance between Chickalah and Dutch Creek was not a short ride on a horse. It was many miles. Chickalah is almost 20 miles east of Danville whereas Dutch Creek is maybe 50 or so miles on the western side of Danville. This is not to say the homes were that far apart but gives an indication of the seriousness with which Andrew thought of Rebecca and his desire to court her. Making such a trip, one would think that Andrew brought his sleeping roll and spent a couple of nights under the stars to make his trip worthwhile.

Andrew Jackson Talley became enamored with this beautiful young lady at about the same time as Benjamin was thinking of marriage. When Andrew Jackson Talley returned to Arkansas, he seemed to have done reasonably well rather quickly. I haven't any idea what the cost might have been for a wagon and a team of mules or horses in the 1880s, perhaps as much as $250.00. I'm sure it was expensive even by today's standards. Even so, Andrew had his own wagon and horses by the time he first met Rebecca Adeline Smith in Dardanelle Arkansas. The story that has been related down through my family is that when they initially met in town, Andrew spent the night in his wagon while the Smith's also slept in their wagon at the trading post in Dardanelle. I suppose they were there to replenish their supplies because you just didn't go to town for a shopping spree even on Saturday in those days…you definitely had a specific purpose and reason.

It has been told, "when Grandpa laid eyes on Rebecca, in the middle of the road in Dardanelle, Arkansas, he fell in love immediately and made the statement, 'I'm going to marry that girl!' " I do not know how long the courtship lasted but Andrew Jackson Talley didn't waste any time. He married Rebecca Adeline Smith on January 1, 1885. This was only eighteen months after he had left home in Tennessee.

The picture on a following page is unique for their time. The original picture of Rebecca Tally was taken when she was sixteen years old and was a tintype. The year of this photo was about 1881 or 1882. The photograph of Andrew Jackson Talley was taken about 1879 when he was eighteen years old. It is also a tintype. I have in my possession both of the original pictures. What is also amazing, simply because I tend to think that the technology was not developed at that time, is the originals are only about two inches square.

The picture combines both individual pictures. However, the one from which these pictures were taken was a single framed picture. The studio photographer had super imposed each of them onto a single photographic plate to make it appear that they were together as if a single picture was taken. I would imagine that it was difficult to do and probably very expensive in those days. The coloration was added at the time, since color film did not exist.

The original pictorial work of my grandparents as a couple hung on the wall at my grandfather's home. It had a large oval, gold colored wooden frame about twenty inches tall and about twelve inches wide. The protective glass was convex, more or less, like a half bubble. The glass stood out away from the picture by at least two or three inches at its highest point of curvature. When my grandparents passed away, the picture became the property of Aunt Lizzie. She had it hanging on the living room wall of her home in Dardanelle, Arkansas when I visited her in 1985. It was in perfect condition.

At my request, Aunt Lizzie allowed me to take the picture outside into more conducive light to take pictures of "the picture" and avoid flash interference and glare on the glass. I used a 35mm camera and propped the picture up in a chair and took a lot of pictures at different settings to make sure that some of them would be developed successfully. It worked better than I anticipated. I took pictures of them together and also of each of them separately by focusing closely. This allowed the pictures to reflect the originality of the photographer's work putting them together in the first place!

It is believed that the picture was not compiled like this until after Rebecca and Andrew Jackson married, which was January 1, 1985. Each of the original pictures was taken before they were married and perhaps before they even knew each other. Rebecca was eighteen years old, almost nineteen when she married. Andrew Jackson Talley had just turned twenty-four years old at the time of the marriage.

I find the difference in ethnic features of my grandparents here interesting and noticeable. It appears obvious that my grandmother is indeed Indian, in fact a quarter breed Cherokee Indian American. Note how her skin appears to be much darker than my grandfather's. On the other hand, he is of lighter skin since he is of Irish descent. Being more than a little bit prejudiced, I find them to be a very good looking and attractive young adult couple even without a smile! It has been said that photos taken in the mid to late 1800s were without smiles because people could not hold a smile long enough to have the exposure take.

My cousin, Wanda Hasten, Aunt Lizzie's daughter, now has possession of this framed picture. She is convinced that this picture is an original and not superimposed as I have related here. Who will argue the point? No one remains to relate the facts of the matter.

Andrew Jackson Talley and Rebecca were married at Walnut Tree, Arkansas, which has since been renamed Waltreak, Arkansas. It was first

Rebecca Adeline Smith and Andrew Jackson Tally. Circa 1885

thought the place of their marriage was at the Council Oaks, near Dardanelle, Arkansas. The Council Oaks that remain are two very large and supposedly one hundred seventy year old oak trees on the Arkansas River in Dardanelle. The Council Oaks have a very important place in Cherokee history. It was here where one hundred twenty Chiefs sat on a log under the trees and signed another of many Indian treaties giving the Arkansas lands to the white men (United States government) on June 24, 1823. Terms of the agreement required the Indians to move to the Oklahoma Territory. This location would have had meaning to the Smith family no doubt, but that isn't where the marriage took place. It was determined later that they married at Walnut Tree, which today is named Waltreak.

The region of Yell County, Arkansas chosen by Andrew and his brother to settle in when they moved from Tennessee, is the hill country of west central Arkansas. It is in the lower or southern Ozark country, as it is known today. Andrew Jackson Talley was to make his home, meet his wife, marry, settled down, have a family, and live the remainder of his life in this area.

James Pleasant Talley occupied the Talley homestead, in Tennessee. James had two sons, Benjamin and Dudley, and a daughter, Evelyn. Upon the passing of their parents, they were the heirs to the property. They sold it and used the proceeds to enter the produce business, Talley Brothers Produce Company in Chattanooga.

James William Talley, the youngest son of Joel and Elizabeth, married Elsie Jane Smith the daughter of Samuel A. Smith, on December 9, 1888. Prior to the marriage, they lived on adjoining farms two miles south of Birchwood. In the early 1900s they lived in the Moccasin Bend area of Chattanooga, farming, and in the Kings Point area. The Chickamauga Dam is built on farmland that was owned by James William Talley and his eldest son, Oscar.

About 1920, James William ("Will' as he was known to all) purchased the James Pleasant Talley properties at Thatcher from his heirs, Ben and Dudley Talley and their sister, Evelyn Priddy. He also purchased additional adjoining acreage until his farm consisted of about five hundred acres. He did not move back to this property until about 1925. Will farmed, operated the store and for the most part reared his family here. At one time or another, nearly all of his children lived on the farm, partly rearing their own children on it. In a state of decay, the 'big house' was torn down and the logs sold to a Mr. Corbitt in Chattanooga for use in building a summer house on Signal Mountain, which later burned. The stone building was torn down in 1930-1931 to make way for a large house on the site, which became the home of 'Will' and 'Elsie' Talley until their deaths.

Their daughter, 'Dollie', and son-in-law, Ralph, were the last owners. They sold the farm to the Church of Latter Day Saints (Mormon) who presently operates it as a cattle farm.

Roark Family

An extremely well researched and written history of the Roark family is found in the book, *Joseph Roark: His Life and Times* by John J. Roark, published by Brown Books located in Dallas, Texas. The first printing was in the summer of 2001. Virtually all of my commentary is based upon this book. The book focuses on the life of Joseph Roark, who is my great great grandfather.

As a young lad, I had heard that my family's background was 'part Irish' from my maternal grandfather's family. I didn't have any ideas how this came about until I read John Roark's book relating to the history of Joseph Roark. This book is very well presented and, after having read the book, I have included a brief review of the troubles in Ireland that caused many to immigrate to America. I have included substantial commentary from the book because I believe it is important for my family to relate to the early struggles for life encountered by families of our complete lineage both in the frontiers of the United States as well as prior to their immigration to this country.

The ancestry of the Roarks is Scotch-Irish.[12] To appreciate this lineage, one has to relate to the history of England and decisions that were made by the kings and queens at certain times. The Scotch-Irish segment of society came into being as a result of English problems with the Irish. For almost five centuries, between 1138 and 1603, the Irish had been a thorn in the side of the British Crown and royal politicians. Characteristics attributed to the Irish throughout the centuries were poverty, clan rule, illiteracy, primitiveness, and hatred of the English.

With the establishment of the Church of England in Ireland, the Catholic faith of the Irish contributed to the friction between the Irish and the English conquerors. The Reformation had not come to Ireland, and the Jesuits in Ireland actively resisted the spread of Protestantism. In order to assume some control over the Irish and reduce the cost of a military force maintained in Ireland for that purpose, England's Queen Elizabeth in 1560 conceived the idea of transplanting hundreds of Englishmen to form a colony in the subdivided Irish "kingdoms". These colonies, however, failed miserably because of the fierce resistance of the Irish and the reluctance of the English to assume the hard work of colonization amid murderous Irish raids. All of Ireland was troublesome, but the biggest problem for Queen Elizabeth lay in Ireland's northern kingdom of Ulster. In 1603, in the last year of her life, Queen Elizabeth saw her armies devastate the Irish in the nine counties of Ulster, destroying crops, cattle, and the homes of the native Irish. The removal of the population to the south, to prevent friction with any English settlers, opened Ulster to a new scheme of colonization.

James I of England, Queen Elizabeth's successor, continued the colonization with enthusiasm. In fact, in 1606, he approved the colony named for him at Jamestown, Virginia. Some months later, King James and his advisors conceived the idea of a similar colony in Ulster. This colony would plant Protestant farmers not only from England but also from the lowlands of Scotland. Land grants for Ulster farms were provided to the Scots along with farm implements to ensure successful crops and weapons by which to protect themselves. Eager to escape the poverty of Scotland and the oppression of English rule, the lowlanders traveled by boat across the twenty miles that separated Ulster from Scotland, and by 1610 the 'Plantation of Ulster' was well underway.

The 'Plantation of Ulster' became very successful for over a century. By the early 1700s, Ulster had established an enterprising export of woolen goods and linen products to England, the European continent, and the American colonies. Manufacturing supplanted farming as the primary economy. During the successful century of growth of the Scots, the Irish lived nearby and thousands of Irish Catholics were subtenants on the Scottish farms. While their faith separated the Irish from the Protestant Scots, both had much in common in that both had known poverty and the lack of social distinction. Both Scots and Irish had been designated as barbarians by the English. With the intermixing of the two cultures, some intermarriage was perhaps inevitable; however, the extent to which intermarriage occurred between the Protestant Scots and the Catholic Irish is questionable. The Scotch-Irish, as they came to be known in the American colonies, were predominantly Scottish in ancestry and Presbyterian in religious faith.

Due to the political climate in England, stirred up in part because the competition of Ulster woolen products with English products, restrictions were put on exports. A drought which lasted for six years, and the religious restrictions by the Church of England in terms of ministers conducting weddings and funerals finally caused the demise of manufacturing in Ulster and brought about economic depression. Opportunities in America beckoned to the Scotch-Irish population.

It is known that at least ten ships brought Scotch-Irish immigrants to New England during the years 1714 to 1716. These immigrants were not well received in this area of the colonies. In 1717, more than five thousand Scotch-Irish immigrants arrived in Penn's Colony after William Penn advertised the availability of cheap land and religious freedom. After the early settlers reported back favorable truths regarding the advertisements, five great waves of Scotch-Irish emigration took place in 1717-1718, 1725-1729, 1740-1741, 1754-1755, and 1771-1775. By the time of the American Revolution, over 200,000 had migrated from Ulster to the American colonies with over ninety percent of these arriving in America through the port at Philadelphia.

The Scotch-Irish people spread out from Philadelphia, moving primarily westward and southward toward the tidewater lands of the south Atlantic regions. The Scotch-Irish on the northwest Virginia frontier, including the ancestors of Joseph Roark, had arrived in the lower Shenandoah Valley by the 1730s. Bryan Roark (ca. 1690-1760), probably a direct ancestor of Joseph, was first mentioned in the court records of Frederick County in northern Virginia on May 14, 1743. The court records on Bryan consistently used what would become the traditional spelling of the name: "Roark." No record remains that Bryan Roark owned land in Frederick County. Also in Frederick County during the same period was Timothy Ororke, Sr. (1700 - 1768), who had by then not Americanized the old Scotch-Irish spelling of the family name. He was probably a nephew or cousin of Bryan Roark. Timothy Ororke, Sr. owned over four hundred acres in the Shenandoah Valley which, at his death in 1786, was left to his widow and his son, Philemon. Philemon lived on the homestead after his mother's death for several years with his siblings and settled permanently in the area of present-day Shenandoah County. The families of Bryan Roark and Timothy Ororke, Sr. were then to settle in different areas of the valley and in different ways. Contrary to the stability and permanent settlement of the Timothy Ororke, Sr., Bryan Roark's family was to push the frontier farther up Shenandoah Valley. His son, Timothy (ca. 1715 - 1780), who was referred to in Frederick County as Timothy Roark, Jr., doubtless to distinguish him from the older Timothy Ororke, Sr., and who gave reason for Timothy Ororke to be referred to as 'Senior,' left Frederick County in the late 1750s to move with other Scotch-Irish settlers farther up the valley.

Such was the consistent pattern of Scotch-Irish migration. Those that had sufficient land settled and remained in a location while those without land moved with their families to the frontier to an area in which to settle and farm. By 1770, Timothy Roark, Jr. was in Botetcourt County near Christianburg in present-day Montgomery County.

Families grew and expanded creating a need for more land. It became seemingly an endless growing frontier and expansionist movement. Communities grew and older families settled in with schools and local government being established. Even so, life was very difficult. There were still marauding Indians to contend with whom resisted the expansion into their tribal hunting grounds.

These early Ororke family pioneers were:

Ororke & Unknown wife
> Timothy Ororke Sr. (1700 - 1768) & Unknown wife
>> Philemon Ororke
>> Michael Ororke
>> George Ororke
>> Jesse Ororke
>> Ann Ororke
>> Rebecca Ororke
>> David Ororke

Little more is known about this family than is printed in the book by John Roark.

The Roark family has its beginnings here in this area and the family roots are tracked in great detail in the aforementioned book written by John Roark. This early pioneering family included:

Bryan Roark (1690 - 1760) & Unknown wife
> Timothy Roark Jr. (1715 - 1780) & Unknown wife
>> John Roark (ca. 1735 - 1800) & Unknown wife
>>> Timothy Roark (1745 - 1811) & Rachel Unknown
>>> James Roark (1740 - 1792) & Unknown wife (1740 - 1780)

John Roark (ca. 1765 - 1785)

Timothy Roark (1767 - 1833) & Sarah Bolen (1776 - 1853)

Joseph Roark (1813 - 1876)

The focus in this review begins with Joseph Roark (1813-1876), my great great grandfather. As you look at this list of ancestors and the line of heritage to me it is incomplete. However, it is known that:

Timothy Roark (1767 - 1833) would be my GGG Grandfather

James Roark (1740 - 1792) would be my GGGG Grandfather

Timothy Roark Jr. (1715 - 1780) would be my GGGGG Grandfather

Bryan Roark (1690 - 1760) would be my GGGGGG Grandfather

Bryan Roark was probably born in one of the colonies, perhaps in Virginia. The various families encountered horrendous pain and suffering as they moved farther west into the new frontier areas. One family member[13] is believed to have been captured by Indians and held captive for about two years. Other family members[14] were massacred on their farm. From time to time, they served in the militia as peace officers and soldiers. Somehow they held on to their religious beliefs and continued to settle and resettle new lands.

After several frontier family relocations, Timothy Roark met Sarah Bolen in 1795. She was the daughter of Joseph Bolen. Timothy was twenty-nine; Sarah, nineteen years old. They married in 1796 after an extended courtship. At the time they married, Timothy was a tenant farmer on land owned by David Crouch.

For a woman, Sarah was well educated for her day. She could read and write and sign her name with good penmanship. Sarah is known to have had a sister, Lucy, who was seven years younger than she. They remained close throughout their adult lives.

On January 17, 1797, Timothy purchased the one hundred thirty acre piece of property which he had been farming from David Crouch. He paid one hundred pounds cash for the property. It wasn't long before their first-born arrived on October 9, 1798. They named him Timothy James after Timothy's father.

Of significant interest was the way in which commerce was conducted by trading. It was done primarily with personal notes. The use of personal notes on the frontier was the most versatile medium of exchange. Cash money was not readily available on the frontier, the buying and payment system was one whereby the parties exchanged notes or purchased goods based on their credit standing. In turn, the credit status of an individual was based upon his past history of making good on his debts. The Roark's had an excellent record in this regard. Notes were widely distributed and accepted. John Roark has aptly described this process in his book, which has been referred to previously.

This practice continued for many decades. During the time of my great great Grandfather, Joseph Roark, there weren't any really reliable banks. By and large, those around were mostly not considered as a safe approach to conducting commerce or for the protection of money and valuables. Paper money generally was not acceptable since the banks themselves mostly printed it. Acceptability of bank notes outside of environs of a community was uncommon and unreasonable. Coins were acceptable provided they were from a recognized mint. However, the coins were mostly made of fine silver and heavy to carry around to buy things or pay debts. Coins were also scarce since the United States did not begin to mint coins until 1794 and then in a limited way.

During the early days of the frontier movement westward, one coin that was acceptable was the Spanish Piece of Eight. It had been used around the world for over two centuries. When England ignored our Founding Fathers' request for silver coinage, America turned to the legendary Spanish Piece of Eight, as it was an officially recognized coin for trade and commerce. This coin was the world trade standard. It was struck from 90.3% pure silver bullion and was extremely popular as a 'Silver Dollar'. It is considered by many as America's first silver dollar. It continued to be legal tender until 1857! Most of these coins were struck at the Mexico City Mint, which was the first mint in the Americas. A lot of the surviving coinage was struck in the years 1772 - 1821. Each coin weighed 27.677 grams and is 39.5 millimeters in diameter, slightly larger than the U.S. Silver Dollar.

During this period in America, the coin was considered legal tender by merchants of commerce, banks for sure, farmers, and merchants. On this basis, George Washington, Benjamin Franklin, Thomas Jefferson, John Quincy Adams, Andrew 'Stonewall' Jackson, Lewis and Clark on their expedition to the Northwest in 1804, or Francis Scott Key in 1815 when he sat down and wrote the Star Spangled Banner at Fort McHenry, no doubt, are people all of whom used this coin to meet obligations.

The Piece of Eight is a large coin. In fact, it was bigger than the U.S. silver dollar minted much later. Because smaller coins were very difficult to obtain in the ordinary course of trade due to their scarcity and lack of mintage, the 'Piece of Eight' coin was often cut into eight 'bits.' Two 'bits' were worth about the same as a United States quarter dollar. To this day, 'two bits' is a common synonym for a quarter. This made the silver coin highly respected and popular in the American colonies and on the frontier.

It is highly possible, when George Washington threw a silver dollar across the Potomac River, the Piece of Eight was almost certainly the coin he threw!

Shortly after the Civil War ended, the Roark family began to feel the urge to move on to new frontiers and relocate from eastern Tennessee, which had been their home for many years. Elizabeth (Roark) Talley's sister, Mary Ann and her husband, Robert Beane Scott, decided to move. Robert was a preacher but also did farm work to assist with meeting his family's needs. It was their intent to move to the Indian Territory, now Oklahoma, or possibly Arkansas where land was cheap and the opportunities were better than in the Salem Community. They lived for four years in McMinnville, Tennessee after their initial move. At the end of four years, they would leave for Fort Gibson in the Indian Territory finally settling in Crawford County, Arkansas, which is north of Van Buren. The relocation of this family to Arkansas was about the time that Elizabeth's husband, Joel Talley was making his initial excursion to Arkansas. It is not known whether these activities were merely a coincidence.

Elizabeth had apparently expressed an intent to eventually relocate to Arkansas near her sister, Mary Ann (Roark) Scott, who was living in Crawford County, and on September 28, 1872 , the Salem Baptist Church on Grasshopper Creek granted her a 'letter of recom-

Joseph and Juda Carr Roark. Circa 1855

mendation' in anticipation of her changing her membership to another Baptist church. Elizabeth at this time knew that her husband and eldest son had died in Arkansas. Either Elizabeth returned shortly from Arkansas or decided not to go, for the church on June 28, 1873 rescinded its previous action on her letter and restored her to full membership. Elizabeth, Benjamin, and Andrew were all listed on the church roster in 1876.

Because life had become very difficult in east Tennessee, other family members set out for better circumstances and opportunities. William M. Roark, about twenty-eight and the youngest living son of Joseph and Juda Roark, who had fought side by side with his two older brothers in the War Between the States, decided to leave home about 1870. He moved to join his sister, Mary Ann, and her husband, Robert B. Scott, in Arkansas. Later, he was to spend time in Missouri. Even later, he would return to Tennessee and the homestead and take care of his aging mother as well as marry.

When Joseph Roark, Elizabeth's father, died on February 15, 1876, Elizabeth received her share of the estate in promissory notes. On March 23, 1876, her brother, James Roark, who was acting as administrator of the estate at the time, provided four notes to Elizabeth in the total amount of $504.65 in apparent settlement of the estate with her. Elizabeth signed a receipt as 'Sarah E. Roark' omitting her married name. She may have chosen to revert to her maiden name since her husband was now known to have died in Arkansas about 1870. The point of reverting to her maiden name is unclear.

In 1880, Elizabeth, who was by now forty-six and a widow with five living children, remained in her home in Hamilton County keeping house with Benjamin (21), Andrew (18), Margaret Ellen (15), and James William (13). Benjamin, the only sibling with an occupation, was listed in the census as a farmer. Some of Elizabeth's neighbors nearest her home consisted of her mother, who was now living at the Joseph Roark homestead with Elizabeth's brother, Will, who had married in 1878 and was raising his family at the homestead; Silas and Martha Jane Conner Witt; her cousin and the son of James and Jerusha Blythe Roark, Joseph Roark, and his wife, Juda Ann (Carr) Roark; and Elizabeth Killian, the widow of William Killian, who lived nearby with her six remaining children, her eldest son, Henry, having settled in Brath County, Texas, with his wife and four children.

Elizabeth Talley continued to live in Hamilton County, Tennessee during the 1880s and attend the Salem Baptist Church. The church, as the focal point of the local community, no doubt guided many of her activities, and in the spring of 1892, the church documents reflect a significant event in her life. The 1892 roster of the church indicates that on April 9, 1892, Sarah E. Talley was 'lettered off', that is, granted a letter to transfer membership to another Baptist church. In the spring of 1892, after her parents had died and after her children were grown, Sarah Elizabeth Roark Talley relocated to Erath County, Texas after marrying Henry Killian. She had been widowed for about twenty-two years.

Liz's new husband was now a rancher near Morgan Mill in Erath County sixty miles west of Johnson Station, where James A. Roark, her brother, had relocated from Tennessee. Jim Roark had known Henry back in Hamilton County, Tennessee and had served with Henry's younger brother Billy in the First Tennessee Calvary. Henry's parents were William and Elizabeth Killian who had farmed 80 acres adjacent to and southeast of the Joseph Roark farm in the Salem Community.

William Killian had received his land in the Ocoee District in 1840 and had held the office of Constable in Hamilton County between 1851 and 1855. Henry was William's eldest son. Henry married in 1853, later lived in Arkansas, served with the Confederacy during the war, and moved on to Texas in 1878. Henry's first wife had died in March 1890 in Erath County leaving Henry a widower at age fifty-seven. He and Liz were married in the summer of 1892 and Liz came to Texas for the first time. At the time of their marriage, Henry was fifty-nine; Liz, fifty-seven.

In the summer of 1894, Liz visited her brother, Jim, in Johnson Station, Texas and enjoyed a two-week stay with Jim and his family. Due to the confining demands of ranching, Henry was unable to accompany his wife on the trip on the Texas and Pacific Railroad from Bluff Dale to Arlington where Jim met the train. It was the first time they had seen each other in sixteen years and it was the first time Jim had seen any of his family since leaving Tennessee. The events that intertwined their lives to meet again in Texas when both Jim and Liz were in their fifties provided a welcomed interlude to life's struggles and tragedies. It would the last time they would see each other.

Smith, Workman and Rider Families

The extended Smith family ultimately had a strong influence in the communities of Moss Creek and Riley Creek subsequent to their relocation to Arkansas. The Smith family intermarried into several prominent community families through their direct descendants. In this regard it will be important to cover the Smiths themselves and their offspring. The Smiths, because of the marriages of their daughters, became part of my family both directly and indirectly. In some cases I am related to a cousin through two different family groups.

Leonard Smith's parents supposedly were of German descent. At one time, they lived in Sweet Springs, South Dakota although he was born in North Carolina. He lived during the period about 1820-1857 in Rowan and Davidson Counties, North Carolina. The original family name was spelled 'Schmidt'.

Family history has it that Rebecca Workman was a full-blood Cherokee Indian taken into the Workman family, adopted and raised by the Workman's. The Workman family had immigrated from Glouchester, England. Henry Workman and Mary Scribner were born in Glouchester in about 1750, where they met and married before immigrating. Both parents passed away and are buried in Davidson County, North Carolina. At least one son, Thomas Workman, was born to this union before they moved from England.

Thomas was to meet and marry Elizabeth Garren sometime about 1797 in North Carolina. Their children by birth or adoption include James Workman, born about 1801, Elizabeth Workman, born about 1803, George Workman, born about 1799, Rebecca Workman, born about 1805, and another daughter born about 1807.

Since a birth record has not been located, it is believed that Rebecca and the youngest unnamed daughter were possibly brought into the family through adoption. A second possibility exists if Rebecca was a half-sister to the other children, then her mother, Elizabeth Garren, would have to have been previously married which would have meant that she was Indian and her previous husband would have had to be Indian as well. The only plausible answer that makes Rebecca the full blood Cherokee Indian is that she was adopted and raised by the Workman family, which then conforms to the family information.

Rebecca Workman married Leonard Smith. They purchased their marriage bond in North Carolina, probably Davidson County, on January 9, 1823 from a bondsman, Turkey Harris with Hy Giles as the witness. At the time they were about eighteen years of age, both having been born about 1805. Leonard was a trapper when he met Rebecca. It would seem that the two could have been attracted to each other based upon the attractiveness of wilderness living and its lifestyle since she was Indian. Regardless, after more than thirty years of marriage, Leonard had apparently settled down and is listed in the local census of 1850 as a farmer.

As stated earlier, Elizabeth is believed to be Native American. Having been taken in or adopted by the Workman family, she took a Christian name. Rebecca's Indian name was 'Shining Star'. Typically Indian names are given or have meaning associated with their physical features or their demeanor, the latter often identifying with their personality. I like to think of the name 'Shining Star' as relating to both her looks and personality. From the little information that is known about her, she seemed to be in support of Leonard; she had to endure many hardships and hopefully did so with a smile; she was there to take care of her Woodall grandchil-

Believed to be Leonard Smith

dren in their time of need. I am convinced she was beautiful just based upon my own grandmother's beauty, which I saw first hand since she was a part of my life for several years.

This union of Rebecca and Leonard resulted in the birth of three children: Elizabeth Evoline Smith, born about 1822 in Davidson County; Obediah Smith, born in 1821 (established by deduction from the Yell County Voters List – 1868); and Thomas E. Smith, born in 1836. The birth dates of Elizabeth and Obediah are incongruous with the information reflected in the Haire Family Bible of Elizabeth Evoline (Smith) Woodall.

Davidson County, North Carolina was formed in 1822 when the area was designated from Rowan County.[15] Fourteen years later, in 1836, Davie County was formed. Again the land was redistricted from Rowan County. Rowan County, on the other hand was formed from Anson County in 1753. This area is where many of my ancestors lived before moving westward to Arkansas.

When the family moved to Arkansas about 1857, Leonard had one free slave who accompanied the family from North Carolina. That 'free slave'

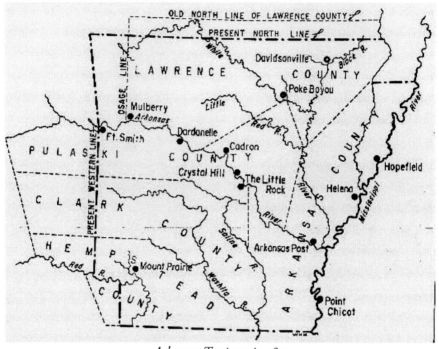

Arkansas Territory in 1819

was assessed a value, in 1861, to Leonard Smith in the Yell County, Arkansas census in the amount of $700.00. Considering the value, one may assume the slave was quite healthy and in good physical condition. How long he was with the Smiths is not of record.

It is believed that in 1857 or thereabout, Obediah Smith and his wife, Marguerite Caroline (Rider) Smith, Obediah's sister, Elizabeth and her family, Obediah's and Elizabeth's mother, Rebecca 'Shining Star' (Workman) Smith, a full blooded Cherokee Indian, and their father, Leonard Smith set out with a wagon train to relocate to Arkansas. Elizabeth's family included her husband, George Woodall absent one son, Alfred Franklin Woodall, born February 15, 1849, who died just before the move from North Carolina. They also had three daughters at the time.

Obediah and Marguerite had two boys, Albert and George, born in North Carolina. Both sons had a disease similar, if not the same, to my mother's brothers. The disease is now known as *osteogenesis imperfecta*. It is a disease linked genetically and carried by the female gender, in this case, Marguerite. Apparently, this was a known issue between the Smiths and

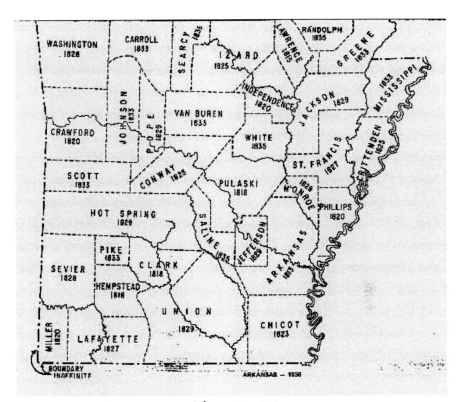

Arkansas in 1836

Riders prior to the marriage since Obediah's family was purported to have opposed the marriage. It must be assumed, therefore, that some evidence existed prior to their marriage that such a consummation could result in handicapped male children. The couple nevertheless married anyway. There has been speculation that this hereditary disease may have been a major factor that ultimately caused Obediah to pursue divorce and marry another woman.

Being a genetically connected disease carried by the female gender, one wonders if other descendants of Adam Rider, Jr. and his wife Barbara (unknown) were also afflicted by *osteogenesis imperfecta*? There were seven daughters and two sons born to this union. Since this disease is female gender carried, it is, by deduction that the two boys, Haules and Ludewig were also afflicted by this condition. Keep in mind that the female passed it on to her male offspring and not to the females. Although the records remain incomplete, it is known that the female children of Adam and Barbara gave birth to at least fourteen females and eleven male grandhildren. Since records have not been found that would establish whether or not either Haules or Ludewig ever married and whereas the females have been determined to have been married, it can be assumed that the males never married because of the probability that they were afflicted by this disease through their mother, Barbara. Based upon this premise, when Marguerite, the youngest, and Obediah were planning to be married, probably in the late 1830s or early 1840s, along with the fact that a number of her sisters had already married and probably experienced the hereditary affliction through the eleven male offspring, that evidence was maybe overwhelming enough for the Smiths to unsuccessfully oppose the marriage of Obediah and Marguerite.

The Smiths initially spent time in the Dutch Creek area of Arkansas. Later they would move to Moss Creek Community and still later to Riley Creek. Moving as they did, it would almost seem as if the Smiths were trying deliberately to remove themselves from civilization because they moved farther and farther away from the beaten track into the hills, woods, and forests. It is a beautiful area with the hills and valleys covered in southern pine and hardwood trees growing in red clay soil. The area is part of the watershed for the Arkansas River system.

"Riley Creek was one of the earliest settlements on the interior of Yell County. In fact Riley became a township which was located on the Petit Jean River, above Danville. The first permanent settlement in this area was in 1829 by Elijah Baker, followed by Joseph McGrady and Henry Evins in that same year. Josiah Hart came in 1830 and the Rileys came in 1831. By the end of the 1830s, some 89 people had settled in the Riley Creek community despite the fact that there weren't any recorded new settlers during the years of 1832 and 1833. By 1844 there were a total of 161 settlers with the largest influx occurring during 1838 – 1841 when 84 settlers arrived."[16] Rapid growth slowed during the next twenty years until the Civil War was over. Beginning in 1866, there was a gradual return of enterprise and growth in this community. This is the approximate time when the Smiths apparently began to think about building and moving to Riley Creek. However, the move did not take place for another ten years or more. Obviously, many land grants were successfully filed during these years.

The first known recorded document of my great grandfather, Obediah Smith, living in Arkansas, is reflected in the 1866 census of Yell County, Dutch Creek Township, page 23. He was fifty-two years old at the time, which would, by deduction, translate to a year of birth in 1814. The birth date is highly questionable since in other census, Obediah is listed with slightly differing ages. He settled on Dutch Creek after a rigorous journey from North Carolina and it seems reasonable because of the Cherokee history in the area and the fact that his mother was a Cherokee Indian by birth. Obediah is also listed in the Yell County, Arkansas Voter List -1868, Dutch Creek Precinct, September 25, 1868 as a farmer.

Obediah became a rather rich man by the standards of his day. He was a landholder of several hundred acres. He cleared a large portion of this land himself, particularly on Riley Creek, so crops could be cultivated and there would be pastures for his animals. He also received a land grant[17] for 158.5 acres through the land grant process from U. S. government signed by President Ulysses S. Grant in 1876. He had applied for four grants in January 20, 1876 but was only successful on the one plot (Section 2, Township 4N, Range 24W).

As a farmer, he cultivated and raised a variety of grains, including oats, corn and barley. He was also a beekeeper. Most of the honey was used in cooking for the family as a replacement for sugar, which was expensive and sometimes difficult to get. Obediah sold the excess honey. He was reported to have bred and raised fine horses, which he occasionally sold for $75.00 per head. On a more personal note, he liked to ride a white steed around his property. Maybe it reminded him of the plantation days when an owner would ride around his property on a fine stallion. Obediah also raised sheep and oxen. Horses were most often used for riding while the oxen were used for plowing the fields and other hard work.

Interestingly, Obediah's father, Leonard, also made application for land grants. Records reflect that he too was successful. He made application for four parcels on the same date, January 20, 1876. He successfully received a grant[18] for one parcel (Section 1, Township 4N, Range 24W) containing 168.36 acres. No recorded disposition of the property is known. Leonard is also listed in the Yell County Voters List 1868, age sixty-nine, occupation is a farmer, and residing in the Spring Creek Precinct as of October 15/16, 1868.

Many stories have been handed down about Obediah. Several of these stories relate to him as having done some devious things. One such act was to try to avoid property taxes on his animals. It is purported that he owned a small island, known as Cane Island, in the middle of Petit Jean Creek about a half-mile south of the main crossing of the creek. When the tax assessor was about to make his visit, Obediah would move most of his animals down onto the island where they could not be seen and more or less show the tax man that he was certainly worth less than he was actually.

As adept as he was at avoiding taxes, Obediah was a talented farmer and businessman. He started his own sawmill on Riley Creek and built a small house on his property. As a shoe cobbler, shoes were made for the entire family by hand. It is said that each pair had to last the recipient one full year before they would be replaced. He was a butcher of sorts, as well. He would kill and cure his own beef. The hides were tanned and used to make the shoes, raw hide strapping for seats and backing for chairs, harnesses for the farm animals, belts, and other things where leather was needed.

Having chosen wilderness living, he had to be adept as a lumberman too. He felled trees and cut the logs used to build the family's log cabin, which I have seen and will refer to many times. Obediah built the first house, or the 'old' log cabin, near his sawmill. This location was about a quarter of a mile away from the place where the 'new' log cabin was to be built. The 'new' log cabin is believed to have been built in the late 1870s since Obediah is living in Dutch Creek as of 1872.[19]

He later built one addition to the log cabin, which basically doubled the square footage of the house. This addition was built from sawn lumber from his sawmill. This is the log cabin where my grandmother was born in 1866. The house later became my grandfather's family's primary residence where my mother and all of her brothers and sisters would be born. The combination log cabin and sawn lumber addition was well built and in full use until my grandfather passed away in 1948. The dwelling during all this time was never painted. Within the year after my grandfather died, the house was demolished and most of the wood salvaged for making a room addition to my Aunt Ollies' home, in the Wilson Community, for use by my surviving grandmother, Rebecca A. Talley. The old log cabin stood for 70 to 80 years and was still in good usable condition along with the many outbuildings.

Obediah probably built most of the other supporting structures (outbuildings) on the farm including the milk house, chicken house, smoke house, blacksmith shop and the barn. We know that everything was completed before 1881 when these items were included in the divorce decree between Obediah and Marguerite Caroline, which was issued on August 10, 1881

Most everyone enjoys a good fish story and my great grandfather had his handed down through the family. It seems that Obediah went fishing in Petit Jean Creek. I do not know what rigging he made up to catch fish, but on this occasion, he was highly successful with his catch. Fishing in this part of the country usually involved what is called a trot-line. That merely meant that you put some bait on one or more hooks tied at several junctures to a long fishing line to which a weight was tied onto the loose end and flung out into the water as far as you could into the creek from the shore. If you were fortunate to have a paddleboat, you could paddle out and stretch the line as taught as possible and release it into the water.

Petit Jean Creek is always muddy water. Some times of the year or during heavy rain run-off, it is muddier than at other times. Once you have placed your line in the creek, the other end is tied to a large sapling or small tree trunk on the bank and then you wait and wait. In fact, many fishermen go away and come back the next day and pull the line in to see if any fish have been caught. If one of any size is hooked, it is pretty easy to know you have a catch. The line will tug, jiggle and pull away resisting being pulled in. If you are going to catch anything in this creek, it will usually be 'mud' catfish or gar. Gar is an ugly and almost prehistoric looking creature. On this occasion, Obediah was very successful. Almost too much! It took great effort to drag and pull this fish to shore and up onto the slippery and muddy bank. After the struggle, the fish weighed so much that it took two men with a long pole pushed through the gills just to carry it! That had to be some kind of catfish. Such a catch no doubt turned into a fish fry with his friends and family in a relatively short time.

Another insight into this man, Obediah, is the story of his purchase of a cut glass butter dish with a cover for my great grandmother Marguerite. This glassware dish is referred to as a 'butter bowl'. Obediah bought it for Marguerite at the trading post in Dardanelle, Arkansas about 1864. Imagine taking such a fragile item and putting it in the saddlebags of his horse and riding as many as forty miles to Dutch Creek without it breaking. It was used almost daily and moved from Dutch Creek to Moss Creek and finally to Riley Creek. Marguerite loved the dish and took very good care of it. The dish ended up in the hands of Rebecca Adeline (Smith) Talley and was given to my mother. When my mother died, it became my prized possession. I haven't any idea how it survived as it has all these years without even a chip. I cherish the dish very dearly and its place in the history of my family.

Marguerite, Obdediah's wife, was said to be not more than five feet tall and was a flaming red head! She had to be of strong constitution to survive the rigors of the frontier in those days. She was reputed to be a good cook, seamstress, housekeeper, mother, and probably helped with at least some of the farm animals as well. As was the custom in those frontier days, she undoubtedly tended a large garden where lots of vegetables were grown for the family's immediate consumption and for canning too. In addition, she was said to be adept at taking cotton that had been picked and picking the seeds out of it by hand. After working the cotton on the spinning wheel, she would put it in a loom and make cloth for making clothes needed by the family.

Another area in which Marguerite gained some notoriety was her ability to plan a highly successful party. She was an acknowledged expert at planning and making wonderful social events. When Obediah would kill a bear, deer, wild bore or turkey or make a nice catch of fish, she would prepare the food with many delicacies including relishes, preserves, and sauces. It is possible that she was the first to make a molasses apple spice cake for which the recipe has been handed down through several family generations. Obediah would invite his friends over to their home to celebrate by having good food and drink.

Marguerite was also a horse lover and thoroughly enjoyed riding horses. Her favorite was a beautiful white stallion. Obediah also loved horses and had a similar stallion, which was said to have a likeness to that of General Napoleon Bonapart's horse depicted in paintings from that era. Several family members have stated that Marguerite was a very kind woman and really loved and cared for her children and grandchildren.

The three daughters must have been extremely active in the family and kept busy learning the various chores inside and outside the house. It has been related through family stories handed down that the three girls had a pet raccoon for a period of time. Obediah apparently killed a mother raccoon and she had this baby. The girls cared for the little animal. Even though the animal was a pet, it apparently had freedom to roam. One day it ventured away from the house and never returned. They didn't know what happened to it but wondered if it had been killed by another wild animal or by a hunter. Perhaps it just enjoyed the 'call of the wild' more than being a well cared for pet.

For reasons unknown to the family, my grandfather and grandmother apparently didn't get along well enough to make a complete success of their marriage. The 1880 census of Rowan County, Salisbury, North Carolina, lists a Marguerite Caroline Rider, married. It can only be surmised now that Obediah and Marguerite had separated as their marriage was breaking up, and she returned to her family in North Carolina for a period of time. Perhaps, too, she was trying to find a way to reconcile their differences by taking some time away to think things through. I suggest this scenario to these distasteful circumstances as a plausible answer for her to have left Arkansas and her daughters even though they were married.

The time she spent in North Carolina could have been relatively short. We know that travel was very difficult at the time. Perhaps she spent three or four months with her kinfolks. Regardless, the relationship with her husband did not improve during her time away or after she returned. After continued deterioration, the marriage eventually ended in divorce. As events unfolded, Marguerite no doubt reflected on the social and Biblical concerns she was burdened with over an extended period of time.

As was the social convention of the time, divorce was not a widely accepted solution to a bad marriage. Divorce was almost unheard of in American society that at the time was intolerant and treated it with disdain to the point that even if there were proper legalities addressed, it would hardly be recognized without some attached stigma. It was strongly frowned upon by churches and by people in society. Furthermore, it was harshly looked upon, by the Christians in the community, as a violation of Biblical principles. In such a close-knit community as Riley Creek, most of its populace were Believers of the Faith. Even so, Obediah filed for divorce from Marguerite as per recorded settlement dated August 19, 1881. The divorce was recorded for public consumption in the *Independent Arkansian*, September 9, 1881.[20] At the time of the divorce, the family was living on Riley Creek, Marguerite was fifty-seven years old and Obediah was about sixty-seven.

Obediah, when he divorced, gave up considerable wealth for his day in both land and possessions. As noted in the Recorded Agreement, Marguerite was to receive the following:

- Land 158 acres in Yell County
- All household and kitchen furniture on the place
- Corn and oats on the place (in the crib)
- 40 head of hogs (enough for the year 1882)
- 14 head of cattle
- 2 head of work oxen
- One 2-horse wagon
- 2 horses
- Part of plows, gear, and other farming implements
- One log chain
- Money with which to buy a stove, say $14

However, family descendants of Andrew Jackson Talley and Rebecca Adeline Smith have stated that their mother told them that Marguerite did not receive all of the items listed in the divorce. In fact in subsequent weeks and months, Odediah's own children, now living on Riley Creek with their mother, Marguerite, would return to the old home place on Moss Creek where Obediah was now living and steal chickens and an occasional pig in order to feed this fatherless family.

Even so, the property tax bills, subsequent to the divorce, continued to show Marguerite as the property owner until 1886, when Andrew Jackson Talley is recorded as the property owner. In an agreement dated January 5, 1886, my grandmother, Rebecca Talley's sister and brother-in-law, Dolcinia (Smith) and Solomon Stanberry, sold their one-third interest in the estate of Marguerite Rider (Smith), who was then deceased, to Andrew Jackson Talley.

In all probability, at least some of Obediah's marital troubles were due to another woman. How long that relationship existed is anybody's supposition. The divorce was granted on August 10, 1881 and he married Jannia 'Pippy' Hunt,[21] age forty-four, on October 31, 1881, less than three months later. Obediah was sixty-seven years of age. At first, some people believed that it was a common-law marriage relationship; however, the marriage was recorded in the Yell County records at Danville, Arkansas, in Book 12, Page 218. The advertisement of the couple obtaining a marriage license was printed in the *Independent Arkansian*, December 9, 1881 as having taken place in the Danville District sometime during the months of October and November. Obediah's spouse's name was given in the newspaper as Mrs. Jennie Hunt.

This entire situation and set of circumstances was so distasteful, disgraceful, and embarrassing to my mother's family, the Talleys, it became buried in secrecy in the minds of many people and was never discussed among family members for many decades. Only in 1980, when one of my second cousins, Georgia Belle (Mayer), was researching records for family history purposes did she inadvertently find the documentation in the Yell County courthouse records. Even after it came to light, family members, that is, the offspring daughters of Rebecca and Andrew didn't want to discuss the matter. It was as if Georgia was trying to cause trouble by 'bringing it up now'. Unexpected to me was the fact that my mother, my Aunt Alice, and Aunt Belle, knew very few details even though they all knew there was a divorce. By now the three sisters lived in Southern California and were available to talk about the events in some depth. It was a difficult topic to discuss and it was evident that they had tried to forget it!

My mother stated that Peggy (Marguerite), lived with my grandparents (Talleys) until the time of her death which she believed to be about three years after Rebecca and Andrew married. The timing then of her death would have been about 1887 when she was sixty-four years of age. Other data reflects her death to be in 1883. If my mother's memory is correct, my Talley grandparents married in 1885, and Peggy lived at least two additional years. The cause of her death was supposedly from 'dropsy' according to my mother. However, it has been learned that Peggy also had a form of very debilitating arthritis. Her condition was such that she could hardly use her hands and was unable to do the many routine things that she had previously done. This had to make her life miserable with the quality of life deteriorating to an undesirable state.

With Peggy's health failing, she left the old homestead and moved in with one of her other daughters leaving the homestead house to Andrew and Rebecca. The move may have been due to the fact that Rebecca was pregnant with her first child and unable to provide adequate care for her ailing mother. For sometime afterward, Rebecca must have had some depressed feelings about missing her mother's funeral even though the impending birth was a legitimate reason why she was unable to attend.

In summary, the Smith family, based upon present knowledge, included the following members:

Leonard Smith - married Shining Star (Full blooded Chreokee Indian) – Christian name was Rebecca Workman

Obediah Smith - married Marguerite Caroline Rider

Albert Smith, was born in North Carolina

Sarah (somtimes identified as 'Sarco') Caroline Smith (b- 6 July 1857, d-8 June 1929) - married David Harrison Johnson 11 May 1882

George Smith (b-1862) believed to have died at a rather young age

Dolcinia Smith (b-1854 married Solomon Stanberry at Dutch Creek, Arkansas

Rebecca Adeline Smith (b-29 November 1866, d-2 may 1950)- married Andrew Jackson Talley at Walnut Tree, Arkansas 1 January 1885

Elizabeth Evoline Smith – (b – November 8, 1822) married George
Washington Woodall (b – January 28, 1818)

Alfred Franklin (b-February 15, 1849)

Rebecca Louise (b-abt. 1850)

Wincy Ann Elizabeth (b- 1854)

Londy Evoline (b – December 26, 1853)

Susan Angeline

Martha Ann Catherine (b – 1869)

Merry Elander (b – March 21, 1862)

It is highly probable that Obediah Smith's brother, Thomas E. Smith, and his family did not relocate to Arkansas at the same time as the other Smiths and Woodalls but made the journey at a later date. Thomas married Elizabeth A. Ward and they had two children, Noah W. Smith and Rusberg C. Smith. Noah, born in 1854 was probably born in North Carolina and Rusberg is thought to have been born in Arkansas.

Just prior to the death of Obediah Smith, my great grandfather called for 'Becky' (then Rebecca Talley) to come to him. It was his deathbed wish to see his youngest daughter. However, his wife Jannia or 'Mia', as some knew her, wouldn't contact Becky until after Obediah passed away. No one ever knew what Obediah wanted to tell Rebecca. Perhaps that haunted Rebecca for years to come. It's possible that he wanted to tell her where some of his wealth was stashed. Whatever those thoughts or expectations may have been, they passed into eternity with Obediah's last breath.

After Obediah's death on Moss Creek, my mother told me the story more than once that people having heard the news came from near and far, in fact as far away as Oklahoma with various kinds of instruments and tools designed to find gold. Apparently Obediah had some kind of reputation about having hoarded gold and silver in boxes and burying it. These people used these items to try to find his hidden gold and silver. Mother didn't really know what these instruments were but described them as 'gold will find gold and silver will find silver.' She further stated, "…the home where he died on Moss Creek was just dug up!" There were holes from digging that covered the front yard and all around the house. After the family members left the farm, people came in and took walls apart and even dug up the well by hand checking for loose bricks that might indicate possible hiding places. Mother also said that Obediah had a hideout place in the mountains near an area that I knew as the Talley Knob. These treasure hunters went up there and dug everything up in sight too! Her final comment on the subject was simply she "never heard of people finding anything for their efforts." According to Peggy, he did hide his wealth in different places. Who knows, maybe he lost track of the places himself!

After hearing that story more than once, I reflected back and wondered where Jannia was during all of this digging. It was her front yard! Had she already made off with the gold and silver? Is that information part of what was ultimately withheld from Becky? Perhaps Jannia wasn't at home to protect her inherited property because she was off making deposits or finding new hiding places?

Prominent People Living During Obediah Smith's Lifetime

General George A. Custer – Died at Little Big Horn Little Big Horn

Daniel Boone - Died at the Alamo in Texas

John Fremont - Western Frontier Explorer

General Santa Ana - Mexican Leader, Won Battle of the Alamo

William Cody 'Wild Bill' - His Wild West Shows Toured the World & Buffalo Hunter

Annie Oakley - Wild West Show Entertainer in Wild West Shows

Meriwether Lewis - Western U. S. Explorer

William Clark - Western U. S. Explorer

Wyatt Earp - Famous Lawman of the West

Thomas Alva Edison - Invented the Electric Light Bulb

George Westinghouse - Invented Railroad Car Airbrake

John B. Dunlop - Invented the Rubber Tire

Alexander Graham Bell - Invented Telephone

George Eastman - Invented Camera Using Roll Film

Richard March Hoe - Invented Rotary Printing Press

Isaac Merrit Singer - Invented Continuous Stitch Sewing Machine

Sam Houston - Fought at the Alamo

Wild Bill Hickock - Western Lawman & Cowboy

Selected Significant Events
Occurring During the Lifetime of Obediah Smith

1815 General Andrew Jackson routed the British at the Battle of New Orleans before the news of the War of 1812 was over.

1815 John Macadam first constructed roads from crushed stone.

1817 Rush-Bagot Treaty between Britain and US to demilitarize the Great Lakes region.

1817 Erie Canal began in the state of New York.

1817 Indian attack touched off Seminole War in Florida.

1818 Cumberland Road opened.

1818 Congress adopted present format of the American flag.

1818 W. K. Clarkson patented the bicycle.

1818 *Silent Night* by Franz J. Gruber and Joseph Mohr was first sung.

1819 US obtained Florida from Spain in the Adam-Onis Treaty.

1819 Alabama became 22nd U.S. state.

1820 Missouri Compromise solved crisis over admission of Missouri as a slave state.

1820 Susan B. Anthony born.

1820 Daniel Boone died in Missouri.

1821 First Catholic cathedral built in the US - Baltimore, Maryland.

1821 Population of U.S. was 9.6 million.

1822 Joseph N. Niepce (1765-1833) invented earliest form of photography.

1822 Louis Pasteur born in Dole, France.

1825 George Stephenson (1781-1848) developed the first steam-powered locomotive.

1825 Erie Canal completed.

1825 A baseball club was organized in Rochester, New York.

1826 Thomas Jefferson and John Adams.

1828 Noah Webster published his *American Dictionary*.

1831 Population of U.S. counted at 12.8 million.

1835 US National Debt was completely paid off

1835 Samuel Clemens 'Mark Twain' born.

1835 The Liberty Bell cracked.

1836 Fall of the Alamo, March 6

1836 Arkansas became 25th U.S. state.

1836 Betsy Ross died in Philadelphia.

1837 Samuel Finley Breese Morse invented the telegraph.

1837 Panic of 1837 begins lengthy economic depression in the US.

1838 There are 1,300 antislavery societies in U.S. with 109,000 members.

1840 There are 2,816 miles of railroads in the U.S.

1841 First immigrant team of 48 covered wagons arrived in California.

1842 US accidentally seizes California then returns it to Mexico with apology.

1843 John C. Fremont crossed the Rocky Mountains.

1843 Charles Dickens published '*A Christmas Carol*'.

1844 Baptist is the first church to split North & South over slavery.

1845 U.S. Naval Academy opened in Annapolis, Maryland.

1846 Mexican War begins when US troops are attacked in the disputed Texas Territory.

1846 Elias Howe (1819-1867) invents the lock stitch sewing machine.

1847 First U.S. postage stamps printed.

1847 Doughnut was invented.

1849 California Gold Rush - gold found at Sutter's Fort.

1850 California admitted to U.S. as 31st state.

1850 U.S. population reached 23 million (3.2 million slaves)

1851 Isaac Merrit Singer (1812-1867) invented the continuous stitch sewing machine.

1852 Elisha Graves Otis (1811-1861) invented the elevator safety 'no-fall' device.

1855 First railroad train crosses the Mississippi River at Rock Island,

Illinois.

1858   First transatlantic telegraph cable laid.

1859   Edwin L. Duke 1819-1890) first to drill an oil well in the US.

1859   Comstock Lode discovered in Nevada.

1859   First US oil wells flow in Titusville, Pennsylvania.

1861   The Great Civil War begins between the states.

1862   Richard Jordan Gatling (1818-1905) invented the machine gun.

1863   President Lincoln declares Thanksgiving a national holiday.

1865   Civil War ends.

1866   Robert Whitehead (1823-1905) invented the torpedo.

1867   First elevated trains ran in New York City.

1867   Chrisopher L. Sholes (1819-1890) invented first practical typewriter.

1869   Hippolyte Mege Moures (1817-1880) patented margarine.

1869   Transcontinental railroad completed at Promontary Point, Utah on May 10 by the Union Pacific and Central Pacific Lines.

1872   Yellowstone National Park created.

1873   San Francisco installed first cable cars.

1873   Great Bonanza silver lode discovered in Nevada.

1874   Joseph Farwell Glidden (1813-1906) invented barbed wire as we know it today.

1875   First Kentucky Derby run at Churchill Downs won by Aristides.

1876   Alexander Graham Bell (1847-1922) invented the telephone.

1876   Karl von Linde (1842-1934) invented the first practical refrigerator.

1876   General George A. Custer and 265 men massacred at Little Big Horn by Sioux Indians.

1876   Professional baseball's National League was formed.

1876   Central Park in New York City was completed.

1877   Nikolaus A. Otto (1832-1891) invented internal combustion engine now used in automobiles and other vehicles.

1877   Thomas Alva Edison (1847-1931) invented the phonograph.

1879   W.F. Woolworth opened his first store in Utica, New York.

1879   Thomas Alva Edison invented the first electric light bulb.

1880   Salvation Army was founded.

1880   First US census to exceed 50,000,000 people (50,155,783).

1881   President Garfield assassinated.

1885   Washington Monument completed.

1885   Karl Bentz (1844-1929) invented the precursor to the automobile.

1885   Rover Safety Bicycle invented first modern bicycle.

1886   George Westinghouse (1846-1914) invented the airbrake for railroad cars.

1888   John B. Dunlop (1840-1921) invented the air filled tire.

1888   George Eastman (1854-1932) invented the first camera to use a continuous roll of film.

1889   Oklahoma land rush.

1890   Yosemite National Park created.

1891   Thomas Alva Edison (1847-1931) invented first motion picture camera.

1891   Dr. James A. Naismith invented basketball in Springfield, Massachusetts.

1892   George W. G. Ferris invented the Ferris Wheel.

1893   Panic of 1893, touched off by New York Stock Market crash, begins second worst depression in US history.

1895   Billionaire banker, J.P. Morgan bails out the US Treasury, faced with a gold drain.

Reflections

As I reflect back on the Smith family, I am astounded by the wealth my great grandfather, Obediah Smith, was able to accumulate with his 'bare hands', particularly when it is considered he was a half-breed Indian. It is hard to say how he was affected by his status in life. Who knows what happened to his wealth? Did his second wife, Mia, steal it from him? Did he allow her to spend it foolishly? Does it make any difference...not at all today! But it is sad to think that after his accumulation, he died a pauper so to speak. He must have had an estranged relationship with his three daughters, partly based upon the fact that Mia wouldn't even honor his death-bed request to see his youngest daughter, Rebecca.

Obediah was buried in an unmarked private location, off a backcountry dirt road, in a location where there was not even a clearing of trees at the time I first saw his grave; a location where hardly anyone would know it even existed. If you found his grave several years ago, you wouldn't come away knowing anything about the man not even his name. When I first saw the grave in 1983, there was no headstone…just a pile of flat Arkansas shale rocks, maybe five of them, stacked one on top of the other. That's all! Did he have some good traits? God knows. He certainly had talent. He made some terrible mistakes for sure. I have no way of knowing, but in all the information that I have reviewed and the stories that have been told about him, never has there been an expression of a love for Christ or that he even considered it. May God have mercy on his soul!

Great Aunt Sissy (Smith) Johnson

Sarah Caroline Smith, born 6 July 1857 in Arkansas, was the oldest of the three daughters born to Obediah Smith and Marguerite Rider. This would be accurate if the Smith family arrived in Arkansas in 1855 as is believed to have occurred. Sarah had red hair like her mother. Sarah Caroline was almost twenty-five years old when she married. Why she had not married sooner remains a lingering question.

Sarah married David Johnson, a gentleman who had been married several times prior. He was forty-five years old, quite eligible, and earning a substantial amount of money from his war pension. He first married Emily Blanche; they were listed in the Arkansas 1870 Census. David and Emily had one daughter, Laura Agnes Johnson, born in February 1874 at Adona, Arkansas and died at Russellville, Arkansas on 6 July 1939. As fate would have it, Laura Agnes was to marry James Ellis Tubbs on 30 July 1893. This marriage brought about family ties eventually to the Talley family. For reasons unknown, David and Emily did not remain together.

David Johnson's second marriage was to June Hamilton on 26 November 1876 (per record on Book B, page 181 in the records at Danville, Arkansas). June was born about 1857. This union produced two daughters, Emma and Viola. At the time they married, it was believed that June's previous husband had been killed in the war. Although it now seems quite strange, more than ten years after the end of the war, her former husband returned home. June left David to return to her first husband.

For David marital bliss seemed elusive. He convinced Sarah Smith to become his third wife. She could probably see herself doing better than most at her age simply because of his pension from the War. She married David Harrison Johnson on 11 May 1882, twenty years after he had been wounded in the Civil War. David was born 26 September 1835 in Virginia and died 22 September 1921 at Danville, Arkansas and is buried at Waltreak, Arkansas.

David Johnson and Sarah Smith seemed to have made a good family life. After Diar and Lillie were born, David filed for two land grants on March 7, 1902. He was successful on one parcel (Section 8, Township 4N, Range 24W) and received a homestead certificate for 160 acres signed by President Theodore Roosevelt.[22]

David Harrison Johnson had joined the Confederate Army as an infantryman when he was twenty-five years old and was assigned to Company 'C', 13 Regiment Tennessee Volunteers, Capt. John H. Morgan's Company on May 16, 1861 at Shelby County, Tennessee by William H. Walker. It remains an unknown fact about David's enlistment as to whether he traveled from Arkansas to join this Tennessee unit or if, in fact, he already was living in Tennessee and later moved back to Arkansas some time after the war. Shelby County is located on the Mississippi River and is the most southwestern county in the state of Tennessee. In fact, the Battle of Shiloh, where David was injured, was four counties directly to the east.

David fought in one of the great Civil War battles. The Battle of Shiloh was waged in two days during the spring of the year. It was early April 1862.[23] The peach trees were in full blossom. Their petals fell to the ground in a carpet of pink. The air was fresh with the hint of the earth awakening from its winter's hibernation. Leaves were beginning to sprout anew with green growth. This was soon to change from such an idyllic setting to one of pungent odors caused by the smoke of rifles being fired and explosions of cannons as they blazed their balls of destruction down on young soldiers. Men cried out in anguish and despair as they lay mortally wounded struggling to draw their last gasping breathe of air. Dead men from both sides could be seen lying in twisted positions with their bodies mangled from cannon ball detonations and rifle shots that riddled their bodies into unrecognizable corpses.

David Harrison Johnson and Sarah Caroline (Smith) Johnson circa 1895

The location of one of the most important battles of the War was in southwestern Tennessee in Hardin County near the state border with Mississippi. The most identifying feature of the local landscape was the little church at Shiloh. In total, there were nearly 95,000 men gathered to do battle and destroy each other. There were generals who had learned their theories of executing a war at West Point. The soldiers firing the weapons and trudging through the trenches were a mixture of varying status economically. They were mostly farmers with a few city dwellers thrown in. Some were veterans of other battles; there were those who had never seen 'the elephant'.[24] This phrase was used to identify those soldiers who had never experienced battle previously. Union forces were predominantly from Ohio and Illinois mixed with others from Iowa, Missouri and a few from other places. Their purposes for being here were based upon their convictions. The Confederate soldiers were from Mississippi, Tennessee, Georgia, Louisiana, Alabama and Arkansas. Kentucky, Texas and Florida were represented as well.

Those of the North believed the overwhelming reason for war was to preserve the union of the states and to eliminate slavery. The gray coats saw it differently. It was an effort to preserve their economic system, which included slavery. It was a God given right and an integral part of the institution of freedom that had brought many of their forefathers to this country less than two centuries before. In all respects, it seemed this war was a war of ideologies. This battle was a confrontation to establish control of the Mississippi River Valley.

Some of the troops began to arrive and position themselves on April 4. Spring showers, common at that time of the year, greeted the soldiers on both sides. The showers were not welcomed. It was difficult for the soldiers to stay dry. The ground became muddy and the roads became rutted as cannons were moved into place. The rain made it difficult to sleep in an already virtually sleepless night of anticipation of what the morrow would bring. David Johnson found himself among this group of soldiers.

It is unknown to the writer if David was one of those fighters who had yet to see 'the elephant.' He was from Arkansas. He was given instructions on the use of his rifle and stand-up position to take when firing the weapon. He was a greenhorn. The general, either Pierre G. T. Beauregard or Albert Sidney Johnston, who ordered his unit into combat is unknown. What is known about the battle was that it was indeed fierce. On April 6, exactly one year to the date after Arkansas seceded from the United States, about 20,000 soldiers died or were wounded. The count was nearly equally split on both side. The Union was able to bring about 25,000 reinforcement soldiers to do battle the following day, April 7, 1862. Rain had continued to pour in torrents during the previous night. The conditions were beyond an infantryman's worst nightmare. Even so they fought the battle anyway. By 5:00 p.m. on April 7 the fighting ceased. The Confederate remnants began their withdrawal to Corinth, Mississippi. The toll of dead and injured was astounding. In addition, General Johnston had been shot in the leg during the battle and, not recognizing the severity of his wound, he bled to death. One of the Northern Generals, William Tecumseh Sherman, had been slightly wounded twice and had three horses shot from under him. The North had won this major battle and was now in a position to move for complete control of the Mississippi River Valley.

David Johnson was one of the wounded casualties of this battle. He may have been injured the first day since he somehow made his way to a military hospital. He had been wounded in his head. He spent most of the remainder of the War in a military hospital recovering. The doctors used a silver dollar as a plate in his skull to repair the damage and let his body's immune system take over the healing process. He recovered and returned home at the end of the War.

David's five brothers also served in the Army of the Confederacy. He had one sister, whose husband served in the Civil War on the Union side. David's death in 1921 was the result of an accident caused when a falling tree from logging operations hit him in the head and dislodged the silver dollar causing a hemorrhage. The Johnson and Stanberry families were loggers. David spent a lot of time watching timber being felled and cut. When David left the confederate military, he had been pensioned (# 25766) and was paid $125.00 per month. In those days, that was a lot of money.

Sarah Caroline (Smith) Johnson, called 'Aunt Sissy' as a beloved nickname, died June 8, 1929 (her headstone records a date of 1939). When she died, my mother's sisters, Alice and Belle Talley walked to her funeral. The place where the funeral was conducted is not known but it was probably at the Riley Creek church, which would have been more appropriate for a walking distance rather than Belleville a town seven miles from Riley Creek. Sarah Johnson is buried in the Russell Cemetery in Belleville, Arkansas. Aunt Alice remembers the time simply because it was prior to her marriage to Albert Tubbs and that date better coincides with 1929.

The marriage of David and Sarah provided a number of cousins that my mother and her sisters were close to during their lives. There was:

Name	Birth	Place	Death
Diar Johnson	9 July 1883	Danville, Ark	
Nettie Johnson	26 November 1892	Danville, Ark	
Levin David Johnson	23 November 1897	Danville, Arks	8 August 1986
Joseph E. Johnson*	21 December 1894	Danville, Arks	17 December 1905
Pride Johnson*	30 September 1893	Danville, Arks	3 October 1895
Lillie Johnson*	23 January 1885	Danville, Ark	22 August 1895

* These three children died at an early age and are buried in the Nebo Cemetery at Waltreak, Arkansas.

Levin Johnson is the cousin that my mother corresponded with for many years and almost up until the time that he died. She was very fond of him. Bunnie was his wife's given name. He lived in the Dallas, Texas area for many years. He had two daughters, Gladys and Ulaine, who lived locally near him during his later years.

Sam Stanberry, David Johnson's nephew (son of Sol and Dolcinia (Smith) Stanberry), described his uncle as being tall, slim, and having a light reddish beard. Sam is also a cousin to all of the Talley girls.

Great Aunt Dolcinia (Smith) Stanberry

Dolcinia, born in 1864, was the second daughter born to the Smiths, as the Civil War was beginning to come to an end. Certainly, it was not the best of times. Bushwhackers were roaming the countryside. Obediah had not yet built the log cabin on Riley Creek. The family was probably living on Moss Creek.

Aunt Dolcinia was highly thought of among the Talley girls and spoken about fondly. She was also a very good storyteller. My mother remembered very vividly some of her stories, which were considered to be highly accurate and real life experiences. Apparently she told her stories with such enthusiasm that my mother had the highest regards for her. No doubt, as most storytellers do, she probably embellished them and made her voice inflections with such action in her presentations that she had everyone on the edge of their chairs with heart-pounding excitement.

My mother related one of her stories to me. It seems when the Smith family moved into the log cabin on Riley Creek (the sawn lumber half of the house had not been built yet) from the house near the old sawmill house, also on Riley Creek. The family's chickens ran wild because a chicken house for them to roost in at night had not been built. The old house was a good quarter of a mile or more from the log cabin. At night, the chickens would fly up into the trees to roost and be protected from predators such as bear, fox, and other varmints. The chickens were difficult to catch during the day because they would scurry away and were pretty adept at avoiding being caught. At night, however, they weren't as active and with diligence and perseverance the chickens could be caught. After the chicken house was built at the new log cabin, Peggy decided that the chickens should be brought to their new home where they would be safer and more controlled. The assignment was given to the two older girls, Aunt Dolcinia and Aunt Sarah to go down to the old sawmill house and collect all of the chickens and bring them home at night. The time chosen was one evening after it had gotten dark.

They arrived at the old place and began to catch the chickens and tie their feet together so they couldn't run off. Naturally, this was uncomfortable for the chickens and they couldn't do anything about the situation but squawk and flop around on the ground and just make noise. Suddenly, before they had caught all of the chickens, they could hear a 'thumping' noise that sounded like it was still some distance away They listened a bit longer and knew that whatever creature was coming, it was getting closer because the 'thumping' kept getting louder. It kept coming! Their hearts started to pound in their chests as they wondered what this noise could be. In another moment of instinct, they grabbed up all of the chickens they had caught and began to run back to the log cabin. They ran as fast as they could! Even so, they could hear the thumping noise and they were excited and very scared. The thumping was getting ever closer. As they neared the log cabin, they began to shout and holler, "open the door!" to anybody who could hear them. They just hoped someone would hear them!

Sure enough, Peggy, their mother, had heard them call and she had the door opened as they stumbled inside, fell to the floor gasping for air, and all the while still holding on to the chickens! As soon as they were inside, Peggy slammed the door closed and put the cross board in place. They were now secure, they hoped, from whatever was chasing them. They stayed quiet and listened. All around the door they could hear sniffing, growling, and scratching that carried on for several minutes. Finally, it ceased. "What was that?" Aunt Sissy asked. The answer came back from their mother, rather simply, "It was a bear." Dolcinia and Sarah were scolded for not having thrown the bear a chicken. Peggy explained that action would have caused the bear to be distracted and stop to eat the chicken and the bear would have stopped running after them. One chicken would be worth the sacrifice for sure. It was obvious that they had been scared out of their wits! Their last second decision to make a run for it had saved their lives!

Among the many stories told, these two, the 'bear' and 'the digging for gold', were the ones that stuck in my mind all these years. I enjoyed hearing Mother tell them over and over again. I know she enjoyed telling them as well. She seemed to sparkle with excitement and become enlivened as she told them. Maybe she embellished them a little bit too!

Aunt Alice stated that her father never visited Aunt Docinia because they did not have a very friendly relationship. On the other hand, he did visit Aunt Sis because she was friendly.

She also told about her father visiting Andrew's sister, Mary Smith, who lived in Chickalah, Arkansas. My grandmother, Rebecca Talley, thought Mary was very stingy. As an example she related this story. One time, she and Andrew visited his sister, Mary. It was the time of year when the peaches were ripe. Rebecca saw the peaches on the tree ready to be eaten and asked if she could have one. The answer was apparently negative...so when Mary wasn't looking, Rebecca reached through the kitchen window and grabbed one from a nearby limb. My Aunt Alice said her Aunt Mary never came to their house for a visit.

Aunt Dolcinia married Solomon (Sol) Stanberry at Dutch Creek, Arkansas. They had at least four children and their offspring included Sam, Elinore, Bessie and Lucie.

Rebecca Adeline (Smith) Talley

My grandmother, Rebecca Adeline (Smith) Talley, was named after Rebecca Wendell of Albany, New York. She was born on Riley Creek, Yell County, Arkansas on November 29, 1866 and died on May 1, 1950. There is some debate about her place of birth. Was it on Dutch Creek or Riley Creek?

When she met Andrew Jackson Talley, the Smith family was living on Dutch Creek. Andrew went there to see her and court her. This predated by several years the family's resettlement to Moss Creek and later to Riley Creek.

Rebecca was a very self-confident young lady. She demonstrated this in terms of her own words about the men she had met in the area. She told some of her daughters that, "I could have had any man I wanted for my husband." This statement would imply that she liked herself, was confident, had pride, was a beautiful young lady, and wasn't bragging because that was the picture of her as she saw her world.

Rebecca loved to dance. Before she met Andrew, she stated that she could dance into the wee hours of the morning. It seemed that she never tired of dancing. That became an issue prior to the time that she decided to marry Andrew. It seems Andrew wasn't a dancer. It could have been his Baptist upbringing. The Baptists' frowned upon and even considered dancing sinful in nature. Andrew would apparently take her to a local square dance and observe but never participate. He told her that when they got married, she couldn't dance anymore. The issue became settled once and for all time when she accepted his proposal for marriage.

Rebecca was a hard worker. As a kid, I still have a vision of my grandmother making soap in the old iron kettle pot in the front yard. It was balanced on three rocks on the ground. She boiled fatty meat scraps to get the grease and collected lye from the fireplace ashes to add to the concoction. I don't remember any other ingredients that she might have used. I only watched her make soap once. I found it interesting.

She worked hard on wash days too. My grandfather would struggle to pull, push, shove and coax to finally get the gas powered washing machine out of the milk house where it was stored when not in use so grandmother could do the family clothes washing. It was a difficult task since the milk house was three steps above ground level. Then he would roll and push the machine to the place in the yard where Grandma wanted it. Then the hours of work would begin. The machine was loaded with water from the nearby well, clothes were sorted and at the appropriate time each pile was dumped into the tub, then her homemade lye soap was added. Then Grandpa would crank on the engine until he got it started. The smoke would billow from the belching of this noisy monstrosity of a machine. With great effort the thing would begin to churn and agitate the clothes. As the clothes were finished, grandma would crank the handle on the manually turned rollers

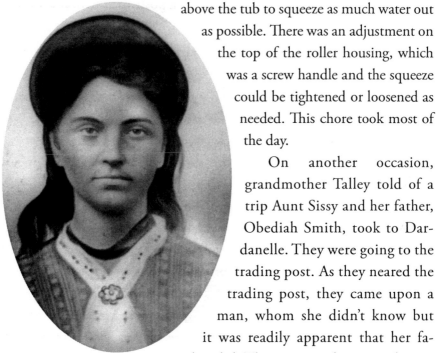

Rebecca Adeline (Smith) Talley
Circa 1885

above the tub to squeeze as much water out as possible. There was an adjustment on the top of the roller housing, which was a screw handle and the squeeze could be tightened or loosened as needed. This chore took most of the day.

On another occasion, grandmother Talley told of a trip Aunt Sissy and her father, Obediah Smith, took to Dardanelle. They were going to the trading post. As they neared the trading post, they came upon a man, whom she didn't know but it was readily apparent that her father did. The two men began to discuss a debt that was owed to Obediah. The debt seemed to be long over due and that aggravated and irritated Obediah. Tempers flared when the man was hardly reconciliatory at all about making repayment. Just as the tempers sizzled and hot words were exchanged between the two men, Obediah within seconds pulled his pistol from the mid-section of his pants and belt and shot the man, supposedly killing him on the spot. Obediah then put the dead man on his horse; lifted the man's young daughter, who had witnessed the dreadful scene, onto the saddle; and slapped the horse on the rump and sent the little girl home with her dead father. Obediah quickly realized what he had done and knew the best thing for him was to return home as soon as possible. For fifteen years, Obediah would not return to Dardanelle for fear of being arrested by the law. Levin Johnson, my mother's cousin, confirmed this event. One would guess that it had been told to him by his mother, Sarah Caroline (Smith) Johnson. Nothing was ever said regarding the impact this incident had on Aunt Sissy. Hopefully, she was in a position where she did not actually witness the shooting.

Although Rebecca could neither read nor write, she was a wonderfully kind person. I don't have any memories of talking with her very much and certainly not for any extended time. What I know for sure is that her children loved her dearly. I felt the same way. I also felt her love for me.

I wasn't always the good little boy I was supposed to be or even thought to be. Once while on a trip from California to visit my Talley grandparents, I got out of hand. I was about seven or eight years old. First, I acted like I was saying words in Spanish when in fact I didn't know one word of Spanish at the time. What I did later was far worse. It was evening time around the fireplace and I had been given a piece of cheese which apparently I didn't like very much. I began to break off small pieces of the cheese and imbed them into grandmother's long grey hair as I passed in back of where she was sitting. It was a terrible thing to do. Back then people didn't bathe on the farm every day and they probably only washed their hair once a week. I should have gotten into real trouble for that act but I don't recall any disciplinary action being taken. Maybe grandmother intervened on my behalf. I do remember Grandmother washing her hair the next day.

Rider Family

Information regarding the Rider family is fragmented and difficult to obtain. Contact was made by cousin, Anne Moore, with Nathan Walker, a descendant of the Rider family in North Carolina. Nathan has had contact with Don and Betty Nees. This couple is directly related to Adam Rider's son, John Rider.

Adam Rider, Sr. is my great great great grandfather on my mother's maternal side of her family. To date, the name of his wife remains unknown. This union, however, resulted in eight children:

Adam Rider, Jr. – b. 1781, Rowan County, North Carolina, d. 1865

Elizabeth (Betsy) Rider – b. 4/11/1786, Rowan County, North Carolina, d. 6/11/1843 in Kentucky

John Rider – b. 1788, Rowan County North Carolina

Catherina (Caty) Rider – b. 4/10/1790, Rowan County, North Carolina

Margaret Rider – b. 1792, Rowan County, North Carolina

George Rider – b. 1794, Rowan County, North Carolina

Barbara (Barbry) Rider – b. 1796, Newton, North Carolina

Christina Rider – b. 1798, Rowan County, North Carolina

This sketchy information at least provides us with a starting point for the Rider family history. Adam Rider, Jr. continues the lineage, which ultimately came down to my mother's family. Information on Adam Rider, Jr. came from the estate records filed in Davidson County, North Carolina.

Adam Rider, Jr. was married twice. Adam and Barbara (family name unknown), his first wife, were married in 1804 in Rowan County, North Carolina. This marriage produced nine children, including my great grandmother, Peggy, who was the youngest. Barbara died in 1853. She and Adam had been married for over forty-nine years. The children included:

Catherina Rider – b. 9/8/1805, Rowan County, North Carolina

Susanna (Susie) Rider – b. 3/18/1807, Rowan County, North Carolina, d. 2/10/1894, Davidson county, North Carolina

Haules Rider – b. 5/20/1809. Rowan County, North Carolina (Records obtained from Pilgrim Lutheran Church.)

Magdalena (Mary) Rider – b. 3/20/1811. Rowan County, North Carolina, d. 11/29/1873

Elisabeth Rider – 3/10/1817, Rowan County, North Carolina (Records from Pilgrim Lutheran Church.)

Susan Rider – b. 9/27/1818, Rowan County, North Carolina

Ludewig Rider – b. 3/10/1819, Rowan County, North Carolina

Sophia Rider – b. 9/12/1820, Rowan County, North Carolina

Marguerite (Peggy) Rider – b. 1/9/1824, Davidson County, North Carolina d. 1883

It should be noted that the family originally lived in Rowan County. The county lines were redefined when another county was created in the state shortly after 1822. The family's residence was apparently located within the boundaries of the newly formed Davidson County.

Adam Rider, Jr. remarried in the same year that Barbara died. He married Rachel Parkes in 1853 in Davidson County. Rachel applied for her dower, which was advertised in the *Greensboro Patriot* newspaper for six successive weeks. Details relating to Rachel such as prior marriages and prior children are unknown. By deduction, it is known that Adam was seventy-two years of age at the time of their marriage. Rachel and Adam had four children:

George Rider – b. Davidson County, North Carolina

Henry Adam Rider – b. Davidson County, North Carolina

Noah Rider – b. 12/25/1858, Davidson County, North Carolina married – Susan (Susie) E. Hughes

Nancy Jane Rider – b. 4/22/1859, Davidson County, North Carolina d. 5/30/1923, Davidson County, North Carolina

Obviously, Adam was an active man. He fathered his last child, Nancy, in 1858 at the age of seventy-seven years! It would appear that Rachel was significantly younger than Adam, since she was obviously within her childbearing years. The children of Adam's first family were fully grown adults, ranging in age from 28 to 49 years, when he married Rachel. Although unknown at this time, it's possible that Peggy, the youngest of Adam's children, could have been about the same age as his new bride. Having a second family was not an unusual development in those days of relatively short life spans especially for women and the absence of medical expertise that is available today.

The following will summarize my heritage as it relates to the Rider family and the family tree branch involving my mother's maternal grandparents:

Marguerite (Peggy) Rider – My great grandmother

Adam Rider, Jr. and Barbara – My GG grandfather and grandmother

Adam Rider, Sr. and wife (unknown) – My GGG grandfather and grandmother

The Woodall Family

Although the Woodall family is not directly related to me in terms of linage, they had significant influence in the lives of many of the members of the Smith family. The Woodalls made the move to Arkansas in the same wagon train as the Smiths. They basically moved wherever the Smiths moved. Their move from North Carolina was anticipated as being a complete new start in life. However, major tragedy struck the family more than once on the new frontier.

The Woodall family included George Washington Woodall, born January 24, 1818 and his wife, Elizabeth Evoline (Smith) Woodall, born November 11, 1822, and their children: Alfred Franklin, born February 15, 1849, who died before the family left North Carolina for Arkansas; Rebecca Louisa Woodall, born August 16, 1850; Wincyann Elizabeth Woodall, born September 15, 1852; and Londy Evoline, born December 26, 1853. This entire family made the trip from North Carolina to Arkansas.

During their years in Arkansas, three additional daughters were born for a total of six. The three born on the frontier were Susan Angeline, Mary (Merry) Elander, born March 21, 1862, and Martha Ann Catherine, born in 1869 was their last child.

Apparently, the parents of George, James Woodall, born about 1798, and his wife Elizabeth (Eliza), born about 1803, were rather wealthy people. They owned some 2,800 acres in North Carolina and decided not to join the traveling party. This couple also had other children including David, Margaret, Jane, John, Thomas, James C., Benjamin, and Ellen. Apparently, none of these children made the journey. George and his family left the plantation life behind to take their chances on the frontier.

There isn't any evidence showing how Obediah got along with Elizabeth, his sister or her family. One would like to think that he had a positive and friendly relationship. The Woodall family referred to Obidiah Smith as 'Uncle Obe Smith.' This certainly doesn't smack of a strong bond. If the family and children, in particular, had referred to him as 'Uncle Obe' my opinion would be different. But they didn't. Just using the last name Smith indicates distance between the families.

The Woodall family was to encounter and be beset with horrendous tragedy after their relocation to Arkansas.

The first problem occurred when George either lost one of his arms or had it badly mangled to the point where it was not really usable. One story says he lost it while fighting in the Civil War. Still another view states that he lost it in an accident. It is unknown as to the accuracy of either of these two stories, neither of which may be true.

A second known tragedy to hit the family was the death of the mother, Elizabeth. It is surmised that she died as a result of complications from the birth of their last daughter. This was a real devastating loss for the family. The oldest daughter, Rebecca Louise, in essence became the little mother to the other siblings. She, no doubt, grew up quickly. Obviously, George carried a very heavy load being a single parent and the only leader in the household. He now had the double duties and responsibilities of motherhood and fatherhood. George was left trying to raise and care for these six little girls. The family lived on Riley Creek close to their relatives and perhaps these relatives assisted with the care of the children thereafter.

There wasn't any way to know what tragedy would lie ahead for this motherless family. As if losing an arm and his wife wasn't enough damage, a third incident occurred which cost him his life.

These were the days of the roaming bands of thieves and robbers on horseback. They terrorized many areas of the South but seemed to concentrate their dastardly deeds in the rural areas rather than towns or cities. They would ride up to any given house to seek money and other valuables supposedly to help the cause of the Confederacy. These bandits were ruthless more often than not. They were known as 'bushwhackers'.

Throughout the South during the Civil War, and for a period thereafter, these bandits or gangs of men were, in reality, marauders of innocent civilians. These gangs robbed innocent peace loving rural people; they injured and harmed their victims often without mercy; set fire to homes and barns causing economic devastation; and even murdered people for no apparent reason as they meandered through the countryside. They also claimed that they were seeking to do harm to those who sympathized with the North. For the most part, it is believed that they were stealing and confiscating money and valuables for their own gain. Proof that such monetary support reached the coffers of the Confederacy cannot be substantiated. Regardless of their reason or purpose, the day came when a band of bushwhackers rode up and paid a visit to George Woodall and his six daughters. They were asking for gold.

This family lived across the road from the old Reed place very near where my Grandfather Talley lived. It was within hollering distance of the Talley family graveyard. George was in essence a poor man, having lost his wife and was having to care for his six daughters as best he could. He obviously told the bushwhackers that he didn't have any gold. They didn't care if he was telling the truth or not it seemed. Did they know with any certainty that George did or did not have gold? Did anything happen to make them think he had a stash? Did his brother-in-law have some role in the situation? Supposedly, the story goes, George Woodall had gold but had it hidden and buried on his farm. No one knows if this was true. Regardless, one story is that they shot and killed him in cold blood in the front yard of his home before his six young daughters. A second recital gives way to George having been taken a short distance away from the house where he was beheaded. In either case, it was absolutely horrible. Since he had a number of children, six by count, it is probable that many or all of them actually witnessed the entire episode. Hopefully the kids were told to go inside out of harm's way. They probably did as they were told but kids are curious. At least some of them either looked out the corner of a window or a crack in the door. It had to be an excruciating and heart stopping event taking place virtually right in front of his little girls. It was indeed a dastardly deed and no doubt caused exceedingly difficult times in the future lives of those little girls. The oldest of the young ladies was about twelve years of age at the time their father was killed.

There is also another twist to this horrible story told to cousin, Anne Moore, by James Jean. Reportedly, some members of the Reed family, which lived close by, saw the entire event unfold. They were hidden from view of the bushwhackers by heavy bushes and peered through the brush to see what occurred. After they felt safe enough, they proceeded to the deceased and found him as expected, dead. Immediately they took the Woodall children under their care until the Smith grandparents arrived sometime later.

It is said that some of the little girls helped the Reeds dig the grave and together laid their father to rest for eternity. I have thought many times how that horrendous incident must have affected and impacted them. It was so ruthless, heartless and such a dastardly deed. Just incredulous!

It took six months for word after the killing to reach their grandparents, Leonard and Rebecca (Workman) Smith who were then living near Morrilton, Arkansas. The Smiths had relocated there temporarily for safety from the bushwhackers. After receiving the terrible and devastating news, the grandparents set out to return to their grandchildren on Riley Creek. Upon their arrival they took the six children into their care. Somehow those little girls did survive the ordeal. The Woodall's must have had a number of extremely good neighbors who were kind enough to see that the children had food and clothing during the time before the grandparents returned. They were probably fortunate that the bushwhackers didn't burn the house. It is hard to imagine such an ordeal! It made me wonder where Obediah and Marguerite were during this time. Did they help the children? Surely they did…they were their own flesh and blood relatives. Perhaps their Uncle, Thomas E. Smith and his wife, Elizabeth (Ward), had moved to Arkansas by this time and he and his family helped or shared in caring for their nieces.

Family information has established the fact that later two of the Woodall daughters, Wincyann and Londy, helped to care for Albert and George, the two crippled boys of Obediah and Peggy. The boys would have been their cousins. Perhaps this was their way of making retribution to their aunt and uncle who hopefully had helped them after the death of their mother and the murder of their father.

As bizarre as it seems, there has been speculation that Obediah Smith rode with this group of indiscriminate bandits over to the Woodall farm and demanded George's gold. If in fact Obediah was a party to the event, he apparently went along with the action and activities because it is said by some that he didn't try to stop it. No one will ever know why Obediah joined in, if he did; maybe it was to protect his own skin; maybe he had some sort of grudge against his brother-in-law. Regardless, it in essence establishes the strong possibility that Obediah participated in or killed and murdered his own brother-in-law. It is a strong indictment of a rather ruthless man who seemingly had a very mean streak in him. Ironically, it is said that most men in the family liked Obediah and that they got along with him well. Supposedly, all of his son-in-laws liked him. It leaves one to ponder if their 'caring for him' was out of fear to protect themselves rather than a genuine friendship.

In the back of the Haire Family Bible dated 1849, from which most of the dates relating to the Woodalls were obtained, these words are noted: "Behold stranger, passing by, once like you, so once was I. Now, like me so must you be. Prepare for death and follow me." The time came when Obediah did meet his maker!

<hr />

[1] This information is a compilation from several sources which data was obtained from cousin Anne Moore. The sources were: *English & Welch Surnames*, Bardsley, 1901, *Early Virginia Immigrants*, Greer, 1912, *The Talley History & Geneology*, G. A. Talley, 1899, *Douglas Register*, Jones, 1928.

[2] Information on Willis Hill Talley was obtained from *The Book of St. Louisians*, 1912, page 586.

[3] *Joseph Roark His Life and Times*, John J. Roark, page 169-172, Brown Books, 2001.

[4] Ibid, page 209.

[5] Ibid, page 209.

[6] Ibid, page 209.

[7] Civil War Soldiers and Sailors System, National Park Service, website: www.itd.gov/cwss/soldiers.htm

[8] *Joseph Roark His Life and Times*, John J. Roark, page 313, Brown Books, 2001.

[9] Ibid, page 346.

[10] Ibid, page 383.

[11] Ibid, page 386.

[12] Ibid, pages 12-16.

[13] Ibid, pages 47-48.

[14] *Massacre of the Roark Family of Tazewell County*, by Emory L. Hamilton, from an

unpublished manuscript, *Indian atrocities Along the Clinch, Powell and Holston Rivers*, pages 79-80 and *Joseph Roark, His Life and Times*, John J. Roark, pages 45-46, Brown Books, 2001.

15 *History of North Carolina Counties*, webpage, which was mostly taken from *The Formation of North Carolina Counties, 1663 – 1943*, by David Leroy Corbitt, NC Department of Cultural Resources, 1950.

16 *Early Settlement in Riley Township*, Yell County, Arkansas, Judy Tate, Arkansas Families.net page 1 and 2.

17 Certificate of ownership as issued by the General Land Office, January 20, 1876.

18 Certificate of ownership as issued by the General Land Office, January 20, 1876, signed by President Ulysses S. Grant.

19 Yell County, Arkansas Voter Registration as of September 25, 1872, page 14.

20 The divorce was published in *Independent Arkansian*, September 9, 1881, page 3, col.4, compiled and reprinted, *Yell County, Arkansas Newspaper Abstracts 1881*, Arkansas Research, by Faye Greenwood Sandy.

21 *The Independent Arkansian*, December 9, 1881, page 3, col. 5, compiled and reprinted, *Yell County, Arkansas Newspaper Abstracts 1881*, Arkansas Research, by Faye Greenwood Sandy.

22 Certificte of ownership as issued by the General Land Office dated March 7, 1902 and signed by President Theodore Roosevelt.

23 Shiloh Silver Maple, www.americancivilwar.com/statepic/tn.html, page 5 of 6, October, 2005

24 *Battle Cry of Freedom*, James M. McPherson, page 409, First Ballantine Books, February, 1989

CHAPTER THREE
My Father's Ancestors

Moudy Family

The earliest known Moudy settler to the new world was John Moudy, who settled in Maryland in 1679. Immigrants with this surname were still arriving as late as 1920. These immigrants came primarily from European countries. According to the *Moudy Family News,* most new arrivals, particularly in the 19th century, located and made their homes in the Mid-Atlantic States. Very few chose to establish themselves in New England.

Based upon my earlier research for the family crest and name search stores, supposedly the Moudy name originated in Germany and was spelled Modi. However, that is basically a phonetic approach, which is not necessarily accurate. My father, William Lewis Moudy, always told me that the name was Welch. So in theory, the name originated in Germany and as pilgrims made their way to Western Europe and settled into some of the English controlled provinces, the name could have been changed into many other forms of spelling including the present spelling used by my family.

Recent statistics compiled relating to the state of Arkansas, indicated that this state was the most populous with 58 separate Moudy families. Over some period of time, I have subscribed to the *Yell County Record,* the local weekly newspaper. In many publications there have been articles in which a Moudy was included. More often than not, I didn't know or have any connection with the particular individual.

The Moudy Clan

The Moudy clan in Arkansas has been traced to Thomas S. Moudy[1] believed to have been born about 1797 in the Holston River area, Washington County, Virginia. Although the names of his parents are unknown, it is known that his mother was born in Maryland and his father in Pennsylvania. He met and married Sarah Ailcy 'Elsie' Dudley sometime around 1821 in Todd County, Kentucky. Elsie was born about 1800 - 1805 in Virginia. Her specific place of birth is unknown.

The Holston River is located in Washington County, Virginia in the southwest corner of the state. It is one of three rivers in this mountainous region of Virginia. The other two are the Clinch and Powell Rivers. Until the mid 1700s, this was strictly Indian Territory. The tribes lived and hunted off the land. From 1750 through the early 1800s, there was a constant struggle between the white settlers and several Indian tribes as they waged battles or skirmishes against each other. It was a very dangerous area and only the hardiest souls could survive. In fact, the Clinch River area, Tazewell County, in Baptist Valley is where most of the family of another relative, James Roark family,[2] was massacred by Indians on March 18, 1780. Indeed, this was a dangerous area in which to live and raise a family when Thomas S. Moudy was born. Research has failed to reveal if a specific reason developed which caused Thomas S. Moudy to move from this area. We do know that he was in his mid-twenties when he moved to Tennessee.

Thomas S. Moudy was a minister and a farmer. In those days, ministers had to support themselves and their families since a church was unable to provide economic assistance sufficient to preclude them from working a second job. Shortly after they married, for unknown reasons, Thomas and Elsie moved from Virginia or Kentucky to Sullivan County, Tennessee. Perhaps Thomas felt the call of God to minister to the souls living on the edge of the wilderness. It is pure speculation, but it is also possible that he wanted to be involved in the evangelism of the Native Americans and, in particular, the Cherokees who were adapting to and accepting Christianity. The Cherokee Nation still owned large portions of land in this area of Tennessee at this time. Thomas could also have been interested in the land opportunities becoming available to all comers. Since he had to be self-sufficient, that would have been important to him.

Thomas and Elsie later moved to Weakley County, Tennessee. This is where their first child, Ambrose Pinkney Moudy, was born on September 28, 1826. In fact, records reflect that Elsie had twins, since a second child, Amanda Elizabeth Moudy, was also born on the date. Other children born in rather rapid succession are: Frances C., in 1828; Rebecca Caroline, on January 12, 1830, also in Weakley County; Mary Ann, about 1831; and a son, William John 'Jack' Moudy, on January 1, 1839 in Tennessee. The family apparently continued to live in Weakley County, although Moudys are included in the census for Sullivan County, Tennessee. [3]Thomas Moudy is included in the 1842, 1844, and 1845 Tax Books for the county indicating that he lived in District 12. On each occasion, one poll was taken. Subsequently, in the years 1846 and 1847 Ambrose Moudy (Thomas Moudy's son) is listed in the Tax Books in the same District 12 and taxed as his father was previously. Even so, records indicate that some of the family also lived in Sullivan County, Tennessee for a period of time. Moudys are listed in the1830, 1840 and 1850 census.[4]

This area of Tennessee is located adjacent to the border with Virginia and very close to Washington County, Virginia where Thomas Moudy was born.[5] Prior to settlement, this entire area was Cherokee Indian territory until the treaty of cessation with the Six Nations was signed on November 5, 1758. Sullivan County is separated from Johnson County by Holston Mountain. The principal valleys are Denton, Holston, Cook and Beaver Creek. The largest stream is the Holston River. It traverses the eastern part of the county flowing in a southwesterly direction. Prior to 1779 the portion of what is now Sullivan County north of the Holston was believed to be in Virginia. Sullivan County was the second county formed in Tennessee.

Shortly before William John Moudy was born, the Cherokee Nation had signed treaties and was forcibly removed from Tennessee and other areas of the east and south. This event, which occurred in 1838, was to become known as the 'Trail of Tears'. Whether or not this event impacted the Thomas Moudy family is not known. Probably in 1845 or 1846, the decision was made to move once more. On this occasion, the move was from Tennessee to Arkansas. They were some of the first Moudys to live in

Yell County, Arkansas.

Ambrose Pinkney Moudy, the first-born, married Sarah 'Sally' Prior Thompkins in 1845. Frances C. Moudy was twenty-three when she married John H. Jones, Sr. on July 12, 1845. Rebecca Caroline Moudy was sixteen years old when she married William Richard Carroll on August 28, 1846 in Trenton, Gibson County, Tennessee. Possibly at that time, the family was already contemplating the move to Arkansas; and Rebecca and William decided upon marriage as opposed to leaving each other. In any event, it is most probable that none of the married children made the immediate initial move with Thomas and Ailcy. Some of them came later to Arkansas and lived a major part of their lives and died in the local area around Chickalah and Harkey's Valley in Yell County. William John Moudy is my great great Grandfather. W. J. Moudy is listed in the Yell County Voters List 1868 as being thirty years old and a farmer residing in the Dardanelle Precinct.

Mary Ann and William would have been about sixteen and seven years of age respectively when Thomas and Elsie relocated to their new homeland. The family first settled in Harkey's Valley, Arkansas. Later, they became an integral part of the Chickalah community. Towards the end of their lives, they lived in the town of Dardanelle.

Thomas S. and Ailcy Moudy appear in the 1850 Census in Chickalah, Arkansas. In 1860, the two parents are shown to be living with Ambrose and Sarah still in Chickalah. Then in 1862-1864, Thomas S. is the Yell County Tax Assessor. Thomas Moudy is among those on the Yell County, Arkansas Voters List 1868 for the Dardanelle Precinct and is listed as a minister, age sixty-six on October 9, 1868. This family patriarch and matriarch do not show again in the records until 1872. Then finally, Thomas S. Moudy is in the 1880 Census for the township of Dardanelle, Arkansas. He is seventy-eight years old and living with Chestine K. Cline and Mary Ann (Moudy) Cline, his son-in-law and daughter. Ambrose (age forty-four and a farmer), the son of Thomas, and W.R. Carroll (age forty-nine and a farmer), Thomas' son-in-law, are both listed on the Voter List 1968 in the Chickalah Precinct dated September 19, 1868.

Thomas must have been quite a farmer. He made the newspaper, the *Independent Arkansian* in August 18, 1876, when he was cited for growing a huge cucumber that was 34 inches in length and 33 inches in circumference and weighed 38½ pounds! What a feat. Even today with modern fertilizers and the attention given to growing gardens I have never heard of one that large.

Land records reflect that William R. Carroll, husband of Rebecca Caroline Moudy, applied for and received three land grants in Yell County totaling 160 acres in 1860 and 1861.[6]

Thomas S. Moudy and His Ministry

There is no doubt about Thomas' commitment to ministry or his dedication to informing people about the saving grace and belief in Jesus Christ. Perhaps he had the benefit of parents who taught him the principles of a Christian walk and the necessity for knowing God's will for his life. Evidence indicates that he was a minister for Christ in Virginia and Tennessee. The most evidence and record of his ministerial efforts are recorded after he had moved his family to Arkansas.

Thomas S. Moudy Circa 1880 (The young lady with him is possibly Hattie Jane Moudy, his grand daughter)

Thomas S. Moudy was a Baptist minister. Many years had passed, in fact almost twenty, before information again appears in print indicating that Thomas S. Moudy is active in church. That is not to say that he and the family were not active during the interim time. It is unknown if he actually began serving the Chickalah Baptist Church, District 4 of the denomination prior to the 5th Lord's Day, 1868. The records in my possession begin on the 3rd Lord's Day,

August 1860. The Civil War may have created some situations where he didn't serve the church or records were not kept.

However, on the 5th Lord's Day of 1868, a number of parishioners had action taken on their status by Thomas Moudy. At this time, Thomas Moudy would have been about sixty-six years old. Other members baptized that day by T. Moudy included, among others, Ambrose Moudy, son of Thomas S. Moudy, who had married Sarah 'Sally' Prior Thompkins back in Tennessee. An interesting fact is that Ambrose was accepted into the church by experience in October 1871. William J. Moudy, a son of Thomas S. Moudy, and Mary Moudy were among others received into the church by baptism. William J. Moudy was received by experience into the church on February 1872. It is unclear as to which Mary Moudy of the family this record relates. It is possible the reference is to Mary Caroline Moudy, the daughter of Ambrose and Sally Moudy. She would have been about eighteen years old at the time. Harriet E. Moudy, my great Grandmother and wife of William J. Moudy, and Harry Moudy were received into the church by confession of faith on this same date in 1868.

William R. Carroll, husband to Rebecca Caroline (Moudy), and son-in-law to Thomas S. Moudy, had been excused by the church but were restored to good standing by T. Moudy on the same 5th Lord's Day, 1868.

There was church action on members of the Harkey family, which was a prominent family in the life of the Talleys and my mother and father throughout most of their lives and continuing even after they moved to California. The Harkey family members identified on the records of the church on this date include Mary Harkey, Albert Harkey, Sarah Harkey, Yell Harkey, Julia Ann Harkey and J. M. Harkey.

Of interest, as well, are other members of the larger related Moudy clan active in the Chickalah Church. For example, the Kirkwoods became active. James Henry Kirkwood married Amanda Elizabeth Moudy in Tennessee. No evidence has been found to date that indicates the time this couple moved to Arkansas or attended this church except for these church records. However the cemetery records of Harkey's Valley Cemetery reflect that James Henry Kirkwood, as the husband of Amanda Elizabeth Moudy, was born October 14, 1824 and died in 1906.

Other church actions dealing with the conditions and circumstances of members of this congregation seem somewhat hilarious in terms of the church of today. Yet in those days, the church was highly rigid with its rules of conduct and was evidently subject to the interpretation of each congregation. Baptists were notorious for self-rule. Certain incidents occurred,[7] some are nearly laughable and far out of step with today's church protocol which are recited below from the records:

- The appointment of Brother Thomas Moudy as the Pastor in February 1872.

- William R. Carroll was one of a committee of three who had to confront Sister Bradshaw in February 1873, regarding a debt that she had failed to repay to Brother W. J. Wiggins. They gave her until April to satisfy the debt.

- May, 1873, Brother Thomas Moudy was absent so the church appointed H. D. Cone as Moderator and W. J. Moudy as Assistant Clerk.

- After the services were over in July 1873, the church called a meeting to take up reports that Sister Chandler had, during services, turned in her seat and with a roving eye, looked back over the congregation. Three church sisters were appointed to talk to her. In August 1873, Sister Chandler came forward and acknowledged that if she had done anything wrong, she was sorry for it. (That wasn't the end; it was reconsidered at the next meeting in September at which time it apparently died.)

- In November 1873, charges were brought that Sister Suggs and Sister Harkey swung their hips in an unusual manner when walking. Sister Ellen Harkey was acquitted at the meeting on February 1874. However, Sister Suggs was not acquitted until May 1874, when she admitted and acknowledged to 'evil walk.'

- Brother Moudy preached at meeting on February 1874.

- March 1874, there was preaching by Elder Thomas Moudy. Also on this date, the church appointed Brother W. R. Carroll and Isaac Lipe to see Brother Thomas Armstrong because he had committed immoral conduct for leaving his seat as Moderator. The two Brothers were to get his credentials and return them to the church. Apparently, a later report indicated that Brother Armstrong had destroyed his credentials. Thomas Moudy was Moderator and William J. Moudy was Church Clerk.

- May 1876 agreed to appoint Clerk, Brother William J. Moudy, to wash feet.
- February 1878, received by experience, Brother William R. Carroll.
- Met on Tuesday before regular Lord's Day service for building repair and for building a brush arbor.
- October 1881, took up charges against Brother Isaac Lipe for unchristian like conduct against Brother W. J. Moudy and Sister Harriet Moudy. (No resolution could be found.)
- Sister Lelah C. Parsley was cited, by the church, for dancing. A visit by members was set to establish the correctness of the report at the March, 1883 meeting. At April, 1883 meeting, she was dismissed from the church.
- July 1883, Sister Harriet Moudy was dismissed for non-fellowship and on Sunday restored for account of mistaken idea.
- At August 1883, meeting Thomas Moudy and two other delegates were to attend the Point Remove Association meeting. The church sent $2.50. (This is the last time Thomas Moudy is mentioned).
- November 1887, W. R. Carroll re-united with the church. Church then called for the lost and found.
- At the meeting of August 1890, the church selected its delegates to the Association meeting and identified A. D. Moudy as the alternate. (This is the last time Ambrose is mentioned in the church activity.)

Some of the actions sound very severe even though some effort was made to investigate reports of perceived misconduct on the part of members. They were definitely literal fundamentalists in their biblical interpretation. Maybe this is where my mother got the identity of the 'hard shell Baptists' as she would sometimes refer to Baptist members. As related above, there wasn't much room to quibble about one's conduct.

My mother was taught, as a child in her father's home, it was wrong or sinful to go to a movie or dance. It was also wrong to wear make-up, drink alcohol of any kind, or smoke tobacco. From the reports above, it is easy to see that looking around in church made it uncomfortable for many and walking apparently in some suggestive modicum was not acceptable behavior.

Thomas S. Moudy certainly lived his life in concert with the way the Christians practiced religion in the 1800s. He must also be given credit for apparently leading a number of his family members to a saving knowledge of Jesus Christ and to eternal salvation. What a great legacy!

William John 'Jack' Moudy, my great grandfather, married Harriet Elizabeth Coose about 1866, shortly after the Civil War had ended. He was twenty-seven years of age. Harriet was born on August 3, 1846 in Grainger, Tennessee, which would have made her near twenty years old when she married William. At one point, this family lived in the Shoal Creek Township of Logan County. They are recorded in the 1882 Arkansas State census. It was noted that a William Pool, a nephew age seven, was also living with the family at this time. This recording seems to be in line with the fact that other Moudys located in this area, including my father's family since he was born in Logan County.

The William John Moudy family made their home in Chickalah, Arkansas for a good portion of their life, though they apparently spent some time in Texas, since their first child was born there. Their children were:

Elsie C. Moudy	born 1855	Texas
Thomas Waldron Moudy	born 4/2/1869	Ark
Will Henry Moudy	born 7/1/1871	Ark
Amanda Moudy	born 1872	Ark
John Quinton Moudy	born 1874	Ark
Nick Moudy	born 1878	Ark
Daniel Moudy	born 1879	Ark
Isaac N. Moudy	born 1881	Ark
Hattie Jane Moudy	born 1888	Ark
Martha Moudy	born ?	Ark

William John Moudy served in the Confederate Army[8] during the Civil War. He was a member of Company D, 15th Arkansas Infantry Regiment. That unit was comprised of men who were all from Yell County, Arkansas. This unit had formerly been known as Hobbs Battalion and later was also identified as McRae's 15th Infantry. He entered the service of the Confederacy on 15 June 1861 in Dardanelle, Arkansas and was sent to Camp McIntosh near Boston Mountain, which is near Bentonville, Arkansas.

Learning about my father's family was more difficult than I ever expected it to be. It seems very few people know very much about the Moudys even though they have been an integral part of the Yell County area for over a hundred years. I can recall, as a kid, living in Belleville and having a number of people with my same last name. Yet my family didn't seem to know them very closely. I wondered, at the time, if I was somehow directly related to these other Moudys. When I was older, I asked about the other Moudy families and my dad's response was, "Yes, we are kinfolk, but I don't know about the family connection." My mother, not being a Moudy for very long, didn't have any idea about the extended Moudy family. As close as families seemed to be, this didn't quite fit the pattern of relations to which I was accustomed.

Thomas Waldron Moudy, my grandfather, married Annie Drucilla Apple and they have family mostly in the Belleville community, which is west of Chickalah and five miles west of the Yell County seat of Danville, Arkansas. This is basically where my immediate family members grew up.

There was one picture, not very large, perhaps an 8" x 10" that hung on the wall of my Uncle Lee Moudy's home in Belleville. It was a picture of five fairly young men and I learned that they were all brothers. I was told at one time the names of each person. With time having elapsed for many years and both Uncle Lee and Aunt Jennie (Buckman) having passed away, I couldn't find anyone who remembered that picture. My interest and pursuit of that picture triggered and fueled my efforts.

I remember that one of the young men in the picture is my grandfather, Thomas Moudy. Another is Dan Moudy, my dad's uncle. They were all brothers but who they are and what happened to their families was not

William John 'Jack' and Harriet Elizabeth (Coose) Moudy circa 1890

known? I turned to my cousin, Doyle Barrick who knows more than anyone still around about the Moudys. As it turned out, he did provide me with some insights for which I am most thankful.

Thoughts about Grandpa Thomas W. and Grandma Annie Drucilla Moudy

by Cousins Doyle and Melba Barrick – (September 18, 2001)

I asked Doyle, since he knew grandpa as a kid and a teenager, "What was Grandpa Moudy like?" The following comments took place over several discussions at several different times during my visit to Arkansas.

I was pleased to know a little bit about Grandfather Tom Moudy and his demeanor. Doyle, was just a young lad but he specifically remembers sitting on Grandpa Moudy's lap at times. Doyle liked to touch Grandpa's hands where he had the scars from having had his thumbs and forefingers on both hands cut off in a sawmill accident. According to Doyle, he could sit for long periods of time just rubbing and touching these scars. I asked him if that seemed to irritate Grandpa at all. He responded, "Don't reckon it did, because he never said anything or pulled his hands away from me!"

Doyle remembers him as a gentleman; very kind and soft-spoken man. Thomas W. Moudy was a large man with a big bone structure. He was an imposing figure, which seems a little out of character in the sense that Grandma was very tiny and of small stature. Their offspring were all rather short, generally five feet eight or nine inches or less in height.

It seems that Grandpa Moudy was rather successful during his life. He owned and operated

This picture includes both sets of my grandparents. Thomas and Annie Moudy are on the left while Andrew and Rebecca Talley are on the right. circa 1935.

the largest sawmill in the area and that was located on Riley Creek. I am unaware of the location of his sawmill on Riley Creek. Since it was the largest sawmill on Riley Creek, it was apparently a successful venture for him. I do not know how long he owned the business, when he sold that business or even why. Perhaps at another time, either before or after or maybe even simultaneously, he owned a general store in the town of Belleville with his brother, Will. Thomas W. Moudy was also the recipient of a land grant which was issued March 2, 1926 under the authority of the April 24, 1829 Homestead Act. He obtained [9]40.84 acres in Yell County located in Section 3 in Township 4 North, Range 24 West of the Fifth Principal Meridian while U.S. President Calvin Coolidge was in office.

Standing left – right: Thomas Waldron, William Henry, and John Quinton. Seated left – right: Daniel and Nick. Circa 1890.

Apparently, Grandpa doted on Doyle. It seems that Doyle, along with his brother, Wayne were tagging along with their father, Chester, and came into Grandpa's store in Belleville. Grandpa Moudy wanted Doyle to dance for him. Doyle was a little reluctant at first but when Grandpa got serious about the reward, it became overwhelmingly convincing that he would dance a jig for Grandpa. What was the reward you might ask? Well, you see back in the late 1920s, special treats were very hard to come by! Grandpa promised Doyle that he would cut him off a big slab of bologna. Now that really sounded good to Doyle.

So without music or fanfare, Doyle started to dance and carry on for a while for Grandpa. Who knows what exactly he did but that doesn't make any difference because Doyle made Grandpa very happy. He had him laughing big-time for a while. After the performance was over, and just as Grandpa had promised, he took Doyle behind the meat counter and got the big bologna tube out and laid it down on the large and tall (it had tall legs under it) sycamore wood butcher's table. There in front of his eyes, Grandpa took a big knife out and cut him that big ole' slab of bologna that he had danced so hard for!

Even as Doyle told the story, you could hear the excitement in his voice and see the gleam in his eyes as he fondly and sweetly remembered the occasion. But Grandpa Moudy wasn't through yet. He knew the young boy needed some crackers with his bologna. They would make your mouth pretty dry, so Grandpa gave him something to drink as well. Doyle couldn't recall what the drink was but he remembered that everybody was happy! I hope this included his brother Wayne as far as the happiness goes, but he didn't really say.

Doyle remembers Grandpa Moudy as a gambler whom apparently enjoyed playing cards and craps. Since the Barrick family lived on Riley Creek during a lot of Doyle's growing up years, Grandpa's gambling generally took place on Riley Creek. It was a somewhat thriving community during these years. Doyle recalls that the location of the local gambling parties was close to the Riley Creek Cemetery. Remembering that Grandpa Tom had his thumbs and forefingers cut off in the sawmill accident, he had to hold his cards and money between his remaining fingers.

During one card game at Riley Creek, Arch Haire, a neighbor to the Talleys, won the pot but while racking in his winnings, he inadvertently, somehow, took some of Tom's money from between his fingers. At least that is what Tom believed. The two argued about it for a little while without resolution. The exchange got pretty heated. They each pulled a gun (pistol) and continued their accusations and denials. Moving behind separate trees for protection in case one or the other decided to pull the trigger, they continued their disagreement. Of course, the other men attending the party were also getting very excited by this time and were beginning to think that someone could end up being killed over the disappearance of Tom's money. These men decided the best thing to do was to talk it up. They said, "There doesn't need to be a killing around here! Remember, someone will end up going to the penitentiary." Finally, with some contemplation, the two men put their guns away and cooler heads had prevailed.

According to Doyle, Grandpa Moudy died at the Barrick's 'rock house' home located in Corinth, a local rural community near Belleville.

I visited that home many times as a kid.

I wasn't around my Grandmother Moudy very much. I went with my parents when they would visit her on trips from California. I don't remember her living any other place than on Uncle Lee's property. Uncle Lee built the house she lived in specifically for her. It was only a couple hundred feet from his house. It is the only place I recall her living during my life. Even when visiting Uncle Lee, which I liked to do, I never felt comfortable spending time down at Grandma's house. She just didn't seem to like kids very much.

Doyle made a statement that grandma was different. His comment was "she was soured on men!" Perhaps Grandfather Moudy didn't treat her right or the way she felt and believed that she should have been treated. Who knows? Maybe she had a lot of idiosyncrasies, which at some point in time became intolerable. Again, who knows? Anyway, Grandmother Moudy was a different kind of person from Grandpa in terms of her charm and sweetness. She would clean her house every day and when she was through, start all over again! She was a fanatic about cleanliness. There was nothing out of place in her house. It was antiseptically clean! She also had a fetish about wearing an apron almost all the time even if she wasn't cleaning her house. Most of the pictures taken of her show her wearing an apron.

The fact that she was different didn't keep Doyle from pulling some shenanigans on her. There was the time when she was visiting the Barrick home (rock house) in the Corinth community. During her visit, Grandma Moudy was helping Aunt Bessie, her daughter, do the family washing. Keep in mind this was during the time of a lot of hand washing using the rub board or, at best, a hand cranked roller for squeezing out as much water as possible from the clothes. There were no clothes dryers in those days so clothes were pinned to clotheslines and left in the sun to dry. Doyle and his brother, Earl, decided that it would be lots of fun to play a game on Grandma. They dismantled the old wall phone from the house and took out the magneto used to crank electric signals over the phone lines. They also got some copper wire to connect the magneto mechanism to the metal wires of the clothesline. They then took the mechanism outside with some long wires and hooked the device up to the clotheslines. Depending on how hard the magneto is cranked more or less determines the quantity of electric current being generated.

By hiding behind some bushes at one end of the lines they couldn't be seen by Grandma but they could easily see her as she would try to hang clothes on the lines. As Grandma would begin to pin some of the clothes to the line, they would crank on the electric magneto to create an electric charge and it would shock her. It obviously wasn't a large charge but he described it as "just a tingle!" The electric bite caused her to jump a little bit and jerk her hand away. As soon as she approached the line again, they would crank the handle and give her another little charge. Again, she would jump back and sort of look around knowing that something was not right! Then she would gingerly tap the clothesline with her fingers to see if she was really feeling something. Feeling no shock, she would be convinced that it was okay to hang the clothes. This went on for quite sometime. Finally, she had enough and she started to look around and found the boys huddled behind the bushes. "Alright boys, was that you doing that to me?" With a sheepish grin, they admitted to their wayward ways. She scolded them thoroughly and went about her business of hanging the clothes. I suppose, since there wasn't any mention of it to their mother at the time, there wasn't any punishment meted out. I guess we have to say, "boys will be boys".

Doyle also told the story about Grandma when she thought that she had heard about a man who had died. It seems that Grandma saw a car coming down the road by her house so she went out to flag it down. She peered into the car and thought she saw a man that she recognized behind the steering wheel. Not expecting to see this man since she remembered that he was dead, she blurted out, "Ain't you dead?" To the question, he replied, "No ma'am, as you can see, I'm still alive I think!"

I asked my mother about Grandfather Moudy. She didn't know the man very well. It appeared from the way she couched her words that he seemed to be a stern man. She felt that he was not always kind to my grandmother Moudy. She added that she thought he was a powerful man in the physical sense. For the most part, it would seem that her comments did not fit in with Doyle's.

On a visit with my Aunt Alice Tubbs in 2000, I asked her about my Grandfather Thomas Moudy. She remembered him and didn't hesitate at all to make her comments. It was obvious that she had a different opinion of him than did Doyle. She stated rather succinctly, "Tom Moudy was a mean man." I asked her why she thought that and she replied, "Your grandmother Annie Apple Moudy was just a little thing…about as big as a whisper. Your grandfather was a big man. He put her head through a fence. He was just plain mean to her!" That was that! She definitely thought of him much differently than Doyle. No doubt he had his good sides as well as those not so endearing.

FAMILY TREE

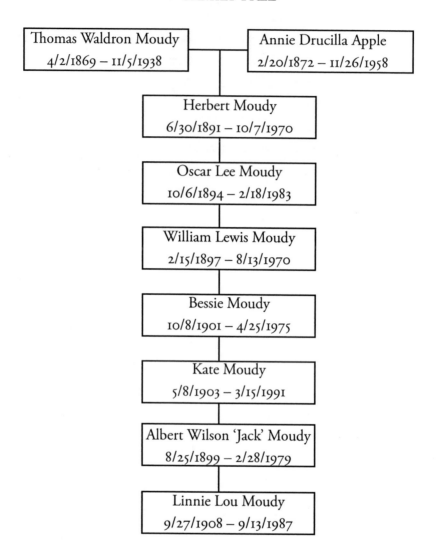

Thomas Waldron Moudy
4/2/1869 – 11/5/1938

Annie Drucilla Apple
2/20/1872 – 11/26/1958

Herbert Moudy
6/30/1891 – 10/7/1970

Oscar Lee Moudy
10/6/1894 – 2/18/1983

William Lewis Moudy
2/15/1897 – 8/13/1970

Bessie Moudy
10/8/1901 – 4/25/1975

Kate Moudy
5/8/1903 – 3/15/1991

Albert Wilson 'Jack' Moudy
8/25/1899 – 2/28/1979

Linnie Lou Moudy
9/27/1908 – 9/13/1987

FAMILY TREE

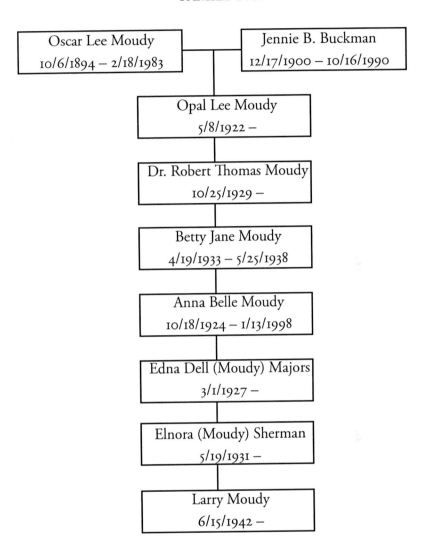

Oscar Lee Moudy	Jennie B. Buckman
10/6/1894 – 2/18/1983	12/17/1900 – 10/16/1990

Opal Lee Moudy
5/8/1922 –

Dr. Robert Thomas Moudy
10/25/1929 –

Betty Jane Moudy
4/19/1933 – 5/25/1938

Anna Belle Moudy
10/18/1924 – 1/13/1998

Edna Dell (Moudy) Majors
3/1/1927 –

Elnora (Moudy) Sherman
5/19/1931 –

Larry Moudy
6/15/1942 –

FAMILY TREE

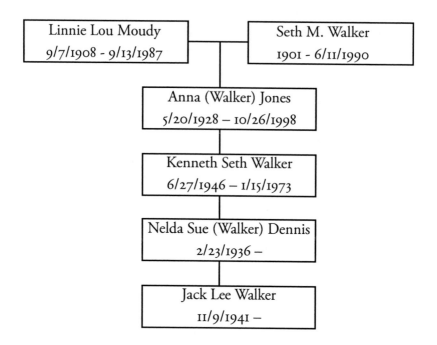

Linnie Lou Moudy 9/7/1908 - 9/13/1987	Seth M. Walker 1901 - 6/11/1990

Anna (Walker) Jones
5/20/1928 – 10/26/1998

Kenneth Seth Walker
6/27/1946 – 1/15/1973

Nelda Sue (Walker) Dennis
2/23/1936 –

Jack Lee Walker
11/9/1941 –

FAMILY TREE

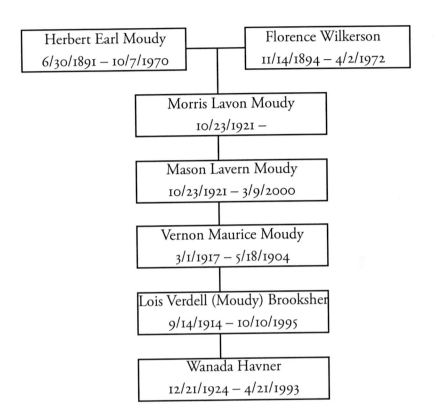

Herbert Earl Moudy
6/30/1891 – 10/7/1970

Florence Wilkerson
11/14/1894 – 4/2/1972

Morris Lavon Moudy
10/23/1921 –

Mason Lavern Moudy
10/23/1921 – 3/9/2000

Vernon Maurice Moudy
3/1/1917 – 5/18/1904

Lois Verdell (Moudy) Brooksher
9/14/1914 – 10/10/1995

Wanada Havner
12/21/1924 – 4/21/1993

Morris and Mason are identical twins.

FAMILY TREE

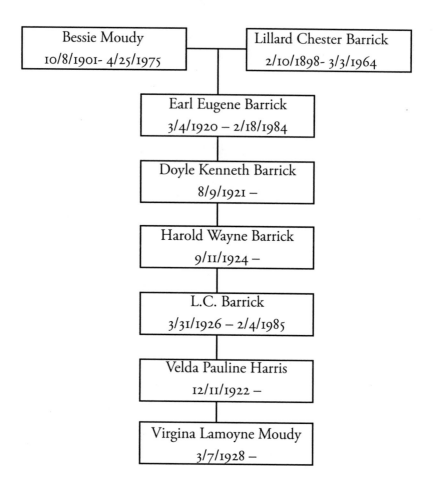

Bessie Moudy
10/8/1901- 4/25/1975

Lillard Chester Barrick
2/10/1898- 3/3/1964

Earl Eugene Barrick
3/4/1920 – 2/18/1984

Doyle Kenneth Barrick
8/9/1921 –

Harold Wayne Barrick
9/11/1924 –

L.C. Barrick
3/31/1926 – 2/4/1985

Velda Pauline Harris
12/11/1922 –

Virgina Lamoyne Moudy
3/7/1928 –

FAMILY TREE

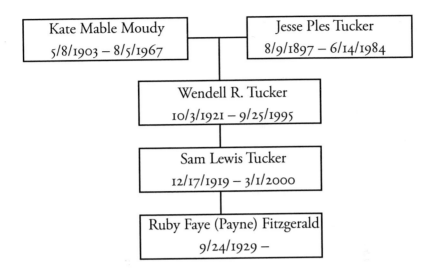

FAMILY TREE

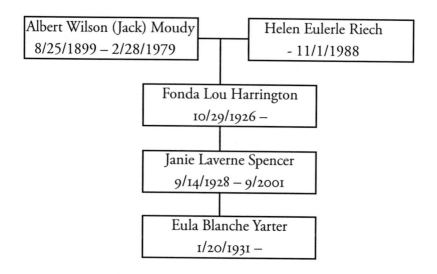

Albert Wilson (Jack) Moudy	Helen Eulerle Riech
8/25/1899 – 2/28/1979	- 11/1/1988

Fonda Lou Harrington
10/29/1926 –

Janie Laverne Spencer
9/14/1928 – 9/2001

Eula Blanche Yarter
1/20/1931 –

FAMILY TREE

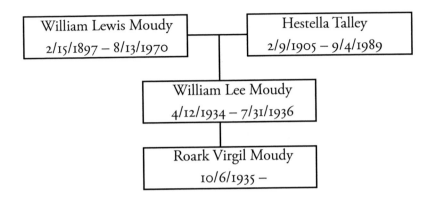

William Lewis Moudy
2/15/1897 – 8/13/1970

Hestella Talley
2/9/1905 – 9/4/1989

William Lee Moudy
4/12/1934 – 7/31/1936

Roark Virgil Moudy
10/6/1935 –

Getting Married – Made Easy

Getting married was a big event on the one hand but treated in an almost too casual manner in some other respects in the late 1920s and 1930s when compared to the social protocols, expectations, and approaches learned from the authority, Emily Post and other scholars of propriety and decorum a few decades later. As my mother related to me, it seemed as if couples who hardly knew each other made the decision to get married. In those days, the couples were typically older when they decided to get married. Courtships seemed to last for a relatively short period of time. The next thing you knew, the couple was getting married. Remembering conversations, which they would get into from time to time, many of my uncles and aunts seemed to have made marriage decisions in this pattern. It was as if a stroke of genius suddenly came upon the couple one day and within a day or two they were married! In many situations, the families had known each other for extended periods of time. Maybe it's not a lot different than today when you think of it. It seems like people don't really get to know one another very well until many years after exchanging their marriage vows.

If you have listened to the stories of your parents or others tell about the "good old days" and the all of the anecdotes, the one story that will usually stand out is 'how they got married' resulting in an intense time of frivolity! Needless to say, they experienced an exciting event in their lives and they usually liked to talk about it. It will most often be a little different than the other stories they tell because it would generally be attended with a lot of laughter and knee slapping with interjecting comments from everyone who attended making a side comment or two and embellishing the tale! At least that was the way it was when my father and mother would get together with their families and assorted friends and talk about yesteryear. It was homespun slapstick comedy at its best. People would grab their sides from laughing so long and so hard! It made no difference as to which person or couple was being described, it would involve 'hard times' and the female being discussed was scared to death of daddy. The big question was, "What will daddy say?" In those days, just as it is today, many young couples just got married and then told daddy. Somehow, these stories, even though they took place in the early twentieth century, had a rather common plot that most of us have encountered or are familiar with in one way or another.

In 1931 my mother had just reached her twenty-sixth birthday and my father had recently passed his thirty-fourth birthday. They weren't really 'spring chickens' any longer and certainly old enough to know what they were doing. Even so, in that period, it was not really that unusual to wait until one was a little older to get

Alice Talley, Lewis Moudy & Hestella Talley. Circa 1931

married. My mother and her parents probably believed that William Lewis Moudy had sown all the wild oats that he was going to sow by this time in his life. My mother was in her prime of childbearing age. Generally, everything made sense for them. Both families were acceptable to each other and in the community. Keep in mind that the real love in my mother's life, Eston Moore, now a miner in Arizona, had been rejected by her father as a viable mate since he had been previously married.

In between his several trips to find work in Kansas and other places, Lewis Moudy had made his way back to Arkansas, rediscovered the road to Riley Creek where the Talley Family lived, and set about to get serious with my mother-to-be, Hestella. His fling with Maudie Lee was over and he was on the prowl, footloose and fancy free. It didn't seem to take long for them both to decide the time had come for marriage. They had dated earlier and now all the elements were in place for the big event.

One week in February 1931, they decided to get hitched. The date chosen was March 10. Early that week, my mother told her sister, Alice, what was going to happen on the next Saturday and swore her to complete secrecy. I do not know what day of the week it was that she told Alice about her plan to marry. Perhaps it was just a day or two before.

Without much fanfare the day arrived. My mother had continued to do her work and chores just as if nothing unusual was about to happen. In fact, she said that she had sawed wood all day that eventful Saturday. She told Alice that afternoon that she "was going to the show tonight with Lewis." She continued her chores even when she saw Lewis driving up the road in a car he had borrowed from his brother, Lee. At the time, she was on her way to the barn to milk the cows. When she finished that work, she proceeded to the house to sort of check things out.

To her surprise, she found her husband-to-be talking to her father, A.J. Talley, and she over heard Lewis asking the question, "Do you care if me and Hester get married?" Mr. Talley was somewhat taken aback and answered, "Okay, but this is really a shock to me!" The news spread rapidly among the family members. It was going to happen NOW! Alice threw a fit, my mother said. I do not know why or for what reason; maybe it was because she did not believe her earlier or because she was not invited to go to the ceremony or maybe she just did not want my mother to marry William. The latter seems most unlikely to me since during my life the two seemed to get along fine.

The two of them hopped in the car and headed for town. Along the way they decided that they would need some witnesses for the occasion. They picked up Grace Phillips, one of my mother's favorite nieces (Ollie's only daughter in her first marriage) and Bessie Moudy, my father's sister, and drove to Danville. By the time they arrived, the town had long ago shut down. It was nearing ten o'clock at night. In this region, the streets roll up at five and six o'clock in the evening without exception. In early March it can often be pretty chilly after the sun goes down. A minister was needed to complete their plans, and my dad remembered that he knew a Reverend Youngblood who lived up the road about ten miles in Havana. They had to rush, however, because the Reverend would be going to bed soon. So they took off for Havana hoping that the minister would still be awake and willing to perform the ceremony for them!

They arrived; knocked on the door! The minister came to the door in his bedclothes. Lewis explained to him why they were there and what they wanted him to do. Reverend Youngblood agreed to perform the ceremony and invited everybody into his home. Bedlam did not break loose, but all in the party were excited that now the event was going to take place! They went inside only to find that one room was partially vacant enough so that the ceremony could be conducted inside. My mother later said that all the rooms were stacked with chairs made from willows. It must have been sort of a bad scene or as she would say, "A sight for sore eyes!"

My mother had a friend, whom she referred to as Aunt Luller Misenhammer, make her a dress just for the occasion. She was not really a relative of the family however. The dress cost sixty cents and her new pair of shoes cost the grand sum of $1.50! Even so, I'm sure she felt very beautiful in her wedding outfit. This was her day in the spotlight!

After the ceremony, they were leaving the same way they came into the house. The front porch of the house was about a foot and a half off the ground. In the dark, it was now nearing eleven o'clock, my dad grabbed a hand thinking it was my mother's to help her off the porch. Instead, it was his sister, Bessie, and my mother had to find her own way off the porch! They always laughed about that part of the evening and Aunt Bessie never let my dad forget it! Life was simple then, I know, I heard the stories. But this must have been one of those occasions when you had to be there to appreciate it in order to see the humor of it all. The story always stops here. I do not know where they spent their one night honeymoon. It could not have lasted any longer because no one had any money and, undoubtedly, they had to work the next day as well.

Other Moudy Family Stories

One never knows what kind of story may develop from a visit with relatives. During my trip to Arkansas in September 2001, I wanted to see my cousin Morris Moudy. I couldn't recall exactly how many years it had been since the last time I saw him. I knew it had been close to four decades. Even so, I felt it would be worth the time and effort to visit with him while we were in Russellville, Arkansas. We stopped at a service station and found his home phone number in the phone book. Doyle didn't seem to be too keen on making the call so I did. Morris' wife, Virginia, answered and she seemed very pleased that we could stop by and didn't hesitate about having us come by. We got the directions and drove a relatively short few blocks from the station to his house. He has lived in Russellville for the last fourteen years.

As a kid I was very proud of him and his twin brother, Mason, who served in the Navy during World War II. I had facts and fiction stored in my mind about them during the war years and I wanted to get the facts straight and direct from the horse's mouth. Both my cousins, Doyle and Melba, had forewarned me that I shouldn't expect too much from him since he didn't talk much any more. They thought that the War and other personal problems had affected Morris in terms of his sociability.

When we arrived, I did recognize him but not instantly per se. I knew who he was because we were at his home. On the street, however, I would not have known him, just to run into him. Morris told us later that he had diabetes pretty badly. He has to take two injections daily to control it. The malady has caused him to become inactive. As a result, he has gained considerable weight. I would venture a guess that he weighs close to two hundred and fifty pounds...far from his slim and trim fighting weight when he was in the Navy.

The introductions were made since some of the relatives had never met each other before. As soon as Morris said his first word, I remembered his voice inflections. I wasn't around him very much as a kid, but for me his voice was very distinct. As he spoke, it was a voice I remembered and it sounded just like Morris. I could have closed my eyes and still have known it was Morris talking. That even surprised me!

As the conversation began, I started asking Morris questions about WWII. I wanted to have him clarify whether he and his twin brother, Mason, had ever served on board a submarine? I had always been under the impression that the twins had served in such a way. He said, "No." I asked what kind of a vessel were you assigned to and with that he seemed to open up. "We served on a four stacker at first (US Navy cruiser). But then the incident of the Sullivan brothers caused the Navy to bring down orders that members of the same family could no longer serve on the same vessel. We started out together on the *USS Southard*. The Navy decided to convert it to a minesweeper (BMS). When the ship was brought in to dry-dock for the conversion, both of the twins were transferred to other separate vessels. Morris said, "I was transferred to the Troop Supply Transport ship, the USS Sheridan. I don't remember what ship Mason served on after that." Morris said he was on board the transport ship during the famous WWII battle known as 'The Great Turkey Shoot', which was one of the biggest, if not the biggest, naval battle with the Japanese during the entire Pacific Theatre. It was the fight for control of the Marianna Islands. Morris said, "We kicked their butts; that's where we won the war! That battle turned the war around for the US." Morris made the statement with great conviction and I knew that he meant every word of it too! After the Turkey Shoot, his ship transported United States Marines to the Island of Guam for the assault on that Japanese stronghold. What I found interesting was Morris' enthusiasm when he was talking about his time in the Navy. He didn't hesitate; it was if it just happened yesterday and was still fresh in his mind. I felt a surge of pride in him. I knew he had paid a price for serving his country.

I asked him to tell me the story about him and his brother meeting up with their sister, Wanada, in Union Station, Los Angeles, California during the War. He said that they were on furlough from the Navy for three weeks. (I think it may have been the time their ship was being converted to the minesweeper since the twins were still together). They were going to catch the train to go home to Belleville, Arkansas. The year was 1943. Their sister, Wanada, had decided to take a trip home to Arkansas and since all trains in that part of California had to pass through Los Angeles, she too was in the Union Train Station. She had purchased her ticket and was waiting for the departure to be called. In fact she was just sitting in the station people watching.

Union Station was a magnificent state of the art station back in 1943.

There are large cavernous waiting areas with very large leather covered seats for waiting passengers. The architecture is incomparable. It is a landmark in Los Angeles and still in use. Wanada happened to look up as the twins entered the station to buy their tickets. Lo and behold, to her unexpected amazement and delight, there were two of her brothers. I'm sure she couldn't believe her eyes. They were supposed to be at sea; fighting the war; trying to help defeat the Japanese. It was incredible! She was beside herself with excitement. They embraced and excitedly established what the reasons were that the three of them had gathered there at the same time. Needless to say, the three of them had a very pleasant and delightful trip home to Arkansas on the train! Perhaps Wanada got caught up on the War and some of the things that had happened to her brothers, whereas, they wanted to know about the folks back home in Arkansas and those living in Oxnard, Ventura and Camarillo, California.

Morris loved to hunt. He told about his squirrel hunting. After he moved to Russellville, he hunted squirrels. He shot fifty-two of them one season. Interestingly, all but two of the squirrels were gray tree squirrels and the other two were fox (red) squirrels! He used to do a lot hunting and I reminded him of the time that my dad, mother, and I were visiting in Arkansas, and he and Mason went out and shot over 100 quail which his mother (Aunt Florence) cooked for dinner (noon meal). I'm not real sure that he remembered that occasion but it happened. I remember that the platter in the middle of the table was piled high with fried quail breasts...nothing else on the platter. In addition, we had homemade biscuits, mashed potatoes and gravy along with that strong dark sweetened ice tea that is made only in Arkansas. That meal was so good. As a young kid I had never eaten quail before so it made a very big impression on me.

At the conclusion of my visit, I had a good feeling that Morris and Virginia were genuinely glad to see us. Doyle and Melba even said, "Morris hasn't talked that much in years!" I could have spent more time with him since he is an avid sports fan particularly of baseball.

My cousin, Doyle, has an unlimited repertoire of stories relating to human nature and its involvement with historical facts, incidents, and life in general. He intertwines this information into verbal pictures of people and their lives reflecting hardships, humorous events, death and other stories. He has lived and observed the rural life in Arkansas his entire life, which now exceeds eighty years. This makes him an authority on the homespun anecdotes that he relates with detail and great enthusiasm. He enjoys telling the stories, some of which directly involve his own experiences while others have been told to him by others. As you listen, you wonder just how much the story has been embellished. Storytellers have a way of doing that thereby making the interest quotient rise considerably higher than it would otherwise be. That's part of the technique of a very good storyteller and Doyle is one of the very best. I could sit with him for hours at a time and never lose interest. There is no limit to how many stories he can tell at one sitting…they come to mind in an endless stream! He is also a self-made local historian. Here are some of the stories he related to me during my stay in Arkansas.

It seems that Doyle's parents, my Uncle Chester and Aunt Bessie went to see another of my relatives, Uncle Seth Walker and Aunt Linnie (Moudy) one day. It was a trip from Belleville to Mount George, a distance of ten or twelve miles. Aunt Linnie was my father's youngest sister. As they drove up in the front yard, Uncle Seth came out to meet them. Aunt Bessie went on in the house but Uncle Chester stayed outside to talk with Uncle Seth. Uncle Chester asked, "How y'all doin'?" to which Uncle Seth answered, "Just fine I reckon, I've been puttin' bees up my pants legs to let them sting me!" Uncle Chester not believing what he was hearing asked the question again. Again Uncle Seth repeated the same comment but explained it further. "Yeah", he says, "I put some bees up my pants leg, several of them, and let them sting me!" Uncle Chester never having heard of such a thing responded, "Well, why would you do that?" Uncle Seth getting a little overburdened and exasperated with all the questions, since he wasn't a man of much talk anyway, replied in such a way that it made Uncle Chester feel as if he should have known the answer. "It helps your arthritis!" Uncle Chester came home and told Doyle all about the conversation. Now we know another home remedy although it may be a bit painful and there isn't any guarantee that it will work!

On another occasion, Uncle Chester and Aunt Bessie were visiting

Uncle Seth and Aunt Linnie at their home near Mt George, Arkansas. It was the cool time of the year in the early part of the winter. Uncle Seth had the fireplace going. But there was something different about the situation. Uncle Seth had a reputation of being somewhat lazy in terms of how some of his relatives viewed him. The strangeness of this situation was that Uncle Seth had a split log about twenty feet long. One end of the log was in the fireplace and the other end was lying across the unfinished wooden floor of the living room and sticking out the front door that was cracked open to accommodate the log! During their visit, as the log would burn, Uncle Seth managed to get up and move more of the log into the fireplace. Uncle Chester thought that Uncle Seth should have chopped the log into lengths that were sized so they would fit in the fireplace and the door could be kept closed. Obviously, everybody doesn't have the same outlook to life or how we approach things!

Another relative of Doyle's was Arch Haire. My mother's family was neighbors to and distantly related to the Haires on Riley Creek. The Haires were closer relatives to the Barrick family. Anyway, according to Doyle, Arch Haire was the most level headed man you ever met. So maybe that had something to do with the potential for a 'shoot-out at Riley Creek!' that day with Grandpa Moudy. Even the intellectual traits, characteristics and reputation of Arch seemed to please and have a positive impact on Doyle, however, he seemed disgusted with Arch's use of snuff. His 'level-headedness' merely meant that after Arch had put a dip of snuff under his lower lip, the snuff would dribble and run down both sides of his mouth equally! One wouldn't think of a snuff dipper as being very fastidious anyway. Doyle's observation was that Arch was an extremist that way when it came to what he was about to eat. At best, his behavior seemed a little incongruous.

These are a few stories whereby I was able to jot down a few notes to jog my memory later. It was difficult listening and making notes simultaneously, as Doyle would start another story just as soon as he was completing the one he was telling without much hesitation. It was like he did not have to think about which story to tell next. It was great! I only wish I could have written down more notes so I would be able to record more of his stories.

I personally don't really know any funny stories relating to my dad. There were stories told and laughter abounded when a story was told among the Moudy relatives. The only one I recall was one which I call the 'bull story.' It seems that my dad, when he was still a young lad, perhaps a late teenager, and some of his friends, perhaps four or five boys, including his brother Jack decided to get even with a bull owned by a local farmer. The group seemed to be very fearful of the bull and always entered the pasture very cautiously. They could not cross through the pasture where the bull stayed without being chased. I'm sure, as most boys would do, they made noise, joked around, teased and genuinely irritated the bull, enraging him to the point of getting his blood pressure up causing him to snort, paw at the ground and carry on with his deep seated frustration! They would entice the bull to chase them and they always managed to escape the potential harm coming at them by climbing over the fence. Having grown tired of being chased, they decided to get even with the bull.

I am not certain that any real forethought was included in their planning but they did come up with some ideas. They pulled the farmer's wagon over close to the fence along the side of the pasture where they could usually find the bull. A four by four post about eight feet long was then put through and rested on the barbed wire fence. The other end was placed on top of the axle of one wagon wheel. Then one of the boys, who had a red handkerchief in his back pocket, tied it to the end sticking through the fence. One of the others helping with the prank had a bright colored shirt that was also sort of red in color. He was selected to go into the pasture to run and dance around. Indeed he attracted the bull's attention and got the bull into raging fever pitched anger so much so that he charged after him much like a bull in a Mexican bullfight. It worked! It worked really well!! The bull zeroed in on that fluttering red handkerchief and charged as hard as he could directly into the four by four with full force bent on full destruction of his nemesis once and for all time and slammed into the post.

There was a major crash as the bull hit the piece of lumber where the red hanky was tied. The instigator of the bull's madness had managed to escape over the fence and out of harm's way. The other boys standing nearby were observers to a horrific collision that caused the wagon to completely turn on its side. The bull was stunned and fell down. The impact had affected him so much that he could not get up immediately. He had been staggered and had a bloody gash on his head just above his eyes and between his horns. It must have been a sight to see! As for the young men, they were reeling in laughter, slapping their thighs and rejoicing in their success at having nearly done the bull in permanently. That event ended when they realized the bull was not dead as he finally got up and slowly walked away no doubt thinking of the next time and expecting different results. The boys seemed very proud of their accomplishment. It was a story to be told many times over!

Apple Family

The Apple family has been prolific in its procreation. I do not have information as to the origin of the first Apple to take the family name. However, the name is known to appear in records in many European countries including Germany, Sweden, England, Holland, Russia and other eastern European countries. Somewhere in this vast region of the world, the family has its roots and many branches.

As for this branch of my family, my father's maternal family was Apple. They made their way to Arkansas from North Carolina by way of Tennessee. Their early beginnings were in Germany. They made the arduous voyage to America primarily because of persecution and war after war. In the early 18th century, many of those seeking a home in the new world were from the Palatinate (Pfalz) region of Germany. It lies primarily on the west side of the North flowing Rhine River. This area was comprised of the Hesse, Rhineland-Platinate, Baden-Wuerttemberg, and the Saarland. Hesse was controlled by Dukedoms Hessen-Darmstadt and Hessen-Kassel while Wuerttemberg was a kingdom. During the Middle Ages this was the center of German life when it was the Holy Roman Empire of the German Nation. In the 13th century, it formed a part of Bavaria. At one time in history, it was divided among forty-four sovereigns. There was the Thirty Years War that ended in 1646 leaving this region devastated by religious conflict. These barbaric activities caused major strife and conflict and inflicted heavy loss of human life as the population of the area diminished from about 500,000 people to only 50,000.

That was not the end to the seemingly continuous devastation and conflict. King Louis XIV of France ordered pillaging raids. Subsequent to the Thirty Years War came the War of the Palatinate from 1688 to 1699. As a consequence of these wars, the victors imposed their religious convictions on the Palatinate four times during this period. Between 1618 and 1700 the area was laid waste six times through three generations. The Quaker, William Penn, made several trips to this region in the 1670's. He found religious and moral people and invited them to settle in America. Land was offered in Pennsylvania for ten cents an acre. From 1708 to 1720, thousands of these Germans came to America and settled in Montgomery, Bucks, and Lancaster Counties in Pennsylvania. It was from this area that they began to migrate to other areas of America initially moving to North and South Carolina.

More specifically, the Apples contributing to my heritage came from Ober-Seemen, Hasse, Germany. This settlement or village first appeared about 400 A.D. The church in the community began about the 13th-14th century. In 1320, Ober-Seemen became an organized community. In the 14th century, it belonged to the ruling line of Van Stolberg-Rossia and was affiliated with Gedern. About 1535, Ober-Seemen with Gedern became Lutheran. In 1565, the Ober-Seemen judicial court was established. In 1626 in Usenborn, Hesse, the census shows empty houses and untended fields. The Plague hit the area in 1627. The Ortenberg Church in the area records forty deaths in three months. Soldiers forced many residents to flee to surrounding villages where they lived in stables or worse. Many of these refugees died from the second episode of the Plague and were buried in mass graves. Like most of the region, after the Thirty Years War, Ober-Seemen had only thirty-two percent of its population survive. In 1748, a large fire destroyed many houses on the present day main street. In 1752, the school was reestablished after having been closed during the Thirty Years War.

The first known generation of the family begins in Germany with Balthasar Appel, who was born about 1610 and died on November 21,

1658 in Ober-Seemen. He married Maria whose maiden name remains un-known. Maria was born in 1612 and died on August 22, 1702 also in Ober-Seemen, Germany. Their children included the following all of whom were born in Ober-Seemen, Hasse, Germany:

Hans Appel – born 1647. Died August 7, 1705 in Ober-Seemen, Hasse, Germany. Married: Margarethe (Widow of Casper Joster) October 21, 1692 in Ober-Seemen, Hesse. Germany

Anna Appel – born February 22, 1651. Died October 25, 1718 in Ober-Seemen, Hesse, Germany.

Christoph Appel – born December 27, 1654. Died September 4, 1655 in Ober-Seemen, Hesse, Germany

Juliana Elisabetha Appel – born March 1, 1657. Died February 22, 1707 in Ober-Seemen, Hesse, Germany

Hans Appel is the line of descendants for my family. He and Marga-rethe (Widow of Casper Joster) had the following family:

Thomas Appel – born March 25, 1697 in Ober-Seemen, Hesse, Germany. Died – about 1765 in Exeter Township, Berks County, Pennsylvania. Married: Maria Catharina Gross – September 14, 1724 in Lutheran Church, Herzenhain, Hesse, Germany. Born on September 24, 1696 in Steunberg, Germany. Died in Berks County, Pennsylvania

Heinrich Appel – born June 1693 in Ober-Seemen, Hesse, Germany. Died – February 5, 1694

Heinrich Appel – born March 13, 1695 in Ober-Seemen, Hesse, Germany. Married: Catharina Thiel. Died – January 20, 1763 in Ober-Seemen, Hesse, Germany

Anna Appel – born March 10, 1699 in Ober-Seemen, Hesse, Germany

Thomas Appel and Maria Catharina Gross both came to America. Catharina's parents were Johann Gross and Anna Maria, family name unknown. She was baptized on February 24, 1696 with her godparents being Maria Catharina and Johann Peter Weber. She and Thomas were to have only two children:

Johann Adam Appel – born September 10, 1732 in Usenborn, Germany. Died about 1810 in Guilford County, North Carolina. Married: About 1760 to Unknown

Anna Appel – born December 13, 1725 in Hirzenhain, Hesse, Germany. Died: July 7, 1733 in Usenborn, Hesse, Germany

With this ancestral line established, the story of my family in America begins in 1749. When Thomas was fifty-two years old, he and his son, Johann Adam Appel, including a Johannes Appel (may have been a brother to Thomas), along with others began their long trip to America. There isn't any record that the two older travelers brought their wives with them, although Maria Catharina Gross did make her way apparently some time later. According to a German National, Ernst Peppel, it is believed that most of the immigrants from the Ober-Seemen villages (upper, middle and lower) formed into larger groups and walked to the city of Hanau on the river Main where they boarded river barges. They traveled westward on the Main, which flows into the Rhine River near the city of Mainz. Here they probably joined into a larger group of immigrants for the trip to Rotterdam. It is believed that as many as twenty stops at custom houses were made on the river trip, which took between four and six weeks. Each stop required an examination and its accompanying expensive delay. By the time Rotterdam was reached, funds of many were exhausted and another five to six weeks layover would be experienced as they attempted to gain passage on a ship.

The voyage to America began from Rotterdam. The ships usually sailed to a port in England, most often Cowes or Plymouth, before beginning the journey across the Atlantic Ocean. Here the passengers went through customs. The ships often waited for one to two weeks for favorable winds. The real ordeal began when open seas were encountered. The voyage would take eight to twelve weeks. The ships were densely packed with passengers but without adequate and proper food and water. Many passengers came down with dysentery, scurvy, typhoid, or smallpox. Children died in large numbers. The weather was also a significant factor with gales of two to three days duration in which the ship rolled so violently that it was next to impossible to stand, walk or lie down. People cried and prayed piteously as they were thrown among one another. Upon arrival in Philadelphia, there was always the possibility that disease would be discovered aboard the vessel thereby causing additional delays in disembarkation. Nearly all of the sailings docked in Philadelphia in late summer or early fall leaving little time for the immigrants to prepare for the severe winters. Furthermore, because the immigrants had mostly spent their small amount of resources traveling to the port city, many arrived as indentured persons. The captain of the ship usually made the agreements as to the years of indentured servitude to be performed. Often it took five, seven or nine years to pay off the cost of their passage fare. These were the conditions faced by my forefathers who made their way to America from Germany.

It was on such a voyage that Thomas Appel and his son Johann Adam Appel left their home for a better life. They boarded the ship *Raneir* sailing out of Rotterdam. The ship's Captain was Henry Browning. It is speculated that Thomas and Johann Adam went to Philadelphia because they had relatives there. The entry recording the arrival of the *Raneir* states that the passengers hailed from Hanau, Wirtenberg, Darmsland, and Isenberg.

The one hundred twenty-six male arrivals among the passengers were required to take the Pennsylvania Colony's Oath of Allegiance at the government courthouse on the 26th of September 1749, the day after their arrival. The family continued to live in the Philadelphia area for several years. Johann Adam Appel is known to have lived in the township of Exeter, Berks County, Pennsylvania, which is located northwest of Philadelphia. On September 14, 1761 Johann Adam Appel was naturalized at Alsase Township, Berks County. Thomas and Johann Adam Appel migrated to Guilford County, North Carolina probably close to the end of the decade of 1770. This statement on records showing he was taxed in the years 1767 and 1768. This would have been close to the end of the mass movement of immigrants into this area of North Carolina and Guilford County in particular. Also, during these intervening years the spelling of the named changed to Apple. Although not proven, the time delay in making the move to North Carolina could possibly have been that they were working off their indenture bonding. Johann was a laborer during this time.

Johann's wife's name is unknown. Their children included:

Daniel Apple – ca. 1761 – 1849. Married: Barbara Loffel (Spoon)

Susannah Catherine Apple – Married: George Williard

John Apple, Sr. – born about 1765 in Pennsylvania. Died: May 1816 in Guilford County, North Carolina. Married: Mary Barbary Waggoner, born about 1765, died about 1842, Guilford County, N.C.

Thomas Apple, Sr. - Married: Christina 'Jane' Parks

Adam C. Apple – Married: Christina Jane

Hannah Apple – Married: Adam Lowman on July 22, 1817 in Guilford County, N.C.[10]

Moving to Guilford County, North Carolina meant that they were locating to a region where a great enclave of naturalized Germans had settled for several years. According to information available, this area of "the German settlement in Guilford County was 28 miles long and 18 miles wide. Many hundreds of families lived here close together." The move was certainly beneficial for Johann Adam Apple. The State of North Carolina made a land grant to him on October 14, 1783 containing 500 acres. Its location was on Buckhorn Creek and the waters of Reedy Fork Creek. After his move to Guilford County, Adam became a surveyor.

Many immigrants followed this pattern of movement to the southern areas which were open to development and settlement. It seems most new arrivals into the Carolinas were initially Scotch-Irish and German immigrants. They tended to cling to themselves in settling communities to make their new homes and obtain land. The distance to the area now known as Rowan County from Philadelphia was about 435 miles and took a circuitous route.[11] Those making the journey traveled on 'the Great Road.' "It ran from Philadelphia through Lancaster and York to Winchester, thence up the Shenandoah Valley, crossing the Fluvanna River to Looney's Ferry, thence to Staunton River, down the river through the Blue Ridge (mountains), thence southward, crossing Dan River below the mouth of Mayo River, thence southward near the Moravian settlement to the Yadkin River, just above the mouth of Linville Creek and about ten miles above the mouth of Reedy Creek."[12] Although there were other routes to be taken, the 'Great Road' or 'The Great Philadelphia Wagon Road' seemed to be more widely used. There isn't any evidence to support the notion that perhaps many of my Apple ancestors made this trek on the Great Road. But there were not many routes to choose for travel in those days.

I have often wondered what it was like to make a major family move during these early pioneer days. I found a very apt and colorful description on a historical web page produced by Guilford County, North Carolina. The writer stated, "These travelers have been described as an interesting procession as they moved slowly southward from Virginia and beyond, principally Pennsylvania. In the lead were cows, hogs, and sheep, kept in line by ruddy men and boys in plain workday clothes of pioneer farmers. Then came the lumbering canvas-covered, horse-drawn wagons filled with simple household goods and meager farming tools. In front of each wagon, holding the driver's reins was a healthy-looking woman. From amid feather beds and cooking utensils popped frowsy heads of children, staring at the wonders of the new world. Hanging to the rear of the wagon bed were feed and watering troughs; and dangling below the bed were water buckets. Under the wagon back and forth into the woodlands trotted the family dog, chasing game by day and keeping faithful watch by night. And always with each group of travelers was the Holy Bible. This great migration took place largely from 1750 to 1770 although some had arrived in the early 1740's and some as late as 1775."

Many Apple ancestors, who moved south settled near Washington, in Guilford County, North Carolina. This area of North Carolina was annexed from Rowan County and Orange County in 1771.[13] Guilford County was later reduced in area when Randolph County was formed in 1779 and further reduced when Rockingham County was created in 1785. Some of the Apple ancestors located into Caswell County, North Carolina which was formed in 1777 from Orange County.[14] Historical cemetery records indicate the community of the Apple family was well established and appears to carry on even today. The Apple family at large is reflected in census records of the late 1800s. As the resettlement fever impacted many citizens seeking free land, so it had its impact on the Apple family groups.

Records tend to indicate that the Adam Apple family attended the Frieden's Church in the late 1700s. Adam had apparently been raised Lutheran or German Reformed in his religious beliefs. He and his sons organized Apple's Chapel perhaps as early as 1803 and it may have begun as a brush arbor meeting. Regardless, records dating to 1825 indicate the existing church split into two groups with Apple's Chapel being formed from the central section. These records also note that on June 4, 1809, Reverend James O'Kelly preached and administered the Lord's Supper at Apple's Chapel. Although unsubstantiated, indications are that the Apple Family was a missionary family. It appears that the youngest son of each generation was charged with the responsibility of starting a new church by donating the land upon which the church was to be built and working to help organize the congregation.

Many of these churches were originally meeting houses for several denominations. Apparently the first was Apple's Chapel on the Apple Chapel Road in Thurmont, Frederick County, Maryland. Peter Apple, who came from Germany in 1717, and Wilhelm Apple organized it. In addition, there was the Jack Apple Church in Carthage, Tennessee. Jack Apple later would become a Senator. He was John Apple's son. Other efforts include Apple Hill Cemetery in Lonoke County, Arkansas, probably associated with a church. There are also Apple's Chapels in Missouri and Indiana. Interestingly, all of the original churches have the same floor plans.

During the years, Adam Apple is reflected in church records in several different ways. First, an article on Apple's Chapel appearing in an issue of the United Church of Christ relates that Adam Apple, Sr. was listed as having received $1.00 from the church on December 17, 1836 "for keeping meeting and school house in decent order for one year." He is also listed in the Church Discipline section – first as a member of a "comity" along with John Apple and Bingham Apple to resolve a dispute between two members on July 2, 1836 and again later on December 7, 1838, as a recipient of discipline: Brother Adam Apple, Sen. according to citation appears and makes concession and promise to amend his way – also informs the church that he has found forgiveness and therewith the church is satisfied.' He appears again in this section on November 23, 1839: "Adam Apple, Sen. charged with drinking spirits in excess this fall. B. Apple to site.

In the Guilford County Court of Pleas and Quarter, May term 1788: "Ordered that Henry Whitsel, Adam Apple, Jacob Hofhinds, Andrew Smith be exempt from paying a Poll Tax for the year 1787."

John Apple. Sr. married Mary Barbery Waggoner.[15] They would be my 4th great grandparents in my linage. The children born to this marriage were:

Catherine Apple – born about 1785, Guilford County, N.C. Married: David Chrismon 16 February, 1803, Guilford County, N.C.

Susannah Apple – born about 1787, Guilford County, N.C. Married: Thomas Heath

John Apple, Jr. –

Peter Apple –

Barbary Apple –

Samuel Apple – born 1795, Guilford County, N.C.Died: June 1868 in Rockingham County, N.C. Married: Eliza Taylor on 23 September 1828

Sarah Apple – born about 1799, Guilford County, N.C. Married: Isaac Jones on 5 December 1815 in Guilford County, N.C.

Elisha Apple – born about 1800, Guilford County, N.C. Married: Sarah Unknown 4 September 1833 in Guilford County, N.C.

Sophia Apple – born about 1804, Guilford County, N.C. Died: Before 1867. Married: John Lee 10 August 1827 in Guilford County, N.C.

Probate for the John Apple, Sr. and Mary Barbary (Waggoner) Apple estate took place in February 1843, following her death in 1842.

Still seeking to improve their lives, some of these individuals and families moved west while land in Arkansas was still available for homesteading. Many of my Apple family ancestors were in this group of Immigrants moving west. They applied for land grants from the United States government in several counties of Arkansas including Yell, Logan and a few other surrounding counties. Some applications were successful. This was made possible when the United States government made the Louisiana Purchase.

Elisha Apple is my great great grandfather. After he and Sarah married and had their family, they left North Carolina. It is not known if their intent was to relocate directly to Arkansas. It is speculated that they moved from North Carolina sometime after their last child, Sarah, was born in 1849. The entire family appears next in the 1850 census of Morgan County, Tennessee. This is an eastern Tennessee county. Elisha died in Tennessee leaving Sarah with eight children some of whom were still very young and not able to contribute to the family's welfare. The cause of Elisha's death is unknown. A sidelight to the 1850 census is that all the members of the family are listed as having been born in Tennessee except for Elisha. This is believed to be in error.

Perhaps because it had been a family aspiration to move to Arkansas or perhaps the expectation of free land attracted Sarah and her fledgling family, she moved on to Yell County, Arkansas after the death of Elisha. The family appears in the Arkansas 1860 census but it is certain that they arrived a few years before the date of the census. In 1857 Sarah received her first land grant containing eighty acres on October 30, 1857. She had filed for the grant in Clarksville, Arkansas perhaps as long as two years prior. With these dates, it is easy to surmise that Sarah buried Elisha in Tennessee sometime in the early 1850s and made her move to Arkansas in the mid-1850s. There seems to be little doubt that Sarah had a very strong disposition besides being an enduring woman.

Earliest records of members of the Apple clan indicate they came and settled on and obtained land in nine different counties in Arkansas beginning in 1857 and concluding in 1923. Sarah Apple, my great, great grandmother is on record as having obtained two separate land patents in Yell County on October 30, 1857 and on March 1, 1860, each for eighty acres.

These two parcels are the earliest on record that were obtained through the land grant process. Two other sons of Sarah Apple homesteaded land in Yell County. They were brothers, David (sometimes known as Davis) and Lewis Apple (my great grandfather). The entire group of Apples, fifteen in count, who migrated to Arkansas were very successful and obtained at least 1,371 acres by patent or land grant from the United States government. Many of them are directly related ancestors.

Known relatives who were successful in obtaining land grants in Arkansas:[16]

Name	Relationship	Location	Date	Acres
Sarah Apple	Ggreat Grandmother	Yell County	October 30, 1857	80
Sarah Apple	Ggreat Grandmother	Yell County	March 1, 1860	80
Lewis Apple	Great Grandfather	Yell County	July 21, 1879	40
George W. Apple	Great Uncle	Logan County	March 22, 1906	80
Evoline Apple	Great Aunt	Logan County	April 15, 1885	37
David (G) Apple	Great Uncle	Yell County	February 10, 1883	40

I have been able to identify and document fifteen applicant surnames with Apple who received land grants in Arkansas. There are numerous other Apple applicants who were successful in thirteen other states.

Many of the Apple families made the Spring Creek Township in Yell County their home. This community is near Belleville. These are the Apple families that are presently identified as directly related to me. Later some of my Apple relatives located and lived on Mount Magazine in Logan County, a neighboring county. In relating stories or information this geographic location is often referred to as 'the Mountain' or 'living on the Mountain'. The Apples were mostly farmers and were very good at raising crops and produce.

My paternal grandmother was given the name Annie Drucilla Apple. She chose to marry Thomas Moudy when she was nineteen. I remember her as being of small frame, short in stature, perhaps about five feet tall, and a very trim and petite lady. She was extremely finicky about cleanliness and as a result seemed to be in constant motion cleaning and re-cleaning her house. Even though it seemed that she had just cleaned the table or stove a short time ago, she was at it again. Visiting in her home was not a restful experience.

Annie had four brothers and three sisters. Some of the children died at a very early age as was the case in many families during that time.

Elisha and Sarah had eight children, all born in North Carolina:

George Apple, born about 1834

Jane Apple, born about 1836

Julia Apple, born about 1839

Lewis Apple, born about 1841 in Caswell County. Lewis Apple married Mary Louisa Patterson – November 18, 1866

Milton William Apple, born about 1843. Married Ellen (Ellender) McBride – October 21, 1868

Elizabeth Apple, born about 1845

David G. Apple, born about 1846. Married Elizabeth D. Hale – October 8, 1868

Sarah Apple, born about 1849. Married Melvin Hale – November 22, 1866

There is a discrepancy as to whether Lewis was born in Caswell County or Guilford County, North Carolina. Cemetery evidence would tend to lean towards Guilford County only because an enclave of Apples lived in that area.

In a relative short period of two years, four of the eight children were married! David and Elizabeth had six children. George and Evoline married about 1859 and had four children: Thomas H., Nancy S., Georgia A., and May Apple. Lewis and Louisa had eight children, including my Grandmother, Annie Drucilla Apple. Milton and Ellender had nine children. Perhaps many young men and women decided that after the Civil War was over, they could now live in peace and begin their families.

Lewis had served in Company F Corp, Arkansas Infantry as part of Coxey's Army.[17] There is some inconsistency with regard to the CSA military unit Lewis enlisted in on June 21, 1862 at Dardanelle, Arkansas. He was in his early twenties. Nancy Gillespie, his great granddaughter has information that it was Cocke's Army. Regardless, the military unit to which he was ultimately assigned was the 15th Arkansas Regiment. Whether or not Lewis saw action previous to an engagement with Union troops on July 4, 1863 is unknown. In this action a CSA contingent was directed to relieve military pressure on Vicksburg, Mississippi. Union troops were occupying an area at Helena, Arkansas located on the Mississippi River in mid-eastern Arkansas and about eighty miles south of Memphis, Tennessee. General Theopolus Holmes led the Confederate soldiers. The attacks of the CSA were driven back. However, Lewis sustained an injury to his shoulder and was captured by the Union troops on this date. He was transported to a military hospital in Memphis, Tennessee for recovery and perhaps treatment of his wounds. He was later imprisoned in a military prison in Alton, Illinois on October 12, 1863. Yet another transfer was made on August 23, 1864 to Camp Douglas, Illinois.

As the Civil War was drawing to a close in 1865, Lewis was transported to New Orleans and became an exchange prisoner of war on May 23, 1865 just three days before General Simon Bolivar Buckner surrendered the last Confederate army also in New Orleans. No doubt Lewis' exchange was a prelude to the final protocol of ending the war. Records are not available as to how Lewis made his way back home or what his physical condition may have been. There is little doubt that his return was a happy occasion because he had survived some of the most terrible conditions men had ever faced in warfare to that time in history.

Two of Lewis' brothers also experienced enlistment in the CSA. George enlisted but for some reason decided the army was not for him and went AWOL. Milton enlisted for the South in June 1863. Where he served is not known. He was discharged in February 1864.

In 1870, census records indicate two Apple families living in the Spring Creek Township, Yell County, Arkansas. One family included Sarah Apple, age fifty-eight, a daughter, Jane B., age thirty-five, David G., age twenty-four, and Elizabeth, age twenty-two.[18] It appears that David is a relative newly wed to Elizabeth and living in this household. The second family is comprised of Lewis Apple, age twenty-six, Mary Louisa, age twenty-five and two children, James E., age three and William G., age one.[19] There isn't any mention of a husband in the family grouping for Sarah. It is believed that she had been widowed previously. These data seem to conform to previous information relating to her land patent filings in 1857 and 1860. In 1872, Lewis is listed as a registered voter in the Spring Creek precinct.[20]

My great grandparents, Lewis (sometimes spelled Louis) and Mary Lou (Louisa) Patterson Apple initially lived in the Spring Creek township of Yell County. Later, they would make the highlands their home on the Mountain in west central Arkansas, near Millard and Liberty and not far from Shoal Creek in Logan County, southeast of Paris, Arkansas. This is the Magazine Mountain area, which is the highest ground in all of Arkansas at about 3,000 feet above sea level.

The mountainous area of Arkansas is aptly described as "the bottoms are walnut, white oak, the red and black oaks, gum, mulberry, hickory, white ash, cottonwood, box elder, and a variety of others. On the uplands are post oak, hickory, cherry, pine, red and black oak, etc. On the north side of Magazine Mountain are found immense quantities of wild cherry, and black walnut, of immense size, from three to five feet in diameter, and straight as an arrow for many feet without limbs. There is perhaps a larger quantity of oak than of any other timber; pine is not abundant."[21]

The children of Lewis and Louisa were Harvey Galeton, George William 'Will', Lou Ellen, Annie Drucilla, Bessie, Markus, James Elisha 'Lish' and Maggie Bell. It is said that Maggie Belle was a "front liner and head turner"[22] wherever she ventured. She had coal black hair, dark eyes, and natural rosy red cheeks with a complexion second to none! My grandmother to be was another offspring, Annie Drucilla Apple.

I do not remember seeing my Grandmother Moudy without her apron. She wore it from sunrise to sunset. I believe it was her signature for her perpetual cleanliness movement. Very few pictures were taken of her without an apron on and even then I'm sure someone had to suggest and coax her to take it off.

Grandmother lived in Belleville, Arkansas in a home built on my Uncle Lee Moudy's property within about one hundred and fifty feet of his home. Uncle Lee wanted it that way so that she could live a good life as best as he could provide for her after my grandfather died.

Because my parents moved to California while I was still a youngster, I was not around my grandmother very much. When I was at her home or we were visiting family and she was present, I seldom saw her smile or seem joyous about anything. I got the impression that she was a rather serious person. Perhaps life had not been what she had expected or hoped it would be. I do not know of other reasons that would account for her demeanor. On the other hand, it's possible my interpretation is very different from others who knew her more closely than I. She was kind to me but I never felt very close to her.

Cousin Melbarene Barrick describes in her writings the workings and daily life of the Will Apple family, Annie's brother, as they worked the family's homestead farm on Mount Magazine. The land had been obtained through his homestead applications. Although Melba indicates that the farm is listed in the National and State Historical Listings, my research has not been able to confirm this fact. Will was an excellent farmer as were most Apple families. Living on the mountain meant that temperatures were always cooler up there by six to eight degrees because of the higher elevation compared to the valleys below. That temperature difference affected the timing of the harvests on the mountain and meant that the mountain crops matured later. The maturing crops could be as much as a month later than those already harvested in the valley thereby creating a ready market for these late crops. The vegetables and fruits were most often sold from this farm into the local communities of Belleville and Havana.

Stories and Information Relating to the Apple Family

During my early childhood years in Arkansas, I recall very little contact with members of my Grandmother Annie Drucilla (Apple) Moudy's family. What little involvement that probably occurred went unnoticed by me at the time even though I was connected to the Apple family. I learned a bit more of this connection after the family moved to California. I feel that lack of association has been a major loss for me since I covet very dearly family connections and relationships.

Great uncle George Willie 'Will' Apple, Lewis' son and brother of my grandmother, homesteaded eighty acres on Mt. Magazine, or as more often referred to as 'the Mountain'. The homestead had been acquired on March 22, 1906. The family raised an abundance of crops on the farm with excess to sell in the local towns and to the resorts on the Mountain. The farm was located more specifically in Section 17, Township 6, Range 24 West in Logan County, Arkansas. The geography of the area is mountainous on a bench which lies about one and one-half miles east north-east of Mt. Magazine highway. It is several hundred feet higher in elevation than the community of Millard and at the ford of Shoal Creek. The home place was a thousand feet lower than the high point on the Mountain with the farm being located about one and one-half miles to Millard, which was the nearest store and school bus stop.

Helen Dean (Apple) Hill wrote about her mother, Irene Apple, who married Alfred Lee Apple, son of Will Apple. "My mother always worked so hard! There was a lot to do, cooking for 8 people, washing on a rubboard and ironing. I can't recall ever seeing dirty dishes or an unmade bed. We cooked on a wood burning stove which had a warming oven. Beside the stove was a shelf for making bread, etc.[23]

When we came home from school, we'd get a baked sweet potato or bread, and onion blades from the garden. We milked 6 to 8 cows and separated the cream to sell. Our horses, Lily and Star-who had a white star on her forehead-pulled the plows in the fields all day, or pulled the wagon to Havana, Belleville or to the lodge on Mt. Magazine, to deliver the produce we sold. One winter we took a wagon loaded with fence posts to Paris. Dad would heat rocks to put in the wagon to keep our feet warm. If it got too cold, getting out and walking would warm our feet."[24]

"Lillie Moudy would give me a permanent each fall before school began and take potatoes, onions, etc. for her pay. The grocery store took produce for our purchases, also."[25]

"We walked 1½ miles to Shoal Creek to catch a pick-up that took us to Rich Mountain School…later we were bussed to Paris High School where I graduated in 1950. During winter, with late daybreak and early sundown and darkness, (mother) she carried a lantern and walked with us to the bus stop on school days and often came to meet us when we needed that light in the late afternoon.[26]

Once it rained so much, the creek was getting very swift and we couldn't get home. We spent the night with Ila Grist and her mother Mrs. Daniels. I know Mom and Dad worried about us, but they knew Ila would take care of us.

In the 40s we had Pie Suppers at Mt. Salem to raise money for Christmas fruit and candy. We had a big Christmas program. Also in the 40s we had battery radios. When our battery was dead, we would walk to Highnights (neighbor) and listen to the Grand Ole Opry on Saturday night. If their radio wouldn't work, Mrs. Hignight would walk the 1½ miles to our house to hear the news, when their son Claud was in the Army."

Nancy Lee (Apple) Gillespie remembers, "People came from all over on Sundays in watermelon season. The front porch was the serving table. The melons were so sweet that drops like sugar water appeared on the halves when they were cut open."[27]

She further described how the meals were approached with a prayer, "Papa Apple (Will Apple) always sat at the head of the table and said the blessing. To this day I remember the rhythm of the blessing, but even then I didn't know a word he was saying (because of his mustache and his head was bent 'way over), but I never worried about it. I knew it was the thing to do and I wasn't the one he was talking to anyway."[28] Food that was prepared for meals is long remembered very fondly by family members by most of us who lived some part or all of their lives around these parts of Arkansas. "We always had plenty of food – ham, bacon, beef, fruit and vegetables. I remember the table of food Grandma Apple always fixed for lunch and dinner, breakfast too. Ham, bacon, gravy, biscuit and red-eye gravy. I would love to have some of those meals again. We had some good times and bad times on the mountain. It's something I will always remember."[29]

Anyone who lived on a farm back in those days enjoyed it when one of their town/city dwelling cousins came for a visit. Most often they didn't know anything about life on the farm. Getting one of the family visitors down in the barn for milking was always good clean fun. This is what Mona (Apple) Schnepp who was living in Portland had to say about her experience (Mona is the daughter of Willie and Jimmie Apple). "Charles, G.L. (George Lee) and Joe took me to the barn to see the cows and to milk them. Well, I couldn't get anything out of them so I said 'How come these triggers don't work!' They thought that was really funny. They were milking and squirting each other, and since I had never had 'cows' milk before, it was quite a shock when I started to drink it. I didn't try it any more."[30]

The Will Apple farm was special to the family and to the area as well. The produce, fruits, grains and other crops grown there made it outstanding. Others who were farmers in the surrounding communities of Yell and Logan counties can recall many of the same experiences in one way or another. Some farmers had a better life than others. Even so, in all my remembrances of hearing stories about the 'good old days', most people seemed to regard that part of their lives as being the best times.

My cousin, Dr. Robert Thomas Moudy (Bobby Tom) passed along a couple of stories about the Apple family and in particular Will Apple. The Will Apple farm was located on Mount Magazine. The mountain is a little less than 2,800 feet in elevation which compared to Belleville that is about 500 feet above sea level. Due to the cooler temperatures at the higher elevation, most of the crops and fruits on the mountain were later ripening. The crop of watermelons on the Will Apple farm always ripened about a month later than those grown around Belleville. The quality of the Apple farm melons was always very good and it seemed that people needed a lift during the 'dog days' of summer after the local supply of melons had tended to wane. Local watermelons grown in the Belleville community were a special treat around the 4th of July when they were especially juicy and sweet. There was a lull of nearly a month until Will Apple brought his wagon load of melons to town. It seems everybody waited for him to bring his mountain melons so they could enjoy another summer treat.

As mentioned earlier, the elevation made coming off the mountain on a dirt road with a wagon loaded with produce or other items was a dangerous sort of trip. The wagons had brakes but they couldn't stop a heavily loaded wagon on those grades. Certainly a team of horses or mules couldn't hold back a heavily loaded wagon on the down slope even with the driver trying his best to pull back on the reins and hold the brakes as tight as he could get them. The locals living on the mountain came up with a good solution, which apparently worked rather effectively. Before beginning the journey down the mountain, they would cut a tree of reasonably good size and chain it to the back of the wagon and drag it. It caused enough drag and resistance that the loaded wagon could be better controlled. Once the bottom of the mountain had been reached, the tree was unhooked and left beside the road. No doubt the trees being dragged made their own new ruts in the road beside those caused by the rains every year. Makes me wonder how big the pile of trees got every year or if anyone came along and cut the trees up for stove or fireplace wood. Will Apple might have used this technique when he made his annual trek to town with his load of watermelons!

Harve Apple experienced a very unfortunate incident. While working in the woods, a branch or limb of a bush hit him in one of his eyes. It injured his eye severely. In those days, doctors were not always readily available and proper treatment was not given in order to save his eye. The infection set up in the injured eye soon impacted his remaining eye. The result was that he lost his sight in both eyes and was blind from that point for the rest of his life. The family lived in the community of Corinth, near Belleville for a period of time. Losing his sight, however, didn't keep Harve from being active.

Harve would walk from Corinth into Belleville on the dirt road. When he got to my uncle Lee Moudy's home, he would have someone there walk with him the few hundred yards further into town. The reason was simply that he wanted help crossing the Highway 10 and the railroad tracks safely. Bobby Tom indicated that he had helped Harve on many occasions in this manner.

Another cousin wrote about Harve and the development of a keen sense of hearing after he lost his sight. It seems that Harve's sister, Ellen, had died.[31] Her husband had remarried but for some reason deserted his wife and family. Unexpectedly one day, Harve, who was now living in Hot Springs, went to the barbershop for a haircut only to hear a familiar voice from the past. He recognized the voice as that of his former brother-in-law, Frank Benefield. Yes, indeed it was Frank, who acknowledged the same when Harve asked him! The conversation continued for a while and subsequent to their happen-stance meeting, Frank decided to return home to his wife, Ted.

Herbert Apple, a son of Harve Apple, it seems was a highly respected and talented man born with dry wit humor. He was a hard worker on the farm, and a person who performed the unusual. For example, he pulled some of his own teeth with a pair of pliers because he believed that he needed dentures. Unfortunately, Herb was to have leukemia attack him from which he could not recover. This poem was written by cousin Melba for Herb:[32]

To Us He Was A Blessing
Lord, please tuck an extra blessing
Into Herb's work-worn hand,
For loving his neighbor as himself
While laboring here in this land.
He had so much work to do,
From early morning 'til late , late,
But if someone else was in need,
His work could always wait.
He had a great talent for talking,
Either to young or to the old.
He talked to the hunter in the woods,
Or to a mother with a baby to hold.
He always had an attentive ear,
If you had a problem to talk about.
And he furnished us so many laughs,
We could never give a full account.
His advice, "Don't neglect your children,
Enjoy them now while you may,
For today you have them with you,
Tomorrow they'll be gone away."
He was a faithful cowpuncher,
He treated each animal with pride.

But he couldn't do all this by himself,
    He had to have Audrey by his side.
Lord, I know he wasn't perfect,
    That's why we need you as an Advocate,
Sometimes it's best if a trial arises
    So we don't stay in the same old rut.
The doctor said his time had come,
    Time to set his house in order.
But in mercy, You blessed him greatly
    By letting him grow two years older.
He was a very sick and weak man,
    But he fought a good fight,
He finished what You had for him to do,
    And he did it with all his might.
He never gave up or even slowed down
    He kept plodding and pushing along.
He even helped cover the church house
    After his strength was already gone.
Now he's gone, and even if we could,
    We wouldn't want to call him back.
Seeing him leave with a smile
    Makes us know he was on the right track.
The world doesn't have too many
    That was made from this same mold,
The outside was a temple of clay,
    On the inside was a heart of gold.
He was a great friend and neighbor,
    He was a wonderful family man.
He will be missed by all of us,
    For we were each a 'Herb Apple' fan.

By Melbarene (Shott) Barrick

Nancy (Apple) Gillespie (granddaughter of Will Apple), told me about her grandfathers.

At the time, the family lived in the community of Corinth. The dirt road from Belleville to Corinth had a small hill to climb just outside of town, which required the team of horses to work a bit harder to get up that hill. The family had become accustomed to the sounds of the wagons and could differentiate between the wagon and team of horses that Grandfather Apple drove versus the team driven by her Grandfather Hayes. In either case, each of them would come along rather late in the evening. It seems that when Grandfather Will Apple hauled a load of produce down from the mountain and made his sales, he would spend the night with the family because of the distance from home. The next morning, he would leave to make his way back home to Mount Magazine, which was a distance of about 17 miles as Nancy Lee remembered.

Nancy related that her Grandfather Hayes was a heavy drinker. She thought he was probably an alcoholic but back in those days it wasn't recognized as such. He too would return home late because of his drinking. The family always knew when he was arriving because he would run his team of horses and get them lathered up, thus making a completely different sound in terms of the horses' hooves and the running of the wagon wheels over the dirt road. What she didn't say was what sort of mood he was in when he arrived!

FAMILY TREE

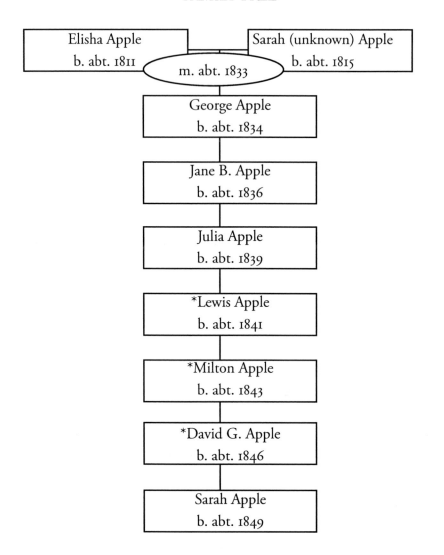

Elisha Apple
b. abt. 1811

Sarah (unknown) Apple
b. abt. 1815

m. abt. 1833

George Apple
b. abt. 1834

Jane B. Apple
b. abt. 1836

Julia Apple
b. abt. 1839

*Lewis Apple
b. abt. 1841

*Milton Apple
b. abt. 1843

*David G. Apple
b. abt. 1846

Sarah Apple
b. abt. 1849

Note: All children were born in North Carolina, probably in Caswell or Guilford County.

There isn't any record that Jane or Julia ever married.

* Served in the Confederate States Army during the Civil War.

FAMILY TREE

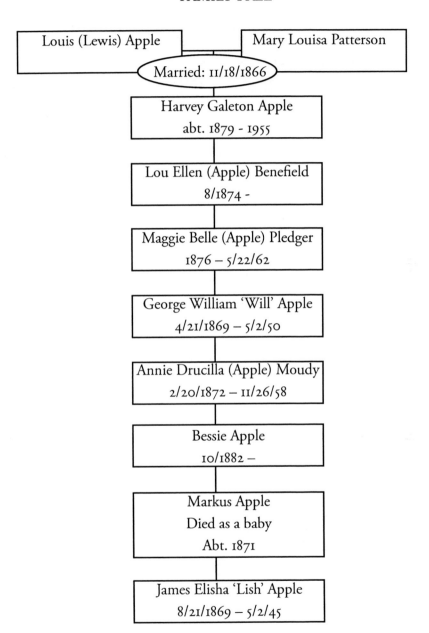

Louis (Lewis) Apple — Mary Louisa Patterson

Married: 11/18/1866

Harvey Galeton Apple
abt. 1879 - 1955

Lou Ellen (Apple) Benefield
8/1874 -

Maggie Belle (Apple) Pledger
1876 – 5/22/62

George William 'Will' Apple
4/21/1869 – 5/2/50

Annie Drucilla (Apple) Moudy
2/20/1872 – 11/26/58

Bessie Apple
10/1882 –

Markus Apple
Died as a baby
Abt. 1871

James Elisha 'Lish' Apple
8/21/1869 – 5/2/45

FAMILY TREE

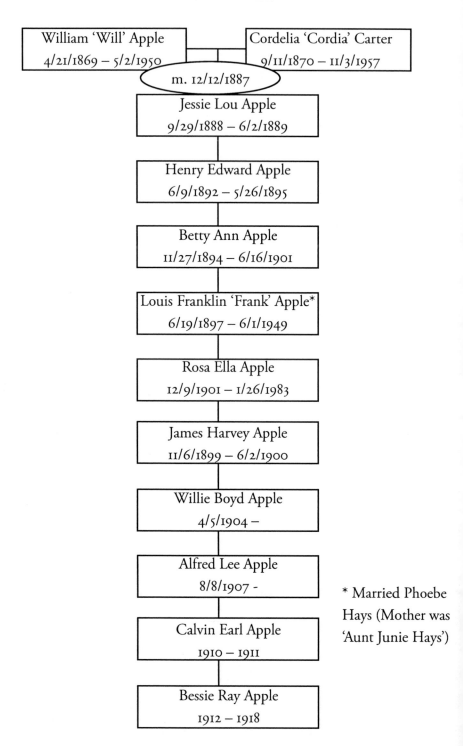

William 'Will' Apple
4/21/1869 – 5/2/1950

Cordelia 'Cordia' Carter
9/11/1870 – 11/3/1957

m. 12/12/1887

Jessie Lou Apple
9/29/1888 – 6/2/1889

Henry Edward Apple
6/9/1892 – 5/26/1895

Betty Ann Apple
11/27/1894 – 6/16/1901

Louis Franklin 'Frank' Apple*
6/19/1897 – 6/1/1949

Rosa Ella Apple
12/9/1901 – 1/26/1983

James Harvey Apple
11/6/1899 – 6/2/1900

Willie Boyd Apple
4/5/1904 –

Alfred Lee Apple
8/8/1907 -

Calvin Earl Apple
1910 – 1911

Bessie Ray Apple
1912 – 1918

* Married Phoebe Hays (Mother was 'Aunt Junie Hays')

FAMILY TREE

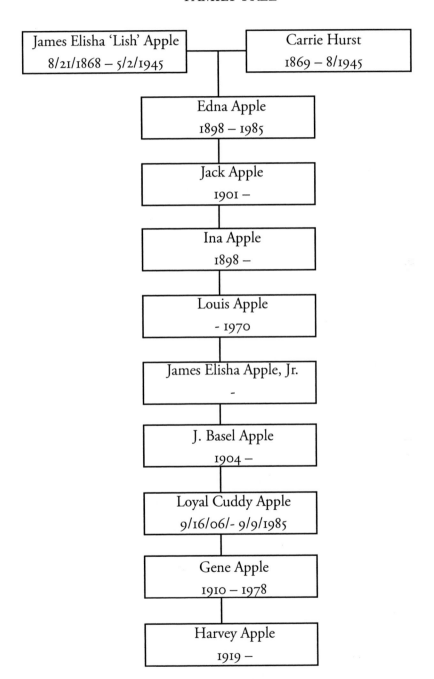

James Elisha 'Lish' Apple	Carrie Hurst
8/21/1868 – 5/2/1945	1869 – 8/1945

Edna Apple
1898 – 1985

Jack Apple
1901 –

Ina Apple
1898 –

Louis Apple
- 1970

James Elisha Apple, Jr.
-

J. Basel Apple
1904 –

Loyal Cuddy Apple
9/16/06/- 9/9/1985

Gene Apple
1910 – 1978

Harvey Apple
1919 –

FAMILY TREE

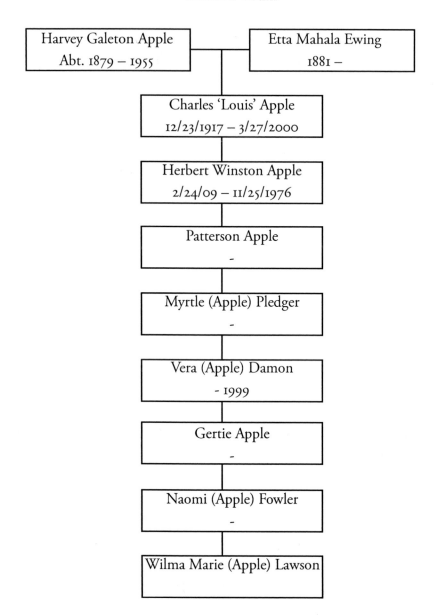

Harvey Galeton Apple	Etta Mahala Ewing
Abt. 1879 – 1955	1881 –

Charles 'Louis' Apple
12/23/1917 – 3/27/2000

Herbert Winston Apple
2/24/09 – 11/25/1976

Patterson Apple
-

Myrtle (Apple) Pledger
-

Vera (Apple) Damon
- 1999

Gertie Apple
-

Naomi (Apple) Fowler
-

Wilma Marie (Apple) Lawson

FAMILY TREE

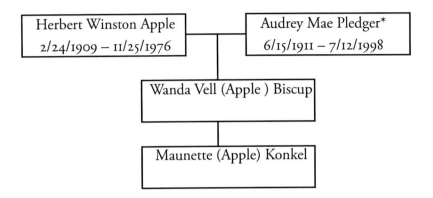

| Herbert Winston Apple
2/24/1909 – 11/25/1976 | | Audrey Mae Pledger*
6/15/1911 – 7/12/1998 |

Wanda Vell (Apple) Biscup

Maunette (Apple) Konkel

* Parents: John Simeon and Willie Austin Sanders Pledger

FAMILY TREE

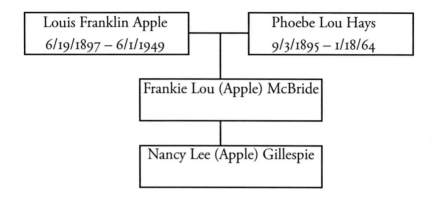

Louis Franklin Apple
6/19/1897 – 6/1/1949

Phoebe Lou Hays
9/3/1895 – 1/18/64

Frankie Lou (Apple) McBride

Nancy Lee (Apple) Gillespie

FAMILY TREE

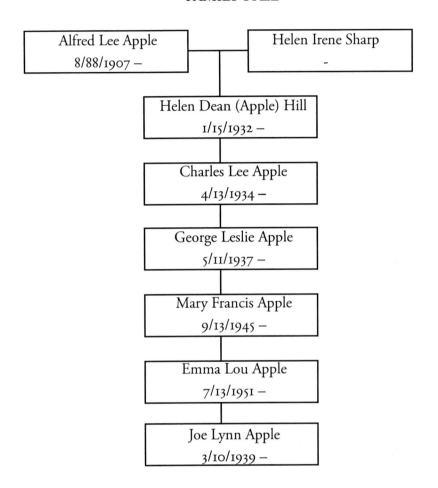

———•·••·•———

[1]   Ancestral information obtained from Ellen Loise Bouton Moudy Capehart, September, 2001.

[2]   Unpublished manuscript, *Indian Atrocities Along the Clinch, Powell and Holston Rivers*, Emory L. Hamilton, pages 79-80.

[3]   1842 Weakley County, Tennessee Tax Book, District 12.

[4]   Sullivan County, Tennessee Census 1830, pgs. 294, 340, 343, 1840, pgs. 128 and 149, and 1850, pgs. 70B and 71B

[5]   Goodspeed's History of Tennessee Sullivan County, New River Notes, pgs. 1 and 2 of 10.

[6]   Bureau of Land Management, Land Patent Certificate No. 8824 containing 40 acres issued 2/29/1888 signed by President Grover Cleveland and Land Patent No. 7058 containing 40 acres issued 5/1/1861 signed by President Abraham Lincoln. An additional 80 acres were received according to the Federal Land Records, Yell County, Arkansas as per Certificate No. 5904 issued May 1, 1860.

[7]   Taken from copies of church records.

[8]   Civil War Soldiers and Sailors System, National Park Service, website: ww.itd.nps.gov/cwss/soldiers.htm

[9]   Copy of Record of Patent No. 975004, issued by the United States of America, March 2, 1926.

[10]   Website found at freepages.genealogy.rootsweb.com/~monticue/index.htm

[11]   *A Colonial History of Rowan County, N.C.,* The North Carolina Historical Society, Volume 16, No. 1, page 5.

[12]   Ibid, page 5.

[13]   History of North Carolina Counties, webpage, taken mostly from *The Formation of the North Carolina Counties, 1663-1943*, by David Leroy Corbitt, NC Department of Cultural Resources, 1950.

[14]   Ibid, page 3.

[15]   *Apple Genealogy*, page 6, Stephen W. Apple and Karen Booth Apple, Gateway Press, Inc., 1992

[16]   Bureau of Land Management, General Land Office Records, Patentee Search, January 23, 2004

[17]   *...And Life Goes On*, 2001, by Melbarene Shott Barrick, page 30 and 31

[18]   1870 Federal Census, Yell County, Arkansas, Spring Creek Township, as of June 13, 1870, page 2 of 11.

19   1870 Federal Census, Yell County, Arkansas, Spring Creek Township, as of June 17, 1870, page 3 of 9.

20   1872 Voter Registration List, Yell County, Arkansas, Spring Creek Precinct, October 21, 1872, page 12 of 42.

21   *Logan County Arkansas – Biographical and Historical Memoirs of Western Arkansas,* Logan County Arkansas Genealogy, www.couchgenweb.com, page 3.

22   *...And Life Goes On,* page 56, Melbarene Shott Barrick, 2001

23   *Wagon Wheels,* Logan County Historical Society, Fall/Winter 1999, Vol.19 No. 2, pg. 5.

24   Ibid, pg. 5.

25   Ibid, pg. 6.

26   Ibid, pgs. 7&8.

27   *Wagon Wheels,* Logan County Historical Society, Spring/Summer Volume 20, No.1, pgs. 4&5.

28   Ibid, pg.5.

29   Ibid, pg. 13.

30   Ibid, pg. 13.

31   *...And Life Goes On,* Melbarene Shott Barrick, 2001, page 60.

32   Ibid, page 63.

CHAPTER FOUR
Proud to be Cherokee Indian

It was well known in our family that we were of Cherokee descent. It wasn't talked about very much in my family but when mentioned, my mother always discussed this fact with great pride. The linkage with a Native American tribe came through the family bloodline of my mother's mother, Rebecca Adeline (Smith) Talley. It was her ancestors who brought the Native American connection into the family.

As I have read, although not extensively, about the Cherokee Nation's history, its trials and tribulations, I find myself sympathetic toward these Native Americans and appalled by the shabby and inhumane treatment meted out by the euro-immigrants, now Americans. It makes me wonder how the white European settlers and the government of the United States could have so despicably treated this organized tribe of people with their own government who always showed respect for other people and had a great love of nature. Perhaps we, as the transplanted people of this Nation, are more tolerant and accepting after the passage of more than one hundred sixty years since the Trail of Tears. If that is true, that in and of itself doesn't rectify or justify what has been done to Native Americans in the last 300 years!

I do not want to diminish the pain and suffering endured by the euro-white settlers as the westward movement progressed. Both groups of people suffered indiscriminate loss of life as the frontier advanced, sometimes without justifiable reason. In reality, it is a sad indictment of both sides that an extended series of conflicts and wars had to be the standard of conduct instead of peaceful co-existence. Regardless, after many efforts to make peace, the conflicts were very devastating and took their toll on both sides. What price progress?

I have tried to think back to my own Native American relatives, the Smith family, and come to an understanding of their surroundings and circumstances. Could the hatred and dispisement between the Native Americans and the settlers been so poignant and permeating as to ultimately cause them to consider relocation and restarting their lives? Did they on a daily basis face the possibility of mistreatment? They may have been recipients of misconduct and experienced moral misgivings because they were considered as second class citizens and social misfits and socially unacceptable to the Euro-settlers and city dwellers in North Carolina.

The Smiths, at least in part, were people of mixed blood with the Cherokee, which was probably worse yet from a societal point of view. Was there constant rejection even as they tried to live and fit into a white man's world? Being that the family was part English and Cherokee Indian, I am inclined to think that this was a continuing saga even after they relocated to Arkansas. Half-breeds were not always treated as humans. In a sense, they were not of God's creation; they did not belong in society. Their migration west also could have been caused by a number of issues that were of political importance at the time.

Having felt the stigma of my own social status in the early years of my life heavily influences where my convictions, sympathy, and pride lie. Back in those days, I did not know very much about my Native American connection; but it was apparent to me at an early age that I was an underdog in this country seemingly made up of the 'haves' and the 'have-nots'. While America has mostly been thought of as a strong middle class country, there have always been a substantial group of 'have-nots' in our society.

Even with this concept of the large middle class status of population in this country, for which America has been proud, I believe the greatest change took place in our country after the Great Depression and World War II. That's when the growth of the middle class really became apparent. Nonetheless, if one is on the lower rung of the social status structure, you are often looked down upon by those above you.

I had a lot of self-pride and happiness within my own family because we were survivors among the down-trodden; however, outside of that warm family cocoon I too felt rejection by society's unwritten standards relating to wealth, education, the clothes you wore, what was in your lunch box, home location, the car you drove and social standing. On that basis, as a kid growing up, I actually did live on the wrong side of the tracks. It was evident in part by the way that I dressed and the kind of work and jobs my parents had to perform. I knew it and my peers knew it. For me, I had no choice but to fight back and prove to 'them' and myself that I had just as good of a mind, level of intelligence, and a desire to succeed as they; and that I could compete in 'their' world.

Maybe my Cherokee ancestors harbored some of these same feelings. Just as relocation gave my family a new start economically in life, perhaps relocation gave them that clean sheet of paper in their life that provided them with the chance they needed to live and compete on the wild western frontier. On the frontier, social status didn't count for anything, but survival of the fittest did. Strong minds and wills along with physical fitness added up to success. In one sense, it was Darwinism for sure but it was also real life. In that regard, they did succeed. Importantly, another aspect of success in most families was simply that they didn't leave God out of the equation for a successful life. My family was not an exception to this belief.

The way the Native American's made friends and voluntarily helped the Euro-settlers when they initially came to the new land of America also makes me proud of them. The Cherokees could have been very hostile as were some of the other Indian tribes. The Cherokees were different. They showed the white people how to plant and grow maize and other edible and useful crops. They shared their wildlife reserves. In general, the Cherokee Indians made life a lot easier for the early settlers.

One cannot entirely dismiss the unfriendliness of some natives. There are some people in life that seemingly one cannot make peace with no matter how hard and extensive the effort that is put forward. In most every way, the Cherokees' were a peace loving people. As time advanced, they adopted and adapted many of the white man's methods, religious convictions and even chose Christian names to go along with their native names. They were industrious and intelligent having created their own written language.

Before examining the treatment of the Cherokees, one must review the circumstances and conditions on the Atlantic coast at that time America was being settled by Euro-settlers. Politically, the correct decisions were not made by either the European settlers or the Indian tribal councils. Some of these were the intrusions into Indian territories that resulted in the confiscation of their lands. Initially, the Indians accepted these incursions since there was little interference or impedance with tribal customs, their living conditions, or their hunting grounds.

However, the time came when the United States government, the Atlantic seaboard colonies, and eventually the states, forced the Cherokee Nation to give up huge land holdings, a piece at a time and over an elongated time frame. This confiscation of land was really masked through the making of several treaties with the Cherokee Nation and other tribes. In general, the governments, regardless of federal or state origin, did not abide by these treaties. Subsequently, the white settlers or the government's authorities broke these treaties. Looking backwards, these were deliberate efforts against the Indian tribes to unduly take their lands. The Cherokee Nation signed or was a party to a number of treaties, which literally divested them of their lands.

1. Lochaber Treaty – 1770
2. Augusta Treaty – 1773
3. Watonga Treaty – 1774, sold land they did not really control to the whites
4. Overhill Cherokee Treaty – 1775, sold all land of central and eastern Kentucky to Transylvania Land Company (Henderson Purchase)
5. Treaties of DeWitt's Corner and Long Island (or Holston) - 1777, signed at gunpoint which ceded all land remaining in the Carolinas
6. Treaty of Long Island (2nd) – 1781, lost more land and confirmed the previous treaty
7. Turkey Town Treaty – 1817, ceded lands in Tennessee in exchange for a reservation in northwest Arkansas
8. Hopewell Treaty – 1785, eastern Cherokee lands ceded
9. Holston – 1791, more of the same

10. Philadelphia –1794, more of the same
11. Tellico – 1798, 1804, 1805, 1806, more of the same with the 1806 treaty ceding 10 million acres
12. Fort Jackson Treaty – 1814, 1816, and 1817, four more treaties signed ceding huge land concessions
13. Indian Removal Act – 1830, loss of protection under the laws
14. Treaty of New Echota – 1835, exchanged their homeland for seven million acres in Oklahoma and $5 million.
15. Treaty with the United States – 1846, established the Cherokee Nation in Oklahoma
16. General Allotment (Dawes) Act – 1887, took away two-thirds of their then remaining land base
17. Curtis Act – 1895, dissolved tribal governments and forced land allotments
18. New Echota Treaty, took away all but one-third of 1% of seven million acres
19. Wheeler-Howard Indian Reorganization Act – 1934, new government of the Cherokee Nation permitted
20. 1961, Cherokee Nation awarded $15 million as compensation for the lands of the Cherokee Outlet.

For more than one hundred years the Cherokee Nation was under great stress and pressure from the white settlers, the Federal and state governments whereby their land holdings were confiscated and generally their tribal customs and form of governance were likewise eliminated from civilization. The final solution of the United States government was to herd them into limited lands, having minimal resources, where maintaining their long established way of life became virtually impossible and more or less imposing the white man's way of life on them.

One only needs to examine the lands occupied by the Cherokee Nation from the 1500s to the early 1900s to understand the impact of the many treaties and the treatment by the United States government along with the intruding white settlers. Always remember that the Cherokee tribe was a peaceful loving people. They had great respect for the land and its natural inhabitants whether animal or human. They lived in communion with Mother Nature and the Great Spirit. They came to realize that the Great Spirit was the white man's God, the Almighty!

The constant harassment and disappointment with broken treaties over an extended period of time had its affect on the Cherokee Nation. After great contemplation, a group of Cherokees in Tennessee, that was 4,000 strong, made still another agreement. The terms of this agreement, forced them to relocate to northwestern Arkansas in 1818 – 1819. A few of them arrived by riverboat by traversing the Tennessee, Mississippi and Arkansas Rivers. Others came by wagon, rode horses, or walked. At the time of their arrival, the Indian population in the new designated area, including the new arrivals, totaled more than 6,000.

Among those choosing this 'voluntary' relocation was one noted Cherokee Chief, Tahchee or 'Dutch.' This group of Indians became known as the 'Old Settlers.' In 1828, the Western Cherokee again made another agreement to exchange their lands in Arkansas for lands in Oklahoma. The area in which they lived stretched from near Russellville, Arkansas on the Arkansas River northwesterly to the Oklahoma border near Fort Smith and north eastward to the White River. The 'Old Settlers' did leave this area about 1830; however, Dutch strongly resisted the move to Oklahoma and instead moved to the Red River valley of east Texas.

Interestingly, the Cherokee Nation according to records of inventory in 1826 revealed some prosperous and wealthy Indians. Many of them had learned the basics of the white man's approach to life and living. They had begun to accumulate their own wealth in white man's terms including purchasing Black slaves and indulging in commerce as is noted below:

1,560	Black slaves
22,000	Cattle
7,600	Horses
46,000	Swine
2,500	Sheep
762	Looms
2,488	Spinning Wheels
172	Wagons

2,942	Plows
10	Sawmills
31	Grist Mills
62	Blacksmith Shops
8	Cotton Machines
18	Schools
18	Ferries

It is unknown if this inventory included the entire Cherokee Nation or merely some portion of it in the Arkansas area.

By law and understanding between the tribes and the Federal government (perhaps misunderstanding), there were to be three groups of Cherokee Indians. The Eastern Cherokee were located in western North Carolina and are not really considered part of the Cherokee Nation since they chose to become United States citizens. An estimated 8,000 live there presently. The Echota Cherokee Tribe in Alabama were also descendants of the Cherokee and protected from removal because they were individual landowners by the 1817 and 1819 treaties. They did not have to relocate.

Presently, the largest group of Cherokee Indians lives on reservation territory in eastern Oklahoma, which was provided by agreement with the Federal government. These people were a composition of Cherokees who were living in eastern Tennessee and surrounding areas. The long and painful journey from Tennessee to Oklahoma began in May 1838 when an army of 4,000 regulars and 3,000 volunteer soldiers under the command of General Winfield Scott initiated the forced march upon these souls. Six hundred forty-five wagons lumbered over frozen ground with their cargo of suffering humanity. Not all rode in wagons because there was not enough room. Many were sick and barefooted. They had been driven from their homes without blankets before the march began. They were put in unhealthy holding areas waiting for the ultimate day when they would depart for their new land. This was the start of the infamous Trail of Tears (The trail where we cried!) of Indians from all Cherokee areas (14,000 after a loss of 4,000 on the trail which are referred to as the 'silent graves') and includes specific groups which migrated separately at different times.

The Western Cherokees, who originally settled in Arkansas (6,000), and the Texas Cherokees driven there by the Spanish of Louisiana and later driven by three Texas militia regiments across the Red River, eventually settled in Oklahoma. Those in Arkansas did not fare well either in terms of the Trail of Tears. There were about 3,000 Cherokees and Creek Indians combined with the majority being Cherokee, being led by Chief Benge, who made the trek to Oklahoma. This group of Indians was one of thirteen who voluntarily made the move under their own supervision. They departed on September 28, 1838 and arrived at their destination on January 17, 1839. Out of 1,200 beginning the trip, 33 died enroute and there were three births. W. B. Flippin wrote in 1899, "Many (of the Indians) were well dressed and riding good horses; fine looking men from their appearance they were half-breeds, while many were poorly clad. Many of the women had only a blanket wrapped around them while those with babies had them strapped in cloth attached to their backs. It was winter when they came to the White River and ice was frozen along the banks, they forded the river and made camp shortly. They built big fires that burned all night. The Indian agent had priced them and brought provisions for those lacking."

"The Trail of Tears came through Baxter and Marion County. The trail was called the 'Old Military Road'. I understand from some of the Marion County history that the road left the Mississippi River near Memphis and went through the town of Batesville, on up near the banks of White River until a good ford was found to Denton Ferry, at a farm now known as the Joe Fee place. This place was known as the Talbert Ford, later Talbert's Ferry. The road crossed Boone County and on into Indian Territory. I am told that because Shawneetown (now Yellville) was such a trouble town, the Indians were sold whiskey, that they bypassed this town on the Old Military Road, going north of it probably leaving the Military Road about Wilkerson Crossing. The other 'Trail of Tears' crossing for Arkansas was up the Arkansas River. There may have been more that I have not read about."

My Native American bloodline and heritage is limited physiologically. Many generations have passed from the time my family had its first half-breed offspring. However, I take great pride in my Native American roots as I do in the Euro-white settlers' contributions and benefits. Today, I am an American and proud of it!

For many years, I have had a lingering desire to better understand that family identity with my ancestors. My grandmother's parents and her grandparents, on my mother's side of the family, relocated from North Carolina to Arkansas in the year 1858 or thereabouts. It is estimated that the trip took three to four months to complete since the wagon train took a rather circuitous route to Arkansas through Alabama.

My Cherokee ancestors were not directly a part of the government imposed resettlement program to Oklahoma. They were probably excluded because part of this family was also Euro-whites. Under such circumstances the family could claim exclusion from the treatment given to full-blooded Native Americans. However, strangely enough, my grandmother's, sister, [1]Sarah Smith, appears to have had a small plot of ground set aside for her in the Indian Territory of northeastern Oklahoma, township 24 north, range 13 east, parcel 1063. This property has never been claimed when family members were questioned about it. To date the information available relating to the family Indian ancestry is incomplete in terms of detail and verification documents such as marriage dates and location for proof as required by the tribal requisites.

Smith Family Relocates to Arkansas

This section relates to the life of the Smith and Woodall families along with their preparation and wagon train trip from North Carolina to Arkansas. It is strictly fictional. I have thought about what it might be like to uproot your family and take them to a place that you had only heard about and did not have any firsthand knowledge or information. This generated the creation of ideas about the process and what it might have been for the Smiths and Woodalls to make the move to Arkansas. To date, not much has been learned about the Smith Family and their past circumstances in North Carolina. The identity of family members who made the journey and those who remained in North Carolina is accurate based upon factual information and data. This information has influenced this fictional portrayal.

My great grandparents, the Obediah Smith family and my great great grandparents, the Leonard Smith family, traveled in a wagon train from North Carolina to Arkansas with others making the same move. There were several wagons and carriages in the group with the exact number being unknown. Obediah and Marguerite Smith had their own wagon. George and Elizabeth Woodall also had a wagon carrying their precious belongings to the land of new opportunity. Some of the family members had been plantation owners in North Carolina and had slaves for many years. Others had been members of the family as they operated the plantations. So what could possibly cause them to leave a seemingly comfortable life for the harsh life on the new frontier? They had undoubtedly lived through tumultuous times laced with personal turmoil at the family level of life perhaps because of social conditions at the time.

Issues, which ultimately brought about the Civil War, were beginning to surface openly and reaching explosiveness when they were deciding to move west. These issues had been developing for nearly two decades. Certainly the Northerners in the federal government who opposed slavery put pressure on the South to abolish this immoral approach to human servitude. It perhaps became a factor in their decision to relocate. The talk of cessation by the South served to further motivate them since war, if it came, would undoubtedly be engaged throughout the Atlantic seaboard and where they lived. War would probably have less of an impact on them personally in the less populated area of Arkansas. After all, moving to Arkansas, a relatively new state in the union, meant that they could continue holding slaves, if they so desired, because it too was a slave state. From an economic viewpoint, the fertile lands that once produced abundant cash crops of cotton and tobacco were being substantially depleted and stripped of their nutrients and their income stream was being continually diminished. They perhaps saw real opportunity in a new land. However, there wasn't any doubt that with slaves to work the plantations it had been a very good life for many decades. That was the magnetism that kept some family members from becoming parties to the relocation. Whatever other issues existed, each family that considered the alternatives made a major decision to either stay or relocate to a new area wrought with new challenges and completely new beginnings. It required significant commitments for each family group.

Although it is not known with surety, it is believed that they probably had only one choice of transportation to their new home. Travel over long distances was difficult in the mid-nineteenth century. Railroads, available in some areas of the country in 1858, could have taken them part of the way to their destination. However, just getting to these few hubs of transportation was a real chore. The cost of such travel was very expensive and did not afford them the ability to take all of the necessities they needed for frontier life. The first bridge to cross the Mississippi River at St. Louis, Missouri was not built until 1857. Although some major roads did exist, travel was mostly over dirt roads with the better roads being topped with gravel. Rivers and streams were forded in shallow areas and ferry crossings used for deeper waters. In all likelihood these facts left them with only one viable method of travel which was with a wagon train group. Group travel provided security and protection from marauders, thieves, and others mindful of assaulting or bringing harm to them. In some areas, renegade Indians attacked the whites whenever an opportunity presented itself. Safety in numbers was indeed important. It would not have been wise to make such a journey alone. Each male would have a rifle or musket and perhaps a handgun stashed in different places in the wagon, carried in their saddles, or stashed in their belts when they were riding horses.

Furthermore, wagons could be loaded, and in fact overloaded, with their clothes, bedding, and some food for family members. A few small farm implements, logging chains, cross cut saws and small animals, chickens and pigeons were brought along too. The only limit was what could be loaded into the wagons. Travel would be slow to say the least but time was on their side.

There had been talk around the plantations and in the towns around Salisbury, North Carolina that new opportunities were available in Arkansas. Subsequent to the Louisiana Purchase in 1803, these lands were made available to those willing to settle in that region based upon the law congress had passed on April 24, 1820, entitled "An act making further provision for the sale of Public Lands". You had to go and settle on it, making it your home. There was also the Act of Congress passed May 20, 1862 "To secure homesteads to actual settlers on Public Domain and the acts supplemental thereto" provided homesteading. The land was described as pristine virgin timberlands with plentiful water from artesian wells, streams and rivers. Wild game was abundant including deer, turkey, wild pigs, quail, wild pigeon and bear. Relocation seemed like a worthwhile possibility.

In early 1857 the decision was made to relocate. It would take several months to plan the relocation details and establish whether or not others might want to commit to making the life changing trip. There was also time needed to get family matters in order. No doubt the decision to relocate would be painstakingly and thoroughly thought through by those choosing to make the move.

During late 1856, several families met on many occasions in their homes to discuss the benefits of relocation and possible destinations. It seemed almost overwhelming to some. There was family to uproot; family and friends to be left behind; and an extended journey of many weeks. Yet there remained for some in the group the magnetic draw of free land; a new start. Once commitments were made, they had to decide what items to pack and when was the best time to make the trip. Many discussions were held for planning purposes. However, in the end, it would be up to each family to decide upon the specifics for themselves.

Another basic question would be the trip and living conditions while on the road. Would it be communal or would each family provide for itself? Perhaps they met at one family's home and then another at different times throughout the intervening months. Except for the children, all of the expected participants had to fully understand their role in the move. The children would be helpers if they were old enough to contribute in one way or another. The trip had to be planned so as to minimize harsh weather exposure. How many people would actually make the trip? Who would be the leader in charge along the way to make critical decisions when difficulties arose? How would they defend themselves from marauders? These were basic considerations. They had to think of the unexpected and unknown problems they would encounter.

Considerable time was spent planning the route that should be taken and how to protect themselves from bands of robbers or thieves along the way. There were also the possibilities of troubles with the Echota Indians who remained on their properties in parts of northwestern Georgia and northern Alabama.

With oxen pulling most of the loaded wagons and horses the remainder, how many miles could reasonably be traversed in a day? Many of the men would ride on horseback the entire trip. How hard could they push their animals? They had to keep them healthy. A good average seemed to be approximately twelve to fifteen miles each day. When the animals were tired, they would take extra rest periods to accommodate them. Each family would have to provide for their own cash needs for the trip. There would be toll roads, ferry costs, pilot fees for fording rivers and streams. They would need to purchase feed from farmers for their animals as well as flour and other staples for their own consumption. Given their belief in God, it was settled that they would not travel on the Sabbath unless forced to do so due to circumstances.

Making plans for a long journey by wagon train in the 1850's was no easy matter. First, there were very few major roads. On the eastern seaboard, there was the 'Great Road' otherwise known as the 'The Great Philadelphia Road', which, traversed from the city of Philadelphia to Savannah, Georgia. In Virginia the Road passed through the Great Smokey Mountains for part of the way then dropped into the valleys and lower terrain of the Carolinas crossing many streams and rivers along its way. Many of the existing roads at the time really began as Indian trails. As the Indians were removed forcibly or by treaty agreement to other lands, they became primary routes of travel for the new world settlers who followed the foot trails. As more and more settlers came the increased usage turned the trails into roads. As new settlements grew, secondary wagon roads in local communities further expanded the road system. As a matter of fact, most roads were not taken care of and maintained except as local citizens and landowners chose to make improvements and repairs. Because of these conditions, many roads became virtually impassible during rainy periods as they would become deeply rutted by wagon wheels and the hooves of horses and mules that labored to pull heavily loaded wagons.

Most relocating settlers put most of their belongings in these wagons including food stuffs, animal grain, drinking water, tools, farming implements, household belongings such as bedding, small pieces of furniture and cooking utensils, and land clearing tools. It took a substantial and well-built wagon with a very hardy and sturdy team of oxen, horses or mules to pull these loads up hills and down and over bad roads for long extended distances. For example, from Philadelphia to central North Carolina the distance was over four hundred miles on these roads. The farther west the pioneers traveled, the less likely they were to find even 'good' roads because of the newness of the territory and its lack of development. Such a move was not for the faint of heart!

At the conclusion of the extensive discussions, the general route of travel decided upon, was southward from Salisbury, North Carolina through the western sector of South Carolina; turn westward into northern Georgia and then into northern Alabama (this was the Indian country); continue the journey by heading slightly northward through parts of northern Mississippi to southwestern Tennessee; cross the Mississippi River at Memphis; then follow a basic route from Memphis to Little Rock, Arkansas crossing the Arkansas River before heading northwestward to a selected territory in Arkansas. This journey would probably take not less than three months and cover about eight or nine hundred miles. On the maps the distance had been measured to be about six hundred sixty miles, but that was the way the crow flies. They estimated another 40-50% distance would be more realistic. Mapping out the journey took time because they weren't familiar with any of these places, never having traveled there previously. Obediah had a good sense of understanding maps and together with his father, Leonard, and his brother-in-law, George, they made detailed plans hoping to not have to change them but knowing full well that could easily happen once on the road due to weather, flooding or other unforeseen difficulties. Maps that were available of all the states they would travel in had been ordered from Thomas, Cowperthwait & Co. in Philadelphia. That was the best they could do.

Their itinerary was planned to take them from Salisbury south through Mecklenburg County to the state of South Carolina. Spartanburg would be the first city they would pass through and then on to Andersonville. There were countless streams, creeks and major rivers to be crossed. The trip seemed formidable. In North Carolina alone there were the Wateree and Catawba Rivers to be crossed or forded. The next rivers to be crossed were the Broad, Saluda and Savannah Rivers in South Carolina. They tried to avoid as many crossings as seemed reasonable by choosing a route to the north in the southern states where the headwaters for many rivers formed. It was a little more hilly but hopefully easier to travel. In Georgia they hoped to replenish food supplies in Gainsville, Cassville, and Rome before reaching the Alabama border.

Once into Alabama they expected to pass through Lebanon, Somerville and Russellville. The rivers didn't appear to be as much of a problem in this area but there would be the Chattuga, Comnesauga, and Echota tributaries to contend with along the way. At Warranton, their plans were to move through the mountain pass and cross over into the Tennessee River Valley. That route would take them along the northern most areas of Alabama and Mississippi making it an easy leg of the journey into Memphis, Tennessee. Their choice of direction would take them through Cartersville and Holly Springs, Mississippi. Once they were ferried across the mighty Mississippi River, they would be in Arkansas making their way to Little Rock. They would get more detailed information in Little Rock about locations in the area where they might settle.

The route was chosen to avoid travel over the Great Smokey Mountains. Furthermore, weather would be a factor but by going through the northern areas of the southern states the weather would be milder. Detailed maps were not available to assist them with early planning. There wasn't any way to know how many streams and rivers they would have to cross. As they ventured into each segment of the trip, they would have to make inquiries and make decisions on the fly. For preplanning purposes, they relied on people who had traveled in the areas and any other information they could obtain. Many travelers returning from the west did not offer much encouragement. Some were unable to cope with the living conditions and were physically sick while some were just plain 'homesick.'

At one of their last meetings with all of the latest information in hand, the final plans were made and agreed to by all travelers. The route selected was to travel south from Salisbury, North Carolina to Charlotte. Continue southward into South Carolina to Rock Hill where they would be able to cross the Catawba River. At that time they could turn in a westerly direction towards Spartanberg and Greenville crossing another major river in the area on the way, the Broad River. To skirt the southern extension of the Great Smokey Mountains, the wagon train would travel in a southwesterly direction to Toccoa, Georgia. Here in a westward trek, they would travel through Calhoun and Summerville, Georgia before reaching the state of Alabama and the growing community of Fort Payne. Beyond this point, the wagon train would travel northwesterly towards Scottsboro getting closer to the Tennessee state line while passing through the counties of Madison, Limestone and Lauderdale. The wagon train would make its first crossing of the Tennessee River in Madison County at Ditto's Landing. Then they would have to contend with making a second crossing of the Tennessee River, probably in Tennessee. It was believed at the time that the best place to make this second crossing would be in the state of Tennessee in Hardin County at a place called Pittsburg Landing. This group of travelers had no way of knowing that in just another three or four years, this location would become a historic location. A great battle would be fought in this area during the Civil War and would become known as the Battle of Shiloh. From there, it would be a straight line for Memphis where the crossing of the mighty Mississippi River would take place. It would be one of the last two major hurdles before they completed their move. Once in the state of Arkansas, the road would make a run to the southwest and they would finally cross the Arkansas River at Little Rock. Then it would be a relative short time before they would arrive at their chosen destination.

The route established meant that the party would be passing through areas where Indians were allowed to remain in accordance with the various treaties between them and the United States government. This would be particularly true in northern Alabama. The Echota Indians were a branch of the Cherokee Nation.

Important was the disposal of belongings that would be left behind. In addition, they realized there were family members who would not be making the trip and whom they would probably never see again. Perhaps for some, it was perceived as their last opportunity to make a new peaceful life for themselves. It had to be a tearful and stressful time, yet there was that spark of hope burning in their bosoms that brought them to expect that the best was yet to come. Some of the family members were older and some were kids; some were moving and some were staying. It was an exciting but difficult time.

It was difficult to understand why members of these families wanted to leave the good life on the plantation and farm. It had been their life for years. For the Smiths and the Woodalls, there had been the convenience of working their slaves with the owners over seeing the farming operation. The Smiths owned 130 acres whereas the Woodalls were part owners of a 2,800-acre plantation. The owners were responsible for running the business of the farm and plantation and supervising the slaves to ensure that all the work was done in a timely manner. They had to make sure that the crops were planted on time and their large gardens were tilled and cared for in order that the family and slaves had food to eat and a surplus left to sell or trade to others. Orchards had to be tended and pruned after the leaves had fallen. In the fall, there was the harvesting of the crops and the subsequent canning and preserving of the many fruits and vegetables throughout the growing season. Yet the question remained, what was so magnetic about the frontier lands that would cause them to give up this life style and move to Arkansas? Certainly this life was an endless humdrum of activity and busyness. It would be even more so in a new land one would think.

Besides tending the fields during the growing months, there was the ongoing effort to insure that clothing was made for the entire family as well as the slaves. Everybody needed work clothes and frequent changes. Spinning wheels whirled and looms were constantly busy weaving the needed cloth. On Sundays, everybody wanted to wear the finest clothes they had when they attended church and social events!

Regardless of the time of the year, animals had to be fed everyday in order to keep them strong and healthy for the rigors of working the fields from dawn to dusk. Open fireplaces heated all of the living quarters during the long winter months, and therefore lots of wood was needed. Trees had to be felled and cut into usable lengths for the stoves and fireplaces then dried so that it would easily burn. The wood had to be stored and cutting it to size made that chore easier. This had to be an almost constant job assignment among some of the slaves because wood was used for everyday cooking of the meals. But when winter was beginning to close in, special attention was made to making certain enough wood had been laid in to meet their needs through the coming winter.

Water was important too. Wells had to be dug as close to the house as possible in order to keep a supply of fresh water on hand for cooking as well as drinking and an occasional bath. Water was also needed to wash the huge quantities of clothing. Often there was a stream or creek nearby that was used for that purpose. This work was all done by hand using rub boards. There was a great array of clotheslines and fences to hang the clothes for drying. Clothes hanging on the lines or spread on fences were not a kaleidoscope of color since dyed cloth was expensive and dyes were limited in those days. It wasn't just clothes either, there was bedding to be washed as well. Water was important in other locations on the plantation. It had to be carried to the fields for the workers toiling in the hot sun and humid climate of the late spring, summer and fall when the harvest came. Water was either transported by hand or wagon to the fields, obtained from nearby streams or from wells that were located strategically around the plantation for drinking and refreshing purposes. Water was critical for the animals as well. Water was carried to the barn troughs for watering of the animals. In the fields, animals were given water at least twice each day with water being brought to the end of a row in large wooden buckets where the animals were given a chance to refresh. Water was also provided for the slaves at that time.

Harvest time meant storing hay in the barns and putting corn in the cribs. This was food for the animals, including the horses, oxen, chickens, hogs and other farm animals that were part of the plantation operation. Corn was the main staple for the farm animals as well as the many people living and working on the plantations. It was cracked and used for chicken feed. More finely ground corn was used as cornmeal for making mash, corn fitters, hush puppies and cornbread. This grain was used to feed other farms animals as well, including the swine, in years when the crops were plentiful.

When the colder months of fall came, there were other important tasks to be done. The slaughter of the swine took place when the weather got cold, usually in early November. It took many slaves who had to work hard and diligently because this was not an easy process. The pigs and hogs had to be killed; then bleed (drained of the animal's blood) by cutting the animal's belly from its throat to its rear and stringing it up on a large tree limb or a pole specially made for that purpose. This process allowed for the entrails to be removed and the animal was cleaned on the inside.

In the final disposition hardly any part of the animal was thrown away. The intestines where used for the skin of sage and peppered sausages, pig bladders became toys for the children since they could be blown up like balloons. The brains were considered a special treat and a delicacy when fried with chicken eggs and that only happened once each year! The slaughter process required that the animal, after it had been bled, be dragged on the ground a short distance, particularly if it was a large hog, over to a long boiling vat of water that had been built in the ground. This was always a dangerous area and kids were constantly being warned to stay away and be careful when close to the vats. The animal, which had been cleaned of its intestines was placed in the vat fully covering the porker in near boiling water for a short period of time until the hair on the animal became soft and pliable enough for a straight edged razor to shave the hair off the animal until it was clean, smooth and void of hair. Often times while the animal was hanging from the tree, with the blood running or trickling from its body, workers and others of such a mind, would collect the fresh pig's blood by the cup full and drink it down while it was still warm. They would swear that it was good tasting as well as being healthy! The entire effort was hard work and could carry on for several days as long as the cold weather held or the quantity of pigs to be slaughtered lasted. It was a very busy time.

After the animal had been cleaned, it was then placed on a table for butchering. Large, very sharp knives were used to dissect the animal. These amateur butchers were actually seasoned veterans and rather experienced about the proper way to carve up an animal. The rear quarters became hams; the sides were cut for bacon; tenderloins were taken from underneath the backbone mid-section area and were a prime cut of meat; the shoulders became roasts or ground up for sausage; the ribs were saved and cooked or roasted; the head was generally used to make minced meat for pies and other delightful dishes. The feet were cleaned, cooked and pickled as a delicacy; generally the tail and the ears were cooked on the hearth of the fireplace in the evenings on the day of the killings as a special treat for the children. The intestines were cleaned and used for stuffing sausage links. However, most of the sausage was treated differently and canned. The effort was not complete until the hams had been cured, often by hickory smoking, and hung in the smokehouse where they would remain until used by the family. The fattiest part of the animal was used to make salt pork by cutting it into small hand-sized pieces and layering them in a wooden barrel with salt and leaving it to cure over time until needed. Sausage was often made into patties or balls, fried, and canned in fruit jars. Mincemeat was also canned in the same way.

The remaining fat of the hog was used to make soap. First, the fatty tissue was cut into small pieces and boiled in a large iron pot over an open fire that held perhaps twenty gallons or more. The big iron pot was balanced on four or five rocks so that it would not tip, since it had a round bottom, while the soap was being made. The fat would separate during the heating process of rendering thereby leaving mostly the cooked skin of the pig, which was referred to as chitlings. The hot rendered fat was then mixed with white lye ashes from the fireplaces or stove. There may have been other ingredients but once the mixture had been thoroughly cooked, it was then allowed to cool, leaving a somewhat hard material but still soft to use, in the bottom of the pot. Once cooled, the soap was then cut into bars, or cakes as some called it, with a big butcher knife. Then it was ready to use. Those skins, which had been removed from the cooking pot weren't thrown away either, they were the pork rinds which became treats for everyone. They were crunchy and crispy and made a great snack.

Plantation living was a unique way of life. It was somewhat routine but brought about a good life for the owners. There was also the social recognition in the community; your friends, most of who would have struggled early in life just as most families had done, were your neighbors. There was also the heritage of your forefathers that had made all of this possible by their striving to gain a new life in this new world of America. Oftentimes, land holdings were split and passed along to siblings upon the death of their parents. Some people had obtained their position in life through the estates of their parents or other ancestors. Yet something gnawed at the very soul of a man to find his own way in life. It was repetitive, in a sense, from an ancestral standpoint but that burning desire to make it on your own could only be satisfied by each individual on his or her own terms. Thus came the decision to make the move to Arkansas.

Thinking about reestablishment in a new land, the individuals themselves had to consider what would be needed while making the trip and their needs upon arrival. The Smiths had decided to sell their other three slaves and keep the one free slave, Gustus, with them if he so desired. The Smiths had treated their slaves well and with respect. Gustus had always treated them with kindness and respect. That was his nature. He never shirked his work and had a cheerful disposition. For the Smiths, consideration had to be given to the necessary accommodations during the trip that should be made for the free slave that they had decided to bring along. No doubt the individual was to be of great help along the way. Being a free slave, Gustus did not have to make the trip unless he had some remaining indebtedness related to gaining his complete freedom. He chose to make the trip.

There were also the decisions regarding the farm animals that were going to be taken with them. Perhaps the discussions had been long and detailed as to why some animals and certain items would be included and not others. A cow would definitely be needed in a frontier setting. Where else would they get milk? The availability of cows was very limited on the western frontier. What about horses? Chickens were needed too. This domesticated fowl was used for the daily diet at breakfast and dinner. Some eggs had to be kept and set aside for hatching and raising more chickens as well. How many pigs should be brought along? Should these be young or newborn pigs to save on weight, space and food? Where should these noisy, grunting and squealing animals be kept? Probably most important of all were the oxen. Should there be one or two pairs? These were very versatile animals needed for pulling the wagons and plowing the fields. These oxen were destined to pull the loaded wagons day in and day out for more than eight hundred miles over rough and difficult dirt roads through rocky and often rutted terrain and cold winter weather that had made the roads muddy and nearly impassible and hot summer conditions when water would become very important. When they crossed streams or shallow rivers, time would have to be taken to not only refresh the animals but allow the wheels of the wagons to soak and swell to prevent loss of the iron rims. Farm implements and land clearing tools would be needed. They would need seeds for future plantings for their gardens and fields as well. There was some hope that the latter could be purchased locally or ordered from an eastern source once they settled. How could they get all of these things together and in one wagon? Space in the wagon would be limited.

There was also the element of the 'unknown', which they believed would be inevitable but obviously unidentified at the beginning of the trip. What contingencies should they include in their plans in order to limit their risks along the way? Most notably, there wasn't enough room to take enough food for each family and all of the animals for a four-month trip. That would be impossible. Therefore, plans were made for some members of the party to be responsible for hunting fresh meat such as shooting squirrels, rabbits, wild turkey, prairie chickens and perhaps a wild bore along the way. When that was not possible or productive enough, they planned to purchase food as needed along the way when their supplies were near depletion, ran out or as they became available. During these days, grains generally were selling for twenty cents per bushel. Farmers would quickly sell butter for the extra money. These purchases could be made from local farmers along the way. Also, there would be the occasional military fort that they would pass but these were very infrequent and far apart. They believed that at the forts they could restock a lot of their needs at the general store. Life on the road would not be easy.

Some of the family members perhaps received their inheritance before they left, knowing this would be their only opportunity to obtain their rightful share. They probably received additional money from the sale of belongings such as clothes, farm implements including plows, cooking utensils and other possessions that could not be taken with them. In any event, being strangers in an unknown and possibly hostile part of the country meant that cash money would talk. How much they brought is unrecorded in pages of time but it had to be the only reliable and available source for commercial exchange when they couldn't barter. The money, consisting of Spanish silver dollars which were still in use, a few U.S. gold and silver coins, and some gold bullion would be stored in a lock-box in the bottom of the wagon and covered with anything that would not draw attention to the location. If they really got into dire straits, they could sell or trade some of their precious belongings. They would need to raise additional cash or barter for goods to get them out of trouble. The anticipation of moving was building day by day as the time neared for their departure to the Arkansas frontier.

The seeds of change had been planted in the minds and hearts of the Smiths, Woodalls and others for many months and now all their efforts were coming to fruition. After all, being Indian or part Indian had played a major role in the decision process for the Smiths. The Indians had been mistreated for more than a century. Their Cherokee culture and ancestors had suffered at the hands of the Federal government, state government, and the inconsiderate white people as well. At one time, their forefathers had befriended the white men who came unexpectedly to their shores. In fact, the Cherokees had helped them to survive the early wilderness life and assisted them as they adapted to the primitive uncivilized world of America. The Indian Wars had been fought and lost. Treaties had been numerous and they had virtually all been broken by the white settlers. Time after time, the Cherokees had been forced to cede lands to the ever encroaching and growing population of white settlers. It was hard to understand how and why all of this had happened and was continuing to occur. They could no longer hunt and fish as they once did. Everything had changed. They were ready to move on.

Even as the departure time was nearing, my great grandfather, Leonard Smith, continued to hear talk among the white population of another possible war. It sounded ominous. He was concerned about the possibility that another war was coming. This war would not directly involve the Indians. He believed this war would probably pit white man against white man. The whites were having trouble within their own government and the political unrest was growing. The major issue was between white brothers of the North and those of the South centered on slavery. The arguments were on both economics and Christian Judeo principles and ethics regarding slavery. Admittedly, it was hard to understand. He and Rebecca had discussed these issues many times. Their ultimate conclusion was that war seemed inevitable. It was clear that whites of the North didn't want to have slavery. Their convictions were very much like the majority of the Cherokees. The white populace of the South had a different opinion. They wanted to have slaves. They believed slavery was proper and needed in order to prosper economically. After all, who would pick the cotton and work the plantations, if slaves weren't available? Leonard and Rebecca were convinced that relocating would remove them from the middle of another war. Indeed, it was time to move.

The departure time was set for 6:00 a.m. early on Monday morning in mid-March. This time was chosen primarily because of weather consider-ations. The winter would be over in the Carolina's and other southern states and the very cold temperatures would, for the most part, be past. There certainly would be rain showers. The plantings in the fields were getting underway and the trees were sprouting their buds. By the time they reached Georgia and Alabama, the fruit trees would be in full bloom. It would be beautiful to see the sights. In addition, arriving in Arkansas in late July would provide warm weather and give them time to seek out the lay of the land and decide where it would be best to put in for the winter to come.

For several days before mid-March, the things to be taken were being collected in one area of the house and on the verandas. Some items would necessarily have to be on or near the top in the layers of packing inside the wagon in order to repeatedly retrieve and use them easily. This included foodstuffs, cooking utensils and kitchen implements such as candle molds, kettle, skillet, boiling pots, pans, rolling pin, biscuit pan, and bedding. Many of the items were made of cast iron and heavy. In addition, there were tools that would be needed and which could be used along the way such as a wagon jack, broad axes, felling axes, felling saw, rip saw, bark spud/chisels, shovel blade, sickle, scythe, rake, fork blade, several planes, and a thrasher fork for winnowing. Marguerite wanted her yarn winder and spinning wheel. Each wagon would need a water barrel hanging on the side of the wagon for drinking water and buckets hung beneath the wagon to water and feed the animals. Certainly Obediah had to pack his powder keg. He would carry his bowie knife in its sheath on his belt. The wagon wheel grease was packed for easy reach. Packing all of these items was painstakingly slow at first. In fact some things were unloaded and re-packed to get it in the right space to save room and balance the load. The wagons had been almost completely packed on the Saturday before their departure since there was a rather strong conviction by most everyone in the community about not working on Sundays.

The Sabbath was a day for resting and going to church. It was the Lord's Day. Many of their neighbors stopped by to spend time visiting and talk-ing with the Smiths, Woodalls, and Riders on that last Sunday. They asked about their trip and explored what they knew about the state of Arkansas. It had only become a state in 1836. Why was it 'the Land of Opportunity?' They wanted to know just what might be happening once they arrived. How will a new piece of property be selected? Will there be people already settled in the area? Why was Arkansas the choice for relocating? Won't this trip be difficult for the small children? Being that several children would be making the trip, the ladies spent time discussing the care of the 'little ones' and the care that would be needed on such an extensive trip. Several of the children, including Wincy Ann and the baby, Londy Woodall, were still in the diaper stage. Their older sister had been out of diapers for a little more than a year. There certainly was justification for the concern of these little children. Elizabeth felt the concern very deeply and strongly; she had already lost her first born, Alfred.

Marguerite Smith was expecting her second child. That brought on an even greater air of excitement but also one of concern. She believed that the baby would be born while they were enroute. The family was aware of a disease that was hereditary in the Rider line that could affect the bone and joint structure of a male child and greatly affect his ability to walk normally. This hereditary condition had been linked to the female gender as the carrier and it would be passed along to male offspring. It would in later years become known as *osteogenesis imperfecta*. Both the Rider and Smith families knew of the condition. It had come to light prior to the marriage of Marguerite and Obediah. In fact, this had become an issue which caused the Smith's to initially oppose the marriage. But here she was pregnant with child and committed to making the move.

Marguerite indeed had some concerns about her condition. One concern had to be whether or not she would give birth to a male child and would it be afflicted. Secondly, the child she was carrying would be born along the way to Arkansas. Those issues alone made the trip seem highly questionable and less palatable for some of the women that afternoon. Perhaps some of the ladies couldn't understand how or why their neighbors would undertake any relocation without taking more than one slave with them to help with all the chores and needs that they would have in the days ahead. Why couldn't they wait to move until after the baby came? That would be the sensible thing to do. These ladies for the most part were well taken care of and were highly pampered living on the nearby plantations where slaves did virtually everything except have their babies. The slaves acted as mid-wives and wet nurses.

The men took time to discuss how their fathers and grandfathers had endured settling in a new land just a few decades previously. Clearing land wasn't easy. However, these new frontiersmen would not have to contend with Indians, as did their forefathers. They re-checked their lists of tools to make sure that important items had not been overlooked or forgotten. These gentlemen respected and loved each other for many years. Their families had been raised together. John Woodall, Jr. had convinced his father to bring a gift of a few 'chews' of his premium tobacco for Leonard and Obediah Smith as well as for George, his young brother. As a last bit of relaxation and endearment, Adam Rider broke out one of his favorite moonshine jugs that he'd brought along for the men to enjoy a nip or two of that home made 'white lightening' before they all went their separate ways that fateful Sunday afternoon.

There were many relatives and long time friends there that afternoon that would never be seen again in this life. It was sad but yet considered a part of life during this time in American history. Many people felt the call to new lands, new frontiers, new places, and the need for new homes. The eastern seaboard areas did not have enough room for everybody anymore.

This was the first round of 'saying good bye'; tomorrow morning it would be time to do it all over again with just the family.

What do you say to anyone, let alone a relative, that you know you will probably never see again? When you are older the inevitable seems more plausible but what about the same issue when you are so young? For the men, it was more wishing them well, shaking hands and giving a hug. With the women it was different. They cried and shed tears as never before. They hugged and held each other and sort of whispered words of caring, love and good fortune in the ears of the one leaving. Then, there were more tears as they made their way through the group of gathered ladies and friends.

The day of departure arrived. The Smiths and Rider families had been invited to spend their last night in the area where they had grown up at the Woodall's Plantation. The slaves had aroused early at 4:00 a.m. that day. They put on their finest starched aprons and began to prepare a wonderful home cooked plantation breakfast in the kitchen house. The guest diners would eat and even gorge themselves knowing such a meal would be their last one like this for a very long time. There was something that everyone liked to eat.

Not everyone could sit at the dining room table so other smaller tables had been carried to the veranda in order to accommodate everyone. Elizabeth Woodall had insisted that everyone have a place to sit and eat this grand meal. The tables were covered with platters of fried eggs. Other platters were piled high with that delicious southern hickory smoked ham. If you preferred bacon, it was there; thick sliced and cooked to a crisp. Missey, one of the slaves tending the cows, had milked four before the sun was up so everyone could have all the fresh milk they wanted. Lola, the main kitchen cook, had made several pans of her beautiful and delicious buttermilk biscuits. She made sure that there was enough red-eye gravy to go around. She had two large pots of boiled black coffee. She knew to be careful serving it because the grounds would quickly wash into the cups if she didn't strain it. Just to make sure that no one was left out of their favorite dish, she even prepared some southern fried chicken with thicken dob gravy. She said to all but no one in particular, "And iffins any left over, y'all are 'posed to take 'em with ya! That's what Master Woodall say. I sho' do hate to see y'all leavin' for that wild country over them mountains yonder. But I knows you wont be hungry fo' a few days!"

By six o'clock, the plates had been cleaned, and it was time for the wagons to move out. John Rider and his brother Cecil scurryied around watering and feeding all the animals that were to make the trip. Thomas Smith was doing his part as he brought the pairs of oxen from the barns over to the loaded wagons and with help put the yoke and cradle in place on their heavily muscled and firm necks and then hooked the pair to the wagon. In the meantime, Leonard and Obediah Smith were busy checking the loads in the wagons making sure all the tie-downs were secure for the chicken coops. Halters had been tied to each of the three cows and then tied securely to the back of the wagons. George Woodall was busy installing the wagon pendulum odometer on the Smith's wagon. This mechanism would record the swings of the pendulum and by multiplying the circumference of the wagon wheel, the distance traveled each day could be calculated.

There was nothing left to do but climb up onto the wagon seat or for the kids to crawl up inside the wagons onto the quilts and cover them warmly against the early morning coolness and to soften the bumpy ride on the rutted dirt roads. Those riding horses swung into the saddles and perched high with straight backs reflecting the confidence of a new world ahead. Again, and for the last time, everyone was busy saying 'good bye' and reaching a hand out to touch and stretching and leaning to make one last hug and giving a kiss for the last time.

The departure was at hand. There wasn't anything else to be done. The wagons were packed and loaded; it was time to leave. It was an early cool spring morning in mid-March 1858 just before the trees of spring, the apple blossoms and dogwoods, began to bloom and the flowers showed their buds for the first time after a long winter. The Smith and Woodall family members making the journey included:

Obediah Smith – Husband (about 41 years)

Marguerite Caroline 'Peggy' (Rider) Smith – wife (33 years old)

Sarah Caroline Smith – Believed to be about one year old

Leonard Smith – Father to Obediah & Elizabeth (Smith) Woodall (about 61 years)

Rebecca (Workman) Smith – Mother to Obediah & Elizabeth (Smith) Woodall (Indian name – Shining Star) – about 59 years

Elizabeth Evoline Woodall (Leonard Smith's married daughter) – age 38 years

George Washington Woodall (Leonard Smith's son-in-Law) – age 41 years

Rebecca Louiser Woodall – daughter (about 8 years old)

Wincy Ann Elizabeth Woodall – daughter (about close to 7 years old)

Londy Evoline Woodall – daughter (baby about 5 years old)

One Free slave – Gustus (Age unknown but probably about 40 years old)

Before the wagons were out of sight, Marguerite was thinking how the tears flowed easily for most of those saying their good byes. She was already remembering how those leaving gathered themselves and finally climbed aboard the wagons. Those remaining climbed up the few steps and gathered around the large pillars underneath the portico. They could see the guide lines draw taught about the oxen and heard the crack of the whip as the command for the oxen to move the wagons was given by Leonard and George. Slowly, the wheels creaked as they began to roll. It wasn't hard to hear the crushing of the small gravel under the iron rims on the wooden wheels as they moved forward. It was a good thing that the oxen were strong animals because it was very obvious that the oxen strained as they leaned forward under the pressure of nearly overloaded wagons. Obediah Smith mounted his steed and moved to the front of the wagons as they began to pull away towards a new land and new experiences. In about one hour, these two families would meet up with the rest of the wagon train on the south side of Salisbury, North Carolina to begin the long journey in earnest. It was indeed exciting but a sad time as well.

In the first wagon and seated were Leonard Smith, driver, and his wife, Rebecca 'Shining Star'. Leonard held the reins to the two pair of oxen. In the second wagon was their daughter-in-law, Marguerite Caroline (Rider) Smith with baby Sarah Caroline and Gustus. Gustus had been in the family since he was born and was well liked. He would be driving the wagon with Obediah on horseback close by. Perhaps on any other trip, Gustus would be perched at the back of the wagon with his legs tucked underneath him on a pile of feed sacks with nothing to worry about but making sure that something didn't fall or roll over on him. Gustus was as strong as a mule and still in his prime of life. Seemed like he was able to carry anything he put his mind to doing. In the third wagon, George and Elizabeth Woodall were seated up front and on make shift pallets behind the spring seat were the three young children, Rebecca, Wincy and Londy. They wanted to have a place in the wagon where they could see out the front and see what was happening as they rode.

For the Smiths, the last two weeks involved some unexpected developments. Their son, and Obediah's and Elizabeth's brother, Thomas E. Smith, had decided not to make the trip. It was a very difficult decision on his part since he was entering manhood and he would have to make it on his own. He had been born in 1836 and being twenty-two meant that he was nearing the age of marriage. An important person had come into his life and he was serious about her. That young lady was Elizabeth A. Ward. She was a year older and had been born in 1835. The fact was, these two were planning to be married in the next few days. These plans had only been completed very recently and they didn't want it to interfere with those moving to Arkansas. They had discussed moving to Arkansas later, within a year or so. Moving to Arkansas and owning their own land seemed like a perfect way to start their young married life together. For now, they would remain in North Carolina and complete their marriage plans. They too, had stood on the portico of the Woodall Plantation home vigorously and enthusiastically waving their good bye!

Marguerite (Rider) Smith was leaving her father, Adam, Jr., and his new wife, Rachel, two brothers and six sisters in North Carolina. Each one was special to her. She wondered if she would ever see Catherine, Susanna (Susie as she was known), Haules, Magdalena (Mary), Elisabeth, Susan, Ludewig, and Sophia again. Marguerite's mother, Barbara, had just passed away in 1853. Her parents had been married for forty-nine years. While her children were still trying to accept her passing, their father, Adam, who was now seventy-four years old, was starting a new family before a year had passed after Barbara's death. In addition, Marguerite was leaving four aunts and two uncles and their families. Another one of her aunts, Elizabeth (Betsy) had died in Kentucky almost fifteen years ago in 1843. These were her kinfolks with whom she had grown up. With most of these people, she had established some endearing and very close relationships and friendships. It was indeed hard leaving family and friends.

Marguerite's favorite uncle, John (age 71) and his second wife, Irene (age 69) stood with their children, Samuel (age 37), Emily (age 35), Obediah (age 33), Catherine (age 30), John (age 29), and Cecil (age 28) and Marguerite (age 25) on the portico and watched their cousin leave with her family. Unknowingly, Marguerite would see some of her cousins again back in North Carolina.

John Woodall (age 61) and his wife, Elizabeth (age 56) felt even more alone. Their first three grand daughters were moving away from them. It would be a difficult time adjusting to life without your first-born and his family. They understood the reasons but didn't like it in the least. They too stood there in compelling silence with knots in their stomachs with their remaining children David (age 30), Margaret (age 33) and Ellen (age 36) watching their oldest son vanish out of sight. This was more painful than they had even imagined. It was hard to see the wagons disappear out of sight. The ladies dabbed their eyes with their handkerchiefs as the last vestiges of their brother's family disappeared from view. They were gone.

It didn't take our travelers long to discover some of the situations facing them. Crossing the first major river, the Catawba, revealed that one could quickly have misgivings about seemingly ordinary things. First they were approached by 'salesmen' on horseback who told them that crossing via the ferry was their most expedient and least expensive option. It would save the wagon train considerable time as well. Before a decision could be made, however, a young man on horseback came up to them and pleaded for them to make the crossing upstream where the water was shallow and slow moving and it wouldn't cost them any money.

An immediate question arose as to the integrity of both. The young lad was bold and earnest about his position and pleading and told a story of thievery and murder by the ferry operator that wrongfully took the life of his father. The salesman slithered away having lost another customer to the young man. What was his charge to be Obediah asked, "nary a cent" said the young man who began to direct them upstream as he had described. Indeed, he knew the river. He demonstrated the depth of the water by riding his horse completely across the river and back for all to see. The travelers watched as the depth of water never reached his stirrups. When he returned, he stated that there was a hard rock bed on the bottom of the river that was virtually flat giving the animals good footing throughout the crossing, and it was an easy crossing for the wagons. Obediah thanked him and gave the young man a dollar and they proceeded across the river.

It had been a valuable and good lesson to learn early on their trip. It was also one that they did not forget as they would see it repeated many times on their journey. In some cases it was strictly a judgment call. For other crossings there wasn't any other way to cross the rivers and creeks except by ferry.

While enroute in Alabama, Marguerite, gave birth to a still-born child, a boy. The wagon train had a temporary delay while they waited to give the child an appropriate burial. They had made the gap just passed Warranton, Alabama having crossed into the Tennessee River Valley when the birth happened. This was slightly more than half-way into the journey and almost six weeks of time had gone by. This was a lesser populated area. It was in the hill country. Obediah decided to ride on his horse a few miles back where they had passed a farm where he might be able to obtain some sawn lumber. There Obediah was able to purchase the needed lumber from a local farmer. In fact the farmer removed it from the walls of his barn. Enough lumber was secured to build the casket for the baby. Obediah and his father, Leonard, measured the tiny little casket and cut the wood to just the right size. The baby's casket was pieced together with tender care. It was indeed a sad time for the family and the several members of the wagon train. George Woodall felt a need, and looked upon the effort as an honor, to dig the small grave. After all, the child was his nephew.

A burial site was selected near a grove of southern pine intermingled with wild rhododendrons with bloom buds nearly ready to burst. Peggy thought this site offered shade in the hot summer months and was protected in large measure from severe winter weather. It seemed to be the only thing she could do for this little one whom God had placed in her womb but took from her before life had been breathed into his little body. The baby was wrapped in its small quilt and placed in the casket. Leonard offered a few words from the Good Book and said a prayer of thankfulness for God's mercy and grace that had been given to them on their journey through life and in the death of this little one taken from them. Such events take a toll on every one of us simply because we can't understand the Almighty's purpose in having us endure such experiences. With his words completed, each person cast a handful of dirt on the little casket as it lay in the freshly dug grave. They had bid the baby farewell in this life. With this final farewell to the little one, they sang the old gospel hymn *We Shall Overcome*. All of the other children of the Obediah and Marguerite union were born in Arkansas.

The journey had been long and arduous but uncomplicated. Stopping every day to find a suitable place to set camp became routinely monotonous. They tried to cook a good breakfast each morning before resuming the journey. They cooked enough food to have leftovers for dinner. Then there was a fire to build as well as finding some good wood to burn so that supper could be cooked. Often supper was a time to munch a cold biscuit or piece of cornbread with a glass of milk, if they had any. Usually someone had been able to hunt wild game for the evening meal or for breakfast. They had learned to eat rather lightly. Enough food was cooked each day to allow for cold food to be eaten as they continued their daily passage of twelve or so miles. That had been a pretty good average for daily distance traveled because it translated into about seventy miles each week, and they never traveled on Sunday.

The animals were holding up very well except for having lost a couple of pigs, which they ended up shooting for food. Being on the road for more than several weeks, the chores and activity within the wagon train had become somewhat routine. There were always two men appointed to stand guard each night. Before turning in for the night's rest, the animals were fed and watered. At the campfire in the center of the circle of wagons, someone always seemed to have a story to recite to the tired and weary travelers. The dancing and flickering of the firelight often acted as a hypnotic potion that caused them to feel the need to go to bed quickly. They were very good storytellers and there was always the question as to whether or not it was a true story. The teller always kept them guessing. There were times too when they just sat around the fire and sang songs such as *Old Susanna* and *Pop Goes the Weasel*. A fairly new song they had learned was *I've Been Working on the Railroad*, which had been written after a few railroads had been built and trains were still unique and seemingly monstrous machines. Early on, some of the kids wanted to know if anyone on the troupe had ever ridden on a train. The adults remained silent after the question until someone decided to answer the question, "Reckon not! Seem pretty dangerous to me!"

While they were in Alabama, the Smith's had decided to have a special dinner. It wasn't too long after the baby had been buried. Leonard was tired from driving the oxen day in and day out. In addition, the family had suffered the terrible loss of the baby boy. He spoke to Rebecca first and suggested that they should take one of the chickens and cook it. He thought that this would bring some life back into the family. She agreed and talked to Marguerite about it. She was apprehensive at first to talk to Obediah but thought so positively about the idea that she did anyway. With some hesitation, Obediah agreed that the idea was acceptable. He didn't want to be contentious with his mother and father.

What a treat for the family. They were tired of stewed squirrel and dumplings and corn mash or cornbread. A few times they had enjoyed roasted wild pig shot during the day as they traveled. The chicken was absolutely delicious and reminded them of meals back home. There wasn't much chicken to go around when the Woodalls came over and joined them but there were lots of biscuits and gravy to share. Indeed, it was a special occasion to be remembered for years to come as the best meal on the entire trip.

Their travels through Alabama were of concern because they knew some Indians had been allowed to remain on their lands because they had chosen to become United States citizens. In particular, the Echota tribe of the Cherokee Nation lived in this area. It had been nearly twenty years since the last major problems with the Indians had been resolved. They concluded that they would just be extremely cautious as they passed through this area. As those days passed, they had no cause for alarm.

The days and weeks continued to pass by but not as quickly as they had hoped for in their minds. The reality was the trip had few problems and unexpected issues to contend with. In general, they had good weather and the usual spring showers. Even these were welcomed since the wagon wheels would soak up the moisture and swell thereby making the iron rims tight again. There had not been any serious illnesses among the parties. The wagons had broken a couple of axles but they were repaired rather quickly. They encountered the unscrupulous pilots at virtually every river and creek crossing. They had learned very fast and early on that generally if your business was being solicited by these trail hawkers, there was a better and cheaper way to make the crossing. Food purchases were found to be extravagant with prices being more than double what the cost should have been. They had to pay toll fares for 'expressways' that didn't really exists but after a while realized it was an extraction tax on them which they couldn't do anything about. Crossing rivers on a ferry was most expensive and could amount to a dollar per wagon. Sometimes they were charged by the number of animals they had. However, they were closing in on an important leg of the journey. In a few days they would see the 'Big River'.

As the wagon train approached the Memphis, Tennessee area, it seemed that all eyes of the eight families in the wagon train were aghast, children and adults alike, as they drove towards the river front docks. They had been hearing stories of the 'Mighty Mississippi' as they ventured through towns and communities along the way in recent days. Here they were in Memphis, a relatively large city for its day. It had been founded in 1819 and the city was nearing 20,000 as its population was growing. Eight years ago, the citizen count was slightly less than 9,000. Just a year ago, the Memphis & Charleston Railroad had completed its line from the Atlantic Ocean to the Mississippi River here at Memphis. Now they were seeing all of the sights of city for themselves.

As the wagons drew nearer to the biggest river they would ever see, they began to hear the hustle and bustle of the river port activity. The blasting of whistles from the ferries and paddle wheelers on the river could be heard clearly. Indeed, they heard the whistle of the train, the screeching of the iron wheels on the track, and the thunderous roar and the bellowing black smoke of a mighty engine could be seen not too far away. Passing them by on the hard packed road were the plodding of horse hooves on the ground and the crunch of dirt and gravel under the wheels of the wagons laden with large sacks of grain being taken to the grist mill and still other wagons returning with another load of cotton bales. This was indeed a very busy commercial center.

But reaching the ferry landing meant waiting in a line of wagons that seemed to be as far as the eye could see. In a short time Obediah rode down to the docks to find out how long the wait would be. The ticket master told him that it was about a four-hour wait. He looked at the river; it seemed almost impossible that a river could be this wide. The ticket master told him that it was a custom that the ladies come ahead and ride a ferry over to the other side and wait for the wagons there. Obediah felt that many of the ladies would not want to make the trip across the river that way and so he did not mention it when he returned with the news. "Soon, he said, you will see the road was right along the river's bank. There is a flurry of activity as people are crossing in one direction and the other as ferry after ferry is busy one trip after the other!" And soon they clearly saw it with their own eyes! Suddenly, Marguerite realized and called out to her sister-in-law, Elizabeth and the children in the next wagon, "Look across the river, that's Arkansas! That's Arkansas! Way over there!"

The river was indeed a wide expanse of water! They had heard that the headwaters of this great river started far up north in some place that at one time was occupied by the French. They also had learned that many other rivers joined the Mississippi along the way, such as the Ohio, Cumberland, Tennessee, Missouri and Arkansas to name a few. Their geography wasn't real good but they had heard of those rivers but had only a vague idea about their existence. That's what made the Mississippi River so big. No wonder it was referred to as the Mighty Mississippi! From here, it continued its winding way to New Orleans and the Gulf of Mexico and that was still a long way down the river.

River life seemed very interesting and different from other things that they had seen or heard about. There were stern-wheelers and side powered paddleboats that plied the river; some going up and others going down the river. There were bales of cotton and sacks of grain stacked on the deck of the boats. Besides the crew, there were also other people on board who seemed to be enjoying themselves and waving to those on shore. Most of the ladies wore hats and beautiful dresses and the men had high top hats that matched the color of their suits for the most part. The children began to wonder what it would be like to ride on one of those boats. Where were those people going? Were they really going to cross this huge river? Indeed they were if they were going to Arkansas!

They approached the docks where other smaller boats were loading and unloading passengers. There seemed to be a whirlwind of activity going on in every direction. The constant drone of whistles could be heard for quite a distance from all directions. They made you want to cover your ears to muffle their magnitude. Too much of this noise and your head would be aching sure enough! Obediah and George stopped a short distance from the docks so as not to be in the way of the people and wagons waiting their turn to board the several ferries working the river. They had to find out what needed to be done in order for their wagon train to cross this river into Arkansas. All of the ferries were steam driven and belched smoke-like several fire places burning at the same time. It was an awesome sight to see all the things that were happening, seemingly all at the same time. For a neophyte visitor, it seemed like total chaos. The larger ferries could load as many as twenty wagons for each trip across the river!

Obediah and George found the ticket master and purchased passage for the entire group in the wagon train at three dollars per wagon. The price was more than they had expected but they did not have a choice. The ticket master informed them that he would try to get all of the wagons in their train on the same ferry so they would not have to wait on the Arkansas side of the river. He said, "You are heavily loaded and the ferry has to fight the down stream currents going and coming. It takes time to be safe." Turn around time was approximately one hour. This allowed time for loading and unloading the ferry on each side of the river. "Make sure the wagons are paired so that their weights are nearly evenly matched so we can maintain an even keel," he told them. "The pilot will tell you which side of the ferry to run your wagon on for balance."

At two o'clock, the crossing began. The Smiths and Woodalls were the first to load the ferry. Riding on a 'big boat' like this one was a first experience for everyone. Some of them ventured up to the pilot's cabin. To them, the height made them feel nearly detached from the water. George noticed that the bow of the ferry was pointing more up stream rather than directly at the docks on the other side where they were headed. The captain overheard him talking and offered a lesson in navigation. He explained that the ferry had to point in an up stream direction to avoid being swept down stream with the strong current of the river. They reached the Arkansas side with excitement still smothering their thoughts and drenching their minds. It was a crossing that they would never forget.

They had arrived; they were really in Arkansas! They stood on the west bank momentarily and watched each trip intently as the others made their way across the Big River safely. As darkness approached, they decided to pitch camp right on the banks of the river. Now they were realizing that their goal was just ahead; just a few more weeks until they would reach their final destination in Arkansas. Where would their new home actually be, they pondered?

Obediah and this menagerie of people arrived in Arkansas and made their way to Little Rock. For several days before moving on, questions were asked of anyone willing to discuss a new location. To the south were the delta lands, low lying, humid and hot in the summer. To the north and west were large forests of great stands of pine. To the northwest was the hill country, somewhat mountainous, lots of streams and creeks and an abundance of wild game. It was some of the highest in elevation in that part of the old territory and new state of Arkansas.

The Smiths and Woodalls chose to make their way to and initially settled in the Dutch Creek community. It was a relatively small community near Danville and Dardanelle, Arkansas. The community may have had some limited importance to the Smiths since Obediah's mother, being a full-blooded Cherokee Indian, possibly provided a remote connection with Dutch Creek.

This community settlement was named after a Western Cherokee Chief named 'Dutch', which in his native language was 'Tah-chee'. At one time, it had been a thriving Indian center. Reportedly, this Indian settlement was considered wealthy and many of the Indians spoke English very well. However, when the Indians generally agreed to move to the Indian Territory in Oklahoma, "Chief Dutch refused. He took his group of Indians to East Texas. These Cherokees were forced to move to the original destination after a bloody battle with the army of the Republic of Texas in the 1840s."

By 1858, the Indians had long since moved on to Oklahoma Indian Territory although there may have been some small contingent of straggler half-breeds still living among the white men. The location of Dutch Creek may have become simply a part of the Indian folklore passed down through the Cherokee tribe. The Smiths probably used Dutch Creek as a temporary living location for the Smith family and entourage to refresh and get their bearings in this new land. There isn't any other known reason for them to have elected to make Dutch Creek their destination location. For some time after their arrival, time was spent getting the lay of the land, exploring the surrounding areas, before selecting and making application for a land grant from the U.S. Government for a permanent place to call home. The Smiths remained in the Dutch Creek community for a few years, as it turned out, before moving to Moss Creek and then Riley Creek as their permanent home.

A New Life in Arkansas

It is unknown how many families making the journey to Arkansas decided to stay in the general vicinity of Dutch Creek or moved on to other locations and opportunities. It is certain that the Smiths and Woodalls did stay and make a new life for themselves in this pristine virgin land which would become part of and known as the southern Ozarks. The final selection for a home was in the community of Riley Creek. Jonathon Logan gave a description of the Riley Creek area from his personal perspective as recorded in the newspaper of the day.

"Jonathon now lives, in what is now called Riley Township, Yell County-then it was in Crawford County, afterward belonged to Scott County, and in 1840, when Yell County was organized was embraced into our territory(sic).

The first mill built in our County, was put up by the Riley's, in his neighborhood, in 1832. It had a big overshot wheel, and was run by a spring branch flowing out of the side of a hill...game was then plentiful. Turkey and deer were too common to be considered game. Jonathon killed 21 bears during one winter by himself, and has often killed as many as seven deer in a day.

Times have changed, these sports have about ended; fine farms have been opened out; Churches and School Houses erected, and civilization has driven out the rude settlers with the game. Riley Township is one of the best sections of country in the State; its located in one of the loveliest valleys the eye ever beheld, and is almost as productive as the river bottoms. Watered abundantly with pure, limpid streams; health and plenty go hand in hand. Thousands of acres of the best land is yet laying idle, and can be bought at very low figures.

We recommend this section to all in want of homes in a good country, among good people."[2]

Obe the Man

Is your curiosity ever aroused about someone you have never met but learned a lot about? Do you find yourself wanting to know more about that person? The person who grabbed my attention as I gathered information, data and stories about many of my ancestors was Obediah Smith. Who was this man!

I do not know if Obe was ever given a middle name. There has never been a reference made to one. My mother's cousin, Levin Johnson, the son of Aunt Sis, described him 'as extremely broad shouldered and muscular, small in stature and had sandy colored hair.' Since his wife, Margueriet, was only five feet, that would seem to fit from a physical standpoint. Such a description doesn't exactly sound much like an American Native half-breed. It must be remembered that Levin never saw Obediah, so his description was probably passed to him by his mother. Other descriptions of Obediah included words or phrases such as miser and very rich. Supposedly, he 'had an eye for the ladies.' Yet it has been said, his sons-in-law were 'close to him'. They evidently liked him because they saw him and perhaps others did also as a 'man's man.' He loved to party and would invite his friends over when he killed and butchered a wild animal.

Remember, too, that he killed a man in cold blood, so his own family related to him as 'having a mean streak.' That was further corroborated with his known failure to fulfill his obligations under the divorce decree with Peggy. Even, his reason for divorcing Peggy is absent validity if indeed it was for the fact that she had crippling arthritis. Furthermore, his own daughters had to steal from him in the middle of the night just to have food after the divorce.

It has been stated also, but not substantiated, that he was a member of the 'bushwhackers' involved in the killing of George Washington Woodall, his own brother-in-law. That murder took place on the Reed property, which he possibly owned at the time. It is factual that he owned the 'old Reed place', at some point, and 600 hundred acres of Petit Jean bottom land including Cane Island, which was in the middle of the creek, about a half mile south of the Petit Jean Creek bridge. Being rich usually, in the locals' eyes, involved a lot of land. We know he obtained a land grant from the government for 160 acres. He also purchased land from Nimrod Kiersey but the acreage quantity and location is unknown.

Obediah become a rather rich man by the standards of his day. He became a landholder of several hundred acres. He cleared a large portion of this land so that crops could be cultivated. The land grant for 160 acres was signed by President Ulysses S. Grant in 1876. As a farmer, he cultivated and raised a variety of grains. He was also a bee tender. Most of the honey was also used for family cooking as a sweetner. The excess honey collected was sold or used for barter. He was reported to have bred and raised fine horses, which he occasionally would sell for $75.00 per head. He also had sheep and oxen. The horses were most often used for riding while the oxen were used for plowing the fields and other hard work.

Many stories have been related about Obediah and various things he supposedly did during his life. Most of them seem to carry a shred of truthfulness simply because of the integrity of the person making the comments. It is a fact that Obediah owned a small island, known as Cane Island, in the middle of Petit Jean Creek in the Riley Creek community at one time. Obediah Smith used the island supposedly to hide his horses from the county tax assessor so he could avoid paying taxes on the animals.

Living in Arkansas, more or less on the American frontier, in those early years was difficult and care was taken to hide valuables around the premises in case of an attempted robbery. Aunt Alice Tubbs related to me about how her grandfather, Obediah Smith, would hide money in the attic of the kitchen of the log house, which he built on Riley Creek. She said Rebecca, her mother, told her that Obediah would go into the kitchen, close the door and climb up where he could reach into the attic. There he kept a very large gourd in which he hid his money and gold. He was very touchy and sensitive about anybody watching him or seeing what he did with his gold. She said that when he came out of the kitchen, he would warn them not to watch where he went or to follow him. He said it in such a way that they were all scared to do anything but follow his directions. Apparently, he would take gold and hide it in the woods by burying it. I can still remember the entrance to the attic, which was just inside the kitchen door to the left when you entered from the porch that was the front outside entry.

Another story has been told by several of the Talley sisters about a terrible murder committed at the hands of Obediah. It has been told that a man owed Obediah Smith $75.00. Obediah met this man inadvertently on a trip to the Dardanelle general store. The man was with his very young daughter, related to be five or six years old, on the outskirts of town or near town. Obediah demanded the money owed to him. The man indicated a willingness to pay but asked to keep enough back, which he would pay later, so that he could have food for his family. This apparently incensed Obediah to the point that he pulled his gun from his belt and shot the man dead on the spot, put his body on his horse along with the young child, spanked the rump of the horse, and sent them home. My mother talked about the incident more than once. She said Obediah had to 'lay low' for a long time because the 'law' was looking for him.

After killing the man, Obediah had friends go to town and buy his groceries, supplies, and pay whatever taxes were owed to avoid the lawmen. He stayed clear of town and law enforcement for some fifteen years. He was fearful of being caught and subsequently being prosecuted.

Obediah was a talented farmer and businessman. He owned and operated a sawmill and he also made shoes for the entire family by hand. He was a butcher of sorts as well. He killed and cured his own beef. The hides were tanned and used to make the shoes and harnesses for the farm animals.

He was a lumberman too. He cut the logs used to build the log cabin, which I have referred to many times. This log cabin is believed to have been built in the late 1860's or early 1870's. He later built the addition to the log cabin, which basically doubled the square footage of the house. This log cabin is where my grandmother was supposedly born. Later the house would become my grandfather's primary residence where all of my mother's brothers and sisters were born. This addition to the house was built from lumber sawn in Obediah's sawmill. The house was well built and in full use until my grandfather passed away in 1948. Subsequently, it was demolished and most of the wood salvaged for making a room addition to my Aunt Ollies' home for use by my surviving grandmother, Rebecca A. Talley. The old log cabin had stood for eighty to ninety years and was still in good usable condition.

Obediah Smith probably built the other supporting structures on the farm including the milk house, chicken house, smoke house, blacksmith shop and the barn. We know that everything was completed before 1881, because these items were included in the divorce decree between Obediah and Marguerite Caroline on August 10, 1881.

Obediah Smith ultimately had a strange resentment to his first wife. Anne Moore, my cousin, thinks this probably came about because she could not bear him healthy male children. This may have been a significant factor and became an important issue which helped him to make the decision to divorce his wife, Marguerite. He did not live up to the provisions as stated in the Agreement of Divorce and caused lots of financial problems for Marguerite and his three daughters, Sissy, Dolcinia and Rebecca. The girls from time to time would go back to Obediah's farm on Moss Creek at night and steal chickens and hogs so that they could have meat. They would quickly kill and cure the meat, can it or preserve it in some manner and hide any and all evidence so that Obediah would never know what they had done or have reason to question them.

As time would pass, the relationship between Obediah and Peggy deteriorated severely. Eventually, they would go their separate ways and end the marriage with a nasty divorce. A precursor to this separation was a serious fight in which Obe used a stick of stove wood to crack Peggy across the head resulting in serious injury. As my Aunt Alice stated, "It split her head open." At some moment during the attack, one of the three daughters stepped into the fray to protect her mother. According to Frances (Threatt) Allissie, her mother, Lilly Gertrue (Talley) Threatt, stated that Aunt Sissy grabbed a fireplace poker and got it red hot and threatened Obediah that if he didn't stop hurting her mother, she would kill him with the poker. She must have demonstrated a high level of anger and intensity with her statements because he stopped his attack on Marguerite. He moved to Moss Creek after that incident. The three daughters cared for their mother and apparently nursed her back to health. It is unknown as to the timing of this physical abuse. Later, after this incident, she made the trip to visit her kinfolks in back North Carolina.

Interesting, he also failed his own sons. Yes, they were crippled by disease, but Sarah and David Johnson were caring for the boys when Obediah died. In addition, some of the Woodall daughters were helpful in caring for the two boys for a period of time. I find that to be a magnanimous gesture on their part when one considers that their Uncle Obe could have been an accomplice in the bushwhackers' murder of their father, George Woodall. One cannot know with any certainty that Uncle Obe may have helped the little girls get along until their grandparents arrived to take them into their care. Such a possibility is at best an unfounded supposition. I don't know how long the two groups cared for the boys, Albert and George. Nevertheless, it is a sad indictment of Obediah to have seemingly abandoned them in such a way. The boys died about 1882.

Obediah was living on Moss Creek with his second wife, 'Mia', in her house when he died. They lived fairly close to his daughter, Sarah, and her husband, Dave Johnson. Janina Hunt, or 'Mia' as some people knew her, had been married twice before. She was born in 1836 in Arkansas and first married Noah Hunt. It is unknown as to whether he died or they divorced. Regardless, she then married her brother-in-law, Lewis Hunt. Later, she married Obediah when she was still relatively young, at age forty-four. This is recorded in Book H, Page 218 of Yell County records.

Much later after the divorce, when Obediah died, Andrew Jackson Talley, his son-in-law, and a friend went to his home on Moss Creek, to see if they could find the 'famous' gourd. Apparently they took with them some sort of device that was supposed to locate minerals and in particular gold and silver. This thing was going to help them find the stash. They never did find anything and gave up. However, she said that her dad always thought that Dave Johnson, her uncle, (Aunt Sis' husband) found the gourd and took possession of it before Andrew and the friend arrived.

Left in his estate were equal amounts of $177.00 for each of his daughters. He also left Mia $177.00. A primary question and the missing link is what happened to all the land holdings and their value? Was he deeply in debt and the lands taken to fulfill the obligation? Did he will them to Mia or did she confiscate them under some rouse? These are questions that will never be answered.

When the details are examined, the picture is not bright or laced with insights that Obediah was a good man. To the contrary, he appears to have been arrogant and defiant, broke the laws of civilized men, mistreated his family and died in disrespect and ill repute. Unfortunately, he made many wrong choices in his lifetime. Never has a word been spoken that would lead one to believe that he believed in an almighty living God. For an unknown reason, he was laid to rest outside of the boundaries of the local Riley Creek Cemetery used for common, respected and noble men.

Marguerite (Peggy)

Peggy's children called her 'Mam'. She was fond of animals and had a dog named 'Watch.' In her later years, she had arthritis in her hands so badly that they became so crippled and drawn up that she could hardly use them. She was known to have a very pleasant disposition.

In Summary

Leonard Smith married Rebecca Workman on January 9, 1828. Rebecca was born in 1805 in Davidson County, North Carolina. Rebecca's parents were Thomas Workman, an Englishman from Gloucester, England and Elizabeth Garren. Rebecca was a full-blooded Cherokee Indian. Her Indian name was 'Shining Star.'

Thomas Workman was born about 1777 from the union of Henry Workman and Mary Scribner. Thomas Workman and Elizabeth Garren were married about 1797 or thereabouts in North Carolina. They had five children, all born in North Carolina in Davidson County.

George Workman	born – 1799
James Workman	born – 1801
Elizabeth Workman	born – 1803
Rebecca Workman	born – 1805
Unnamed Workman (female)	born – 1807

The family members are buried in unknown location(s) in Illinois.

It is without confirmation but highly possible that Obediah Smith's brother, Thomas E. Smith, may have made the trip with the wagon train. More than likely, he and his family arrived at a later date in Arkansas.

Thomas married Elizabeth A. Ward and they had two children, Noah W. Smith and Rusberg C. Smith.

Rebecca Adeline Smith was the third daughter born to this union while they lived in Arkansas. It is known that Obediah and Marguerite had two boys, Albert and George who both had a disease similar, if not the same, to my mother's brothers. It is now known as *osteogenesis imperfecta*. It is a chromosome linked disease carried by the female gender, in this case, Marguerite. The disease affects the body's capacity to stand upright in a normal position and affects the joints as well. Depending upon its severity, some people can stand and walk but with great effort and in a somewhat disjointed manner holding onto railings or using walking sticks for support. Apparently, this disease was a known issue prior to the marriage of Obediah and Marguerite since Obediah's family was purported to have opposed the marriage. They nevertheless married anyway.

---

[1] Cherokee Nation Map - Applications For Allotment, 1899-1907, Indian Territory of Northeastern Oklahoma, Township 24 North, Range 13 East, parcel 1063.

[2] *The Independent Arkansian*, July 21, 1876, compiled and reprinted, *Yell County, Arkansas Newspaper Abstracts 1875-1879*, Arkansas Research, by Faye Greenwood Sandy._

CHAPTER FIVE
My Mother's Immediate Family

I loved my mother deeply. Although I cannot compare her to other mothers, I can sincerely hope that other mothers are as good to their offspring as she was to me. I couldn't have asked for a better mother. She was the next to last child to be born into the Andrew Jackson Talley and Rebecca Adeline (Smith) Talley family. She was named Hestella Talley. She was never given a middle name. As she grew up, her family and friends never called her by her given name, instead, they called her 'Hester.' Her brothers called her 'Hash.' Because she didn't have a middle name, she was often asked when filling out applications and other documents, "What is your middle name?" even after having stated previously that she didn't have a middle name.

In the late 1800s and very early into the 20ᵗʰ century, agrarian life was the norm. Much of America was yet to be developed and the industrial age was just beginning. Huge areas of land were still untamed wilderness and yet to be homesteaded by the new American immigrants under laws passed by the United States Congress. In order to convert these lands into tillable productive crop acreage, forests were cleared, settlements sprung up, and the influx of people grew rapidly or so it seemed to them at the time. As expansion progressed westward, there was the intrusion by European white settlers onto lands once freely roamed by the American Indians. It was a land managed by Mother Nature. These settlers brought with them the pioneering spirit and the desire to own a piece of land and that alone was enough to drive them to the frontiers for nearly the entire 19ᵗʰ century.

Mother's grandparents and her immediate family were participants in the development of the frontier in several states and especially in the states of Tennessee and Arkansas beginning in the early 1800s through 1870s. Both her paternal and maternal grandfathers' and grandmothers' families homesteaded some of these lands. They moved from one location to another so that they could own land, clear it with the expectation of earning a living off the land and raising a family while enjoying life as much as possible in rather harsh times. It was a tough economy and a lot of sweat to say the least. Achieve any kind of success generally required large families with numerous offspring with a focus on sons. It was the norm to give birth to your own farmhands. It made a lot of sense at the time because it was most difficult, if not virtually impossible, to obtain hired hands to work most any place and especially on the farms. The settlers were all doing the same things like clearing land, planting crops and raising and caring for their animals. Farmers could hardly make a living to support their own families let alone pay hired workers. The children would learn the total requisites about running and operating a farm and eventually get married and move out on their own and the cycle would repeat itself.

The help of additional farm workers was only needed for relatively short periods of time during the year, primarily at planting and harvest times, another reason they were in short supply. Most farmers learned how to function with just their family members under these conditions. Farmers then didn't have irrigation; it was all dry land farming. Having to depend on the weather made farming a very risky business at best. If it didn't rain, the crops didn't develop. On the other hand, if there was too much rain, the crops could be ruined. Hailstorms could cause severe damage to the plants no matter when it came. Rain at harvest time could also be disastrous. In addition, this was natural farming without insecticides. The array of potential problems must have seemed formidable at times. Regardless, they carried on because this was their life and without or having very limited education, what else could they do? Generally, the males were taught to hunt and farm while the women were taught to cook, sew, care for the children, garden, wash and iron when necessary and most importantly, have babies. Unlike the high class ladies of the South who seldom lifted a finger to do much of anything, a stout and physically strong woman was usually successful on the frontier.

Large families meant plenty of available workers. In reality, the family performed all of the chores and required work on the farm. In my mother's family there were thirteen children born to Andrew Jackson Talley and his wife, Rebecca Adeline (Smith) Talley. Just getting married and staying together was no easy task either. No doubt the intention was to have a lot of laboring hands to work the farm. However, bearing large numbers of children had its affects on the wives and many of them died at a relatively young age due to complications no doubt caused by their several pregnancies. For many of them it must have seemed their destiny was that of being a life-long incubator for they were giving birth to one child and then another almost continuously. In a different way, Grandpa Talley's expectations didn't turn out as he wanted even though he fathered lots of children. He and Rebecca never produced able-bodied male children. That left the females of the family to do all the chores on the farm, including heavy labor.

Comments made by Aunt Alice provided a varied slant on some of these intertwining family topics. I have consolidated Aunt Alice's comments with some of those made by my mother, Hestella Moudy, over the years. I visited on July 30, 1999 with my Aunt Alice Tubbs at her mobile home located in Lockeford, California. Also with us that day was her oldest daughter, Geraldine Balash, and my wife, Beverly.

Aunt Alice Tubbs,[1] told the story of my Grandfather Andrew Talley getting married to my Grandmother Rebecca. The way she described the situation, Andrew Jackson Talley, almost immediately after their marriage, left Rebecca for a period of three days. No one knew where he went or what he did during his absence. Knowing the family did not talk about such matters very openly and certainly not extensively when they did, the issue was probably never discussed thereafter. Even so, they were married for more than sixty-three years and seemingly very happily as they raised a large family of thirteen!

One can ponder the issue as to a reason that Andrew Jackson Talley would choose to leave his young bride at such an early time in their marriage. Did he learn something that he had to rationalize away? Did he learn something about his father-in-law, Obediah Smith, that made him second-

Rebecca (Smith) and Andrew Jackson Talley, circa 1920

guess the kind of family he had gotten involved with and was now a member? Certainly, he knew Rebecca's father had divorced her mother only four years before. He would have had to know that her father had remarried after a troubling divorce long before he and Rebecca married. In those days, with the stigma attached to divorce, did he suddenly have second thoughts? It would seem reasonable that he would have been told about the murder Obediah had committed many years before, but had he? Perhaps he saw himself having to take on more responsibility with his mother-in-law than he had bargained for since she was crippled so terribly with arthritis and basically unable to care for herself. Who really knows? Those facts are buried on Riley Creek!

During this time, my mother's Aunt 'Sis' (Sarco [has been in some records, possibly an Indian name] Carlene or Caroline and is also a combination of **Sar**ah **C**aroline) and Aunt Dolcinia Smith married. Rebecca was the last to get married on January 1, 1885. When Rebecca married, her mother, Peggy (Marguerite), who had been living with her on the homestead, left to live with Aunt Sis on Moss Creek. The log cabin home had been given over to Andrew and Rebecca to occupy. Within less than a year

Peggy died. Rebecca could not attend her funeral because she was nearing the time when she would be delivering her first child. In October 1885 she delivered a stillborn baby, BF (Frank) Talley. Considering what had happened earlier, her mother's death was apparently a traumatic experience for Rebecca. Here she is a new mother, her mother has now passed away at this critical time in her life when most mothers readily assisted with the newborns in the family, and she was probably still struggling with her father having divorced her mother.

While discussing Rebecca, it should be noted that she was recorded in Yell County, Arkansas as being a 'witch'. This was not the kind of witch that one could get 'strung up' for as in New England but one who used a 'witching stick' to find underground water where a well could be dug successfully. She was apparently very good at doing this kind of thing, a reflection of her reputation and expertise. In addition, she did have a strange aspect to her witching prowess since she was known for being able to heal 'bone felons'. These were growths that occurred generally on people's hands that supposedly grew from the bone and probably looked a lot like a cyst. According to Aunt Alice, people would come from near and far for her to treat them. The procedure was very simple. Rebecca would grab hold of the finger or part of the hand where the 'bone felon' was growing and squeeze it as hard as she could for as long as she could which was when the strength in her hand gave out. Supposedly there were many who told the story of being healed in this manner. Sort of makes one wonder why others did not do it if it was that simple.

As for the family of Andrew and Rebecca, the first two of five boys, were stillborn. The other three survived and lived fairly long lives. These three, Robert Thomas (Tom), William Lester (Billy), and Virgil White (Buddy) each had physical defects from birth, which prevented them from becoming significantly productive in the family. It was later determined that they were born with *osteogenesis imperfecta* which was a defective gene carried by their grandmother, Marguerite Caroline (Rider) Smith and believed to be the reason Obediah Smith's parents opposed his marriage to Marguerite. This disease seemed to affect their legs and feet primarily. Billy and Buddy could stand and get around by using a cane but with some difficulty. Tom had to crawl and was virtually immobile. Billy and Buddy would grow vegetable gardens and did some wood carving, or 'whittling' as it was known, on small sticks of wood. Otherwise, they led a simple passive life. Never did I see my grandpa or grandma mistreat any of the 'boys' in any manner whatsoever. If they sassed or talked back, he would certainly correct them just as any other child. Visitors arriving at the Talley place would often bring them candy and other treats. I'm very sure this was a lifelong disappointment for Grandpa not to have any male counterparts in the family to work the fields of the farm or pass along the family name. This latter point was a very important issue in most southern families and, in particular, southern males.

With the lack of physically fit brothers, my mother and her five sisters had to do most of the hard work that would have normally have been done by men. This became the main reason my mother was unable to complete more than the eighth grade in her education…she had to work on the farm and the work for survival came first in the family. The same can be said for her sisters as well. It was for everybody's benefit and welfare. The older sisters also helped out with caring for the younger children in the family as they were born.

My mother related this story to me about her birth on February 8, 1905. Rebecca, her mother, was about to give birth; her time had come. There wasn't time to get a doctor from town seven miles away. Besides, the roads were virtually impassable due to the ground being frozen solid and a big snowstorm was heavy upon them. My grandfather was sent to get the 'granny woman', or mid-wife, Mrs. Jackson, to assist Rebecca with the birth. The old woman lived about a mile away from the old Talley log cabin and home place. This would have put her house about where Merlee Reed 's house was when I was a kid. My mother said that Mrs. Jackson lived in the old Trentham place. (This was confirmed as being the Trentham family home by Aunt Alice when I visited with her in July, 1999). Mrs. Jackson, being rather old and somewhat feeble, couldn't stand upright. Besides the footing was treacherous for anyone since the ground was frozen with ice and snow. Mrs. Jackson was very fearful of falling and breaking her limbs. However, with the help of my grandfather, Mrs. Jackson was able to push

The Talley Family except for Thomas, Lester and William. Left – right standing: Ollie, Lillie, Belle and Elizabeth. Seated: Hestella, Andrew Jackson, Rebecca Adeline and Alice. Circa 1915

herself with his assistance in her rocking chair to the log cabin. One must keep in mind that there weren't any sidewalks or paved roads! There was a lot of distance that had to be traversed in this manner. Much of it was either uphill or downhill and not much flat ground in between. The log cabin itself had not been weather boarded or chinked yet so the log cabin had lots of cracks between the logs where the cold frigid air came whistling through trying to make frozen sculptures out of anything in its wake! It was extremely cold.

No doubt there were many thoughts about the new baby and how it could survive these conditions. Anyway, when my grandfather and Mrs. Jackson arrived, at her direction, he immediately built a big fire in the fireplace and kept it roaring throughout the birth process. Sheets and quilts were hung in the room along the walls for as much protection as they could provide and particularly where the drafts of cold frigid air were ripping through as if trying to freeze the very soul of the about to be newborn! The sheets did help keep the blowing snow out sufficiently enough that the birth occurred without major trauma. Hestella Talley was born and had been

Hestella Talley, age 14

named by whom other? Mrs. Jackson, of course!! No one knows where my mother's name came from or the reason for the selection. Mrs. Jackson liked it obviously.

Ludy, one of my mother's older sisters, died at a very young age which my mother thought to be around two or three years old (records show that she was three and a half years old). It seems that Ludy climbed up in a mulberry tree and ate some berries. The family always believed in doing that, she ate a poison bug or was bitten by a poisonous spider in the process. That very night, she awakened from her sleep and was very sick. In fact, she died before morning came. My grandfather was grief stricken over her death and it affected him for a long time thereafter.

Another of my mother's older sisters died when she was about thirteen. Her name was Mary Asilee. Supposedly she died from a 'congestive chill'. That too was a tough loss for the family.

For the most part, the Talley girls had to learn to sew, cook, can everything on the farm, clean house, wash clothes, which wasn't an easy matter when you did it with a rub board, iron clothes with irons heated on the stove or near the fire place, make feather beds and pillows, quilt, knit, and crochet as well as help with the slaughter of the hogs, kill chickens for meals, feed the animals and the chickens, milk the cows, and perform hard labor in the fields during the day. They became very good at their chores and crafts.

My mother made several quilts, which I still have in my possession. She made quilts from scraps of material from old dresses, flour sacks, shirts, pants, and leftover cuts from her sewing activities. Usually the quilts were colorful but were not color coordinated as is often seen in the 'decor' quilts found in shops today, even those made by hand. Obviously, they followed the particular pattern she selected. Even so, the quilts served their purpose and that was to keep us warm on cold winter nights and that was most meaningful anyway.

Hestella Talley, circa 1926

I remember Mother making dresses for herself sometimes along with the old fashioned bonnets. At times, she knitted house slippers from yarn she had been given or purchased on sale. She also made clothes for her dolls from leftover cloth scraps from her other sewing endeavors.

Aunt Lizzie, her sister, was a very good quilter as well. In the early 1980s, I asked her to make two quilts so that my two daughters, Leslie and Jacquelyn, could have a remembrance of her skills and something directly from someone in my mother's family. The designs chosen were the *double wedding ring* and the other one was the *flower garden*. They were colorful and coordinated in their theme. My daughters cherish them as family heirlooms.

Even though life seemed to have dealt the Talley girls a devastating blow, during my life I never really heard any of them complain about their plight in life, at least not to us children. They left you with the impression that life was good but tough. In fact, they had nothing but love and praise for their 'Mama' and 'Papa' as they would refer to them affectionately.

From my mother's recollections, I know that her "Papa was a very strict disciplinarian." Most of the time their recreation consisted of having watermelon feeds and going to the Riley Creek swimming hole in the summertime. These were usually co-ed activities but Papa had to know every detail before he would let them go. She described the swimming hole as a large natural pool of water in Riley Creek, which was about twenty feet deep. Over hanging the swimming hole was a very large oak tree limb to which they would tie a long rope. On the side of the bank, one would grab the rope and swing out over the water to a spot where you wanted to drop and splash into the water. She stated that there were often as many as twenty or more young people there on these occasions. As she would describe her fun, one could easily sense the memories and excitement, which she held and felt on those days of yore!

Another event, which was of great delight were the homemade ice cream feeds. Such a social outing would probably not seem like much of a major event or treat for most of us today, but it was back then. When you stop and think about it, there was no electricity to their homes and, therefore, no icemakers. All of the ice needed for that purpose had to be specially purchased in town and brought many miles covered with toe sacks and old quilts to keep it from melting away during the trip home. This was a large block of ice. It then had to be chipped into small pieces with an ice pick so that the pieces would fit into the ice cream maker. There were probably some volunteers for the ice chipping job just to cool off a little and slip a chunk in their mouth when no one was looking. After that, it was time to start the process of making the delightful treat. First, the desert's ingredients were mixed and poured into the freezer canister and the lid tightened. The chipped ice was placed between the canister and the bucket and alternately layered with coarse salt. Then the hard work began of cranking the freezer by hand for about thirty to forty minutes. Whoever did that work was sure to be hot and sweaty but the results and benefits were worth the effort for everyone. Usually there would be young

A social outing, dressed to the hilt and having fun. Standing left – right: Ike Red-wine, Lizzie Talley, Albert Tubbs, Lee Horn (hat over eyes), Lillie Talley, Belle Talley, Alfred Tarkenton, Viola Hobson. Sitting left – right: Levin Johnson, John Tubbs, Ollie Talley, and Aunt Sarah (Smith) Johnson. Circa 1916

men taking turns cranking the freezer until each tired then rotated to wait another turn. For a long time, we made homemade ice cream on our family outings because it was soooo gooood! That's what most in attendance would say. To me, it was okay but, in my opinion, didn't compare to the store bought ice cream. You see, the home made ice cream always had ice chunks, or crystals, in it and the store bought didn't. It was smooth and creamy. It was Grandpa's fault, he had ruined my taster because he almost always bought me an ice cream cone in town when I rode in the wagon with him.

Because of religious convictions in those days, my Grandpa Talley would not let his girls dance, wear lipstick, or dress in any way that would smack of provocativeness. My mother was not permitted to attend a 'picture show' as movies were called in those days. A highlight each year was attending the county fair. Even that was not an automatic given. Generally, Grandpa had to be begged; and the girls almost always needed help from Grandma to gain his permission. Together they would 'work' him so that they gained and secured his permission to go the fair. She said this didn't always work, however. They usually got to go…but not every time. Usually there was a price to pay, such as a given quantity of work that had to get done and then they could go. A little bargaining going on, I guess.

One thing that they seemed to do more than would be expected was to take a lot of pictures. This was particularly true of the young people. My mother had several albums of her 'old pictures' some of which I have used in this historical review which were taken in various places but always in a rural setting. Interestingly, you can see people dressed up in their 'Sunday finest' with seemingly no place to go in particular. Maybe that was the fun of it, just getting dressed up and showing off their best attire. At other times, they appear to have 'just walked out of the barn' so to speak. They obviously enjoyed the camera bugs and the occasions when there was some reasons for taking pictures or perhaps just no reason at all. Almost all of the pictures had to be sent off by mail to the Fox developers in Dallas, Texas. So it took a while before they could get to see the results of their poses and pranks. This activity was referred to as *kodaking*.

When they were old enough to have dates, which my mother talked about as if it started about the time they were twenty years old, very tight reins were kept by Papa on where they were going, how long they would be gone, and who else was going along, etc. Sounds like the same hassle that I got in high school many years later! Aunt Alice said that their mother talked to them especially when they started dating boys. Possibly the strictness and high degree of discipline affected some of the Talley girls later in life since some of them had multiple marriages.

The Talley Girls' Love Lives as viewed by Aunt Alice

Aunt Alice made the following comments when I visited her in 1999. Aunt Alice didn't believe that any of the Talley girls were happy with their choice of husbands. To her knowledge, none of them married the man they loved. She tended to believe that the real cause of that were her crippled brothers, especially for her. In one sense, it seemed as if it was virtually a curse upon them.

I concur with her observation. That could very well have had an over-riding influence in the decisions that many potential suitors may have made. It was a similar consideration when their grandparents on the Smith side married and Obediah's parents opposed his marriage to Peggy for this very reason. There was fear that the genetic inheritance of the offspring might be affected by the defect. In reality, this might have been a similar issue that the Talley girls were enmeshed in with their possible suitors.

It's always good when you can ask questions first-hand and get answers straight from the 'horse's mouth' so to speak. So it was when I made my visit to see my Aunt Alice. We had a wonderful visit that day; her mind was still keenly sharp at her ninety-one years of age! She had no hesitation in her voice. She knew what she was talking about almost as if it happened yesterday. Therefore, her answers to my questions were very responsive and direct…she didn't 'beat around the bush' with what she had to say. I recall her preface statement before answering some of my questions, "Well, you asked for it, and I'm going to tell you!" Some of her answers even made me think that I was going where I shouldn't have gone. But in all honesty, my questions were innocent; things that I could no longer ask my own mother and Aunt Alice knew the answers to my questions. I loved her for it! What a lady!

As one can well appreciate, when you hear a story told by one person, it comes out one way. Then you can hear presumably the same story told by a different person and it is different. Maybe not significantly different but that can happen too. More often, the story gets expanded or told from a very different perspective and therefore you get a varying slant on the details. I found that happened to me when I heard Aunt Alice reflect on an event as compared to my mother's version. That's really no different than the four Gospels as they relate the actions and events of Jesus' time and life here on earth before His resurrection in some respects. By the way, I'm not making a comparison of my writings to the Biblical writings!

According to Aunt Alice, Aunt Lizzie was very friendly with Ed Thre-att. Lillie told Grandpa about their association and he forbade Lizzie to see Ed again. Ed was riding on his horse by the fence surrounding the field where the girls were working in the corn one day. Ed waved at Lizzie and she waved back. Lillie told Grandpa about the 'hand waving' event and he gave Lizzie a terrible beating because of it. Ovid Phillips was working on the farm at the time. He saw what had happened and with some conviction about the beating given to Lizzie, he said it went far beyond what he believed was necessary. He asked Grandpa, "Don't you think you have beat her enough?" With that, Grandpa stopped.

After all was said and done, Lillie married Ed Threatt although she had been serious about Albert Tubbs before he went into the army in World War I. Albert enlisted in August 1918 and was discharged in December 1918.

Aunt Lizzie ended up marrying Bill Mehle. They had several children. He died from pneumonia in 1943 and is buried at the Riley Creek Cemetery. Bill's death seemed to start Aunt Lizzie on a multiplicity of marriages as she sought solace and comfort in her loss.

Aunt Alice stated that my mother, "Hester, was in love with Roy Buckman. He had given her the money for a wedding dress and ring. She was having the dress made and Alice was going to the drug store in Belleville to buy the wedding ring. Roy's father gave him $50 and sent him to California and that was the last she heard of him until he was near death. He wrote to her asking her to come and see him. We were living in Oxnard, California at the time, near Hester, and she asked Alice to go with her to see Roy. Alice agreed to make the trip but can't remember why they didn't go. Hester wore Roy's ring ever since she bought it." My mother had lost the diamond and the band was worn so thin that I was afraid that it would possibly cut her finger and I was able to convince her that she should take it off. She had worn that ring for more than fifty years. I still have the ring.

"After Roy left for California, Hester dated and was ready to marry Eston Moore. They were attending a party one Sunday afternoon when another girl that Eston had been seeing drove up in front of the house with her brother. He left the party and got in the car with the young lady and her brother and that was the last she saw of him.

Hester Talley ultimately married Lewis Moudy but left him in the early years of their marriage. He was a drinker and gambler. That became old and unacceptable to my mother after a while, so she left him. After the separation, Lee Moudy went to her and offered to buy her a housekeeping set if she would go back to Lewis. She did. Some time later, she had to go to the Russellville Arkansas hospital for surgery. Aunt Alice thought it was for female problems. Aunt Alice believed that Lee Moudy convinced the doctor to do a tubal ligation while she was in surgery so there wouldn't be any more children. Aunt Belle suspected this and discussed it with Hester."

My mother took a different approach to her life after marriage. I don't know if she decided that she had 'made her bed and chose to lay in it' as some people certainly made such decisions. One viewpoint could have been that it was her religious convictions that she chose to stick with her plight. Her choice was a bit different in this regard than some of her sisters' choices. She never chose divorce as the solution. Instead, she steadfastly prayed that my father would one day give his heart to the Lord. Years later he did. It is certain, as a boy and through my adulthood until her death, she never uttered a word about having problems with any of her sisters' separations and divorces. However, she lived with her heartbreak for her true love throughout her life, I'm sure of that fact.

"Belle dated and became pregnant by Tode Jones, but he would not marry her. Grandpa Talley convinced him to give $300 for expenses. Belle continued to live at home but it was not a happy time for the family. Hester (age fifteen) thought that Belle had done a terrible thing and, according to Aunt Alice, Hester and Belle did not speak to each other for five years. Things were so bad between the sisters that chores were divided so that they did not have to work together. Ollie and Hester would do the milking one time then Alice and Belle would do it the next. Alice, who was 12, helped Belle take care of baby Dora and this upset Hester. She told Alice that she (Alice) would have a baby, presumably out of wedlock, of her own within three years. Belle married a man by the name of Franklin just to get away from home. After two years, she divorced him and came back home. What finally started the sisters talking again was when Hester was almost bitten by a rattlesnake. She was so upset about the incident that she talked to the first person she saw…that was her sister, Belle.

When Belle married Franklin, she moved to Greenwood, Arkansas. Belle took housekeeping jobs so that she could take Dora with her. That marriage ended in divorce. She then met Albert Smith and married him. There were problems in this marriage but she had other children by this time and stayed with him so the children would be taken care of. After the children were out on their own and Albert had passed away, she married Luther Chapman and later moved from Missouri to California and they lived next door to my family at 1075 Stroube Street in El Rio, near Oxnard, for several years until his death.

Aunt Alice stated that the happiest time of her life was when she met her first sweetheart, Huston Thrasher. She had gone to Belle's to help out when Jack was born and met Huston there. He worked on the railroad with Albert. After Huston left, and Aunt Alice returned home they wrote to each other almost daily. She stated that she just lived for his letters.

"They corresponded for three years and during that time she never told him about her three brothers. He surprised her one day by showing up unannounced when they were getting ready to go to the field to plant sweet potatoes. This was the first time that he saw the boys (her brothers) and nothing was said, but he was very quiet. He went to Belle's house and' waited for them to finish their work. Albert Smith told Alice at that time that she might as well say goodbye to Huston. She went to Belle's to talk to him but still nothing was said. When they finally parted, Alice kissed him and told him that she knew she would never see him again. When Geraldine, her first daughter, was about a year old, Alice had a letter from Huston asking forgiveness for what he had done. She wrote back that 'only God could forgive him.'

Aunt Alice did marry Albert Tubbs but later told Gerry, her daughter, that she never loved him, just married to get away from home. Gerry states that, "My sister and I never saw any affection displayed between them except they did kiss goodbye the one time when she (Alice) took the train to Arkansas. She took a leave of absence from her job and spent five weeks in Arkansas to help move Grandma Talley from the old home place to Ollie's house in the Wilson Community after Grandpa Talley died.

Ollie first married Ovid Phillips and they had one daughter, Grace. He had worked for a while at the Moudy sawmill but was working for Grandpa when Lizzie got her beating. He is given credit for stopping it.

Ovid did not like to work and this caused some problems. Alice cannot remember hearing about his death, so she thinks they may have divorced. Ollie then married Oscar Moore. Together they had a very nice family.

Alice (Talley) Tubbs and Albert Tubbs, circa 1940.
Oxnard City Library

All my life I have held to a strong belief that my mother's family was a wonderful and supportive family. I do not mean wonderful in the sense of an easy and laid back kind of life style. It never happened that way. In some ways just living, for my mother and her sisters, was a hard life in those days performing duties and work on the farm which was usually done by men. I remember my mother telling about the visit from one of Andrew Jackson Talley's brothers or cousins (Uncle Willie) and how he sort of 'jumped' on her father for the way all of his daughters had to work. He thought it was almost disgraceful that women had to work like that. Hard work does not necessarily tear at the root of a good and solid family's way of life. Now that I have reached my senior years, I believe, and it is solely my opinion, that I have learned and now understand better the rigors of life which my mother and all of her sisters experienced. Life wasn't easy for them.

For example, Aunt Ollie, being the oldest of the children who lived a full life-time, sort of became the 'mother' to some of her sisters simply because my grandmother for years was busy having children nearly on a production line regularity. One has to remember that this was in the late 1800s and early 1900s and my grandfather was still trying to make ends meet and raise a family large enough to really help out with the total work-load on the farm. Remember too, it wasn't an easy life financially. There was the growing and raising corn, cotton, hay, gardens for home usage, sorghum, fruit trees, feeding and raising animals for milk production and butter, animals to work the fields and animals for table use, and chickens for their eggs and edible meat were all part of the way of life. Any excess in any category could be sold and the money used to help pay the bills or saved for a rainy day.

With this kind of background, I found, rather expectantly, that most of the things, which happened to my aunts is reflective of the times in which they lived. Virtually unexpectedly, I discovered that more than one of my aunts were married and divorced; at least one of them had a baby out of wed-lock; one was married at least six times; some remarried after they lost their first husband in death. My mother never remarried after my father died. Maybe it was due to her age; maybe her marriage having been concluded had already produced enough experiences for one lifetime. It could have been that it was her remembrance of what she had missed with her first true love that caused her not to remarry or even consider it as an option. Health was no doubt a contributing factor to her decision as well.

Perhaps, the six Talley girls' problems at home caused them to be driv-en to move on and start their own families and new lives. Yet, they did not marry early like the young people of my era or some of them today. It became apparent in my discussions with Aunt Alice that life at home wasn't a bed of red roses and blue skies between the sisters. Nonetheless, I attribute some of the interactions to their young ages and lack of maturity that would normally exist in any large family. There is always the mix of personalities as well. There seemed to be reconciliation between them in later years. There weren't any family reunions per se but there were the vacation visits for those living in California and returning to Arkansas. During those respites, there wasn't any visible evidence of past grudges or hard feelings, just gladness to see each other.

I asked my Aunt Alice if she could give me one word, which would best describe each of her sisters and her parents. Of course, she couldn't do it with one word; but she did it rather succinctly as follows:

Dad – "Good man and a good dad. He was kind to us. Didn't believe in courting – just go out and get married." (Sort of reminded me of what he seemingly had done with Rebecca). "Nearly beat Lizzie to death one time. Lillie was jealous of Ed Threatt. Ed came riding his horse one day by the stream close to the house and Lizzie was in the field and Lizzie waved to Ed. That made Lillie upset and she told Papa and Lizzie got a beatin'. Lizzie and Lillie never visited in later years because of this incident."

Mama – "She would always talk to us especially when we started dating boys. I remember the times when I was sick and she took care of me. At 9 years old, I had yellow jaundice and pneumonia, I was very sick. I miss her and all of my family…my sisters and mother. She couldn't even write her name; always marked her name with an 'X'. She worked very hard."

Ollie – "She was second mother to me. She made all my dresses and combed my hair for school."

Lilly – "When I was little, I worshipped her. However, after the Ed Threatt incident I had ill feelings about her and it wasn't the same."

Lizzie – "I didn't know her very well. She was more of a loner."

Belle – "I felt sorry for her. I did everything that I could for her. She had Dora out of wedlock. I washed her clothes and hung them by the fireplace. Belle had gotten pregnant by Tode Jones. His family paid $300.00 to help out. It was the worst experience in my life."

Hester (Hestella) - Belle and 'Hess' lived in the same house (parents') for five years and never spoke. She said that I would have one like Belle within three years. However, they began talking when Dora was 7 years old when Hess was almost bit by a rattlesnake. Hester ran into Belle and Dora and began to tell them excitedly about her incident. From that time on they started talking."

Belle – "When she married, she ran away with Clifford Franklin to Greenwood, Arkansas. She got a job housekeeping for a while. Then she came home and started going to church. She later married Albert Smith. Albert had left his first wife due to his love for Belle."

I asked Aunt Alice did she remember the happiest time in her life? She responded, "It was when I had my first sweetheart. I wanted to hear (get mail) from him every day. His name was Houston Thrasher. He worked on the railroad. Everyday, she would go to the mailbox to get her letter from him. He wrote me nearly everyday. Another happy time for her was when Belle had Jack and I went to stay with her during that time."

Auntie stated that within two months after she married Albert Harrison Tubbs, she ran away. She was upset about the way the household was being allowed to operate with her husband's relatives. They got into raiding her kitchen and did not put things away and she was not accustomed to living that way. So, after giving fair warning to have things change, and they didn't, she decided to leave Uncle Ab. At the time, she was pregnant with her first daughter, Geraldine. She headed down the dirt road walking without much money. She heard a car coming down the road and quickly hid behind some trees and bushes until she could see who was in the car. It was Burl Patton and May Rue. Seeing them, she quickly returned to the road and flagged them down and asked that they take her to Havana to her sister Ollie's' home. That was a distance of about seven or eight miles. For fifty cents Burl said he would. I don't know if she stayed with Ollie very long…probably not because her husband would have come looking for her. It cost $2.50 to ride the bus to Fort Smith, Arkansas, which she borrowed from Ollie. When she went to the bus station, she found that the bus had left 10 minutes ago. She was so disappointed. That changed quickly when the bus station manager told her that if they could get into his car quickly they could catch up with the bus and she could still get on it. It worked! She had also received money from a cousin in the amount of $16.00. She ended up in Seymour, Texas where her uncle, Benjamin Talley, lived. He had a son, Robert. Apparently, her Uncle Benjamin was very ill and soon died. She stayed on with her cousin, Robert for two months. The Talleys ran a boarding house. As time went by, her husband, Albert 'Ab', sent her $16.00 to ride the bus to come back home in Arkansas. When she went to get her ticket that morning, she was a nickel short. So she begged the ticket agent to give her the needed nickel. After some time and consideration, he did. She had her ticket! The trip back to Arkansas was eventful. In Oklahoma, there came a cloud burst and it rained so hard it washed some of the roads out.

The bus trip could not continue. That night she had to stay in a hotel which cost her fifty cents, and that was about all she had. The next morning, the bus company (probably Greyhound) put her on a train to continue her journey to Belleville, Arkansas.

FAMILY TREE

Andrew Jackson Talley 10/11/1861 - 4/30/1948	Rebecca Adeline Smith 11/29/1866 - 5/2/1950

BF (Frank) Talley - still born 10/11/1885 - 10/11/1885
unnamed boy - still born 9/14/1886 - 9/14/1886
Mary Asilee Talley 10/19/1887 - 2/4/1901
Robert Thomas Talley 11/15/1889 - 4/29/1957
William Lester Talley 11/16/1891 - 3/28/1951
Virgil White Talley 6/5/1893 - 11/16/1972
Ollie Mae Moore 3/5/1895 - 11/25/1975
Luela (Ludy) Talley 1/20/1897 - 6/12/1900
Sarah Elizabeth Shinn 11/21/1898 - 3/18/1992
Lillie Gertrue Threatt 6/20/1901 - 3/20/1990
Arie Belle Chapman 6/13/1903 - 2/14/1993
Hestella Moudy 2/9/1905 - 9/4/1989
Alice Francis Tubbs 1/23/08 – 12/13/2003

FAMILY TREE

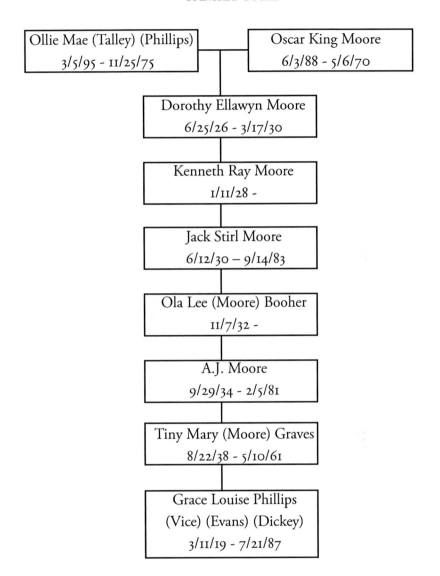

Ollie Mae (Talley) (Phillips)	Oscar King Moore
3/5/95 - 11/25/75	6/3/88 - 5/6/70

Dorothy Ellawyn Moore
6/25/26 - 3/17/30

Kenneth Ray Moore
1/11/28 -

Jack Stirl Moore
6/12/30 – 9/14/83

Ola Lee (Moore) Booher
11/7/32 -

A.J. Moore
9/29/34 - 2/5/81

Tiny Mary (Moore) Graves
8/22/38 - 5/10/61

Grace Louise Phillips
(Vice) (Evans) (Dickey)
3/11/19 - 7/21/87

Gracie's father was Ovid Phillips. Grace was married three times: Steve Vice, Arthur 'Monk' Evans, and Alfred Randall Dickey. The latter's grandmother was Clyde Harriet (Moudy).

FAMILY TREE

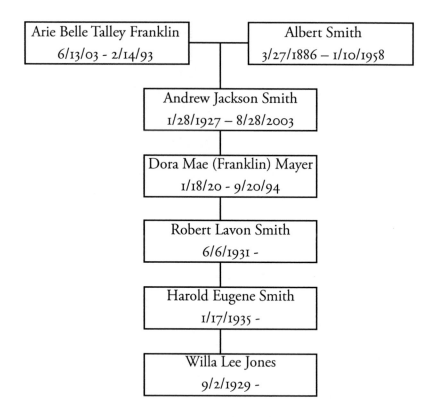

Arie Belle Talley Franklin	Albert Smith
6/13/03 - 2/14/93	3/27/1886 – 1/10/1958

Andrew Jackson Smith
1/28/1927 – 8/28/2003

Dora Mae (Franklin) Mayer
1/18/20 - 9/20/94

Robert Lavon Smith
6/6/1931 -

Harold Eugene Smith
1/17/1935 -

Willa Lee Jones
9/2/1929 -

First husband – Clifford Franklin (1/18/1895 – 8/8/1975) married 2 June 1924, divorced 24 November 1925. She then married Albert Smith on 26 July 1926. Her third husband was Luther Chapman, who died 12 December 1970.

FAMILY TREE

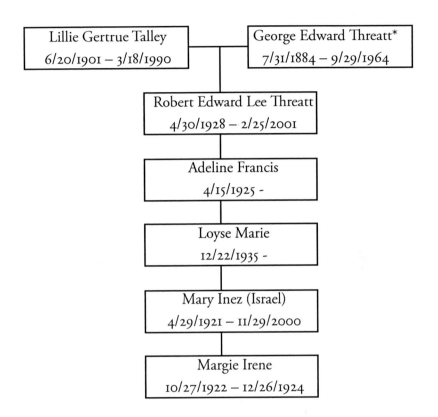

| Lillie Gertrue Talley | George Edward Threatt* |
| 6/20/1901 – 3/18/1990 | 7/31/1884 – 9/29/1964 |

Robert Edward Lee Threatt
4/30/1928 – 2/25/2001

Adeline Francis
4/15/1925 -

Loyse Marie
12/22/1935 -

Mary Inez (Israel)
4/29/1921 – 11/29/2000

Margie Irene
10/27/1922 – 12/26/1924

*This was his second marriage. First wife was Nannie Threatt (7/13/1884 – 5/3/1916) who died of burns.

FAMILY TREE

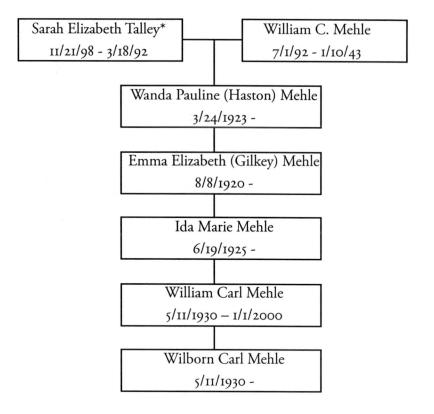

| Sarah Elizabeth Talley*
11/21/98 - 3/18/92 | William C. Mehle
7/1/92 - 1/10/43 |

Wanda Pauline (Haston) Mehle
3/24/1923 -

Emma Elizabeth (Gilkey) Mehle
8/8/1920 -

Ida Marie Mehle
6/19/1925 -

William Carl Mehle
5/11/1930 – 1/1/2000

Wilborn Carl Mehle
5/11/1930 -

*Aunt Lizzie had six marriages :
#2 Lelon Isom 'Dick' Williams, divorced
#3 Fleet Stevison,- divorced
#4 Ed Shinn, died
#5 John Owens, divorced
#6 Utah Bates, died

FAMILY TREE

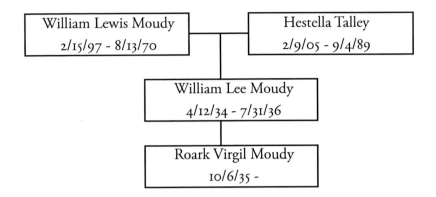

FAMILY TREE

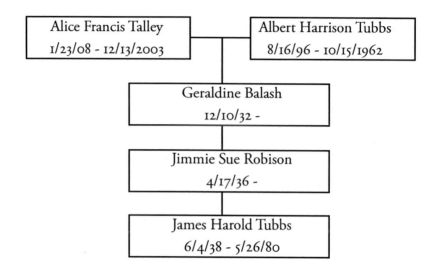

| Alice Francis Talley | Albert Harrison Tubbs |
| 1/23/08 - 12/13/2003 | 8/16/96 - 10/15/1962 |

Geraldine Balash
12/10/32 -

Jimmie Sue Robison
4/17/36 -

James Harold Tubbs
6/4/38 - 5/26/80

A. J. TALLEY FAMILY
DATES OF MARRIAGE

Andrew Jackson Talley	to	Rebecca Adeline Smith	January 1, 1885
Sarah Elizabeth Talley	to	William C. Mehle	July 19, 1919
Sarah Elizabeth Mehle	to	Lelon Williams	Unknown
Sarah Elizabeth Williams	to	Fleet Stevison	Unknown
Sarah Elizabeth Stevison	to	Ed Shinn	Unknown
Sarah Elizabeth Shinn	to	John Owens	November 9, 1957
Sarah Elizabeth Owens	to	Utah Bates	May 19, 1965
Ollie Mae Talley	to	Ovid Phillips	May 5, 1925
Ollie Mae Phillips	to	Oscar King Moore	August 21, 1925
Arie Belle Talley	to	Clifford Franklin	June 2, 1924
Arie Belle Franklin	to	Albert Smith	February 26, 1926
Arie Belle Smith	to	Luther Chapman	Unknown
Lillie Gertrud Talley	to	Edward Threatt	April 16, 1919
Hestella Talley	to	William Lewis Moudy	March 10, 1931
Alice Francis Talley	to	Albert Harrison Tubbs	February 9, 1932

The question was raised about how far her mother and father had ever ventured from home on Riley Creek. I previously believed and estimated that it was probable that my grand parents had traveled not more than a one hundred miles, if that far, from Riley Creek. Aunt Alice stated that her parents had gone to McAlester, Oklahoma on the train to see Ed and Lilly Threatt. To her knowledge, that was the farthest away from home that they ever ventured.

After my grandfather died in 1948, Aunt Alice went to Arkansas to help Oscar Moore tear down the sawn lumber portion of the old homestead so the lumber could be used to construct a room for her mother, Rebecca, to live in at the Moore's home near Havana, Arkansas. Their home was located in the community of Wilson and about five to six miles from the old homestead on Riley Creek.

I didn't know some aspects of issues which arose regarding my grand-mother's relocation to Aunt Ollie's because I had never heard the story previously. When my grandfather died, Aunt Lilly and her husband, Ed Threatt, were living in the sharecropper's house on my grandfather's property. This was part of the arrangement between family members in their attempt to take care of their aging parents. Many of the sisters and their husbands had taken their turn at caring for the Talley parents and the farm. However, it seems that most of the sisters thought that Ed was not on the 'up and up' about the whole situation. As it turned out, he wasn't and Aunt Alice learned about it firsthand.

The children of the Talley's were caretakers of their parents at various times through the years and also sharecroppers. Aunt Alice and Uncle Ab had worked the property for several years. Obviously it was very hard work with very little wealth to look forward to in the future. They decided at one point in time that it was in their best interests to move to California and join my parents expecting to improve their life. In leaving, it was agreed that Uncle Ed and Aunt Lillie Threatt would become the sharecropper and take care of the parents and the three boys. A warranty deed was drawn up stating this. Hestella Moudy and Ollie Moore, two of the daughters, witnessed it. This document was also signed by Grandpa and Grandma, who made her mark 'X' since she could not write.

After Uncle Ed took control, he cut and sold much of the timber for $3,500 and kept most of the money even though it did not belong to him. Aunt Lillie was supposed to be cooking for the grandparents and the boys (three brothers). Instead, she would help Uncle Ed with his farm work and Grandma had to do the cooking if any was to be done. After Grandpa died, Uncle Ed and Aunt Lillie moved in with Grandma and the boys. However, this did not improve their living conditions or circumstances. It seemed that Aunt Lillie would cook breakfast for all of them and then leave with Uncle Ed to go work in the fields. Food that was left to eat later was cold. Aunt Alice said that Uncle Ed was a mean man and that Aunt Lillie was afraid of him. She felt that Uncle Ed was responsible for the mistreatment of the remaining family.

Aunt Alice traveled back to Arkansas within a year for the express purpose of getting Uncle Ed off the property. Aunt Alice went to talk to both of them but Aunt Lillie left leaving only Aunt Alice and Uncle Ed to discuss the problem. Grandma and Aunt Ollie were in an adjacent room fearful that Uncle Ed was going to harm Aunt Alice. This is when Uncle

Ed took his pistol out and laid it on the dresser in an attempt to scare Aunt Alice. She told Ed that his tactic wasn't going to work. She further stated that she was here to talk and not shoot anyone. Her message to Uncle Ed was simply that the arrangement was not working out with them living there and that they were not taking care of Grandma and the boys as they had agreed to do. He had taken, according to Aunt Alice, all of my grandfather's money. He still wanted more of the property after his death. Aunt Alice, during the conversation, mentioned that grandma had $1,000. In the end, she learned that Ed did not know about the $1,000 but it was too late and he demanded that as well as the cows, corn in the barn, mules and pigs. She agreed that he could have it. With that, Ed stated that he would move out. It was an accptable ending to a terrible situation that had developed.

What she never told him was that Grandma had some war bonds still in her possession. Ed never got the bonds. She and Belle took the war bonds to the bank for safe keeping and eventually signed them over to Ollie to help build the room for their mother to live in until she died in 1950. Grandma signed the bonds with her 'X' and that money was used later to help pay for the care she needed while living at Aunt Ollie's home where grandma was relocated in the Wilson Community, near Havana. There she would spend the rest of her days.

Uncle Oscar Moore, Aunt Ollie's husband, with Aunt Alice helping him, tore down the newer part of the Talley home place and used the lumber to build the addition at Aunt Ollie's.

The remaining property was sold. However, in her opinion, Oscar Moore practically gave her father's bottom land near the Petit Jean Creek away...meaning the value he received was less than the real market value she thought it was worth. On the one hand that seemed to be a bit of an irritant but on the other hand, she was pleased that Aunt Ollie and Uncle Oscar would take proper care of the Talley girls' mother.

According to Aunt Alice, in later years, Ed Threatt lost his faculties and apparently became mentally incompetent. She said Aunt Lillie committed him to a hospital in Ola, Arkansas, where he could be cared for physically and mentally until he died.

Another story, and I cannot recall how it came about, was the early part of the winter of 1947 when Aunt Alice, Uncle Ab, and my parents returned to Arkansas for the express purpose of killing hogs, butchering and putting up (canning or curing) the meat to be used for the Talley parents over the next year. She never stated whether Ed Threatt was there to help with the effort. Of course, being the caretaker, he should have been.

I asked Aunt Alice when her family came to California? She wasn't sure of the date but thought it was 1941 or 1942. I know our family came to California in 1941 just before World War II started and they didn't come until after my family arrived and had settled. I think, on that basis, her family arrived in California in 1942.

Another family, which lived in the old Trentham's place near my grandfather's farm, was the Reed family; Merlee, Calvin and their daughter, Irene. I didn't know if they too were somehow related to my family. I personally remember them as being a friendly family. I have always assumed that they were good neighbors to my uncles and aunts who worked as the caretakers and to my grandparents as well.

My cousin, Melba Barrick, writes very descriptively about life on Riley Creek. I have included some of her writings and information about this area because it reminds me and closely follows my own remembrances and experiences as a boy living in the Riley Creek Community. This is also the area where her husband, Doyle Barrick, my cousin, was raised as a youngster.

"They settled in the Riley Creek Community of the long, long ago. It is still there today but it has experienced some drastic changes. No doubt, this was a friendly settlement, in the midst of virgin timber and lots of good, cool, clear water.

With a good cross-cut saw and a sharp chopping axe, they soon felled enough trees to erect a log cabin. Sometimes using clay to chink the cracks between the logs to keep the north wind from howling through the wall. Using a fro then they split wood and made shingles to roof it with. With the help of their good neighbors, they soon had a place to call home, a table to put their feet under at mealtime and able to stretch out on at night... and usually tired enough to go right to sleep and maybe dream pleasant dreams. Rising early in the morning, they'd split rails for a fence. Later on they might replace those around the yard with pailings and have a picket fence. Eventually those around the pasture might be replaced with barbwire. Then they (usually the women) would set out a few Flags (Iris), some buttercups, and maybe a lilac bush. They'd find a good rich spot for Hollyhawks, then a running rose on a picket fence. Landscaping finished, they'd take a hoe and scrape every blade of grass out of the yard, but there would always be a broom handy and the yard was swept at least once a week. During the molting season, when the chickens began to loose their feathers, it had to be swept more often.

Every family had a cow, for milk and butter, a fattening hog, for ham and bacon, a few chickens for eggs and chicken dumplings. Of course they had a rooster that flew up on the gate post every morning, bright and early, and crowed his most melodious crow. He was the Cock of the walk. With him around, who needed an alarm clock?

The community soon had several dwelling houses, a school, a church, a Community Hall and a large number of families.

The Riley Creekers had sawmills. That and farming were their chief money-making projects. There were logs to cut, there were logs to skid. There were logs to be hauled to the mill and be cut into lumber. When the lumber was sold each worker got his share for what he had done.

Some farmed new grounds that they had cleared. They planted mostly cotton to bring in cash, but they had corn and hay for their animals. After it was garnered, the corn was thrown into the corn crib for horses, hogs and chickens. The corn sheller was in the corner of the crib. After shucking the ears they'd shell some for the chickens. Those old hens would watch for them to go to the barn and they'd come running. Some of the corn grains were "looked" (bad grains picked out) and taken to the grist mill and ground into meal. This was for cornbread to go with potatoes and beans for dinner and supper, or cornmeal mush for breakfast, served with cream, butter and sugar. Cornbread was especially delicious if it had cracklings in it. You could crumble this into a glass of cool sweetmilk, or a glass of buttermilk, with little flecks of butter floating around in it, and it would hit that hungry spot every time.

The cracklings was the fat of the hog when it was butchered, and cooked down into lard, the grease poured into five gallon cans, buckets, crocks or stone jars, and the settlings in the bottom of the pot were the cracklings.

Some of the good ears of corn were shelled for hominy. This was made by soaking the corn in lye water. The lye was made from ashes taken from the fire place that had been placed in the ash hopper. This was to remove the eyes (husks) from the corn. Then it was washed several times and cooked in the wash pot outside. Then season a hot dish of it with bacon drippings, and it was most delicious to the taste buds.

Soap was made from this lye and meat scraps. Lye soap would make their clothes white, and be used for shampoo, it made their hair shine. Then vinegar was needed for a rinse to make their hair smell clean.

Hay was cut and stacked around a pole (hay stack), or thrown into the barn loft (hay loft) with a pitch fork. This was loose hay, and it was for cattle after Jack Frost had visited a few times and the green grass could no longer be found.

Those big, fluffy, white cotton boles were picked in anything from a "toe sack" or "gunny sack' to a big long six-foot "cotton picking sack". Many times little tots, if wasn't a grandma at home, had to go to the cotton patch. They might pick a few handfuls and put in Mama's sack, or they might chase lizards or a cotton tail rabbit, but sooner or later that little fellow would get tired and sleepy. Mom could always tell what her child was wanting, and she would let him get on her sack and ride, pretty soon his grumbles were replaced with a smile and he'd be sound asleep.

Sometimes the cotton-picker would come across a little-rotten ended watermelon that had been planted in the cotton. Even though broken open and eaten with little dirty hands, it was such a welcomed break in the monotony. And sometimes there'd be a wild apricot that had been frosted on and was all shriveled up, but tasted so good!

That cotton sack would get very heavy before reaching the wagon where the scales were, and find how many pounds had been picked. After the wagon with high sideboards had been filled, the cotton was taken to the gin and baled. Then it was sold for cash. Sometimes this money had to last until time the next fall. Material was bought for a dress for the women folk and overalls for the men and boys. This money was also used to buy flour, salt and sugar for the kitchen, and a few other bare necessities. And of course they couldn't forget the coffee beans that they ground in the coffee grinder to make a pot of strong, black coffee to dunk their golden brown biscuit crusts in.

These farmers always had a sorghum patch (field). Some of it was used for cattle feed, while some was made into molasses for the family. It was good to eat as syrup with butter or red-eye gravy (made where ham had been fried, by pouring the grease off and adding a little brewed coffee) with hot biscuits. Sometimes they'd make taffy candy on rainy days, or sometimes they'd have a candy pulling party. They'd raise popcorn and peanuts and made yummy popcorn balls. Dad would take his axe in the springtime and chip bark from a sweetgum tree and the kids would pick the resin, or wax, that ran out of the tree and chew it for gum. Some would even pick stretchberries from sawbrier vines and mix it with their wax and have their own Bubble Gum. Just like store bought! Well, not quite.

They had bee gums (hives) and raised their own honey. They'd sew a veil on an old hat and it would come down over their shoulders so their face and neck were covered. They'd get the smoker and put rags in it and set them on fire and they would smolder. The smoker was like a bellows and when it was pumped smoke came out and this was to ward off the bees, and they'd take out big golden cakes of honey. After being extracted from the comb it was ready to be put on the table, and it was food fit for a king to eat. Then the honeycomb was melted down into beeswax and was used to resin their bows. They were very much independent people

Riley Creek School was for the little Primer kids (today we call them Kindergarteners) on up until they were ready to quit school and help bring in some income, or go on to Belleville High School. This Riley Creek School was a one-room building at first, and had only one teacher to handle all the grades. Their salary was very small. It didn't begin to compare with the patience they had to cultivate. But to make up for it they had a strong paddle that was administered to the same ones over and over again. Many stopped their book learning at this level, while others went on to further their education. A few even pushed their way on through college. At one time Belleville had an Academy. Where else could Belleville have gotten such a pretty name except from the beautiful belles that attended this school? Long ago, even doctors were educated there (so I've been told).

The land on Riley Creek where the church was erected was donated to the Methodist people, but after the building was up and they were in business to see some souls saved, the church was for anyone who wanted to attend, no matter what denomination you might have preferred. It was for spiritual growth and fellowship gatherings with both God and man. Overalls and gingham dresses were good enough for anyone. They were not going to church to be noticed but they were going to worship the Lord. The little girls who were fortunate enough might have on patent leather slippers that had been shined the night before with a cold biscuit. But their feet might be cramped since they went barefoot most of the summer. The ladies wore sunbonnets if they didn't have umbrellas. They might even have on their Sunday-going-to-meeting apron. The boys slicked their hair back, probably put Rose oil in it, and helped dad harness the horses and hook them up to the wagon.

The adults had a spring seat, the babies had a pallet (a quilt spread out in the wagon bed), but the teenagers sat in the back-end with their feet dangling out. That was fun! Every now and then one of the boys (or a tomboy) would jump out and ride the coupling pole. Down the road they went bumpty-bump, sometimes singing and keeping time to the rattle of the wagon or the clipity-clop of the horses' hooves. After hearing a quite lengthy message on "Hell, fire and brimstone" they all spread lunch and ate fried chicken and potato salad (picnic menus haven't changed all that much). After the baskets were all filled with leftovers, and all the news and gossip had been exchanged, the horses had been turned around and they headed for home.

Every summer they had a revival. Souls were saved and the angels in Heaven rejoiced. These sinners, saved by God's grace, were baptized in Riley Creek, their lives were turned around and they began a new life.

There was a cemetery beside the church. What better place to lay their loved ones than by the church they loved. This land was donated by Uncle Dan Arnold, probably a love offering.

They had a Community building, called Liberty Hall, which was used for both business and social gatherings. It was also used for a schoolhouse before they erected the school building. And those who belonged to the Lodge (I suppose Masons) met there.

On Sunday afternoons, in the spring and summer, they had baseball games. It was usually played on the smoothest pasture they could find. The majority of spectators were fathers of sons playing, or sons of the fathers participating. It was a time of sport and socializing. Occasionally the Community had a pie supper if they needed to raise money for some project. Each pie was sold to the highest bidder, and sometimes it went pretty high if a young beau desired a certain young lady's pie (because she ate with whoever bought her pie) and the bidder would go a little higher each time. And if that interested lad didn't have enough money to keep bidding, he sometimes had to stand back with his hands in his pockets eyeing the two, not wishing for a piece of pie, yearning to hold her hand. Was it fair? Well, maybe not, but remember the object was to raise money for a worthy cause.

They had singing schools to teach those who were eager to sing better, and had a voice for doing so. Then sometimes they had Saturday night singings and shared their talents with others. If they didn't have a piano they had a tuning fork so they could get the right pitch. Either way, they had good singing and entertainment.

They knew that "all work and no play makes Jack a dull boy" so they had parties sometimes. Games like Spin-the-bottle, Strange-questions-and-crooked-answers and Gossip, were played in a house if it was too cool to be outside. But when Springtime rounded the corner, and the moon, with a special glow, smiled down on the lads and lasses, games of an outdoor nature took over, like Drop-the-handkerchief, Blind-man's-bluff, two-deep, etc.

They enjoyed square dances, the old as well as the young. These old farmers might plow hard all day but still be able to shake-a-leg at the sound of that music. Music was furnished by fiddle, guitar, and mandolin, and the beaus could swing their belles to the "Doe-ce-doe".

There were no radios or televisions, just good old plain entertaining. On week nights, after the chores were done and supper was over with, the kerosene (or coal oil) lamps were lit and dad sat down with the Kansas City Star to see what was going on in the rest of the world, while mom patched his overalls where he'd hung them on the barbwire fence, or she might be sewing a quilt.

They had quilting bees formed by all the ladies in the Community. They would take cotton, loose scraps from the gin, and card bats until they were light and fluffy. The lining was tacked into the quilting frames, the bats spread evenly on it, then covered with the quilt top. It might be a nine patch, or a string quilt, for a cover on a cold winter night, or it might be a fancy wedding ring for some young girl to put in her hope chest. By mid-afternoon the quilt would be finished, taken out of the frames and hemmed.

If someone needed a barn, then the men all got together and had a barn raising, all on the same line as the quilting bee. Neighbors were near and neighbors were dear. Today we hardly know who neighbor is, we live such a busy life, everything is push-button, too, but there are so many buttons to push. And we panic when one gets stuck." [2]

It is important to remember the 'closeness' of the families, which lived in and around this community of Riley Creek. They lived and made their homes and raised their families there. In reality, they did things together because getting around wasn't easy; you walked, rode on horseback or traveled in a wagon. Traveling by these modes meant that distances were pretty limited. In the early days of my mother's childhood, automobiles did not exist in this part of the country. I doubt if anyone could afford one. Even if they could there probably wasn't any desire to spend what little savings they might have had on a 'contraption' like that!

In general, social life was centered about families. The families included the Talleys, Smiths, Haires, Wells, Farmers, Redwines, Bannisters, Haneys, Johnsons, Barricks, Trenthams, Tubbs, Reeds, Horns, Misenhammers, Pattons, Stanberrys, and even the Moudys, and the Buckmans, to a lesser extent because they lived in Belleville. Over time, as one would expect, the offsprings of these families intermarried. Many of the families became related through these marriages and then they had their own families. It is here, in the second and third generations, that they began to leave the rural way of life. Their parents passed on, and financial conditions became a predominant factor (depression) which caused them to more or less scatter to the four winds. Efforts were made to keep track of many of their childhood companions, particularly first cousins, but eventually many of these contacts were lost and they too passed on to their eternal reward. Those of us who remain can only record something in writing which reminds us of 'those good old' days of yesteryear.

Today, I look back and know that my great grandparents helped to clear the frontier lands of America. My grandparents helped to develop these frontier lands into an agrarian society of highly principled and basically strong Bible believing people. My parents left that way of life for the 'milk and honey' and the pot of gold at the end of the rainbow, which they hoped to find in California. I am left to marvel at all of their sacrifices and the fact that I have become the beneficiary of their endeavors. My pot of gold was an education and a good way of life very different than theirs sans their struggles. My descendants continue the pilgrimage of life knowing someone else before them paid the price for their ability to have the enjoyment of life, which they experience today.

On Riley Creek, I learned of a gravesite which I visited in 1983 for the very first time. My Uncle Lee Moudy who told me about the gravesite took me there. This information was a shock in one sense to me. I had never heard a single word about such a grave from anyone in my family, previously. Keep in mind that until that moment, I didn't even know my great grandfather's name or anything else about him. Uncle Lee said he wanted to show me this family gravesite since my great grandfather, Obediah Smith, was buried here with his second wife and a child, which he didn't know the origin or family relationship.

I knew the road and location since I had passed close by many times. It is off the side of the dirt road just a few hundred yards past the old Haywood Haire place on Riley Creek, which is on the way to my Grandfather Talley's old home and farm where I lived for short periods of time. I had passed the location while riding in the wagon with my grandfather and on daily school bus trips. After moving to California the family passed the location many times more when we spent time in the area on vacation. No one had ever uttered one word about it! I was stunned! Uncle Lee and I had walked many paces off the road when he stopped and pointed to a pile of flat rocks a few feet in front of us. There were maybe five or six rocks stacked on top of one another and fairly close to a rather mature yellow pine tree. "That's it, son." Uncle Lee suggested that I have a fence put around it to protect it. I had the feeling later, that Uncle Lee had shown me that gravesite because he knew that I didn't know anything about it and his time for living was getting shorter. It was his way of 'letting me in on some things' before he passed on and perhaps no one else could or would tell me about it. A few years later, I was talking to Anne Moore and she was excited because she had learned of the grave. She informed me that there were several relatives buried there including:

- Obediah Smith
- Jannia Smith (second wife)
- Marguerite Smith (first wife)
- Franklin Talley
- Baby Boy Talley (both infants and from the union of Andrew Jackson and Rebecca Talley)

Since that time, I have worked with Ann Moore and had the area cleared and a headstone put in place to show the names of the known buried at this time. We worked with James Mitchell, the landowner, and gained his permission to lay the headstone. Cousin Anne believes that it is likely that other family members are buried there.

Charlie and Mary Smith were the parents of Albert Smith who married Aunt Belle. There is not any known relationship with the Smith's of my grandmother (Smith) Talley's family and this family of Smith's. This couple was married in Ohio, moved to Virginia, then to Oklahoma, and finally located in Arkansas. Albert is the gentleman who married Belle Talley after her first marriage failed.

Londy and Ranford Wilson were great grandparents to Sam Dickerson. I have learned that Sam is a distant cousin of mine. He lives in Van Buren, Arkansas. This comes about through the Woodall clan, when George Woodall married my great grandfather Obediah's sister, Elizabeth Evoline (Smith) Woodall.

The Talley family also has a tie to the Gilkey family through my cousin Emma (Aunt Lizzie's daughter) who married R.V. Gilkey. An unrelated but interesting twist comes from Sam Dickerson (another of my distant relatives) who has stated to Cousin Anne that the Navy discovered that he had some form of sickle cell disease at the time he was processing through his induction while joining the U.S. Navy during WWII. It is known that this disease originated in some parts of the eastern Mediterranean Sea countries such as Greece, Yugoslavia, Serbia and other Slavic states along with Africa which is the most predominant of the group. Cousin Sam has tried to find out its origin for himself but without success. Since he is related to the Gilkey family in a more direct blood line, he believes that it came through the Gilkeys. His reasoning is that the Gilkeys were known to have owned slaves at one time in their history. And since Sam has no known relatives from the Mediterranean area, he believes that it had to come through the slaves owned by the Gilkeys. Anne Moore stated that she has written letters to the Gilkey family and hasn't received as much as an acknowledgment nor will any member discuss it with her. Searching through the cemetery burial records of Yell County, Arkansas, some records do reflect a number of blacks with the family name of Gilkey. This fact, standing alone, doesn't prove anything.

Anne Moore has a letter from Uncle Willie Talley. She says that Uncle Willie Talley owned and operated a boarding house in Seymour, Texas. Robert had a son, Robert Roark Talley, who married Mable (maiden name unknown) and eventually moved and lived in Beachwood, N.J. Later, when they retired, they moved to Florida. The boarding house referred to in my writings is the same one in which Aunt Alice Tubbs lived when she first got married and left her husband, Albert Tubbs, for two months. I have a picture of it from my mother's collection of photos.

My Aunt Alice

On my mother's side of the family, I was most fond of my Aunt Alice because I spent the most time in my young years with her family. At birth she was named Alice Francis Talley. She was the youngest of the Talley girls. My mother was just three years older. Aunt Alice was born on January 23, 1908 at Riley Creek and passed away December 13, 2003 at the age of ninety-five years.

She was to marry Albert Harrison Tubbs, born August 16, 1896. They married on February 9, 1932 in Danville, Arkansas. Uncle Albert was always called 'Ab' by his friends and most of the relatives. I always enjoyed being around him as I was growing up. He was friendly, carried a smile most of the time, and had a story to tell. I liked him very much and he treated me kindly. Uncle Ab's father was James Allen Tubbs and his mother was Laura Agnes Johnson. Through his mother's family, his great grandfather was David Harrison Johnson, which made his great grandmother the same lady as Alice's aunt, Sarah Caroline Johnson. I remember that Uncle Ab had a brother, Allen Tubbs, who lived in Visalia, California for many years and drove a large double trailer fuel tanker truck all over the San Joaquin Valley. My mother and dad would stop by to see them when we were on trips to the northern San Joaquin Valley.

One trip to Arkansas that I remember vividly occurred before my Aunt Alice's family moved to California. It was the time when my parents visited them while they were farming and taking care of the Talley grandparents. They lived in the 'caretaker's house' down close to the road and were sharecroppers. There was a large dirt half circle driveway from the road to their house and back to the road again. The school bus made its last stop here for kids attending the Belleville school, so the half circle made it easy for the bus to turn around. This visit, however, came at Christmas time and kids were out of school. The year was probably 1942. It was very cold and it snowed probably about six inches, enough so it stayed on the ground very easily.

The fireplace was roaring as one pine log after another was placed on the fire as we tried to keep warm. To the left of the fireplace in the living room was a window. I don't remember who did it, but probably Uncle Ab took a box outside, could have been a wooden orange crate, and propped it up on one end with a stick that had a string tied to it. He lifted the window just very slightly; just enough so we could pull the string through the sill when it was time. Then he placed a bit of cracked corn, normally used to feed the chickens, on top of the snow inside the area where the box was balanced on the stick. My cousins, James, Jimmie Sue and Gerry and I waited. It wasn't long before a friendly beautiful red bird, a cardinal, paid us a visit. The corn looked pretty good to the bird, so under the box he hopped and immediately, the string was pulled which pulled down the stick propping the box up and trapping the red bird inside. I do not recall what we did with the red bird. I believe that someone went outside and caught the bird, dressed it and it was roasted on the fireplace hearth. I'm almost certain that we didn't turn it loose. Sounds pretty gruesome now and I'm sure we would not do that kind of thing today.

Within a relatively short time after that visit, Aunt Alice and Uncle Ab moved to California. It was during World War II and they lived in Oxnard. Almost everyone in the community worked for the U.S. Navy at the Port Hueneme Seabee Base some five miles away, and I believe that's where my uncle worked. Aunt Alice worked for the Federal Housing Project in Oxnard, where my mother also worked. Together they worked cleaning houses in the project by washing walls, mopping floors, and cleaning the kitchen and bathroom areas and getting the place ready for the next tenant to move in. It was hard work to say the least. After the war, Aunt Alice got a job working at Camarillo State Hospital as a cook until she retired. This was a state mental institution.

My Uncle Ab and Aunt Alice bought a house on "D" street in Oxnard. I still remember the house. It sat back off the street and was about a block from the Oxnard recreation center and fairly close to the Haydock Grammar School my cousin, Jimmie Sue, and I attended. It was within several city blocks of and fairly close to the housing project located to the west. This made it easy for me to spend time there with my cousins. In my youngest years in Oxnard, I was probably closest to them of all my cousins. I had supper with them many times. My Aunt Alice was always good to me. I loved her very much. Later they bought a house near the Assembly of God Church that my family attended in Oxnard. The house was almost across the street from my Aunt Kate (Moudy) and Uncle Jess Tucker's home. The last move I remember they made in Oxnard was to Cedar Street. That was the same street where my girl friend lived, Janice Elliott. Many times when I visited one of them, I paid a visit to the other as well. It was convenient in that regard.

One of the things I miss most, at my age, is not being able to visit Aunt Alice and my cousins over the past several years. She relocated to the San Joaquin Valley, near Galt, California to be near her oldest daughter, Gerry. My cousin, Jimmie Sue, moved to northern California several years previously and has lived in that area most of her married life. Cousin James lived in Santa Cruz, California for a few years prior to his death.

Other relatives on my mother's side of the family also made their way to California. Kenneth Moore related his story to me. Kenny graduated from Havana High School when he was seventeen years old. The community is just five miles up the road and west of Belleville. That was in 1945. Either World War II had just completed or was nearing the end. Economic conditions were terrible in Yell County. Hardly any work was available especially for a recent high school graduate without experience to speak of except having worked on his father's farm. They lived in the Wilson community. Kenneth felt that he no other options but to go to California. He had a sister, Grace living in Southgate, a city within the Los Angeles megalopolis. It was difficult to find work even in this location. He met up with another cousin, Andrew Jackson Smith, who was likewise trying to find a job. They heard of opportunities in Salt Lake City, Utah.

They made a decision that together they would hop a freight train and make their way to Salt Lake. When they left Los Angeles, they didn't have any money with the exception of 'one thin dime.' It was winter but in Southern California the weather is still very warm or moderate temperatures at its worst.

These two 'freeloaders' riding the 'fast freight express' made their way to northern California and headed east over the great Sierra Nevada divide. They would board any freight train that was going in the right direction. They finally crossed the Great Salt Lake and almost immediately knew they had made a huge mistake. The weather in Salt Lake City was absolutely freezing and completely miserable. Winter in this area can be very cruel and life threatening. In fact Kenneth said, "I've never been so cold in all of my life." They were more or less begging for handouts just to stay alive since they did not have any money. Somehow, they made their way back to Los Angeles safely but very tired and hungry. It had been a hard lesson and a tough introduction to the West Coast. Both of them lived many years in the Southern California areas and were successful in finding work.

CHAPTER SIX
Social Life on Riley Creek

During the late 1800s and through the 1930s, rural life was rather simple and uncomplicated from our current perspective. At the time my ancestors were living, they undoubtedly considered their lives complex and even complicated. It was a period of great and significant changes in our country. Inventions were being developed at a very rapid pace. Our basic body of knowledge was multiplying at an exponential rate ... even so life indeed remained tough and hard.

Riley Creek in many respects was a self-sustaining but somewhat isolated community. In a general sense, things that were happening globally were not nearly as important as local news and developments. Local developments had a direct impact on the life of farming families. The land cleared of forests, for the most part was red clay soil and somewhat rocky and nearly void of nutrients in a short period of time. The sandy loam of the creek bottoms was deep in nutrient rich topsoil that had washed down and collected in the low lands when the areas were flooded. The bottom lands were prime agricultural properties but there wasn't much of it in the Riley Creek area.

Since the farmers mostly owned and tilled the red clay land, growing crops was a really tough enterprise. To make matters more questionable, these farms were all dry land operations. That is, they did not have irrigation systems to supplement watering crops when the spring and summer rains did not materialize. Sometimes the farmers lost their entire crop due to drought. When there was crop failure, it generally affected the entire community. The weather was not selective. Little use was made of insecticides. Regardless, they were survivors and had seen many years of this kind of living and nothing much really fazed them when things didn't go well. They always knew there would be a tomorrow. The locals of the community had a respect for one another and held out a helping hand to those in time of need. It was like they were in this life on Riley Creek together as one larger family.

In many respects, it was a man's world. For the most part, women were considered the weaker sex and weren't expected to do what the men did. However, looking back, I believe that the women of that era have an excellent point for argument. They worked the inside jobs for sure and did them extremely well. On the other hand, women seemed to be merely incubators for creating newborns. In this setting, it is easy to see why my grandfather, A.J. Talley, had to be disappointed when all of his able bodied children were girls. He did not have the expected help to run his farming operation. This was indeed a dilemma. He did not have a real choice to make except to have his daughters help with the hard outside work on the farm. His brother, Ben, chastised him on his only visit, for having his daughters doing men's work. Ben thought it was awful to the point of being disgraceful!

Virtually every family had the women of the household performing more chores and duties on the farm than any female city dweller was accustomed to or expected to perform. Besides their 'field duty', the Talley girls learned to cook, sew, mend, quilt, can produce and meats, crochet, knit, wash, iron, plant gardens, care for children, go to school when they could and make time for social life. Based upon the various alternative choices which we make routinely for our entertainment today, theirs would have been very sedate and considered uneventful or maybe even boring for us … but when you heard them talk about those times, you would not have thought that to be true at all. It was good, clean, wholesome fun and they loved to tell the stories repeatedly when they were together!

Going to the county fair was the event of the year. That was top billing and ever so exciting! Movies were just starting to come into the social life of rural America. Remember these were the silent movies and in black and white film! Movies weren't readily accepted in the minds of strong Bible Belt Christian believers. Films were thought to be of the 'devil'. To go see one was sinful! To go to a movie labeled one to be a flagrant liberal and less than understanding of Christian principles. A virtual heathen!

This concept reminds me of my own mother's attitude and convictions towards television when it was introduced to the masses in 1947. She was convinced that it was sinful to watch it because it reminded her of going to the movies. I had great difficulty relating to television in any similar way to her thinking. Over a period of years, she did change her viewpoint. She eventually purchased her own television!

So what was left to do to have fun for young and old alike in those days? Church was the mainstay and center of activity in the community. If you think about it, these people and families worked with each other when they needed each other's help; they went to school together; they visited and socialized with each other. They really got to know their neighbors and, in fact, the whole community! Everybody knew everybody. Who needed newspapers or telephones? News and information got around pretty quickly. Every time the church doors opened, the community went to church. There was only one church so there wasn't any denominational choice to make. Regardless of your personal denominational preference, you still went to the local community church; the alternative was to stay home.

There were cake and pie socials as well. This may have been more of a contest than any one realized. Just as we have dessert socials, during the evening, word gets around to those gathered to "try Betty's special strawberry pie, it's out of this world; it's to die for!" The same thing happened back then with one difference, these were the young and eligible for marriage. The ladies were up for testing their cooking skills! If you were good at it, you were more in demand. No doubt, their attire was on display from a skill standpoint as well that afternoon or evening. For the most part, the young ladies made their own clothes with a little help from their mothers, as needed, and in particular when it came to special dresses. Perhaps the mark of a successful event for a young lady was when she did not have to take any pie or cake home after the party and someone or several made some nice comments about her attire!

Very rarely did they have an ice cream social. It was very difficult to keep the ice, which was necessary to make that favorite dessert, from melting. Someone had to go to town to get the ice at just the right time, buy enough of it that as it melted away before using it there was actually enough left to make the ice cream. It could be a little tricky in terms of timing particularly in the hot months of summer. But this was considered to be a real treat and everybody loved it!

Another favorite summer activity was the watermelon feeds. My dad like to go into the field and thump melons until he found the 'right sound' and then pick however many melons were needed. He usually had to sample some of the melons right there on the spot by breaking them open and eating only the heart of the melons. These were not seedless melons and, therefore, the heart or center of the melon was the sweetest and had the fewest seeds. They would cool the melons before eating them by putting them in the cool flowing water of a stream or lowering them into the wells for several hours in a large bucket or small tub.

It goes without saying that during the summer months there was always the old swimming hole down on Riley Creek. No doubt there were others in the area as well but my mother always referred to this one. The kids would get together and go swimming mostly on weekends or on days when they weren't tied down with chores or work to do. My mother liked to tell of her future mother-in-law going to the swimming hole with the kids. Annie Drucilla (Apple) Moudy could not "swim a lick" so she would get in the water with a bucket turned upside down to trap the air and float. The kids were always scared to death that she would fall off or turn over and drown. You will recall that the swimming suits of that day were non-revealing and had long legs and usually full length arms. The idea was to show nothing and avoid sunburn at all costs. Seemingly very different than what we experience in our 'swimming holes' in our backyards or on the beach today!

Weddings were not the "big billing events of today". They were very cost effective and didn't require a lot of planning. Notice of the wedding was almost based upon 'spur of the moment' decisions for the most part. From the stories that I have heard, there wasn't really any time to send out invitations and invite family, neighbors, friends or relatives from near or far to come over to the shindig and join the festivities. In fact, I have hardly ever heard any stories told about having a celebration. Once in a while those "in the know" would give the newly weds a charivari. This event happened after the couple had gotten married and was a mock serenade and the group would parade around the house on the outside banging tin pans, blowing horns, hitting kettles or anything they could find that would make a lot of noise. When they couldn't find anything to bang on, they'd shout, bellow or whistle just to disturb the newlyweds. Sounded like it was rather a raucous noisy event! In my mother's family, she received some gifts later including some quilts and dishes, pots and pans and other items of similar nature when she got married. So in reality, weddings were apparently not considered high on the list of social events except perhaps to your very closest friends and relatives.

Courting was somewhat limited in terms of time but there was some of it. The story was told regarding a date my mother and dad had before they were married.[1] It seems 'One night they went to an entertainment event, which was a 'play party' at someone's house. She was sitting in a chair, when someone distracted her (deliberately, of course) for some reason causing her to get up from her chair. It was planned, I'm sure, because someone called her across the room. When she returned to her chair someone had placed a raw egg in it. She did not notice it and sat down right on the egg, breaking the shell and, of course, making a mess. Her natural reaction was to throw up her hands and scream. Everyone knew she was easily embarrassed, and they loved to see her get tickled and blush. And so she did.' It seemed everyone enjoyed the fun of the prank pulled on her!

After she and my dad married, they soon bought a cow, a few chickens and a pig to "fatten out" for butchering. Early one morning, while Hester, as she was called, was making biscuits, Lewis picked up the milk bucket and headed out the back door for the barn, but after getting outside he decided to pull a prank on her. He went around the house and knocked on the front door and said "Hey Lou!" Hester answered in her loud, somewhat shrill voice, "He's out at the barn milking." She thought it was their neighbor, Marvin Dyer. He knocked again and yelled, "Hey, Lou!" She thought he didn't hear her so she told him again, even louder, that he

A social event – Amy Lee Misenhammer and Levin Johnson wading in Riley Creek.
Circa 1925

was milking. After he knocked and called for a third time, she was kind of "put out" because he couldn't understand, so she opened the door and said, "He's out in the barn ... Lewis is that you? I do wish you wouldn't do me that way!" She was aggravated at him, but he was enjoying her state of aggravation.'

Another story involved both my mother and her younger sister, Alice.[2] "Like the other girls, she had to work in her daddy's fields. One spring after getting the weeds chopped out of his cotton, Ab Tubbs hired her and Hester to help him get his cotton hoed. Hester did all right, but I guess Alice either left weeds in the row or cut down too much cotton, or maybe whiled away too many hours, anyway something unsuitable occurred because she didn't please him and he fired her. But later on he must have repented because he took her on permanently when he took her for his beloved wife."

If you notice in these old pictures, they show the people dressed up as if there was some major activity to be attended. Nevertheless, you see the young ladies and men sitting on the ground or on bridges, at the base of a tree and on farming implements and what have you. It is amazing to me how dressed up they are in their finery. Some of the men's clothes do not

Right to left: Hestell Talley, Minnie Bannister, Mamie Misnhammer (married Cecil Moudy) Betty Bannister, Lula Reed, Unknown, circa 1929

look like they fit real well. They could easily have been hand-me-downs from older siblings. You also have to realize that all those Kodak locations where they gathered were dirty and dusty and their clothes were certainly going to be soiled. Seemingly, they paid no attention to that issue. Taking pictures on a Sunday afternoon was referred to as going *kodaking.*

It is apparent that a lot of time was spent in those days just plain 'talking' to each other and enjoying each other's company. They told many stories and more often than not, they embellished stories which they had heard at some time from their parents, sibling brothers and sisters and friends. You just sort of got the feeling that there was never much complaining being carried on. There was always some prank that had been pulled on somebody that brought a lot of laughter. All of them knew that there would be another gathering tomorrow!

Those were well loved days of yesteryear for my parents, my aunts and uncles. It was just plain good clean fun, inexpensive and wholesome. Riley Creek was a closed community by some standards but the enclave was active and protective of one and all and of each other. I'm glad I got the chance to have a small taste at the end of that era.

Uncle Willie's Visit

In the late 1800s long distance travel for most people was laboriously difficult. There were not many railroads and certainly the cars were not in such stage of development to enable travelers to conveniently depend upon them as a timely mode of transportation. Even so, iron horses were the mode for long distance travel. The airplane was yet to be invented. As the century turned, this all changed very rapidly. Perhaps in 1928 or 1929, Uncle Willie felt he could stop off and visit with his brother, Andrew Jackson Talley. He had not seen him in at least forty years. This was his first trip to the Talley homestead. My mother was twenty-three or twenty-four years old at the time of his visit and it was two or three years before she married. Uncle Willie, who was the baby boy of the Joel Talley family, had apparently been to Texas to spend time with another brother, Benjamin, and was stopping here on his way home to Tennessee. It was summer time and a Sunday when he arrived in Danville, Arkansas.

As the story was told, Uncle Willie arrived by train in Danville. He asked around to find someone who knew "Uncle Jack" Talley. You have to remember, on Sunday, everybody went to church and I'm sure that made Uncle Willie's task that much more difficult. He was able to hire someone with a wagon to take him to Riley Creek. He later made the statement, "Thought we were never going to get here!" He had to ride probably ten or more miles in that wagon to which he was obviously not accustomed. In fact he was used to cars and trucks, he said. To get to the Talley residence, he probably would have ridden past the country church were my granddad was attending Sunday worship services. Regardless, he made his way to the Talley homestead and was awaiting the arrival of his brother from church. Back in those days church just didn't last for an hour ... it could be several hours if the preacher got to 'feeling the spirit moving'.

For reasons unexplained, Lewis Moudy showed up at the Talley's sometime before church was over. He had a car, which probably belonged to Uncle Lee Moudy. He was asked to go to the church and bring Uncle Jack Talley home. He was further advised and instructed to not tell him anything about Uncle Willie's arrival. Uncle Willie was, in fact, playing a game of identity and wanted to see if Andrew could recognize him. Lewis

Uncle Willie and Girls: Elizabeth, Alice, Uncle Willie, his wife, Lillie, and Hestella Talley, circa 1932

probably had some trouble not making any disclosures, but apparently was able to withstand the inquisitions of my grandfather.

They drove into the yard, and Granddad got out of the car and went up on to the porch to greet this visitor who had interrupted his Sunday worship. They shook hands without Jack Talley really recognizing who the visitor was, and so Uncle Willie asked, "Who do you think this is?" To which Granddad replied, "Let me see your eyes." Upon making his inspection and observation, he announced, "You're a Talley, you must be my brother, Will!" Recognition took place because of a peculiar marking in the eyes of the Talley family. Each of them had little gray or brown spots in the cornea of their eyes. It was a unique family trait and Granddad had recognized that feature in Uncle Willie.

Uncle Willie stayed two weeks. He had a lot of catching up to do apparently. Granddad and Uncle Willie would talk into the night each evening. The whole family was enjoying his stopover. During his stay, Uncle Willie observed the girls doing all the chores around the house and working in the fields doing a man's job. He did not like that at all and chastised his brother for allowing that to happen. He thought that was terrible for them. No one knows what Uncle Jack's response was but after Willie left the girls continued doing all the things they had normally done before he came.

During his stay, Uncle Willie decided that he did not like his brother's mustache. He told Uncle Jack that it made him look at least ten years older. So, one day, he had him sit down in one of those hand made chairs of oak frames with cow leather strapping for seats and backs that were kept on the front porch. Then he got some soap, the old mug brush and lathered it up real well. He had someone get the straight edge razor along with the leather strap and sharpened it up. Now every thing was set. I don't know if he had drawn an audience by this time or not but he proceeded to shave off Andrew's mustache. He surprised everybody by announcing that he was going to shave it off. No one could believe that Granddad would let him do it … but he did. After it was over, Uncle Willie said, "See, I told you it would make you look ten years younger." From that day forward, Granddad never grew another mustache or beard.

In 1943, Lizzie, my mother's sister, went to visit Uncle Willie in Tennessee after her first husband, William 'Bill' Mehle, had died. She took the train on this trip. Uncle Willie told her to wear a red ribbon pinned to her dress so that he would know her at the train depot. She did and had a wonderful visit with him and his family. She felt that they were quite wealthy and owned lots of land compared to her Talley family.

My mother's recollections included the facts that Uncle Willie lived near Chattanooga, Tennessee and that he had twelve kids. They were well educated. One became a nurse in Washington, DC, another became a doctor, one was a lawyer, two others were farmers, and one married a Chambers and lives in Alabama (this latter one could be a mix up with my Granddad's sister, Margaret, who married a Chambers and lived in Alabama. She had a daughter named Alma). She couldn't remember any other particulars.

As fate would have it, Granddad didn't see any of his brothers again before he passed away in 1948.

Grandma's Elderberry Wine [3]

It seems that the Ollie Moore family (my mother's sister's family) was visiting Grandpa and Grandma Talley at their home on Riley Creek. The Moore boys were playing and having a good time running and climbing in the trees or investigating other things that seem interesting to young boys on a farm. At some point, Kenneth, Jack (Junior as most of us called him) and AJ (that was his name) came across Grandma's elderberry wine that she had made.

For the most part it seems, no one knew that Grandma made wine of any kind. Perhaps the Moore boys did not really know what it was that they had found in its hiding place somewhere in the house. Whether or not all of them participated in the decision to take it outside is unknown. Did one of them have a taste and think it was pretty good? Regardless, they took the container of wine and sneakily went outside where they would not be seen very easily. At the Talley farm that made for a wide variety of places.

As fate would have it, the three boys found that the wine was not half-bad, so they drank all of it. It's hard to tell how much they consumed since Kenneth is the only one still living who was a participant and he claims memory failure to any of it! Maybe it was in a bottle or a fruit jar; maybe it was completely full or only partially full. Maybe Grandma had used some it in her cooking or maybe she would just occasionally take a little nip of it to assuage her own desire for a bit of relaxant. It must have been good because after its consumption, the three boys were a bit giddy.

Before the visit was over, Grandma discovered that her wine was missing and for reasons unknown felt that the young boys had stolen it (and consumed it). Perhaps she had become suspect due to their behavior and she probably asked them if they had taken the wine and no doubt they denied it. They were not convincing so she began to chase them. The boys ran into the house and hid under the bed. But Grandma thought that old bed just might be a good place for those three boys to hide. She was right! She took her broom and tried to hit them. Being older, she could not bend down and really get her licks in. When she would try one side of the bed, the boys would merely slide over to the other side and she could not hit them. This jostling escapade went on for several minutes without any satisfaction on the part of Grandma.

Aunt Ollie finally heard the commotion and to her dismay found the boys giggling and laughing under the bed with Grandma standing with broom in hand looking somewhat disgusted over the whole matter. Aunt Ollie announced," There has been enough of this fooling around and it is time to stop!" Whether Grandma thought the comments were for her or the boys, we do not know for sure. Nevertheless, Grandma put her broom down and the three young lads came out from under the bed looking rather sheepish with grins on their faces. Whether the response came from the fact they had 'bested' Grandma or they were still feeling a little tipsy and light-hearted from the wine only they will ever know for sure.

Catherine Rogers wrote about life and living in the community of Riley Creek.

"South of Monrovia – Parkersburg the road crosses the Petit Jean River, the Riley Creek Church stands about one mile south of the river. The church faces the Riley Creek Cemetery. A stream south and east of the cemetery, flowing toward the river is Riley Creek. One of the first townships made in the county was Riley. It was a large township extending as far west as Waveland. Today the area included in the Riley Township is greatly reduced. Riley Creek School was in the township known today as Reed-Keathley.

Riley Creek District #77 was made in 1885. It was made from Macedonia. There had been a church built in the community many years prior to the school's formation. The first school was built near the first church which was southeast of the Riley Creek Church and Cemetery. The first post office for the community was Manning, named in honor of an early settler. Manning was east of the cemetery some distance. In 1893 the postmaster was James Black. In 1902, the post office of Manning was dissolved to Danville.

Two who taught at Riley Creek during the 1890's were W.F. Hough and T. M. Montgomery. Some of the later teachers were Elmer and Myrtle Frazier, Ralph Dennis, Ila Suggs, Willie Suggs, Lillian B. Fair, John Denton, Pierce Bristow, Faye Watkins, Mutt

Whittington, Leo Bowerman, Joe Wheeler, Olean Buckman, Joe McCall, Irving Wells, Edgar Green, Cecil Moudy, Mel Pearce, Elsie Scott, George Denton, Lillie McReynolds, and Boyd Keathley. (This is the school where my grandfather, Andrew Jackson Talley was superintendent during the year 1915).

In 1918 two of the directors were M. L. Farmer, and C. F. Misenhamer. Some of the other families of those days were the Sherrels, Farmers, Haires, Jeans, Reads, Talleys, Pattons and many others.

Cold lunches from molasses buckets were enjoyed as kids shared cookies, baked sweet potatoes, and fried pies. There were no toilets for years. The school children, like many other rural schools, used the privacy provided by nature – the bushes on the hillside. Later a toilet was provided for the girls.

After a period of years, it was necessary to build a new schoolhouse. During the rebuilding, school was for a time in the church house across from the cemetery. Arvil Haire was about eight years old at the time. There was a woven wire fence with a barb wire top around the cemetery. "I went over the fence to get a ball, but the seat of my pants didn't go." He explained that when books took up, the teacher sent his class to the blackboard. The twittering and giggling among the students prompted the teacher to send Arvil to his seat.

Once a thunder-storm came up and lightening struck the tree just outside the school. Kids screamed and crawled under seats and some cried. The teacher appeared outwardly calm but the students knew she too was scared.

After students finished the eighth grade, many dropped out of school but some went to high school in Belleville. The Petit Jean River sometimes got out of its banks and parents took the kids in wagons. Amilee Hancock remembers a time when the wagon bed floated while the river was being crossed

The Riley Creek church house continued to be used after the school was consolidated. In 1933 there was a District Singing Convention there when 600 attended. It was said that about 400 were inside and half that number were under the trees outside.

Riley Creek School consolidated with Belleville in the early 1930s. The old school house was for a time used as a dwelling. The place where the building stood is approximately where to-day's home of Floyd McInturf stands. The farm is owned by James Mitchell.

Those who have loved ones buried in the Riley Creek Cemetery continue to care for the graves. Since the late 1940's the building has stood idle. Few live in the community today and they attend church elsewhere. Riley Creek, one of the earliest settlements in the county, is a fond memory to those who recall the place of sing-ings, parties, church and school. Many who return to Yell County to visit, drive by the old church and live in memory of the days of Riley Creek School."

1   Copied from *Barrick Roll Call*, Melba Barrick, 1993, pg. 33.

2   Ibid, pg. 35

3   Cousin Anne Moore told me this story on my visit to Arkansas, September 19, 2001.

4   *Readin', 'Ritin', 'Rithmatic*, Riley Creek, pages 12-13, Catherine Eikleberry Rogers, 1981.

CHAPTER SEVEN
Collected Family Recipes

These recipes are a collection from different family members and friends of my mother. Most of them have been used in my family or by my relatives for as long as I can recall. They are by no means an all inclusive collection of favorite foods which I enjoyed as a kid. In fact there are some I wish I had reserved to writing, such as my mother's baked yeast buns. She had a way of preparing and cooking them that seemingly cannot be duplicated. Even to this day, my children remember eating them at her house.

'Moma Talley's Apple Spice Cake' is special in the sense it has been in the family at least since the 1880s or 1890s. Anytime the Talley's girls visited each other, they often mentioned this cake. Without exception, they all liked it and thought it to be the best. I ate a piece of it once and enjoyed it very much even though I am not a serious fan of apple anything. It was very tasteful.

I am pleased to include some of the recipes I collected.

Real Mincemeat

Ingredients:
Bags of dried fruit (one each) use 1 lb. bags:
    apricots - 1 bag
    apples - 1 bag
    peaches - 1 bag
Plum or grape juice - 1 quart
Apple vinegar - 1 cup

Pork shoulder - 2 to 3 lbs.

Lemons - 3 to 4 whole lemons

Sorghum molasses - ½ gallon

Raisins - 2 lbs. (do not cook)

Sugar - 4 to 5 lbs.

Spices: ginger, allspice and cinnamon

Process:

Cook meat separately in water. Season with salt and cook until meat is tender. Let cool thoroughly.

Cook fruit separately until tender.

Save meat broth to use later.

Grind fruits and the entire pork shoulder including the lemon skin (rind) and meat fat for seasoning.

Mix all ingredients fully and be sure to use the meat broth.

Season to taste with the spices.

Mixture should be thick.

Cook to a point of boiling. STIR CONSTANTLY!

Put in jars for canning and follow canning instructions for fruit.

A quart of this mincemeat will make one double covered pie.

Source: Laura Haire made up this recipe and gave it to my mother. She in turn told it to me on July 2, 1984.

Moma Talley's Apple Stack Cake

Ingredients:

1¼ cups melted Crisco shortening

1 Jar of sorghum (approximately 2⅓ cups)

1 tsp baking soda

1 tsp ginger (do not exceed 1 tblsp)

1¼ tsp nutmeg

6 large eggs slightly beaten

1 cup brown sugar

5 lbs. all purpose or self-rising flour (regardless use baking soda)

3 – 4 lbs. dried apples (Can substitute 15 – 20 lbs. of Granny Smith fresh apples)

Process:

1. When Granny Smith apples are used, peel and core, slice rather thinly and add ½ cup water; then cook on medium heat. Season with cinnamon, brown sugar, and nutmeg to taste. Cook until most of the juice has evaporated. Note: The old time dried apples used in Arkansas are not available in California, which is why the Granny Smith apples are used. The Arkansas dried apples would turn a golden brown and had a completely different flavor than those available now.

2. Melt shortening in a large skillet; add sorghum and baking soda on low heat. Mix well and let cool.

3. Beat the eggs and spices together.

4. Combine the eggs and spices with the sorghum mixture. Mix well.

5. Place the five lbs. of sifted flour in a large mixing bowl. Make a well in the center.

6. Gradually pour in the sorghum mixture into the well mixing as you go in the well.

7. When the combined mixture reaches a still cookie dough consistency, roll it out to a ¼ inch thickness.

8. Use a dinner plate (or smaller size) for a pattern and cut out cookies. Should make 7 – 9.

9. Place each cookie on a buttered or greased cookie sheet and bake at 450° until golden brown. Cool on a wire rack.

10. With selected cake plate, place a layer of the cooked apples on the bottom of the plate. Place one cookie on the top of the apples. On top of each cookie place a layer of apples about ¼ inch thick. Alternating, place more cookies and apples until the stack is completed. Save enough applesauce to cover the top and the sides of the cake.

11. Cover the cake and store in refrigerator for about one week.

12. The cake is now ready to be served.

Chow – Chow

Ingredients:

Head of fresh cabbage - 1 large

Green tomatoes, fresh picked - I gallon bucket full

Onions - 8 large

Bell peppers - 8 large (can use mixed colors)

Anaheim Chile peppers - ½ lb. (small hot yellow variety)

Long green chile peppers - 6 long peppers

Cucumbers - 2 large (do not peel)

Apple cider vinegar - 2½ cups Sugar - 1½ cups

Pickling spices - approximately ⅓ cup

Process:

1) Grind all vegetable ingredients into a large pan.

2) Drain almost all vegetable juice from the pan.

3) Place pan with vegetables on stove on **LOW HEAT**.

4) Mix thoroughly.

5) Add vinegar and sugar (can add more sugar to sweeten to taste).

6) Place pickling spices in a rag and tie so that the spices do not mix with other ingredients. Place in pan with other ingredients.

7) Stir mixture frequently making certain that it is well mixed as it cooks.

8) Let mixture come to a boil and continue to mix ingredients. Let boil for 3 minutes. Keep vegetables on the slightly under-cooked side so they are crunchy.

9) Have sterilized jars ready and immediately pack and seal jars. Will make approximately eight pints. Do not pack with very much juice.

Zucchini Piclkes

Ingredients:

Zucchini Squash - Enough to fill 3 quart jars when the squash is sliced across.

Onions - 2 large

Bell peppers - 2 large

Water - 1 cup

Salt - ⅓ cup

Apple cider vinegar - 4 cups

Sugar - 3 cups

Turmeric powder - ¾ teaspoon

Mustard seed - 1 tablespoon

Dill seed - 1 teaspoon

Celery seed - 1 teaspoon

Process:

1) Slice the squash, peppers and onions and place in a large one gallon container.

2) Mix the ⅓ cup of salt thoroughly in the 1 cup of water and pour over vegetables.

3) Let mixture stand for 2½ to 3 hours. Cover.

4) After soaking, wash vegetables in cold water and rinse completely. Drain well.

5) Mix the cider vinegar, sugar and all other spices in a separate container and bring to a rolling boil. This container should be large enough to also hold the vegetables later.

6) While in a rolling boil state, add vegetables. **DO NOT COOK.** Just heat and be ready to fill jars.

7) Have sterilized jars and lids ready.

8) When vegetables are heated, pack into jars and seal immediately.

9) Makes approximately 6 pints.

Mom's Chocolate Pie

Ingredients:

Milk - 1½ cups

Sugar - 1½ cups

Eggs - 2 large

Butter - 1 large heaping tablespoon

Cornstarch - 2 heaping tablespoons
Cocoa - 2 tablespoons
Vanilla flavoring - 1 teaspoon

Process:
1) Separate egg yolks from whites and place in separate containers.
2) Beat egg yolks thoroughly and add milk.
3) Add and mix cornstarch, sugar, butter and cocoa.
4) Cook mixture in pan until it thickens, then add vanilla flavoring.
5) Pour into baked pie shell and top with meringue
6) Bake for 15 minutes at 325° F and until brown.

Make Meringue:
Beat the 2 egg whites thoroughly and until stiff to stand. Then add: 4 tablespoons of sugar and ¼ teaspoon of cream of tartar.

Pecan Pie

Ingredients:
Eggs - 3 large
Sugar - 1 cup
Karo, dark - 1 cup
Pecans - 1 cup
Salt - to taste
Vanilla Flavoring - 1 teaspoon

Process:
Chop nuts
Beat eggs thoroughly in a bowl large enough to hold all ingredients.
Add sugar, salt and Karo and mix.
Mix in chopped pecans and add vanilla flavoring and mix to get consistency.
Place into baked pie shell.
Have oven preheated to 325° F and bake for 30 to 35 minutes.

Zucchini Bread

Ingredients:

Zucchini - 2 cups, grated.

Eggs - 3 large

Corn oil - 1 cup

Sugar - 2 cups

Baking soda - 1 teaspoon

Baking powder - ½ teaspoon

Salt - 1 teaspoon

Cinnamon - 3 teaspoons

Flour - 3 cups sifted

Nuts - 1 cup finely chopped (your choice)

Process:

1) Beat eggs completely in container large enough to contain all ingredients
2) Add in all other ingredients and mix thoroughly.
3) Pour into loaf tins. Contents will be enough for 2 loaves.
4) Preheat oven to 325° F.
5) Bake for 1 hour.
6) Serve when cooled.

Salt Pickles

Ingredients:

Cucumbers or zucchini squash - enough to fill selected ceramic container

Chili peppers - 2 to 4 depending on quantity of pickles to be made

Salt - Mix with water to your taste (should be similar to regular food)

Grape vine leaves - fresh picked and preferably tender for best flavor

Water - enough to cover all ingredients

Process:

1) Wash grape leaves thoroughly
2) Fill container with salty water you have prepared (to taste).

3) Slice cucumbers by quartering and halving enough to fill container to within 2 inches of its top.
4) As you are filling, add a chili pepper occasionally.
5) Place some of the grape vine leaves in the mix of cucumbers as you pack them.
6) Place a thick grouping of cleaned grape leaves on top of the salty water after having added the cucumbers.
7) **Make sure that the grape leaves are also covered completely with the salty water.**
8) Cover container with a cloth that is tightly secured.
9) Let set at room temperature for about 40 hours. Check occasionally for coloration of the skin of the cucumbers. When the green skin begins to have a tinge of yellow, they are nearing the pickling stage.
10) Pickles should be crisp and crunchy when ready to eat.
11) When pickled, remove from salt brine and refrigerate. If left in the salt brine, they will become soft.

Cranberry – Orange Nut Bread

Ingredients:
Bisquick - 2½ cups
Sugar - ½ cup
Flour (Gold Medal) - ¼ cup
Egg - 1 large
Milk, whole - 1 cup
Orange peel - 2 tablespoons of grated peel
Cranberries - ¾ cup finely chopped
Nuts - ½ cup finely chopped

Process:
1) Heat oven to 350° F
2) Grease box loaf pan (9 x 5 x 3 inches)
3) Combine and mix sugar, flour, bisquick, egg, milk, and orange peel; beat

vigorously for ½ minute.

4) Stir in cranberries and nuts.

5) Pour into pan and bake for one hour or until wooden pick comes out clean.

6) Cool thoroughly before slicing.

7) Wrap in aluminum and refrigerate until eaten. Can be frozen for long storage.

8) **Note: do not use self-rising flour.**

Source: Lil Lemoine (Neighbor in Pomona mobile home park)

Hummingbird Cake

Ingredients:

3 cups sifted all-purpose flour

1 tsp baking soda

½ tsp salt

2 cups sugar

1 tsp ground cinnamon

2 large eggs

¾ cup vegetable oil

1½ tsp vanilla flavoring

8 oz. can crushed pineapple (do not drain)

1¾ cups chopped pecans

1¾ cups of mashed bananas

Process:

1. Combine first 5 ingredients in a large bowl and mix lightly.

2. Beat eggs.

3. Add beaten eggs and oil to mixed ingredients. Stir until dry ingredients are moist – do not beat.

4. Add vanilla, undrained pineapple, pecans, bananas and stir mixing well.

5. Pour batter into 3 greased and floured cake pans.

6. Bake at 350° for 23- 28 minutes or until an inserted wooden toothpick is

clean when withdrawn.

7. Cool in pans for 10 minutes and remove to let cool completely.

Source: From cousin Wanda Hasten

Cream Cheese Frosting

Ingredients:

1 cup of butter or margarine softened

1 8 oz. pack cream cheese softened

1 16 oz. pack powered sugar

1 tsp vanilla flavoring

½ cup chopped pecans

Process:

Cream the butter with the cream cheese.

Gradually add the powdered sugar.

Beat until the mixture is light and fluffy.

Complete the Cake

Process:

Select cake plate and place first layer of cake. Frost top of layer.

Place second and third layers adding frosting each time.

Frost sides and top of cake.

Sprinkle chopped roasted pecans on top.

Berry or Fruit Cobbler

Ingredients:

<u>Filling:</u>

6   Cups of berries or fruit

¾   Cup sugar

1   Tablespoon cornstarch

2   Tablespoons butter

<u>Crust</u>:

1 ½ Cups white self-rising flour

1 Tablespoon sugar

6 Tablespoons butter cut into pieces

2/3 Cup of heavy whipping cream

<u>Topping</u>:

1 Tablespoon heavy whipping cream

1 Teaspoon sugar

Process:

<u>Filling</u>:

1. In large bowl, mix fruit, sugar and cornstarch. Mix well.
2. Pour into 12 x 8 baking dish or other shallow 2-quart casserole dish.
3. Heat oven to 350°.
4. Dot with two tablespoons of butter.

<u>Crust</u>:

1. In large bowl combine flour, 1 tablespoon sugar, and mix well
2. Add butter; cut into flour with pastry blender or two knives until the mixture is about the size of small peas.
3. Add 2/3 cup heavy whipping cream. Mix with fork until moistened adding additional cream 1 tablespoon at a time if needed.
4. Shape dough into a ball.
5. Roll out on a lightly floured surface to 3/8 inch thickness.
6. Cut with knife or three inch biscuit cutter into 8 pieces.
7. Place on top of berries. Brush dough or biscuits with 1 tablespoon of cream.
8. Sprinkle top with remaining 1 teaspoon of sugar.
9. Bake at 350° for 40-50 minutes or until crust or biscuits are golden brown and thoroughly cooked. Cool slightly.
10. Serve while still warm.

Options:

1. Serve cobbler with ice cream.
2. If cobbler is cooked in a deep dish, additional biscuit dough can be made (depending on the dough needed for the crust). It can be cut into strips about two inches long and **placed into** the berry/fruit filling and cooked with filling. This is an old fashioned way to make a cobbler. All other aspects of the cobbler remain the same.

CHAPTER EIGHT

Tough Times for Tough People— the Great Depression

I was born during the Great Depression. That was on October 6, 1935. William Lee 'Sonny', my brother, was born in 1934. Given these birth dates, we were bonified Depression-era babies. No matter how one looked at it, having babies contributed to the increasing family load and strain by causing more economic struggles with more mouths to feed. This was especially true for young married couples having families with these conditions. Without government assistance and work programs there would have been even worse conditions and fewer survivors. It was into this economic climate I was born although I didn't know it was a terrible economic period for our country.

As a child, you just woke up in the morning; mom gave us something to eat. There was never a question as to how much food you got. There was never any question related to whether you liked the food or not. You ate what was put on your plate. Since hunger was never too far away, you tended to clean your plate very thoroughly. There weren't any scraps for the dog; it had to fend for itself.

There wasn't the convenience of a nice hot bath or shower before going to bed in the evening or starting your day off with a hot shower in the morning. A bath once a week was the best you could do and then it was with water heated on the cook stove and poured into the galvanized tub which was also used for washing clothes and other needs. Each day, when I was small, soon after I had gotten dressed mom would wash my face and hands, wet my hair, part it, and comb it for me. I did not get clean fresh clothes everyday but she made me change if I had gotten my clothes soiled during the previous day. Needless to say, that probably happened more often than not! Keep in mind that all members of the family did not have more than two or three changes of clothes to our names.

On my visits to Arkansas, I found that the humidity is very high during most of the summer and it can get very cold during the winter months. Being born in October was a very nice time of the year. It is the 'in between' month or so when the weather is very beautiful and the colors of autumn are on display in the hill country. Often, when there is an Indian summer, the splendid weather carries over well into October and it is just a beautiful time of the year. I don't really know if these were the conditions when I was born but I like to think that it was nice weather much as I have described. My mother never told me anything about such circumstances however.

My birthplace was Belleville, Arkansas. It was and remains a small rural town on Highway 10 several miles south of the Arkansas River and in the hill country located in the north central part of the state. The actual house was still standing when I made my last visit. In the mid-1880s, Belleville was considered a thriving community. In fact [1]it was the youngest as well as the second largest town and commerce center in Yell County. In its early history, [2]during a period of twelve years, about 300 inhabitants lived in its environs attracted by its scenery, mineral waters, healthfulness and other natural advantages. Mr. William H. Fergeson was the first settler and he built a sawmill in 1872. Still others followed in the next twelve to fifteen years establishing drug and general stores, grist mills, cotton gins, the Belleville Hotel and the Belleville Academy. The academy started in 1873 was for boys and girls with the curriculum designed to prepare the students for work or further education at the college level. It was a unique institution in its day. According to Uncle Lee Moudy, the town at this time was a mile or more from its present location towards Spring Creek. The town burned completely and was rebuilt on its present location.

My earliest recollections of life in Arkansas are at the age of about three or four years old. Except for the early months of my life, I lived my life as an only child having lost my brother when I was yet in the cradle. I do not remember my brother, William Lee "Sonny" Moudy, because he died of rheumatic fever when he was about two and a half years old. At the time, I was about seven months old. All I know is limited to what my mother told me about him and what tidbits of information others said at one time or another.

It was always said that William Lee was a quiet little boy. My mother stated that he had 'soft leg bones' and therefore, she was instructed by the doctor to give him cod liver oil. I do not know if that helped or not, she never said. I do recall seeing a picture of us together in the front yard of a farmhouse. Perhaps it was at our own house. Regardless, I was bundled up and sort of lying in a rocking chair outside the house (probably for lighting so the picture could be taken) with a country dirt road in the background. A lawn or grass could not be seen. The ground was bare: just plain old dirt. In the picture, Sonny is looking at me and holding the arm of the rocking chair. It was the only picture that my family had of Sonny that I know of. That is sort of surprising to me since my mother was such a real *kodaking* young lady.

The realization, at an early age of four or five years old, that I was an only child left me to occasionally ponder and wonder why I had no brothers or sisters like other families. Oh yes, I have heard about missing all of the fighting and arguments that peers can have with the other off spring. It may seem good to say that I never had to deal with those issues but I am not so sure. Maybe some would relish that thought but for me, I feel as if I have missed out on a significant experience in my life. That fact, in and of itself, is distasteful to me. I wish that I could have had those relational building experiences that only brothers and sisters can provide. I am not saying they are all fun and that troublesome problems do not arise. But think of the learning that goes on in finding solutions and building for the future when you live in a family of several brothers and sisters! There isn't a price tag that can be put on that. It is priceless in value. Missing out was not over bearing nor did it ever become a major focal point of my life. But it remains as an empty compartment of my life through this very moment. I truly regret that I did not have the companionship of family members, other than my parents, which most other children enjoyed in their families.

Being born and beginning a life in the hill country of Arkansas did not confer any special advantages upon a child in 1935. There are those who would say it was an economically disadvantageous time. It was after all, the middle of the Great Depression. Life itself was at best a sinister struggle of major proportions. My father worked on a part time basis whenever and wherever he could find work. He took odd jobs working for anyone, including relatives, who offered a job whether for a few hours or a few days. Permanent jobs were very scarce and limited to only a few people such as farmers, store owners and other commercial establishments. There was not any debate about selecting a job…you took what you could find and get…and you were doggone happy to get it, whether you had experience or not. Often times, the pay received was given with foodstuffs or produce from a garden because that was just as valuable as money. When you were paid, it was always in cash because banks were not completely trusted then as they are today. The cash put food on the table or helped pay the rent with those earnings. There was never any money left over. In fact, there was never enough money!

My father along with his brother, Albert 'Jack' Moudy, tried to buy and sell cattle and other farm animals for a while during the Depression. They would drive their pick-up truck along the back roads in the country and buy a pig or a cow and before the day was over, try to sell it to another party for a quarter, fifty cents or a dollar or two more than they had paid for it. That is a hard way to go. I do not know how long they tried to broker animals this way. I do know that they were not very successful doing it and gave up their efforts after a while. It wasn't possible to support two families with that kind of work.

Each year there were a group of men, including my father, young and older, that would head for Kansas and the wheat fields during harvest time. The venture involved catching a ride on the freight trains that passed through town and make their way to their destinations. I don't know where they went in Kansas. My dad never mentioned it by name, he just referred to it as the 'wheat fields out in Kansas.' I do not know if it was the same place every year or if they heard about work someplace and headed there.

Catching the freight train was a dangerous practice. Many would-be hitchhikers were severely injured and occasionally killed trying to hop a freight train. In essence, these men lived the life of a hobo for a few weeks each year going to, working, and returning from Kansas. This ride wasn't about just getting on board the train either. Once on board, the rider had to avoid the train crews who searched the boxcars and other places trying to find these 'free loaders'. If they were caught, they were subject to being beaten and sometimes turned over to the police depending where their location was at the time. On the return trip, they had to be wary of thieves who tried to steal their money or highjack them. The trip back to Arkansas could be more of a hassle than going to Kansas in the first place. My father made this trip four or five times before he decided there had to be a better way.

The harvest time only lasted a few weeks at most. Living conditions were terrible. My father said that he had slept on haystacks at night covered with cardboard or an old coat. Some of the hired hands were given meals but most often he had to scrounge for any other food. The farmers paid them as little as they had to pay. Most of the men saved their money. He stated that they were fortunate to get their clothes washed once a week!

The work itself was hard and very dirty. Steam tractors or mules were used to pull the cutters and combines. Clouds of dust swirled about the men all day as the equipment climbed up one incline and down the other side of these vast prairie farms. They wore nose scarves or tied handkerchiefs over their noses and around their necks. Hats were worn to protect them from the hot summer sun. The crops were all grown under dry farming conditions. My dad said that it always seemed like they were miles from nowhere. They wore kerchiefs to filter and clean the air somewhat and help them to breathe easier. Their eyes and lungs would still fill with dust causing them to cough a lot. After taking their handkerchiefs off and before washing their faces, they had the countenance of an unmasked bandit. The workers would wash their faces and try to clear their eyes several times a day. Many of the transient workers got fevers from the inhumane conditions. My father broke his ankle on one summer trip trying to push hay into the feeder for bailing. He was lucky. He only broke his ankle but he didn't lose his foot. Without reservation, I am certain this incident contributed strongly to his decision to forego more trips to Kansas.

At home, people got by through their own labors and lots of sharing.

Planting big gardens and canning the excess food which could not be eaten at the time was for self-preservation. Neighbors and family members alike shared in whatever they had grown. In one sense, it was nearly a society of communal living in a highly positive way. Each person did their best; each family unit did its best and together, and the community made it through the tough times. It was the only way to survive the dreadful circumstances everyone was being subjected to in life. Neighbors, friends and relatives helped each other. When it was time to slaughter the hogs for the year, several people would meet at one farm and then another farm a few days later to slaughter and prepare the pork for curing or canning. 'Help out work' was available all the time but of course one did not earn any cash for that effort. Often times, a worker got paid in produce or meat. That helped too, in terms of survival.

An interesting side note is that these people didn't necessarily complain about their plight in life. It was just a difficult and hard life they had to live. They were not given a choice. I don't remember anyone blaming God for the plight in which they found themselves. They continued to build and strengthen their faith in the Almighty that someway somehow they would emerge as survivors. Somehow they found ways and means of finding enjoyment or entertainment throughout the tough times. Life was in reality pretty simple. It was a real special treat, for example, to pop popcorn, take time to go swimming in the creek on a Sunday afternoon, or even bake a cake. Sounds very unsophisticated and that is true, it was! It was wholesome and satisfying at least to some extent!

A delightful treat was to be invited home after church on a Sunday afternoon with friends or relatives and have the farmer's fare, southern fried chicken, (a freshly killed pullet from the yard that someone chased down, gutted it, pulled the feathers and singed the pin feathers off and cut it up for frying). Added to the meal were freshly made biscuits or cornbread usually cooked in an old iron skillet. After the fried chicken had cooked, the leftovers in the skillet were used to make fried chicken gravy, which was most often referred to as 'thicken dobb'. There would always be a couple of vegetables such as fried okra and boiled whooperwill peas, crowder peas with bacon drippings for seasoning and mashed potatoes. To drink, there was fresh whole milk almost straight from the cow, except that most often the milk had gone through a separator process and a lot of the cream was removed and then the rich milk that remained had been cooled in a bucket let down in the water well, or strong ice tea without ice but loaded with sugar. To top it off there was a piece of yummy pie or cake for desert. What a meal!

Now, you say, anybody could live on that and you are right. Remember, however, that a meal such as this was a special meal…a Sunday dinner (which to us today is very large late lunch) and not an every day meal. As a side note, I recall that every one usually got one piece of chicken. The adults had first choice and the kids got whatever parts of the chicken were left on the platter. I can still taste that good golden brown and crunchy 'just right' chicken. Oh man, it was so very good. It was always cooked through and through. Every kid would eat the meat as clean as a whistle off the bone. Then you sort of sucked on the bone a little longer because it was so flavorful. Usually, the kids got all of the chicken gravy and biscuits that they wanted. My favorite piece of the chicken was the 'pulley bone.' That was the very front of the breast and all white meat. We no longer get chickens in our stores cut up the way they were butchered back in those days. For many years, however, my mother bought whole fryers in the market and she cut them up the good old way! I always got my pulley bone!

The kids' entertainment after dinner was to play by climbing trees and playing games such as tag or hide and seek. Sometimes there would be a rope swing hung from a tree limb. Remember too, there were not many used tires to tie to the tree limbs since cars were still relatively newly invented machines. This was especially true in poor rural areas like this part of Arkansas. If you did not have a tire, there was usually a large limb with a piece rope tied to it then a good sized stick tied to the loose end of the rope. It worked just as well.

The adults spent hours usually on the front porch trying to find shade and talking about this and that. Telling stories was a great past time. The latest political issues in Washington D.C.; what was going to become of this world in which they were living (often the discussion centered on the world conditions, which were getting worse and worse and hopefully Jesus was coming soon!); local events, anticipated weather, how the crops were coming and if it was going to be a good year or not for the crops, or more often than not stories about pranks that had been pulled on some one at sometime. Pranks and good times were to be remembered because they were some of the few things which brought rays of happiness and laughter to them. Before too long, it was time to get into their wagons or climb on their horse and head for home because there were chickens to feed, hogs to slop, and cows to milk before it got dark. So off they would go heading for home and another week of hard work and hopeful of another Sunday to come when the socializing would be repeated.

Those who lived in town did much the same things with one difference…they did not have farms to work on necessarily. That meant they were always looking to find work one way or another. Full-time work was indeed a rarity; most often the work was part time, a few days of work or a project to work on until it was finished. The government started several large extensive projects during the Depression era under the leadership of President Franklin D. Roosevelt. A federal government organization was formed to establish and administer large building programs such as roads, bridges, dams and even buildings, which was known as the WPA. Those letters stood for Works Progress Administration, later changed to Work Projects Administration.

My father worked on the WPA in Arkansas for a while. He told me he earned fifty cents for a full day's work and was very glad to get the work and the pay! I don't know if the project was completed or the type of work he did, which was most likely manual labor, played out. He never said. I am sure that he was happy just to earn some money in some very tough and trying times.

---

[1]   *Town of Belleville*, Yell County, Arkansas, Judy Tate, Arkansas Families.net, page 1.

[2]   Ibid. page 1.

CHAPTER NINE
Breaking the Bond of Entrapment

From the crash of the stock market in 1929 to the beginning of the United States involvement in World War II is considered 'The Great Depression' era. There were 'soup lines' on the streets of New York City and probably in most major cities throughout the country. President Herbert Hoover had campaigned using the motto of 'a chicken in every pot' for all of the people. However, it was President Franklin Delanor Roosevelt who actually started putting a 'chicken in every pot'. There were beggars asking for a food handout in numbers that had previously never existed. Many men could not take the pressures of the moment and lived the life of hobos traveling from town to town and from one stop to the next. Families were malnourished and in some cases near starvation, unable to get the nutrition they needed. Health failed many people for lack of medical treatment. People more than ever before were susceptible to disease. It was not that men and women did not want to work, they did. The problem was simply that there wasn't any work to be had. Work was extremely scarce and when work was available, it seemed there was a stampede to get it. Always, there wasn't enough work for those wanting to work.

Fortunately, the federal government started the Work Projects Administration, a work program focused on extending and building the infrastructure of the United States. Thus, a lot of new construction got underway. The program contributed extensively to the building of this great nation and, in fact, put it in a position to protect itself and help its allies in the coming World War II that was just over the political horizon. For certain, it made lots of jobs available for the masses. Families moved to places where they had opportunity and could get work. Now these were not high paying jobs but it was better than starving. I'm talking fifty cents per day...not per hour! Men took the jobs and were very glad to get the work. Of course, the buying power of the dollar was substantially greater than it is today. Regardless, families were still struggling to stay alive. Now there was a difference. People had hope for better things to come. That period of struggle and strife made an indelible imprint on many people. Even today, we still refer to people with a 'close to the vest' approach to life as having a 'Depression Mentality'. We see someone saving things that most everyone today would never think of saving and an automatic question is raised as if it were a given, 'Was that person born during the Depression?' I continue to see that happening today where a friend of mine saves (takes home) all of the unused napkins from our lunch table every day...he was born several years before the depression but still lives it affects on his life. They avoid debt if at all possible and have a propensity to always be preparing for a 'rainy day'.

Many people did not trust banking system during this time because of the great stock market crash in 1929. Gold was still the monetary standard. Many banks went 'belly up.' There wasn't any Federal Depositor's Insurance Corporation to cover depositors' losses when banks failed until a few years later. People tended to hoard their money, gold, or silver at home in lock boxes, safes, under the mattress, or in coffee cans planted in the yard or some other hiding place. Gold was considered better than money. The federal treasury backed up the paper money with gold with a fixed price value of $35.00 per ounce. The certificates were issued as gold or silver certificates. At the time, these currency bills could be redeemed for actual gold and silver. Although these certificates have long since ceased to be circulated, there are some of them, which remain in the hands of collectors because of their uniqueness. However, the United States Congress subsequently passed legislation taking the country off the gold standard, which allowed the dollar to float on the world money markets. The point is, during this time, if you had money, you kept it somewhat secretively and for as long as you could possibly hold on to it. That rainy day was just around the corner! However, in reality, it had arrived a few years before and people were merely trying to survive the best way they could.

As I said earlier, I was born in the middle of the Depression. Therefore, even though I had firsthand experience with life at that time, my age helped me tremendously because I do not remember how difficult life really was. Therefore, the Great Depression left me with few scars. I recount a lot of what happened in my family from the depictions given to me by my parents and relatives. What little I recall from my experiences during that time was dulled by childhood. That is, one tends to recall the good things in life a lot better than the tough times especially as a kid. Nevertheless, my parental training was directly related to the Depression Mentality and some of it rubbed on me. I do know for certain that the Great Depression was not a panacea for life in general, that is for sure!

One of the first affects the Depression had directly on me was always an admonishment from my mom to 'clean my plate.' That meant to eat everything put on your plate…don't leave anything. I got so good at it that I would take a biscuit or a piece of bread and sop up my plate after having eaten all of the solid foods. In fact, it would look as clean as it was before my mother had put any food on it in the first place. Why was that important? It was very basic. We didn't always know when there would be a next meal. Even today, I still have a tendency because of that training to literally clean my plate. I am conditioned much like Pavlov's dog but for a different reason!

Living on a farm, was perhaps a little better than being a town or city dweller. You could grow your own food with a large garden. In the fields, animal feed or edible crops for human consumption could be grown. Almost every farmer had a cow or two and chickens with a new brood coming along as needed. All of the table scraps, if any, were saved in a 'slop bucket' and went out the door as food for the pigs. There wasn't any money; it was as scarce as 'hens teeth'. There was usually some food, however.

There were times in our household when a meal would consist of a piece of day old (or more) cornbread and a glass of milk. The milk might be sweet milk or buttermilk. I do not know when redeye gravy was first created. It was a carryover from the frontier days. I do know that when ham or bacon was cooked, the drippings were never wasted. The drippings were mixed with coffee, when possible, and served as redeye gravy to be sopped up with a biscuit or cornbread. To have a piece of meat was a real treat and most often at my grandfather's house that would be pork of some kind. There were those occasions when there was no food in the house. The cupboard was bare. My mother told me that she has mixed flour with water and fried it and that was our food for that meal. I suppose it was a lot like a pancake of sorts. We were really living high when we had molasses to go on it! She often praised the Lord for what He provided and the way He provided. It seems, somehow or some way, an individual, a friend, neighbor, or relative would bring something to eat to our door. There wasn't any other way to get food. If the garden produced more food than you could eat, you canned it. That was after sharing with your neighbors and relatives. When you canned, you reused fruit jars and the rubber seals over and over again until the seals were no longer usable. Canning was very important to our survival.

Home remedies were prevalent on the frontier. Their use had been developed by the Native Americans and the early settlers. Medicine had progressed significantly from those early days and into the Depression period. Yet, if you didn't have money, you couldn't buy prescription drugs. Family doctors came to the sick. Nobody in rural areas went to the doctor's office. Doctors traveled on horseback or in a buggy and made house calls. Knowing the circumstances of the patient, family doctors often prescribed what we would consider today to be home remedies. Many seemed to work while others probably did not help very much if at all. Patients probably more often than not got well on their own doctoring of home remedies as the sickness ran its course. Yet, country folks had a high regard for doctors and treated them with great respect as if they were next to God. My mother had several of these home remedies which she used on me especially during my childhood. I have taken castor oil for many illnesses and on many occasions. I took paregoric as a tonic for something I don't even remember. I think her favorite prescription was making a poultice by putting Vicks vaporub on a soft clothe after she had sprinkled it with turpentine or kerosene. She would then warm it over an open flame making certain the medication was evenly distributed and then, with safety pins, pin it to my chest under my tee shirt while it was still warm. This was the treatment for a chest cold. It cleared up your nasal passages and actually felt good when it was warm on your chest. In a few hours or a day or so, you would start coughing up the phlegm. Generally, it seemed as if you would cough your head off before you got well. Interestingly, I still do a version of that remedy today when I rub the same Vicks salve on my chest or on a cloth and apply it to my chest when I have a bad cold.

There were other problems that depression people encountered. One was the weather. Farmers depended upon the seasonal rains to grow their crops. This was dry land farming. Almanacs were used to try and determine the best time to plant and whether the moon and stars were properly aligned to establish their conviction that it would be a good year for crops. If the rains did not materialize, the farmers would not have much of a crop, if any. This brought about additional stress and chaos. The greatest drought occurred in Oklahoma. 'The Dust Bowl', it was called. The drought spread into other geographic regions in a slightly less destructive manner but it nevertheless had its disastrous impact. My relatives in Arkansas did not fare well in this regard either.

It was under these conditions that people struggled to survive. Many were consumed by the situation and circumstances, lost hope, and did not survive.

These are many of the reasons why my father traveled to the Kansas wheat fields during the harvest time. Ultimately, those trips and the experience is why he went into business to scrape up a buck or two by going into a partnership with his younger brother, Jack. In the end, the horrible economic conditions were why he worked on the WPA for fifty cents a day. There was no choice. It was a means by which my mother, father and I survived until the decision was made to move to California and leave our home in Arkansas along with most all of our loved ones.

First efforts to break out of these conditions happened in May or June 1937. After the death and burial of my brother, Sonny, in the Riley Creek Cemetery, my parents decided to move to California. The motives were the same as always…to find work. I learned my initial trip to California was via a pick-up truck driven by Lloyd Barrick. In those days it was not illegal to ride in the bed of the truck. My cousin, Edna Dell (Moudy) Majors, told me that my family was on its way passing through Fort Smith, Arkansas, which was about seventy-five miles west of Belleville. Her father, Lee Moudy, was doing business in Fort Smith and saw the vehicle passing. There was no tarpaulin to cover the back and he was fearful for those sitting in the truck bed encountering bad weather. So he had them pull over and wait while he purchased a tarpaulin cover for the bed of the truck. Theodore Haire was also making that trip. He had just graduated from high school. Perhaps everyone pooled their resources to pay their way. I was on board but I do not know whether I sat or laid on a pallet or blanket for the trip.

Our destination was Berinda, California in the great San Joaquin Valley. There, both my mother and father got work picking grapes and cotton. They scrimped and saved; it was difficult to save any money. Within several months, my father was able to buy a car. That car provided transportation to the ever-changing locations encountered by itinerant farm workers as they followed the seemingly endless harvests of cotton, fruits, and nuts up and down the Great Valley. They went where the next harvest would happen or was already underway and where they could get work. Living conditions in the migrant worker camps were terrible. But being molded in the crucible of a tough life in Arkansas had made them hardened soldiers of survival. They knew how to cope and they did. It was not a panacea of success or a cornucopia of life however.

In 1938, my Uncle Lee Moudy, somehow tracked down my father, by telephone, to tell him that their father, Thomas W. Moudy, was dieing and to return home immediately if he wanted to see him alive. Without giving it a second thought, my parents quit their work, packed what few belongings we had in the old car and headed for Arkansas. There wasn't any question about whether or not they should return. It didn't make any difference regarding what you were doing in terms of your work, either. In those days, it was a family tradition to return home when someone was dieing. It was almost unforgivable, by other family members, if you didn't come home under these dire circumstances. In those days, death was a preemptive issue under any condition…everyone had to come home immediately! This was the way my parents' families looked upon death and

Lewis & Hestella Moudy, my parents, with me at Dos Palos, CA, while they were migrant farm workers in the San Joaquin Valley. Circa 1937

burial. Be there unless you are dieing! The family packed its few belongings and got in the car and headed east.

There was car trouble on several occasions along the way. The last breakdown left the car in such condition that it was no longer drivable, so my father sold the car in Oklahoma and bought bus tickets for the remainder of the trip to Belleville. My Uncle Lee Moudy met the bus when we arrived and informed my dad that their father had already passed away. They had held up the funeral so that we could attend.

Such an event can be seriously disruptive to the economics of a family. The belief was that it was easier to start over than to miss out on a loved one's last moment in life. Perhaps there was some issue to be reconciled or a last statement to be made between two people. It was looked upon as a last opportunity to 'speak your peace.' It was a time of grief but also a time of reunion and renewal. Making the trip was a necessity but in the back of their minds they expected to return again to the new life within a short period of time. When you are among relatives and friends who love and care for you, it is a warm atmosphere. There were talks of staying on in Arkansas and staying close to home rather than being out in California, which for many seemed to be the other side of the world, so far away. Most of my parents' relatives had never been to California…never carried a thought or harbored a desire of going. It wasn't home no matter what the magnetism happened to be. There was nothing like home in Arkansas. The result of this logic and persuasion was that my parents decided to stay on in Arkansas, at least for a while.

Life was not much different than previously. My parents struggled day after day to make ends meet. We first lived, and this is my earliest remembrance of Arkansas, out towards Spring Lake across from what was known as 'old town' near present day Belleville. It was in back of Doc Grayson's home. I do not have a lot of recollections of my dad being home very much. I recall my mother raising ducks and geese. There was a very small stream, which ran through the back yard and the ducks and geese were always in or around the water. It might have been breeding time or just a cranky old goose, I don't know. What I do recall is that I was out probably agitating or chasing the geese around when one of them decided that she had enough and turned on me. I was just a little tike of about three and a half or four years old. The goose snapped on my finger and I thought she had taken my finger off. My mother ran out the door when she heard my anguished cry and saw me crying and looking at my finger. It was bleeding. That old goose had nailed me. Mom took me in the house and wrapped it in a piece of rag and tied it. I do not think we had any alcohol to put on it. My finger soon got well and the incident was forgotten.

This house is the place where I remember climbing up in the peach tree growing near the back side door. The tree was probably thirty feet tall and adjacent to and overhanging the chicken house. The tree was at the very edge and inside the garden fence. That was the first tree that I can remember climbing.

I could climb up in that tree and get on top of the chicken house and survey the garden and the ducks, geese and chickens running around. I recall watching my mother picking the feathers from the ducks and geese to make feather pillows and mattresses for the bed. She would chase one of them down, pin it under her arm or between her legs so that it could not bite or snap her and pull the smaller feathers. Those birds would squawk and screech like you never heard. I am sure they were scared for their lives and it probably hurt a bit too! When it was over, they looked almost sickly. As you can imagine, they did not preen their feathers for a while. I sort of thought of the process as proper payback to that old goose that snapped me!

Living about a mile or so from town meant walking to church almost every Sunday down the old dirt road in our Sunday best with my mother holding my hand. Sunday best wasn't much for us in those days. My mother always said that Jesus wanted us to look our best and be our best at church. We went to the Assembly of God Church in town. It wasn't far from the brick school (I would attend it later), which we walked past each time. I liked walking to church in the spring because there were beautiful wild flowers that grew along the road. Along the way were clumps of bearded iris that were light purple in color and, often standing as tall as I, Black-eyed Susan wild flowers too. As a kid, plants, and particularly flowering plants, were always interesting to me.

As a curious boy, I spent quite a lot of time just picking flowers apart

The town of Belleville, AR as it looked in the year 2000. Major differences today include paved roads and a new post office on the left forefront; otherwise not much has changed as compared to my childhood days. Uncle Lee Moudy once owned the building in the far back left.

trying to understand how they were made and how they could grow from those little tiny seeds was fascinating. I would pull off a petal at a time until there were no more petals. The petals seemed to grow in a row but sometimes they did not. I would smell them. Some did not smell all that good. I usually had that powdery stuff (pollen) all over my hands. That wasn't a problem because I could just rub it off on my pants. Perhaps that was the period of time when I learned to like flowers. It has been a lifelong enjoyment of mine!

Perhaps a year or so later, we moved into town in Belleville, next to the blacksmith shop on the main street. It was about a block or so down from the large general store in town, which Uncle Lee Moudy owned later, but

probably not at this time. This was like a small apartment house, single story with maybe four units. We lived in one of the front units. There was not a lot for a boy of almost five to do there. I spent time looking into the blacksmith shop and watching what they were doing. It was interesting but sort of smelly like something was always burning. The man would heat metal in a furnace until it got red hot then take it out and pound on it with a big hammer. Sometimes, he would put the metal back into the fire or stick it in a pail of water. Then I could hear the sizzle as the metal created steam and cooled. It was a dirty old place. I also played with my dog and my little red wagon. I don't know how or where I got the Wagon, I'm sure that it wasn't new.

My dog liked for me to pull him in the wagon. There was a ditch along the road in front of the house and I would pull the wagon into the ditch until it was over balanced and would turn over. My dog would bark like crazy until I turned the wagon back upright so he could get in again and start the game all over.

Before too long, a matter of a few months maybe, my grandfather came in his wagon with the mules and all of our belongings, clothes, some furniture and other things were put in the wagon; and my mother and I traveled to Grandpa Talley's farm on Riley Creek. We were moving to grandpa's farm! I had just started to school in the first grade. We did not have kindergarten. That was 1940. My dad was returning to California to find work again. My mother and I were to stay with Grandpa and Grandma Talley until he sent for us.

I remember being ill one morning. I did not feel like going to school. The part that I recall most that day was what my mother did for me to make me feel better. I apparently did not feel like eating my regular breakfast. But somehow, my mother had a remedy for that which she had probably learned as a little girl. She got a cup of hot black coffee. At Grandpa's house no one ever put cream or milk or even sugar in coffee. It was meant to be drunk as hot as possible and the blacker the better. I really did not like the taste of it black because to me it was somewhat bitter. Even so, my mom got a cup of the coffee and put some sugar in it. To my surprise, she put some of the coffee in a saucer, blew on it to cool it down and then put the crusty bottom of a biscuit in it and soaked it for a minute or so. Next thing I knew, she was feeding it to me. It tasted good. It really tasted good! I think that was about all that I had to eat for that day but it did make me feel better.

Late the following spring, the day finally came when my mother and I boarded the train for the trip to California. In the meantime, I had started school, riding the big yellow bus everyday from Riley Creek with Herman Patton the bus driver. Grandpa's place was the last stop on the route. It was the turn around point on the route. At school in Belleville, we were given cans of grapefruit juice and a few other staple items from time to time as food supplements for the poor. This was a food program from the federal food programs during the days of the Depression that remained. Life still was not easy but it was better.

It was while riding the school bus every day that I noticed a 'special' young lady in my first grade class. She rode the same school bus, too. Her name was Mary Beth Harris. Think she had a sister who was older. I always felt a little extra pulsation of my heart when the bus stopped to let her get on. She was close to being the last one to get on the bus while I was always the first one on with my cousins Gerry and Jimmie Sue Tubbs. I never as much as held her hand but as a kid barely five years, I liked her. Maybe that was my first crush on a girl.

I did not realize it at the time, but when my dad left Arkansas that time and my mother and I followed a while later, it would be the last time my family would have a permanent residence in Arkansas. We were leaving for the 'promised land, the land of milk and honey' as my dad always said when he referred to California. We had been freed from bondage forever…at least that's what we believed.

CHAPTER TEN

Migration to the Land of Sunshine, Milk and Honey

My father had been in California more than six months. He had gone to live and be with his youngest brother, Jack, while he found work and got back on his feet financially. Uncle Jack Moudy and his family had moved to California some while before and from the reports, we got in Arkansas, he was doing pretty well. This tended to encourage other family members to want to make the trek in order to improve their lives. Some thought seriously about it but did not make the commitment. My dad had been in California for several months when he decided that it was time for my mother and me to join him. This was an exciting time for me. We were going to California!

The day before my mother and I were to leave on the train for California, Uncle Lee Moudy drove over to Riley Creek in one of his cars that he used for renting and taxi services. He helped us load our few meager belongings, which were packed into cardboard boxes and one old suitcase, into the trunk. I don't recall where the suitcase came from…a hand out or loan from someone no doubt. We said our 'goodbyes' to grandpa and grandma and got into the car for the seven mile trip to Belleville. I do not remember anything on the trip to town, I am sure that I was too excited anticipating the train trip to California.

We would be spending the night at Uncle Lee's and Aunt Jennie's home and going to the train station the next morning. Their house was only a quarter mile or so from the train depot in town.

The Train Was One Way Out

Those iron behemoths; goliaths of machines! Some of those big steamers weighed in at more than one million tons! They were incredibly durable and had the equivalent energy of many thousand horses. They pulled loads, which actually extended on the steel ribbons for more than a mile. Yes, even to a little boy of five, they generated both a fascination and fear as they belched black smoke and hissed huge billows of steam from their innards. They made horrible screeching sounds as iron wheels rubbed against steel rails on rounding curves or when the brakes were applied. The cars would sway to and fro as a ship with drunken sailors on board. It was a sight to see.

In Arkansas, one did not get to see trains very often. You could hear the lonesome drawn-out shrill sounds of a whistle in the hills of my grandfather's farm and that was at least seven miles to the nearest set of railroad tracks. It seemed to echo and ricochet off the many hills as it bounced its way to the farm. Even that far away, one could plainly hear it. As a small boy, I never once anticipated getting to ride on such a vehicle. But one day, through no choice of my own, the time came to take a ride on the Rock Island Line.

My mother had received some money from my dad in California, telling us to buy tickets and come to California on the train. It was in the late spring of 1941 when I was almost six years old. The day came and the excitement reached its zenith for me. Uncle Lee Moudy drove one of his cars to Grandfather Talley's farm on Riley Creek the day before we were to leave. We spent the night at his home in Belleville. That afternoon, Aunt Jennie fried a chicken and cooked some biscuits. This was some of the food we would take on the train. In addition, Uncle Lee brought home some bananas and apples along with a box of vanilla wafers from his store for us. He packed all the food, along with a jar of Grandma Talley's canned sausage balls, in a box. We were ready for the trip now. We had food in one box and some clothes in some others.

That eventful day arrived. Uncle Lee drove us down to the train depot that morning. It wasn't very far from his home, maybe a quarter mile. We got up at dawn, which was about five o'clock. A couple of hours later, I remember going down to the train depot in Belleville. As soon as we arrived, the stationmaster began barking out orders by telling us to stand over there (some place) out of the way. He was a little stern ... maybe thought I was one of those misbehaved spoiled brats. I wasn't! I couldn't wait for the train to arrive. The time of day, in this rural community, was long after everybody had gotten up, had breakfast, and was working or ready to work. That still meant that it was only about 7:30 in the morning.

Standing in the station, you could hear the train coming as it drew near. At first it seemed some distance away with its lonesome whistle blowing every once in a while. Then there was a sort of rumbling to it and even the station's frame building started shaking as the train got closer. While still a fair piece down the tracks, the engineer pulled the control for the whistle as he neared to clear the many dirt road crossings of cars, wagons and people and to let everyone know to get out of the way. That was a whole lot louder than I'd ever heard it before. Shortly afterwards, all you could hear was those squeaking and screeching brakes as the engineer tried to stop the monster.

Once it stopped, there was a bevy of activity. A few bags along with some mail pouches were taken off and others, including my mother's suitcase and some of our boxes that had been placed on the cargo wagon were loaded into the baggage car. It really did not take very long. The conductor took our two boxes of food and my mother placed them under a seat in the coach car where the conductor told us to sit. Then we returned to the door and said our 'good-byes' to Aunt Bessie and Uncle Lee but were quickly hustled to our seats by the conductor. The trainmen were indeed in a hurry! Almost as soon as we climbed the three stairs and set foot inside the coach, the engineer gave two short toots on the whistle and the train began to move. We waved to Uncle Lee and Aunt Bessie as we left the depot not knowing what was to lie ahead of us or if we would ever return. It seemed to me like the Engineer had been watching us during the entire stop and pulled the throttle as soon as we boarded ... we had not even reached our seats yet! It was about nine o'clock in the morning and I had been told that the trip would take about three days. Slowly at first, the train began to move; then it was wobbling and jostling from side to side as it began to pick up speed.

Within a few hours, after making many stops, we arrived in Fort Smith, Arkansas and we had to disembark to board another train that was going to take us to California. I didn't understand that fully back then because I thought the train tracks would take us to any place we wanted to go. So why couldn't the same train take us to California? Much later I was to learn that railroads owned certain routes and those were the ones they could travel on to conduct their business. I learned later that there were short line and long haul railroads. That seemed to make sense. That was why different trains had different names. Later that day, my mother broke open one of the two boxes she had carried on board. It was the one filled with food and now it was time to enjoy the goodies our relatives had prepared for us. Besides, we could not afford to buy anything, including food. We had no more money. We felt good though about going back to California. I would get to see my dad again, and Uncle Jack and Aunt Eulerle (Reich) Moudy and my cousins, Fonda, Laverne and Eula. They lived in Camarillo, California.

For the most part the trip was uneventful until we got to either Barstow or San Bernardino, California. The train was delayed for over one day while floodwaters subsided. I believe that the Santa Ana River had overflowed it banks. There had been a major storm that brought substantial flooding to the area. The train was not allowed to pass over the bridge until safe passage seemed assured. When we did make the crossing, we moved across that bridge, which did not have any side rails like the train bridges in Arkansas, very deliberately and extremely slowly. As I was unable to see clearly while sitting in my seat, I stood up during the crossing to have a better vantage point. It was a sight to behold!

As I looked out the window, water was rushing and gushing in every direction, frothing white, yet muddy and dirty looking as it seemed to boil. It was just almost touching the bridge we were crossing, so close that it seemed like it would be fairly easy to just reach out and touch it. There were pieces of trees and branches and debris caught on the abutments. The conductor said we were moving at three miles per hour. It was scary. Passengers all around were making comments about the depth and speed of water and showed great concern about our safety. With no more excitement, we made it to Union Station in Los Angeles where we again changed trains to complete our journey to Camarillo, California. I have had a love for trains since that trip.

Arriving in Camarillo, a drastic change in scenery and weather was noticed immediately. Compared to Arkansas, it was very different. There were lots of lemon and orange groves surrounded by giant eucalyptus trees, used for wind breaks, beginning about a block away from where we lived. The eucalyptus trees gave off a strange but likeable odor which was obviously new to me. However, I liked the strange sweet smell of the citrus trees when they bloomed best. The air was permeated with the fruity citrus flavor when the bloom was on. Up the hill, there was a huge Catholic church bigger than any church building I had ever seen. It is still there today, avoiding the demolition crews as new freeways were built through the area many decades later. Now it does not appear to be as huge as it was back then.

Camarillo was a sleepy little town with primarily citrus workers living in the local area. There was also a walnut packing shed, as we referred to it, down the road a short distance adjacent to the railroad tracks. English walnuts were processed there during the harvesting of these nuts from the numerous groves that surrounded the area. Other than a gas station or two and a restaurant, there wasn't much remaining. Highway 101 was the main street through the town and it made its way east up the Canejo Pass to Thousand Oaks. Highway 101 east as it left Camarillo was bounded on either side by huge and very tall eucalyptus trees. They had been there so long that the top parts of the trees converged and completely shadowed the highway making a sort of 'tree tunnel.' It was shady and cool during the hot summer months. Many of these trees remain standing today on one side of the freeway. They continue to remind me of many years ago when things were very different than they are in the world I now live in.

Our first place to live was across the street from where my Uncle Jack and his family lived. It was basically a small sort of rental farm labor type of house. Every thing was on a small scale, the kitchen had a small dining table, a bedroom, bathroom, and I don't remember a living room. Noth-

289

ing to brag about but it provided shelter. My cousins, especially, Eula, took me to the little village grocery store just down the street less than a block away. It was a hole in the wall and looked as if it had been there forever. It probably did not offer a big variety of foods but it was crammed full of groceries and appetite whetting candies, sodas and ice cream and Popsicles for the kids in the neighborhood. The store was 'quick shop' for the locals who lived in the area when they forgot something at the big grocery stores. Inside, it was very small and crowded with canned goods and boxes of cereals, fresh bread, a handful of fresh vegetables and an ice cream freezer. In the heat of summer, it was a cool place to go. When I could, I would beg my mother for a nickel so I could buy a Popsicle, an ice cream, or candy bar. On other occasions, my cousins, usually Eula, would ask me to go to the store with her and she would buy each of us a treat of some sorts. It seemed to me that my cousins had all the money in the world. From my viewpoint, they got to buy whatever they wanted anytime they wanted. My aunt Eulerle never seemed to question them when they wanted some money. I do not know if she ever asked them 'how much' they wanted, she seemed to just go to her purse and hand them some money.

The Moudy family members were not large people and were never heavy or exceedingly overweight. Perhaps the only exception to that was Uncle Jack Moudy. He was a great cook and loved to cook as well as loving to eat it! Good cooks are always sampling their dishes before serving their entrees! Uncle Jack was no different. I still recall many of his baked turkeys that he would cook to celebrate Christmas or Thanksgiving.

Uncle Jack also had the male hair traits of the Moudy's. Most of them had very little hair as they got older except around the edges of their heads and they did not have any hair to speak of on top of their heads. All of my dad's brothers were that way.

California was new and very different from Arkansas. Except for a few foggy mornings, there was sunshine almost every day. I liked that very much. At least the first part of what my parents had told me regarding California was true; it was a land of sunshine!

The trip to California was like a trip to freedom. We were living proof of surviving the Great Depression. From that time on, our family life would improve economically...not dramatically but nevertheless a new and improved state of existence. We had survived the Great Depression!

When we arrived, my father had a job working in the citrus industry caring for the orange groves in the local area. It didn't pay very well, but the needs of the family could be met if there was economic scrutiny on how the money was spent. My mother referred to it as watching our pennies and I think literally that is exactly what it was for our family. Within a few months, President F. D. Roosevelt announced the attack on Pearl Harbor and that would further change our lives forever. My father quit the groves after getting a job with the Navy at Port Hueneme.

Highway 66 played an important role in the lives of the migrant farm workers and the impoverished people who made the move to California. Many after arriving in the Golden State, easily got homesick. This Great Depression built highway would be well-traveled by many of the poor migrant people who had moved to Southern California and the San Joaquin Valley, the 'fruit bowl of the world.' Many of these travelers, after making the rather tortuous trip to the promised land, would move back to whichever state they had come from only to decide their decision was a bad judgment call. They would then turn around after a relatively short period of time and return to California. Many families made more than one such trip. The trips were made with the best of intentions and expectations. Even so, economics of the time dictated their ultimate decisions to remain in California. People from a number of states followed this cyclic tripping whether they were from Arkansas, Oklahoma, Tennessee, Texas, Missouri and several other states. This road was a tale of woes and heartache, of heat and frigid cold, of auto breakdowns, an occasional 'Good Samaritan' story of rescue and revival, which showed that the belief in the basic human spirit of kindness and caring was still in existence even when you were poor and destitute.

The City of Chicago was a collection point for many eastern travelers wanting access to the West Coast and all interim points. For the first twenty-five to thirty years of the 20th century, there was no 'good way' to get to the Pacific Coast region of the country. Highway 66 was built to solve this problem. It was a ribbon of concrete that traversed into the

Southwest from the Chicago area down through Oklahoma City and then turned virtually due West all the way to Los Angeles. Travelers from the South would make connections for the trip West in Oklahoma City. It was a major highway building accomplishment back in the 1930s and contributed widely to the growth of the West Coast.

Highway 66 was romanticized in many ways including songs and books being written and historians in later years recording unique tales of life along the great highway. Today, sections of this two-lane road, a precursor to today's freeways, are memorialized and preserved in local areas. There are celebrations to recall the good old days of years gone by and the commerce it brought to many small and strange out-of-the-way and seemingly forlorn places. For many entrepreneurial types, it was an economic gold mine. You would see signs, "No more gas for 40 miles!" In some desolate places, you could even buy a hamburger; this was the big thing! If you had a lot of money, you could even get a hot roast beef sandwich with mashed potatoes and gravy. In my case, I felt fortunate to get a hamburger once during the day on our trips because we might only stop when we needed gasoline and then would have hours of driving in between. We did not even make potty stops where real toilets existed. It was often a road side stop without even a cactus or small bush to hide behind. Try that in the wintertime when it is freezing!

In my teen years, I remember Nat King Cole's famous version of "Route 66". It was written during the swing music era and made a lasting impression on me. In the song, several cities along the way are mentioned including Chicago, LA, Flagstaff, Kingman, Barstow, and San Bernardino to name a few...and don't forget Winnona! The Nat King Cole Trio gave it a good beat and it became a very popular piece of music.

I recall Highway 66 very vividly because I traveled it so many times with my parents on trips to and from Arkansas. Crossing the desert areas was boring with endless miles of sagebrush, cactus and treeless barren mountains. It seemed like to me nobody would ever want to live in the non-productive isolated sand piles. But they did! Since we did not know what smog was, there was none. Just a little haze could be spotted once in a while on a trip like that. There were rivers; but they were almost always dry. Made one ask the question why were bridges built out here? I was told that it really did rain once in a while and that flash floods were common with big gully washers. As a kid, I knew about floods.

Riding in the car, on Route 66, a slow climb would be made to the top of a hill. Hardly anyone traveled more than about fifty miles an hour. It had to be slow because we had the car fully loaded with things and people. I do not recall ever making that trip without some one or more riding along making their way 'home'. The guest passengers helped pay for the gas too. Once on the crest of the hill, as far into the distance as one could see, the highway would stretch like a flat straight ribbon with one stripe down the middle until it narrowed and disappeared into the next set of purple, red or brown mountains. At dusk or in the night, a city in the distance stood out like a neon mecca calling and magnetically attracting one and all to rest, eat, and sleep. What a comforting thought after riding all day without the benefit of air conditioning! In the summer, the windows of the car had to always be rolled down and the hot wind seemed like it would scorch your face or skin when it blew on you. We thought that we had arrived when we had water coolers that hung onto the side windows. This marvelous invention dripped water onto fibrous material until it was saturated which allowed the incoming air to cool as it passed to the inside of the car through the water saturated material. That really helped to lower the temperature a lot!

If there were enough drivers we drove all day and all night. Stopping at a motel was out of the question. Those off-in-the-distance neon lights sparkling and glistening were exciting to see for a kid. They were varied, vivid, colorful and bright with all the colors of the rainbow and generally appeared to create endless running motion. The lights would flash, run up and down, or around in circles, act like the lights were chasing each other and then disappear from view for a split second. Blink your eye and they were back again. They were on the right and on the left; they were all over the town. This is how I remember Albuquerque, New Mexico and a few other places. For the most part, civilization in the desert areas was very isolated. Tripping on Route 66 could be very monotonous for a kid used to jumping, running and playing every day for hours at a time.

The Navajo Indians and their hogans along the highway in Arizona and New Mexico made quite an impression on me as well. They would sell their blankets and jewelry from 'trading posts', which were really just stores. Some of them spread their articles on blankets on the ground in the summer in the hot sun to offer them for sale along the highway or off to one side of the stores. It was not real interesting to me but I did wonder how they made their wares. Never saw very many people stopping to make a purchase back then. Now I wish that I had a few of the items as a keepsake of days gone by. This includes the artistic blankets and silver turquoise jewelry. I see the jewelry today and realize how expensive it is and what artists these indigenous people were during those times. Then, the turquoise was real and not manufactured like a lot of it today.

The farther East we traveled, the greener the land and fields began to appear. It may have been prairie lands but it was good to get away from the desert. Back in those days, I didn't see any value in the desert. That was Route 66, a federally built concrete ribbon of two-lane road that impacted our family directly and changed all of America permanently. I still love to think about those days! When an opportunity arises nowadays, I take detours to drive a part of the old Route 66. Sometimes I see a scene on the road, an old building still standing, or a sight of flat land; it reminds me of yesterday!

I cannot recall how many times we made this trip but it was plenty to be sure. Enough trips that I became familiar with many of the sights along the way. There was never time to do any sight seeing. Our trips were always tiring and every attempt possible was made to drive as long and as fast as we could so that we would have that much more time with our relatives and friends once we arrived in Arkansas.

Many of the trips were for the same reasons as previously mentioned. Somebody had died and we were going to the funeral or someone was seriously ill and about to die. Sometimes the trips were for more or less 'Good Samaritan' reasons…some relative needed help physically to care for them or help with the farm work. There were times when we went to Arkansas for Christmas, and this was one of the few times when it was really a vacation. Winter trips were always tough trips because the weather was miserably cold most of the time and driving conditions were poor. Our time to be away from home was always short lived because of my parents' work and my school enrollment. Most of the time, we drove Route 66 and returned the same way because it was a good road and the shortest distance. When the winter weather was bad, we would take the southern route through Phoenix and Tucson, Arizona, then to El Paso, Texas and straight through to Dallas, Texas and Texarkana, Arkansas. Then we would turn north traveling through DeQueen, Arkansas to arrive in Belleville. That route was slower and longer and almost all desert. It could be extremely boring. I often wondered why any people would live out there at all or why they would even want to live in the desert since it was seemingly such a desolate place. It never failed to baffle me.

Time in Arkansas was always spent just going from one relative's to another. There was never time to consider what the kids wanted to do with the many cousins in the different households. The idea was to see as many relatives as possible so that none of them would be upset with the family because we did not come by to see them. On one such trip, however, I had more fun than usual in terms of kid fun. While visiting my Aunt Ollie Moore, in the community of Wilson, near Belleville, I had a chance to go horseback riding. My two cousins, AJ and Tiny Marie (Tince) asked me to go. I was inexperienced when it came to riding horses. But they assured me that I could do it…bareback riding. So off we went down the road and up the little incline towards the Wilson Church where my Grandfather Talley's funeral would be held in a few short years. I was having a real fun time until my cousins decided it was time for us to head back towards the house.

Horses, I found out can have a mind of their own. They know where the barn is and the faster they can get there, the better for them I guess. Anyway, the horses decided they should run back to the barn and just not walk at all. I was unable to maintain the rhythm of the running horse I was on. The bouncing became exaggerated to the point that I fell off. For some unknown reason I had enough sense to grab the horse around his neck with my left arm and lock my right hand onto my left arm and hold on for dear life. I must say in reality it was for dear life! Tince noticed my predicament and tried her best to stop the horse from running but that didn't work out until we arrived at the gate where the horses were pastured. I think back on the incident and wonder why I did not fall off completely or why the horse's hoofs did not kick me or stomp on me in some way…but the fact was that I escaped unscathed! I still to this day do not know why the event never scared me, but when the horse stopped and I let go, I never thought of it again as a potentially serious accident.

My mom and dad no longer discussed whether they should consider staying in Arkansas anymore. That question seemed to have been settled once and for all time. All of us loved to make a visit but our home was now California. I always got a kick out of the way my dad would say, " California," especially when he was excited. He would pronounce it 'Cal – la – forn –i-a! We had become acclimated to the climate of the Golden State. It also helped to have a number of transplanted Arkies in the local communities. These families visited with each other and sort of picked up the social life where it had left off in Arkansas. When the War started, even more families and friends came to Camarillo, Oxnard, Ventura, Santa Paula, Somis, El Rio, Port Hueneme and other local communities. Everybody was doing better than they ever had in Arkansas but for many comers the nostalgia for 'home' could not be forgotten or overcome.

When the War was over, many transplanted people picked up their belongings and packed their bags, emptied their bank accounts and headed back. Many had spent the War years earning good money. By nature and due to their upbringing, most were savers not spenders. They were still counting on that rainy day coming. For many of them, they had saved more money than they had ever dreamed of having so going home meant that they could enjoy life much better than those years of the Great Depression that had been left behind. The Arkies and Okies had survived! Thank God!

Within several months after our arrival in Camarillo, my father was hired at the Port Hueneme SeaBee Base, a naval installation. It played an important role during World War II in training military construction personnel in the use of heavy equipment such as road graders, bulldozers, carryalls, trucks and other vehicles. There were many thousands of enlisted men engaged in this type of work during the War throughout the South

Pacific. They built aircraft runways, constructed new facilities and bases, repaired captured Japanese bases to be used by our armed forces throughout the island hopping of the Army and Marines.

During the war, my father worked as a driver of vehicles on their way to the war front. Great convoys, sometimes inclusive of 200 to 300 vehicles, would be formed at Port Hueneme and travel up the coast to San Francisco and down the coast to Long Beach and San Diego. The workers drove the vehicles to places such as San Pedro Harbor and Mare Island later to be shipped trans-pacific on supply ships to the war theatre. Most of the time the convoys traveled at night so as to go undetected by Japanese Navy submarines believed to be sailing off shore in our coastal waters to spy on our military activities. The vehicles had 'eye-brows' on their lights to prevent reflections or refractions of light skyward to be seen from above by aircraft. An eye-brow was a piece of metal, thin, curved and half-moon shaped to fit on the top side of the headlights of the vehicles. This activity went on from 1942 until the end of the war.

The civilian population paid a price during the war in a different way. They supported the troops in a most dedicated way. Besides the civilian commitment to the work of the war effort they sacrificed food off their tables. This support was centered on food and fuel rationing. The necessities of life were put on hold more or less. If you had a car, owners could only get new tires at specific times after so many miles were driven and then a special permit was required. Gasoline was in short supply as well. Gas could only be purchased with 'stamps.' Run out of stamps and you could not get any more gasoline until you received your next month's allotment. There were those who worked the black market and under some conditions, if you knew the right person, a limited quantity of gasoline could be obtained in that manner. Of course an exorbitant price was paid for it.

Food was a very burdensome issue as well. Fresh meat was very scarce as was butter and other dairy products, except for cheese. Food stamps were issued for specific food items, namely sugar and other similar staples, which limited how much one could purchase. This is the time when margarine became popular to replace butter. Mother would buy the margarine which was creamy white in color and contained in the box was a packet of orange-yellow coloring. At home, she would mix it all in a bowl until it looked to be nearly the same color as regular butter. It wasn't as good as butter but we became used to it. During the war years is the time that we learned to appreciate spam, a canned pork meat more or less eaten of necessity but in reality did not taste bad. Even though it was already cooked in its can, my mother still thought it best to fry it! Fresh eggs and sugar were in short supply. Some items were sold in limited quantities to prevent hording. I believe a lot of mothers became very creative in their cooking during those years as they tried to prepare good meals for their families with some disguise and culinary artistic magic! At the La Perla Market in Oxnard where we shopped, fresh meat was very difficult to obtain. Yet, wives would shop early in the morning to be there when it opened just in case there was fresh meat to be bought. It was always a pleasant surprise to find fresh meat in the counter case. If a shopper came later in the day, and some did not have a choice because they worked, forget it, the supply had long since been sold.

The irony of all this rationing, particularly the gas and tires, was it still did not prevent family members from making their treks to Arkansas. How did they do it? If a trip was planned, gas stamps were saved for months, just a few extra above those needed to buy gas to go to work each week. Friends who could spare a few would sell them. The black market also played a role in the overall effort as well. Obviously such trips had to be planned well in advance of making the trip.

After the war ended, my father continued to work at the base. By this time, however, he had learned a new trade. He learned to fire and control boilers that supplied hot water throughout parts of the naval SeaBee facility. It was a good job for him since he had a very limited education. He was protected from the weather elements since it was inside.

Income was always an issue and my father continued to work double jobs when he could. Most of these extra shifts related to the seasonal packing operations for fruits, walnuts, and citrus. I remember that he took a job as a janitor so he could work evenings at my old Roosevelt Grammar School. Once he took a job driving a trash truck. The route he serviced was out on the beach strand to the west of town, then known in Oxnard as Hollywood by the Sea. On another occasion he worked at the Sunkist

My family – Hestella (Talley), William Lewis and Roark Moudy, June 24, 1945

Lemon Association packing plant in Oxnard as a night watchman. I often went with him to work on the evening jobs and assisted him with his work and duties. I liked to do that and I think he liked to have me along. I also help him with his trash truck route during the summer months when I was out of school. That was the only job that I did not like. It embarrassed me to think that some of my friends in school might see me doing that work. I did it and it helped my father immensely…and I never saw or met any-one I knew while doing it! As a night watchman, I thought the work was kind of creepy. Walking through a big dark warehouse filled with boxes of lemons and having to 'punch-in' at the different stations along the way to prove you were doing your job. Every hour he had to make the rounds. This task was repeated throughout the night. For me, it was boring.

But here we were in the land my parents had long sought as their ref-uge from the hassles and strains of life a few years before in Arkansas. The escape had been very successful by their standards.

CHAPTER ELEVEN
Setting My Compass

It is on the one hand easy to write about my life. I am not a person with a highly regarded history of personal accomplishments. I can't lay claim to having done anything truly magnanimous. On the other hand I haven't lived my life in such a way as to attain fame or to accumulate a fortune. What I have done is to enjoy my personal life in a wholesome way, performed my professional work with honesty, dedication and loyalty, and made my family the highest priority of my life. It was basically an integral part of my person. No one had to tell me to do it; I did it because it was the right thing to do and I wanted to do it.

In school, I learned early on and firmly believed that a person could become whatever he wanted to be with lots of hard work and by applying himself. I had a teacher or two say that in class. It was an idea that stuck with me as I began to work and earn money, buy a few things on my own and even save some money ... never very much but it was an important experience in my life.

After the Great Depression and the World War II had ended, this idea became even more imbedded in my mind. I was learning to apply these ideas in the crucible of life in everyday living by watching my parents continuously struggle with the economics of life. Their way of life was an extension of the belief that many people had experienced and suffered through the Great Depression. Now as they moved into a time in their lives when economics began to improve, due to new jobs and opportunities created by the war effort, they were still paralyzed by the thought and in some instances, virtually believed the expectation that tough times would return and prosperity would not last very long. My parents never directly taught me this concept of 'hard work and save'. It was our way of life. It was a survival technique. Saving money was a good idea but never materialized as much of an accomplishment for my parents. Economically, they struggled all their lives.

It became a philosophy for people of this era because they believed and had become convinced that a new peaceful world order was being built and that the holocaust caused by the "War of Wars" would never occur again. It was a new ray of sunshine in their otherwise uneventful lives of work and more work to make ends meet. Of course, many of these same people thought the same thing after World War I as well. I felt people were more convinced but with restraint and caution after World War II that there would finally be a good life in which everyone could have plenty.

Peace had come at last! You could own a home, buy a car, have children and just live the good life. Making a 'good living' and establishing roots meant owning a home, which you could call your own. In other words, eliminating some of the struggles of life that had plagued the working class for so long and finally the time to extinguish the horrible pain and strife in these peoples' lives had arrived. After the War, work remained fairly easy to find if you wanted to look for it. In Oxnard, new two bedroom homes were being sold for the outrageous price of $4,000.00, just outside the Federal Housing Development where we had lived throughout the war years. The Navy Seabee Base at Port Hueneme was still going strong with lots of work opportunities because the 'cold war' was beginning in the late 1940s. As always, there was work available on the many produce truck farms and seasonal crops grown in the area. In reality though, Oxnard was still a sleepy little town of 15,000 people in the early 1950s. It had more than doubled in population from when the War started.

As a young boy, I enjoyed roller skating. I'm sure this came about because I learned to roller skate on the many residential sidewalks of Oxnard. I had those skates that clamped directly onto my leather soled street shoes and could be tightened with a skate key. These skates could also be adjusted to fit a variety of shoe sizes. We lived in the downtown area of Oxnard near the corner of 4th and 'B' Streets in an eight-unit apartment. It was a block from Roosevelt Elementary School that I attended for three years.

Oxnard City Library where I spent many hours and enjoyed reading books.

The main streets in town were 'A' and 5th Streets. The city park was at Fifth between 'B' and 'C' Streets. I skated downtown, through the park, past the City Library, to school, and throughout the neighborhood areas. There were blocks and blocks of good sidewalks to skate on. If I wanted to ride a scooter, I would go over to my friend Howard Pringle's home. I had met Howard in school. He lived near Third and 'D' Streets near the Catholic Church. I would trade off my skates for his two-wheel push scooter. His father owned a shoe store in town and Howard always had great toys to play with. We would play for a couple of hours before I knew it was time for me to return home.

It was at Howard's home that I first played with electric trains. Trains became a life long love affair for me probably because of my train ride to California and also getting to play with Howard's Lionel train set up. We spent hours doing various fun activities of this nature.

I first noticed the roller rink while selling newspapers on the street. By the time I was nine or ten, I began to go to the rink. The skating rink was located about a half block north of the intersection of Fifth Street and Alternate 101 Highway in a main part of town. Saturday afternoon was the only time I could go. My mother encouraged me to go for some reason. I never quite understood her logic since the skating consisted of everybody skating in one direction and then the announcer would reverse the direction; then it was girls only; boys only; mixed pairs, and other innovative approaches to skating. All the while, an organist (recorded or live) played music throughout the afternoon. I definitely liked to skate, but I questioned why my mother thought this was acceptable and other activities were not. For example, skating to music with a girl was similar, in my view, to dancing to music. I asked her what the difference was between skating with a girl and dancing with a girl when I wanted to go to a high school dance. Mother had her reasons but I could never understand or appreciate her view. Nevertheless, she exercised her influence on me to the point I attended only a limited number of dances during my high school years. Even then, I had this sort of guilt feeling hanging on for the evening's activity. Interestingly, she never 'put her foot down' and said that I couldn't go to the dances, she just made me feel like I shouldn't. I was never able to reconcile her position despite the fact that I always felt her intentions were good.

As I progressed through elementary school, I attended grammar school at Roosevelt Elementary for almost three years. I loved Dorothy Deathridge one of my teachers there. She was an excellent teacher for me and I learned a lot especially wanting to read. She made stories come to life with excitement. That experience made me want to go to the library around the corner from the apartment house where we lived. I would spend hours down there reading a lot of adventures written by Pearl Buck. I liked Mrs. Deathridge for another reason. She made me feel like I was no different from the other kids who came from a higher economic status. It was a good foundation building time and experience for me.

For the next two years, we moved to Port Hueneme where I attended school for just a few months before my dad qualified for government housing in Oxnard, and we moved to the Project. I attended most of the fourth grade at Anacapa Elementary School, which was part of the Project development and a temporary school. The following year everyone in that grammar school had to attend Haydock Grammar School, which was perhaps the equivalent of eight to ten blocks away and outside the Project. It seems somewhere along the way in life, boys notice girls and vice versa.

In my case, I noticed a young fifth grader, Arlene Hyde. She lived the opposite direction from my house but I got to the point where I would walk her home nearly every afternoon from school. I think we may have held hands but I do not remember that we ever kissed. We were just special friends and liked each other more than some of the other kids in our class. After grammar school, we lost track of each other. I do not know what happened to Arlene during our junior high years; but she did attend Oxnard High School at the same time as I did through her junior year. At that time she got married. A long interval took place and I did not see her again until I attended a 50th year class reunion. I did not recognize her until I saw her nametag! Then I could not believe that it was her. She lost her husband and was back living in Oxnard once again after an extended absence in Missouri. I remember having a crush on Merlene Wilson while I attended Haydock Grammar School.

Besides going to school, what else did a 'city' boy do to stay busy in Oxnard in the mid to late 1940s? Oxnard was simply a farming community located on the Oxnard coastal Plain. Every place you looked there were lemon groves. At one time, it was supposedly the lemon capital of the world until Santa Paula, a smaller town more inland in Ventura County laid claim to the title. The land that was not devoted to citrus groves was heavily involved in 'truck farming'. The truck farms grew many seasonal vegetable crops repeatedly throughout the year. There were table and canning tomatoes, celery, lettuce, strawberries, and cabbage, all crops which were readily harvested and sold into the huge Los Angeles produce market which was only about sixty miles away. Some other vegetables were grown on an annual basis such as lima beans and English peas. Sugar beets played an important role in the local economy. They were grown locally and were also shipped in from other areas of California, such as the Imperial Valley, for processing at the Oxnard sugar beet factory. When it was in operation each year, the entire town could smell the sweet odor that permeated the atmosphere. Some liked the smell and other people didn't. Needless to say, everyone got used to it or suffered through the sugar production seasonal run. Fortunately, the plant was located in the southeast part of town and the prevailing westerly breeze from the ocean helped many residents endure the processing season.

As for myself, I always found a job doing something. No one told me to do this, it was a notion of my own and I think my parents appreciated it. Most of the time, I sold the *Oxnard Press Courier* walking the streets. Then I got a bicycle delivery route for the same paper. Then I was offered a route with the *Los Angeles Examiner*, which later merged and then it became the *Herald Examiner*. I purchased a motor scooter and the *Los Angeles Times* gave me a delivery job with the largest route around town. That was the premier newspaper delivery job in town.

Whether you were a young teenager or an adult, a seasonal job could be secured with a little patience and tenacity. After all, this locale was a small version of the scions of the San Joaquin Valley identified in many of the writings of John Steinbeck. Parents worked as did most, if not all, of the offspring in the family. In between harvest times there would be limited periods when work in the fields was more difficult to obtain. In those periods, young boys found other things to do. I hoed lima beans and white washed young citrus tree plantings to protect them from rabbits and squirrels gnawing on them. That was mostly in the summer when I got to work two jobs at the age of eleven through sixteen. I had a paper route in the early morning and another job most of the daylight hours.

Belonging to the junior group of the International Order of Odd Fellows had its benefits. One adult sponsor owned extensive property between Camarillo, Oxnard, and the El Rio community. The property he owned included the hills, now known as Las Posas Estates just west of Camarillo on the north side of Highway 101. Some of this property was being converted to lemon orchards. But the vast majority of it was open undeveloped raw land covered with sagebrush, beaver tail cactus, and other natural flora and fauna plants of this region of California. This part of his land was alive with cottontail rabbits, rattlesnakes, birds, and ground squirrels. He invited any of the juniors over to his place to shoot our guns and hunt when we wanted.

Usually three or four of us teenagers, thirteen to fifteen years old, would trek over to this property from Oxnard. Since most of us lived in the government housing project, it was a rather lengthy hike to the hunting area. Generally we did not follow the streets and roads except in town but took short cuts by walking through lemon groves and cut across fields. During these years, Highway 101 was merely a two-lane highway and not heavily trafficked. Keep in mind we carried our .22 caliber rifles along with our boxes of ammo out in the open. Not one of us ever discussed the potential dangers of what we were doing. No one ever challenged us about carrying rifles in the open or taking specific safety precautions. It was if we knew those kinds of things even though we had never really had any formal classes about the subject of safety, shooting, cleaning and caring for a rifle. It would be impossible to do such things nowadays without a police officer stopping you and probably confiscating your rifle, and who knows what else. To obtain a rifle, you just simply went down to the local Auto Supply store and made the purchase, no questions asked. You did not need to apply for a gun owner's license or have a waiting period before you gained possession of the rifle.

My boyhood teenager days of the late 40s and early 50s were fun in most respects. My three cousins, Fonda, Laverne, and Eula Moudy introduced me to the music of the swing era. Every time I went any place in the car with them, the radio was blaring the tunes of Frank Sinatra, the Andrew Sisters, Nat King Cole and a host of other popular vocalists. The Big Band era was still trying to hang on. Band leaders like Benny Goodman, Tommy Dorsey, Jimmy Dorsey and Glen Miller's Band, Les Brown and 'His Band of Renown' and a host of other lesser known bands were still playing on the road but not like they were in the early 40s and during the War years. You heard Al Jolson less and less with his famous "Mammy". I was glad that Al Jolson was fading away in popularity because my family had neighbors living across the yard in the housing project that just loved his music. They had a record player and nearly every evening my family and six others got to hear him sing very loudly. No one was excluded! The volume was near deafening and each evening it was the same record. My mother thought the record was the only one they owned. By the mid 50s the preeminence of 'swing' was really starting to slide into the background as 'rock and roll' was becoming more popular.

For the younger generation Fats Domino and his 'Blueberry Hill' was

Left – right: Cousins Laverne, Fonda, and Eula Moudy, circa 1946

coming on strong. And not too far down the music track was 'The King', Elvis Presley. Even so, at most dance parties during my high school days, the last dance song usually played for the evening was Glen Miller's *Moonlight Serenade.* You were expected to reserve this last dance of the evening with your favorite girl, and preferably, that most often was your date for the evening. It was slow and groovy. Whether you knew how to dance or not, you could stand on the dance floor and lean this way and that to the slow rhythmic music. I did not go to many dances – but I loved the music.

As fate would have it, I did get to see three of the famous swing bands in 1955 live at a "War of the Bands" at Keesler Air Force Base at Biloxi, Mississippi. The bands included Tommy Dorsey's, Jimmy Dorsey's, Les Brown's and a local (very good) band from New Orleans. These bands played nearly four hours continuously! The only time the music stopped was when the bands changed.

Growing up under these conditions came with ease in many respects but not without incidents, which sometimes seemed very difficult and continued to mark me. On the social side, I liked to interact and felt comfortable talking to the boys and girls in my church and a few others in high school, but only after getting to know them. Being bashful among the opposite sex, I did not open up easily even though I would talk with them. The girls attending our church and their families were from similar backgrounds to that of my family's. They came from poor working class families; their parents were not highly educated; they lived a simple life and life was lived tight to the vest. Many came from southern or mid-western states. Most came from farms and knew hard work. They worked hard and they loved and worshipped Jesus in church nearly every time the church doors opened. Looking back, it is easy to understand that liking or even later dating a 'church girl' was much easier for me to do than exposing my background to an 'unknown high school young lady socialite' whom I had met in a hallway or classroom and who most often lived on the 'right side' of the railroad tracks. I thought that Myrna Brown, Barbara Brown, Joyce Lake, and Lois Holmes to name a few, were knock-out good looking. I could not come close to getting up enough courage to think about asking them for a date. I'm sure part of it was the fear of rejection. It was not that I did not like my family's heritage; but there was an imagined stigma on my part that we did not cling to the same rung on the social ladder as the parents of many of my high school classmates. My family, for the most part, still lived from hand to mouth.

Growing up as a teenager was very different and not as difficult then as compared to the exposure and experiences that young people encounter in today's world. I am glad to have grown up in the 40s and 50s. I came across a description that a friend and co-worker, Charles McDonald, sent on the e-mail (in 2002) and it identified a lot of the elements of how life was in those two decades for a young person. Unfortunately, the writer is unknown. I have included it here.

The 1950s

Were you a kid in the Fifties or earlier? Everybody makes fun of our child-
hood! Comedians joke. Grandkids snicker. Twenty-somethings shud-

der and say "Eeeew!"
But was our childhood really all that bad? Judge for yourself:

In 1953 the US population was less than 150 million people...yet you knew
more people then, and knew them better...
And that was good.

The average annual salary was under $3,000...yet our parents could put
some money away for a rainy day and still have a decent life...
And that was good.

A loaf of bread cost about 15 cents...but it was safe for a five-year-old to
skate to the store and buy one...
And that was good.

Prime-Time meant 'I love Lucy, Ozzie and Harriet, Cecil the Seasick Sea
Serpent, Gunsmoke and Lassie...so nobody'd ever heard of ratings
or filters...
And that was good.

We didn't have air-conditioning...so the windows stayed up and half a
dozen mothers ran outside when you fell off your bike...
And that was good.

Your teacher was either Miss Matthews or Mrs. Logan or Mr. Adkins...
but not Ms. Becky or Mr. Dan...
And that was good.

The only hazardous material you knew about...was a patch of grassburrs
around the light pole at the corner...
And that was good.

Most families needed only one job...meaning Mom was home when school
let out...

And that was good.

You loved to climb into a fresh bed…because the sheets were dried on the clothesline…
And that was good.

People generally lived in the same hometown with their relatives…so 'child care' meant grandparents or aunts and uncles…
And that was good.

Parents were respected and their rules were law…children did not talk back…
And that was good.

TV was in black-and-white…but all outdoors was in glorious color…
And that was certainly good.

Your Dad knew how to adjust everybody's carburetor…and the Dad next door knew how to adjust all of the TV knobs…
And that was very good.

Your grandma grew snap beans in the back yard…and chickens behind the garage…
And that was definitely good.

And just when you were about to do something really bad…chances were you'd run into your Dad's high school coach…or the nosy old lady from up the street…or your little sister's piano teacher…or somebody from church…all of whom knew your parents' phone number…and your first name…
*And even **that** was good.*

Unknown

I think the comments are accurate and reflect my remembrances of growing up in that era. It was a good and wholesome way of life. There are many other statements about the family that I could add to the description above because the immediate family as well as my family at large had such an important role in the life of the offspring.

A highlight for me as a young teen occurred while I was in the Boy Scouts of America. In Oxnard our troop (the only one at the time) was troop 212. It was not a large group of boys but it was a good group. We had good sponsors and leadership. I did not diligently pursue rising in the ranks or gaining a large number of merit badges. I did the necessary things like learning the Boy Scout oath, tying knots, building fires, and learning about camping. We made several camping trips into the Tahacchipi Mountains north of Ojai and east of Oxnard into the Santa Paula and Fillmore areas. The Ferndale Ranch area north of Santa Paula was a prime hiking and camping area.

As 1950 approached, and the world had started to settle down after World War II, the scouting organizations from around the world decided that a world National Jamboree would be held at Valley Forge, Pennsylvania. It was considered a huge honor to be asked to attend. For whatever reason, probably because I was the troop leader, I was selected from my troop. It cost money and I did not have any for that kind of trip. Lee S. Barnes, was a member of the local Rotary Club, took on the task of helping me accumulate the necessary funding. The scouts called him Lee. Lee was a real help to me and worked directly with me to make certain that I got to make the trip. He told me one time he was the Olympic pole vault champion in the 1924 competition. Fifty years later, I looked him up in the Olympic records for 1924 and verified that indeed he was an Olympic champion! He saw to it that the Rotary Club made a direct contribution and all the members of the troop sold special souvenir lead pencils in their respective neighborhoods to help me. I probably had friends, relatives and people who did not even know me buying more pencils than they could ever use. A few of my relatives made contributions to my cause. I do not recall the amount of money needed for the trip but the amount was raised and I was very appreciative. The preparations were thorough in terms of practicing for the contests such as knot tying, building a fire, setting up a tent, and any number of other activities once our group reached Valley Forge.

The train was entirely filled by boy scouts from Southern California. No other passengers were on the train. It began a journey around the full perimeter of the United States that would take thirty days to complete. This included the week's stay at the campout. We made touring stops in Seattle, Washington, Glacier National Park, Montana, Chicago, Illinois, Niagara Falls, New York, New York City, Philadelphia, Washington D.C., Atlanta, Georgia, New Orleans, San Antonio, Texas and then returned home. There were more than 50,000 scouts in attendance from all over the world at the National Jamboree in Valley Forge, Pennsylvania. During the Jamboree, General Dwight Eisenhower made a speech to the scouts. It was really a political platform but many of us did not realize it at the time. He was beginning his campaign for the President of the United States. Most of us knew him as the great general that led the allied troops in Europe during World War II. He was well received. During the trip, I wrote a few articles for the local newspaper, *The Oxnard Press Courier*, which were published. That was the first real trip I had ever taken other than the many trips to Arkansas. It was an eye opening experience and most educational for me. I will never forget it.

In my teen years, dating was rather simple in those days. It was a movie (a drive-in was the 'in-thing') or an athletic event at the high school. Very rarely did I go to a party, even though invited. I felt awkward and ill at ease because I did not know how to dance and would never think of drinking any alcoholic beverages like many of my classmates. I had no car and no way of earning and saving enough money to get one. My father was always good enough to let me use the family car for dating when I was going to an event or I was 'coerced' into attending some special school or church function.

This is the way it was for me growing up within the Pentecostal denomination. There were real strict rules about dating, drinking alcohol, dancing, smoking, swearing, or going to movies. One did not breech the faith! If you did, your life was subject to retribution by the Almighty God … and your parents as well in some sort of way! Breaching the Faith was not acceptable behavior…not for any reason. If you did partake in those activities, it was the belief that you had 'backslid', you had lost your faith, and the only way to gain the good graces of God was to repent by asking His forgiveness and then turn from your ways. Through God's mercy and love, he would accept you back into the family of believers of the faith. Not all denominations believe this is the way God handles your lack of commitment and waywardness.

Taking a young lady on a date was fun despite the fact that I felt insecure inside and probably had some inhibitions to go along with all of the other problems of a teenage boy. I do not recall being turned down by any of the young ladies when I asked for a date. Believe me, it took lots of courage for me to get up enough gumption to ask in the first place. I tried not to think about the possibility of being turned down. I don't want my comments here to sound like a litany of numerous dates. That was not the case at all. Each young lady I dated had an impact on me in a variety of ways. Some were just good friends and remained that way. Others caused me to have more than a passing interest. Finally, one came along in my young life that was extra special and I married her.

The one girl that attended church and that I got to know was Rena Jo Lively. She lived in Somis, quite a distance from Oxnard, probably about twenty miles. I think she was a year or two younger than I. She attended Ventura high school. My dad was good enough to let me drive the car and we dated for a while but it waned after a while because we lived so far apart. My mother liked Rena Jo and seemed pleased when I would go out with her. I brought her over to our house several times during the couple of years we dated. Rena was a nice young lady. Her older sister, Claudia, took care to make certain that she was proper at all times. If my memory serves me, their mother had died at an early age and they had a single father parent raising them. He was an exceptionally strict disciplinarian and her sister watched after her very closely as well. Perhaps the father told her to watch after her sister, I don't know. I felt that he must have liked me to let me take his daughter out for as long as we dated. I must say, however, we always abided by the rules he had set on times to be home and where we were going.

Needless to say, I was very fond of Rena. Just cannot really say that I was ever in love with her. Perhaps under the right circumstances, I could have fallen for her. One day, after returning home from the Air Force, I passed Rena on 'A' street on the south end of town near the five points intersection in Oxnard. She recognized me in my car and proceeded to make a U-turn and catch up to me. I did not see her until she had pulled up along side my car and honked. Rena had always been a hard worker and drove nice cars ever since she started working after high school. She was in a brand new Chevrolet hardtop! I pulled over and parked along side the curb and she got out of her car and stood along side and we talked for quite a while. I learned that she had gotten married and divorced since the time that we dated and I had put in my time in the Air Force. She had no children. I knew that she had gotten involved with a guy who rode motorcycles and that was never a strong point with me. For some reason, those kinds of guys were just not the type I could make friends with or feel comfortable around. I just didn't respect them and their reputations. In my mind's view, she had been ruined by that experience and would be very different than she once had been. That made it real tough for me to have any interest now.

She was a beautiful young lady for sure with a great figure but my bias regarding her being a past 'motor cycle momma' was too much for me to swallow. More than anything, it was the crowd that I associated with that group. In my books, they were hard, tough, ruffians. They were the pre-hell's angels of their day. But that was only my opinion. Much to my surprise, she was rather forward with me that day which was very different compared to the way she was a few years earlier. That was out of character for her. She had been a quiet individual but would talk and converse with most people in a reserved manner. I do not know to this day why we ran into each other that day...just happenstance I guess. But before the conversation was finished, she wanted us to immediately elope to Las Vegas and get married. My God, I could not believe it. It had been more than five years since we had seen each other! I politely declined and told her of my desire to get an education. I have never seen her again although a friend later told me that she married a pilot stationed at Oxnard Air Force base and moved somewhere in central California.

Being back in Oxnard again after four years in the Air Force was a big change in the pace of life for me. There were things I wanted to forget and others that brought back fond memories. As I reflected, I could not get Janice out of my mind. There was a sweet and sour taste of lost teenage love. It was all about the one young lady that meant the most to me as a teenager. She was a young sparkling freshman when we met in high school. I was two grades ahead of her. It was at the beginning of my junior year, when Janice Elliott was a freshman. We met briefly and inadvertently on campus one day early in the first semester. She was a knockout picture of beauty, as I remembered her, at the time. Young but certainly very good looking! It was obvious that we thought and felt some mutually convergent feelings about each other…at least for a while.

Within a short time, I was convinced that she was the girl for me! She was blonde and vivacious with a gorgeous figure. She was a good conversationalist and we were always laughing about things that were happening on campus and with our friends. I thought that she was a lot of fun. We enjoyed being together. It was still early in the school year and one morning as the students were arriving and getting ready for the first class of the day. I was crossing 5th Street from the housing project to attend class when I saw Jan and her girl friends stop at the curb and get out of a car. Jan's mother apparently brought them to school each day. However, I had not noticed them arriving at school previously. I wondered if that meeting was deliberately planned or was it happen stance. There I was, meeting her mother, Ruth! Already no less and we had not even really been on a date! Campus meetings never counted on that score. I probably stuttered and stammered to her mother but was as courteous as I could be. To this day, I have no idea what I might have said that morning. I suppose it worked out okay because Jan and I were to become more acquainted and even 'go steady' for almost the next three years. Within a few weeks, we began to do everything together. Our laughs and fun together never subsided. My parents liked her too. She would come to my house and I would spend time at hers.

One thing extremely tasty that I enjoyed was her mother's incredible black walnut cake. She baked it from scratch. It was just outstanding and very delicious. Every time she baked that cake (or others I suppose) she would always give me a piece if I was there. I would practically gulp it down, it was oh, so good! As I think back, I probably embarrassed her mother and myself gulping down that cake but I didn't know it, thank goodness! To this day, I have never tasted a cake like that one! Just this past year I spok to Ruth about her cake but she does not recall such a cake, so maybe I just dreamed it up. Even if my memory has failed, whatever it was that she fed me, it was superbly delicious.

I was occasionally invited to take day trips with the family in their beautiful new Hudson Hornet. One such trip was to the Santa Barbara area and I rode in the middle of the front bench seat. I got to know her father, Willis and her brother Mike somewhat. Mike was a handsome looker as a young lad. I don't recall, but I think he might have been a couple of years younger than Jan. All of my life, I thought that they were a beautiful family and felt accepted by them.

When the day came in 1954 that I was leaving for basic training with the Air Force, I left my prized possession, my first car, my black 1947 Chevy convertible with its red leather interior and white top for Janice to drive and take care of for me. By this time we had been dating and 'going steady' for nearly three years. I knew that I was deeply in love with Jan. She was my first true love. I was beginning to think that I wanted to marry her at a future date. I never mentioned my expectations to her; that might have scared her out of her wits. Such was the blind love of a teenager perhaps.

Off to the military I went with my buddies. There is not any doubt in my mind that our separation became part of our downfall. If she was not feeling the same as I, it would have happened anyway. That is how I rationalized my ultimate loss of the relationship with her. No one will ever know that's for sure. As a couple, I came to believe that it was pretty simple; we were not meant to be. That is life in reality, filled with unsuspecting turns; some are great and some not so good. We all survive!

There are all kinds of stories that absence makes the heart grow fonder. It did not for Janice. Before I came home on furlough for Christmas, in 1954, she had already changed her feelings about me. In fact, while I was still in basic training she had written me one of those typical 'Dear John' letters. I have to say, it really hit me hard. On my Christmas leave, we met very briefly at her work place so that I could retrieve my class ring and probably a few other trinkets that she no longer wanted. As I think back, she blew me off before I was even in technical school. By the time I arrived for basic training, she was apparently dating other guys. From what I heard, her dates were not with guys having the best reputation. At least that was how I viewed it in my mind. But I was not in her shoes and who am I to judge another person! I distantly knew one guy in particular that she had fallen for. When I heard that news, it ended our relationship probably in both directions for us. I continued to correspond with Ruth, her mother, for quite sometime afterwards but that waned over many months as my duty stations changed and I slowly recovered to find that the world hadn't stopped turning.

Until the 'turn off' occurred, I can honestly say that I had been absolutely 'true blue' to her. Other girls didn't matter to me regardless of their beauty or family stature. I didn't see Jan again until I was discharged from the Air Force, back home and in college. I was back in college again and I attended a basketball game at Ventura Community College. A friend of hers was in the stands with her and they saw me. The friend, Phyllis Damaron, came over and stated that Jan was there and wanted to see me so I went over and spoke to her. She looked different to me. She had one child. I don't recall why she was at the game since to my knowledge she didn't attend the college. Possibly it was a social outing. Our greeting was very casual but somewhat distant. I didn't really have much to say to her because of how badly I felt she treated me. In my view she was history. She had hurt me deeply and seeing her only refreshed some good and bad memories. I think her parents had moved to Ventura by that time. That was in 1958 or early in 1959. I haven't seen her again since that occasion.

Interestingly, in the last couple of years we started to communicate again. I learned that Jan remarried. This time, she told me that she found a really nice person, Norman Harrold. They now live in Oregon near Medford. Establishing an acquaintance again with her came as a real shock to me. Without forewarning and much to my surprise, one day in 2002, I received a letter in the mail from her. I was dumbfounded. How could she know where I lived? Turned out, she had her husband find me on the

Internet. The return address on the envelope was Glendale. I worked in Glendale and had for several years. Who was Jan Harrold? When I opened it and began to read, it registered...Janice Elliott. Then I thought, how could we have missed meeting just by chance during all these years if she lived in Glendale? We probably would not have recognized each other if we had met. I looked again at the envelope; the return address was not Glendale, California but Glendale, Oregon.

Since then, Jan and I have exchanged letters several times on a periodic basis. We have exchanged pictures of families too. After seeing her pictures, I am almost certain that I would not have recognized her if by chance we had met face to face on the street. I have written her mother as well. I do not know her reason for making the contact. She merely said in one of her letters to me that she thought that we should be friends once again at this stage in our lives. It was a pleasant surprise. I appreciated her efforts to contact me. Life has its pleasant and not so pleasant twists. Our relationship has had both!

While I was in the Air Force, I met Margaret Dupree through a friend of mine, Emile Wolf, who was a native of New Orleans. He had lost his mother and father earlier in his life and his sister, who was considerably older by some twenty years, had actually raised him. Emile's niece was in nurse's training at Charity Hospital in New Orleans. At the time, there were fifteen of us airmen from Oxnard stationed at Keesler Air Force base at the same time. I have long since forgotten many of my fellow airmen except for a few in the group including Ray Benefield, Eugene Nunes, Bill Duncan, Art Cox, and Frank Reeves. The group of us did a lot of things together during off-duty hours. On weekends, many of us would travel to New Orleans and hang out. Sometimes, Emile's brother-in-law, who had a big band, played at the Roosevelt Hotel and for many of the sorority parties at Tulane University. The belles of the university did not cater to military personnel. Those activities never accomplished anything in terms of meeting some interesting young ladies. Then Emile got the bright idea one day that he should have his niece set all of us up with blind dates with some of her fellow student nurses.

This contingent of airmen, twelve to fifteen strong, traveled to New

Orleans on the appointed weekend and arrived at Charity Hospital. We met in a rather large conference room with the beaus and belles on opposite sides of a long conference table. All the young ladies were on one side of the room; all the flyboys on the other side (we were not dressed in our uniforms) and the whole scenario seemed a little strange and uncomfortable at first. I think each group just stood there looking and wondering which one is my date? It was a time to survey the potential but the time was short lived. I am sure both sides were sizing up the other as to the possibilities. The niece had made out a list matching, sight unseen, a guy and a gal. I do not know if Emile had talked to her at an earlier time but interestingly the sizing was good. There weren't any 'Mutt and Jeff' combinations. It was weird how things developed and worked out, but interesting to say the least. One young lady's name would be called and the matching escort's name would be revealed. I had never been on a blind date before. I didn't really know what to expect. My name came up about half way through and I got a big lump in my throat and a rush of adrenaline. "Roark and Margaret" Gulp! There we were and then we paired with another couple for the evening.

Greetings were more or less nonchalant but courteous. After all, the guys were strangers to the young ladies as they were to us. We spent the evening walking and seeing the sights in the French Quarter. The two young ladies directed us to a French coffee shop and I tasted my first beignet. There were to be a number of firsts in this entirely new atmosphere. It helped me forget there had been a Jan in my life too! It turned out to be a very nice and fun evening for the four of us. Many of the couples were to date many more times after that initial contact. Later all of us airmen talked about the evening having been a great success. For the next six months, Margaret and I dated pretty regularly. Then it was time for me to ship out to March Air Force Base, in Riverside, California and I left Mississippi and Margaret behind.

Margaret's parents lived in Houma, Louisiana. She was a very attractive young lady and indeed a southern 'Belle' of French descent. Margaret was stunningly beautiful. She had very dark eyes and hair with a beautiful smile, which showed, off her gorgeous white teeth. She was well versed in the cultural aspects of courtesies and with my Southern heritage, I was able to adequately accommodate her expectancies. I sort of surprised myself since I didn't have any formal training in proper etiquette. I just used common sense that my mother had taught me. Margaret never once complained about my manners.

Much to our complete surprise, the day came when my buddy, Frank Reeves, and I were invited by our respective belles to Houma, Louisiana, their hometown, for a weekend.

Frank Reeves and I had no way of knowing what had been planned for that weekend. We arrived Saturday about mid-morning in a car we had borrowed from one of our airmen buddies. It turned out that Margaret's parents had moved out of their home with plans to let us two flyboys spend the weekend there. I could hardly believe it! I felt this was over doing the hospitality a bit! They made doubly sure that we understood that we were to make ourselves at home. On Saturday evening, they had a huge barbeque party at Margaret's sister's home. It was an incredible barbeque with lots of pork ribs and chicken as well as many other fine dishes that southerners prepare. There was spicy hot boiled shrimp and crayfish. We had jambalaya. There was roasted corn and black eyed peas and plenty to drink. It stayed very orderly during the entire event even though there was plenty of beer and liquor. Being a 'tea totaller' that party was quite a different experience for me. I must say that I enjoyed meeting all those very down to earth, friendly people. It seemed that each and every one of them wanted to get some detail about the school we were attending and the type of work that we would be doing upon graduation. I tried my best to explain it but it was very technical. They pressed the issue by asking many questions. I also learned that Margaret's father was a County Supervisor in their parish.

As the late afternoon began to approach darkness, the two young ladies announced to the family and friends gathered that we were leaving to go see a drive-in movie. It was a very warm evening so the windows of the car remained down for fresh air throughout the drive and after arrival at the drive-in. Within a short time, the mosquitoes arrived in force. I represent desert to these small blood thirsty insects and when they find me they call all their friends and have a feast. These critters had found something new for their dessert and it had a California flavor! The two young ladies were immune to the pesky buzzing and biting mosquitoes but I wasn't. I had bites all over me in a relatively short time! I felt as if I was a spastic of some kind trying to futilely fight them off. I suffered but made it through the evening somehow and without untold damage. The two young ladies had many laughs as Frank and I engaged in the life and death struggle with the mosquitoes. Even so, we had a great weekend and I came back to the base looking like I had a bad case of the measles. As I have thought back over the events of that evening and later, I came to the conclusion that Margaret was introducing me to her family on a more serious note of which I was unaware. I never picked up on it at the time.

We dated steadily until I left for my new assignment. I remember the first time I left her, on my furlough trip to California. I was boarding the train in New Orleans for my trip home on the Southern Pacific's Sunset Limited a few days before Christmas. With one of her close friends, she stood outside the coach car with tears streaming down her face and told me to have a good time but to come back. That scene was to repeat itself in another five months when I was reassigned to my permanent duty station. By then she told me that she loved me. We corresponded for some time afterwards. I let the relationship die.

I was scared to death at the time that if I got serious with her, my parents would not approve. I am now convinced that my logic was faulty and wrong. The reasoning, at the time, was directly related to our religious upbringing and differences in our faiths. She was a devout Catholic and my family was heavily involved with the Assembly of God Church, a protestant church. Even though both denominations believed in Christ the Son and God the Father, and the Holy Spirit, there were substantial differences in the respective worship of members as well as theological differences. The methodology of worship was very different. I felt that my parents would never accept her because of their understanding or lack thereof regarding the Catholic faith. I later came to believe my parents would have approved anyone I chose for my mate. Infrequently, I was to think back and believe that they would have accepted Margaret because of her kindness and genuine concern and caring for people. My mother's health was not good and Margaret often wanted to talk about someday being able to care for her. I know Margaret would have done a great job because of her registered nurse training. As time passed, I regretted having let the relationship die. She would have been a wonderful companion to me. We got along extraordinarily well.

I was to meet Emile several years later, about 1965 when he and his wife visited my family when we lived in Diamond Bar in Southern California. He told me that Margaret became a registered nurse, married, became a chain smoker, and lived at that time in the Carolinas.

I enjoyed the company of several other young ladies from time to time during my four-year tour of duty. I even had some other blind dates once I arrived at March Air Force Base in California that I wished I had never accepted. They were incredibly different than the first one I went on. These dates were so bad and undesirable that I wished that my 'buddies' had never thought of such maltreatment. I did not deserve it!

As all young men ultimately do, I began to explore life and establish an understanding for myself as to what my life was about and by what principles I should live by. My upbringing, my parents efforts to guide me and the teachings of the church had unknowingly taken seed in my heart and I soon realized that my convictions closely aligned themselves with the basic teachings which I had been taught and had preached to me for years. My parents, church members, preachers and my aunts and uncles who lived by the "Good Book" had taught me the real principles of living a Christian life. But that was not before I had tried some things out for myself. All of us find our own way.

Experience life yourself for yourself; don't take someone else's word for it. That seems to be ingrained in every individual regardless of who taught us. I'm somewhat certain that most every young man and woman do not start his or her life with that as a deliberate expectation. Being cut loose from our mother's apron strings, we quickly discover an insatiable appetite to find out things for ourselves, spread our wings, and see what the 'real' world is really like from which we have been shielded particularly if we have had Christian parents with Christian values. It is also one way to prove to yourself that God indeed has a Plan for your life.

I didn't stray too far from my early teachings as a young man and even when I did the conviction was always present. My guardian angel seemed to always be whispering in a wee small voice to my conscience giving me direction. I really didn't stretch my wings at all until after I joined the Air Force and even then, it was a slow process. I was a 'good guy' and really didn't enjoy carousing around, getting drunk, or making a fool of myself like some of my high school and Air Force buddies. I always liked and wanted to be in control of my faculties all the time. I didn't like show-offs and didn't want to be one myself. I didn't fully appreciate or understand God's unconditional love for me and somehow felt with absolute certainty that such behavior would serve to bring God's wrath upon me and somehow taint me in a personal way with those who loved and cared for me.

I would have been labeled or described as a 'nerd' or a 'goody goody two shoes'. I would have been ashamed if my parents learned that I had committed acts of that nature. In today's society all of these kinds of things and even more are considered the more normal behavior especially for non-Christians but I still cannot endorse it. Without any doubt, I was out of step with my peer group in those days. Maybe I'd even be the 'designated driver' of today's crowd. This never bothered me because in most respects, I felt comfortable with myself.

When I joined the US Air Force in 1954 on a voluntary basis, I was nineteen years old. I joined on the 'buddy system.' This meant the Air Force would guarantee that my buddy, Eugene Nunes (Gene) and I could stay together through technical school. Gene and I had been friends in high school, in the Marine Corp Reserve, and had worked together at Booth's Texaco Station at Fourth and 101 Boulevard in Oxnard until the time we joined. I was absolutely clean in every way even though I had begun to be exposed to a widely differing life-style in the U. S. Marine Corp Reserves while still in high school.

Almost as soon as I turned seventeen, I joined the Marine Corps Reserves. This unit was the 67th Infantry Battalion. Many of my high school friends were enlisting. It was the 'in' thing to do. We had meetings at the See Bee base at Port Hueneme every few weeks, probably like once a month. In the summer, we had two weeks of training. The first year our two weeks were spent in basic training at MCRD (Marine Corps Recruit Depot) in San Diego, California. The next year, our two weeks were spent at Camp Pendleton, near Oceanside, California. That year the concentration was on amphibious landing and live fire with M-I carbines and Browning automatic rifles. I earned my sharpshooter's medal and felt pretty good about that accomplishment. However, I learned that crawling on your belly in beach sand and muck was not really that much fun.

Before joining the military I had never tasted alcohol or smoked – just never had the desire. In the military your basic exposure begins, and it can be a rude awakening for some young men. The

Pvt. Roark V. Moudy
United States Marine Corps Re-
serves, July 1953

choice is to sit back and watch the action or decide that the alternative of participation is best for you. It is a rude awakening when your commanding officer or drill sergeant personally introduces himself to you in basic training. That event becomes the starting point of your introduction and exposure to some previously unheard or rare verbal expletives. They may choose to call you every name in the book just to see your reaction. You are definitely in momentary shock and shaking in your boots. Mentally you are in utter dismay that another human being would talk to another that way. The main question in your mind is 'what did I do to deserve this?' The answer may be nothing, just nothing at all! In other words, you are in trouble for having done something or not having done something that you were supposed to do. It is probably best to have never provided such a reason in the first place yet sometimes it can be unavoidable! But who controls that? In basic training your life is not your own. You belong to the United States government and your drill sergeant.

I had always been a pretty good observer and listener. As life unfolded in the Air Force, if I had a choice, I participated in what I wanted and left the rest alone, particularly in boot camp and basic training. That was pretty easy for me to do. Perhaps it was because I had a dear mother at home praying for God to protect me every day. I believe that He did answer my mother's prayers and had my guardian angel protecting me all the time.

My first introduction to 'breaking the rules' happened in basic training. Keep in mind that my mother had embedded in me the wrongful nature of drinking and I made a decision not to contend the issue. Furthermore, Christian principles do not teach that it is sinful to partake of alcoholic beverages; but the teaching is that it is wrong to become drunk. Even with my mother saying many prayers for me, virtually by 'command' I tasted an alcoholic beverage for the first time in the Air Force. Beer was introduced to me when we marched back from a week on bivouac while in basic training.

We were nearing the end of our training. It was one of the hottest days of summer on the Texas 'desert' near San Antonio at Sheppard Air Force Base. The training lasted almost three months. That particular day everyone was dead tired and incredibly thirsty. As a favor and reward for 'doing a good job' on bivouac, the Commanding Officer announced to our squadron that we were marching straight to the 'beer garden' for some cool refreshment and that the cost was all on him before going back to our barracks for that most enjoyable extended hot shower for which all of us were waiting! Everybody cheered wildly and applauded. I had never tried beer but everyone said I would like it. I didn't even like the idea of drinking it because it had alcohol. I received my bottle of beer and tasted it. Never had a drink of ice-cold horse urine before!! I had tried beer, but throughout the rest of my life, I have never really cultivated a taste for it. Mixed alcoholic drinks were sometimes tasty – but I never got drunk. I stayed in control of my actions.

On smoking – it was a nasty habit; tasted terrible, burned my tongue, and gave me horribly bad breath. Cigars were worse! Again, it was easy for me to stop smoking when I wanted to because I did not enjoy it. That was not the case for many other young airmen who really got hooked on nicotine. For good reasons, it was the clean life for me and I am proud of

Roark V. Moudy, United States Air Force, 1954

it. God has blessed me for it, I believe.

Once out of basic training at San Antonio, Texas I was enrolled in technical school at Keesler Air Force Base in Biloxi, Mississippi. Life in the Air Force took on more of a routine work job. However, the work was going to school 'full time' to learn how airborne radar and radio systems operated. This was the only subject taught each day. I went to work (class) every day at 6:00 pm and finished my day at midnight then went to the mess hall for breakfast. Then back to my barracks for sleep about 2:00 a.m., and get up in time to make noon lunch. Study and relax in the afternoon until we had roll call and marched off to training class again. This was the cycle. Normally it was the routine for five days a week. Off duty hours were usually on Saturday and Sunday except you had to pull KP (kitchen patrol –wash dishes, mop the floors, get food stuffs out of the cooler or freezer, etc.) once a month. The training was intense but was still my cup of tea because understanding electronics and all of the various circuits came very easily to me. There was substantial electronic theory in the curriculum. Our first area of study was the navigational radar system known as the APN 9, which had been used on the B-17 and B-29 aircraft during World War II. Then it was on to the KC-97 systems, which included the APN 13, APN 20, APN 69, and identification, "Friend or Foe", systems. My one year studying radio electronics in junior college gave me a head start in class. I did very well in the course curriculum and graduated in the top three of my class of twenty airmen. I was never told whether I was at the top of my class or the third rated. It didn't make any difference. What was important to me was being in the select top group because the top three received the permanent assignment base of their choice. That fact was related to us the day our class started. I chose March Air Force Base because of my father's declining health. I did not know then that the base was part of the Strategic Air Command. I chose it because of its geographical location.

Being assigned to March Air Force base in June, 1955 was good for me because I could visit my ailing parents fairly easily since they lived up the coast in Oxnard, a few hours drive away. When I did not go home, I would often be invited to go home to visit with other airmen who came from the Southern California area. Sometimes I'd go fishing in the San Bernardino Mountains with my fishing buddy, Jerry Olsen.

Occasionally, I would be invited with a friend to go on a date with a friend of a friend whom I had met. That wasn't often … thank goodness.

I wasn't too keen on that arrangement. Worse yet were the two occasions I lost my mind and accepted a "blind date" arranged by a real barracks buddy! I'm surprised at myself that I ever went on a second one! Worse yet!!! That blind date was the absolute worst that I had gone on … and yet I went a second time as a favor to my airman friend. Obviously, I did not learn anything the first date, which had to mean that I was really stupid, or my friend was a very good friend! It was not the latter. I remember her as the girl with skin that reminded me of the feel of a snake that I had touched as a kid. It still gives me the shivers to think about it and I still remember how her arm felt when she touched me. I worked overtime trying my best to stay away from her.

There were two groups of airmen with whom I seemed to associate with while at March AFB. One group was a really rowdy bunch and the leader was Butch Sassy, whose father was supposedly the mayor of Pomona, California at the time, and Dick Bassett, who was a 'lush' from the Sacramento area. Now, these two could have become the town drunks in Any City, USA. They could really put the beer away. I think I was the designated driver and caretaker for these two whether we were on a date night or not. To this day, I cannot understand how I would have become friendly and buddied around at all with these two characters even though we did work closely together in the radar repair shop. Another factor was that we lived in the same barracks together. They seemed to have a motto of 'work together, play together' so I got invited to many events in Pomona and other local places. They were totally out of character for me. For whatever reason, they seemed to like me even though I did not drink with them. I guess they counted on me to keep them out of trouble somehow.

The second group was much more civilized and a really nice collection of rational people. I like to think of them as the typical citizen USA. These airmen went to a lot of parties in San Bernardino where they dated many young Catholic girls from St. Bernadine's High School. The families of these young ladies were very nice to us and we had good clean fun. My real good buddy, Joe Boyd, who would later live with my mother and father, spent a lot of time with this group and got me somewhat involved even though neither of us was of the same religious conviction as the young ladies.

As my military life continued unfolding, I started to occasionally attend the Riverside First Baptist Church in 1955. Late that year I purchased a car, a 1951 Ford Victoria. In that day, this was a classy hard top convertible. Mine was a light blue with white top and a lot of chrome all over. It looked good and was a good car. I began to attend church off and on. My attendance at church became more regular during the early days in March, 1956. Church attendance was often interrupted, however, for very long periods because of my TDY (temporary duty station) trips. These assignments were for two weeks to three months at a time to distant bases in the Pacific Basin, including Honolulu, Hawaii, Anchorage, Alaska, the Island of Guam, Japan, and a strange stop at Lockborne Air Force Base in Columbus, Ohio. These Temporary Duty Stations in far off places were unusual and often required me to work twenty-four to seventy-two hours at a stretch without sleep when the big birds (B-47s) were flying sorties or training missions. As a young man, it was easy to recover from that kind of duty. Besides, I had enlisted to 'see the world' and I was doing just that. In between trips, I began to date a few of the young ladies who were active in the young people's group at church. There were activities such as a sip-n-sing to attend after Sunday night church. This was where you could meet people. I dated Noma Cowan, Phyllis Wood (Beverly's cousin), and a couple of others from the church. It was quite a while before I was to take Bev on a date.

By now, my personality had changed; I had gained a lot of self-confidence and could hold my own with people with whom I made contact the first time. I no longer had to 'get to know them' before having fun, laughing and talking with most anyone. I had always been quite a tease and liked to play practical jokes whenever an opportunity came along ... but only if I felt comfortable with that person. Based upon my shyness and being somewhat reserved not many people would learn this about me for quite a while after meeting me. Perhaps because of this role reversal in my life, I could somehow attract some of the 'good lookers as well as the ugly ones'. I'm not saying, by any stretch of your imagination, that I had my way with girls. I really didn't believe or feel that I did. That would be far from the truth if I said that I did. My mother had taught me to respect the female gender. After all, I was from the South, and I had gentlemanly responsibilities to perform regardless of the circumstances or situation. It was always important to me to be a gentleman around young ladies or in any crowd. I disdained the loudmouths and the vociferous and verbose characters who tried to gain the attention and establish a territorial foothold with any young naïve, eligible, but unknowing female.

By the age of a little more than twenty-two, I began to start looking at girls more seriously. On one occasion, I remember my mother asked me if there was anyone in my life with whom I was serious. That was a little embarrassing to me in the sense that I didn't think it was really any of her business and besides, I'd choose a mate when I was good and ready. But she was my mom and she could ask any question of me she wanted. She had wondered why I didn't date some of the eligible girls from the church in my hometown. That was pretty hard to do simply because I couldn't get to Oxnard very often. In addition, that would put me back into the rigid religious environment that I now felt freedom from. Besides, those girls, if they were still around from my old high school days had to be 'problems' if they had not already gotten married, I thought. In addition, at the time I didn't like the Pentecostal image those girls carried. You know, no make-up, no movies, basically … no nothings! I never told my mother any of those things in response, however.

It was in Riverside, the city closest to March AFB, that I met Beverly Humphrey at the First Baptist Church. Bev had two boyfriends that she was always locked into: Ralph Shannon and Jerry Kechter. When she wasn't dating or going steady with one, she was with the other. I thought she was cute and I liked her personality. She was talkative to say the least but always friendly. She seemed to be well liked by her peers. I thought it would be fun to just go out on a date with her sometime. But she was tied up. Besides, she was quite a bit younger than I. At the time we met, she was sixteen and I had reached the ripe old age of twenty. Even so, she was always 'in between' her two boyfriends, when I was out of town some place on a TDY so there was a long interval before we were to have that first date. Perhaps it didn't have a lot of influence, but 'flyboys' did have a reputation in the community which was less than wholesome I was to learn later. Airmen had been at March since the 1930s. The truth is, and in the final analysis, I'm not sure that Bev would have chosen voluntarily to go out with me. If it hadn't been for her mother, Rubye, we might have never had a first date! Her mother apparently thought I was a cute boy and suggested that she should try to date me. I did not know this at the time of course. In 1957, after having been at March AFB for well over a year, Beverly and I finally had our first date. I cannot recall where we went or what we did. It could have been to an after-church social or perhaps to a movie. I am also certain that it was a double date.

There is one aspect, from a guy's point of view, that became apparent to me after reaching maturity and that is what parents' today caution their own children about. Perhaps mothers are better to their daughters about selecting the 'marriage partner of choice' than fathers. I believe, in my day, those kind of issues were not generally discussed in depth...at least not as likely as perhaps they are today. (They were never part of any family discussion that I ever had.) That is probably not a true statement in the higher levels of our society where, at least in the past, family histories and bloodlines take on major significance. At least that seemed to be very prevalent through part of the 19th and most of 20th centuries. It was never an issue for me simply because I considered myself as just a 'poor boy from Arkansas' trying to do the best that I could. It was my feeling that my parents had one day 'just decided to get married.' That's more or less what my grandfather had expected of my mother's choice of a mate. Today, success in marriage has the best chance when any and all issues can be discussed openly and thoroughly. Parents can and should assist their children in learning about life and coping before serious consideration is given to marriage.

From my limited focus and perspective, I wanted to select a mate from a good Christian family, who liked children, and was a good homemaker. Even these subjects were not explored in any serious vein between Bev and me when the time came to be serious regarding our future possibilities together. It's sort of scary to think back and know that this is more or less how it all started and culminated in marriage. Has it changed today as compared to the decade of the 1950s? I'd like to think so but I have serious doubts about how much attention it really gets. Maybe it's because we become blinded by the belief that we are in love and we can conquer the world without giving any real thought to the world or how we are setting out to conquer it! In addition, our hormones get revved up to the red line which blinds us, often causing mental paralysis in this regard.

For Bev and me, our dates and activities centered around three things. There were movies (drive-ins) and two drive-in restaurants in Riverside, Ruby's and Kings, and going to church. In the summer, there was the beach several miles away. The two drive-ins were where all the

Miss Beverly Ann Humphrey, age 17

kids would hang out and cruise through to see or spot someone you knew or to see who they were dating on any particular night. The other place to go was Fairmont Park in northwest Riverside, which was located very near the Santa Ana River and near a road which later became the 60 Freeway. In the park, back in the mid-fifties, there was a lake where boats could be rented and lovers and friends could paddle their boats around the lake until you got tired or the proprietor wanted to close for the night. It was sort of like an amusement park with some arcade games and refreshments available. It was fun to go down there once in a while. That part of the park is closed today and the lake is not what it used to be. In fact, the lake dried up completely and is no longer a recreation area like it once used to be.

Occasionally, we would go the local San Bernardino Mountains to Arrowhead, Blue Jay, Big Bear or Crestline. It was usually for a drive with other friends or couples. Sometimes during the summer, the church would have church camp programs and many of the youth would attend. Bev attended several of these activities up there. During the encampment, I would wander up to the mountains one or two evenings to see her and some of her friends spending the week up there.

As time went by, our relationship began to take on new meaning for both of us. She was to graduate from Riverside Polytechnic High School in 1957 and go on to college. She was very interested in music and in particular vocalization. She had a very clear and soft soprano voice, which was always on pitch. Bev was a real student of music and took it seriously. Her parents had provided lessons for many years. She chose to attend Westmont College, a Christian college in Santa Barbara, California where she could continue her music studies, among other subjects. The start of the fall semester of 1957 was the beginning of her college education. The end of her first semester was also the end of her college education! She liked to boast about it only taking her one semester to get her education whereas it took most students four years to get theirs!

At that time, I still had about nine months of my enlistment to complete. Our relationship was not what I would consider as a mad passionate falling in love on the first date or anything like that. I enjoyed her company and her many friends, some with whom we double dated. It was obvious that there was something special in our relationship and how we responded to each other. We always had good fun, enjoyed good food, liked to eat out and other activities and experiences such as going to the beach. However, most of our activities were basically focused at church or were family oriented. That fit in well for me with my convictions and up-bringing. In addition, being in the military didn't provide very much money for dating expenses! Dinner out most often meant going to the 'El Sarape' Mexican restaurant on Market Street.

She worked the summer of 1957 at Sears and Roebuck and saved her money to get ready for college. It was truly a sacrifice on the part of her parents to enroll her in this private school. In late August or early September she left for Santa Barbara, California.

Beverly and I did not really talk about our marriage or how many children we wanted in our family or whether she would have a career. We didn't discuss whether she would ever complete her college education. As for me, I basically announced that it was my intention to return to college and obtain my degree after I completed my tour of duty with the Air Force. I thought it was just the right thing for me to do as well as being a good idea. Being in the military meant that I was eligible for the GI Bill to help offset some of the costs of my education and that was definitely an encouragement to me. I knew that I would be the first in my family to try to complete a college education and that was a positive challenge to me as well.

Bev started at Westmont College in Santa Barbara in the fall of 1957. We wrote to each other quite often and it turned out that we missed each other probably more than either of us expected. She completed one semester before returning home to go to work. It was during that semester that I drove to Santa Barbara to visit her. During that weekend, I proposed to her that we get married. She accepted and we looked ahead and planned for June 1959 as our big day! I say 'we' loosely since it was really she and her mother who became intensely involved.

After Bev's semester, she returned home and began working at California Electric Power Company, which was then located in Riverside, to earn money and save for the costs of a wedding and setting up housekeeping. Later California Electric Power Company moved to Rialto, California near San Bernardino and Colton. In the meantime, we had our engagement party at the "Copper Penny' at the Riverside Shopping Center on Central Avenue near Magnolia. Other establishments have long since replaced it. The strip mall no longer exists.

During this period of time, I finished my active duty with the Air Force on July 14, 1958 and returned home to Oxnard. There I lived with my parents. In the interim period of time, they had moved from El Rio, a small community northeast of Oxnard, where we lived at the time of my enlistment in the Air Force to live in 'Colonia' area, which was the City Housing Project for low income families and the primary barrio community in the city. In the fall of 1958, I enrolled once again at Ventura Community College to restart and begin my college studies once again. The college had also moved. It was now located on a new campus east of the City of Ventura on Telegraph Road and much closer to Montalvo, a community about half way between Oxnard and Ventura.

Not really knowing the major course of studies I wanted to pursue, I decided to try engineering. Previously, I had been enrolled in industrial electronics before I joined the Air Force and I thought this would be an extension of that subject matter at a higher level. There were other required courses in the engineering field in which I had to enroll. I remember taking inorganic chemistry from Dr. Beane and algebraic calculus ... two subjects, which I really enjoyed. In fact I took two semesters of calculus and chemistry. I remember Dr. Beane asking when we met each other crossing the campus at the conclusion of my last semester, if I was going to major and get a degree in chemistry! At the time, I thought 'no way'! It was fun but it was definitely a solid subject which I worked hard to complete and maintain a 'B' average. I completed that year and was ready to transfer to a four-year college. I chose California State Polytechnic College in Pomona because of its proximity to Rialto and Riverside. Now our wedding date was looming large...June 27, 1959!

I can honestly say that at this stage in my life that I had never been to a big wedding. I was to learn rapidly that having a large church wedding was no easy task in terms of planning. The effort had been going on for many months with minute details relating to everything and it was hard work. There was a bedlam of activity. Bev and her mother were deciding what kind and style of gowns for the bridesmaids, her wedding gown, and the type of fabric, color coordination choices, the style of tuxedos, music and selection of soloists, songs to be chosen, the cake, the invitations, the guest list and how large it should be, transportation arrangements, where to go and where to stay on a honeymoon. It was a mad house from my perspective. I remembered how easy it was for my parents ... yet here we were with a mountain of incredible details of everything, which needed to be done. Regardless of my response to this overwhelming display of project management, Bev and her mother were in their heyday!

And don't forget the need to select a place to live after we were married. We decided on the city of Rialto because Bev's employer had moved there from Riverside and it was close to where she worked. In addition the location was reasonably close to California Polytechnic Pomona where I was to attend college for the next three years. In fact, Cal Poly was about thirty miles west down the freeway towards Los Angeles. It was also close to her family and that was important to them and to her.

The wedding, although stressful and tiring, was a superbly orchestrated event, which brought her parents, relatives and friends a lot of satisfaction. As for my family, my father had never worn a tuxedo before (or since) and I think my parents and my few relatives reacted in much the same way that I did…overwhelmed! When the Day came, it unfurled like clockwork. I think someone could have used a stop-watch to time everything. In addition to the incredible logistics, there was time for well deserved recognition. If you stop to think about it … her mother got to choose her daughter's spouse, did a lot of sewing and planning for the wedding, and had a controlling hand in the food and its preparation. Rubye got her well-deserved recognition being the mother of the bride!

What do I remember about this whirlwind of activity? First, I wanted it to be over quickly. I was nervous! Yet I wasn't. I had never done anything like this before. There was such a whirlwind of action that I did not have time to think about it. I remember seeing Bev in her gorgeous pale green wedding gown as she walked into the sanctuary. She was really beautiful! She had chosen a gown that 'was her' and she was beaming. Then I realized that the church was full. The 600 people took up every pew in the building. It was a packed house! Being that the wedding was in Riverside, there were only a handful of my relatives and friends in attendance. This was a show for the Humphrey family and what a show it was! As it turned out, the wedding ceremony and reception was a marathon of extended fatigue for me. It followed that detailed plan of action that Bev and her mother had put together. I remember my knees got soooo tired when we were kneeling for the prayer and a song to be sung. Then there were pictures and more pictures, upstairs and downstairs in the sanctuary.

It was such a blur for me that as years went by, people whom I would swear I had never met before would make a statement that we had a lovely wedding and they remember this or that! Silently, I would ask myself, "Were they at the same wedding where I got married?" There were several tables piled high with gifts. I had never experienced anything like it before.

As I look back, I think for the most part nothing out of the ordinary or unexpected took place until we left the reception. My Air Force buddy,

Leonard Williams, from the San Diego area was my best man. He drove the car for the traditional ride and horn blowing trip through town. As it would turn out, there were unsavory so called friends, among others, John and Marilyn Duke gained entrance to our room at the Dunes Motel in Riverside. This was the location we had chosen for our first night since we didn't have a flight out of Los Angeles until the next morning. These culprits gave a very feeble excuse that we had forgotten some of our wedding gifts and they needed to put them in our room for us. I have to believe the clerk was paid off somehow! They proceeded to block bathroom doors with chairs, wet all of the toilet paper, rearrange the bed and furniture and generally raise havoc. They stayed well beyond their welcome. The wedding was over about 9:00 pm. After the traditional parade around town, all the horn blowing, and the extended meaningless conversations in our room with this group of friends, I think we finally got to bed, beyond dead tired by about 2:30 am.

Leonard Williams, my best man, and Earlene Ada Gould, my sister-in-law who was matron of honor, were back early the next morning for the sixty mile drive to the Los Angeles International Airport so we could catch an 9:00 a.m. flight to San Francisco. This was the place we had chosen for our honeymoon and also because that's about as long a trip as I could afford. I don't know for sure who did it, but a real special friend spread Limburger cheese on the head of the car's engine so that when it heated up, it would burn the cheese. It was absolutely horrible to smell and smoke was every where. It didn't seem like it would ever burn off before we would be sick from inhaling the stench. Somehow we made it to Los Angeles International Airport with the windows down and hanging out to get fresh air. Fortunately we made it to San Francisco without further incident. We were now married and had spent our first night together! I had survived the ceremonial aspects of being married!

Now, my life would take on new meanings and experiences. I was to learn that my life had changed forever!

As newlyweds, you really begin to get acquainted. Dating was just the introduction. You find out things that you did not really know or pay much attention to before the marriage. For example, Bev's mother was trying to

Roark V. and Beverly Ann (Humphrey) Moudy
Riverside First Baptist Church
June 27, 1959

teach her some elementary things about cooking. I had noticed Bev in the kitchen when I was over at her house, but I never realized that she did not know how to cook. So when we began our life together the menu consisted of tacos. We had tacos virtually every night for a few days it seemed. When I asked about it, I found that was her specialty and that was about the grand sum of her cooking. So as a good husband I began to do some cooking. I am not a good cook but I had to learn to some extent when my mother was ill for a long while. I could cook a roast, vegetables, soups, hamburgers, make sandwiches, bake a basic cake or pie. It wasn't anything fancy at all. For me, it was survival food when I had to fend for myself.

After showing Bev some of my expertise, she quickly picked up on it and expanded her own repertoire. However, because of my effort, I always told people, tongue in cheek, that I taught her to cook. I didn't really. Bev loves to experiment with her culinary skills and is a superb cook and baker. She could duplicate anything published in *Bon Appetit* or *Sunset Magazine* in taste, flavor and beautiful presentation.

I also learned that Bev did not like to sew. She knew how to sew; she had taken a class in high school. Her mother was an excellent seamstress. My mother could sew well enough to get by. I was used to having torn pants repaired or buttons sewn on. I soon became grateful that my mother had shown me how to sew on buttons. Given the fact that Bev did not like mending; I could hang a pair of pants out to have a button reattached and they might hang there for a week or more. She had other higher priorities. I would get tired of waiting and do it myself. I think that was her plan all along. Once in a while she would feel guilty about the situation and pitch in and do it, especially when she would see me going to get the needles and thread!

One aspect that I always appreciated about my wife was her penchant for cleanliness. It sometimes bordered on extremism in my opinion. Everything had to be picked up, hung up, put in the cupboards or in the closets. Even to this day, if I leave a glass on the counter after having some water and expect to use it again within a few hours, it will be gone, out of sight; it's in the dishwasher! She is the clean-up kid!

It sounds like I'm complaining; but I'm not! I sort of like it that way just not to the extreme that she does.

Bev has always made statements about me that I am too slow. I like to think of myself as deliberate. My kids heard these comments for so long that they started referring to me as the 'two toed sloth', a notoriously slow creature. You can't win them all, so I just ignore the comment.

We have had our ups and downs, as all marriages do, but we learned to work together and it has been a very good life together. She has been my stalwart supporter and has loved me unconditionally. Even if her mother picked me, I picked her and I'm glad I did!

CHAPTER TWELVE
Waking Up to Reality

I t was August 27, 1939. It was hot, just like her parents remembered the Texas panhandle. But this was California; in fact Brawley, California! Not the panhandle at all!! Even so, Beverly Ann Humphrey was born in California and has loved to proclaim her start in life as a native of the state. At the time, she joined her father, Earl Byrd Humphrey, her mother, Rubye (Wood), and her older sister, Ada Earlene to make a family of four. Needless to say, mom and dad were two proud parents.

The Depression was coming to its close but life still was not easy in rural California and especially in the farming communities of the Imperial Valley. Earl worked long and hard as an auto mechanic. He was one person I considered to be a 'fix anything mechanical kind of man.' He loved everything mechanical. World War II had already started when the family decided to move to Riverside, California. There were several reasons for the move. With the war, work was easier to find and other family members lived there but some remained in the Coachella and Imperial Valleys too. Living conditions could be improved by the move. No doubt, the move must have seemed like moving from the farm to a metropolis, considering the size of the two communities of Brawley and Riverside at the time. As time moved along, many more of Rubye's family, the Wood Clan, came to live in Riverside. I fondly refer to them as the "Wood Clan."

My first real contact with the family occurred in 1957. It was an interesting time in my life but it was inundating. There were many family gatherings and on each occasion there seemed to be an endless string of relatives with one after another being introduced that I had never met before. I'm poor at remembering names and this made it even more ridiculous for me to even try to recall many of them let alone the whole group. Each time there was a family gathering, more family members were introduced to me as 'family'. I began to think it would never end or someone was putting one over on me about the number of relatives! There wasn't any way to imagine how large this family really was in numbers. It seemed almost as if they were increasing exponentially.

Occasionally, additional family members would arrive for visits from Texas or other places in California and without exception, there was always someone coming up from the Imperial Valley! It would be impossible for me to tell you how many years it took after we were married that I began to think that I had met nearly all of her relatives. With such a large family, friends and acquaintances cannot be left out of the equation either. Without exaggeration, there were multitudes of people at every event. To this day, I'm not sure that I have met all the relatives! This is getting ahead of the story, however, because our relationship did not get started for sometime after my arrival in the Riverside area.

I first saw Beverly during church services at the First Baptist Church in Riverside. I arrived at March Air Force Base in July, 1955 after completing the airborne radar technician's course in Biloxi, Mississippi during the previous nine months. I had chosen March AFB because it was close to Oxnard, California where my parents lived. That was important to me since my father's health was beginning to fail. I felt that in an emergency, I would be able to go home and help my mother. It gave her some comfort as well.

As had been my life's custom, I began to attend church in Riverside. As a young flyboy, it was important to find a 'good church' to attend. That meant a church where I could hear a good message, have a social outlet, and where there were lots of pretty girls. My initial impression of the church from that viewpoint was that indeed there were lots of pretty girls but they were rather distant and snobbish towards 'out of the locale invaders by way of the military' or any man in a military uniform for that matter. After all, World War II had been over ten years ago and the skirmish in Korea couldn't compare to The War. Without well defined military objectives in Korea, there weren't any real military heroes, and a military uniform didn't have much impact on beautiful young ladies. For a fact, it was detrimental to being able to even approach some young ladies and start a conversation. For that reason alone, most of us shed our military uniforms for 'civies' garb before leaving the base. To some extent, the parents seemed to be more accepting of service men, I think, because of their experience and linkage with service men during World War II.

I did meet a few of the young ladies of the church and eventually dated three or four of them. That first summer, I met Sally Hannah from Denton, Texas, who was visiting her younger sister, Nancy Smith, who lived in Riverside. These two sisters had been separated after their mother had died. Sally had been raised by her father in Texas whereas Nancy had been raised by her father's sister in Riverside, thus the difference in their last names. Sally had just finished her junior year of high school. I managed to have a few dates with her going to the beach on a few occasions, some local parties, and other activities during her summer visit. I enjoyed her company a lot and thought quite highly of her. Her stay seemed shorter than I would have liked but she had to return to Texas for school. The following year, I was invited to take a trip down to Denton to meet her parents and spend a few days there. Nothing serious ever came of our relationship. However, she did call me once and tried to reestablish a relationship with me but I no longer felt compelled to entertain that idea. It is hard to have a long distance relationship.

Being assigned to the Air Force's Strategic Air Command, my squadron always seemed to be on alert or moving out on TDY (temporary duty station) somewhere in the Pacific Basin for a period of two weeks to three months. Continuous assignments of this nature made it hard to get consistently involved in the church and its programs where young people were active. On a few occasions I did try to date Beverly. She was, however, most often going steady with Ralph Shannon or Jerry Keckter. If she was 'in between' boyfriends, I was on TDY. If I was in town, she had reconciled with her boyfriend(s). This went on for about two years. Finally, her mother stepped into the life of this struggling teenager and helped her to make a decision about her relationship with her boyfriends. Her mother thought that I was a good looking kid, I guess, so she suggested that she should have a date with me...if she could get one! During this period of time, I had virtually given up on ever having a date with her. She was too locked in to Jerry.

As I would find out later, Jerry was somewhat of a tightwad. He would rather spend his money on his car than on Beverly and entertainment. He knew what was important for himself but that was not satisfying to Beverly. This fact along with a little coaxing from her mother, she finally decided to give me a break. We had our first date in 1957. I do not recall the specifics of our first date probably because I had the feeling that I was filling in until her boyfriend came to his senses. During the evening, it became obvious that she had been tracking my social activity around town. She asked me about one of those blind dates I had; she even knew about that event in some detail – which I must say made me sick because the date was such a loser. The girl was one of her acquaintances in high school. I had done it as a favor for one of my Air Force buddies so that he could go out with his girlfriend. On a positive note, the one thing she took notice of from that early date was that I did spend money on my dates…if I had it. Money was sort of tight being in the military. There's not much to begin with and at the end of every month I was lucky if I had a few coins in my pocket. I lived from one paycheck to the next but I was not a spendthrift. I also helped my parents financially so I didn't have a lot to spend.

Because I was a gentleman and paid attention to her and spent some money, she seemed to be more positive about me than I had expected. We had a good time together and she was fun to be with. We enjoyed each other's company. That summer was a good summer with respect to our relationship. We hung out at Ruby's Drive-in and went boating down at Evans Park. There were also church activities and camps. I didn't attend any camps but I did go up to Crestline a couple of times when she was attending camp. The more we were together, the more we seemed to enjoy each other. She finally told Jerry that she was through with him and they were just friends from that time. In the fall, I left for an extended tour of duty in the Far East at Anderson Air Force Base on the island of Guam. She was starting her senior year of high school in the fall of 1957.

Beverly was a gregarious young lady. She always seemed to be in on the fun and group chatter. She conducted herself well and had a beautiful smile. I learned that she could sing as well and heard her sing in church. That always made her father practically burst his buttons he was so proud of her! Her mother was always very nice and friendly to me. She made me feel comfortable and welcome. I got invited to their home for a few of her mother's delicious home cooked meals. That was indeed a treat for me especially if you have eaten food prepared in the military kitchens. Beverly's entire family made me feel very quickly that I was not a stranger in their midst. I really did appreciate that reception. Since the family's roots were in Texas, I assumed that their treatment of me was merely an extension of that southern hospitality.

I learned about her love for dancing and how much fun she had going to dances with Ralph. He was obviously a good dancer and that made me think that my two left feet might become a hindrance to our future social life. As a kid, I was forbidden to even learn to dance by my parents because of my family's religious beliefs. I did not know at the time that Bev's interest in dancing was in conflict with the Baptist's beliefs. Even so, her father permitted her to attend dances at school. After all, this was a changing world and some of my early convictions were beginning to change as well. Rightfully, differences had to be challenged by me and then I was left to arrive at my own ideas and conclusions. For Bev, dancing was just an expression of fun and exercise. I think she could have become a 'dancing mimi' if she had wanted to go that way. I also think her father tolerated her dancing or 'looked the other way' because his daughter was such a great committed Christian otherwise. I say that because he was a deacon and a member of the board of trustees at the church for many years. Interestingly, we didn't do much dancing which was no doubt a let down for her. We did attend some of her school dances during her senior year, however.

During the summer before her senior year, Bev worked at Sears and Roebuck in downtown Riverside in the credit department. She was earning money to help defray expenses when she left for college. She was a hard worker and finding a job never seemed to be a problem for her.

Bev seemed to have her head on straight and was a very nice young lady. She enjoyed meeting people and people spoke very highly of her. It only seemed logical that we would find as much as we had in common. I could see that her family wasn't wealthy but they were better off than mine. Perhaps that would not become a hindrance. Our relationship continued to grow prior to her leaving for college.

Both of her parents worked for some time just as mine worked. Rubye worked at the University of California – Riverside as a cook in the commons. She was an excellent cook and knew what a well-balanced nutritious, meal was all about. Her techniques were similar to my experiences at home – good basic meals. I enjoyed sitting down at her table. Earl was an excellent mechanic. He worked repairing and rebuilding automobile engines for many years. Then he took on the more sophisticated diesel engines in the heavy moving equipment and power generation fields. He had a book of knowledge on the mechanical puzzles that kept him in demand in local shops until he was in his late eighties in age. He was a great father and treated his two daughters very tenderly. Never really saw him lose his temper or embarrass anyone.

Bev and I corresponded fairly regularly after she left for college. It left a vacancy in activity for me. However, it provided an opportunity for me to get to know her parents better. Rubye would invite me over for dinner occasionally and I appreciated their hospitality very much. I recall on one occasion, I was sick with the flu and her mother insisted that I stay over and sleep in Bev's bed. I didn't feel well so I agreed. As fate would have it, I started to feel a little better the next day and began to snoop around. Built into the headboard of the bed were some cubbyholes and in those locations were treasures and keepsake items she had saved. I enjoyed reading some of her letters and looking at pictures for a while. Sometime later I told her what I had done and, needless to say, she was none too happy about it.

Our two families had a lot in common including limited educations, both in the lower middle income level of American families, attended church regularly and that was an important part of their social life and had a strong belief in God. Bev's parents had moved to California's Imperial Valley a few years before my parents but in the same time frame, which was part of the Depression. The parents of both families worked hard and had a strong work ethic. Admittedly, Bev's family was better off financially because they were homeowners whereas mine were renters. They owned good running cars and so did mine. So on the economic strata were we comparable. I was not overstepping my social boundaries. I tend to think these facts convinced me that Bev and I would be good marriage partners.

The only drawback was that she did not know how to cook for beans!

CHAPTER THIRTEEN
Those Incredible Flying Machines

There are many times when I hear an airplane fly over the house from our local airport and I will comment, even when nobody else is around, "There goes someone having fun today." Every time I look up into the sky and see an airplane on its way to some place, I remain in awe of such a machine ever being developed. How does it ever get off the ground? How can air hold up an airplane that is so heavy? Even yet, after having studied, in a brief sort of way, aerodynamics, it remains a mystery of theories in so many respects. It just has to be one of the greatest inventions of mankind! Flying is exciting and thrilling as a passenger, as a member of a crew, second seat, or as the pilot in charge.

When I go flying in an airplane, the whole world changes for me. I am insulated from the issues of daily life and I can give my total concentration to making that machine do what I intend. I have used flying as an escape hatch many times. It is work but very relaxing to me although some would beg the question, "How could it be, when you have to be aware and concerned about so many things simultaneously?" That is indeed a good question because a pilot is responsible for having a safe flight under any and all conditions. Your eyes are constantly surveying the horizon for approaching or crossing aircraft. You listen over your radios for conversations of other pilots and what they are doing because it could affect what you do relative to your flight plan. In addition, if a pilot is flying by visual flight rules (VFR) he is always scanning his instrument panel for information, such as compass headings, oil temperature, altitude, fuel mixture and consumption, engine RPMs, checking ground directional indicators such as VORs, and landmarks for verification of your course and flight progress. It does keep a pilot busy; but if you enjoy it, it is a good busy. For me it was a diversion from the hassles of being a corporate officer and manager and the related daily challenges that brought stress and headaches. Flying was something to look forward to anytime I could climb into an airplane.

My First Airplane Ride

From the time I was a youngster in Oxnard, I have had a love affair with airplanes. I have no way of knowing how I really got interested in aviation. As a small boy, I recall my father and mother telling the story of our family's first airplane ride. By that time in their lives, it had become a rather hilarious story to them and they would both delight in the re-telling. They never mentioned the type of airplane or whether there were many passengers. However, one got the impression that there were more than just our family on board.

The ride took place at a local fair in or near Dos Palos, California about 1937. My parents were migrant farm workers. They didn't seem to ever have any extra money. No doubt, it was a bit of a struggle just to go to the fair let alone think of taking an airplane ride. It had to be very expensive. I was around two years old at the time. As they spent time at the fair, the hawkers were trying to attract people to their particular show or activity.

It seems that my parents became engaged in conversation with one of these hawkers about taking an airplane ride. Naturally, there was the immediate refusal and the reason given for not doing it was probably not related to money but just a simple comment to avoid taking a ride along with not having to admit their money was limited. Anyone looking at my mother and father, these migrant farm workers, had to know who they were and what they did for a living. Just look at their clothes. If that wasn't enough, listen to the way they talked. They sure weren't from California! For the most part, my parents were uneducated. Even so, they were good people; pure in their hearts; most of them relied on their religious beliefs to carry them through the hard and difficult times of living and life itself. They knew heartache in what seemed like a very dismal world. Perhaps the best thing they had was each other.

No doubt, my mother and dad had gone to the fair to get away from the daily routines that every migrant farm worker encountered day in and day out. There were grapes to harvest or cotton to pick. There were clothes to wash and a baby to care for. There was the every day question of what will we eat today or for this meal. Often the outlook was bleak. It was a dull life with little hope of a lifetime of success. The major theme was simply survival. Life indeed was a struggle and therefore any diversion was a huge event. So it was with the fair.

Take an airplane ride? Probably the highest either one of them had ever been off the ground was when, as youngsters, they climbed trees on their farms. That might be as much as twenty or thirty feet off the ground. I am sure they both asked how high did that machine fly?! Being 2,500 or 3,000 feet off the ground just did not seem to be something ordinary people ought to be doing. No doubt there were concerns about what it would feel like to take off and land. Was it scary or frightening? Airplanes seemed to make a lot of loud ear piercing noise when the engines were running. They had already heard and seen the airplanes take off and land at the fair. Perhaps neither of them dared to think of the unthinkable. What if we are up there and the engines just quit?

On the other hand, they had never been in an airplane. Perhaps they wondered what it would be like. Maybe it could be exciting and fun! The hawker no doubt egged them on and even grew impatient after a while. That was always a convincing tactic. Possibly, he could almost see the wheels turning as they tried to make a decision. Buy a ticket or not? You go…no, you go! Another plane just left…buy a ticket now and you can be on board the next one. The hawker might have sensed that my mother was the most vulnerable to the final decision 'to go or not to go.' He began to challenge her womanhood. Was she a piker or not? Now in the thirties, no one wanted to be known as a piker. A piker was a person who speculates in an overly and extremely cautious way. That was a word poor people could not stomach. It made them sound cheap and indecisive. They were not cheap just because they didn't have any money. Neither were they to be considered to be of suspicious character. That was a real slap in the face if you were to be called a person of that nature!

Nonetheless, that seemed to break the straw that had, to that point in time, kept the camel's back from breaking. In no uncertain terms was she going to stand there and be considered a piker. No way! A good hawker tries to prevent his targeted prey from realizing that they are being taken until it is too late. He had to have been very good in the case of my mother and dad. To this day, I can't conceive of either one of them being taken in to do something that neither one of them probably really didn't want to do. That point can only be debated however. The final step was to bargain about the cost of the flight. Money was obviously an important issue. Price the trip too high and it's out of the question. How it all worked out, I can only surmise. My mother told me that I rode free. In other words, I didn't take up a seat on the airplane since my mother held me. If I recall correctly, they ended up paying two dollars for the flight.

Both my mother and father were probably too busy wondering and worrying about their decision to take the flight to have noticed how many other passengers there were on board. I know that I asked them. The only response that I could remember was simple 'there were a lot of people.' Now that could have been seven or eight or who knows maybe twelve or fifteen. The way my dad talked about the airplane, I got the feeling that this aircraft had two engines. At this time in aircraft development, a Ford Tri-motor would have been a strong possibility since that aircraft was just being recognized and popular. It probably wasn't an aircraft any larger than a tri-motor. Therefore, I think it was probably a Ford Tri-motor airplane but it did have three engines not two as my dad thought. Now if you were sitting in your seat and looked out the window, you would see only one engine mounted on each wing. With the cockpit area closed off, it would be impossible to see the third engine which was nose mounted. If you didn't look carefully, you might have overlooked this third engine. I have tried to think of other aircraft that might have fit the very brief description but nothing else comes to mind. For a while I thought that maybe it was a Canadian made DeHaviland Beaver but that plane would have had only one engine yet could carry seven or eight people. No one will ever know and it is not important.

The plane was loaded and, after some cranking on the starter and belching of smoke and sputtering, the engines roared to life and started and they sat there on the tarmac as he ran through a check list of some type before the pilot taxied the aircraft down the apron to the run-up area, conducted his pre-flight, moved onto the runway and began the take off. All of this activity seemed to be conducted in a routine manner which it should have been.

I have wondered what was going through their minds as they sat in their seats during the pre-flight check. Perhaps, my mother may have asked my dad, "Do you think we should have done this? The hawker said we would enjoy the trip and it would a short flight, I hope he was right! Lewis, how does your stomach feel, do you feel okay?' My dad's reply to this barrage of questions could have been, "Just relax, you got us into this. Didn't you see some of those passengers getting off the plane, they were smiling and seemed happy. I think it's going to be okay. Just look out the window and enjoy the scenery. We'll be back before you know it!"

The flight seemed to be uneventful and apparently going well until it became a little bumpy. Those not accustomed to flying are generally unaware that air has bumps in it even though one cannot actually see the bumps. The bumps can only be felt and then only after you have had the experience of hitting the bump. This phenomenon can be unnerving to the new or infrequent flyer and traveler. According to my dad, everything was fine until my mother got excited. She looked out the window and could see that we were 'a long ways up' in the air. That was a new and un-usual sight for her. She thought the cars looked like little bugs and that you could hardly see people. Obviously, my dad had to see the same views as well. However, combine the height or altitude with hitting the air pockets and it caused the ride to become even more exciting to her. No doubt, she might have had a fleeting thought that the airplane might crash if it hit too many bumps. What actually happens when there are 'bumps' is that the sun's heat, especially in the summer, warms the ground and then becomes reflected heat from the ground back into the air in a vertical column and with a concentration of unstable action. This activity is particularly strong over desert and very warm areas. Convection air currents would have been common at that time of year. These currents, which are rapidly rising at different rates of speed, are dependent upon the terrain and the heat reflection. This causes updrafts which the airplane flies through as it travels. This action causes the plane ride to feel bumpy. The affect is sort of like a car riding over a series of potholes in the road.

If one is already nervous about making their first airplane flight, anything about which a person is a bit more uncertain can make the stomach uneasy and the heart palpitate and beat faster than normal. An individual can experience nausea along with intense perspiration if the condition exists for very long. I do not know if my dad had any of those symptoms, but he made sure that every body knew that was the way my mother reacted. Knowing my mother, she probably became somewhat vocal as the bumps were encountered. Many people do! I have heard them shout out 'whoopee' as if they were riding a wild bronco!

At this point it seems my dad became a bit impatient with my mother since he blamed her for my reactions. He always said that I started to cry at that time simply because she was getting too excited. Although there wasn't any vomiting, or injury of any kind, it seemed that all the passengers were glad to be back on good old solid ground.

So it was, I had taken my first airplane ride at the age of two! I am sure that it would have been my last if my mother had anything to say about it. Gladly, it was not to be my last.

Developing and Maintaining an Interest in Airplanes

Other than this particular airplane excursion, flying was never spoken of in my family except to tell this story. It was like we knew airplanes existed but they were a very strange, dangerous, and peculiar mode of transportation. There was just minimal interest in airplanes in my family. By the time World War II started, I was six years old and I had not been around airports or airplanes at all. About this time my father took a job near Port Hueneme, California at the Naval SeaBee Base close to Oxnard. By 1942, housing was very difficult to find since many people were moving from the southern and eastern areas of our country to California to work in the defense plants and help with the War effort. The government helped the cause by building a complete federal housing development to shelter defense workers. There were literally hundreds of these four-plex housing units made available strictly for government workers and their families. My family was lucky enough to obtain such housing and at reasonable rental rates. The northern boundary of this development in Oxnard was Fifth Street across from the local high school and very near the small local airport to the west. In fact, the field was only a little more than a mile from where we lived in the project.

Like most kids, we played in the streets and playgrounds of the complex. The Navy took control of the local airport and developed the facility into a training base for a variety of carrier destined pilots and aircraft. There were airplanes constantly flying overhead in the landing patterns. It was just routine during most of the day to see plane after plane making a landing followed by another and another. These pilots were very young, green and inexperienced aviators fresh from cadet school. They were there to better learn the idiosyncrasies of their aircraft and to practice, practice, and practice! They had to master landing their fighter plane on the deck of an aircraft carrier in order to be sent into action. None had seen front line action when they arrived at Oxnard except for the instructors. As soon as one group completed the school and its training, another group would arrive and the action would begin afresh. This seemed to occur about every couple of months. In one group or squadron there would be Avenger aircraft; in another, Corsairs; then the Thunderbolts or P-47s. There were also AT-6s that would arrive. The only thing constant about the base was the change in aircraft and the pattern they flew for landing.

Obviously, these pilots were still learning about flying and becoming familiar with their aircraft as they sharpened their skills. In the Pacific, they would encounter the Japanese enemy in dogfights so they needed to be sure of their feel for each aircraft. As a result of pushing them to their limits, there would be engines that ran out of fuel or maybe a fuel pump stopped or something else went wrong while in flight. We kids could look up and see the pilots with their goggles and leather head covers as they flew the down wind leg and turned onto the base leg part of the landing pattern before turning 'final' to squeak onto the runway. We would often wave to the pilots but most often they didn't acknowledge us because they were so busy trying to configure their airplanes for their impending landing. After all, this was a matter of life or death.

By seeing and watching so many airplanes every day, my friends and I became very adept at knowing when a pilot was in trouble. Fortunately, there weren't many crashes. When we knew an airplane was going down into one of the local lima bean fields due to problems, we would quickly jump on our bikes and peddle like crazy to get to the crash site and arrive most often before the Navy emergency crews arrived. Fortunately, the pilots were not seriously injured very often. They would be out of the aircraft and surveying the damage when we arrived. However, these young cloud tormenting air jockeys seemed to remain very calm and collected about the disaster and their plight. Most often, the emergency landing was made with the wheels up and there would be several rows of the farmer's beans taken out by the impact of the wings and fuselage. The nose of the plane was usually partly buried in the soft ground with its propeller bent backwards over the cowling of the engine which sort of gave the airplane a sad and disgusted look. That was how the pilot felt as well, I'm sure! I never learned if these crashes affected their careers in any way

In those days I was more interested in the airplanes and not so much the pilots. Looking back, I now know that many of the pilots never returned home to their loved ones. They would be killed in action against the Japanese. I really never had an idea then as to where they were being reassigned once they finished their training. No doubt some of these pilots were assigned to aircraft carriers such as the Yorktown, Enterprise, Philippine Sea and many others. They were the elite airmen chosen to support the battles in the Pacific Theater for Midway Island, Iwo Jima, Guam, Coral Sea, Philippine Sea, Guadalcanal and the Solomon Islands, among many others. They fought bravely under horrendous odds on many occasions. I pay full tribute to those gallant souls who flew over my house day after day and fought in the War of Wars so that we could keep our freedom. So many gave their full measure of life!

My involvement with airplanes and the neighborhood went on until the War was over in 1945. Much to the renters' surprise, after the War, the housing project with its many tenants remained intact and dwellers took other jobs as the defense industry in general closed down. The local aviation enthusiasts and town authorities saw a private use for the training base and within a year or so, it was converted from a military base to a civilian county airport. It became known as Ventura County Airport. Now that really did change things for me. I could go to the airport and get up close and look at the airplanes. I could talk to the people who knew how to fly them. I was becoming more interested in this exciting idea about flying in an airplane.

My fascination with airplanes seems to have had continuity from the time I took that first airplane ride with my parents even though it didn't seem to be all that successful. I believe the reason was plainly that I was too young to remember any of the displeasures of that event. By the time the War ended, I was approaching ten years of age. I had worked from the time I was seven years old selling newspapers as a street walker barking out 'Oxnard Press Courier' all over town! For a kid, it was seemingly a good time; for the older folks it had been a horrible experience but they could now rejoice that it would never happen again.

During the War, the front pages of the newspapers were covered daily with news about the European and Pacific Theatres and the various battles taking place. Often times, the news was several days late in reaching the papers. It seemed like every time my family went to church, someone had a son that they hadn't heard from for weeks and they were deeply concerned. Since it was a small church, there were the occasions when someone was heart broken; they had received the terse news announcing that their son, husband, loved one or boyfriend had been killed. It was indeed sad and unmistakably brutal. So indeed it was a wonderful day when we heard that the Germans surrendered! It was even better news when the announcement came on the radio and in the newspapers that the Japanese had agreed to peace!

The air traffic at Ventura County Airport could never compare to the days when the Navy pilots were training. It was very quite as if it had fallen asleep. At least, I got to look up every once in a while and see a small private airplane taking off or landing. A few crop dusters operated out of the facility. After another year passed, arrangements were made with Pacific

Southwest Airways to provide passenger service to our community and the coastal cities between Los Angeles and San Francisco. It was a 'milk run' but that was especially exciting news. I was really excited about that because I had never seen a big airliner up close! Now they would be flying regularly into our airport.

I remember the first time that I saw the airliner coming in for its initial flight into Oxnard. It was about one o'clock on a bright sunny day with absolutely clear weather. The big bird was bright and shiny with the sun reflecting off its aluminum skin. It was arriving from the east and it just seemed to float along almost as if it wasn't moving. Slowly but surely, it came down from the wild blue yonder. In those days, there wasn't any smog and very little haze so you could literally see for miles. The plane crossed over the fence and I could hear the tires squeak as it touched down on the runway and a plume of black smoke momentarily blasted into the air. The spectators could hear the engines slow down as the big plane reduced its speed, settled onto the runway, and the tail rotated gently downward until the tiny wheel at the rear touched the runway. This bird was a Douglas DC-3. A tail dragger of great proportions! It was a real workhorse during the War serving as troop carriers and supply transports.

Down at the far end of the runway, the plane turned around and headed our way. The engines sounded smooth and synchronized. In those days there weren't any automatic passenger walkways to be rolled up to the plane to keep the passengers out of weather. In fact, there wasn't even a ramp with stairs to walk down. When the pilot shut down the right engine (the side where the passengers disembarked) the door at the rear of the fuselage opened and dropped down. It had its own steps built-in. The steward came down the steps first to assist the exiting passengers. In the meantime, a local airline worker was busy unloading and reloading baggage and mail from the underbelly of the plane's many compartments. Only three passengers got off and only two climbed on board. It only took about five minutes for all of this to happen.

The next thing you knew, the pilot and captain of the bird was cranking up the silenced engine on the right side. The passenger door was already closed and the ground crew was backing away to keep from inhaling very much of the cloud of smoke being expelled by the laboring and sputtering engine working to start up. As the engine caught on and smoothed out to a steady roar, the DC-3 slowly made its way to the east end of the airport runway; sat there motionless for a few seconds. Then it turned onto the runway with its engines screaming as the props bit into the heavy sea air, gently blowing in from the Pacific Ocean, and began pulling this lumbering giant faster and faster down the runway. The tail came off the runway first and the plane was left to roll on its two main landing gears. I watched ever so closely as it lifted off the runway very gracefully and almost imperceptibly at first. I stood there watching as it headed up, banking slightly in a north westerly direction and flew out over the ocean.

As it disappeared from sight, I wondered about where the plane was going and where the people on board were headed. It made me wish that I could have been going along for the ride as well. Who could possibly know, maybe some day I could do that too…only I would like to be the pilot! It seemed sensational for me to see all that happened that day. I never forgot the event. There would be many other days when I would watch the same sequence of events. I never tired of it.

Working and selling newspapers provided me with a small amount of money for my own use. Rather frequently, I bought hamburgers at Rolley's Diner, near 4th Street and the 101 Highway before I picked up my afternoon papers since the paper office was across the alley from Rolley's. More often than not, I bought my own clothes or at least helped my parents. The day came when I had saved up enough money to purchase my own bicycle down at the Western Auto store, which was next door to the Bank of America near the corner of 4th and 'A' streets.

I thought that bike was the cat's meow! The bike had a light built onto the front fender; a double bar across the center where a housing had been mounted to contain a battery powered horn. Best of all it was red and white with white sidewall tires. It sparkled in my eyes. I loved it and was very proud of it. I also ventured out to the airport occasionally on that bicycle. There I watched those private pilots do the work around their airplanes. Some of them gave lessons and taught people to fly. They even noticed me hanging around looking and watching what was going on. One day, one of them who had seen me many times came over and asked me if I liked airplanes? I said, "I sure do mister! I want to fly one some day." He responded with a statement that 'maybe someday I could go for a ride with him.' Was I ever excited! I wondered over and over again when that day would come. I could never tell my mother about it…she'd kill me! She seemingly didn't like airplanes very much ever since the ride at the fair, more than ten years before. Airplanes were scary and somehow dangerous to her!

On a day when I had just about given up hope, that same pilot saw me and invited me to come along right then for that ride he had talked about. Wow, I couldn't believe it! A ride I had dreamed about. I was so excited. It didn't seem real. But I learned a lot that day. There were a lot of things to do in order to fly an airplane. Jeff had me follow him around the airplane. He said he was doing a pre-fight check to make sure everything looked okay and was in good working order. He even checked to see if there was water in the gas tanks. After about ten minutes of checking, he said, "Okay let's get in the airplane." He got in first and then had me get in and he closed the door and secured it by locking it. He fastened his safety belt and then he helped me with mine and he stressed the importance of always keeping it fastened. Then he started to turn dials and flip switches. I heard strange noises and then he shouted out the little window, "Clear," looked all around the area and then reached for the starter switch. The engine wined for a few seconds, coughed a couple of times, and began to run. I noticed that the pilot didn't take his eyes off the instruments as he checked some of them, tapped a bit on another one, then picked up the microphone and announced he was moving to the run-up area. He pulled the throttle a little and the engine purred louder and faster and the craft began to move. I noticed that he guided the airplane with his feet on the pedals. We turned onto the apron and moved to a spot just off the end of the runway. He set the brakes, just like an emergency brake in a car, and began to really make the engine run fast. He would turn a little switch and watch an instrument…said he was checking the magnetos. After a little more time, he let the engine idle and told me we were ready for takeoff. What a day!

He pulled the throttle a little and the plane moved forward and he turned it onto the runway. The nose was pointed up in the air but down the centerline of the runway and then he gave the throttle another pull and the craft lurched forward as he moved the controls and began to pick up speed. It wasn't long until we were up in the air and I could see for miles. There were lots of lemon orchards and fields of vegetables. I easily recognized them since I often rode my bike to all these places. As we climbed, the cars and the people got smaller and smaller. It was an amazing sight and I loved it. It was everything I had thought about all those years watching from the ground. Jeff pointed out different landmarks to me but I could already identify with them for the most part. I could easily follow where we were in terms of the vicinity. I saw my school and the lemon packing house where my mom worked. We flew over to Saticoy and up the Santa Clara River almost to Santa Paula before taking a heading back to the Oxnard airport. When we started to land, we flew over the town area and straight over the high school and landed at the airport. The flight had lasted about an hour all told. But I was ecstatic. I wanted to tell my parents but I dared not…maybe someday I could but not now.

As an early teenager, my friend Kenneth Stearns', who lived in the project next door to my cousin, James Tubbs, brother was interested in model airplanes. He always seemed to be working on new models or fixing his old ones. He was older than we were but he still showed us what he was doing and that was interesting to me. He was a very good painter of his models and I always thought the paint jobs were superbly done and in metallic kinds of colors. I always knew when he was working on his models as soon as I entered the door because I could smell the airplane glue, paint and dope used on the models. That exposure to model building eventually became an integral part of my life as I, too, became an enthusiast for a period of time. I built a model P-40 Spitfire while I was on Guam spending a three month TDY. I also went down to watch various models fly that were built by airmen who were club members on permanent duty stationed on the island. Later, I bought a model helicopter when I went R&R (rest & relaxation) to Yakota Air Force Base in Japan. Without explanation, I have yet to get it in flying condition even though I have had it for a number of years. This activity also helped me maintain an interest in flying airplanes.

Sometimes on weekends, there would be model airplane enthusiasts at the Oxnard High School on the old grass football practice filed. It was a pretty hard surface and often there would be several model builders there with their airplanes. They would take turns flying the models around the grounds. Once in a great while, one would crash. That was heart breaking for the owner. He had spent literally countless hours building the wooden structure, installing the radio controls, balancing the craft, selecting the right engine to power the model and painstakingly painting it. These model planes were works of art!

I recall a U.S. Navy officer who brought a multicolored red 1930 something racing model bi-winged airplane in which he had installed a radial engine. It was the first such model airplane engine like that I had seen. I was so anxious for it to fly. I waited around until it was his turn. I wasn't leaving until I saw it fly. The flight started off perfectly; good take off and climb out; flew a couple of loops at high speed; then the pilot took it over close to the cedar windrow that protected the field from the afternoon sea breezes, where a gust caught it and it dove straight into the grass of the field at about a forty-five degree angle and disintegrated into a zillion pieces and caught fire. I remember the model maker running over to it and kicking the radial engine out of the fire and lamenting as to what went wrong. He was completely disheartened over the accident as were all of his model builder buddies.

During my high school years, my enthusiasm didn't wane but I was sort of pre-occupied with work, going to junior college, and my girlfriend, Janice Elliott. I had learned over the years that flying was expensive and I really could not afford to do that and get an education too. I still liked flying and would look up in the sky most every time that I heard an airplane flying in the vicinity. I felt that my dream was out of reach at the time. I was not financially able to pursue it. Even with that realization, I never lost my love for flying. It held a fascination for me like a piece of metal is attracted to a magnet. The tug was always there.

Chapter Fourteen
The Military Makes a Flyboy

Air Force Life Convinced Me That I Could Fly

While still in high school, many of my school mates were joining the Marine Corp Reserve unit located at Port Hueneme, California on the SeaBee base. I don't know why they were making such a decision but when I was asked to come and join by a friend of mine at school, I did. That was in 1952 and the Korean War was going on. My Reserve Unit was the 67th Special Infantry Company, USMR. I had spent two summers going to reserve training exercises. In 1953, I put in my two weeks at the Marine Corp Recruit Depot in San Diego going through the rigors of basic training and then learning to shoot an M-1 rifle at Camp San Onofre near La Jolla, California. During the summer of 1954, school was barely out and we were on our way to Camp Pendleton, near Oceanside, for field training and extensive beach landing assaults while under live fire ammunition. We trained more on the M-1 and Browning automatic rifle with static and pop-up targets. I qualified for sharpshooter with the M-1. It was after that training when I was invited by my fellow marine, school buddy, and co-worker, Gene Nunes, to 'go active duty' with the United States Air Force. Gene and I had worked together for about two years at Booth's Texaco station on the corner of 4th Street and the 101 Highway in Oxnard. On July 15, 1954, we volunteered and joined the United States Air Force. I could have joined other military branches and thereby not have had to commit to a four-year enlistment. But the Air Force was my only choice. At the time of my enlistment, it never crossed my mind to apply for flight school. I was very proud of being in the Marine Corp Reserves and had come to believe in some of the brainwashing that goes on in the Corp. At this time, however, I was momentarily preoccupied with getting out of the United States Marine Corp Reserves and avoiding foxhole duty in Korea. I had been studying electronics at community college and wanted to pursue that field. Being in a ground pounding outfit did not offer that opportunity.

By the time I had completed almost two months of basic training at Lackland Air Force Base, near San Antonio, Texas, a second Lieutenant visited our Basic Training Squadron and inquired if any recruits would like to take a test to get into flight training. Apparently there was a need for pilots. A few of us accepted the invitation, not more than four or five. I knew some of my buddies did it just to get out of three days of training in the hot summer Texas sun. I did it because I thought this was my chance to learn to fly. Let the Air Force pay for it. I could be flying the best and latest souped-up jet fighters in the world. I really thought that this was my lucky day! The Air Force was training fighter pilots for F-4 aircraft then and that was really exciting for me.

The next week, about five of us left basic training and ventured over to the testing facilities as instructed. They had informed us already that the testing would last for three solid days. It was not going to be a cakewalk for sure. I hadn't any idea about the type of information that would be in the test. We were told that there would a written part, a hand-eye coordination part and a physical part. I was a bit intimidated by the extensiveness of the testing. After all, I had only one year of Junior College when I enlisted. I had been an above average student but not a top scholar. I liked school and did my best. I did my homework because I wanted to do it. I knew it would help me in the long run. That's what my parents had taught me and told me many times. My mother was always my great encourager. She was virtually obsessed with the idea that I would get a 'good education' as she referred to it. That was something that both of my parents had missed out on when they were young. My mother was able to complete the eighth grade; my father, only the third grade. I never looked down on them nor was I ashamed of them for their lack of education. They, in a sense were forced to quit school because of economic hardships of their respective families. I also knew their basic motivation was to see me succeed.

The testing began. The written part came first. It was a series of word and comprehension retention problems. The tests started at eight o'clock sharp and lasted until noon. We had a short break at mid-morning. It picked up again after lunch and concluded at 4:30 p.m. I was exhausted but felt reasonably good about the tests. Testing began again the next morning at the same time. The focus was now on hand-eye coordination. One test involved holding an electric stylus in one hand and trying to hold it on a metal spot on a turntable about the size of the head of an eraser pencil. The turntable would stop and start, slow down, speed up, go like crazy for a few seconds and stop again. This repeated itself several times. During this time, if you made contact with the stylus on the little spot, an electrical connection was made and a meter behind the scenes racked up points for your efforts. Other types of hand eye coordination exercises continued for the remainder of the day.

On the third day, our time was devoted to taking a thorough and extensive physical. Everything that had ever happened to me had to be listed and discussed with a flight physician. A significant time was spent testing my eyes. There were color blindness tests, reading tests, tests to see how close I could focus on something sitting on my nose. It was an exhausting physical and extremely thorough. We were told that we had to have 20/20 vision uncorrected.

After that day, I reflected back on all that had occurred. I did not have any idea whatsoever that I had passed or failed even though I knew that I had done my very best. All of us were told that our tests would be graded and evaluated. In about three months, we would be notified of the results. All of us knew that by that date, we would all be reassigned to a technical school for additional training and we had no idea as to which base or school we would be assigned. How would we really find out if we had or had not passed the test? We were assured that we would be notified regardless of where we were assigned. It was off to Keesler Air Force Base at Biloxi, Mississippi where I was enrolled in airborne radar technical school for the next nine months.

I had been in technical school for about two months when a letter came one day. I opened my mailbox and saw it, I could not decide whether to open it or not. I was anxious. Within seconds, I opened it and began to read, "You have passed the test requirements and are fully qualified for entry into flight school. You will be notified when you are assigned a class. If you have not been given a class assignment in one year from the date of your eligibility, you are automatically disqualified. If you desire, you may reapply at that time." Hip, hip, hooray! I passed. It was incredible! I could not believe it! I was so happy and excited. I had just been given all the confidence in the world. I just knew that I would get a class assignment before a year's period of time had passed. I was on top of the world. I wrote home and told my parents about the developments.

What I didn't know about was my mother's reaction. I thought that she would be very proud of me. Never once did I have any inclination that she would not be excited for me. As I learned later, she was petrified. All she could think about was crashing airplanes and war. She was beside herself about these developments. I learned later that she got down on her knees and began to pray for me. Knowing her, she probably summoned all of her friends and other prayer warriors to pray that I would not get a flight school assignment. I wasn't to learn about this tactical effort until my tour of duty had been completed more than three years later.

On my side of the effort, I continued to hope for a school assignment. The year passed and my assignment never came. I was told that I could go down to the testing center at March Air Force Base, Riverside, California and take the tests over again to reestablish my eligibility. I did. It was the same extensive testing all over again. I passed again. If I had known what my mother was doing, I probably wouldn't have told my mother again. But I didn't, so with elation I related my success again. She didn't say much. She seemed proud but her enthusiasm was somewhat lacking. I didn't realize what was going on. So, I waited another year…another bail out by the Air Force on my assignment. There wasn't much hesitation on my part to try again. So off to the testing center I went. This was getting to be old hat. Passing tests and physicals was no longer a strain. You bet, I did it again…and waited. It wasn't hard to detect a pattern here. I just wasn't going to get an assignment to flight school it seemed. I was willing to fly anything with wings even those slow multi-engine transport planes! Honestly, it no longer had to be a near supersonic fighter…I'd go for anything! I had become completely convinced that I had what it took to learn how to fly an airplane. In fact, I was certain that I could become a very good pilot. It still had all of the allure for me that it had seemingly always had only more so now.

In the meantime, I was flying irregularly with the United States Air Force in an electronics support effort for a squadron of B-47s of the 320th Bomb Wing and supporting a squadron of KC-97 aerial refueling tanker aircraft that did mid-air refueling of the B-47s. I was an airborne radar mechanic responsible for fixing the 'black boxes' used in navigational radar, identification – friend or foe equipment on board and bombing radar systems. I was assigned to the 320th Armaments and Electronics Squadron with my home base at March Air Force Base. I loved the assignment and environment. Being able to be around airplanes routinely all the time was exciting for me.

Just watching the professionalism and perfection of the flight crews was exhilarating for me. Each member of the crew had a job to do just like us enlisted airmen. But there was something special about being an officer and assigned to an aircraft as part of the flight crew. They got to see and be in the 'wild blue yonder'! Living with that connection day in and day out reinforced my desire to make flight school.

The B-47 was an impressive aircraft. It looked sleek and powerful. The tandem canopy provided incredible visibility – wide-open views inside an unobstructed Plexiglas bubble.[1] Its long sweptback wings drooped very noticeably but were prevented from touching the ground by the use of outrigger wheels that retracted in flight. The landing gear was a tandem bicycle type undercarriage consisting of two main landing gears or 'double wheels' one set being somewhat forward and below the canopy with the second set near the mid-section of the fuselage. It had six jet engines and could operate for combat purposes at 38,500 feet flying at 557 miles per hour. The bomb load capacity was 22,000 pounds.[2] It was America's first all-jet bomber. Even as large as this aircraft was, it could dive from altitude and descend at 6,000 feet per minute by deploying its aft-rear main gear and extending its outriggers to act as dive brakes. The Air Force purchased more than 2,000 of these airplanes from the Boeing Airplane Company.

By 1957, a year before my enlistment commitment was completed, the U.S. Air Force's Strategic Air Command (SAC) had a force of 224,000 personnel operating 2,700 aircraft including 127 B-36s, 243 B-52s, 1501 B-47s, 742 KC-97s and 24 KC-135s.[3]

The KC-97s were the main type aircraft used for in-flight refueling during my tour of duty. These tanker crews and support personnel received comparatively little public acclaim despite the fact that aerial refueling is dangerous and requires close and difficult maneuvering and operating with a high degree of precision during refueling. It is dangerous. A safe operation requires a high degree of skill on the part of both the tanker and receiver crews. Think of two very large aircraft flying at over 300 miles per hour with the tanker plane having four aspirated engines and a ceiling of about 20,000 feet with a jet bomber swooping in from altitude and somehow becoming physically hooked together for only a few minutes. The tanker plane pilot is flying his machine as fast as he can while the bomber pilot is flying as slowly as possible trying to avoid stalling and all the while a boom operator is trying to make a flying boom fly and fit into a 5-6 inch opening on the top side nose of the bomber from approximately 17-25 feet away. Its one thing to refuel in daylight but the technique had to be done at nighttime as well with visibility problems, weather problems, wind issues and delivering fuel at near 600 pounds per minute under pressure. That's what it was all about! We did it often and many times as if it was a cinch routine. It wasn't!

When, as is done so often, the refueling is carried on at night, in bad weather, under radio silence, and sometimes within range of enemy defenses, it is extremely hazardous. The skill of the crews and the frequency with which refueling occurs have dulled public appreciation of the difficulty of the operation. In stark contrast, no one appreciates the tanker crews more than the receivers, for tankers have saved countless aircraft and crews over the years.

My unit was part of the global defense system of the United States identified as the Strategic Air Command, 15th Air Force which was commanded by General Curtis LeMay, a diminutive 5'-5" cigar chewing, butt knocking commander out of headquarters in Omaha, Nebraska. That was the command center for the Strategic Air Command. I only saw him once during my military career. That was when he landed his B-52 at March Air Force Base on a Friday evening late, about 8:00 p.m., completing a non-stop flight around the world.[4] The B-52 had been in the air non-stop for 45 hours, 19 minutes and had traveled 24,325 miles averaging 530 miles per hour. Politically and militarily, it was his way of telling the Russians that the U.S. could hit Soviet targets anytime that the need existed. It was a mission with major political significance at the time and it had been successful. Anyway, instead of leaving for my week-end, I had to stick around and wait for his plane to land so that I could fix the APN-69 radar system that had malfunctioned on the final leg of his historic flight. When I arrived on the ramp to make repairs, he came bouncing down the stairs with his staff and got into his command car limousine without fanfare. He seemed to be all business.

General Curtis LeMay, historically was the second to command the Strategic Air Command having succeeded General George C. Kenney on October 19, 1948.[5] He is credited with bringing the Air Force to its zenith in terms of a worldwide force of power and fast response capability. He was extremely interested in training of personnel, performance, and evaluation of performance. He expected excellence in everything. It has been said that not everyone liked General LeMay but his results could not be refuted. He is also credited with modernizing the primary delivery systems (aircraft) equipment and the related support equipment for intercontinental airborne warfare. One of his most important accomplishments was the development of mid-air refueling techniques for the U.S. extension into a global fighting force through the air. Through SAC's strength, it became the deterrent to the Soviets creating more havoc than they did during the long years of the Cold War. This constant vigil and show of strength caused LeMay to declare, "there would be no more Pearl Harbors." The Cuban Missile Crises of 1962 is a good example of SAC's impact on the leaders of the Soviet Union. Subsequent to that event, Nikita Khruschev stated, "all during the negotiations over Cuba, he could not get the thought of orbiting B-52s out of his mind." General LeMay retired in 1965.

"The klaxon alert horn shocked me awake.[6] I glanced at the clock. Three fifty-five a.m. I scrambled into flight suit and boots, and then ran down the alert facility corridor out into the night to our alert truck. Freezing rain brought me further awake. The navigator and I tumbled into the truck. The co-pilot drove the 100 yards to the dark B-47 sitting on the ramp. As I climbed the entry ladder, our crew chief started the ground power unit, applied power to the aircraft, and then manned the fire bottle. I put on my helmet and heard the wing command post transmitting the alert message in code. As I started the engines, the navigator called, 'Exercise Cocoa Message Working authentication.' The co-pilot and navigator confirmed authentication, then I taxied toward the runway. Visibility was very poor but I saw 11 other alert bombers and tankers falling into line. We crossed the runway hold line 11 minutes after the klaxon had sounded, then taxied back to our parking space having demonstrated once again that the SAC alert force could get airborne in less than 15 minutes.

During the Cold War, the Strategic Air Command constantly maintained more than 300 aircraft on alert as a deterrent force. SAC exercised the force, day and night, to insure responsiveness in all conditions. Crews averaged more than one week out of three on alert. While on alert, we received daily briefings on operations, weather, and intelligence, studied assigned targets, or trained in simulators. We ate and slept in the alert facility. On Sundays, families brought lunches to an area adjacent to the alert facility.

After a Friday changeover to the replacement crew, we were off until Tuesday afternoon. One month out of three, we deployed to England for alert duty. On average, SAC crews spent forty percent of their lives on alert or deployed until the end of the Cold War."

In this book there is a picture of a crew running from a truck towards an aircraft clearly marked with the SAC shield (probably a B-52). The caption under it reads, "This scene of an alert crew racing to the aircraft was repeated thousands of times over the years. The crews never became jaded. Any one of the alerts could have been the real thing, signaling a nuclear first strike by the Soviets with all the terrible implications that had for the world-and for every individual crewman's family. It was a sobering time, when the airman going to war had a greater chance for survival than the family he left behind."[7]

Indeed, SAC was the shield and deterrent for the United States and our Allies from the great Russian bear and through its efforts served the cause of peace in the world through its intercontinental capability to deliver nuclear weapons to any part of the world and, in particular, to the Soviet Union and its allies for more than four decades. This global force was a culmination of part of the political idea of George F. Kennan,[8] historian and diplomat, best known as the architect of 'containment.' This was America's cornerstone policy in dealing with the Soviet Union for forty years. I was proud to have served SAC and my country during this period of time. I truly believe, it was through our country's alertness, power and strength militarily that the Soviet political structure finally collapsed late in the twentieth century. Certainly, President Ronald Reagan helped push its demise over the precipice.

I mentioned earlier that I serviced General LeMay's personal B-52 aircraft. That was one of the few times that I made it to the flight line since I spent most of my time in the shop running sophisticated electronic test equipment analyzing the maladies of the black boxes brought in from the flight line. That was my job and I liked it for more than one reason. In the summer months the inside of an airplane would get very hot parked on the tarmac in a semi-arid desert environment. I mean really hot sitting in the hot sun all day. Inside the fuselage temperatures could get as high as 140 degrees Fahrenheit. Many of my poor buddies who were assigned to the flight line were either hot or cold all year it seemed. I enjoyed an air-conditioned work area with a constant temperature. It had to be that way because of the electronic gear I was working with in a testing condition.

On another occasion when I was on the flight line, I was doing some work on a B-47 when a tractor pulled up and attached to it were four small trailers. The trailers were like metal cradles with a drab green can that didn't appear to be quite as big as a fifty-five gallon drum. That, however, could have been misleading because of the relationship to the large aircraft fuselage, which it was near. This was not an ordinary drum. It was different. It had many bolt heads showing as if it was hard to hold together.

It seemed there were dozens of bolts and nuts. I had never seen one of these objects before so I asked the crew chief what were those things? Being taken aback a little, he said, "Haven't you seen those things before, they bring them from across Highway 395 from the bomb dump. That's an atomic bomb!" Oh my! Suddenly my knees felt a little shaky and they started to get weak. I was very ill at ease being that close to one of those horrible monstrosities. It gave me a very eerie feeling. I wanted to hurry up and get away from these destructive devices. Sure I had read about the ones dropped on Nagasaki and Hiroshima and that made it even worse. I knew these bombs were more powerful than the 'Big Boy' dropped in WWII. It didn't make any difference if I was back in my barracks and out of sight from the device, I'd be blown to smithereens just the same as if I was straddled on top of it and if for some reason it exploded. I wasn't really thinking in terms of reality, obviously. Thank God, that was the only time that I ever saw 'the bomb', but I knew from that point forward that what SAC was doing was very serious business.

Not all duty performed was an issue of high alert. I remember standing on the flight line at March AFB and watching with great pride and enthusiasm as B-47B 51-2314 took off.[9] That bird was our 320th Bomb Wing entry into the 1955 Bendix Race involving equipment and crews from several bomb wings in speed competition and navigation exercise from March AFB to Philadelphia. It was an exciting event and was one way to boost morale not that we needed it. The course distance was 2,337 miles and our entry averaged 589 miles per hour over the route! I do not recall if our Wing won the event but the officers were very pleased with the results.

Having been permanently assigned to the Strategic Air Command, my Bomb Wing made many relatively short-stay trips to other duty stations throughout the Pacific Basin. These trips were referred to by the military as TDYs meaning 'temporary duty station.' Usually, the assignment might last for a minimum of two weeks but not more than three months. It was the Air Force's way of completing its commitment to join the Air Force and 'See the World.' However, there were more sinister issues. Generally, these TDYs involved 'playing war' against the Russians. Simulating the conditions under which our unit would be operating in case of war. The birds would fly many sorties (missions) sometimes twenty-four hours a day. Being around such awesome aircraft, crews and support personnel made me feel proud that I was helping to defend our country. I usually flew in the KC-97s with the electronic analytical and test equipment from the shop and being transported to the temporarily assigned field and then return the same way. Often times, particularly on our way 'home', we would fly a sortie and refuel a B-47 or two before taking our compass heading for home. I do not know how many of these trips I took but they were numerous and frequent. I doubt if one half of my assignment time at March AFB was actually spent on that base. This version of the Air Force's slogan of 'see the world' was for me limited to the Pacific Basin sector of the world. There were several TDYs to Elmendorf AFB (Anchorage, Alaska), Hickam AFB (Honolulu, Hawaii), Anderson AFB (Guam), Yakota AFB (Japan) and one trip to Lockbourne AFB (Columbus, Ohio). My daily activity and just being around aircraft helped me to maintain my long time interest and excitement in flying.

These TDYs could be extensive in terms of the personnel required to support and maintain the aircraft. Most often, however, the electronic support group was rather small. Most of the time, the same personnel made the trip. The group was chosen by Master Sergeant John Rodney Richardson, a career man who had served in World War II. He expected nothing but dedication and performance from the crew that he selected. The rest of the group most often consisted of Joe Boyd, Jack Haff, Harold Stitt, and Gonzalo Grenados. Other airmen made the trips having different duties and responsibilities but all having one objective in mind and that was to keep all the birds flying for every aspect of the operations.

I was proud to have served in the Air Force at this time. I felt like I was doing something positive to protect my country and to deter the Russians. I never viewed my four years of experience as an endangerment or risky. Years later, it seems more risky than I ever realized at the time. Flying in the Alaska area was very risky because of the proximity of the Russian Mig-15 fighter patrols over the Bering Sea. That body of water does not provide a lot of separation between the U.S. and Russia. It was not uncommon to encounter fighter scrambles on both sides when any aircraft came unreasonably close to the other's border. Part of the political strategy was testing each other's surveillance and identification systems. It was a gut check on reaction times!

We are all very aware of the Russians' attitude about their borders and the unprovoked attacks on aircraft of other countries throughout the Cold War. Perhaps the only reason, I didn't have any experience of that nature was the proximity of the two giant military forces of the time and the belief that such a military act would provoke an atomic holocaust. Years later, I truly believe it would have caused such a holocaust if such an event had occurred then. The U.S. had nuclear weapons loaded on most all of our B-47 bombers on every mission. They were not flying for the fun of another sortie. In a matter of minutes, they would have dialed in their compass headings and could have been on their way to Moscow and other critical military targets. That was a nervous time, believe me! As it is known now, the USSR would have never survived as a country. Probably most of the U.S. bomber forces would not have survived either. Who knows what might have happened to our country? The Mutual Assured Destruction (MAD) theory was often discussed by politicians. This theory said that if either country was attacked by the other, both countries would be destroyed from the face of the earth by either blast destruction or radioactive fallout consequences. Given the vastness of such horrible proportions, other populations would have been impacted as well. Thank God, it never came to that point!

Cold War military personnel were never engaged in combat as we know history records in World Wars I and II. There were no purple hearts or battle stars for bravery handed out to U. S. Military personnel who fought the Cold War. Instead, this was a war of détente, political skirmishing, blustering by our enemy, the Communist countries of Eastern Europe, displays of military might and continual improvement in destructive delivery systems. The United States' focus was the Soviet Union and vice versa. We saw Communism as a threat it to our western democracy. As far as America was concerned our goal was to ultimately prevent actual war if at all possible through strength of our military. It was a 'war' in which the United States had no previous precedence. It often seemed as close to war as two countries could be without actually having a war. The intricate balance of power, with its ebb and tide, weaved fear of a massive atomic bomb strike into the hearts of all Americans. Subsequently, we learned that the Soviets had similar feelings and that our global strike force of the Strategic Air Command had contributed mightily to the fact that the world did not have to contend with mass destruction in any country. That was the essence and reality of the Cold War!

I am not certain what appreciation the general citizenry ever felt about the role the 'Cold War' warriors played in maintaining the peace for America. It was a silent war in many respects. Parents, relatives, wives, and loved ones knew we serving in the military, but never really knew what we were doing because, in part, it was secret and servicemen were told we couldn't talk about. There were no headlines in the newspapers relating to military maneuvers, actions taken, or deployments and yet it was the norm for those of us serving. Our service cannot be compared to The World Wars I and II servicemen who lost their lives in battle, but in this silent war, we lost aircraft and crews who were performing their duties. Many have said that World War I was the 'mother of all wars.' It probably was that indeed. Yet, often I have spent a nanosecond thinking about what could have happened to our country and even the world if the Cold War warriors had not given their service. Even though more than fifty years have passed since this War began, people still do not have any appreciation for what was accomplished by the effort of containment. Perhaps some day they will.

Being part of the Strategic Air Command, meant all of us were on constant alert, twenty-four hours a day, five days to seven days a week. The tactical alert was sounded on the base by blowing an 'air raid' type siren that could be easily heard all over the base and beyond. When it sounded, it brought a gigantic sense of urgency to 'move out!' all over the base. There was no time to waste! Married airmen living off base took what they needed and started driving or riding with others to the base to begin the ritual. For me, I had to report immediately to my normal and routine duty station in the electronics shop, then go to the base armory and draw out my carbine rifle and Artic gear which was already packed in a duffle bag.

The next step was to proceed to the infirmary where we were checked to see if we were up to date on all of our inoculations. If we needed some, the corpsman gave all the injections on the spot. It was a horrific time for the few guys who had trouble with injections. As we stood in line waiting, they would fret and stew about it all the way to the medic station. Some guys didn't mind it at all. For me, it was okay; I did not like it but I didn't mind it. On one occasion, the airman two positions in front of me needed two shots. To get the shots, you had to undo your military green overalls and drop them down to your waist and take off your t-shirt because the injections were given in the fatty tissue under your shoulder blades. The medic jabbed the two injections at once into the airman's shoulder and before he could withdraw the needles, the recipient started walking away with the needles dangling and bouncing around with blood oozing out. The medic called out for the guy to come back but the airman wanted to know 'what for?' The airman in front of me couldn't take it and passed out right on the spot! Fortunately, I did not need any shots that day.

Next I reported to my electronics shop post where I worked everyday. There aluminum boxes, which were approximately 4'x4'x8', housed virtually all of the test equipment. This equipment was permanently mounted inside the box for expediency of a fast departure. Then as fast as possible, I packed up all of my portable test equipment (some of which could also be packed into the large aluminum boxes); buttoned up and sealed the boxes, and helped carry them to a loading area where they were moved by truck to the ramp area for immediate loading onto the KC-97 refueling aircraft. We stood by the aircraft until the flight crew arrived. The captain would take roll, give us some instruction, and all of us would load into the aircraft. Many times these were practice exercises. Nothing further happened and we would then have to reverse the entire process. On most occasions, the captain would at least fire up the engines as if we were proceeding to the take-off position. At other times the aircraft would go through the routine run-up as if it was taking off.

On other occasions, there were times when we would actually start to make a take-off roll down the runway and be at full power picking up speed for takeoff when the order would come just in time to abort the takeoff and return to the tarmac. We never knew what the outcome would be on any alert. Each and every time, we had to perform as if it was the real thing. Of course, there were many times when we actually became airborne and made our way to some distant airbase. When we did take off, usually, we didn't know where we were going until a couple of hours into the flight. Then the captain would give us the word over the intercom.

One of the most irritating aspects of the alerts was simply never knowing when one would occur. Most of the time, it seemed to happen in the middle of the night. The timing was anywhere from 11:00 p.m. to 3:00 a.m. If you had been out for the evening, it was a killer because it seemed like you had just gotten to sleep. If it was on a weekend, you were supposed to leave a telephone number where you could be reached. Surprisingly, it worked quite well since our personnel were very conscientious for the most part.

Having a somewhat stress filled kind of assignment didn't leave a lot of time for relaxation…but we managed a few laughs on occasion. On one of my TDYs to Elmendorf AFB, I learned to snow ski. I had never been on skis before. My buddy and co-worker, Gonzalo Granados, and I decided to venture over to Fort Richardson, which was the adjacent Army Base in Anchorage. The military services there shared many recreational activities. Because we were in Alaska, we wore artic gear all the time so we didn't have any problems with the cold freezing temperatures. We had to have someone help us put the skis on and show us how to move around by side stepping. It was difficult at first, because we couldn't keep our balance. After seemingly conquering the basic balance issue, we decided to take the rope tow up to the first level and try to make our way down the slope designated for first time skiers. We made our way from the end of the rope tow to a vantage point to decide how we were going to make our way back down to the bottom without killing ourselves and others. While we were standing there, I noticed an individual ski up to within ten yards of us. As I stood there I could see he was a two star general. I couldn't believe it. I tapped 'Greco', as I called Gonzalo, and said there is a 'big general' standing right next to us. He first ignored my comment, so I tapped him again and pointed to the 'big cheese that had just swooshed in.' About the same time as he turned his head to look, Gonzalo lost his balance and fell down!

377

We both laughed about how the general had really shook him up to the point he lost his balance!

As we made our way down the slope, we encountered another one of our squadron's crazy airmen. It seemed every TDY produced something incredible to talk about for weeks and months to come. One of the lower ranking non-coms, John Hall, had never been on skis before as well. However, he was a daredevil of some renown. How he made his way to the top of the slopes we never learned. Once up there, he then pointed his skis straight down the mountain and started hollering as loud as he could, "Look out! Look out!" He did that all the way down. Well, there was more havoc caused by people trying to get out of his way than you would see in a couple of weeks of normal skiing. He made it down the hill without falling but he didn't know how to stop! He managed to maintain his balance somehow as he skied over the last foot of the rounded roof of a Quonset hut used for an office that was peering out of the snow pack. Somehow, John managed to stop on the other side a few feet further and in a sitting position with his skis dangling off a sheer fourteen foot drop where the snow plows had cut a road for vehicle traffic. It was a sight to see and we did our best to scramble and skid, fall and pick ourselves up but finally arrived where John had stopped. He was laughing! He was not hurt and appeared to be viewing the snow covered mountains in a relaxed sort of way. Needless to say, it took Gonzalo and me several extended minutes to get down to where John landed and check to see if he was okay. He was! He just laughed about it and thought it was thrilling. I think he and many others thought it was exciting but for entirely different reasons. As for Gonzalo and me, we made more trips to Fort Richardson before returning to March AFB, and learned to ski reasonably well for a beginning skier.

On another TDY to Alaska, John pulled another of his episodes. Our barracks were two story frame structures. At the front were two entries. There was one on the ground level and the second level had a small landing and ladder to be used in case of fire. On the side of the building, about three quarters of the way back from the front, was the main entrance. It seems that John and his buddy drank too much and, being in a playful mood, decided to play tag. They would run in the main entrance on the side, climb the stairs on the inside and run out the second level onto the landing and climb down the stairs. This went on for several rounds until John failed to negotiate the fire escape stairs at the front. He fell from the second level but managed to land in a large snow bank. As usual, John didn't have a scratch. He didn't even go to the infirmary for a check up. After it was over, we all laughed about the event as another one of his shenanigans. He had survived again!

Some of our extracurricular activities were educational. One such trip was while we were in Alaska. A group of us took a trip down toward the Kenai Peninsula, along Cook's Inlet to view the Portage Glacier. I had never seen a glacier before. The ice blue color of the ice was unusual, different, but beautiful. We observed big chunks of ice floating that had broken away from the glacier body. The guide provide information about the glacier, we took some pictures and boarded the bus back to the base.

The aurora borealis didn't light up the sky on Guam, but that didn't stop John from finding another way to entertain us. Our rest and relaxation area was Taragey Beach on Guam. It was a beautiful and peaceful beach area with any number of coconut palms trees scattered all over. Once in a great while, a coconut would fall and hit and make a near miss of some unsuspecting sun bather and you could hear a cry of dismay as they decided to move to another location to avoid another possibility of being hit. The lifeguards would gather the coconuts and anyone could go over and crack the top off and drink fresh coconut milk. The local Guamanians and imported Philippine laborers worked the beach. The beach was located on a long and wide beautiful beach with a large lagoon beyond which was a reef. The ocean waves would break over the reef continuously. Supposedly the drop off at the reef was several hundred feet into the ocean.

John wanted to go diving off the reef and play with the huge manta rays that frolicked in the water there. After some negotiation, over a period of days, he convinced one of the locals to take him out to the reef. While out there, John supposedly hitched a ride on a 150-pound manta ray. The Guamanian didn't know that John had brought a knife along with the intent to kill the ray. He got underneath the ray and began to stab the ray to the alarm of his accompanying local. You see the local knew that the waters all around Guam were filled with a wide variety of huge sharks. The Guamanian tried to get John to leave the ray alone but he ignored his pleas. Instead, John killed the ray and then was working to get it up and over the reef so that he could show off his prowess to his squadron buddies. As it turned out, he almost lost his life to the sharks since they smelled the blood from the wounded ray and began to circle in to determine what was happening. Somehow, they both escaped and made it back to shore with the dead ray in tow. All of us told him what a jerk he was and the Guamanian was extremely upset. They had escaped death but now what would you do with a dead 150-pound ray? Nobody wanted it. To this day, I don't really know what happened to dispose of the ray. Some said it was thrown off the cliffs on the south side of the islands where the island's garbage was dumped. There, the ever present sharks would have quickly disposed if it. I wouldn't have believed this ever happened had I not been there to see it with my own eyes. John obviously lived a different life than most of us airmen but his antics kept us entertained!

During my Air Force stint, I met two guys with whom I would maintain a lifetime friendship. They were Joe Boyd and Jack Haff. We haven't always stayed in close touch with each other but periodically Joe or Jack would call me. They have both come to visit me in California and on each occasion we have had a great time together just recalling some of the TDYs, incidents that happened or people we knew. It was fun to learn how their lives had developed and turned out. Both were divorced and had at least one child. Now they were living alone and seemed to like the 'adjusted lifestyle.' Joe went on to college and university to get an under graduate degree in geology, then his masters and later his doctorate. He worked in the oil industry for several years traveling to many countries of the world. Of the three of us he was more of an academician. He spent time teaching at the University of Mississippi. He now does some consulting work but spends a lot of time on his farm east of Dallas, Texas.

Jack Haff was in flight school when he was discharged from the program, getting caught in educational qualification cutbacks. He subsequently joined the California Highway Patrol but soon grew tired of that since he felt it was a boring job. He then joined the San Jose, California police force and he retired after twenty-three years. During that time Jack sustained many injuries including being shot, experiencing a severely broken leg in which plates and rods had to be inserted, and other less severe injuries. He served on the swat team, rode motors, and served duty with patrol cars among other things. Upon retirement, he joined the U.S. Marshals and served in that capacity for another nine years before finally retiring in Spokane, Washington.

Gene Nunes, with whom I joined the Air Force, was assigned to a SAC base in Florida near Orlando. Most of his TDYs were to England. He married a local young lady while he was still the military service and remained in the South. I lost contact with him.

It was early in 1958, and I was nearing the end of my tour of duty. My enlistment was going to be up near mid-year and prior to my annual flight school disqualification. I would be discharged in July with my flight school eligibility running until October. I had become upset because the Air Force didn't seem to give any credence to my long time standing as a qualified flight school candidate. My prospects of getting to fly in the Air Force had diminished substantially. If only I could get into flight school, I would get to fly fighters or transports. Man oh man, how I wanted to do that. I looked at pictures of all kinds of military aircraft and wished, but it didn't help nor did it happen.

A few days before I was to muster out of the military, my Squadron Commanding Officer (CO) had to have an exit interview with me. That was protocol. Oliver C. Buschow, Major, USAF called me into his office and he began to thumb through my personnel records. Suddenly he stopped and said, "I didn't know that you were qualified for flight school!" With some degree of sarcasm I retorted, "I have been for three years, why didn't you know that?" 'Ollie', as his squadron airmen referred to him, mumbled that he didn't look at personnel records all that much. Then with surprise, he said, "If you want to reenlist, I can get you down to flight school in 60 days." Now that was a real blast to me. How could he get me down there in that length of time when I have been trying for three years? It was then that I realized there was a higher authority working on this case. There was obviously a political element that I didn't know about.

That was very disillusioning to me. I felt let down and betrayed. I had always thought assignments were based upon merit and available openings in the school and not whom you knew. I knew in my heart that I could be a good pilot. In fact, I believed that I could be an excellent pilot. I loved to fly. My dream to fly was still nagging at me. It tugged at my inner most passions. Now it was seemingly being destroyed. I thought for a moment, should I reenlist and take a chance? I would have to sign up for six more years. Should I go for it? I mulled over the possibilities. My better judgment prevailed and I replied, "No sir, I don't think I will do that. I want to fly but I want to finish my education. I'm going to go back and complete my college education." Maybe some day I can learn to fly.

Major Buschow wanted me to commit to staying in the Air Force. I had a good record and was an excellent airman. He continued to bargain with me, "After all," he said, "it's a cold cruel world you are going to be facing out there! It's a tough life." I thought, little do you know about having a tough life! You need to know my family and what we came through to survive. I really did believe him that I could have a class assignment in a short time because of the political aspects of the military. By now, it was too little too late for me. I would not forego my dream for an education. I signed my papers and mustered out of the Air Force within a few days, never to regret my decision.

When I arrived home, I told my parents about my discussion with my commanding officer. I told them that if I had chosen to reenlist for six more years, I could have gone to flight school. With only a slight hesitation, my mother announced, with a significant degree of confidence and relief, to me that she, " had prayed me out of going to that school." I was astounded! In many ways I knew and could understand the power of prayer. She indicated further that she thought flying was very dangerous. That was the real root of her problem…she was obviously still afraid of airplanes from way back in 1937. There wasn't anything for me to say. She had been part of the plot against me and my desire to fly. I could understand her position on the matter. With her loss of my brother, she was adamant that she did not want to lose another son to the angel of death. She had good reasons for her conviction. I never argued the point.

In the past few years I have read a few books on World War II. Living on the Pacific coast, that theatre of war was a natural historical magnet for me since I experienced first hand many 'flyboys' training for missions to come against Japan. The book, *Flyboys,* written by James Bradley, tells a tale of the horrors and destruction of war and its impacts and affects on humans fighting on both sides. It reflects the history and strategy of war and its indescribable horror on the command level as well as the airmen's combat in battle, which translates into fear, hope, and prayer of those on the home front. I know my mother's concerns for me were completely real. I am blessed that she cared that much for me to have prayed for me the way she did. I believe God heard her prayers and answered them.

In another realm, I am grateful for being lucky. I reached manhood during a peaceful time without wars involving actual combat in the world. I am the lucky one who didn't have to fight during the tremendous up-heavals caused by war. World War II weaved itself into the very fabric and soul of virtually every American. There wasn't any family left untouched by the war as loved ones were lost, sons, husbands, wives, fathers and mothers, cousins, nephews or friends. Yes, indeed, I am one of the fortunate ones who did the most honorable things a man can do…serve his country honorably! I thank God.

My Desire for Flying Hangs On

Years went by and my thoughts of flying were put far back on the back burner. I was busy with college, then my family and my career. I was trying to build a home and a professional career. I would talk about the past and my interest once in a while when some of my co-workers would discuss the subject of flying. Other than that, it became a moot point.

Almost twenty years later, I was working at Fleetwood Enterprises in Riverside, California. Life had been very good to me. I had surpassed all of the professional goals and objectives I had envisioned and hoped for the day I graduated from college. Somehow I had managed to have some spendable income that was above and beyond my usual monthly bills. In 1975, one of my fellow managers came by my office and asked if I was interested in taking flying lessons over at the local airport. My heart skipped a beat. He went on to state that if four of us took lessons at the same time, we could have a special rate. It didn't take long before I consented to be included in the group.

Fundamental Fixed Wing Flying Lessons...and More

At Riverside Municipal Airport, I started out taking Piper Aircraft flying lessons in a structured environment geared to my work schedule. My instructor indicated that I would have to have about forty hours of flight time before I could qualify for a private pilot's license. That's when my dream started to reappear. I ate it up. Dreamed it, read it, studied it and flew any time I could. I couldn't get enough of it. It was superb. I loved it!

I started out in a Piper Cherokee. It was a fixed wing, landing gear and a fixed prop as well. Training went very well. I transitioned into single engine high performance aircraft. That meant that the prop was a variable pitch and the landing gear retracted among other things.

As is the case with many student pilots, they think they are ready to solo long before their instructor thinks they can. Earl Crittenden, my instructor, made me wait and wait. Finally that one day came as we were doing 'touch and goes' when Earl said as we were landing, "Pull over by the control tower and I'm going to get out and watch you. Take the airplane around the pattern and land and then come back and pick me up." I was absolutely elated. I was not nervous at all; I knew that I could do it; in fact I wanted to do it; I had wanted to do it for what seemed like a rather extended time. Earl was cautious and that was good. I took the plane up and did exactly what I was supposed to do. What a relief came over me. I was overjoyed. My heart was pumping faster than usual! I did it!

After your first solo flight, the custom is, for the male student pilots at least, to have your shirt actually cut off your back with scissors by your instructor. He then writes something on it, signs and dates it and it becomes your souvenir. I still have the signed piece of my orange colored shirt framed and stored away. I proudly displayed it for a long time in my office among a lot of flight paraphernalia. It was an accomplishment that

I will never forget.

Flying had almost become an obsession for me. I tried to learn about as many different propeller type aircraft as I could. I was still a short time flight hour's pilot. Nevertheless, I asked Earl one day if I learned to fly twin engine aircraft, would that count towards my time to get into instrument flying. He was quick to assure me that my time would count. So I began training for multi-engine airplanes. Basically, it was more of the same training that I had received in single engines except that I had two engines to be concerned with all the time. I took my training in a Piper Aztec. It seated six people and had a thick leading edge wing, which made the airplane very forgiving and easy to fly.

There were dissimilarities between single engine aircraft and the twin-engine airplane other than the number of engines. In the case of the Aztec, it had counter rotating props. Quick reactions were required in case of engine failure on take-offs especially since the plane's characteristics caused it to roll over and nose-in upside down. If you failed to recognize the problem, the airplane had a tendency to quickly rotate over and become upside down in a split second and pile in nose first, usually resulting in tragedy. You had to recognize the problem quickly, shut down the power and maintain control to avert crashing.

I remember one day when I was flying a training session and had just about completed all of the maneuvers and turned to head back to the airport. I was still flying out of Riverside Municipal Airport and had been out to the designated practice sector in the Lake Matthews area east of Riverside. Everything seemed normal. However, I noticed that Earl was on the microphone and talking in a very low, subtle, incomprehensible voice, on a different channel than I was tuned to so I could not hear the conversation. He also turned his head and looked out the right window as he talked. I kept on flying, going through my routine procedures and preparing to land. The routine preparation for landing included checking all of the instruments, pulling flaps, reducing power, releasing the landing gear, and checking for the green light indicator. I had three green lights, which indicated that all three wheels were down and in the locked position for landing.

Earl hadn't said a word to me in quite some time. As the airport came into clear view, I noticed that there were several fire trucks adjacent to the runway on which I was about to land with their flashing lights on. That was not normal. I commented to Earl, "I wonder what is going on…I've never seen the emergency trucks out here before." Like a bolt out of the blue, Earl calmly says, "We have an engine fire on the number two engine!" I couldn't see it from the left side pilot's seat and there was no indication on the instrument panel of a problem condition. I had kept right on flying as if nothing was wrong. Besides, this aircraft was supposed to be able to self-extinguish an engine fire automatically. Obviously that system had not worked to perfection.

I squeaked the tires as we sat down on the runway and watched the trucks as we swiftly passed them while slowing down. I didn't do anything any different in terms of flying and landing the airplane those last few seconds. After I had reduced power, slowed down and was turning off the runway, I could see the fire trucks were tracking with us. However, Earl readily announced that the fire was out on the engine. He said the emergency system had extinguished the fire and that there was nothing to worry about. That was the end of that event. I don't really know for sure that there ever was a fire. Perhaps, it was a training technique to see how I would react in an emergency. I don't know. Earl never cleared up the point. I know that it didn't have much of an impact on me, and I continued my training without incident in the twin. By the time I had accumulated 112 flying hours, I had trained, taken my tests with the FAA examiner and obtained my multi-engine license. Earl told me I was the shortest time multi-engine license holder he knew. That statement made me feel good. I liked learning with Earl. He had been very thorough and made sure that he knew that I knew the subject material and performance criteria of each and every airplane that I trained in with him.

Shortly after completing the multi-engine training, I became inquisitive again. I was feeling good about my flying experience. My enthusiasm was growing and I wondered why I hadn't started flying a long time before. I was looking for another airplane to learn to fly. As I was completing a solo excursion about two weeks later, I noticed a group of whirly birds parked on the apron. As I walked into the flight school office, Earl was coming out. In passing I said, "Earl if I take lessons in a helicopter, will that count towards my time for an instrument rating?" "Oh, yes!" was his reply. Earl didn't want to start me on instrument training until I had accumulated 160 hours flight time. I was working on it for sure!

Learning to Fly Whirly Birds

Earl Crittenden did not fly helicopters. He turned me over to another instructor. I liked my first instructor, W.R. Ferguson. He was a military veteran but trying to catch on with the airlines. I learned during my initial training that instructors were very fluid…they didn't stay around too long. It seemed they were always in transition.

To pre-flight a helicopter is very different than pre-flighting a fixed wing aircraft. You still check on fuel levels and look for anything unusual. The two keys to checking the helicopter is to make sure the 'Jesus' nut is in place and secure and that the tail rotor blade is not cracked or starting to crack. If it has cracks, the craft is not flyable, period! Even though I was learning helicopters for the fun of it, I found very quickly, helicopters are a very serious undertaking.

Flying a helicopter is nearly like trying to balance yourself on the very top of a large ball while having various forces trying to knock you off or lose your concentration so that you fall off. It is very different from a fixed wing aircraft. Importantly, however, it is quite a thrill because of the maneuvers that such a craft can facilitate.

I took my basic training in a Bell 47G3B1. Compared to helicopters of today, it was an ugly duckling. This aircraft had been used in Vietnam and later by the United States Forest Service. It had fuel tanks mounted just behind the bubble canopy on both sides of the airframe. The tail rotor was geared directly to the main rotor. The tail rotor turned fifteen times for each revolution of the main rotor. There weren't very many instruments to check and they were very basic. There was an altimeter, an RPM gauge which showed the speed of the main rotor with a second shorter needle indicating the tail rotor speed. In addition, there was a fuel gauge and an engine temperature indicator. The pilot and one passenger sat in a clear

Plexiglas bubble with full vision except directly to the rear. There wasn't any need for brakes on this aircraft.

To give direction to the helicopter, the 'stick' between your legs could be pushed sideways, forward and backward. This was the attitude control. To make it climb or descend, the pilot pulled the 'collective', which was a long handle on the left side of the pilot's seat that could be pulled up or released downward. This action caused the helicopter to rise and descend because it affected the 'bite of air' made by the main rotor blade. Attached to the end of the collective was the accelerator. It required a twisting action much like a motorcycle. Finally, the two pedals controlled the tail rotor's movement. Pushing one pedal and releasing the other caused the helicopter to turn to the right or left. This all seemed to be quite logical until I realized that all of my limbs or extremities were continuously in use all the time during flight.

It was summer. In Riverside, summer means hot. That was also the reason to take the doors off the Plexiglas canopy bubble for air and cooling. However, in the summer, bugs like to fly and make nuisances of themselves to the focused and concentrating student pilots. With the cockpit doors off, the bugs had free reign. They definitely took advantage of their unchallenged freedom to be very irritating pests. There I was, bugs seemingly crawling all over my face and itching like crazy and I couldn't turn loose of anything to scratch and relieve my irritations. For the first couple of lessons I went bonkers. However, perseverance prevailed and eventually they no longer had much of an affect on me.

This helicopter required the pilot to maintain a main rotor speed of 1,500 rpm regardless of the attitude or speed of the craft. As much as possible, normal landings were always performed at a 45° glide angle. When the pilot was right on the angle during descent, the main rotor blade would 'pop' loudly with every rotation, You didn't have to look at any instruments to know that you were doing things right.

Flying helicopters tended to remind me of pilots of the early days when they flew, so to speak, by 'the seat of their pants'. That meant that they 'felt' the airplane. They did not have very many instruments and what were available were not very reliable. Weather forecasting was more of a guess than a science. They seemed to do what their senses conveyed and followed their convictions of the moment. Their planes were held together with wire, wood, and canvas. They listened to the engine and its peculiar sounds; they heard the rush of wind through the prop and over the wings; they flew by landmark recognition; they flew their machines with feeling and instinct. They were relentless in their pursuit of the skies and perfecting their skills and flying machines. In a helicopter, with limited instrumentation, I often thought of those early pilots and to some extent felt I was replicating some of their experiences in a limited way. I liked it!

I read every thing I could get my hands on about helicopters and related manuals. At that time there just was not very much written. I was like a sponge trying to absorb everything. As fate would have it, I began to see one instructor after another fly with me for a couple of lessons and move on. The instructors seemed to be playing 'musical chairs' with me. After several instructor changes, I began to think that I would never finish this course. Each new instructor wanted to fly with me to determine how far along I was in my training. There was Joe Pagan, Jim Taggart, and B.R. Smith. That got to be old stuff...over and over again just to start over again.

Finally, on my fifth instructor, I was introduced to a local police helicopter pilot named John Obarri. He thought of himself as being a pilot of all pilots. He was all business but with a 'know it all attitude.' He was arrogant. During my first flight with him, he announced that he was going to teach me the 'backwards autorotation'. I quickly responded to him that the maneuver was not in the book. He just as quickly responded that he knew that but he was going to teach it to me anyway. Well, okay, I didn't have anything much more to say about it since I had no idea what it was or how it was to be performed. It seemed strange that we would do something that wasn't in the book. He said the flying conditions had to be right for him to show it to me.

Helicopter pilots are taught autorotations. If the engine power is ever lost, the helicopter can be brought down to a safe landing without injury or damage to personnel or equipment by executing this maneuver. It is a necessary and integral part of learning to fly helicopters. It is, needless to say, a tricky and serious but most important segment of training.

I continued with my training and learning. I was anxious to complete this phase since my police instructor wasn't any great pleasure for me with my personality. We were just two very different people. Finally, one day the wind was blowing like crazy out of the west and I was nearing the completion of the course. Mr. Know-It-All announced that today was the day for learning the reverse autorotation. I was sort of hoping that he had forgotten about it…but he hadn't!

I had practiced autorotations over and over again. They were getting to be second nature to me. I practiced them in my sleep. I read about them. My instructor would take me out and we would practice them over and over. But now it was time to learn something brand new. I didn't know what to expect.

My instructor first demonstrated the maneuver before I could try it. That was okay with me. We headed into the west wind which was blowing at about twenty-five knots or more. He explained, over the headphones, what he was doing. He was looking down to establish a suitable landing site for an emergency autorotation. He indicated that the idea was that we had overshot the best spot to land and that we had to get 'back' to it, thus the backward autorotation. He then put the helicopter in a nose high attitude and reduced power letting the wind blow us backwards all the while descending. When we had 'backed up' far enough, he nosed the helicopter over in a downward direction and performed a normal autorotation. Well, that's not such a big deal, I said to myself. I can handle that and so demonstrated to him that I had learned the technique.

Within a couple of weeks, I took the FAA exams and obtained my rotocraft-helicopter license. As it turned out, that would be the last flying license that I would actually pursue. Not long after completing my license, I had the opportunity to fly a French Aerospacial turbo jet helicopter. It was one of the most modern aircraft in the world at the time. To my amazement, it would climb vertically at fifty feet per minute without having to pull collective. I couldn't climb at all in the Bell without pulling collective. The cabin was virtually soundproof and most luxurious. It was a real treat to fly it.

I had other enjoyable flights such as a charter flight in an Aero Commander, a twin engine turbo prop, when I flew second seat from Upland to Orange County Airport to Willits, in northern California and the reverse return trip. I still remember the call numbers…sugar, sugar, 18 (SS18). This identified to the air traffic controller, the aircraft number SS18 in a controlled air space. That is how we could identify our plane from other aircraft in the area. Tripping like that was a real kick. That plane had an impressive vertical climb speed. Because of noise restriction at Orange County, our climb out rate was over 2,000 feet per minute. I didn't know the airplane had that kind of power or capacity to do it.

I have flown in Lear jets (second seat), twin prop Aero Commanders (older models than the one above) and Cessna singles and twins. I do not remember one really bad flight… as far as I was concerned they were all great!

Much to my surprise on my sixtieth birthday, my two daughters gave me a flight certificate to fly a simulator at 'Fighter Town USA' in El Toro, California. I was so surprised, appreciative and excited. The instructions indicated that I could take along one other person. Arrangements were made and Alan Aufhammer, my son-in-law, and I drove down to the facility. It was a real showcase for trying out simulators and just having some fun.

There were close to ten types of aircraft to choose from and I selected the F-14 Tomcat, a fighter jet. At the time, it was a real hot aircraft as the mainstay of the aircraft carrier attack vehicle of the U.S. Navy. We were given a rather short review on the key elements of trying to fly this high speed subsonic jet in the briefing room. It was supposed to simulate a 'mission' concept and was well put together. After putting on the flight gear, which included coveralls (navy type) and the helmet with inside earphones, we were taken downstairs to the various simulators. As soon as the canopy closed, I was talking to the air traffic controller, the engines were firing, and I was being given directions to the runway. It was very realistic with motion being integrated with the flight controls. A safe take off was made and then a couple of 'touch and goes', some terrain flying, target practice and then a chance to try water based aircraft carrier landings. The landing was fine but I did have to work at it. My landing wasn't smooth but I did 'stick it'. After hitting the deck, what I forgot was where the brake control was located and with power at an idle we slowly, very slowly, edged ever closer to the end of the landing deck as I frantically pushed the brake peddles to try to stop the aircraft. That failed miserably and finally on the screen we plunged over the side into the deep blue water! I was totally embarrassed. The brake control was on the left side sort of like an emergency brake on a car. However, on all the aircraft that I had flown to that time, the brakes were the 'toe' portion of the rudder controls. After that, I told Alan that it was his turn to fly, which he did with aplomb. It was a fun time and an experience that I will never forget!

I enjoyed flying and continued to fly for a while. However, the expense of flying was increasing rapidly and I decided that I could forego such a hobby and past time. After all, I had completed a lifelong desire to learn to fly. No one could take that away from me. I still enjoy flying whether it is on an airliner or private plane. My love for it will never leave me.

There are times, even now, when I think of the exhilaration and adrenaline rush associated with what it would feel like flying a fighter plane in a combat situation. My daydreams remain related to the World War II dog fights when it was man and his machine, his ability to fly his machine better that his adversary and winning. As I envision such an event, I sense the call of the wild blue yonder, and flying through holes in the clouds, smiling and laughing with Mother Nature and hoping it is not my last flight here on earth!

I truly thank God for allowing me to have had such an exciting experience in my life!

1   *The Great Book of Bombers*, page 312, Salamander Books Ltd., 2003
2   *The Air Force*, The Air Force Historical Foundation, Hugh Lauter Levin Associates, Inc. 2002, Pages 65 -66, 72.
3   Ibid, page 65.
4   *Vulcan, B-47 & B-52*, Stewart Wilson, page 151
5   *The Air Force*, The Air Force Historical Foundation, Hugh Lauter Levin Associates, Inc. 2002, Pages 64 - 65.
6   Ibid, Page 69
7   Ibid, Page 69
8   *Los Angeles Times*, Diplomat Was Architect of U.S. Cold War Policy, Jon Thurber, page A1, March 18, 2005.
9   *Vulcan, B-47 & B-52*, Stewart Wilson, page 101.

Chapter Fifteen
Education...
the Way to New Horizons

I have always wanted to learn. There has never been a time in my life that this idea wasn't pertinent. It didn't matter if the learning took place in a formal classroom or in a show and tell situation with a miner, pilot instructor, reading an instruction manual or a fishing guide. I was born with an innate desire and expectation that it was good to learn everything you could. There wasn't anything too hard to learn and understand. The more difficult it was merely meant that one had to apply oneself more intently and vigorously. I felt like an empty dry sponge waiting to be saturated with new information. It really did not matter what the subject matter was, it was all interesting and I was willing to make the effort to learn. I just soaked it up!

Beginning the Learning Process – Remembrances of "Home"

Perhaps more than anyone, I loved and respected my grandfather, Andrew Jackson Talley. He was a role model even though he probably never knew it. I only spent time with him for a short period of my life before my family moved to California. It was a very short time frame when I think back about it, from about 1939 to mid-1941. In the intervening years before his death, I only saw him briefly when we traveled to Arkansas for a vacation or a family reason such as critical illness. Some seven years after we moved to California, he died. He died in 1948. I am certain that listening to my mother, her sisters, and others talk about my grandparents further influenced me. I just know that all the people who met him had the utmost respect for him and my grandmother. He had a way about him, which let people understand and feel that he appreciated them. If you didn't know him well, people would address him as 'Mr. Talley.' If they had really gotten to know him, those in the community called him 'Uncle Jack,'

My grandfather Talley's home was on a farm some seven miles, by dirt road, from the little town of Belleville, Arkansas where I was born. I have traveled that road by wagon, school bus and car on many occasions. Almost all the streams, with the exception of the Petit Jean, had bridges without side braces or guards over which we crossed. These bridges were simple in construction and had rather limited clearance from the water level since the water for most of the year was very slow and meandering but almost always running unless the summers were very dry. If there was a hard rain, these streams and creeks would easily overflow and even wash out a bridge once in a while. The one crossing that always made me feel uneasy and uncomfortable was the one over the Petit Jean Creek. This was a steel bridge with girders and thick wooden timbers (boards) placed on the bridge floor as structural cross members. During the crossing, it would shake, groan and creak as the weight of the vehicle shifted during the traverse. The bridge approach angled up steeply from either side onto the bridge section, which was elevated high above the creek. It looked a lot like some of the older railroad bridges, which are still in use today in some areas. In California, this creek would have been referred to as a river. The water in Petit Jean was always muddy and somewhat slow moving. It was a great place to catch catfish! On a lucky day, you could catch a 'blue channel' cat as opposed to the 'mud cats' that didn't taste as good.

I often wondered where the Petit Jean River (Creek) got its name. It didn't seem to fit in with other names for streams, creeks, mountains or just people. [1]According to tradition this river derived its name from the following circumstances: When the Territory was under the dominion of the French, a party of explorers or hunters visited the head of the stream, having with them a small man whose name was Jean in French, or John in English. Petit means little, in French, and being a small man they called him Petit Jean (Little John). While there the explorers had a fight with the Indians, and Petit Jean was wounded, and afterward died from the effects of the wound as the party was returning down the river, hence the name

Petit Jean River.

I do not remember all the creeks and streams we crossed on the way to my grandparents' home. But some of the names I recall besides Petit Jean Creek were Deadman's Creek, Bailey Branch, Little Riley Creek and the creek near the Haire's family place which was Riley Creek. Beyond Grandpa's farm there were other creeks including Moss and Dutch Creeks but they were up and over the mountain. Many times in the late winter and early spring months, all of these streams would flood and passage was made very difficult because no one could actually see the road. You just sort of knew where it was and the driver made his way rather slowly and with extreme care. The water on many occasions was over the running boards of the car. I remember the water coming inside the car on one occasion.

There were many times when it was rather difficult to get to Grandpa Talley's farm. In rare instances, the road became completely impassable due to floodwaters in the bottom lands of the Petit Jean. I've prepared a map, which denotes the roads traversed in making the trip from town to Grandpa's home. There is another map that relates to the farm property layout itself.

Grandpa's place was a great area for a young boy to explore the "out of doors" and farm life in general. At my age of five and six, during the years 1940 and 1941, there wasn't a lot of work for a small boy on the farm. Thus, I had a lot of time on my hands and I used it to learn about nature and plants and see what goes on at a farm to keep it operating in order to sustain family life. I didn't really think of it in that way then because it was only later that I would realize how important those times were to me.

For the most part, Grandpa was a self-sufficient family man. He grew lots of corn and cotton; he sold much of it. Some of the corn was stored in the barn for the animals (pigs and mules) and chicken feed throughout the following year. All of the work was done manually, including planting the corn seed. Plowing the fields was done with a single plow pulled by a mule or a team of mules with Grandpa walking behind holding those long leather reins which passed through the horse collars and on to the bridle and the bit. These leads were used to control and direct the working animals. These leather lead straps were held in his gloved hands and were sometimes wrapped

Belleville And Vicinity

1. Corner house where I was born.
2. House in back of Dr. Grayson's where I lived when I started school.
3. Log house built by my great grandfather, Obediah Smith.
4. House used by my grandfather's daughters while they were caretakers and helped on the farm.
5. Burial place (family cemetery) of my great grandfather and members of his second family, including his wife. There are also Talley family members buried there.
6. Haywood Haire home on Riley Creek.
7. Riley Creek Church and school (one room) where my mother and her sisters attended school and the family went to church on Sunday.
8. Riley Creek Cemetery where my brother and many members of my mother's family are buried.
9. The Wilson Church where my grandfather's funeral was conducted.
10. Belleville Park where 4th of July and other celebrations are held.
11. My Aunt Bessie and Uncle Chester Barrick's home in Corrinth.
12. Corrinth. A community where my family lived for a while. It was located across the road form the Castleberry home near Danville.
13. The place where we lived in town for a short period which was next door to a blacksmith shop.
14. Uncle Lee and Aunt Jennie Moudy's home. My grandmother Moudy lived next door on the same property.
15. Uncle Herbert and Aunt Florence Moudy home.
16. Aunt Ollie and Uncle Oscar Moore's farm and home.
17. Scruff – the black community where Lee Cole lived when he was working for my Uncle Lee Moudy.
18. Dr. Grayson's home – the local town doctor.
19. "Old Town" Belleville was located here before it was destroyed by fire and rebuilt at its present location.

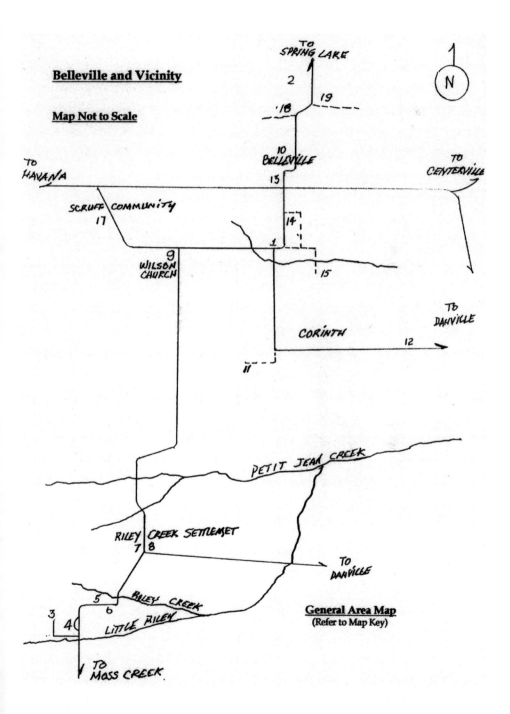

Belleville and Vicinity

Map Not to Scale

TO SPRING LAKE

N

TO HAVANA

TO CENTERVILLE

SCRUFF COMMUNITY

BELLEVILLE

WILSON CHURCH

CORINTH

TO DANVILLE

PETIT JEAN CREEK

RILEY CREEK SETTLEMET

TO DANVILLE

RILEY CREEK

LITTLE RILEY

General Area Map
(Refer to Map Key)

TO MOSS CREEK

Riley Creek Homestead

1. The location of the log house built by my great grandfather Obediah Smith and later expanded with sawn lumber by my Grandfather Andrew Jackson Talley.
2. Combination smokehouse and chicken house.
3. Wash house
4. Blacksmith Shop
5. Main vegetable garden
6. Peach, apple and plum orchard
7. Tobacco garden of Andrew Jackson Talley
8. Storm and food cellar
9. Barn
10. Hog pens
11. Expanded hog pens
12. Very large persimmon trees
13. Location of molasses mill
14. Large oak trees in front of house
15. Second house for caretaker (usually a daughter's family lived here in later years)
16. Caretaker's barn
17. Caretaker's smokehouse
18. Dirt road to old saw mill

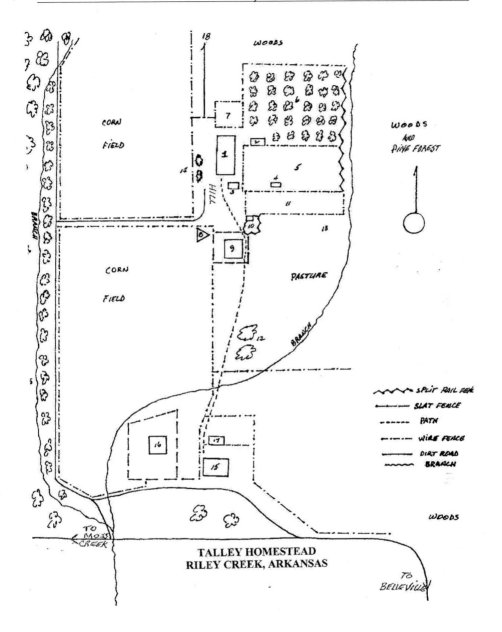

**TALLEY HOMESTEAD
RILEY CREEK, ARKANSAS**

The Wash House was all that remained in 1970

around his wrists and forearms and he carried a big switch, which he would use to get the mule to do what he wanted if 'talking' didn't work. I can still hear him calling to the mule or mules and occasionally yelling as he worked planting the cornfield close to the house.

Harvesting of the corn was done by hand as well! A wagon would be pulled along the rows and the ears would be plucked and thrown into the wagon for the trip to the barn where it was stored in bins. Hay was grown for the mules and cows and was also used in the barn areas to keep the dirt floor clean and orderly. It, too, was stored in the barn up in the loft. Most of the time, the animals ate the natural grown grasses in the pastures, which grew all year except in the winter months.

Grandpa kept his barn pretty clean although it could get messy when it rained for a day or so. The hay was scattered around on the dirt surface to absorb the droppings and urine from the animals. The smell was unique in the barn in the sense that it was a 'clean odor' but you definitely knew there were farm animals around. In the summer months and rainy season, if the barn wasn't cleaned out and fresh hay brought in regularly, it could get fairly 'ripe' if the temperature heated up very much. Because of the sloping terrain around the barn, the barn floor drained well and stayed pretty dry even in the worst times of the year.

From the map of the property, you can find the cellar just down the hill from the barn along the road leading up to the house. The cellar had been dug and burrowed directly into the red clay hill. The cellar was used to keep certain vegetables cool and at a fairly even temperature, which assisted in maintaining their freshness for a lot longer period of time. Potatoes, squash, peanuts, apples, sweet potatoes were among the items that were put in the cellar. Canned goods were also stored down there. It was big enough to use as a safe haven in case of a tornado. Rather than stay in the house, the family could go to the cellar and have a better chance of survival. I do not remember going to the cellar for that purpose, but on a couple of occasions, that possibility was discussed when it looked like a big storm was coming in. That really meant there was a possibility of a tornado.

Directly in back of the house were orchards. Far down beyond Grandma's garden "Indian red" peaches, apples, plums and pears grew. In most cases, there were at least a couple of varieties of each fruit. These were methodically canned in "Ball" or "Mason" fruit jars every year. It was a real chore but had to be done. Usually, one or more of my aunts would come to Grandpa's to help my grandma do the work. It was tiring, hot sweaty work and done over a wood burning stove.

One must remember that this was in the very late 30s and very early 40s. At Grandpa's there wasn't any running water or electricity. Every time more water was needed, someone had to go to the well in the front yard and draw it with a bucket tied to a rope on a pulley. That water was always cool even in the hot summer months. This same well was used to preserve milk by lowering it into the water in capped buckets to keep it cool until it was used. Drinking water was kept in wooden buckets on the front porch with a dipper made from a certain species of long necked gourd that my grandma grew in her garden. This gourd grew with a long handle and was planted along the garden fence so there would be a place for the gourds to grow and hang down. This made the "handle" grow straight. As I look back to our propensity for cleanliness and sanitation today, I marvel at how many people would drink out of that old gourd and no one seemed to get sick! Occasionally, someone would be a little "persnickety" and ask for a cup or a glass. No one seemed to mind however!

As I indicated, there was no electricity on the farm. In the evenings any lighting in the house was done with 'coal oil' lamps, otherwise known as kerosene lamps. In larger rooms, there might be two or three lamps. The flame would flicker as the family would sit and talk. Being a kid and not always following the conversations taking place, I would watch the patterns created by the flickering fire in the fireplace or the flicker of the lamps as silhouettes would dance on the walls. One could imagine seeing any number of creatures or objects as I looked at the walls. All you had to do was use your imagination; it was fun entertainment and helped to pass the time.

Living and working everyday on the farm made it difficult to stay clean. It was sweaty and mostly dirty work. There was dirt everywhere. You walked on it; you walked in it and maybe kicked a rock or clod causing a cloud of dust, which quickly enveloped you. In those days, no one expected a clean set of clothes each day before going to the fields.

Talley Homestead

After all, you were probably going to do the same thing you did yesterday. Grandpa changed those blue denim overalls once or, at most, twice a week. Usually Granddad, wore a light blue denim long sleeve shirt. If he was going to go to a meeting, some place like church, he had a black 'dress' coat (jacket) that he'd put on and wear on top of his overalls. Grandmother and the ladies generally wore long dresses. For Grandma, her dress was always close to her ankles, while my mother's and her sisters' were about half way below the knee. They wore aprons to protect their dresses from spills and splashes while working in the kitchen and other places. If they were outside in the summer, they would wear a heavily starched bonnet. Usually, Saturday night was reserved for a bath for everyone. Had to get ready for church tomorrow, you know!

Living and working on a farm makes for a lot of dirty clothes for a family as large as Grandpa's. Grandma used to begin her washing by putting the clothes in huge kettle pots in the front yard filled with water and heated them with burning wood. Sometimes, the smoke would just sort of move wherever she moved around that big pot. She'd tell me "smoke

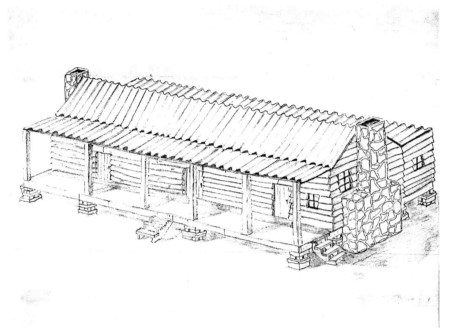

Talley Homestead: Note the log cabin portion compared to the sawn lumber portion of the house. (Freehand drawing by my grandson, Collin Aufhammer)

always followed beauty!" She used a big stick to stir the clothes around as they were soaking and being cleaned in boiling soapy water. Clothes, which were less soiled, were washed by hand using a rub board. This was backbreaking work, bending over that rub board for hours. The clothes were rinsed and hung on the line to dry. I can't imagine the amount and difficulty of the work that my grandmother did back in her time. It seems incredible now as I reflect back.

Things improved significantly, however, when Grandpa bought Grandma a washing machine! Now that was a 'big deal', a real big deal!!! I do not know if he bought it in town or ordered it from the Sears Roebuck catalog. It probably did not make any difference to my grandmother.

Now this washing machine had an engine, which was kerosene powered. It was seemingly noisier than those far off trains we could hear echoing in the mountains from time to time as they passed through Belleville. To make matters worse, the contraption smoked many times worse than the biggest campfire you have ever seen. I could hardly see Grandma as she worked! It appeared as if someone had set off a smoke bomb and she was in the middle of it. You could see her and then you couldn't as the smoke drifted. I don't know how Grandma could stand it. I couldn't. It was choking to say the least. It made me cough and sneeze; then I had trouble breathing. It could almost cause nausea because it smelled horrible with that kerosene and oil burning.

But every washday, Grandpa would drag that machine out of the milk house into the front yard for Grandma to use. Once the clothes were washed, she would turn the machine off and use the hand crank to roll the clothes through the ringer, adjusting the pressure several times to try to match the thickness of the clothes in order to squeeze as much water out as possible. This allowed the clothes to dry faster. After the washing was done, the soapy wash water from the washing machine was drained directly onto the ground since it was just dirt anyway. Most often the ground was bone dry, especially in the summer so the water soaked into the ground real fast. The soapy water brought a refreshing and welcome drink to the rose bushes along the fence. She was happy because it made her life a lot easier. She loved that new fan dangled machine.

Grandma made her own lye soap too. I don't really remember the details. I do know that she made it in the big old iron pot that sat out in the front of the house on the ground beyond the inner yard fence. I think she used lard and a lot of ash from the previously burned wood that had been used to heat the cook stove and fire place ash residue too. She would 'cook' the ingredients and then let it cool. That would cause the soap to solidify into a soft beige or tan color in the bottom of the old pot. After it was cooled and had solidified, she would take a big butcher knife and cut it into rather large bars. These bars were much larger than any you can buy in our stores today. They didn't have any perfumed smell nor did they look particularly appealing, but they could really make you clean! Today, we'd probably think of it as being a somewhat harsh soap.

The farther one would venture away from the house, the more of nature one could experience. The Talley Branch was only a couple hundred yards from the house. I spent many hours down there looking and watching the birds and squirrels in the big oak trees. I would see an occasional cottontail rabbit hopping along the fence around the cornfields and, very infrequently, a snake would slither past. I never liked snakes and I would quickly scurry away to a safer area when I saw one. They scared me!

At the Branch (Little Riley Creek), I liked to hop across the water by stepping on rocks or just jumping when I could. There were crawdads to be found in the stream and water bugs and other creatures under some of the rocks in the water. Lift a rock and likely you could see a lot of bugs scurrying about to find a new hiding place. You had to be careful with those crawdads though, because they could really pinch hard if they grabbed onto a finger!

Many very large sweet gum trees grew along the Branch. By looking around the tree trunks, you could usually find enough sap or tree resin to scrape off and chew. It was really quite good and tasty and was nature's chewing gum. You could probably chew it for maybe ten minutes and then it would start to harden. But the supply was virtually endless!

Once in a while, Grandma would want to cook squirrel and dumplings for dinner. That would be a great dinner for me because I loved squirrel and dumplings. I knew that I could probably go down by the Branch with Grandpa to shoot one of those gray squirrels living in the oak trees for Grandma to cook. You see, Grandmother Talley would ask 'Jacent', as she lovingly called my grandfather, to go down to the branch and get a squirrel for dinner (noon). That was the big meal of the day because people worked so hard. Then Grandpa would ask me to come along. When he asked, I thought, "Are kidding me? Sure, I want to go!" What a delight that was for a boy of five or six years old to be with his Grandpa, whom he looked up to so much. That was both figuratively and literally. He was well over six feet tall. He would get his relic of a small bore rifle and grab a shell or two and off we'd go. So Grandfather and I walked together down to the branch and where huge old oak trees lined the little stream. I usually assisted with the success of the hunt by telling Grandpa where I'd seen the most squirrels playing in the trees. When we stopped under the trees, it was important to be very quiet. He would then load one of the two shells that he had brought into his rifle and we waited patiently. We had to stand real still and stop talking and pretty soon the wild life would start to come out and survey their world and begin the process of looking for nuts and acorns and other goodies to eat or store for the winter. This would occur in a relatively short time after we intruders had arrived and the noise had nearly disappeared except for the birds chirping in the trees.

The squirrels seemed to sense that danger had passed. As they slowly began to come out of hiding and spring back into action again, Grandpa would pick one out. They were now unsuspecting and back at their very playful roles, jumping from one limb to another; sitting and staring; flipping their bushy tails around; seemingly chasing one another. They were back doing the playful things that we expect of these little creatures. I watched Grandpa carefully. After a while Grandpa would see the 'right one' and he would raise that trusty old single shot 22 caliber rifle to his shoulder, point it and slowly and smoothly squeeze the trigger. BAMM! We had the main course for our dinner! The one that Grandpa had picked out tumbled out of the tree. I don't ever remember Grandpa taking more than two shells with him on these hunting expeditions because he only used one!! It became 'dinner time' for us with squirrel and dumplings made by Grandma in her big old stewing pot. It was really a very tasty and delicious meal too! I'll never forget those times.

Sometime in 1885, my Grandfather purchased a 12-gauge shotgun. The brand name was *Nitro Hunter*. I had never heard of that brand before I actually saw the gun. He also owned a 22-gauge rifle. My cousin, Andrew Jackson 'Jack' Smith, told me that when he was about fourteen years old, he was at Granddad's home one day and Granddad showed him both the shotgun and the 22 caliber rifle. He asked Jack, "Which of these guns do you want when I die?" Jack quickly responded, "The shotgun!" So when Granddad died in 1948, Jack inherited the shotgun. I had seen the gun as a kid and when we went squirrel hunting at Grandpa's house, but I never knew that Jack had received it. I only found it out in 1998 when I was visiting Jack at his home in Oxnard and he told me that he had it. I was very excited to learn that it was in his possession. As usual, I wanted a picture so I asked Jack to take a picture of it and send it to me. A couple of years later I was at his home again and I had my camera with me and he got the gun out again. I took several close-up pictures of it and others with Jack holding it.

The brand name and logo are inscribed on the plate of the gun. The words of the logo are artistically scripted. This model or manufacturer's logo is also inscribed very clearly on the butt plate of the gun and is much easier to read. The gun is a single barrel with a single bead near the end of the barrel for aiming and lining up with the target. The barrel is thirty-two inches long and the overall length is forty-seven inches. The gun indicates that it is trademark registered but without any number or reference to that effect.

Cousin Jack Smith with GP Talley's shotgun

The side plates to the trigger housing function to protect the moving parts inside, as with any shotgun. They were chrome plated originally but the chrome shows significant wear. The housing is a reinforced breach, which Grandpa referred to as a 'cannon breach' and Jack understood that to be heavy reinforcement and a good safety feature. The gun is also 'choke bored', which probably refers to the gun being of a 'full choke' design. Jack believes that the gun probably sold for about $8.00 when it was new and would have been worth half that amount used. We do not know if it was used when Granddad purchased it. Jack stated that after he received the gun, which would have been in 1948, he would go bird hunting with his brother, Robert (Bob), in nearby woods and fields where they lived in Missouri.

As I held the gun in my hands, I could not help but recall my two or three trips to the branch, a small stream, I made with Grandpa to shoot squirrels. The branch was down the hill directly in front of the house, perhaps five to six hundred yards. Going down the dirt road to the branch on either side were the fields where grandpa grew his corn crops every year. At the branch, you could turn to the right or left. Going left took you down to the main road that would be taken to go to town. We turned right. This road, I was to learn from Doyle Barrick, was at one time the old stage coach road. Not too far up this road, it crossed the branch. But before getting to the branch, there were many very old, large and beautiful oak and sycamore trees. I am sure that many families of squirrels lived in those trees. It was fall and the trees still had most of their leaves although they were well on their way to completing their color array of red, gold and orange of autumn. Grandpa had asked me to come along with him. That invitation made me feel really good. I liked being with my grandpa.

Needless to say, I am very pleased and proud that Jack chose the shotgun and that he kept it and has taken good care of it all these years. Knowing how hard the work was on the farm, as my mother had explained to me many times, Jack's two week tour of duty alone made him the most eligible to receive the shotgun!

Jack has taken very good care of the shotgun as evidenced by the condition of the stock and metal parts. The bluing is still quite good; the stock is well preserved and shows limited wear marks or dings. I felt very honored and pleased to be able to hold the gun and to get to see it again after all these years had passed.

Before finishing my visit with Jack that day, he told me a rather sinister story about an experience that he'd had after he received the shotgun. It seems, in Missouri, he'd take the gun and go bird hunting, often with his younger brother, Bob. One day, they were out hunting in the woods and it seems some other hunters took some unusual shots at them. They were not hit but certainly became very concerned about the whole situation. They took refuge as best they could out of sight of these two 'would be' hunters. They watched as the two men moved on. Even so, Bob was certain that the shots taken at them had been deliberate. Bob tended to want to retaliate but Jack didn't think that was the right thing to do. However, the incident bothered them immensely. A while later, Jack and Bob decided to call it quits for the day and go home. As they emerged from the woods, they saw the other two hunters walking ahead of them down the same road. They were both sure that these were the same two who had taken shots at them earlier. Bob immediately began to talk about getting closer to them and giving them some of their own medicine. Before taking the law into their own hands, Jack said, "What are we going to say if in the papers it says these two were shot, we can't tell our momma and daddy a lie! We'd have to tell them, we did it." Bob listened to Jack and ultimately gave in to the wisdom of his older brother. They walked on home and never took their revenge nor did they learn for sure if the two men were the ones who actually shot at them. Needless to say, they were plenty sore about it!

What happened to the remaining 22-gauge rifle? It turns out, as I learned on a trip to visit my cousin, Kenneth Moore, in Chandler, Arizona in 2004, that grandpa gave him the rifle. I also took a picture of him holding the rifle. I could tell he was very proud to have it, as any of grandfather Talley's descendants would be. It was a Meridian Model 10, 22 caliber, single shot and would fire both long and short ammunition.

The corn brought in from the fields and stored in the cribs of the old barn was used to feed the chickens and and other farm animals. Mounted and attached to the side of the chicken house was a corn sheller. In order to feed the chickens, one would go to the barn and select an adequate number of ears of corn and take them to the chicken house where they could be shelled and cracked in one process.

The hard dried corn ears of were fed in at the top of the outside wall mounted apparatus and with the crank handle turning, the ears would pass through and the grains of corn would be removed from the cob. The cob would go flying in one direction and the cracked corn would fall out the bottom into a pan or sack. As a kid I liked to do this. Of course, the chickens would hear the noise and gather around because they knew it was near the time to eat. They would cluck and walk around close by and sometimes a couple of them would get into a little fight. When it was time to feed them, the cracked corn was thrown onto the ground and you no longer heard any clucking going on, just chicken heads bobbing up and down as they scrambled to get their share of the corn!

Between the vegetable garden and the pigpen was Grandpa's blacksmith

Kenneth Moore with Grandpa Talley's 22-caliber rifle, October 2004

shop. I never saw him work down there, but I spent hours, ever so often, pretending to be working and making something. There were so many tools. I didn't have a clue as to what their purpose was in making or repairing farm tools and implements. In town, I had lived next door to a blacksmith shop for a while. I remember looking through the big old doors when they were open and seeing fire, smoke, and red hot pieces of metal. If you stayed around long enough, you could hear the hammers pounding on the cherry red metal and the sizzle of hot metal being dunked in the quenching water buckets and the resultant hissing as steam would rise from the process. It was always dark and smelly in there, strange for a young boy but still interesting. I never saw a finished product so I never quite understood what they were supposed to be doing in there.

Naturally, no one ever invited me in to see more closely what was going on. So it was, when in Grandpa's shop, I could put on those big ole black dirty gloves, pound on the anvil with any hammer I chose and take the baffle and 'stoke the fire'.

On the farm, any gate I could open was acceptable to my grandpa so long as I always closed it behind me. I could go to the barn, to the garden, to the pasture, to the old sawmill site, or to the cellar down the hill from the house and the barn. I loved it! I could go any place with no one to say 'no, you can't do that'. I remember coming back from a branch excursion one afternoon about three o'clock in September. This is about the time of the year that the muscadines ripen. I loved muscadines. Grandma would make a cobbler that tasted oh so good to me. Anyway, on the left side of the road grew several muscadine vines along the fence and virtually every

Talley smokehouse and chicken house

time I passed by, I'd pick one to see if they were ready to eat yet. Much to my delight some tasted pretty good on this particular day. All of a sudden, I looked down and on the ground around the vines and there were ten or twelve tarantulas crawling and moving in all directions. I had never seen them there before. I started to quickly make my move to escape but instead picked up a long stick and began to play with these creatures. They were hairy all over and I thought they were really ugly and scary. Needless to say, I never picked any more muscadines without an adult with me. My mother made it worse when I told her about my experience and she scolded me and said that tarantulas were poisonous and could jump three feet. That convinced me to stay away from then on. Subsequently, I learned that her facts are supposedly inaccurate but, regardless, to this day, I still have a strong dislike for tarantulas.

I didn't go to the old sawmill site very often, maybe twice in my life. There was not much left of the old buildings and nature had significantly taken over to reclaim it from civilization. Any pieces of equipment had long since been carted off by salvage bidders or others who made legitimate purchases of it. What I never knew until 1995 was that the old sawmill was owned and operated by my Great Grandfather Obediah Smith in the 1870s and perhaps early 1880s. What was left were the remnants of old rock walls and small pieces of scrap metal scattered around one confined area. It could have been a repair shop area. I also noticed that vegetation didn't grow well in a couple of areas. As I think back to that time, I surmise that there were chemicals used or perhaps saturated soil from oil spills or drippings that prevented nature from making a complete reclamation of the grounds.

My cousin, Jack Smith, when he was fifteen years old, worked on Grandpa Talley's farm for two weeks. In 1942, Jack helped with the harvesting of the corn, and cut wood for the winter months to come, which included splitting wood for use in the wood burning cook stove. In Grandpa's front yard, I remember stacks of wood like those that Jack spent time cutting during his two weeks on the farm. In late fall, the wood was gathered and the sawing, chopping and splitting began. There would be wood piled up all around. When the wood supply was running low, Grandpa would get into his wagon and go into the woods for more. The yard had to be nearly full of cut wood before there was enough to last through the long winter months. Cut wood was stacked up like cord wood along the front yard fence on the inside and the outside of the fence as well as the yard outside the fence which had row after row of chopped wood stacked up about five feet high. Shorter pieces were used for the cook stove and the rest went into the fireplace. When you were asked to 'bring the wood in', you knew which stack was used where, based upon its length. This ritual was repeated yearly. I am sure that Grandpa was especially pleased to have Jack's help at such a crucial time of year. There isn't any doubt that Jack worked hard.

The stove and the fireplace were the only methods of heating the house. As you can imagine, the amount of wood needed for the winter season was enormous. Every evening the fireplace would burn and die out and that's when the big heavy feather bed mattresses and the homemade quilts were most welcomed to keep us warm in bed. Some of the wood was very heavy with pinesap or resin and was cut into very small long-stemmed pieces called 'kindling'. Kindling was especially useful in getting a fire started quickly because the pinesap would catch fire very quickly and burn intensely. The stove fire was made early in the morning hours just before any daylight had shown on the cold mornings of winter. The stove wood was brought in from the many stacks in the front yard and kept in an old wooden box sitting on the floor next to the cook stove the evening before. Lighting the kitchen stove was Grandpa's job. He did it religiously. The stove was used for preparing breakfast and for the dinner (noon) meals only. It was never lit for the evening meal.

Another highly memorable event at the farm was the annual slaughter of the hogs and pigs. This meat was one of the main staples for the family on the farm. It provided ham, sausage, bacon, and source for home made mince meat and even a pigtail to be roasted on the hearth of the fireplace! This was an extremely busy time to coordinate and make every thing happen in proper sequence. The event included both family and many neighbors. It could last two or three days depending upon how many animals had to be processed. I remember very vividly how it all began. I sat on the fence of the hog pen and watched with great interest and tried my best to stay out of the way. The fence was a cross stacked wooden fence in a zigzag design.

Today, the process I am about to describe would be considered cruel to animals and in some circles would probably be unacceptable. It was a way of life back then. Every farmer did it. Survival was first and most important.

First, a pig or hog was herded into a tight pen where the animal could not move around very much. One person was selected to be the executioner and used a 22-caliber rifle to shoot the animal between the eyes. Death came very quickly. Immediately, the animal would slump over on the ground. Then it would be pulled and dragged to a nearby tree where a pulley and chain had been attached to a very strong limb of an old oak tree. The pig or hog would be strung up with its head pointing down to the ground. Then the animal was cut and bled until virtually all the blood was drained. To bleed it, the throat and underside were slit with a sharp knife. The blood fell onto the ground and soaked into it. As gruesome as it sounds, now as I write this revelation, one and sometimes more helpers would hold a cup at the point where the blood was running in a stream and allow the pig's blood to drain into the cup and drink it while it was still warm. That was most repulsive to me!

When the blood flow was reduced to slow methodical dripping, the animal would next be moved to hot boiling water vats, which were heated by burning wood and buried in the ground. The animal would be moved by several men and placed into the vats for a short time. Keep in mind that the larger hogs could weigh as much as four hundred to six hundred pounds. Every pig and hog was shaved with a straight edged razor to remove all hair. It was then lifted from the vat and put on sturdy tables. The women took over to finish the cleaning, cooking and canning process. With the precision of a doctor with a scalpel, they used sharp butcher knives and a saw to cut bones and dress out the pork. A man usually did this, although some of the women did it too. Sides of the animal were used for bacon and were cut into slabs and sent to the smokehouse for sugar and hickory smoked curing. Fattier parts of the animal were cut into one to two pound sections and placed into a barrel in which alternating layers of meat were covered with salt until it was full. Then a lid was fastened on top and it was sent to the smoke house for curing. This became salt pork to use in cooking for seasoning or sometimes just to fry and eat. The hind quarters were cut away in whole sections and sent to the smokehouse for sugar and hickory curing to provide that good old country fried ham for breakfast and 'red eye' gravy. The hams were always hung from the smokehouse rafters by bailing wire to prevent rats and mice from having an incredibly enjoyable feast. Bacon was also protected in this manner.

The meat from the animals' neck and shoulders was ground for making sausage. There was an art to making good sausage because you had to get the right amount of fat in the mix and the proper quantities of spices, particularly sage and red pepper. Usually one person was known as a good sausage maker and was delegated that chore. The sausage would be immediately fry cooked and placed in the canning jars and processed for future use. The head and neck would be used to make mince meat by grinding it and mixing it with raisins, nuts, dried fruits and cooked. It too was packed into jars and canned. Later, it would be made into pies for special occasions. Finally, the feet would be cooked and canned with spices to provide pickled pigs feet. As strange as it may seem, the bladders, after cleaning could be blown up as balloons. The tails and ears would be roasted on the hearth of the family fireplace that night before going to bed as a special treat for anyone who wanted it. This could only occur on the day of the animal's slaughter.

Going down into the pasture in the late fall of the year could produce a major treat for anyone making the trek. That's where the giant persimmon trees grew. When the fruit was really ripe, it would fall from the trees and you could make your selective picks and eat as many as you wanted. There was always competition from the some of the farm animals for these fruits. The fruits were extremely sweet and very, almost mushy, soft because they were tree ripened. When the weather was near freezing, these fruits could be even tastier because of the ice particles formed with the juice of the persimmon. They were eaten right on the spot. Persimmons could be gathered and used for puddings, cookies, and breads. I made many trips to those trees and stopped many times on my walk from the school bus to Grandpa's house. I found it to be worthwhile every time!

One place I never got to visit while it was in operation was the molasses mill. It had been dismantled and disappeared before I was born. My mother worked the mill, along with her sisters, and so she was very familiar with it. Making molasses took place in late September and October every year. She remembered there was lots of activity going on with wagons loaded with fresh cut sorghum stalks being unloaded, wood being burned to heat a large vat, and a mule continuously moving in a circular pattern with its harnesses connected to a long wooden pole to which the mashing wheels were attached to squeeze the sorghum cane stalks to get the juice out. The juice would drain into a barrel for future cooking.

The molasses mill was designed and built by my grandpa. It consisted of a press with two iron wheels, which Grandpa had purchased. The wheels rotated in opposite directions through which the cane stalks were fed to be smashed and squeezed. The mashed stalks, which my mother called 'pummies', would be stacked and left to decay throughout the following winter. Then in the spring this decayed material was used for fertilizer by spreading throughout Grandma's big garden. The natural juices were collected in a catch basin below the two wheels. The sorghum juice was green in color before it was cooked. These juices would drain into a barrel from the collection basin. The wheels of the press were rotated by a mule tethered to the long pole which then continuously walked in a circular direction during this squeezing process. This was the routine all the time the press was in use.

A pipe was installed underground from the press to the barrel. The press was elevated compared to the barrel to allow for gravity feed into the barrel. From the barrel, the juice was piped into the cooking pan, which was made of copper and was approximately four feet by ten feet and about four inches deep with several compartments or dividers across the four-foot width. The pan was built on top of a wood burning fire pit and was tilted slightly downhill. A valve on the exit side of the elevated collection barrel controlled the juice entering into the pan. As the juice entered the hot pan at the top end, it began to cook. It would continue to cook as it migrated through on its way to the other end of the pan through each compartment. At the far end of the wood burning pit was a stovepipe flew built to allow for adjusting the heat and air draw to control the draft and ventilation – temperature control. The fire was hottest near the stove-pipe. As the juice drained through the compartments, it got hotter and the cooking sorghum molasses would foam up vigorously at first. Grandpa would skim the foam off continuously until the molasses, which was down near the bottom of the pan, would no longer foam.

To skim the foam, Grandpa took a big coffee can and attached it to a stick five to six feet long. He had put holes in the closed end bottom of the can. By picking up the foam, the molasses would drain back into the pan leaving only the foam. From time to time, he would stir the juices as they cooked until they got near the lower end of the pan or until all the foam was removed. After that, he didn't stir the juice any more. The foam was thrown down on the ground as he walked back and forth collecting the foam. (My mother said that the foam collected in a low spot one time and the hogs ate it and got drunk!)

After the molasses finished cooking, a plug was pulled at the end of the pan and the molasses drained and collected into a new galvanized wash-tub. Apparently this was important to my grandpa, because my mother said he bought a new washtub every year. From the tub, the molasses were put in one-gallon jugs, one-gallon metal cans or sixty gallon wooden barrels depending upon the desires of the farmer. The firewood for the molasses season was special and important as well. Grandpa would select prime pine with lots of heavy pine resin in it to use for the pan fire. This would of course have a higher BTU rating for producing higher heat.

My mother said if the girls helped with the molasses, they were given a chance to go to the county fair. This usually turned out to be my mother and her sister, Alice, who would carry the 'pummies' away from the press and pile them so they would decay. She also added that they (the girls) could go to the fair that year if they all pitched in and picked a bale of cotton on Saturdays. That was a lot of cotton ... five hundred pounds of it!

Some of the cane used for molasses was 'ribbon cane'. It was considered 'white molasses' because of its light "bronzy" color. The area farmers who wanted their cane processed would bring in the cane and stack it in separate piles all around the mill to assist in identifying their own crop. When they were ready for processing, they would move the cane into position for loading into the masher. My grandpa would operate his mill for five days each week for about four to five weeks each year. The cost to the farmer was to split the molasses fifty-fifty with my grandpa. He was considered to be the best molasses maker in the entire area. The molasses received in like-kind payment was always sold by my grandpa in gallon jugs or in sixty gallon wooden barrels. He generally sold most of his crop since people would come from as far away as fifteen to twenty miles!

While cooking of the cane juice was in process, the vat would be drained at differing levels to obtain the light high colored amber molasses, which was supposedly the best quality in the batch. The medium and darker molasses were taken later in the cooking process. As the progression continued, the molasses migrated to the lower level of the vat and this stage of cooking was considered the lesser in quality (too dark). While still boiling hot, the molasses would be poured into a variety of containers and sealed. They could be stashed or stored for future use as syrup or in making various desserts.

In a typical southern family, molasses were used as a breakfast food on biscuits. Usually, the molasses was heated with a generous portion of home churned butter melted into the pot together so that one did not have to add butter at the table unless you wanted more butter. This preparation makes the molasses a little frothy on top. But it smelled really good, sort of like very slightly overheated brown sugar. When they hit your taste buds, the taste was absolutely incredible! As a boy nothing ever tasted so good! I do not know if I could have observed any more of the molasses making process had I been there and had my own vantage point, but it was extremely interesting to me hearing my mother tell me about it.

After the molasses season ended at Grandpa's farm, Mr. Charlie Misenhammer would hire him to dismantle his molasses mill and haul it down in his wagon to the Misenhammer place on Moss Creek to process Misenhammer's crop of sorghum. This took about a week and Grandpa would stay there the whole time. The Misenhammer sorghum was grown in the bottom lands in rather rich soil. My mother said that in a general way the sorghum juice would take on the color of the ground in which it grew. If the soil was light in color the juice would be light. If it was dark, the juice would be darker.

Grandpa Talley processed molasses for as long as my mother could remember. From her recollection, he had always had a molasses mill. However, in 1930, when my mother was about twenty-five years old he stopped. He was about sixty-nine years old at the time.

In the fall of the year, wild growing blackberries and muscadines (wild grapes) would be harvested and canned. This was an exciting time for a kid, particularly, if you liked sweets. This was the place to be without a doubt! You wore old clothes to go pick berries, because you knew that you would get berry juice on them and it would never wash out. You could not simply wash it off your hands; it had to wear off. Sometimes it would be several days before that happened. Grandpa would put many buckets in his wagon and drive the 'team' of mules out to his selected locations where he thought a lot of berries would be ripe and ready for picking. He had probably already scouted them out. On these trips, you just rode into the pine forested mountains without any trails to follow. I was glad Grandpa seemed to always know where he was at any given time. You never get lost when you were with him. The berries had to be picked at different times depending on when the blackberries and huckleberries (similar to blueberries but with a stronger taste) were ripe. These trips could be nearly all day affairs if the berry crop was abundant —did we ever pick berries! At first, I would eat more than I put into the buckets. Since the berries were vine ripened, they were really delicious. But by day's end and often before, we had all the berries we wanted and needed and back to the house we would go. It was time for Grandma to get to work!

The berries would be washed several times to clean them and then they would be canned in fruit jars for use later. Oh, they were so good!!! Some were saved by Grandma to make her famous and delicious huckleberry or blackberry cobblers. Also in the fall, the peaches got ripe. She cooked an incredible fresh peach cobbler as well. The cobblers just seemed to melt in my mouth and tasted so much better with the heavy cream that Grandpa had saved from the milk separation process.

The muscadines were either eaten raw like grapes or cooked and made into jelly. There is a special way to eat muscadines. You don't just pop one into your mouth because the skins are tough and somewhat bitter. The way to enjoy them is to take the 'vine end' and point it into your open mouth then, using two or three fingers, just pop the inside of the grape into your mouth. That's the sweetest and tastiest part anyway. The muscadines found in Arkansas are mostly of the bronze variety and are native to America. They grow wild or as cultivated crops throughout the southern states. Generally, this fruit grows in small clusters of five or six grapes. The grapes, like the berries, were made into homemade jams, preserves and even wine. It was not uncommon for Grandma to make cobblers using those fresh muscadines or berries. They could be a little bit tart at times but they were always put away by anxious eaters and there weren't ever any leftovers!

Until December 18, 1983, I never knew that my Grandpa Talley ever did anything of a questionable or dubious nature that might raise eyebrows. However, he was not perfect even though in my mind he was close. His questionable activity was simply that he made whisky and peach brandy during Prohibition! Perhaps this issue should not even be of concern since at the time in his life he was not a Believer. His still(s) operation was located down by the blacksmith shop. It appears that he did an excellent job of camouflaging its location. You see there was a neighbor man by the name of Willie Underwood who was referred to as the 'snooper' in the local community. He was a nuisance as he tried his best to find out where Grandpa made his spirits. Willie lived on the west side of Backbone Mountain in the Moss Creek community. Apparently, he would come around un-announced and start his search by looking around my granddad's place trying to find where his still was hidden. He never did find it!

Grandpa got paid $20 per gallon for his peach brandy and corn whisky (moonshine). A Mr. Schoate, possibly a sheriff in the county, from Danville, was my grandpa's protector from the law. In fact I was told one time that he was the law! Buyers and officials from Little Rock would come to Danville to pick up their orders. Supposedly, his peach brandy was so good that "it made your lips smack and stick together", at least that is how my mother described it. I don't know if that is the mark of quality or not but that was the way she described the brandy to me trying to emphasize it would have been very hard to make it any better than Grandpa's!

For those who wanted his product during Prohibition, Grandpa would leave the whiskey and brandy at designated and different drop locations in the local area. The customer would pick up the order and leave his money. Later Grandpa would return and find his money in the hiding place.

Grandpa kept some of his whiskey in a trunk in the house. This was used for health and medicinal purposes. If Grandpa wanted (needed?) to have some of it, he would light the whiskey with a match and it would give off a blue blaze. When the blaze died, he would drink it. He operated the still before he became a Christian. Making whiskey was to become a very important issue in his life.

Apparently, he worked late in the day or even into the night making his whiskey and brandy. It seems on one such night, he believed that Asilee, his daughter, 'spoke to him'. He was certain that he had heard her voice. In three days Aslie came down with a congestive cold and died. This was in February 1901. Grandpa decided a few weeks later to make another batch of his whiskey. He returned to his still and this time as he worked, he heard another voice which he was certain was like Becky's (Grandma Talley). He was so convinced that Grandma was calling to him that he stopped his work and went to the house only to find everyone sleeping soundly. At this point, he became convinced that God was really talking to him! He returned to the still that night and poured out all of his mash and stopped making whiskey and brandy. He never made it again!

This just did not set well with most of his customers. In fact, the law (sheriffs) from both Danville and Little Rock came to see him and tried very hard to get him to start it up again. He was told that he made the best whisky in this part of the country. They said that they would pay him any price. Nonetheless, he could not be convinced because as he put it, 'he was living for the Lord now!'

My cousin, with the 'ghost writer' name of Country Gal (Anne Moore), wrote in the local newspaper about whisky making in the 1920s and she provided a bit of a slant on this illegal activity.

"I was reading about stills and illegal whisky back in the twenties, seems at one time there were as high as 5 to 6 stills on the ridge between Cedar Creek and Spring Creek.

The sheriff back then was heard to remark that unless a complaint was lodged he left them alone. Times were hard and this is how they supported their families, and if he arrested them the county would have to support them and we were a poor county."[2]

What had happened, you see in the meantime, before the sheriff came back to try to convince Grandpa to restart his still, was that a preacher had come to visit the area and held a brush arbor meeting in the Riley Creek community. Grandpa attended the meeting. At that time he became convinced that he should give his heart to the Lord but he did not want to be one of those 'shouting and hollering Christians'. Ironically, when he was 'saved', he said he found himself shouting but he was very happy that he had become a Christian anyway!

My mother believes that if Grandpa had been in business today, he would have made a lot of money. She thought very highly of her father. He was inventive as evidenced by his design and building of the molasses mill. He also cut lumber (hardwood) from his property and made his own highchairs by hand for both my brother and me. He also made chairs and tables for use at his home. People liked him and he enjoyed discussions. Apparently, he was a gregarious type of individual.

My kids have always been told of my having to trudge through the snow in the winter to go to school. I do not know if they believed it or not, but it was true. I do not remember exactly at what time I had to catch the school bus but it had to be around 6:30 a.m. Grandpa's place was the last stop on the route home or the first one in the morning. To get to the bus stop, I had to walk through the corral at the barn, down through the pasture following the fence, down to the sharecropper's house and a short distance out to the road in front of that house. It was a distance of about a quarter to a half mile, at most. Indeed on some occasions, the ground was covered with crunchy and almost squeaky fresh snow and it could be very cold. My mother or my grandmother always packed me a lunch. For my lunch, I would usually get a couple of biscuits stuffed with a sausage. Sometimes I would get some dried fruit or a homemade cookie. Once at school, I was given some fresh fruit, like an apple or an orange, and some milk. That was it and I was glad to get it.

Mother said that her father, as she remembers him, during the last few years of his life, as having stooped shoulders and that occurred even before he stopped making molasses. It is a Talley family trait to some extent to have sort of rounded shoulders.

Near the time of my grandfather's conversion was also near the time that my mother became a Christian, was saved, and committed her life to Christ. It was a lifetime decision for her. She was also baptized at this time.

What Was Life Really Like at Grandpa Talley's Home?

Grandpa liked to smoke a corncob pipe during his time to relax. Each time one would "burn out", he would just go down to the barn and make himself a new pipe. I learned to do that too… on my own of course. I never ever smoked one of them though. One aspect, at the time that I thought was rather different was Grandpa had his own "tobacco garden." That's all he grew on that plot. It was on the north side of the house and all fenced in with thick honeysuckle hedges. The vines growing on the fence in the spring and until the late fall kept the tobacco garden well hidden from view. It was hard to see what was going on in there. As I ventured all around the place, I often wondered what was going on inside that fence.

From the window on the right side of the fireplace I could get a glimpse of the far end of the plot. All I ever saw were small plants growing. My mother told me that Grandpa would order his tobacco plants out of a catalog each year and plant them. In the fall, he would cut the tobacco leaves and dry them by hanging them on the rafters of the long porch. When the leaves were "just right" he would roll some of it tightly to dry to be used for "chews" and the rest would be used in his pipe during the next year. He and my grandmother both dipped snuff and each of them would use an old coffee can for a spittoon ... oh yes, sitting on that front porch, rocking or sitting in one of Grandpa's homemade chairs, just "chewin' and spittin', how good could it get!

While sitting on the front porch in the late afternoon, you could hear the leaves on the three big oak trees, in front of the house, rustling as a breeze would gently disturb their quite silence. There was nothing more tranquil. It could be just a relaxing time leaning back in one of Grandpa's old chairs and resting or almost nodding off. Once in a while, depending on who was sitting on the front porch, some interesting conversations and discussions on a wide variety of subject matters took place. I could only listen with my big ears and try to understand but my attention would begin to wander as the details of the issues were debated. It could cover the water front on politics, religion, crops, the weather, the biggest snow ever, the coldest winter in the last ten years, what should be planted next year, the fact that two lonesome train whistles blew on the same day last week instead of one (I knew about that because the sound easily echoed through the mountains from some seven miles away), or the roar of a airliner miles up in the sky that occasionally traversed the clear blue cloudless sky. Everyone wondered how they flew so high and sometimes how they could even fly at all. It seemed like any and everything was talked about sitting on that front porch or around the fireplace at night!

Another important activity on that front porch was making butter. Whole soured milk would be poured into a tall ceramic crock churn (pot) which was maybe 28" tall and had a wooden seated lid on top with a hole in it. A paddle, which was a like a broom stick with a couple of flat pieces of wood fastened to the end would be placed into the churn with the handle sticking out of the hole in the lid. The person churning would lift the paddle (inside the churn) and push it with some force into the whole soured milk, which contained significant quantities of animal fat (butter). As the agitation process wore on, the butter would begin to separate from the milk to some extent. Once the churning was completed, the churn would be opened and the butter collected and squeezed to get all the milk out. Sometimes, my grandmother would make beautiful designs on the mound of butter. The residue in the churn was buttermilk and still contained little chunks of butter that were very tasty with cornbread for supper.

After the evening chores were completed, which included milking the cows, feeding the chickens and "slopping" the hogs, it was time to eat supper. The meals served every day were breakfast, dinner and supper. Dinner was the main meal. Never were there any 'in between' snacks. I think this resulted in the concept of cleaning your plate at every meal.

Breakfast was prepared very early every morning. My grandma was up every day by about 4:00 but not later than 4:30 a.m. My grandpa had already been up at least by 4:00 a.m. getting the wood burning cook stove going. The stove had a large water reservoir and as soon as the fire in the stove 'caught on' it was heating the water and simultaneously heating the coffee pot. The heated water was used for other purposes, including washing dishes. Grandma took coffee beans and ground them fresh everyday with a hand grinder. She had a collection of coffee grinders, which I assumed was because you might not have been able to sharpen them very easily or get new blades or something like that. She stored them high up on a wall shelf in her kitchen. She had quite a collection of them.

Water had been drawn the evening before from the well and poured into the stove reservoir. In addition, the wood needed for the cook stove had been collected from the numerous stacks of cut wood in the front yard and placed in the wood box in the kitchen along with kindling wood by the stove. This kindling wood would catch fire easily and quickly and begin burning the cut wood. It usually did not take long for everything to get going. Breakfast was usually served at 5:30 a.m. and never later than 6:00 a.m. Most always throughout the house, you had already smelled the wafting odors of sweet hickory ham or bacon frying through the partially opened doorway coming from the kitchen long before you knew it was nearing the time to eat! That alone heightened your senses just like Pavlov's dog and could easily cause you to awaken with your mouth watering. You did not want to be late for a meal because no one ate anything until all were present and accounted for at the table. When you got up and had put your clothes on, there was a wash basin or pan on the front porch (except in winter) where you could wash your hands and face to get the 'nappies' out of your eyes then douse your hair with a little water and comb it with your fingers so that you would look sort of presentable at the table. Until the wash pan on the front porch with the water for washing would actually freeze over at night, it stayed out there. When you broke the ice and washed your face, that was a real wake up call!

The dining area consisted of a very basic homemade table with wooden benches, picnic style on either side. Of course Grandpa made the table and the benches too. At each end where Grandpa and Grandma sat, they got to use the homemade chairs he made of oak and hickory with the backs and seats utilizing strips of cowhide about one inch in width being woven into a crisscross pattern. These chairs were more comfortable than the benches and seemed to never wear out.

On the table at breakfast would be a huge platter piled high with fried fresh eggs out of Grandma's old cast iron skillet. Usually there would be about a dozen and a half to two dozen eggs fried medium hard on that platter. Another platter would typically be filled with a combination of ham, bacon and sausage. Still another platter was loaded with fresh baked buttermilk biscuits. There were various jams, preserves and jellies on the table from Grandma's orchards that she had made the previous fall. Usually, there was molasses, as described earlier, honey, if Grandpa had time to rob a bee hive or that red eye gravy. Needless to say, there was that pone of butter that Grandma had decorated ready to be sliced and slid inside your hot biscuit. To drink, there was always farm fresh sweet milk, water and coffee.

Coffee was made in an old grayish color porcelain coffee pot. The best that I remember, the grounds were just dumped into the pot and boiled until the coffee was done. The grounds were allowed to settle in the bottom. You drank it black too. If you didn't pour it carefully, you would find coffee grounds in your cup. The only time I got coffee (with sugar) was when I was sick and I got to soak a biscuit crust (bottom) in some hot coffee. I learned to love coffee that way!

In case you don't know, red eye gravy is made from the renderings of frying ham, removing most of the grease, and adding some black brewed coffee to the drippings in the frying pan. Red eye is served hot and usually poured on the hot homemade buttermilk biscuits. If you preferred, it was very acceptable to 'sop' up the remains of the red eye that had been spooned onto your ham as if it were *au juice*.

There have been all kinds of stories told about the rooster crowing at dawn on the farm. I think Grandpa's roosters were trained to start their 'cock of the walk' serenade or 'it's time to get up' call on the fence post as soon as they heard the creaking of the floor slats going into the kitchen every morning. That was before daylight! Grandpa was never one to tiptoe any place. Don't know why they couldn't be like other regular roosters and start crowing at dawn …I always thought they were supposed to awaken us! Not the reverse.

Dinner consisted of many vegetables including green beans, butterbeans, whippoorwill peas, black-eyed peas, okra, corn, greens (either mustard or sallet, which were wild greens picked at certain times of the year), and red potatoes (my father always called these "arsh taters" meaning 'Irish potatoes', I guess) from the garden or from the laid-in supply down in the cellar. Meat could be freshly dressed such as southern fried chicken or any particular special main dish that Grandma or Grandpa had a craving to eat, including squirrel, rabbit or catfish from the Petit Jean. There was always cornbread for this meal and the 'pone' would be made large enough to have sufficient leftovers for supper. Very rarely was there any beef, simply because it wasn't available. Becky, as Grandpa called Grandma, would cook a cobbler, pudding, cake or pie for dessert. To drink, we always had sweet milk, buttermilk and water. Grandma always timed her 'call to dinner' early enough that if you were working in the field you could make dinner timely. All she did was go out into the front yard where a large bell hung from a twelve-foot high pole. She would pull the chain and make the bell ring several times so that everyone in the field could hear it. It was loud! I think you could easily have heard it from a mile or more away as the sound bounced and ricocheted off those hills.

Now if you have never tasted southern fried chicken cooked in an iron skillet, served with farm fresh mashed potatoes, gravy and homemade buttermilk biscuits … you haven't lived yet! On the farm, you just couldn't get any fresher chicken. If Grandma decided that she was going to cook chicken, she or someone would go into the yard and pick out a nice sized young fryer. It could be a little tricky catching those fryers because they were more easily spooked and could run fast as they darted here and there. But chasing 'em into a corner area made snatching one a bit easier and you could generally grab one, one way or another. At times, you might end up on your nose in the dirt but who cared. Once it was caught, that chicken would squawk loudly…but only for a short period of time. The catcher had only to grab it around the head and swing the chicken in a circle much like a rope lariat until you were left with nothing but a chicken head in your hand! That chicken would flop and flip and jump with the blood squirting out all over until the life in it was gone. I guess that's where the old saying came from about 'running around like a chicken with its head off!' The chicken would be put into boiling water briefly and then the feather plucking began. That could be a tedious job because you had to get all the pinfeathers out. Then the chicken was gingerly held over an open flame to burn the real small pinfeathers off the bird. Generally, the chicken would have been gutted before the singeing and cleaned and then cut up into its various parts for cooking. Nothing but the head and feet were wasted. Even the short soft feathers were collected and saved for the feather beds.

The butchering of the chicken was done a little differently than is typically done in super markets today. In the breast section, Grandmother always cut the "pulley bone" out first. It was cooked separately as another piece of the chicken just like a leg or wing. That was always my favorite piece of chicken and when I had cousins around, we'd sometimes have to decide who got the pulley bone to eat. In an iron skillet, the chicken would cook to an absolute golden brown…sort of crispy. Bring on the mashed potatoes and gravy made of the settlings from cooking the chicken and

Riley Creek School – 1915 with 68 students.
Grandfather Andrew J. Talley is the Superintendent and stands at the far right in
his overcoat. Five of the six Talley girls are present. Right –Left: Hestella, row 1, #7,
Alice, row 2, #18, Lillie, row 5, #1, Elizabeth, row 4, #13, & Belle, row 4, #17.
Note: This picture of the Riley Creek student body includes many friends of the Tal-
ley family who lived and attended the local one room school. All of the following
people are identified in the picture and all are listed Right to Left:
Row (all girls): 1) Della Reed, 2) Mary Lee Sherril, 3) Clare Smith, 40 unknown,
5) Lula Reed, 7) Hestella Talley, 8) Ora Belle Reed, 9) Chessie Jones, 10) Lora Belle
Barrick, 11) Amy Misenhammer, 12) unknown
Row 2: 1) Charlie Haire, 2) Tommy Jones, 3) Fred Vandiver, 4) Aubrey Arnold, 5)
Otho Tucker, 6) Minifred Holder, 7) Arvle Haire, 8) Calvin Kimbrough, 9) un-
known, 10) Jess Reed, 11) unknown, 12), unknown, 13) Clyde Vandiver, 14) Mamie

Farmer, *15) unknown, 16) unknown, 17) Alice Talley, 19) Etta Barrick, 20) Myrtle Vandiver, 21) Freda Smith, 22) half face unknown, 23) Ida Smith, 24) Hester Jones, 25) Gracie Tucker*

Row 3 *(five boys on right): 1) Hugh Misenhammer, 2) Edwin Kimbrough, 3) Gloyd Davidson, 4) Roscoe Reed, 5) Johnny Jones, (Left side all girls): 1) Lillie Talley, 2) Carrie Reed, 3) Effie Reed, 4) Mae Barrick, 5) Elva Farmer, 6) Gracie Arnold, 7) Anna Kimbrough*

Row 4: *1, Andrew Jackson Talley, 2) Pierce Bristoe (teacher-highest), 3) Ray Larson, 4) Edridge Reed, 5) George Jones, 6) Lawrence Reed, 7) Sylvester Jones, 8) Ervin Wells, 9) Homer Misenhammer, 10) Rea Tucker, 11) Arthur Farmer, 12) Raymond Tucker, 13) Elizabeth Talley, 14) unknown, 15) unknown, 16) Elva Davidson, 17) Belle Talley, 18) Merle Kimbrough, 19) Mae Reed* it was hard to get your fill! Gravy went on the mashed potatoes and the biscuit…you know, 'load it up'!

This was one of my most favorite meals. My mother learned to cook her chicken the same way and she could do it just as well as Grandma. She was a very good cook. Still have her old iron skillet too.

The pulley bone was special for another reason. The person who got to eat it was lucky for sure. However, after the meal that individual usually chose another person to actually pull the pulley bone. The idea was to get the best piece (biggest) of the pulley bone and that would bring you good luck! I don't know if that was something somebody made up way back when but it was always fun anyway.

Supper was light. It consisted of 'leftovers' from the other two meals. But mostly it was buttermilk or clabbered milk put in a glass into which you crumbled the remains of the cornbread from dinner. If there was any chicken or other meat left over, you might get a piece of it. That was it. Healthy, simple and light but you never over ate so you slept well.

In the cold or cooler evenings of the year, the fireplace was started early. Grandpa really knew how to build a good fire. It literally roared as it quickly consumed the pine knots filled with resin and started the hard-woods burning. If you stood too close your clothes would get very hot to the point of feeling that they were nearly ready to burn.

Grandpa always had some rich pine kindling wood to get the fire going. I loved the smell of that pine burning; it had a fresh pine scent to it that one could never forget. That old fire, once it got going, would roar, snap, crackle and pop! The embers would pop right out on the floor or even sometimes onto your clothes since he didn't have a screen for protection. The old wooden puncheon floor (floor made out of split logs which had been roughly dressed) had lots of dark spots where embers had popped out and burned before they were put out or just burned out on their own. Everybody came to the fire place in the evening to finish the day before retiring. The chairs were all arranged in a half circle around the fireplace. If someone was cooking a special delectable delight, such as a pig's tail or a sweet potato, they were placed on the hearth to cook during the evening. This was time to be spent in conversation and activity around the fireplace and could last for several hours but every one was in bed by 9:00 p.m. always ... and then you went to sleep! During the time around the fireplace, Grandpa never missed an evening of reading the Bible and discussing God's love, salvation or one of the miracles Christ performed. He firmly believed that calamity was going to strike the earth at any time and that mankind's' deeds would only wax worse and worse. These beliefs caused him to be very intrigued by prophesy on the 'last days' and the Book of Revelations. Mind you, we did not spend the entire evening talking about the Bible but it was never left out of any evening's conversation. Grandpa wanted to hear others' views on the many issues of the world and the politics in his day.

Andrew Jackson Talley was a staunch Christian and made his way to the country church at Riley Creek every Sunday as long as he could get there. That was very important to him and he taught his family to do the same. He was identified to be a 'hard shelled' Baptist, as my mother described him. To this day, I do not really know what that means. This small country church was also the Riley Creek School. It was a one-room building and all grades met in this one room at one time. My mother and all of her sisters attended this school. None of them ever finished the high school curriculum in Belleville but my mother did complete the eighth grade at the Riley Creek School. My grandfather was the School Superintendent for a while but I do not know for how long he served. I have a picture of him with the student body, which was taken in 1915. At the time, he would have been about fifty-four years old. In the picture, he looks as if he took the job very seriously and appears to be quite stern. My mother and some of her sisters are also in the picture. My cousin, Jack Smith, gave this picture to me.

I remember being at my Aunt Alice's house in Arkansas during Christmas one year, when she and Uncle Ab were the caretakers and sharecroppers for my grandfather. They lived in the house down by the main road where you turned off to go to Grandpa's house. It was probably around 1942. The winter was very cold and there was a good snow on the ground. Uncle Ab stoked the fireplace constantly trying to keep the cold out and inside warm. At this time of year, there is always some effort to recognize the Christmas season. A tree cut from the forest was set up in the main room. It was decorated with popcorn that had been strung on a thread and draped around the tree. At other times we took red and green art paper and cut pieces into strips all about the same size and glued them together into a chain. There may have been some tinsel that gave the tree a little more of a celebratory look. Sometimes crepe paper was used to make rope like decorations that were also strung on the tree. It was simple but exciting for all of us. That one Christmas was no different from the ones in the past, in terms of what our parents gave us for Christmas. We kids got our usual red net mesh bag with an apple and an orange, some walnuts, pecans, brazil nuts (back then for whatever reason they were called 'nigger toes' which today is very political, extremism and incorrect) and a couple of pieces of hard 'Christmas candy' that was very pretty with its patterns and designs and tasty, too. This candy was never chewed but broken off and placed in your mouth to dissolve and suck on 'til it was gone. The object was to make it last as long as possible. That completed the treats. The bag was always tied in a hard knot at the top and took some time for small hands to get it opened. One had to save the bag because we could play with it later. That was it! If we didn't like a particular treat, we traded with someone to get something we liked. We cherished the Christmas treats and looked forward to it each year. We didn't know any other traditions then. There were no presents or exchanging of gifts. No one could afford them and it wasn't traditional for our family.

There were so many ways in which Grandfather Talley's farm was a basis of education for many of his grandchildren. It was a practical education. He was also interested in formal education evident by this relatively 'unschooled' and virtually uneducated father having his own children attend school even though they weren't able to complete a high school education due to economic circumstances. He served in a very public capacity as the Superintendent. With my mother's continuous effort and desire for me to get 'a good education', I benefited from her loss, I'm sure.

My comments may seem strange to you today, but that was the way life was then. I have not exaggerated what I remember. These memories are coddled in the caverns of my mind as if they happened just yesterday. In other ways, they seem very distant and far as if fading into a world of oblivion and are giving way to the world I now live in. There isn't anyone around anymore to add new stories from the past and neither is there any possibility of adding new experiences from that era now long gone. This time frame was the end of an era and the beginning of a new one. It was the passing of one generation and giving way to a new. It is a time I'm glad I saw, lived and today I will forever treasure it. Then too will my generation pass! My children and my grandchildren will have their time on the stage of life and they will remember...the way it was.

---

[1] *Logan County Arkansas – Biographical and Historical Memoirs of Western Arkansas,* Logan County Arkansas Genealogy, www.couchgenweb.com, page 3.

[2] *Tales From Belleville, Yell County Record,* July 23, 1997, by Country Gal

CHAPTER SIXTEEN
Career Path: the Efforts and Struggles

Vince Lombardi, famous coach of the professional football team, the Green Bay Packers, once said," The difference between a successful person and others is not a lack of strength, not a lack of knowledge, but rather in a lack of will."

I worked hard in high school and college in terms of my studies and a job. My studies were always interesting and exciting even in grammar school. I thoroughly enjoyed attending school and learning whether the subject was history, variety of mathematics including algebra, geometry, solid geometry, trigonometry, and algebraic and trigonometric equations of calculus, chemistry, government, social studies, shop classes, physical education, and health. They were all good learning experiences. Perhaps the one subject I had trouble with was taking Latin. I didn't have any reference point. At this time I couldn't visualize where I would ever use Latin. I didn't know anyone who spoke Latin or used it daily, so why should I take it as a foreign language? I didn't know at the time that it was a root language so I transferred to Spanish. I never failed a class in high school although at the university, I took a typing class, since it was a requirement and barely got through the class. My fingers didn't connect to my brain in an expedient way so I could never exceed twenty-nine words per minute. I got a 'D' in the class, my worst grade in college. It definitely embarrassed me even though I graduated with honors.

Before getting too far into my formal education, you need to understand what it was like finding odd jobs and working at a young age in a farming community. That was part of the educational process too. You could quickly determine if a particular job was something that you wanted to do the rest of your life. That easily became a 'no brainer.' There weren't any factory jobs for teenagers below the age of sixteen. In fact, the only factory in Oxnard, California was the sugar beet factory. So a teenager worked in a store, gas station or in agriculture.

Most of the work I did was in agriculture in the surrounding areas of Oxnard. Lee Barnes, who helped me with the Boy Scouts, worked with or knew the Wallace family that owned and operated the Caterpillar Agency in Oxnard. Victor Wallace was the patriarch of the family and was developing and planting new lemon groves in the Somis area of Ventura County. During the summer months, my parents and I would hoe lima beans. The farmers were very particular about the job their hired hands did simply because it was the weeds that had to be chopped and not the bean plants. It may have been during this time that Victor and I became acquainted. Somehow, I made a contact with the Wallace family, and Victor, through Lee, hired me from time to time to do work on his ranch. It was a good job for a kid of sixteen. I drove a tractor, cut weeds, and white washed the trunks of the young citrus trees. This is the same Wallace family that my girlfriend's father, Willis Elliot, worked for at the caterpillar agency in town.

At the end of each day, Victor had me knock on his front door and he would have my check waiting for me. One evening, after having given me the check, he wanted to talk. He began to ask me questions, like, "Are you going to go to college? What do you have in mind to study?" He told me that I was a good worker. Then he made a statement that stuck with me ever since he said it, "You will make a good businessman." I didn't think much about it at the time. I reflected back on his statement later, even before entering the business curriculum in college, and wondered why he made that observation. What did he see that made him think that way about me? It was a bit eerie to think that he could envision that in my future at such a young age. Ironically, he was correct and I did enjoy being in business in the corporate world whether it was large or small business.

Early in my senior year of high school, I was able to get a regular routine job that didn't depend on the weather or harvest timing of crops. I was hired as a grease monkey or service station attendant for Boothe's Texaco. Working in a gas station in the early 1950s was very different from today. Customers never pumped their gasoline, a service station attendant did it for them. Everyone working in the station had to wear a Texaco uniform. The long sleeve cotton shirt had the Texaco star insignia patch on it above the left breast pocket. The pants were a heavy duty woolen and had to be dry-cleaned. All of the attendants purchased their own uniforms. The attendant was taught to give every customer the complete 'around the car' quality service regardless of the quantity of gasoline they were purchasing.

This work was done in sequence every time. The customer was greeted at the driver's side window where the order for gas and other services was taken. The service was given in a sequence with the next step being to wash and clean the driver's windshield; then move to the rear window and wash it; open the gas cap and begin filling the tank until it was filled to the quantity ordered by the customer, complete the windshield cleaning on the passenger's side, move to the hood and have the driver release the latch and check the oil, water, battery fluid levels, power steering fluid, brake fluid, radiator hoses, and fan belts. Anything needing service was then brought to the driver's attention when there was a cost involved and a determination made to fix it or wait until a later time. Owners seemed to really appreciate this kind of service even though it took some time to complete. I think people were not in such a hurry then as they are now.

On the lubrication rack, oil was changed and filters replaced; when wheel bearings needed to be cleaned and repacked with greased, it took time. Wheels were taken off the car and the bearings pressed out, rinsed in kerosene or other cleaning fluid, then placed in an apparatus that fed heavy grease into the bearing powered by an air compressor. Naturally, it was a dirty job with dirt, grime and grease getting on your hands. Fan belts and radiator hoses were changed and sometimes the car was hot from the engine being run for a long time. Doing a grease job was relatively easy because the grease joints were mounted any place where there were two moving mechanical parts. A lubrication chart provided information and instruction to assist the 'grease monkey.' Cars were cleaned and polished in the lube bay as well. If the paint was somewhat oxidized, the car was hand washed with kerosene or white gas, then washed with soap and water, and dried with a chamois. Then a car paint cleaner was applied and wiped off.

The final application was the polish and hand buffing. In most cases the car looked bright and shiny when the work was completed, almost as if it was new again.

One evening, I was working the station by myself, which was a routine for the younger attendants. A man came into the station and wanted to sell a nice ring with a stone in it. I wasn't about to pay him any money. However, he kept harassing me to give him some money for it, said he needed some cash. At night the cash drawer had very little cash in it. After more discussion, I unlocked the front door to the station and showed him the fact that there was very little cash. About that time, I had a customer drive to the pumps and I had to attend to his needs. Inadvertently, I left the door open and while I was distracted, the guy opened the cash drawer and took all the twenty dollar bills, dropped the ring in the drawer and left. When I went to ring up the latest transaction, I could see what had happened, I immediately called the owner, Jack Boothe, and told him what had happened. He didn't sound too disturbed about it and said he would report it to the police in the morning. I was pretty shook up about the incident but nothing more ever came of it. I did learn a valuable lesson about cash, security, and unscrupulous people. Incidentally, the ring was worthless. It wasn't a ruby stone at all…just cut red glass.

Probably the most irritating event for me occurred one afternoon when it was raining 'cats and dogs.' Nothing was going on in the lube bay because people weren't venturing out in the rain. The four of us were standing around in the front part of the station taking turns with drive-in customers at the pumps. There was only one row of pumps with one side being under the canopy and the other on the open side. My turn came and sure enough a big old black 1930 something LaSalle four-door sedan car drove in. Wouldn't you know it, the driver chose the uncovered outside lane of the gas pumps. He probably didn't give it a second thought that the pump hose could reach across the car. Besides that, the driver wanted twenty cents worth of gas! I could not believe it. I don't think he could drive a mile on that much gas in that machine. I had to show good service and do all the things I had been taught because the owner and the others employees were inside watching and laughing at what was going on. They really broke up laughing when they saw me pump twenty cents worth of gasoline! The only good thing was that I didn't have to wash the windshield or windows, but the guy did want his oil and water checked along with the air pressure in his tires…all for twenty cents worth of gas! By the time I was finished, I was almost completely soaked by the rain! That story was retold many times during the next several weeks at the station. I felt like all of our regular customers knew the story of what had happened. It always got a laugh at my expense.

I appreciated the job at the gas station and tried to do my very best. It was a very good learning experience for me. It helped me to earn and save enough money to buy my first car.

In high school, I really didn't know what I wanted to do for a career. I knew that I didn't want to be a 'grease monkey' for the rest of my life since I had worked for over a year at Boothe's Texaco gas station. When I entered Ventura Junior College (now community college), the course of study that I selected was a two-year course leading to a technical career in radio electronics. I decided on that course even though I had taken college preparatory courses in high school. I just liked the subject matter and doing something with my hands and it was technical.

After a year in college, I joined the U.S. Air Force and continued my studies in electronics. I did a pretty good job in this technical field so when I returned to civilian life in 1958, I knew it was back to school for me. I enrolled once again at Ventura Community College in electronic engineering, a four year curriculum. I again loved the learning process. It was more difficult in the sense I had to contend with the sciences more than ever. I learned that I was an above average student in most subjects but never in the top echelons of the grading. I generally made 'B' grades. Occasionally, I'd get a 'B+' or an 'A-.' If it was a class I needed but didn't want to spend a dedicated amount of time, I'd take a 'C.'

I completed my course work at Ventura Community College in 1959 and transferred to California Polytechnic College at Pomona, California to continue my studies for a bachelor's degree. This move coincided with my marriage on June 27, 1959. My studies, after the transfer, were basically a continuation of my engineering major curriculum studies. I loved geometry, algebraic and trigonometric equations in calculus. Throw in all the statistics courses and I was enjoying college! However, later in my first year at Cal Poly, I came to the realization that the zenith of engineering was in Southern California where it was a hot bed for space project work. This was indeed the space age. If you were an engineering major and you wanted to succeed at the higher levels of the profession, you had to be a top notch 'A' student. Companies did not recruit anyone not achieving this. It was then I realized that I could not achieve what I wanted in life as an engineer. My above average grades wouldn't allow me to accomplish my goals to really be more than very good in my chosen field of endeavor.

What were my goals? I never sat down and wrote anything out on paper. Just sort of followed my instincts, but I'm also sure the Lord guided me. My aspirations evolved over a period of time. I had decided that I wanted a better life than my parents had experienced. That meant making more money than anyone in my family ever had previously. It related to a 'higher standard of living' as well. It was like washing away the stigma from my youthful days when I felt my peers looked down on me as being from 'across the tracks.' That always upset me because I felt within myself that I was just as good a person as they but without their social standing. I wanted to be respected for who I was without the attachment of 'he comes from over there' someplace. I have never had aspirations to be a highly visible person or reach some lofty acclaim as a means of personal gain or recognition. My joy in my fields of endeavor has come from teaching and leading others to be successful and all the while forging a team effort and atmosphere. This was my incentive.

I made an appointment with a campus counselor to take an interest examination. Within several days I returned to get the results. It was shocking in some ways but certainly not in others. The counselor told me, in an unnoted voice of comedic kidding, my test scores were off the graph and that I should consider becoming a mortician! I was stunned beyond words. I didn't know what to say. I still didn't notice that he was kidding me. After all this was my career and that was serious business. I thought silently, that profession might be at the very bottom of my list. Being around dead people was not my heart's desire! Then I finally noticed his smile and I'm sure he had seen the disbelief on my face. "Roark," he said, "One score in one area is not the way we interpret interest tests. We must look at groupings and you look like you are best suited for a business career," Wow, that was a relief! He continued, "I think you like math a lot so it seems to me you would be very good in accounting. I recommend that you transfer to the School of Business." I heeded his advice and changed my course of studies and have never looked back.

My Bachelor of Science Degree was completed in Accounting. Since I had a lot of engineering course work, I had a minor in engineering. I graduated in June 1962. While in the business school, I was fortunate enough to have three separate internships during my summers and during my senior year, which had a requirement for an internship during the mid-quarter. My first internship was with the California Telephone Company, which had recently moved to Victorville, California from Rialto. Since we lived in Rialto, I commuted daily to Victorville to work. It was a good experience for me. There was a myriad of detail work having to do with the company's assets. It was referred to as a Depreciation Study. Every telephone pole, switching station, truck, office, and all other assets had to be listed by location, date of installation, its service history, and current depreciated condition. It literally took all summer to complete it and write the report.

My other two internships were with Arthur Andersen & Co. in their Los Angeles office. At the time, this certified public accounting firm was one of the major 'big eight' firms in the United States and was also moving on the international business scene. It was a very prestigious company to be associated with and had a conservative reputation in its industry. The firm was highly selective in their employment process. I felt extremely fortunate to be able to work with the firm. My first engagement was for the summer between my junior and senior years. The second opportunity was the winter quarter of my senior year. I did very well and was offered a position as a junior auditor in the Commercial Audit Department when I graduated. I was on cloud nine. I had become only the second student from Cal Poly Pomona to be offered full time employment with the firm. The first was my friend and car pool rider, Don Huennekens. My class was only the second graduating class in accounting from the college, so that became a feather in the institution's cap as well. Another of my closest friends in college, Roger McEachren, was in my graduating class and was hired in the Small Business Department of Arthur Andersen & Co. Roger had the top grades in our class.

As an aside, Arthur Andersen & Co. has fallen into great disrepute in the year 2002 for its role in supposedly not performing its audit functions properly. I am at a complete loss as to how this could have happened based upon my experience with the firm in the period 1961 through early 1967. Audit rules and regulations were so rigid and strict, there wasn't any room for poor performance with any client audit regardless of whether the business was small or large, whether it was a listed or unlisted company. Partners and managers stayed around because they did their work well, were dependable, and dedicated. I felt privileged to have been able to work with this firm of superb professionals.

In the last few days before graduation at Cal Poly, I recall sitting in a study room and all fifteen accounting majors were discussing what we expected to do and how much money would we hoped to make. When it came my turn, I told them that I had an offer from the CPA firm, which most of them already anticipated. I further commented that since I was going to work with a starting salary of $575 per month, I would think of myself as being on top of the world if I could earn $20,000 annually. I probably sounded sort of braggadocios that day but I was very excited about the future. That seemed like a target almost impossible to reach at the time. Little did I know how my world would turn over the next several decades.

Each year, the firm gave me a strong positive performance review and a corresponding raise. Other new recruits seem to come and go but I was still there getting bigger and more difficult audit assignments. I had a chance to meet the presidents of companies, their financial officers as well as operating managers during the progress of the audits. I really enjoyed working the commercial audit staff as opposed to the small business audit group. There wasn't anything wrong with the Small Business group but I enjoyed the big companies and the complexities of the many consolidations of subsidiaries and divisions in them. In the commercial side, I had a chance to see how the very large and complicated companies functioned. There were always cutting edge accounting issues to contend with and resolve. Just recognizing the problem was important at my level. If the issues were of major significance, the final decision was made by the managing partner in the local office. If it was going to be precedent setting, the decision went all the way to headquarters in Chicago to the home office to the partner in charge of that specific industry specialty.

In my third year with the firm I was assigned to the largest job originating out of the Los Angeles office, it was Teledyne, Incorporated. It was a relatively new company on a fast growth track. The power man behind the growth and direction of Teledyne was Dr. Henry Singleton. He was seeking to build a major corporate conglomerate. When I was assigned to this audit, the company had already bought almost fifty companies in the past couple of years. They were then 'dismantled' and the product lines that Dr. Singleton wanted were retained and the remainder of the purchased company was sold off. In the period of time I was on the job, seventy-five more companies were purchased and ultimately revamped in the same manner. This meant many 'purchase investigations' in addition to the regular annual audit work. After a while, I was spending six months of each year on Teledyne work. During the audit period, it was extremely intense with long hours. Teledyne was located in Hawthorne, California at the time and we lived in Diamond Bar, California. It was about a forty-mile drive to work each way. The problem was the working hours and the lack of freeways to get there and back home easily. Getting to and from work each day was a real accomplishment over the busy streets of the sprawling metropolis of Los Angeles.

Back in 1964 to 1967, the 10 Freeway was the only main thoroughfare from the Pomona Valley into the downtown Los Angeles area. There was no 60 Freeway or a 57, 91, 710 or 605 Freeway. Outside of the 10, the drive was on surface streets. I thought it was congested then! Now it is many times worse even with the added freeways!

During the audit season, I worked until midnight or as late as 2:00 a.m., then drove home and I was back on the job by 8:00 a.m. Driving time was over an hour each way and often longer. This was my schedule for seven days a week during most of the audit. I had become the senior-in-charge on the Teledyne engagement. It was part of the fast track for promotion. I had become one of the chosen few in the firm for my experience, age and work ethic. Every year after the audit season was completed, the firm would throw a golf tournament and recognition party for the worker bees. My claim to fame for three successive years became the 'individual with the most overtime' in the office! It was good for my bank account but not so good for me physically or for my family life.

Leslie and Jacquie were growing like weeds and I never could get enough time to spend any quality time with them. It bothered me very much. I never wanted this to be the way my kids would grow up. I remembered how many times I had missed my dad as a kid growing up when I had a basketball game or some other activity. He was never there; he had to work. Not once in high school did he or my mother ever see me play a competitive game. I felt as if I had really missed out. I knew there wasn't another good alternative because my dad had to work every day. There were times when he worked two jobs just so the bills could be paid and our family was not extravagant by any stretch of the imagination. But here I was letting the same thing happen to me with my two daughters. This was not going to be the way it ended…not the same thing that happened to me!

The day came that offered an opportunity for change. I did not even entertain thoughts about pursuing a career change until after a long and difficult contemplation about my career needs and expectations. There was a wedding that Bev and I attended in Riverside. My long time friend, Eddy Honacker and his wife, Jean (Cooper), were there too. Eddy and I had met while in the Air Force at March AFB. We had palled around together, double dated, and gotten married about the same period of time. After the wedding, as we were about to part company, I mentioned to him that if a good job opened up at the company where he was working, to let me know. Eddy was employed by Fleetwood Enterprises, Inc. at the time. I was unaware that Fleetwood was an audit client of Arthur Andersen & Co. Within a matter of a few days, maybe three, I had a call at my office in Los Angeles. It was David Totten, General Manager for Fleetwood. I already knew Dave. He, too, had worked for Arthur Andersen and was a CPA. He told me about his conversation with Eddy and wanted to know if I was serious. He said he had a position as Assistant Corporate Controller and I could have it. I never dreamed there would be this fast a response!

Dave asked me to come out and talk. That was in January 1967. I made the trip out to Riverside, California to the company's headquarters. This facility is located near Van Buren and Indiana in the southeastern section of the city. The facilities were okay but certainly not modern or very impressive. During the visit, I met other personnel, Jack Dahl, and Jerry Kelly, who both had worked at Arthur Andersen & Co., so it sort of became 'old homecoming day' for me.

Before the interview concluded, Dave Totten made me an offer of employment. At the time, I did not know very much about Fleetwood's compensation program except that management made a lot of money. I was put into shock when Dave indicated that my compensation would be a flat $800 per month and, if every thing worked out, I would be able to join the bonus program after one year of employment! That statement put me to thinking, I will have to take a pay cut to join this company. My annual review would be coming up very soon at Arthur Andersen & Co., and the scuttlebutt from the managers in the office indicated that I would be making close to $1,200 monthly after my raise. So, by making the move to Fleetwood, I would be taking about a thirty percent cut in pay but with an upside potential. This was cause for thinking and contemplation. After discussions with Bev, I made the decision to change jobs. This would eliminate overtime; I would have a regular schedule for work; there would be less travel; and, most important of all to me, now I could spend time with my two daughters. I called Dave after a couple of days and told him that I accepted the offer but that I would need three months to wrap things up with Arthur Andersen & Co., because of all the jobs that I was supervising during the prime audit and tax season. Dave agreed that I would begin work in May.

Much to my surprise, when I told the Personnel Manager with Arthur Andersen & Co., Larry Pitroff, he seemed to accept it but said he would call me in a couple of days and talk to me. Always in the past, when a staff auditor made a commitment to leave the company, that was it. The deed had been done. Larry did call me and made arrangements for lunch. He proceeded to tell me that 'I might be making a mistake. He wanted me to know that I was doing very well with the company. He suggested that I might want to reconsider where I was going with my future.' These meetings were repeated almost every week or so for the next three months. The conversation always worked its way around to discussing the firm and my career. Finally, I think Larry decided that I was not going to change my mind. I had been 'wined and dined' by the firm and I wasn't changing my position. At our last luncheon date, Larry shocked me. He said, "Roark, the firm likes your work, you are on the fast track here with your future. As you know, when anyone resigns from the firm, it has been a policy since the beginning that the employee could never return to the firm. In your case, an exception has been made. If your new employment does not work out to your satisfaction, the partners have made an exception to the rule. They want you to come back to work with Arthur Andersen & Co.!" I knew the rules, and he was right. I couldn't quite believe what I was hearing! This was incredible news. It gave me a new boost in confidence. I really did like the firm and enjoyed the work and professionalism. I felt like I had learned an incredible amount in a relatively short five years. I really hated to leave, but I knew that I owed it to my family and myself. In May 1967, I ended my career in the certified public accountancy field and began my future in line management of mostly manufacturing companies.

At Fleetwood Enterprises, I would get my baptism into the everyday world of manufacturing. Fleetwood was young and had just gone public. It was on a fast growth track. Its two major product lines were recreational vehicles and mobile homes (often referred to as factory built housing). My first assignment was in the accounting department as the Assistant Corporate Controller. I enjoyed the work and it certainly wasn't as demanding as my past days as an auditor. Within a year, I was approached one day just before lunch by Jack Dahl, Treasurer, Jerry Kelly, Vice President of Finance, and Dave Totten, General Manager of the company. This was a 'force to be dealt with,' they were the 'controllers' of this business, the 'young turks' of their day. All three walked into my office together on that occasion and said they had something to discuss with me.

According to them, the company was going to be divisionalized. There would be two divisions; one, the recreational division; and the other, the mobile home division. They wanted me to be the recreational division general manager! I had no experience at operating or controlling any kind of business. Almost immediately after the shock had passed I blurted out, "I thought that I was doing a good job here in accounting!" They assured me that I was doing a good job. "Well. I'm just a numbers jockey; I've never been in line management before!" We know that too, Roark. We are convinced that you can do a good job in this new position, they said to me. "Well, I need to talk this over with my wife, can I give you an answer tomorrow?" Needless to say, I was excited and also concerned about leaving accounting from a career standpoint. This would be a complete change for me. My accounting could help me for sure; my engineering would be helpful also; but what about people issues and operating a business? I had managed my audit crews well and got my assignments in on time and within budget so I thought I was doing okay in that realm. They told me that I'd have a team to work with and cover the specialty areas such as production, sales, and purchasing. Maybe I could do the job. Bev and I talked about it that evening trying to cover the pros and cons of the new position. Finally, I decided to go for it. I accepted the position the next day. That decision made my basic career in line management become reality. It would serve me well for the remainder of my working days.

The announcement was made in the company about having divisions and the two teams that had been put together. The Recreational Vehicle Division team was comprised of myself as Division General Manager; Eddy Honaker, Purchasing Manager; Bob Schiffermiller, Production Manager; Bud Schreiber, Sales Manager. The divisions were organized this way as well as the management teams within all the production plants in each of the divisions.

The Recreation Vehicle Division inherited eight plants located throughout the United States. These plants were generating $12 million in sales each year at the time. I believe that the mobile home division had about twenty plants and perhaps combined $20 million in sales. The housing group also generated 90% of the company's profits. I had not paid attention to the detail of profit generation 'as a division' while I was in the accounting department. There the focus was on each operating plant. These facts were available at the time of my decision to take the position. Furthermore, it didn't cross my mind that such a drastic segmentation of profits existed even though I had been in the accounting department. We had just always looked at the company as a whole. Now there were some real issues with which to contend.

I got my team together with the idea of putting together a business plan to make the division successful in a realistic way. It wasn't going to be easy. Within a month, I got the real shock of my life. Dave Totten came into my office four or five weeks after the reorganization and tersely revealed to me that the Board of Directors had made a decision to close down the RV operations because the company was not making any money. That blew me away! How could they do this, we had not even gotten an opportunity to prove what we could make happen in this division. I was upset to say the least. It seemed grossly unfair to all of the team. I told Dave that as well. I said, "You have got to give us a chance; we're putting together a business plan. I think we can prove to you and the Board that we can be successful!" With that Dave said he would seek the approval of the Board. The decision came back that we had thirty days to present our plan of action.

The team hustled like never before. We discussed all possibilities of what each plant could do from a sales volume standpoint. How long would it take? What new models would be required to help us achieve our expectations? We worked hard and it all came together. The day came for me to make the presentation to the Board members. I was about thirty-three years old at the time. My plan was clear and precise. It was bold. It had a lot of fluff in it too, but we thought it could be achieved. The bottom line was that in five years, the RV Division would reverse the positions of profitability within the company. Whereas, the housing group generated 90% of the profits heretofore, the RV Division would reverse that position. I don't really know if the Board believed that or not, maybe they saw our sincerity in wanting to try to make it happen. They might have even figured that if we were only half as successful as we envisioned, that would certainly be acceptable. It well could have been the team had a false sense of future success and we just didn't realize that our goals couldn't be reached! Regardless, the Board made the decision to let us keep on operating…and we did! The team never knew if the Board's action was merely a measure to pacify the four of us.

The irony of it all is that the RV Division did grow rapidly. The housing group had some problems with low growth and the RVs did in fact overtake them. As a matter of record, the prognostication came out as presented to the Board…only in three years instead of five! During that time, RVs added four more plants and we started up the motor home group. We acquired the Pace Arrow Motor Home Company and that became our entry into a new expanding market and a way of travel for many Americans. The Division originally had the travel trailer brand names of Prowler and Terry. We added the Wilderness brand to the product line-up in a different price range. Our national market penetration was improving every month! It was a great time to be involved in this industry's rapid growth. All of us were in high spirits, having a ball and reveling in our successful efforts.

As a result of this success, my personal advancement and compensation within Fleetwood was moving ahead very nicely. At the end of my first year of employment, I was admitted into the 'bonus' compensation pool. These earnings were on top of your monthly $800 'beans on the table' pay that every employee in management received. Even the President got the same $800 a month. I remember my first bonus check. It was for $1,500! It didn't compare to the long time participants but it was a start. Neither was it computed on the company's profits, as were the others, it was just a 'token of appreciation' for having made a sacrifice to come to Fleetwood. Bonuses were paid quarterly based upon profitability. I remember one quarter, just a couple of years later, my bonus amount was $25,000 and I took the check by my parents' home in Pomona to show my dad. He had trouble understanding how much it was. I tried to explain it to him and after talking about the amount, he wanted to know if that was my pay for a whole year! It was hard to explain how the system worked. He was very happy about it all anyway.

I experienced substantial professional growth at Fleetwood. It was a fun filled thirteen years. In that period of time, the company expanded from a handful of plants to seventy-two facilities in the United States and Canada. I was promoted from Division General Manager to Vice President of Operations for the entire company and then into senior management in the position of Executive Vice-President and member of the Board of Directors. In each new position, I learned more and more about the philosophy of the company and how to manage a large business that was now listed on the New York Stock Exchange. Many acquisitions of companies took place as we expanded our product line up into other types and price ranges of recreational vehicles and mobile homes and factory built housing. We built the company vertically as well as horizontally. We brokered our own lumber business and furniture requirements. In the thirteen years, the company grew from some $20,000,000 in revenues to more than $800,000,000 in sales.

Not all aspects of my professional career have been void of problems. I relate this event in my life simply to say that horrendous disasters can occur in one's life but it is important to understand and stay focused on the fact that if you have a belief in God the Almighty, He does have a plan for your life. When these circumstances come, do not lose hope because in God's time there are better days ahead. As my income had increased at Fleetwood, so did my spendable income. I now was looking for investments for my surplus. I had been taught at an early age to save money for that 'rainy day.' Some members of the management team would find investment opportunities and share them with others on the staff. It was always optional as to whether you chose to invest or not.

In the late 1980's an investment came along that involved straddle transactions of United States government bonds. The basic concept was to legally convert current income into long term capital gains and thus be taxed on a much lower tax rate. Several mangers and officers of Fleetwood were interested, including me. We received the prospectus and read it thoroughly checking the IRS code for compliance. We read the legal opinions of prominent law firms. Since many of us had started our careers in public accounting at Arthur Andersen & Co. we called tax managers and partners and discussed the compliance, propriety, and legality and how it would actually work from an investor's standpoint. Without exception, we were convinced that indeed it was a legitimate investment vehicle. We had very thoroughly done our 'due diligence'. For three years investments were made and sold.

As the straddles began to work, after the proper holding period, one could choose when to sell certain bonds in one given year in order to insure a loss and reduce current income or to experience a capital gain taxed at the reduced rates. An investor had to project the rate of interest in three months segments and then make the investment decision. Everything seemed to function properly until the Internal Revenue Service decided to viciously attack all straddle programs regardless of whether government securities were involved or not and unilaterally decided that these transactions were improper. Then everything became an issue. There were more than 2,000 investors primarily located in San Francisco, California, Atlanta, Georgia, Washington D.C. and Dallas, Texas.

The IRS filed suit. The investors, believing that all standards of investment had been met, hired a bank of lawyers to defend our position. Depositions were taken in all the major cities. Expert witnesses testified on our behalf. The government had its own witnesses and lawyers. It was a 'free for all'. Our lawyers, as is always typical of lawyers in my opinion, initially stated that there wasn't any way the investors could loose. But as time evolved over a three-year period, the odds fell from 90% down to 50%. The legal fees kept accumulating. Tax returns continued to be filed on the premise that the investment was legal and proper. In the meantime, the IRS sent letters and statements about the interest accumulating. At that time the interest rate was standing at 20%! During this time, if an investor wanted to 'pay up' and wait for a tax court decision, the IRS wouldn't let you do that. You settled and lost any opportunity for recovering your payment or you watched the exorbitant interest accumulate to the decision date. As the trial neared its conclusion, the judge, who had been involved in the case from its inception came down ill with serious back problems supposedly and had to resign from the case. The newly appointed judge indicated that he would make a determination within six more months. In the meantime, interest continued to compound so much so that now the interest was greater than the initial settlement with penalties that had been offered by the IRS. They were throwing the book at us and not showing any leniency whatsoever because we would not settle. The IRS was going for the jugular and nothing less would do than to extract the last pound of flesh from every participant. It was inhumane the way the agents treated you even when you tried to be cooperative. They were out for blood! There weren't any give and take negotiations by the IRS in this case.

The Tax Court found every investor guilty. It was an unfounded decision based upon the tax laws of the time and seemed to prove simply the fact that the United States government decided that it didn't like the tax law permitting straddles and pursued it at the investor's cost and significant loss. I tended to think that the lawyers representing the defendant investors took advantage of the situation as well. They tried to keep the investor community fighting the IRS just to earn more fees. After the decision, legal counsel wanted to appeal the decision. Some investors chose to follow the appeal. For me, the writing was on the wall. I had to cut my losses, suffer the consequences, and pay the bill. That is the choice I made and the right one in my opinion. The financial cost to my family was nearly unbearable. The IRS had taken all of our accumulation. At first I was absolutely devastated. I had judiciously tried to make sound investments and maintain a balance of stocks and cash for over twenty-five years. Then it struck me, the Lord is in control so don't be frustrated. I was reminded to feel good that I had the capacity and capability to totally settle with the IRS without any impact on our home equity! I felt that at my age, which was approaching fifty, I could still start afresh and reach some degree of independence financially. All was not lost…just a few hundred thousand dollars. I never felt guilty in any way because I had always tithed what God had provided. As it would turn out, it was a lesson well learned that made me know that God indeed had me in His hand. I trusted Him to see me through.

It reminded me of God's faithfulness to us if we only let Him lead us in His paths. I haven't any complaints after these many years. God is good.

John Crean, the founder of Fleetwood, had differences with the then President Jack Dahl. He was one of the 'young turks' of the times. Something went wrong between John and Jack and in quick time Jack resigned

his position. Among a lot of the
staff there was speculation that
I would become the next president. I, however, never had that
feeling. It seemed John was bent
on having one of his 'old timers'
at the helm of the company and
did not want to chance another
young 'turk' in the making. He
appointed Bill Weide, my Vice
President of Real Estate. It was
tough for Bill because he was
not a natural leader; he was
not a visionary. He had been a

Roark V. Moudy, June 1981

public accountant (PA). He had to be led by the hand to read company
reports. The most disappointing aspect of it for me was that Bill wanted
to run the company by committee of three. This committee consisted of
himself, Glen Kummer and me. Bill's appreciation of Glen was inescapable
because Glen had made his way into Fleetwood management from plant
operations as a purchasing manager. Glen was a good man and I had, in
fact, selected him to fill each position as I vacated it. As time elapsed, Bill
and I developed philosophical differences relating to moving the company
in the direction of housing developments. This would provide spaces on
which to place our manufactured houses and move the company into the
real estate development business. I don't know if Bill disapproved of the
direction or John chose not to do it. Regardless, I found myself leaving
Fleetwood within a few months.

When I left, John Crean invited me down to have dinner with him at
his San Juan Capistrano Ranch just off the interstate 5 Freeway in San Juan
Capistrano. Much to my surprise during my visit, I learned that John had
become a Christian. In fact he and his wife, Donna, had made a commitment. As the evening closed out, John stated that I would be like a lot of
other former Fleetwood employees and, in a short time, I would be back
with the company! I never saw myself as ever coming back to Fleetwood

and it never materialized.

I have always felt like a person should be in a continual mode of learning. Fleetwood set the standard for me to learn teamwork, operate a manufacture business under stress, duress and good times. I had been able to put into action a lot of basic knowledge learned while growing up, including a consistent work ethic, utilized some of my education in accounting and engineering from college days, and the practical experience as an auditor of many manufacturing companies while with Arthur Andersen & Co. It had been a great run for me. From a personal standpoint, I had been able to spend more time with my family and my compensation had been such that we could live comfortably and take some vacations that I would probably never have taken had I not worked at Fleetwood.

While at Fleetwood, I had gotten to know Doug Caffey. He lived in Upland in one of the old landmark homes at Euclid and Nineteenth Streets. Doug was a very friendly sort of fellow and had been highly successful selling real estate. Sales of any kind that he put his mind to seemed to breed nothing but success. In the late 1980's, he came up with the idea along with another individual, Bill Nickolai, to start up an oil exploration and drilling operation using a shell company registered and publicly owned in the state of California. These two individuals purchased a significant majority position in the stock for a nickel per share, and reactivated the company. They then contributed certain personal assets into the business, including oil properties owned by Bill, in exchange for stock. From that point forward, it was a matter of selling drilling programs and getting more investors into the company. Initially, Doug made contact with several Fleetwood employees through me, before I ever left Fleetwood, who were looking for investment opportunities.

Since I had left Fleetwood, Doug suggested that I join the company in a position of corporate development. It was a new company, the compensation was lousy but the stock offered seemed like a generous offer. I took the position. Soon I was out selling oil drilling programs for leases Transierra Exploration Company had purchased in Louisiana and Texas. Some were more successful than others and some were not successful at all. Initially, the success rate was very respectable but then it began to fall off as many leases turned up as dry holes. Even the development of successful leases turned into losers as the dry development wells exceeded the producing wells or played out too soon.

That caused Doug to turn to alternative opportunities, one of which was pay telephones just after the telephone industry was deregulated. Doug traveled the country making deals to buy pay phone technology by exchanging stock. It was truly a disaster in the sense that Doug was not a technician, didn't understand the values related to an exchange, and failed to nail down the details of each agreement he did consummate. It was my job to come along and pick up the pieces and learn from the sellers what the deal really was, which most often varied significantly from Doug's information. It was a horrible and distasteful position for me since I had to reconcile differences between Doug's view and the seller's view of each deal. I felt like the janitor in the china store sweeping up the trash after the bulls had just run through the store. After a while, I couldn't take it any longer and I resigned so that I could move on to some thing more satisfying.

Once again, my long time friend, Eddy Honaker, lent a helping hand. He was still at Fleetwood and, being in purchasing, knew a lot of suppliers and their needs. He suggested that I should consider roto-molded plastics manufacturing. I thought that sounded good because I would be back in manufacturing again. I took the position of General Manager at El Monte Plastics.

It soon became evident that the business needed help. More than anything else it was a family feud involving a fifty-fifty split ownership where two sisters could not get along and their husbands were being dragged into the situation. It was Virginia and Gene Kite versus Bill and Peggy Burmingham. Virginia tried to avoid conflict whereas Peggy seemed to thrive on it and deliberately irritated Gene. On the other hand, Gene was the genius behind the technical part of the business and also a pretty good salesman. Peggy had tried to run the business and was a master at manipulating the finances and hiding expenses. Gene knew enough to feel that he and Virginia were being taken advantage of financially. Gene always wanted some kind of financial investigative effort from me to find out what Peggy was doing with the company's money. Peggy was always resisting or trying to throttle my investigative efforts. It was cat and mouse games all the time.

As I had time, I did some audit work and ultimately found that there really was fraud taking place. Cancelled checks and the related payees showed that Peggy and Bill had confiscated or misused more than $500,000. The money had been invested in boats, condominiums, real estate partnerships and other investment opportunities not in the company's name but in their names personally.

Gene decided and more or less forced Virginia to go with us to see a lawyer, Jeffrey Linden whom I knew, and present the evidence. I suggested Jeff because I had known him professionally for several years. I trusted him, and I had worked with him on corporate matters over the years. The appointment was made. During the interview and review, the lawyer finally said, "There is enough evidence here to send your sister to prison for at least twenty years!" At which Virginia replied, "I love my sister, she stole from me out of our chest of drawers when we were little girls but I couldn't send my sister to prison, she's my flesh and blood!" That basically concluded the meeting. Gene was very angry about the final outcome and how his wife had handled it.

Given the result, it became apparent that I couldn't keep the two family groups from fighting; it probably had always been this way; it wasn't going to change. Peggy even sensed her 'victory' I think. She came into my office one day shortly thereafter and suggested that maybe I had completed my efforts and role at El Monte Plastics. I didn't disagree. I was tired of the situation.

My benefit was that the two parties could at least sit down in the same room together and converse without it becoming a shouting match. They had become more civil in their dealings and disagreements with each other and the business was growing. This had been a project on diplomacy for me, as well as operating and learning a new business under very trying circumstances. At least I had the satisfaction of 'scraping the business off the rocks.' It had been an experience very different than any other I had known.

Several years earlier, I had met a man who served on the Board of Trustees at Pomona First Baptist Church with me. Lou Tepfer was a crude sort of man who had been very successful in business running an aerospace metal machining shop. It was not a big business, annual revenue was about $4 - $5 million. The company made specialty parts for aircraft programs for Douglas, Boeing, McDonald, Northup, and several other aeronautical companies involved primarily in the defense industry. However, the drawing card for me was that he wanted to sell the business and I was potentially interested in buying a business. He had expectations of moving to northern California on Lake Shastina where he was building a huge new 15,000 square foot home on an island in the lake that he had purchased. He thought that it would be good for me to come in and learn the business and then decide as to whether I would pursue a purchase of the business.

Lou was always very cordial and good to me. He did have a very hot temper and sometimes it was uncontrollable. It was very common in the office for him to lash out at someone in a very loud and vociferous sort of way. He never apologized to these employees, including his own daughter. One day, after such an outbreak he came into my office and said, "I guess you heard that? You know it is not personal, especially if I did it to you." I said, "Yes I did Lou and I've heard it before. You need to know that if you ever did it to me, it might not be personal but you would never have a second opportunity to do it to me again!" Lou never did talk to me that way, ever.

After a while, I had learned the business pretty well. It was solely oriented towards the defense industry and that industry was not doing well. The real question was whether it would continue to decline or stabilize at a business volume that would allow a new owner to pay off the related debt of the purchase price. In addition, Lou had established long term personal relations with a lot of the buyers. He never indicated if he provided any kind of favors to them but it was happening routinely in that industry at that time. Based upon these conditions and circumstances, I decided not to buy the business although I think Lou would have treated me fairly.

Within a relative short period of time after making that decision, my older daughter Leslie was working in Pasadena for a periodontist. One of her clients was a gentleman by the name of Carl Newell. He came in for his appointed treatment one day and began talking about his business and his need for an experienced General Manager. Even though she was not well versed in business, the more he talked she became convinced that the work he was describing was the kind of work that I did. She told him so. At that, Carl stated that he would like to talk to me. She came home excited to relate the story to me and gave me his business card. I was not actively looking for a job, but I said that I would call him.

A couple of weeks went by and Leslie came home from work and nailed me right away. She blurted out, "Dad, you are embarrassing me!" I didn't have a clue as to what she might be referring to. So I said, "How could I be embarrassing you?" She quickly responded, "You said you would call Carl and talk to him and you haven't done it!" She was right. I promised that I would indeed call Carl right away.

I had a brief conversation with Carl explaining that I wasn't really looking for a new position. Well, that didn't matter. Carl wanted to talk to me anyway so we set up a time to meet at his office. Carl was a tall, slender man and a very good talker and conversationalist. Before I knew it, we had talked for about three hours and I had enjoyed the entire time with him. He was a technical type and needed a business manager, which he readily admitted that he was not. In addition, he was an avid fisherman and so was I. We had both grown up working throughout our lives. I was mechanical enough that I understood all that he talked about. His business was floundering and he needed help. I knew at that time that Carl and I could work together. I would run the business operation and he would take care of the technical part of it. It was a good combination.

Within a couple of weeks I began my new work at Carl W. Newell Mfg. That was in 1989. Things went very well. I got control of the business issues, established some procedures, put cost controls in place, implemented a cost and inventory control system, created a procurement system that would purchase our materials and supplies at competitive costs and within a year the company had begun to turn a profit. I felt good that I had scraped the company off the rocks with the help of my other managers, and Carl seemed to appreciate the work that I had done. To show how positive he was about the turn around, the next year, he purchased a car for me. Bev chose a used Mercedes E300 that was about two years old with low mileage and in excellent condition. I could have kept the car but, when I left a few months later, I didn't think that was right, so I sent Carl a check to reimburse him for it.

It was late November 1991 and I received a blind call from a headhunter. He obviously had information about me by the way he talked. John Carroll wanted to know if I would be interested in a change I employment. I politely rejected any discussion or consideration. However, John was most persistent. In a few days he called me again and stated that I should at least listen to what he had in mind. That would be prudent on my part he blurted. He was right in that regard although I explained that I was very happy at Carl Newell's. I finally agreed to meet him for dinner and hear what he had to say some three weeks later.

The nuts and bolts of the situation were that he was talking about a company that I knew about; knew the deceased owner well; and knew the family. I knew the product as well. Jim Wilden had been developing an air operated double diaphragm pump since my days in the Air Force. I knew he was successful with his efforts and had actually seen several prototype units in his garage in Grand Terrace near San Bernardino when I dated his daughter, Marilyn. I liked Jim, although he walked to a different drummer than most folks. I would see him in the intervening years at social events and we would catch up on how things were going. Jim was a pilot as well and we exchanged our activities as avid flyers too. In the meantime, I was to learn that Jim had passed away a year or so before from cancer. The company needed help.

I listened while John Carroll explained all of this information to me. I then told John that I had my reservations about working for friends. There were stories that floated among your contacts and peers that working for friends didn't have positive results and ended in conflict. I had never really worked with people that I had been reasonably close to before. He assured me that the family wasn't interested in operating the business and that I would have complete control of day to day operations. It sounded good but I was not fully convinced.

Then John Duke called me just after Christmas to come and visit him in Oregon and talk things out. I made the trip. John Duke emphasized to me that the family's expectation was that in a period of five years, they wanted to sell the business and forget about Wilden Pump and Engineering forever. The family wanted someone with the skill to grow the company so that it could be sold for about $300 million. It was now at slightly over $50 million in sales volume. John felt that if the company could reach about $100 million in annual sales, the goal could be reached. After all, it was the dominant company in the world in that industry. John said they wanted me to be the President and Chief Executive Officer and that I would sit on the Board of Directors. It sounded very legitimate to me so I agreed, if we could work out an employment agreement, I would come to work.

I wrote out my requisites for the agreement and gave them to the company's lawyer, John McElearney, as John Duke had instructed me to do. What I did not know then was that the lawyer had wanted the position of President, which had been offered to me. That became a serious hinge point later. An agreement was worked out but not in the way that I had first laid out my expectations. The lawyer always had reasons why my approach wouldn't work and, therefore, it had to be done his way. I didn't do my due diligence because I trusted the family to treat me right. I blew it! Live and learn!

I reported for my first day of work in February 1992 and met my management team. They had met previous to my arrival and apparently had extensive discussions about my relationship with the family and from their perspective, it was not positive for me. However, they were cordial as could be expected. As they sat around the conference table, I asked each one of them what their goal was in life. Two of them, Chuck Marco and John Allen said they wanted my position. I thought that was good and that I could mentor them if they were really up to the task. They emphasized that they needed a decision maker, which had not existed since Jim passed away. That was a reasonable expectation from your leader. But obviously, they were there to question my qualifications as a leader. There would not be a 'vote of confidence' until I showed them my abilities to be their leader. I knew this was going to be a tough assignment. Even so, I didn't have any equivocations or regrets for having made the move. I knew that I could do the job. There wasn't anything mysterious about this company or its team. I would have to convince them to work together.

When I interviewed with the family, I was told that the company owned 44% of the world's market in this industry; and that the growth continued but at a slower rate because the industry growth had slowed down. I was to learn that the business was a real mess and, more significantly, major infrastructure for normal business operations was completely absent. Not only was the business not what I had been led to believe that it was but the management team didn't know how to manage or what teamwork really was all about. They each had little 'fiefdoms' with very high walls around themselves. It seemed they did not want anyone to know what they were doing and could care less about their fellow managers. I began to question the facts that I had been given. I questioned the correlations relating to their areas of responsibilities and the coordination and teamwork that were so vividly absent.

My approach was to have management meetings every week and ask each manager to submit any items, problems, issues for discussion, all of which were needed for the agenda. For several weeks, the agenda was comprised of topics that I put on the listing. Not one topic was submitted by another manager. I had enough of this nonsense and with exasperation I announced that we would no longer have meetings unless they had subjects that they needed to discuss. That helped in a minuscule way but it did get off the helplessness that seemed to abound. Were they testing me? Did they know how to manage? I took more inventory of the team. I stated that the team needed to work and pull together. As it was we were not going any where. It was time to have a planning meeting and budgeting session off campus. Each manager had to work on and make an oral and written presentation of how he saw the company moving, the goals that needed to be set, how long it would take us to get there, what was the expected cost of the effort and what other resources would it take to accomplish the effort successfully.

At the meeting, I started off with a state of the company review. I had information that showed we were not as good as what the family believed. First of all, Wilden Pump didn't own 44% of the global market. Instead it was only 28%, but still a substantial position in market penetration. It remained the largest in its industry despite the errors in facts and faulty information. Secondly, the company was growing at a declining rate of 4.2% whereas the industry was growing at an annual rate of 15% compounded annually. Our lack of infrastructure was evident. We didn't have a quality assurance group; we didn't have any electronic technology planning for world-wide communication and data processing; our engineering department consisted of one college graduate six months out of the university; there wasn't any product development capability or capacity; production was performed on relics and dinosaur machines of the past with very little automation; efficiencies were sorely lacking. It became very obvious that I had been dealt a bad hand with a major rebuilding job to do.

It is difficult for any non-management owner removed from the day-to-day operations to fully appreciate the difficulty and effort needed to turn a company around. In my opinion, the owners had not recognized the deterioration of their company even before they hired me. For years, the family had benefited from the momentum built into the company by the initial patents of a new product and the building of a new industry by the father of the two daughters, Marilyn Duke and Evelyn Freed, and his wife, Naomi. The survivors of his death were interested in the business as a basis of wealth but their gratefulness was encapsulated during an interim period by the declared dividend, which was substantial every year, until the company could be grown larger for the final sale and ultimate payout. There isn't anything wrong with that approach to ownership but it can be so myopic relating to their immediate income stream that issues which are important are not focused upon and neglected by the owners at management's expense. Another perspective is that negative outside influences can gather positions of strength which affects the owners and prevents them from achieving alignment with the goals and objectives set about by management to make the operation successful to meet the owner's objectives, which in this case was to grow and sell the company.

Another issue which raised its ugly head was nepotism. In many privately held companies such employment problems are faced and adequately dealt with without the need to interfere with management. When offspring, who are not qualified to perform the job's functions, are employed it disrupts the manufacturing process and operations, requires an inordinate amount of time to teach methods and ways to perform a duty and correct errors in judgment which results in costing the company in untold ways. That same time would have been best served doing functions required to promote the business. Yes, there is a waste of money; but there is also the impact upon other employees. They know the kid is getting special treatment because he could not otherwise qualify and get the job. That affects the morale of all other employees. In one sense the kid is viewed as a spy there to absorb all that is wrong and report. If management is doing its best the spying is a direct line to getting good information back to the owners. However, what if it is tainted or skewed in an unfavorable light, which is not completely truthful? What can management do? Just tolerate it, hope for the best and keep focused on moving forward.

One thing that draws attention and immediate focus is compensation. That take home paycheck is very important to every employee. If there is a hinge point for an employee, that is it! I remembered my experiences in Fleetwood with incentive programs which were extremely positive. I had witnessed first hand its impact on business operations and the attention that was paid to details often forgotten in most companies. If it is an all-inclusive program then everyone is dedicated to expansion of the business, minimizing costs and maximizing bottom line. After making detailed studies and developing methodologies and getting my management team to buy into it, I proposed an all-inclusive incentive plan to the board of directors. The plan actually included every employee from the janitor to top management. The foundation was growth and a sharing of improved profitability between the employees and the owners. If there was not profit improvement between years, there was nothing generated to share with the employees. Furthermore, if the basis of the incentive calculation became excessive in the eyes of the board, they reserved the right to lower the ratio of sharing. I received the blessing and 'go ahead' from the board.

Each group of employees had a separate methodology that was used to calculate bonus incentives. For production employees, extra compensation was earned based strictly on their productivity. Incentives were calculated based upon hour standards. Employees were paid by the number of pumps, and their related value, produced as compared to the employee's regular hourly compensation. If the production value was higher than regular hourly pay, they received extra money weekly. If their regular hourly payroll was higher than the production value, they were paid that amount.

The production pool was also charged for all warranty costs based upon the fact that they had failed to build and properly test the pump before it was shipped and sold. They generally earned a 20% bonus weekly.

Sales personnel received annual incentive compensation based upon the increased and expanded business that they had generated. Regardless of what one accomplished last year, the company was only willing to reward them for what they did this year in the way of additional business above and beyond that of the prior year.

Management was paid incentives based upon the overall success of the company. In addition, clerical personnel were included as a portion of the management pool. Each manager's responsibilities were reviewed and graded as to the participation rate in the incentive program.

This has been a rather simple description of the basics of the program but it was well received and accepted by all of the employees. The incentive programs were introduced and they did incite the employees to higher levels of productivity and efficiency. The entire effort came together and the company reestablished its growth rate as a leader in the industry. In five years, the company's annual revenues had grown 60% from $53 Million to a programmed $84 million. Gross profitability improved from the low 50% range to just under 60%. Net profits likewise moved higher and had a higher ratio of growth than did the gross profit rate. All of the incentives were paid from the improved earnings results.

All of the deficiencies were corrected within the first two-year period. It was a strenuous task. The company was able within itself to implement the international quality program known as ISO 9001, which was a great accomplishment. The engineering department began to develop several new products, which were successfully introduced into the market. We earnestly sought feedback regarding our product from dealers and users then changed the product somewhat, but not as much as it could have been.

Not everything was perfect. I made mistakes for which I paid a price. The effort that I put in was draining on me physically and mentally and was never truly appreciated by the Wilden family. Sure they saw the financial statements each month but not one of them had ever run a company day in and day out. They were always the 'good guys' and never had to experience the trials and tribulations of understanding what had happened to their company nor could they have put it back on a rapid growth track. I don't recall a single suggestion to improve their company. In the end they were highly rewarded from the growth, gains and improvements made to the company in a very substantial way. I had put into action many of my business theories and philosophies and they had generally worked very well. I learned that trusting in managers not recruited by a leader meant that they had no loyalty or allegiance to an incoming leader. I was an outsider whom most of them didn't really ever accept even though all aspects of the company had made significant strides of improvement. Without exaggeration, it was a very difficult task to overcome and one that I never intend to try again. My employment contract was established for a five-year period, which was the time frame John Duke had hoped would be the period needed to build up the company and sell it.

About three years later a market investor called me at home to inquire about Wilden and I learned an elevator company in Missouri had bought the operation. He wanted to know what I thought the value really was of Wilden when I left the company. He stated that the corporate owner had paid in the neighborhood of $270 million for the business and had to write off some 25% of that value within a short time. My response was simply that if the business had continued in the direction it was going with new products coming on stream and perhaps a critical acquisition or two, it could easily have been worth $300 million. That statement seemed to indicate that subsequent management had not done the job that could have been carried out for greater success.

Long after my departure, I met by chance a Wilden employee at a hobby shop. He came to me and introduced himself. At least five years had passed since I left the company. During the course of our conversation he stated, "The best times in the company was when you were President." I have had several other current and former employees randomly run into me on the street and make voluntary comments to me that the best time in the company's history was when I was there and in charge of its operations. Those statements made me feel good and I realized that the rank and file employees had appreciated me more than the owners ever had! With the employees, I succeeded in gaining their trust and faith. I had their welfare and the company's productivity as the centerpiece of my efforts to drive the company to new heights. It worked and worked well!

After six months of regaining my frame of mind and energy, I returned to Carl W. Newell Mfg. where I will probably remain until I decide to retire.

The variety of companies and positions which I held throughout my career were stimulating to me. With each one I learned new aspects of business. They were each valuable lessons in terms of ways to approach and work with people, strategizing and implementing business plans, making exacting assignments with people in order to achieve success, holding managers accountable and then sharing the fruits of the team's labor and accomplishment with appropriate rewards. Finally, it is unacceptable to stand on your laurels and accomplishments; you must continually improve and meet competition head on. New products and cash flow is the life line of every company!

The most rewarding position in my career that I experienced was at Wilden Pump. It was an unexpected major challenge because the company was not doing nearly as well as I was lead to believe during my interviews with recruiter, John Carroll. The significant additional challenge was the lack of a cooperative management team and new product development. Management direction was sorely lacking far beyond my expectations upon arrival. However, by slowly convincing the management members to become a team and work together, we overcame many issues and problems and became very successful.

CHAPTER SEVENTEEN
Making Time for Family

B ecoming a father can be discussed and talked about but it cannot not be completely understood or appreciated through some detached conversation. It's the experience that counts!

Back in the 1960s, hospitals and doctors had very different ideas about the birthing process even to the point of making the mother-to-be decide beforehand on the one person who could visit her room during the hospital stay. It was a terrible situation for the mother, the father and the in-laws as well. Why did there have to be one choice? Ridiculous, certainly! Especially when you see the attitudes and circumstances with which childbirth is now handled in the hospitals. How time changes things.

I was in my last year of college when my first-born made her entry into this world. The pregnancy was not planned. In fact, neither of our children was planned by us. Obviously, Bev and I didn't plan parenthood well, but God knew all along how it was to be. As it turned out, what we expected or wanted didn't really matter. God's gifts to us were welcomed indeed.

I can truthfully say that I have enjoyed my two daughters immensely from the days they arrived. I hated to see them grow up. I hated to see them leave home for college. I knew they would get married but I also knew they would never be coming home again on a permanent status in all probability. I liked having my daughters around. They were fun to be around. Life was never the same once they found their way to the university. But that too is part of the plan God has for our lives.

From the time they were young enough to understand playing games, we played a variety of table games. Both Leslie and Jacquie were very good competitors. One of the first games we played was *Memory*. It was a good exercise in developing a good memory because you had to recall the positioning of the two matching tiles. I never just let them win. They became very good at the game on their own initiative. Many times, they would beat me and they always beat their mom. It was a big event when either of them beat their dad. Other games included monopoly, checkers, dominos once in a while, and a variety of card games. One game, which I never could play very well was *Nerts*. I was too slow. Jacquie was very good at this game. She and her mother would almost always fight it out for the winning score. This still goes on to this day.

Working for Fleetwood Enterprises during their younger years, I had access to recreational vehicles, both motor homes and travel trailers. In fact, I bought a Terry travel trailer for camping purposes. Camping trips to the mountains and the beach area parks were very common and rather frequent. Many of these trips included the Ireland family. Because of my work, I usually came down on the weekend. Everybody seemed to enjoy the outdoors with Mother Nature and getting away from home routines. Trips were made to several state parks such as Doheny, San Juan Capistrano, Sequoia National Park, the local mountains, and down around Temecula, California.

Camping trips were not the only trips we took. As a family we were fortunate enough to have traveled in Europe and the Far East. Each trip had its own special times and events. Some made us laugh nearly deliriously while other situations led us to near tears. In Paris, while visiting the Eiffel Tower, Jacquie had to visit the restroom and unknowingly did not have any money on her person. When she was about to leave the restroom, a lady working in the facility wanted the equivalent of twenty-five cents for using a towel. The lady would not let Jacquie leave until she had deposited her passport. When she returned to us and told us the story, I was furious at both of them…the lady and Jacquie. I had heard about passports being stolen and that was my foreseen vision unfolding, whereas Jacquie and her mother just wanted to pay the lady and move on. We accomplished the latter.

On the same trip, we were visiting the Louvre, France's National Museum. I love museums and can spend considerable time enjoying the many attractions whether it is paintings, furniture, jewelry, or sculptures, especially from the antiquity periods. We began our tour in a wing filled with paintings. It was a long marble domed cavernous structure with brown leather sitting benches throughout with various artists' works beautifully displayed on the walls on each side of the hallway. This wing was perhaps a couple hundred feet long. Before too long, I noticed that the other family members were not observing the art with me. They seemed to have vanished. As I cast my eyes about the sparsely populated hallway, three small figures appeared to be resting and almost reclining on one of the benches at the very end of the wing. They had left me without even giving notice of their intentions. I thought our trip was to include some culture and learning but I learned it was more for entertainment.

We soon left the Louvre for other activities, including Notre Dame Cathedral, the Home of the French Foreign Legion, tomb of Napoleon, and the Arc of Triumph in our limited acculturation. And shopping, oh yes, on the Champs-Elysées, where else when you are in France! However, that experience was not as interesting or successful as the ladies had anticipated. The French clerks did not like or appreciate the Americans 'sorting and looking' through their racks of clothing as is done in the States. These workers were very disrespectful and impolite and it was obvious that they did not want to oblige or cooperate with us Americans, so we left to see and do other things. One aspect of our visit in France was wonderful French cuisine. Those who waited our tables seem to want to make our meal enjoyable and delightful. After some other less forgettable experiences with the French, we were most appreciative to leave the country.

In England, we viewed Buckingham Palace, saw the changing of the guard, toured Windsor Castle, visited the birthplace of William Shakespeare at Glen Upon Avon, viewed the royal Family Jewels display on the River Thames, and saw the House of Parliament. The highlight of the visit was to have lunch at Herrod's, the famous department store. I was more than surprised that shopping was not the highest priority since I had three females in tow!

Our lunch was to be a bit different than what we experienced in the states. Bev is adventuresome and is always seeking new foods and unique dishes; for me, I want to select something to eat that at least looks edible, appears as if it most probably would be tasty, and has some visual attraction with the presentation. Herrod's had four or five floors and on each floor was at least one place to eat. There was a very nice sit-down restaurant on the top floor, while the other dining areas were basically cafeteria style operations. Bev chose the cafeteria style eatery. I do not recall exactly what each of us ordered but it went something like this: Bev ordered an apricot pork loaf dish; turned out it was cold and the fat had congealed which formed part of the cooked pork loaf. She was not satisfied with her selection. It was terrible in fact. My two daughters ordered an Indian cooked turkey leg which was pink in color. They had not noticed until they sat down to eat that near the base of the leg of the fowl, the small pin feathers had not been removed. That ended their noticeable hunger immediately. I ordered something more Americanized even though I no longer recall the dish, perhaps it was a sandwich of sorts. I do vividly remember that all four of us ended up sharing my small meal and deciding that on trips of this nature, exploration definitely is what not to do in most foreign countries.

I spoke of visiting a castle. The fact is, we visited more than one. On our tour of one much less renown than the Windsor Castle, Bev was leading the hike, Jacquie, Leslie and I followed up the many stairs inside one of the turrets of the outer fortress wall in order to get an advantageous view at the top for some pictures. Behind and following us by perhaps a dozen stairs were five or six Orientals. Along the climb we noticed that the air was somewhat stale and very little ventilation except for a few infrequent peep holes. Leslie was having a gaseous problem that day and, unaware that the Asians were following so closely behind, she relieved herself much to my dismay. The polluted air caught up with us and caused us to speed the rate of climb to reach fresh air and avoid suffocation. The Asians soon encountered the gaseous chamber and began to chatter very loudly and quickly amongst themselves. At the top, we all cleared our lungs, breathed a sigh of great relief and Leslie was hilarious; she said she had 'paid me back' for my past such sins foisted on her in certain circumstances. Meanwhile, the Asians exited the turret and continued to obviously reflect upon their experience inside the turret which made all of us react more so for having caused the turmoil among eight to ten people. We never forgot the occasion and I'm certain the Asians didn't either!

A few years later, and prior to the Chinese taking over Hong Kong and Macao and just prior to Jacquie's wedding to Alan Aufhammer, the family decided to make a trip to Hong Kong and see some of the Orient. We invited Alan to accompany us on the trip along with another friend to keep Leslie company. This trip would be more or less a shopping spree than a sight seeing adventure. We had many fun times trying on clothes and jewelry and looking at the variety of merchandise the stores offered. I think Leslie maxed out her credit cards but did not regret any aspect of shopping until afterwards when she had to pay them off! As a group we sampled the Chinese dumplings and other short order foods. We especially enjoyed a dinner one evening in a restaurant where locals dined. The establishment was in what appeared to be a dingy sort of place upstairs and off the local street. We were told the food was very good so we decided to go for it. As we neared the top of the stairs, waiters were passing through double swinging doors as rapidly as they could maneuver with trays of food that had obviously been cooked in another area. At first we were skeptical but through limited English and sign language we were seated in the very crowded dining area. The floors were wooden, things seemed to be clean but it didn't compare to a classy restaurant in the U.S. We noticed as we waited to place our orders with the waiter the many trays of roast duck that were constantly coming out of the swinging doors. That was the special of the evening so we decided to go with the flow and had an extremely enjoyable meal and evening. Everything was very delicious, as we had been told it would be.

During our stay, we took the hydroplane boat, which ferried about two hundred or more people between Hong Kong and Portuguese held Macao, which was really a gambling center.

Thereafter, we bussed and crossed into the southern part of mainland China and toured for a day. We visited a school and a three-story concrete open-air market place. The school was named in honor of Dr. Sun Yat Sin, a famous educator of his time. It was obvious that they didn't have the modern conveniences of the American classrooms. The market was especially different. There wasn't any refrigeration to keep meats and other products. Animals, particularly chickens, were kept alive until slaughtered. It was dirty and appeared unclean throughout but it was the best they had apparently. The floors all had drains in the cement so when the day was over, everything was hosed down with water and left to dry until the next day when the scene was repeated. The water from all the building just drained onto the dirt and ground outside the building. We were glad to be returning to Hong Kong later that evening. It was an eye-opening experience for all of us, and made us appreciate what we have in the good old United States of America!

Leslie Ann (Moudy) Collins

You were my first born!

Leslie was the first grandchild for my parents and the second grandchild for Beverly's parents, Rubye and Earl Humphrey.

Because of the hospital visitation limitations, and because I was still in college, we decided that it was probably best to have Rubye, your grandmother, be the selected visitor to the hospital during your mother's stay. Her parents lived in Riverside and were relatively close by the hospital. At the time, we were living in Rialto, which was about ten miles north of Riverside. Even though I would have preferred to have been able to visit at the hospital, there weren't any other choices.

We had chosen to live in an apartment in Rialto after we married for at least two reasons. First, it was close to Bev's work at California Electric Power Company. Secondly, it was within easy commuting distance to California Polytechnic State University near Pomona, California, about twenty-five miles to the west.

As the time drew near for Leslie's birth, I became even more excited, thinking how great it would be if we could share the same birthday. We could celebrate our birthdays together. I'm sure that part of the reason I felt that way was because my Uncle Lee Moudy and I had the same birthday, October 6. For whatever reasons, we had always had a special bond between us and I attributed at least some of that to our sharing the same birth date.

As a new-dad-to-be, I never worried about Leslie's birth. I seemed to have a calmness about the coming event that everything would go well. My primary hope was that she would be born healthy; that she would be a perfectly sound baby, and that there would not be any complications. Thank the good Lord, that's the way it happened.

It was late in the afternoon on Sunday, when your mother reported that it was time to go to the hospital. Your mother said the one thing she remembers was that I did not want to miss classes so, therefore, she had to have you on a weekend. Leslie was born on October 8, 1961 at about 7:40 p.m. Dr. Robert R. Johnson was the attending physician. Unfortunately, a few years later, Dr. Johnson was to die in a small airplane crash.

Attending school everyday meant that I got to 'baby-sit' you when I got home while your mother finished preparing dinner. That was really 'play time'. You were a truly delightful baby and loved very deeply. I loved to lay you on my thighs and knees and gently bounce you, and talk to you, and tickle you so that you would begin to coo and laugh out loud to my delight! In fact, you would almost laugh so much that it would almost reach a point of being out of control. We had a ball almost every night. Oh, how I loved you!!! You were a very good baby. No fussiness; just a good natured little lady! You brought a lot of joy to our lives.

Taking care of you was never a problem because your mother and I shared duties such as diapering, feeding and bathing you. We took you to church virtually every Sunday. Quite often, we would visit with friends after church or go to 'Nana's and Popee's' home for lunch. We always enjoyed showing you off to anyone who took time and would listen. We never grew tired of having you in our lives.

I began to teach you things very early and needless to say, you were an excellent mimic. The first thing I taught you was how to make a buzzing sound by putting your lips together and forcing air and spit through them. You always made me laugh when you did it at first. I was to regret that later when you demonstrated it for me while I was feeding you baby food (green beans). You covered my face and most of my shirt with a big mouth full so much so that I had to stop and clean myself up before continuing with your meal. After you did it, you were so proud of yourself! You just smiled at me as if to say, "Dad, I did it just like you showed me!" You were very proud of yourself. For a split second, it wasn't a smiling or laughing matter…but then it was after a minute or so. Your mother cracked up at what had happened when she looked at me and saw you smiling. I must give her credit, she did help me get cleaned up and wiped my face off.

You weighed in at 6 pounds 9½ ounces and were 19 inches long. Not a big baby but a nice size. I'm sure your mother appreciated that fact. You carried a lot of baby fat and were a plump little girl with rolls about your legs and arms. You had a chubby little face too. We thought you were the cat's meow!

Both of your grandparents were very proud of you. Your Nana and Popee got to see you more than my parents who lived in Oxnard, almost a two hour drive from our home. That made me feel badly because I wanted you to have a good relationship with your Grandma and Grandpa Moudy. Grandparents had been a great influence in my life and I wanted you to be able to enjoy that aspect of life as I had early in my life with my parents as well as your mother's parents. It wasn't until 1968 that you really had a chance to spend any time with them. That was the year they moved from Oxnard to Pomona to live in the mobile home. By this time, you were already seven years old and I felt that they had missed your 'baby years' and the love and influence they might have had on you. As a grandparent, you become very aware about the importance your influence can have on your grandchildren. The early years are the most formative years of a child's life. Whatever is taught or passed along at that time lasts for a lifetime! I know that because of my own Grandfather Talley. His time with me was relatively short, but he made a huge and lasting impression on me. Things that remain in my memory to this day are things that I recall he did with me when I was only four and five years old.

Since I have had a penchant for learning, it was always fun to see you learn new things. Your very first step! Wow! Either your mother or I would hold your hands up and help you to walk at first. Then the day came when you thought you could do it on your own. You took your first step, teetered for a moment, and decided to sit down and think things over again. We were very happy to see you doing that because you had a problem with your hip sockets when you were born. They were not completely formed so you had to wear a metal bar brace that caused your legs to stick straight out and spread apart. It was our first encounter with a possible serious problem. The diagnosis was correct and the treatment worked perfectly so you were able to discard the brace after a few months. It gave you an advantage that very few other people have…you can sit on your own feet tucked under you and turned toes-in without pain. No one else in our family can do that like you do! It still looks painful to me whenever I have seen you do that.

When Jacquie came to our house, you didn't know what to make of her but you didn't like her. In fact, you wanted to know from your mother if Jacquie could go back to the hospital or from wherever she had come! Jacquie had the colic and cried a lot, sometimes seemingly for hours almost non-stop. We carried her on our shoulder, we cuddled her, your mother would sing to her; we would run out of options and because she was tired and worn out, she would fall asleep. Those were trying times for all of us and I'm sure for you especially. Eventually, with a little coaxing, you accepted her. I have been most fortunate; now there were two very precious little girls whom I idolized. Still do!

Since dads are not usually into dolls, I subconsciously tried to get you to play with trucks and other toys more than the prissy little girl things that are generally the focus of your attention at that age. The take was not effective, however, and you never became a tomboy. I was glad that you didn't because that was never my goal.

As a boy, I had several dogs and I thought it would be good for you and Jacquie to have a pet to play with and learn to love and enjoy as I had. Both you and Jacquie were scared to death of any animal, cat or dog, regardless of how small they were in size. If there was a big dog around, the two of you were absolutely terrified! We had a neighbor in Diamond Bar, California, where we bought our first house (2315 Tellgate Drive), who lived across the street. That lady was Nancy Rhinehart. She was a nice lady but could be rather vociferous at times on our little short cul-de-sac. Nancy bred miniature poodles and our thought was that would be an ideal dog for the two of you…small, could live inside and you'd learn to play with and love the dog and get used to animals.

When Nancy was ready for us to make our pick of the litter, we went over and saw the puppies. One was larger than the rest. He obviously was the first one to eat his dinner every day and probably was nursed the most. Nancy called him 'Sherman.' I don't know why she called him that but I assumed it had an association with a Sherman tank…he pushed his way to the food before the others in the litter. When we got Sherman home, we decided that we didn't want that name for the dog. You and Jacquie decided that a good name would be 'Pepe.' That's how Pepe got his name and that was a good name for a miniature French poodle. At first, you and Jacquie were a little afraid of Pepe even though he was so small. To the two of you, he might as well have been a Great Dane! You didn't like him 'nosing around' and putting his cold wet nose on your legs or hands. You sort of wanted to pet him but that was a bit strange. In a short time, you did adjust to him. You and Jacquie became good buddies with Pepe. He was you first pet.

Pepe was not an ordinary dog. He became a member of the family. He got special food and never had to eat table scraps. For me personally, I had never before had a 'house dog'. All of my dogs lived outside. Being a poodle, Pepe didn't shed hair and he was clean. We grew very attached to him and he lived for almost seventeen years. He had become diabetic and he died of an overdose of insulin. We buried him in that backyard of our home at 1679 Quince way in Upland. I dug a grave for him and we put his favorite little red doggie sweater on him and laid him to rest. It was a sad day or two before we carried on without thinking about him as much. We all cried when he died!

You were three years old when we moved to Diamond Bar in October of 1964. We had been living in Sierra Madre after leaving Rialto because I was working for Arthur Andersen & Co. in downtown Los Angeles. Within a short time, we moved to Pasadena on East Washington Avenue. Your mother worked for the Jet Propulsion Laboratory in Pasadena. Judy McEachern would baby-sit you while we worked. During this time, we began to attend the Pasadena Brezee Nazarene Church. On one occasion, you became very ill and ran a very high fever. We took you to the hospital because we couldn't get it under control. You were in the hospital for several days and lots of our church friends prayed for your recovery and came to the hospital to visit you. We were scared. Over a period of a few days, you began to improve after responding to the treatment and finally we were able to bring you home. It was frightful having to leave you at the hospital at night. We worried about you constantly. The good Lord was with you and we were so thankful that He saw fit to give you back to us. That was in 1964.

Judy McEchern was Roger's wife at the time. They were long time residents of Pasadena. Roger and I were classmates at Cal Poly. We maintained our friendship when Arthur Andersen & Co hired us both. He was hired into the Small Business Audit Department. They had two children, Randy and Susan. Several years later they would relocate to Boulder, Colorado. Still later, they would divorce and Roger returned to California and worked with me at Transierra Exploration Corporation. A few years later when that was no longer a viable position, I invited him to come to Wilden Pump and Engineering Co. as the Controller. Roger and I have been good friends in excess of forty-five years. He married Leah after his divorce and now lives in Glenwood Springs, Colorado.

It was in Diamond Bar where Leslie first went to school at age five. The school was just a few blocks up the street, Sunset Crossing Road. You would walk with your mother to school every day. Your best friend was Julie Inman. You two were bosom buddies and almost constant companions. Often you two ganged up on your little sister to mistreat her, exclude her from your games or cause chaos of some kind. That caused Jacquie a lot of consternation and dismay. You and Julie were about the same age. It was during the time we lived here that Julie's mother died. Fred, Julie's father, worked as a Los Angeles City motorcycle policeman. He usually worked from mid-afternoon until late into the evening. As a result of his schedule, your mother baby-sat Julie everyday. It was like she was practically a part of our family. We fed her; she spent the evenings with us, and then went to bed. A few hours later her father would come home from work and pick her up out of bed and take her home, which was just down the block.

When there was a special occasion or event, such as Mother's Day or Easter, you needed a new dress. Your mother spent considerable time searching for the same dress in the sizes that would fit both of you. Finding the identical dresses was sometimes difficult for two reasons. First you were a blond and Jacquie had red hair so color that suited your mother for both of you caused extensive shopping. Secondly, the two of you were three years apart so there needed to be two different sizes. You can see in some of your childhood pictures what I am talking about. After all was said and done, you both always made me very proud because I knew that both of you looked beautiful! There was never any doubt on these occasions as to you being sisters or that you belonged to the same family. No matter where we would go, people would always make comments about how nice and pretty you both looked. You were two beautiful daughters and loved dearly. In fact, I knew that the two of you were the apple of my eye!

Early on, Nana and Popee always stated that they only wanted girls in the family. In my mind, that was Popee's way of paying back the world for the fact that he never had a son. Perhaps I was wrong in this revelation. As time went on, he convinced me that he truly liked having only girls around. I still believe, however, if he had of had a son, he would have loved him just as much as he did his daughters and grand-daughters. Obviously, he and Nana were pleased to have their sons-in-laws keep the record intact of only having girls in the family. That string was only broken when you and your sister had your children!

You were always an excellent student throughout your school years beginning in grammar school through the university. You took school seriously and tried to do whatever your teachers told you to do. To me, it seemed that you overloaded in terms of studying your homework assignments. I think you knew the answers backwards and forward. But you were certainly conscientious about it and got good grades. Things that affected you were tests and having to give oral reports in your classroom. That was definitely nervous and queasy stomach time. You would fret for days over upcoming tests or if you had to make a presentation in front of your class. I don't think that ever changed for you throughout your entire formal education process.

I liked to tease you. When I would take you to school, particularly junior high, I would let you out where all of your friends were hanging out. You'd take a few steps from the car and I would honk the horn sometimes and wave good-bye to you. I thought it was funny because it embarrassed you so much! You didn't like it because your friends all laughed and you, in fact, did feel embarrassed. I really didn't know why it embarrassed you because I took you to school in my 911 Porsche or the new Cadillac. Those were snazzy cars in those days!

I think one of your most disappointing experiences was in Upland High School when you tried out for cheerleader. You have always been somewhat reserved about yourself particularly when in public...not as much when you were among friends. You practiced your routines and had them down pretty well. In fact, I thought that you would make the team. As fate would have it, you didn't. I felt your disappointment. Your mother had gone down to watch the tryouts. She was sure that the judges were highly prejudiced. It was not a good day on that occasion.

During your early dating years, your boyfriend was Jeff Thrasher. You met him at church since his family attended Pomona First Baptist also. He was a handsome young man with dark hair and a great smile. His family lived in Diamond Bar. I think you dated Jeff for all your years in high school. He was a very likeable person from your parents' viewpoint. However, as you neared the completion of high school, our concern was simply that Jeff didn't seem to have your drive or initiative. We did not believe that on that basis you would be a happy young lady if you were to get serious with him. You had such a strong desire and expectation to go to dental hygiene school and get a degree. Jeff had not found his direction in life yet. As it turned out, you went off to college and eventually decided that there were other fish in the sea to catch.

It is a fact that you seemed to always know what you wanted to do for a career even when you entered high school as a freshman. That was, you planned on becoming a dental hygienist. You never wavered from that objective. That was most unusual for a young lady in high school to have made such a choice at such a young age and stick with it. I was always proud of you for such discretion and conviction. You had a real knack for medical terms and terminology. Your science classes seemed to be a delightful experience. I'm not saying that they were not difficult. They were. You just seemed to thrive on all science topics. It was impressive for me to see that you were so dedicated to your course of study. I was always so proud of you in that regard. I was never in that position as a young man at your age to know exactly with such certainty what career path I wanted to follow. Your successful professional studies always made me think that you could have, if you wanted and had the desire, become a doctor of dentistry. I recall talking to you about it. Your response was simply that you didn't want the responsibility of it. That was a very meaningful answer for me. You had accomplished what you set out to do and you had achieved. So why continue your efforts when you wanted to begin a new life after college! I am so very proud of you, Leslie.

Throughout your time at the university, you met Mike Banducci, who was in dental school studying to become a doctor. You hooked up with him during your final two years at USC and continued dating and working for him after you graduated for some time. Mike's family was of Italian ancestry and his mother, from comments you made to us, did not want Mike to marry anyone who was not Italian. Ethnicity was never a strong issue for your mother and me in terms of who you and Jacquie dated or would possibly marry. We wanted the best for you and the few times we were with you and Mike we did not see him caring for you in a way that made us believe that he cared for you in such a way as to make for a good marriage. We just never thought Mike was the man for you. We weren't trying to tell you whom you should pick for a mate, but we were more than a little bit concerned. It was not an especially calm and settling time in your mother's and my life.

You and Mike parted ways and the search was on for Mr. Lucky. It wasn't exactly your cup of tea to be on the prowl, so to speak, but you found your way. Jacquie had already gotten married and for some reason I was beginning to feel that was putting pressure on you. It was just an observation I had and I didn't want you to feel that way.

After some period of time of working, purchasing your own car, and feeling the freedom from school and having your independence, you found Don Collins, a handsome young man full of energy and pursuing a business

The Collins Family
Left – right: Leslie, Mackrnzie, Donovan, Kiley & Don (standing)
September 2000

career in the bond trading market. Before too long, you two decided to make your relationship permanent. The two of you have three beautiful children and needless to say they are half of the apples of your mother and father's eyes. There is Donovan Roark, Kiley Elisabeth and Mackenzie Nicole.

A few years after Don and Leslie were married, he was having a conversation with his mother-in-law, during which she apparently got on the subject about the best day of his life. It probably caught him off-guard because his response became a point for which he has often been reminded. He had encountered the curse of 'not thinking before speaking' and knowing your audience. Don didn't stammer or stutter when he answered without a hint of hesitation in his voice, blurting out "Well, it wasn't the day that I got married! You know, girls grow up thinking about that day all their lives, but boys don't." Without letting him gather his thoughts because he could see he had made a near fatal mistake and was turning several shades of red with embarrassment when Leslie chimed in with, "Well, thanks a lot!" They were not smiling back at him. He could plainly see that his *faux pas* had not set well with the two females. I don't recall having heard any of his additional comments or even if he tried to make amends that day. It was probably best that he not further complicate the issue without additional deliberate and considered thought. Who knows what Don was thinking that could compare with the day that he got married? Perhaps, he wasn't thinking! Maybe he was trying to recall a high volume day in the bond market or the crossing of the finish line in a competitive sailing race, a water skiing feat he pulled off, a big fish he hooked or something else of small importance, who knows? He was in with the barracudas now! Immediately, Bev challenged him on his recital and inquired why it was not the day that he and Leslie were married? The price for his *faux pas* has been and continues to prey on him even to this day. It will forever or until she dies. His loving mother-in-law will not let him forget, since it re-enters their conversations with infrequent regularity.

Leslie, you have always been a special part of life ever since you came into our lives. You are special as an individual to me, your mother and your family and you will always be!

Jacquelyn Denise Moudy

"Jacquie", she announced one day, not "Jackie", was the way she wanted to spell her nickname and what she wanted to be called as her own unique moniker. That didn't really surprise anyone in our family. Jacquie was full of life, one way or another, beginning the day she was born at the Huntington Memorial Hospital in Pasadena, California. The exact date was February 8, 1964. She was most welcomed by the family when she arrived. She was a beautiful little lady but with one more main reason being simply that she had red hair. That was indeed an important family tradition for her maternal grandmother's side on the Wood family. It seems they had been blessed with redheads for many generations…so Jacquie didn't let them down!

For years I thought Jacquie was named for Jacquelyn Kennedy, the wife of Jack Kennedy, President of the United States. Jacquelyn was a very popular First Lady. She was noted for her fashion and trend setting style while she was living in the White House. She was constantly in the newspapers with some new designer dress, hairstyle or new hat. Later I learned the truth of the matter only to find out that her name was selected by her mother simply because she liked that name. That was a good reason but was not quite as noteworthy as I had imagined it to be earlier.

The day you were born was very exciting. I was hoping for almost the same result with Jacquie's birth as I did with Leslie. That is, I was hoping that she would be born on either my mother's or my father's birthday since they were both in February. She arrived the day before my mother's birthday. It was obvious that she was showing her independence even before she came out of the womb. Well now, within our immediate family, we could really have a birthday party and celebration with three dates in February!

In short order, we were to learn that Jacquie had colic, or something very similar, from the day she was born. This ailment was to stay with her for the next six months. It was a difficult time for this little baby girl. Needless to say, it had its affects on the other members of the household as well. She finally out grew the problem and it was certainly none too soon! Now she was able to resume a modicum of normal babyhood. During all this time of her irritation, it seemed to bother Leslie. She inquired more than once about the possibility of returning Jacquie to the place she came from, wherever that happened to be. Fortunately for all of us, including you, we were able to live a more conventional life subsequently.

It was only about eight months after your birth that we decided to buy our very first home. We chose a Dean Developer home in Diamond Bar, California. We needed the room with two children and a collection of meager belongings that was growing with every birthday and each Christmas. The move seemed to bode well for our Jacquie. She began to grow by seemingly leaps and bounds. Besides that, it was becoming most apparent that you were a complete and incredible bundle full of energy from the time you awoke in the morning until the clock had ticked your bedtime. Lethargic was never going to be a part of your vocabulary or action level! Everything you did was with a high degree of energy and enthusiasm. There wasn't anything that frightened you to the point of blunting your spirit so as to keep you from trying or actually doing anything. It gave me passing thoughts about a dare devil mentality and I was hopeful that you would never reach a stage of 'dare you to do anything' because I was convinced you would at least try it!

At the age of four, you were given, along with Leslie, a new pair of tennis shoes. The brand name was *Jumping Jacks*. That was just the ticket for you. You must have thought that you were superwoman when you had them on. You would jump and jump and then jump some more! You always needed an audience so when I was home you engaged me for extended sessions of jumping. You wanted me to see you jump far. You wanted me to see you jump high. You used our terrazzo entry as your runway for practicing. The entry-way was about four inches high off the living room and kitchen floor and probably four feet wide with an iron railing on one side and the wall on the other. To watch you, I had to sit in a chair near the dining room (combo kitchen) table. That was your idea because you wanted me to see the entire action. You usually liked to jump high first so you would start jumping over and over again thinking you were really jumping very high. You were a pogo stick of sorts. You made me laugh!

Many times Leslie would be a spectator but most of the time she was a participant too. Even if your mother was preparing dinner, you often called her attention to your performance, with the command, "Watch me!" You never seemed to run out of energy just jumping. I'm sure your best effort produced a high jump of at least four or five inches off the floor but it might as well have been six feet! When you really got wound up, you would get so excited and yell and scream with your little voice at its highest pitch. You would have so much fun that Leslie would join in too. Pepe, our dog, wanted to participate too. He didn't fully appreciate what was going on so the result was most often he would get in the way and you would shoo him away. He never stayed away too long because everybody was having fun except for mom in the kitchen and she was busy. After jumping high, it was time to run and jump far as if you were doing the long jump in a track event. Believe it or not, your longest jump was probably two feet off the end of the terrazzo. I always had to see your entire performance, you made sure of that. Those were great times which I will never forget!

Your Dad didn't want to leave you out of the boy toy items, so I bought you a truck just like I did for Leslie. For whatever reason, you just never had a liking for them as your sister did. At an early age, it was obvious that you were very sharp and quick to learn almost anything. Along with that sharpness came your emotional roller coasters. One minute everything was okay. In a matter of a few seconds that could all change and disaster reigned on your little world. When you were happy, you were on the top of the mountain. When unhappiness struck, you and Chicken Little held hands and watched the sky fall on you both! That ruined your parade to say the least. I have to say however, that as quickly as the weather changed for you, it could easily get back to 'normal' in short order. The emotional outburst was usually over as quickly as it had arrived. Never having been around redheads very much, I attributed those antics to being high strung and high tempered as redheads had been depicted in comics, movies, and elsewhere. That seemed like a legitimate explanation to me. What else could it be? After all, I had learned to cope with your mother slamming cupboard doors when she boiled over!

It became obvious very early that you were exceptionally sharp mentally. I liked to say that you were as sharp as a tack. You had a sense of alertness so that very little escaped your perception. You seemed to have the ability to anticipate things as well. You also had superb hearing. It seemed that you could hear sounds that none of the rest of us could hear. Even though you were very young, it was evident that you needed to have a lot of action going simultaneously. That fact was a bit disconcerting to us, your parents, for a while until you were tested as a teenager and the results explained to us. Your mother and I took you to the Johnson O'Conner Research Foundation in Los Angeles for testing. It turned out that you were the kind of person who needed four or five projects going on simultaneously in order to function well. Many people don't even handle one project at a time well, but you were different. Even today, that is part of your personality and it has bode well for you. I just don't know how you do all that you choose to do! I think it is a great attribute for you and makes you very unique.

You enjoyed competition; and, as a result, you were a great competitor. When you had a chance to do something that would be difficult for someone your age, it was like, "Give me a shot at it!" By the time you were age four, our family was heavy into the game *Memory*. You, Leslie and I had very good memories. The keen competition made the games close between us. Your mother was almost certain to score dead last. Regardless, when it was time to play, she was a good sport and joined in and had fun participating and watching you and Leslie play if nothing else. The older you and Leslie became, the more competitive the games were each time. Your mother liked to say that 'Dad always won.' That wasn't true. What she should have said was simply that I didn't let you win…you earned it! Indeed, there were many times when you or Leslie would win. When that happened, it brought on this big celebration. Those were really fun times and are some of the activities that are my fondest memories. What was really interesting was that you never once complained that all of the family members were older than you. It seemed that you liked the game, too, because you were always ready to play any time the game was brought out.

Your mother began your charm school lessons early. Before we would go anyplace, your mother took the time to make sure you were dressed properly. Then it was time to comb your hair and then get the curling iron out and put some 'curlies' in it. This was the start of your beautification and charm school, I guess. Proper dress was very important to your mother. She wanted you to be well dressed and groomed for each and every occasion. I also think you liked the recognition it brought to you as well. Polishing of your social skills began when you joined the National Charity League. During the three or four years of high school, you and your mother spent a lot of time together attending different functions and events. You seemed to like that sort of activity while Leslie didn't.

You were more than ready when the time came for you to start school. There wasn't any apprehension or hesitation about going. You didn't like it when Leslie got to go to school and you couldn't. You just couldn't understand why you couldn't go to school the day that Leslie started kindergarten. When your day came, you were more than just excited; it was a great and joyous day! An occasion to be remembered!

There wasn't any doubt that you loved school. You must have done what your teachers told you to do because your teachers generally liked to have you in their classes. At least early on that was the case. Then there were those few teachers that made comments later from time to time that seemed to indicate to us that you intimidated them somehow even at your young age. That seemed ridiculous and amusing to me. Why couldn't a professionally trained adult teacher cope with an obviously ambitious grammar school child? You were not misbehaving at all; you were simply exercising your inquisitive and inquiring mind. That's what you are supposed to do in school…learn!

It seemed that the teachers were frustrated at your insistence on getting answers. This was particularly true in your fifth and sixth grade classes. After a while, it was rather apparent that your teacher had a personality clash with you probably because of your astuteness and strength academically.

You were a very good student and took your studies seriously. In elementary school, almost every year, you would be tested for the accelerated academic education programs. It wasn't until high school and college that you actually participated in those fast paced special learning classes and programs. You always made your grades and succeeded in achieving a high grade point average. Your academic accomplishments made me very proud of you. From your father's point of view, you were truly a gifted young lady and you learned very quickly. That was important to me since I had to work hard to get my grades and even then I could never seem to get much higher than a B+ average as a student in high school and college. Attending the 'open house' each year was always a joy; we knew that your teachers and instructors would give us a good academic report. Your efforts carried on through high school and the university.

Having friends was socially important to you. You had the ability to attract many of them. Other kids were attracted to you as well. You had more friends than I could shake a stick at. You brought them home with you from school beginning at an early age and that trend continued through high school. Your mother enjoyed that activity because it meant that she could prepare treats of one kind or another, mostly fresh baked cookies, for you and your friends almost every day. Generally, you had three or four kids with you when you arrived at the house and had something planned for the group to do. I was hardly ever home at that time but when I was, I knew you were having a good time from all the screams, shrill sounds, and laughter being made by everyone.

In 1970, we moved from Diamond Bar to Upland to an old landmark home located at 2370 North Euclid Avenue. It was an old craftsman home built in 1920. Our family had become acquainted with the Ireland family through church. In a short period of time, Michelle Ireland had become your bosom buddy and best friend. The two of you were basically glued at the hip. Your mother and Elaine Ireland, Michelle's mother, had also found a special friendship and become virtually inseparable when they weren't busy. This friendship resulted in the two families doing many things together, including shopping, going to the beach for the day, having vacations together including a trip to Mexico, going to Palm Springs for a day in the sun, spending a week at the beach in our travel trailer and sometimes just hanging out together. When there were events or activities that only the parents could attend, we had baby sitters for all of you children together. The time period was from about 1968 through about 1975 or 1976.

You knew that I liked sports and I think you pushed yourself to become interested and involved in part to please me. That was a good reason, if it was true, because I was proud of you for making the effort. Sports on TV didn't interest you, however.

As a junior high school student, you decided that you wanted to play soccer in the local city recreational league. I thought it was great but admittedly, it surprised me. Soccer involved a lot of running and required physical stamina. I thought that would be good for you. Every Saturday morning during the season you had a game. I'd go down and watch you play. You seemed to enjoy the sport and played hard. You had never done anything like that before and after the season was over didn't engage in this kind of activity again. Your involvement made your father very proud of you. After each game, I'd take you home dead tired and exhausted. Once in the house, you'd head straight for the big over stuffed chair in the den and sort of curl up and rather quickly fall sound a sleep for an hour or two. That was your recovery time. At the end of the season, you gave me a three-inch picture badge with you in your purple uniform. I still have it. It was my reward, or trophy, and I considered it very special. Attached to the button was a white ribbon imprinted with the words, "That's My Girl". I will always cherish that badge!

During your high school years, you continued your interest and involvement in sports in the sense that you tried out for the Cheer Leading Team. It was just a super exciting time when you learned that you had made the team. Your mother and I attended all of the try-out sessions at the gymnasium. I was so proud of you! I was very happy for you and thought it was so neat because you had tried so hard to practice and you had to make up your own routine. There were your 'yells', steps and jumps and all the other elements of your program. You practiced with other classmates who were also trying out. During those hours of working things out there were lots of laughs, yelling, and squealing all done with the high pitched voices that girls have at that age in our back yard. The vocal activity brought about by going over the routines many times would reach a crescendo when one or more missed some cues now and then. I think I even recall an argument or two. I know for a fact that some of you took some hard falls occasionally and you had your share. The one I specifically remember was the one where you cracked your elbow very hard and injured yourself. That didn't stop you for long. You really put things together well and I definitely felt that you did deserve to be selected. It was really extraordinary to say the least. That was a special time so vividly etched in my memory.

I mentioned earlier your need to stay busy. It was easy for you to have several projects or activities going on simultaneously. In fact you were bored if you didn't. You excelled under those conditions. That type of environment was unique to you. Your non-stop conduct made us become concerned for your health, so we made an appointment to have you tested in Los Angeles relating to your personality traits and interests. The test results, the counselor indicated, showed that you did need to have multiple projects going and that was the 'norm' for you. As parents we thought you were just pushing yourself too hard and more or less 'driving yourself into the ground'. This information changed our entire outlook. I thought what an incredible characteristic to have in one's repertoire! That testing had brought long sought answers and understanding regarding your high level of energy. It has stayed with you amazingly, even through today. It may not be quite as evident as it once was but the action still continues. You are an amazing woman! Your father still likes to give advice, and here it is…don't push yourself too hard or too far, you are not as young as you used to be, you know!

All young people have romances, boys and girls. You had your share in high school. I know because your mother and I lived through them. There were several tough times for your father to say the least simply because you were my daughter. Fathers see their little girls as they grow up and they always think of the need to protect them from the 'enemy.' Who is the enemy…any male. Dads have to try hard to accept the fact that their daughters will be going out on dates. I think you attended every dance and party while you were in high school. When there was a costume party, you always had creative ideas about what to wear whether you were in character or out. Most every event meant that you had to create a theme or idea for you and your date and dress accordingly. You always demonstrated your imaginative results with verve, creativeness and enthusiasm.

It was so exciting when you received that phone call at 10:00 p.m. on a Saturday evening and someone at the University was calling to inform you that a scholarship was waiting for you. What made it highly motivat-

Left – right: Claire, Jacquelyn, Alan, Collin & William Aufhammer
with Chocolate Labs – Talley and Woody
November 2004

ing was simply that you had not applied for a scholarship, The University's computer had run your grades through the system and you popped out as qualified academically for the scholarship! You were also invited to take an accelerated course of study in literature in which you enrolled and seemed to thoroughly enjoy it even though there was a lot of work involved.

It was that sad day when we took you to the campus of the University of Southern California. Our baby daughter was off to college. That left two empty nester parents who missed you greatly. Our house was very empty for a long time as the adjustment took place.

Once your studies were completed, in reality, you didn't come back home. You made an extended effort to find work in a financial position in the Los Angeles area. It became a discouraging time in your life since offers weren't piling up at your front door. Your mother and I encouraged you as much as we could. I know that didn't make it any easier but I commend you for never giving up your effort. After some thirty-six interviews, you were hired by Public Storage, Inc. Your career in business did not last too long because you had met Alan Aufhammer before graduating and the wedding bells tolled soon thereafter.

One of the most memorable times of my life was when you called me up to ask, "Dad, would you be upset with me if I quit work?" I believe that it was after you and Alan had gotten married. Without comment, I was surprised in a sense by your question but I appreciated you asking and your sincerity. You further explained that you knew that a lot of money had been spent on your education. Even so, your mother and I would always opt for your happiness and so I replied that, "It's okay with me so long as you and Alan can afford to do it!"

You and Alan have given us three wonderful grandchildren. They make up the other half of the sparkles in our eyes. We love them dearly beginning with Collin Littlepage, Claire Hamilton and William Roark. We are indeed blessed.

You were loved when you arrived, you were loved during the good times and the not so good, and today you are still loved, more than ever, and you will always be loved. You are a very special and beautiful lady! I love you deeply!

CHAPTER EIGHTEEN

Niches of Special Interest—
My Hobbies

All of us develop areas of interest during our lifetimes that we enjoy. These areas can cause us to have an extreme desire to pursue a particular subject for a period of time and then in some instances, interest can wane almost as rapidly as it came. Other times that special subject may prove to last a lifetime. I have always enjoyed new areas of interest. Many of these areas could have become my avocation such as my flying airplanes and geology.

Gardening

There has never been a time in my life when I did not enjoy gardening. I say that even though in more recent years I have done very little of it. As a child, my mother and dad always made a vegetable garden. We lived in some cramped places where space for any kind of gardening was at a premium. It didn't matter how little space, my mother had to at least plant flowers even if there wasn't room for vegetables. I think she got the interest from having lived on the farm. She would get my dad involved with gardening too, although I never thought he enjoyed it like she did. Once he got into the job of gardening each year, he would become energetic about tending and caring for the growing plants. He made sure the garden was watered, fertilized, and the weeds were cut down.

When I was in my teen years, we lived in the El Rio community near Oxnard. This area, then, was as rural as you could find in the Ventura-Oxnard area. The houses were built with large lots maybe as much as an acre. Our rental house was small and didn't take up a lot of the property so that left an enormous area for gardening. Down in the back part of the property, I had large cages with built-in nests so I could raise pigeons. I think I inherited them when we moved in. So, when the desire struck to have fresh squab for dinner, I would just go down and take two or three and dress them so my mother could cook them. The accumulated manure was used for fertilizer in the garden.

My parents had as much as a half acre devoted to gardening. Each year, many rows of corn, cabbage, cucumbers, peppers, banana and zucchini squash, radishes, tomatoes, sweet potatoes, beets, red potatoes, and green beans were planted. My dad would get up early in the morning and begin sprinkler irrigation. It took a long time to water such a large garden. He would water one section for an extended time with the big rain bird sprinkler. Then he'd shut the water off and move the sprinkler to a new area and continue the process until the entire garden had been adequately watered. It might take as long as a couple of days so it was a slow process 'to do it right.' The weather in Oxnard was generally cool and that helped tremendously by allowing the water to soak into the ground and refresh the growing plethora of plants. Some of the vegetables would grow so plentifully that we gave relatives and neighbors a lot of the crop. Even then, my dad would place some of the produce in lug boxes on an old wooden table next to the road and people would come by, see the little signs, stop and purchase the vegetables on the honor system.

My mother and dad would spend hours upon hours in the kitchen each year as the various crops were harvested. They made chow-chow from the cucumbers, peppers and green tomatoes. The corn would be pulled when it was ready, cutoff the cob and cooked with seasonings or made into creamed corn. Food was always canned in fruit jars, either quarts or pints. The tomatoes were peeled and stewed then canned. Some were put through a sieve by mashing them, which resulted in tomato juice. Green beans were also canned along with peaches from the few fruit trees we had in the yard. Most of the hard surface squash, such as the banana squash, would be placed in a cool place without much deterioration for several months. Cucumbers were made into a variety of pickles and canned.

My mother was big on homemade pickles. She loved 'salt pickles.'

She would mix a salt brine in an old ceramic 4-5 gallon jar. Pack the sliced quartered cucumbers in the brine, add some spices for flavoring, such as chili peppers to 'kick it up a notch' and cover the mixture with fresh grapevine leaves. A dishcloth was then placed over the mouth of the jar and tied down so that it was covered but could still breathe. The process would take maybe a week or more before the pickles were ready to eat. I still recall the taste. The pickles were so firm and crunchy and tasted very good!

A lot of the work of canning the vegetables entailed using a hand cranked food grinder. If I didn't know how to handle the fruit or vegetables, mom or dad would show me how and that became my job and my contribution to the process. In the meantime, they were scalding and cleansing the glass 'mason' jars, rings and lids getting them ready. In some cases, the fruit or vegetables were being cooked as soon as I had completed the grinding. Once the food was in the jars, the rings for sealing and the lids were put on. The filled jars were then put in water, spaced so that they did not touch, and cooked for a prescribed number of minutes to kill any and all bacteria. The jars were then allowed to cool and you could hear the 'lids popping' as the jars were sealing. Finally, they were removed to the pantry for storage until needed.

Since we lived in an area where there was lots of 'truck farming', many vegetables were plentiful throughout most of the year. After the main harvest had taken place, the farmers allowed people to come onto the fields and pick what was left. That was one way we had of cutting our food costs. At different times of the year, there were tomatoes, strawberries (for jam and preserves), lima beans, apricots, English peas, carrots, squash and other edibles. To me, it seemed like we were canning all too often.

It was in this kind of family living where I learned to garden and really appreciate its many attributes. I learned to grow vegetables as well as flowers. My mother truly had a 'green thumb.' I think she could grow anything, including a dead stick if she put it in the ground! Often she would see a plant growing and ask if she could have a 'start' or a 'sprig', as she referred to the plant she wanted to propagate. Then she'd just break off a stem or small branch from the plant, wrap a wet rag or paper around it, take it home and literally stick it in the ground, and pack the dirt around it. In a short time, evidence of new growth would appear like magic. Others would complain to her because they never seemed to achieve the same results even though, according to them, they did the same thing and in the same way. She always had marvelous results.

I, too, love to see plants grow and thrive. In the past, I have spent a lot of time having a vegetable garden. As my available time has become shorter because of my work schedule, I have had to curtail and finally eliminate vegetable gardening. Flowers and shrubs have become my primary focus and even that is very limited. I love the bright fresh start of spring and all of the annuals. The blooming season seems to bring new life to a dull and fading winter time. Flowers and blooms, in general, bring so much color and enjoyment compared to the dull winter months. The intensity and variety of color is motivating to me.

The shrubs and flowering plants that I prefer the most are azaleas, rhododendrons, pansies, roses, especially tea roses, iris, both bearded and Dutch, all kinds of daffodils, camellias, certain species of geraniums, rinoculus because of the vivid colors and length of blooming season, and sporaxis, among others. Many of the species are bulbs and require a late fall planting here in California if they are to bloom in the spring.

I have visited the 'Flower Fields' down the coast near Oceanside just off the Interstate 5 freeway. It is an incredible sight to see hundreds of acres of blooming flowers in extremely vivid colors as ribbons of flowering rinoculus cover the hillside in an array of splendor. It is virtually a rainbow of coloration growing in the ground. People come by the busloads just to see the sight. I think God gave us flowers as a way of cheering us along life's pathway and to lighten our loads. They offer a moment of solitude just to see and contemplate the handiwork of the Master.

Flowers also bring a sense of good cheer due to their special aromas. Roses are my favorites in this category. Many roses do not have any depth to their smell or bouquet which leaves us to appreciate the exquisite beauty they offer. Regardless of the flower, I love a wide variety of color.

Mineral Collecting

I was never a student of geology. In fact, I never took a class on the subject. However, I seemed to have an innate interest in terrain and rocks. This interest lay dormant for many years. Rocks, for this reason, held somewhat of a fascination for me. As I traveled in various countries throughout the world, I would see a wide variety of rocks and rock formations in natural landscapes and I would wonder how the differences came about. Yes, I knew it was God's handy work…but what made the various displays so different interested me. What caused these formations to occur was truly fascinating.

Through the church that I attended, the First Baptist Church in Pomona, California, I was to meet a Dr. Robert (Bob) Feldmeth. Bob was a professor of biology at the local prestigious Claremont Colleges. He was also a well versed Bible scholar and became our Sunday school teacher. It was through this association that I became good friends with Bob. In fact, I was later to consider him to be my best friend.

Bob was highly intelligent, savvy, well educated in the field of sciences and a very interesting individual. He was a biologist specializing in plant and fish life in a salinity environment. He made many field trips with students or on special assignment. Bob had made extensive studies of pup fish often found in underground streams and rivers in the desert areas. He was highly sought after for consulting to businesses trying to develop housing along the California coastal zone, which had become rigidly controlled by the state environmentalists. The demand for his services, I believe, was because he was extremely well versed on the regulations and environmental subjects and told the truth about issues. Basically, he just loved nature and could talk about the flora and the fauna and the terra firma in almost any area where he traveled on the North American continent infinitum.

One day, unexpectedly, he called to see if I was interested in taking a field trip to a borax mine near Boron, California. This is an area in the Mojave Desert northeast of Los Angeles. He and his wife, Judy, were going and I could come along. They were going to collect some minerals and crystals, if they could find any. I decided to go along even though, as I told him, I don't know anything about the subject.

As it worked out, we arrived at the U.S. Borax mine on a Saturday about mid-morning. The mine was not operating on a weekend. At the gate the guard told us we could visit the borax storage piles but that we would have to be escorted by a company vehicle, both going and returning. As I scanned the surrounding area, I saw what appeared to be several enormous piles of dirt, maybe a hundred feet or more in height and, once on top, probably a hundred yards square! This is where the company was stockpiling its mined ore or raw material supply. Along each huge pile of ore was a dirt type ramp from the bottom to the top that allowed ore trucks and vehicles to drive to the top.

Once on top, Bob instructed me to look for anything that was shiny as if faceted, clear and not opaque, unusual in its appearance, and could have color so long as it didn't look like dirt. That sounded pretty easy. He and Judy went their way and I went mine. No matter where you were on the plateau of the pile, you could see each of the few people up there. There weren't very many, possibly eight to ten. One couple, I noticed, was down on their knees and bent over with their noses close to the ground with a magnifying glass looking at the dirt at close range. I wondered what they were looking for and thought maybe that's the reason I can't see anything 'unusual', I don't have a magnifying glass. I ventured over by them; they were friendly and readily acknowledged my presence. They were from the state of Washington and told me that they were looking for a very small crystal and this was the only place they could find them. The crystals were used in their classroom for teaching purposes. They showed me some of their sample findings and through their glass I could easily see them but they were really miniscule to the naked eye. That didn't excite me very much.

I continued my trek to find something on my own and, hopefully, more worthwhile. I found some colored material that sort of looked like blobs of glass in a burnt orange and light blue color and irregular in shape. I thought it was pretty but didn't have any idea how it got there but I saved it. Ever once in a while I found a few pieces here and there. That didn't really excite me very much either.

I saw another man arrive by himself. He seemed to know what he was looking for and ambled all over the place intently looking and stopping to dig around ever so often. He soon had worked his way near me and I was closing in on Bob and Judy. The four of us converged at the same time in the same place. We were to find out that this individual was from Connecticut and had been in the area on business as an engineer for the last week. He said that he came out to California about every five years and always came to the Borax stock piles to look for crystals. He hadn't found anything yet but seemed to remain enthusiastic that he would find some specimens. He promised if he did find anything of interest, he would call us. The three of us stayed in that spot and shared a lunch that Judy had prepared. By now, it was nearing one o'clock and we were hungry. The little picnic of sorts hit the spot!

About an hour later, the engineer from Connecticut called to us. When we arrived, he had found a large ball like object, perhaps two feet in diameter, irregularly shaped, and clear as glass, except that the mass appeared to have numerous cracks and fissures in it. The first thing I thought of that it reminded me of was crushed ice that had started to melt and then had been refrozen into a sort of ball shape. All you had to do was crack off a few pieces and put them into your coke or ice tea! The engineer had a gad and began to use it to break the ball apart. He was so excited to have found the piece, and we were too!

He selected a number of beautiful pieces of the crystal that he had broken off and afterwards told us that we could have anything left…that was our signal to collect virtually all the rest of the pieces. The engineer said this material was Colemanite, a member of the borate family of crystals. What we didn't know, or at least I didn't was that if left exposed to the air, oxidation would take place as the water was leached out and the pieces would turn completely white on the outside as if they had been whitewashed. These crystals had a lot of water in them and that helped the oxidation to take place rather rapidly within a few days. Needless to say, that was the highlight of the day.

As the day wore on, I was also able to find a lot of Kernite and some Ulexite crystals, which were also members of the borax family of crystals. The colored material that I had come across earlier was slag from the processing operations that had been dumped on the pile and was really just glass. Little did I know at the time, but this outing set the hook in my mind and created an interest for the rest of my life…I like rocks and have become a mineral collector over the years. To further deepen my interest in rocks, Bob invited me to a night class where jewelry making, three dimensional objects, such as spheres and rock carving were taught. From those two experiences, I was ready to become a true 'rock hound'!

It has been many years since that first trip to the borax stock piles. I have become highly selective in the minerals which I collect. Not everything interests me like it did at first. In the beginning I wanted a specimen of every new mineral that I came across. I suddenly realized that I was running out of room and I wasn't ever going to be the Smithsonian Museum nor did I intend to be. Without equivocation, my wife agreed on that issue. That's when I began to focus on the hexagonal crystal family. This group of crystals includes a number of semi-precious gemstones as well as some precious gemstones. They are my favorite crystal group to collect. The hexagonal crystals include amethyst, citrine, quartz, emerald, aqua marine, and heliodor, along with a wide variety of tourmaline crystals. For the most part, these crystals cannot be found by rock hounds. They are found through hard rock mining and mostly in other parts of the world than the United States.

Among the crystals in the hexagonal family are the tourmalines (no longer an applicable technical description of these crystals but they are commonly called that by people), also known as the 'rainbow crystals' because of the wide variety of colors. These crystals are peculiar for their vertical and horizontal zoning. With vertical zoning, as many as three different colors can appear in the same crystal, such as the 'watermelon' crystal. To see it from the top, the outside rim is green, the next inside layer or zone is white and the interior, or center, is a beautiful red color. Horizontal zoning is not as spectacular to me but is equally impressive because the crystal changes colors very definitively as it grows vertically. Some are totally translucent while others are opaque. The basic varieties includes shorl (opaque black), rubellite (red), indicolite (blue) and elbaite (green), dravite (brown) and uvite (clear). I have tried to collect these specimens in the matrix rock which is their natural condition when found by the miners as opposed to cut stones which are used in jewelry and are highly polished. I like to see God's handiwork as He made these minerals with each one following a specific order and design.

I have had a lot of fun and have seen many many varieties of crystals from all over the world. I have attended many shows from the local California area to the world's largest gem and mineral show in Tucson, Arizona. I have shown my collection in the local shows and the Los Angeles County Fair as well as the California State Gem and Mineral Show. I am pleased with my showings and ribbons that I have received because it takes a lot of hard work and study to make the displays and to properly label each specimen as to the location where it was mined, the technical name of the material, the chemical identity of the material, and then make the presentation display so as to create a focal point and make it pleasing, informative, and having enough but not too many specimens. I have learned a lot from my rock hounding experience and met a number of really 'down to earth' people.

At class, I met a lady, Lydia Deets, who has kept me interested more than anyone in rocks. In fact, she and I formed a partnership for the express purpose of importing 'Mexican coconuts' or geodes from Chihuahua, Mexico for the benefit of the local Glendora School District. We have chosen to do it, not to make money, but to help the junior high and high school kids learn about rocks and minerals at an early age. Perhaps it will incite them to become geologist, mining engineers, or geo-physicist or open the door to a career in jewelry making or stone faceting. It has been a wonderful way to spend time and learn about a subject previously foreign to me.

Coin Collecting

I can remember my dad always finding coins on the sidewalk when he was walking in town. I don't know if he looked down all the time as he walked. I don't think so because that doesn't register with me. He'd bring the coins home and 'save' them in a little coin purse he had for that purpose. My mother taught me to save coins with my first 'piggy bank' when I was still in grammar school. My interest in coins was a very natural process for me.

I never toyed much with the idea of collecting coins as a hobby until one day, while working at Fleetwood Enterprises, my Vice President of Real Estate Development, Bill Weide, asked what I was doing for lunch. There was nothing in particular or of any importance so he asked if I wanted to go to the Bank of America in downtown Riverside and see if they had any 'old money'? I thought that could be an interesting way to spend a lunch hour so I went with him. It was obvious that he had done this sort of thing before. He knew the manager and he asked him if he had any old money that had been saved. John, the banker, replied that he thought one of the tellers had some and directed us to one of the tellers. She had indeed been saving it. She had primarily paper money, some of which dated back to World War II and was stamped with the word "HAWAII" in big black letters on several of the denominations of bills. Needless to say, that's what he was looking for. Bill bought them all by exchanging current bills for them. I was to learn later that the woman had been saving them for some time and was about ready to buy them herself. Bill selected the bills that he wanted and offered me the rest of them, so I bought them from him.

Within a few days, Bill was back in my office and was asking if I saved the annual U.S. Mint series of coins. I said, "No." He offered me an order form. I then began to order and collect the annual proof and uncirculated sets of coins from the Mint every year. I have been doing that every year since.

That caused me to become more aware of coins, when they were minted, where they were minted and to some extent identify with the rarity of coins. I began to collect a few commemorative coins. Although I do not have a lot of coins, I like to find the ones that reflect on my interests such as some of the Olympics, USO, World War II, etc.

More recently, I have been giving coins to my grandchildren in hopes of getting them interested in collecting. The 50 States Quarters program by the Mint has been a big assist in that direction. They are all saving the state's quarters as they become available over the ten years mint period.

Some of my favorite coins are the old Morgan type silver dollars, such as those minted in Carson City, Nevada from the silver mined in the Comstock Lode. I seem to connect history to these old coins regardless of when or where they were minted, and treasure the fact that they are so old and wonder how they survived all these years. It is exciting to hold or look at an old coin and contemplate where it has been and think of the possible notable people who may have held the coin or the thousands of persons within whose hands it may have passed as they conducted commerce. A coin is also a piece of art as well as history!

Certain coins are no longer minted, such as the St. Gaudiens double eagle gold coin which I believe is an extremely beautiful coin. Some numismatic specialists believe this group of coins to be the most beautiful ever minted. I have also had an affinity for the lady liberty coins. Finally, the coin which is very special to me was the Indian Head silver dollar issue by the mint in limited quantities in 2001. It was an enlargement of the old 'buffalo nickel' long since out of mintage. Unfortunately, I have very few of these coins.

For fun when my daughters, Leslie and Jacquie, were young, I liked to flash paper money in front of them and let the mint mark show, such as 'A', 'B', 'H', etc. These capital letters, one printed on each bill, established the mint where it was printed. If they knew or made a correct first guess as to the mint identified on that particular bill, I would give the bill to the one making the correct answer. As time passed and with each successive 'viewing', they had virtually memorized every mint mark and knew most of the twelve federal mint symbols in the country. I loved to play with them that way but I'm not so sure they enjoyed it, especially when one of them was not winning. I will say that they got to be pretty good at identifying the various mints very quickly. I don't recall when we stopped doing that exercise. Maybe it was when they went to college and I was short on money!

My daughter, Leslie, began to save pennies in an old five-gallon Arrowhead Puritas glass water bottle with her a boyfriend, Jeff Thrasher, in high school. She left the water bottle in the house when she left for college. I still save the pennies that I get as change from the stores and I have continued to put pennies in the bottle. This has gone on for more than fifteen years. One day about a year ago, I had my grandchildren, Willy, Claire, and Collin over and we dumped all the pennies out on the floor and counted them. The present count is up to 17,030. The big thick water bottle is so heavy that one person cannot lift it from the floor. I'm sure it would cause a hernia! One day it will be full (about 2/3 now) and we will decide what to do with all of the pennies. Somehow, I think my grandkids will be involved!

Saving coins as a hobby is resourceful and fun. It isn't as forceful a method for saving money as planned deposits in a bank from your paycheck but over time it does add up. They certainly don't grow due to interest rates. Their value at any given time can fluctuate with the market price of precious metals such as silver and gold. Their face value is limited. For the collector, there is an intrinsic value of beauty and, in most cases, some historical significance that causes one to maintain an interest in coins and keep on collecting them.

Fishing

Although I never considered fishing as a hobby, it has been of special interest to me for virtually my entire life. I don't think my father taught me very much about fishing but he, too, liked to fish. As a youngster, he took me on some of his fishing trips even though, for the most part, I never had the opportunity to try to catch fish with him. I watched what was being done and learned a lot about fishing in that manner. I vaguely remember going fishing once in Arkansas in the Petit Jean Creek. The only fish that I recall being caught that day was a blue channel catfish that probably weighed two or three pounds.

After we moved to California, my father did mostly salt-water fishing. It was about a ten-mile drive over to Ventura where he liked to fish off the pier. It often seemed like a waste of time to me. Once in a great while, Dad would catch a small halibut that would weigh about ten or twelve pounds. That was the only time it got exciting to me. On other occasions, he would drive down the coast on the Alternate 101 highway to Santa Monica and take the half-day boat out for fishing in Santa Monica Bay. He focused his efforts mostly on bottom fishing and catching halibut. Most often he was successful on these trips and would catch a twenty-five to thirty pound halibut. He would take me on these trips with him but I never fished. I prowled around on the boat finding various nooks and crannies and staying out of trouble. I liked riding on the boats with the sea breeze blowing in your face but I didn't care too much about the 'fishy' smell of the boat.

Another place where my dad liked to fish was at Port Hueneme off the sewage dumping area. A very large pipeline had been laid for disposal of sewage and it was secured from the impact of waves and storms by huge granite boulders on it and around it. Fishermen would climb along the pipeline to a spot where they thought they could catch fish and also felt safe from the thunderous pounding of the ocean's waves. I was never allowed to go out on the rocks with my dad. I had to spend my time around the car and find something to occupy myself for hours at a time. Now, that was boring. I went with my dad simply because I wanted to be with him anytime that I could since he worked so much.

On one of these excursions to Port Hueneme, my dad was deeply involved in his fishing and not paying attention to the tidal activity. Suddenly, without warning, a huge wave just seemed to explode and envelope the vicinity where he was standing. The force of the huge wave knocked him off his feet and hurled him into the rocks with great force. According to his statements afterward, he was left momentarily dazed and unconscious but the cold ocean water revived him quickly and he tried to regain his footing when he realized that he was bleeding profusely from his forehead. He had lost all of his fishing gear but that wasn't important. He knew he had to get to the doctor as rapidly as possible. He called to me before he even reached the car and I was trying to find a rag of any kind for him to apply to his forehead to restrict the blood flow. He couldn't drive the car because of his condition. It was up to me! There was a problem with that expectation; I was too young to drive and I had never had a driving lesson. But I felt I could drive because I had watched and seen for a long time how my dad did it. There wasn't a choice at this time…I had to try. I did everything as I had learned in my mind and it worked out pretty good. I got him to the doctor, who happened to be our family doctor. Needless to say, I was very scared during the ordeal.

I have forgotten how many stitches he needed but it was several and the doctor did take good care of him. I don't think the doctor was much of a 'plastic surgeon' as we know them today because my father had a very noticeable scar on his forehead for the rest of his life; but he had survived!

After this incident, it was easy for me to understand why he wouldn't let me go out on the rocks. It was dangerous to the point that he almost lost his own life.

In my memory, I recall only one fishing trip that involved fresh water. One summer day, our family and that of Uncle Jack Moudy decided to go to Lake Sherwood and some would go fishing while the young ladies would travel down to the hot springs for sun bathing and swimming. Those who didn't want to do either stayed on shore talking and visiting. They also fixed the food for the picnic. I got to go in the boat to fish. It was better than the other choices I had. We spent several hours in the boat that day but I have no idea as to our success. The best I recall, the fish were probably sun fish, such as perch or crappie, and maybe a catfish or two and the count was very small!

After I got to be friends with the Japanese family next door, I was occasionally invited by the Hosaki family to go on some of their day fishing trips up the coast to the Carpenteria area. Jimmy Hosaki was my age. He had a younger sister, Helen, and two older brothers, Joe and Frank. Their father was an astute surf fisherman and the boys were very skilled at that type of fishing, too. I learned to catch octopus on these trips. Jimmy Hosaki was one of my best friends when I lived in the Federal Housing Project on Federal Avenue in Oxnard. When on these excursions, he would stick his hand underneath the large rocks that were partially buried in the sand on the beach where the waves gently washed ashore. In these crevices, where it was dark and where the waves just sort of lapped up gently against the rocks, lived the octopus. These creatures were collected throughout the day and put in galvanized buckets filled with salt water to keep them alive until we returned home. These trips were always interesting and a good learning experience for me. This approach to getting fish was very different from how I was accustomed to fishing.

These experiences are recited merely to convey what is perhaps my birth right to the enjoyment of fishing. I don't know why I would have had any interest in fishing by just going along for the boat ride or staying close by when my dad was fishing but some how I have seemingly always had an affinity for fishing. I love to fish. I loved the openness, being out in nature, as well as trying to learn the techniques and gaining an understanding of fisheries and fish habitat. It used to be that you would not hear a phone ringing all day; you had time to just relax and enjoy the sights to and from the fishing areas. No one told you that you had to do something. It was just good clean fun.

My father-in-law, Earl Humphrey, also loved to fish. I had to laugh when he told me that he could put a line in the bathtub and fish all day and have a great time! But he was serious about his enjoyment of fishing. Based on his love for fishing, I don't think his statement was far from wrong! I have also heard it said that 'the worst day of fishing is still better than the best day at work!' That I can agree with.

I began to pick up on fishing 'again' while I was in the Air Force at March AFB in the mid to late 1950s. A good friend of mine, Jerry Olsen, who was from Wisconsin and assigned to the same A & E Squadron, loved to fish. He would ask me to go trout fishing with him up into the San Bernardino Mountains. When we got time off from duty, we would make the trek up to the South Fork of the Santa Ana River and fish. Since the natural reproductive cycle for the trout had been broken years before, we would check the local newspaper listing and determine when the Fish and Game Department was going to make their plants. That way, we were pretty much assured of a bountiful catch. There were other trips when we would venture off to some other location, after having heard a fish tale of some success, and find that someone had over sold us on their story. For instance, we fished Jenks Lake, which was on the long back road to Big Bear Lake, and left the lake without being close to a limit.

There was another preposterous trip where we climbed out of the Jenks Lake area and up the side of Mount San Gorgonio to Dollar Lake. That was a real test of survival and an extremely difficult climb to about 8,000 – 9,000 feet, which was still some distance from the summit. It turned out to be just a huge rock pile. When we finally arrived at the lake, after almost five hours of climbing, you could easily have thrown a rock across the lake; there was not any vegetation whatsoever, just water in a big rock hole.

Therefore, if there were any fish in the lake they couldn't grow to any size because they didn't have any feed and a very short growing season because of the heavy winter snows and the cold weather at that altitude. The lake was frozen over for almost half the year. Later, we were to learn that the U.S. Forest Service had worked with the Fish and Game Department and made a plant of trout up there by helicopter about three years previously. We didn't catch a single fish. But we did enjoy a cooling off period while we ate our lunch. Our trip down the mountain was relatively short as we took a straight line down the side of the mountain never trying to walk the trail. That was our last trip to that area.

After my service time was completed and I had married, I made several trips in the 1960s to the high Sierra Mountains in and around Bishop and the Mammoth Lakes area for trout fishing. Mostly, I fished Lake Sabrina, South Lake, North Lake, the various Intakes (man made water holding ponds used by the California Electric Power Company to generate hydroelectric power), June Lake, Silver Lake and some of the local streams. I have been up to these areas on opening day, May 1st, when the water would collect in the eyes of the fishing rod and freeze to the point you couldn't reel in your line. When that happened, you gently tapped your fishing rod on a rock close by or on a tree limb to knock the ice off! Mostly, I caught rainbow trout but in some areas, the larger brown trout were more plentiful.

When I was employed at Fleetwood, I continued to make trips to the high Sierras but that was usually limited to opening day for the trout season when it was so very cold and often before the snow pack had completely melted. I recall fishing at Silver Lake in the High Sierras. There was a campground close by where the recreational vehicle was parked. I had purchased some crickets in Bishop, California on the way up to use for bait hoping to catch brown trout. Many of the older people who fish the lake were trying to catch rainbow trout and do 'lazy man's fishing'. That is, they sit in the folding chairs on a nice spot at the edge of the lake, cast their bait out with a float attached and wait for the fish to jiggle or pull the float under the surface of the water. It is a rather inactive way to fish. I am a much more active fisherman. I like to keep trying different things with bait and depth to attract the fish and cause them to react and attack my bait.

On this particular trip, I passed shoreline fishermen on my way to the bridge where a stream fed into the lake. The water was very clear and quickly became rather deep. With waders on, you could gain a little advantage over those without them. It was a beautiful place where the brown trout like to feed on the natural bait brought in by the flowing stream. In addition, the browns had a difficult time resisting a fresh cricket and in a short time I had caught my limit. On my way back to the campground, I had to walk past the shoreline fishermen and they noticed and commented on my nice catch of fish. Needless to say, we had a very enjoyable lunch eating the fish.

Later in the afternoon, I was bored and made a bad decision to go back and try catching more brown trout. Again, it was a very successful trip to the bridge and I caught another limit. Much to my surprise, as I was returning to the campground, a lady called to me from one of the camp sites, "Aren't you the one that caught that limit of fish this morning?!" With a great degree of guilt I replied, "Yes I am, would you like some of these?" The fact was that I had broken the law because a fisherman was only allowed one limit of fish each day in California. She had caught me red handed! She said, "No thanks, just leave some for us!" I walked away with a very sheepish look on my face. From that point on, I never took more than the limit of the day or 'in possession' on any fishing trip.

Snake River - Wyoming

Some of my best fishing in the great outdoors occurred during my tenure with Fleetwood. Our supplier of steel and aluminum was Kaiser Steel, which at the time was headquartered in Oakland, California. The company would invite some of us company personnel on a fishing adventure to the Jackson Hole area of Wyoming. First, we would fly into Denver on our own; then an executive Gulf Stream II corporate jet would take us to Jackson Hole. Kaiser would put us up in the Jenny Lake Lodge at no cost for two or three days for a time of recreation. Your choices were fishing on Jenny Lake or on the Snake River, tennis, golf, hiking or just relaxing. It was always in early October when the winter weather was just arriving.

The days were generally comfortable with the nights being rather cold. Usually at night, bears would make a run through the cabin area trying to find free food and making quiet a bit of noise. No one was ever attacked by the bears but you made sure you weren't outside when they were on their rampage!

I always chose to fish the river. Bill Weide, my Vice President for real estate and plant construction, usually made the trip with me. I recall my first such venture. I had never done any fly fishing before and didn't have a clue about technique or anything else relating to fly fishing. Somehow, I was teamed up with a veteran fly fisherman from Connecticut. He was sort of a salty old fellow. We were up and out of the lodge about 4:00 a.m. because our guide wanted to be on the river at 5:00 a.m. He met us at the lodge with his pick-up towing his trailer and hauling the boat. He was on time and he worked his planned schedule like an engineer running a passenger train.

We arrived at the launch site and, of course, by then the guide knew I was the neophyte and needed some instruction before heading downstream. First, he had me watch what he did and how he did it. We were going to use dry flies. So I had to practice the primary technique of using the rod to keep the fly in motion until I was ready to release the line hopefully in a general target area. He showed me how to apply muslic to the fly to help keep it somewhat impervious to the water. After no more than three or four casts, from the dark shadows to my left I heard the old salt yell, "He's got the idea, let's go!" As we settled in the boat and started down the Snake River, I was sitting in the front of the boat, the guide in the middle so he could give instructions and directions as well as guide the boat through the best fishing holes, while the old gentleman sat in back. By the time the sun was up, I had the casting down pretty good so I thought. Within another hour, neither of us had a strike. It was then the guide let me know that I needed to cast the fly within a foot of the logs near the river bank that were partially sunken in the river or right in under the logs or other debris as we passed them while floating down river. I hadn't tried to do that because I was fearful of getting snagged on the near-sunken tree trunks and limbs. The guide said that would be okay. So I tried harder to do what he was telling me. All morning long we fished without even one strike. Even the old salt was having his troubles so I didn't feel real bad. It was fun but I do like to hang a few fish!

As we floated, we saw moose munching on the grasses growing in the shallows of the river. They would put their head down in the water and get a mouth full of fresh green grass and pull it out of the muddy earth all the while their mouths were expelling the water. It made it look like a very messy way to eat but they didn't seem to care. We also had an incredible view of America's bird, the beautiful bald eagle, only twenty feet or so above our heads as it glided majestically up the river on the invisible currents of air searching for food, especially fish. The eagles are expert fishermen and have an amazing ability to collect fish to feed their young primarily due to the superb eyesight. This eagle had a wingspan that looked to be nearly eight feet. I have never been that close to such a beautiful wild bald eagle before or since. It was a majestic sight.

At lunchtime, the guide put in on a sand bar and told us to continue fishing. He pointed out where he wanted me to fish while he prepared our lunch. In my waders, I was standing thigh deep in the water at a place where there was slow and fast water. The guide told me to cast upstream and let the fly float on a natural course through the fast current. As I did it a large beautiful cutthroat trout came charging up out of the water attacking the fly! I couldn't believe it! It was spectacular and unbelievable. I was so shocked by the events that I missed setting the hook and lost the fish.

The guide had been watching me the entire time and made some comment about being ready the next time. He yelled to me to try the same thing again...I did. The same thing happened again except I was ready for that monster. I hooked him and the fight was on. I played him like I had done it many times before and finally wore him down so that the guide could get the net under him. I had landed a very nice fish. It was an absolutely gorgeous specimen.

The guide asked if I wanted to keep the fish. I said, "No, I don't have a way to keep it or cook it on this trip." It pleased him greatly that I had refused to keep the fish. 'Catch and release' is the best way to preserve the spawning size fish for the future. It's good conservation. Before releasing the fish, the guide took a picture of me with the trout and measured it. Turned out it was 25" long! The afternoon was better. Seemed like the noontime experience got us going. Each of us caught out limits and had an absolutely wonderful day on the river.

Unknowingly, that evening at dinner, the best performers in the various activities were recognized. Much to my surprise, I won the Jenny Lake Lodge tankard for the biggest fish on the river that day. However, a few weeks later, I was surprised even more when I received a phone call from one of the Kaiser Managers telling me they were coming down to Riverside from Oakland to award me the trophy for having caught the largest fish on the river during the entire retreat! I was taken aback needless to say. The trophy was quite large and I kept it for many years. It was a day I would never forget and here I am some thirty years later or more writing about it.

Salmon River - Idaho

My fresh water fishing experience would be incomplete if I failed to make a few remarks about steelhead fishing on the River-of-No-Return, the Salmon River in Idaho, otherwise known as the Middle Fork of the Salmon River. I have made several trips into this wilderness area. A few times we would fly in with bush pilots in small planes. When there were problems at the airport, we have taken jet boats up the river fifty-five miles to the ranch where we fished. Both modes were excitingly different. The jet boats could move through deep as well as very shallow water, up relatively small rapids, with the drivers on the lookout for the 'can opener' or sharp rock of major proportions slightly submerged under the surface of the water. If a boat hit one, it could open up the aluminum shell of the boat just like a can opener and it would quickly sink in the rapidly rushing and foaming water of the river. It could be dangerous if the navigator didn't know the river or what he was doing.

Flying with the bush pilots was more exciting to me. First their equipment appeared scary because of its appearance. That is, the headliners were flopping in the breeze while the plane was sitting on the tarmac with the doors open. The next thing I noticed was the undersides of the wings. They looked as if someone had taken a hammer and deliberately dented the entire bottom sides of the wings…all of them! The fuselage was not excluded either! Who ever did it didn't miss one square inch of surface. My first trip into this fishing area had its special issues and concerns before we had left the runway.

In the fall of 1969, six of us drove from Boise to McCall, Idaho to make the trip into the back country. I only recall one of the fishermen on this excursion, Dale Skinner, President of Fleetwood Enterprises. Dale didn't like flying at all and especially in small aircraft. I noticed the condition of the airplanes when we walked out to the aircraft…Dale did too! That immediately put him into a state of near panic. First of all, Dale was a tall man, perhaps six foot five inches, sort of balding, wore thick glasses, and had a big mid-westerner smile and brogue. The doors were open to the aircraft as supplies were being loaded to take with us. In one plane was loaded a 55-gallon steel drum of a petroleum product. It hadn't been lashed down yet. There were boxes of food supplies in the other airplane. These airplanes were Cessna 182s; a high wing and a good flying airplane. Soon the seating assignments were made. Three passengers and a pilot along with all of the supplies were making the trip in each airplane.

Before passenger loading into the planes, I noticed Dale wasn't in the group. What happened to him, I wondered? I went looking for him and found him off to one side and three or four airplanes down the ramp. I noticed that he was just putting something back in his coat pocket, when he turned to me and said, "I needed a little encouragement and fortitude!" He had just taken a swig of whisky from his flask. That was his way of coping with his present circumstances.

We departed McColl without incident and headed for Mackay Bar, Idaho. It was the last ranch before the actual Idaho wilderness area and just beyond the James Ranch. I was selected to ride second seat up front beside the pilot. That was an unexpected special experience for me since I was interested in aviation. We took a course heading straight for the mountain range to the northeast of the airport with a very slow rate of climb speed, maybe fifty feet per minute. That didn't bother me until we began to close in on the mountains. The old bush pilot had made this trip hundreds of times no doubt but this was my first. I sensed that we weren't going to clear the peak ahead of us so I asked if we were okay with respect to the needed clearance. With confidence he said, "Oh yes, we're going to make it," and he just kept on watching the horizon. Well, he was correct; we cleared the peak by not more than 500 to 700 feet. To me, it was too close for comfort.

No sooner had we cleared the peak, when ahead of us was a very steep drop off into the Salmon River canyon. It was an absolutely gorgeous sight. It seemed pristine, as if untouched by anyone but Mother Nature. This is one of the deepest river gorges on the continent. To my surprise, we started dropping down into the canyon. Now we had tall mountains on either side of the airplane. I was looking straight out the windows at the green forests of ponderosa pine and Douglas firs. Among the trees were white splashing and misty waterfalls as the water was cascading and finding its way down and into the river. From the air at that time of day it appeared to be a silver mirrored ribbon nature had brought from the past. The river itself looked beautiful and almost peaceful at this altitude with its white water rapids and gorges winding its way for a thousand miles to the Pacific Ocean.

Within forty minutes after entering the canyon, we reached a place where the river makes a virtual 90 degree turn and of course the pilot banked the Cessna accordingly. The down wing was on the port side and the pilot took his hand and pointed downward and announced to me that we were passing over the place where we were going to land. We had arrived at Mackey's Bar. I looked past his body and out the window and could only see a house with a barn…no landing strip! He kept talking, "If I don't make a 180 here, I have to fly twenty-five more miles up the river before I can turn around." Again he made a very sharp bank to his side of the aircraft and made the 180 degree turn. Then he nonchalantly described the landing that he was about to make as a 'completely blind landing.' At the moment I was in complete agreement with that statement because I had not seen a landing strip anyplace and I could not even see the house or the barn. He was heading straight into the river and was cutting power with full flaps and we were going down! Now this maneuver really had me on edge and probably everyone else on board but the pilot. As he maneuvered the Cessna 182, he made a slight left turn just as we slipped past what appeared to be a huge landslide that had made its way directly into the river and immediately hit a dirt work road adjacent to the corrals and the barn. I suddenly realized why the undersides of the wings on the Cessna were so beaten up, we were kicking up rocks and stones like you couldn't believe and the dust was comparable to the largest dirt devil ever stirred up. Almost as soon as the dust started to settle, the second plane came roaring in with the same results as we experienced.

Makey's Bar was an actual working ranch. When the ranch hands weren't doing their routine work, they were helping the fishing guests by dropping them off at various locations for steelhead fishing along the river using the jet boats, helping with breakfast or taking us on little excursions. All of the guest fishermen slept in the former bunk house, which had been modified for better accommodations. It was acceptable but not a great facility. Around the main house were some apple trees laden with the fall crop. The nights were very cool but it warmed up very comfortably during the day at that time of year. The food was very good and a pleasant atmosphere and ambiance prevailed. It was indeed western all the way!

A couple of days into the trip, two of the ranch hands, who also assisted with the boats, asked some of us if we would like to take a short trip up river and visit an old abandoned mine. I was for that since the fish were pretty scarce. On the way back from the mine the drivers had decided to stop at a well kept group of very small buildings on the river. The place was fenced neatly and had a nice sandy beach in front built up by river sand deposits over time. The location was on an almost ninety degree turn the river made. It was on this trip and stop over that I met a legend of the wilderness, Sylvan Hart.[1] This gentleman was a complete throwback to the American west early frontiersmen.

Sylvan had lived a major portion of his life on the river and in this wilderness area. He told the story about how he came to this part of the River-of-No-Return in 1920 from a Midwestern state after being jilted by his sweetheart, a schoolteacher. He was a fairly young man at the time. The only time Sylvan ever left the river after his relocation was when World

War II started and he felt it was his obligation to serve his country so he joined the U.S. Navy. As soon as the war was over, he returned to the river and has spent his life there. It was only by his invitation that I visited his facilities and that in and of itself was a real life highlight for me.

In the wilderness, it is important to think of safety as much as possible with respect to fires and floods. This precaution caused Sylvan to scatter build. He didn't build one building as we do in today's construction for his habitat instead he built separate 'room buildings.' By that I mean, Sylvan had a building for his kitchen, another for his bedroom, and another for his den or entertainment area. Separation was primarily for fire safety purposes. If one building burned, he wouldn't loose everything. Each building was built about four feet off the ground on stilts, except for his kitchen. The reason was simple, to keep high and dry when the river flooded. His property was fenced and located on one of the wide sweeps of the river, which created a large sand bank in front of his property sort of a nice beach. He was very proud of his existence. In fact, Sylvan got dressed up when he learned he was to have visitors. That was a real sight to see…a mountain man all dressed up! In many ways, he looked as if he was a displaced warrior from a Viking warship! He stood perhaps five and half feet tall and weighed perhaps one hundred and sixty to seventy pounds. On his head, he wore a hand pounded and shaped bronze metal helmet that he had made with a buckskin chin strap and cow horns mounted on top. It was well made and a perfect fit. He had chosen a long sleeved red plaid flannel shirt. He wore black bear skin shorts held up by big red snap suspenders. Finally he had high top work shoes with metal hooks for lacing them up. Around his neck hung a unique and rather lengthy necklace that came almost to his waist. He had made the necklace from collected ornaments such as bear claws, mountain lion claws, rather large beads that he had made from deer antlers which were all strung on a deer skin leather lace. He looked quite fierce as if he was ready for battle. His personality and friendliness quickly overcame any visual fierceness cast by his attire. By the time he took us on a personal tour of his 'home' he had everyone in the palm of his hand as he described his handiwork and the features of his 'wilderness haven'.

In the kitchen, there was a small wood burning stove, a small table and chair where he ate his grub. The room had a couple of small paned windows for light and a kerosene lamp. All of his pots and pans, as well as his dishes were made of metal in the same manner as his helmet. He had personally made them by cutting and pounding metal he had obtained from the old abandoned mine that we had previously visited. He had done a very good job with everything. On the window sill was a large bottle about the size of a large deli dill pickle jar. The contents looked very strange and he sensed our interest so he explained. The jar contained two near full-term unborn baby mountain lions. He had unintentionally killed the mother lioness and found the fetuses and decided to preserve them in formaldehyde. He was very proud of this possession although, being a conservationist, he was quick to point out that he would not have shot the lioness had she not been raiding the rations he was storing for the ensuing winter. In the bottom of and underneath the floor where his small dining table stood, he had built a cellar to store his home grown vegetables during the winter months. Having the storage here was convenient for cooking.

The den or entertainment area was really a glassed-in hot house. It had a built-in barbeque pit made from river rock. He had some eatable plants growing in there. The window panes could be opened or closed for ventilation. The last point of the visit was his blacksmith shop. It was well equipped in terms of hand made equipment. Every machine was hand powered. He had a hand cranked lathe, a boring machine, hand drills, and augers. The coal to stoke the furnace came from the old mine a couple miles up the river. He made bellows, pliers, hammers, and quenching buckets! It was quite a sight. Now I could see how he made his pots and pans and, of course, his helmet. The biggest surprise came when he stated that he made his own guns. It was incredible. There were black powder blunderbusses, long rifles, and hand guns (somewhat oversized). He had a number of such weapons and he actually hunted with them. He was a real mountain man living off the land. He never left the area and actually homesteaded his place on the river. He got his mail through the Mackay Bar ranch hands, just down river where we were staying, when they went to town. It took five days in a jeep to make the round trip drive to town over land and he had no reason to go there.

He seemed to enjoy having visitors but there also seemed to be a bit of sadness in his demeanor. He went on to elaborate and said at one time he did get married and he and his wife had a son. They divorced and after a period of time, he convinced his son and his family to come and live in the wilderness area on his property. The unfortunate part was that his grandson somehow fell and was seriously injured and passed away after some time. He couldn't forgive himself for that event feeling that if they had never come his grandson would still be alive. He had built what appeared to be a rather beautiful home (one building) for them to live in. He had cut the timber and did all the work himself. There was a welling up of tears in his eyes as he spoke. I knew it was painful for him.

At the time I met him, Sylvan Hart was in his seventies. Shortly after my visit, *National Geographic* paid him a visit and wrote a rather extensive article on him in the publication of *Volume 137, No.2, February, 1970*. I had never met a man like Sylvan previously and I never really expect to meet another. He was one of a breed that has all but disappeared. Incidentally, the fishing that year on the river wasn't very good. We went for steelhead and out of a group of ten or twelve men, only a half dozen fish were caught.

Saltwater Fishing – South of the Border in Mexican Waters

About 1987, I made my first long-range deep sea fishing trip. A neighbor down the street from me in Upland, Dave Shobe, a contractor by profession, invited me on an eight-day trip out of San Diego aboard the *Royal Palaris* sports fishing boat. A group of local businessmen interested in fishing got together every year to make this trip. I had never been on such a trip and I was a complete neophyte needing all the help I could get in preparing for the trip. I needed rods and reels and, since it was nearing my birthday, Bev arranged through Dave to purchase three new custom rods for me with my name on them. The trip turned out to be a wonderful experience and I was hooked on saltwater fishing for the rest of my life. It was on this eight-day trip that I caught my first tuna, a yellow fin that weighed in at 100 pounds! We found a school of these fish and worked it until the sun went down. Man, was I ever tired when I finally landed that fish! It would be a few years later that I would learn that I didn't have the right equipment for that species and size of fish! No wonder it took me almost two hours to land it. I had a lot more learning to do regarding this 'stand-up' approach to tuna and wahoo fishing!

It was not until 1989 that I began to really learn about saltwater fishing. I had begun working for Carl W. Newell. He was an avid fisherman for both fresh water and saltwater. Carl also owned a manufacturing company that made the famous Newell graphite saltwater fishing reels. Obviously, it didn't take long for us to begin discussing our fishing experiences and our love for fishing. In terms of saltwater fishing, Carl was a great mentor for me. He knew a lot more about fishing than I did. In a relatively short time, he invited me on one of his annual albacore trips, all expenses paid through the company. It was a four-day trip out of San Diego.

To get ready for the trip, he wanted to teach me a little bit about casting and the rigs needed for the various species of fish we would probably encounter on the trip. Carl had a casting technique whereby one hand was on the reel (spool) and rod while the other hand was on the end or butt portion of the rod. The live bait or lure was put in motion by swinging it and as it began to make its outward arch, the rod and reel were swung over the top of the shoulder almost as if throwing a baseball. It took awhile to get used to it but it did work. In fact Carl was written up in one of the west coast sport fishing magazines with pictures demonstrating his method. Carl also believed that you need several rigs prepared and ready for the inevitable chance that specific things happened at sea very quickly when the fish are biting. When you heard "Hook-up," yelled out no one had time to change reels or tie on the 'right' hooks. The action was starting. The size rod was very important. A 20 pound rod was a 20 pound rod much like a golfer's five iron is always a five iron. So a fisherman needed a 20, 25, 30, 40, 50, 60 and 80 pound rated rods. Each had the basic monofilament line to match the size rod in poundage rating. The concept is to match the rod and line to the size fish that is being caught. That way the fisherman stands a much better chance of catching fish. If the fish are very difficult to catch, then down size the monofilament line by ten pounds and try that. Because most fish can see exceptionally well, it may be they are seeing your larger diameter line and are skittish about nailing your bait. Downsizing improves your possibilities for a hook-up but makes you play the fish with less aggressiveness.

On certain trips, you had to double the number of rigs made up because you needed one for live bait and another of the same size for wire leader to fish for wahoo. Finally, Carl had read a lot of material about the smelling sensitivity of fish. He learned that a hound dog smells a hundred times better than a human, but a fish smells a thousand times better than a hound dog! That tells a lot about what scent you may have and whether fish detect it and like or dislike your personal smell. Did you use a perfumed soap to wash your hands? How about that shaving cream you spread all over your face? Did you finish it off with your favorite 'smellum good' aftershave lotion? Did you use cologne? I learned quickly that this seemingly minute issue made a big difference in catching fish…both fresh water and saltwater. So how did you circumvent the problem? The simple answer was to rub the worst smelling lotion on your hands that came bottled from Berkley. It had an odorous putrid smell. Carl even had a can of the stuff close by the bait tank and often doused his live bait in it before casting out. It smelled so bad it seemed some fish surfaced to just find out why we weren't the live bait they were waiting for and jumping in the water! If you didn't have any of the canned stuff, then just get some fish entrails and rub your hands well and enthusiastically with them. That works, too, but not as well as the bottled gunk.

Temperature of the water, I learned, was another important factor. At first, the deep sea trips seemed to me to be time spent aimlessly wondering around on the ocean without purpose. I was wrong. The skipper was looking for specific water temperatures because it is known that fish of various species follow ocean currents that maintain a specific temperature. That is common to their habitat. Interestingly, it also applies to fresh water fishing. For example, when the hot sun bakes a lake for a while during the day, some fish will move to deeper and cooler water to stabilize their body temperature.

Finally, the last thing was the right technique used to bring a fish in after the hook-up. Many ocean fish have certain habits when they are first hooked that telegraph to the fisherman what species he has hooked. There are other indications that inform the fisherman about the species being fished. After the hook-up, I learned that it was important to 'keep their head.' That meant keeping the pressure on the fish with the line taught so that the head was always pointed in towards the boat...don't let them turn and make a run unless you haven't any choice. Keeping the rod up at an almost 90 degree angle from the fish at all times keeps direct pressure off your line and maximum pressure on the fish and your rod so the fish works harder and, hopefully, tires more quickly. To keep the fish's head, a pumping action is used in a rhythmic sequence much like keeping time to a song's beat. As you pump, the rod comes up and, if your line and reel brakes are holding, you are actually dragging the fish towards the boat; then as the rod is released downward, the fisherman takes one or two strokes on the reel bringing in the line that has some very slight slack. It takes strength to do this for an extended period of time and often the fight between man and a large fish can last for more than an hour without any let-up. This is referred to as 'stand-up' fishing and the most physically strenuous type of big game fishing.

Prior to the development of the 'short rods', such a battle between man and fish could last at least a couple of hours with a tuna weighing in excess of 150 to 200 pounds. The long seven foot and eight foot rods were like rubber bands. One has to only identify with the science theory of leverage to understand the problem of the long rods and the fight with the fish. The shorter the rod, the fisherman gains the advantage. As a result of this research by Carl W. Newell, eventually we were fishing 200-400 pound tuna fish with four and a half foot rods. This was unique in the industry. It is more difficult to cast with the short rod but if the fisherman is 'fly-lining' live bait, the current takes the bait and minimal casting is needed.

My trips out of San Diego were always oriented to catching albacore, big eye tuna, yellow fin tuna, blue fin tuna, wahoo, and yellow tail fish. On the long boat journeys from San Diego, which were three days and nights in each direction, it was common to see literally hundreds of playful bottlenose dolphins swimming along with the boat a hundred yards or less off the port or starboard sides of the boat. They could swim for miles and miles. When they got up very close to the boat, within twelve to fifteen feet off the side, you could watch them takes turns leading in the front position while the others in line behind drafted much like in auto racing. As they would tire and need to rest, the lead dolphin would pull out and fall back to the rear position. They just seemed to be playing and having fun. I found it most interesting and entertaining.

For a while, it seemed every trip on which I ventured out to sea was extremely unique. The old salts would say, "You'll never see another day like today!" or "I've never seen so many mahi mahi in my life!" On another trip the comment that stood out was, "I've never seen a school of blue fin tuna held for six hours before!" These trips produced some fond memories for me and my companions. Usually, we were on board a vessel that was the best or next to it from the San Diego fleet. That meant we had a superb crew, excellent food, and great fishing. I think the trip that sticks out most in my mind was a twelve day trip to the Revilla Gigedo Islands which lie approximately 350 miles southwest of Cabo San Lucas, the southern most point of Baja California. The islands we fished were Clarion, Roca Partido, and San Benedicto. We had a crew of eight and twenty-four fishermen. The final count was twenty-seven tons of fish that we brought back to San Diego. That was in November 1994. It was on this trip that I caught the largest fish that I have ever caught...a 183 pound yellow fin tuna. I landed it at 9:30 p.m. after about one hour and forty minutes of coaxing and coaching from the crew. It truly wore me out but I was extremely happy. I caught the fish on 100 pound test line with a 200 pound rated leader on which I had put a live 'salami' (about a five pound live Mexican mackerel) and 'fly-lined it.' I had been soaking (letting it swim where it wanted and where the water currents took it) it for about thirty minutes when the big tuna hit it. What a thrill!! I knew I had what I was fishing for as soon the line was taught.

If it is such hard work, I have been asked, why do you like to do stand-up fishing? Big game fishing is indeed hard work. While you are on a fish, it is just plain hard work and a lot of sweat. The fisherman must be attentive and constantly aware of what his fish is doing or trying to do. Others on the boat are still fishing and as your fish moves in the water, you must maintain a straight line between you and the fish and the boat. That means moving on deck constantly and avoiding the lines of the other fishermen. That's not always easy as you get your fish closer to the boat. You are hollering to each fisherman, "over" or "under" depending on how your line is in relationship to the fisherman you are attempting to avoid. That takes skill, patience and a keen awareness on the part of both fishermen.

Roark Moudy with 183 pound yellowfin tuna caught off Clarion Island, Revillagigedos Islands, Mexico November, 1994

Your reward begins to manifest itself when you see 'color'. Your fish is coming up from the depths and you can see it, a silver flash, as it begins the 'death circle.' The circle gets tighter as the fish nears the surface of the water. Then you or a deckhand calls for the gaff and you know you have almost completed the task of landing a big one! Once on deck, you see this beautiful creature that has given its best in a gallant effort. They are colorful, majestic creatures of the oceans, strong, and propelled by incredible muscle strength, designed for speed in water. Catching giant tuna is indeed special for stand-up fishermen. You are pitting your equipment and strength against the fish's raw power. Fighting tuna is unique because they are the only fish from the deep that can regulate their body temperature and continue the fight from the time the hook-up takes place until the gaff has been applied. The fisherman does not always win these fights either.

Saltwater Fishing – North Pacific

The fisheries of British Columbia to Alaska are teaming with sea life. There are the common appearances of the 'killer whales' or Orcas. There is an abundance of the five salmon species, halibut, lingcod, red snapper and rock fish. The trips I have enjoyed to this part of the world are different from the trips to the south. First, although not a significant factor, is the weather. It's almost always cooler and often rains as compared to Mexican waters where the weather is hot, full sun and humid. In the North, there is also an abundance of the food chain for the growth and survival of the ocean's creatures.

On many trips, the fisherman will see many land based animals such as bears, deer, elk, and bald eagles. I love to be in a boat and view God's creation in its natural habitat. You generally have to look carefully in the brush to see the elk and deer. On the other hand, the bears and bald eagles are active during the day trying to snag a meal. On one trip to Black Fish Sound in British Columbia, I was in the boat making our way to the fishing area when we came across a brown bear swimming across the channel. In that position, he is virtually helpless. The guide decided to have some fun and came along side the swimming bear and with a paddle pushed his whole body under water. Of course, the bear was sputtering and gasping for air when he came up and seemed to give a look that said, "If I ever catch you in the forest, I won't have any mercy on you!" We left him to his destiny and went fishing.

I have fed the great bald eagles rock fish that I have caught. In fact, on one trip, a test was performed to see how much weight the eagle could carry in its talons. It was on my first trip to British Columbia with one of my best friends, Bob Feldmeth. Dr. Bob was a professor of biology at the Claremont Colleges and literally a living encyclopedia on salt-water creatures. He also knew a lot about geology. He specialized in the study of salinity life of fish and plants. I always had fun with him. It turned out this particular eagle's capacity was right at five pounds of fish at one time.

On this trip, we traveled to Rivers Inlet, British Columbia. As we made our way to the fishing grounds from the lodge (without a guide), we noticed an eagle sitting atop a tree at one end of a very small island. It was his territory alone. He defended it against all intruders as we witnessed one day. He was always perched there because it gave him an advantageous view of his territorial fishing grounds. Eagles have very keen eyesight and can see fish swimming near the surface from long distances. Then they swoop down and pick up their unsuspecting prey with their strong talons and take it back to their nests for their young. Incidentally, bald eagles mate for life.

Bob and I decided to have some fun when we passed the eagle's perch that day on our way back to the lodge. We would save all of the rockfish that we caught and feed them to this eagle on our way back. It turned out we caught and saved five rockfish. It was about five p.m. when we arrived at the point of the eagle's island and he was home surveying his kingdom. We shut off the boat's engine and began to drift. We tossed one of the smallest dead fish overboard and waited. After we drifted several feet from the fish, the eagle made his move. He leaped from his perch atop a Douglas fir tree, spread his wings and glided down for the swoop. Just as he reached the fish, he extended his talons, bent his tail feathers downward to slow his flight speed and picked up the fish. Away he flew to the nest to deliver his catch to the young hatchling and its mama.

Within a stretch of three minutes, he was back on his perch again. We threw out another fish, slightly bigger than the last. The eagle repeated his actions. By the time we threw out the largest fish, which weighed about four to five pounds, we were having fun watching the effort. Again the eagle made his move. This time the weight of the fish was more than he could pick up. He tried to hold on but soon had to give up the fish and dropped it as the flight drag on his body was bringing him down to the point where the very tips of his wings were splashing in the water! We were no more than fifteen or twenty feet away. He didn't give up however. He flew back to his roost and sat there gathering his strength for a new assault. He must have waited five minutes when suddenly, off the perch he flew and swooped down for one more try. He seemed to make sure there wasn't any mistake this time. Yet the load was obviously very heavy for the bird. He struggled hard and labored to gain altitude and slowly but surely climbed out and headed for the nest. He had done quite a day's work in about fifteen minutes! We continued to provide some delicacies for the eagle family each day we were there.

Bob and I made this trip in late May. We didn't have an appreciation for the timing of salmon runs so this was a learning experience. We were to find out this was very early in the season and salmon fishing at this time of year is very sketchy at best. We thought it was a little strange when we arrived and there was only one other person at the lodge to fish. The other people were members of the crew getting things shaped up for the real fishermen who would arrive in another week or two. Only one guide had arrived at the lodge and the other person, a lady who was fulfilling her husband's dream fishing trip, hired him. Bob and I were on our own.

Salmon fishing involves a lot of trolling and having your bait properly set up so that the bait rotates in a three or four-foot smooth circular motion as it is towed behind the boat. The depth to be fished is set by down riggers attached to your fishing line. It takes a while to get the hang of it but with patience it can be accomplished. Bob and I had fished diligently for three days and didn't have anything to show for our efforts. Fishing for the King salmon meant we needed to fish about twenty to twenty-five feet off shore and about that deep in the water, almost on the bottom. We followed the shoreline into and out of all the little inlets and bays as we had been instructed without success. No strikes. Nothing.

As we were making our way out of an inlet near the stepchild eagle's nest, I told Bob to stop the boat. I was hung up on a rock or submerged log. I tried to pull it loose when all of a sudden my line took off. It went zipping past our boat and out into the open ocean water! Bob was scrambling trying to get the boat going so we could follow the fish, but the fish was taking my line faster than Bob could get the boat to move. I started yelling that, "The fish is going to spool me!" Bob says, "Yeah, he's headed for Japan!" Just before I was to be spooled the fish stopped. Bob continued moving the boat towards the fish and I was reeling the line in as fast as I could when the fish decided to make another run…this time straight back at the boat. I couldn't keep the line taught. It was flying loosely in the breeze. Now the situation was reversed. The fish passed directly underneath the boat along with the attached line. Bob was trying to turn the boat around again and I was stumbling around in the boat trying to stand up and trying to keep up with the movement and direction of the fish. I almost fell out of the boat more than once!

My efforts seemed to be of no avail. By now my rod was bent under the boat in the direction the fish had gone. All of a sudden, a big bang and my rod snapped into two pieces but I still had the fish on! Then it was Bob's turn to scramble. Bob first tried to hold the two pieces of the rod together and let me try to reel and drag the fish in. That did not work very well. Bob almost fell out of the boat.

This clown act continued for several more minutes before we had things somewhat under control. I was carefully reeling in the fish with the broken rod, all the while trying to keep pressure on the fish. For the next several minutes Bob had settled down and was regaining his composure. For some reason, a miracle happened I suppose, I don't know how but I managed to land the fish with the broken end of the rod dangling. As the fish surfaced, I tried to maneuver it close to the boat so Bob could net it for me. Bob stumbled and crawled around on the boat until he got into position and finally netted the fish for me. We both had a great rush of adrenaline and let out a war whoop simultaneously and "high-fived" each other a couple of times.

What we did not know was that the boat with the lady and the fishing guide had watched the entire episode and nearly fell out of their boat grabbing their sides with laughter as the two neophytes tried to land their first King salmon. It was the only fish caught during the five days we were there. The guide told the lady that Bob and I were very lucky to have landed that fish. We were given a 'tyee' pin denoting that we had caught a large sized King salmon. It is an Indian word supposedly for 'big fish.'

Looking back today, I would have to agree! How big was it? It weighed in at twenty-five pounds. It was the first King salmon I caught. I was proud!

As soon as they became members of the family, I learned quickly if my sons-in-law were recreational fishermen, hard core fishermen or boat riders. Since Alan Aufhammer was the first, he was the first to be confirmed one way or another. I invited him to join me on a salmon trip to the west coast of Vancouver Island, British Columbia to the little hamlet of Bamfield. I had assembled a group of about fifteen fishermen. I think Alan enjoyed the tripping and the camaraderie. As the second day began at 5:00 a.m., Alan was not on the dock and no one seemed to know where he was at the time. He had not joined us for breakfast. I jogged back up the pier and drive from the docks area to the lodge and found Alan asleep in his bed. "Aren't you going fishing with us?" I asked. He replied, "No, I don't think I will this morning, I'm going to sleep-in and maybe read a little and then I'll go out this afternoon with you after you have come in for lunch." This isn't intended to be any kind of a negative statement about my very fine son-in-law, which he is, but needless to say he has never pleaded or begged me to go on another fishing trip!

I took my other son-in-law, Don Collins, on a trip to Alaska. We were traveling to the Kenai Peninsula and the Kenai River with John Duke and some of his family and friends. This area is the home and spawning area of the largest King salmon in the world. The record fish weighed in at about one hundred pounds. We flew into Anchorage and drove down to Soldotna, Alaska. We fished the river for two days and I caught one King that weighed in at about thirty-five or forty pounds. In addition, after spending the day on a boat in the river, the pink salmon were running so, in the evenings for a couple of hours, we fished for pinks. They were so thick along the banks that you could feel them hitting your line and hooks but they weren't biting. If you could have fished with a treble hook, you could have easily snagged a limit but that technique was against the law.

On the third day, we took a float plane with our party of ten across Cook's Inlet to another river to catch Silver salmon. The float plane flight took about half an hour. It was bad weather…rained all day, but the fish were biting. Besides catching fish, we were entertained by a grizzly bear believed to be about five years old. To start our fishing effort, we were dropped off at a location on the high side bank of the river and about fifty yards from a sandbar in the middle of the river where there was a confluence of the river with a smaller stream. Perhaps seven or eight fishermen were on the sandbar fishing. Our location was perhaps eight to ten feet above the river and about a couple hundred feet downstream from the sandbar. The river itself was maybe thirty or forty yards wide where we were going to fish. We immediately noticed that there was evidence of bears having worked the bank area where we were located with tracks, scat and berries all around. That didn't exactly make us feel secure. In fact, we were rather nervous throughout the day. However, the fishing was very good and that distracted us from our concern about the bears.

Within a couple hours, I noticed two men several hundred yards down river hollering and rapidly jumping in the river making their way to the opposite bank from us. They crossed over safely but within a short time a bear was following them. Then next thing I noticed, these two fishermen were making their way upstream towards us on the opposite side of the river, with the bear still following them. They made their way to the sandbar group of fishermen. The bear arrived a short time later but stopped directly across the river from us

It was a brown bear, as known in Alaska, but in the lower forty-eight we know it as a grizzly bear. He was eyeing our fish that were laid out and lined up on a washed out depression in the riverbank. The bear looked at our fish for what seemed several minutes as if weighing the possibility of taking our fish versus the sacked fish on the sandbar. One of our guides thought that it was a young bear, maybe three to five years old, because he still had the white tuffs of hair on the tips of his ears.

After studying our catch for a rather lengthy period of time, the bear must have decided that the sandbar fishermen had more to offer even though we were closing in on our limit of ten fish per fisherman. Suddenly the bear stood tall on his hind legs and sniffed the air and started to move in the direction of the other fishermen. They began blowing whistles at him like crazy. It didn't matter. It was as if the bear was saying, "Those whistles don't bother me, I want your fish any way." So off he trudged to the sandbar as the fishermen scattered in all directions. Some headed for the bank and some waded out into the river. All of the fishermen left their catch behind on the sandbar.

The bear didn't waste any time at all. He immediately grabbed the plastic bags containing the fish catch of each fisherman and carted them off the sandbar onto the bank opposite us. He meticulously took one bag at a time. Sometimes, his paws or teeth would split the bag and he would drop one or two fish along the way to the location of his cache. He didn't waste any fish, however. He came back and picked up each one that he had dropped or that had fallen out of the plastic bag. The bear was indeed going to have the feast of his young life!

The overhead sound of our plane arriving, after descending through the rain and heavy overcast skies, interrupted our fishermen's' comedy just upstream. Simultaneously, our shuttle boat arrived and picked us up for the return trip up the river to our plane and the flight back to Soldotna. The timing was great as some of us were contemplating a visit from the bear with his next act. As we turned upstream from the confluence, I looked back at the sandbar and saw the bear sitting on his haunches seemingly enjoying watching the fishermen now wading and fishing in the river and sort of saying to them 'Here I am, hurry up and catch me some more fish!' I was very thankful the bear had decided to descend onto the sand bar rather than choosing to cross the river and take our collection of fish! We had a good time because all of us caught our limit of fish even though all of us were pretty much soaked by the rain.

The next day we drove down to Homer, Alaska for a halibut trip. Once on board the boats, we had to travel about an hour and half from the port to the fishing grounds. The weather was great, a perfect day. The boats were relatively small taking only four fishermen each. My son-in-law, Don Collins was discussing fishing with the skipper, who at the time was eating a banana while we were underway. The skipper proceeded to tell Don that halibut could be caught with a banana peeling as bait. Of course, never having used such an item for fish bait before, Don was given to a huge dose of skepticism! We had been on location for more than an hour and it seemed every time bait was put overboard, a halibut weighing from fifty to sixty pounds was hooked. It was getting somewhat boring even though we had a limit of two fish. Each of us would reel in fish after fish and release them because we were trying to land a 'barn door' halibut. That is a halibut that seems as big as a barn door and weighs any where from two hundred to four hundred pounds.

It was during this monotony that Don asked where the banana peel was. The skipper pointed to the trashcan. Don put the whole thing on his hook and lowered this unusual bait to the bottom. Within seconds he had a strike but was so surprised that he missed setting the hook. He reeled in and saw that he still had about half of the banana peel intact. The skipper, watching this young up-start fisherman said, "Throw it in again!" Without hesitation Don threw the bait in again and within seconds he had a hook-up. He actually caught about a fifty-five pound halibut on half of a banana peel! I would not have believed it had I not saw it with my own eyes! What a great day of fishing. Again we had our limits of fish but left without a barn door!

I love to fish more than I like eating fish. There is a certain attraction there for me. I have spent many hours and even days on the water of beautiful lakes, rivers, streams, and on the ocean trying to outsmart the fish. Getting a hook-up gives me an adrenaline rush that is hard to describe. It is better than the best golf shot I have ever made; it is better than any basketball game that I ever played; it is deeply embedded in my memory. It is just an absolute thrill.

I have mentioned some of the places where I have fished already but here I will summarize those that are stuck in the cudgels of my mind as having been special fishing trips for one reason or another:

Middle Fork of the Salmon River, Idaho

Snake River, Wyoming

Rogue River, Oregon

South Fork of the Santa Ana River, Southern California

San Gabriel River, Southern California

Kenai River, Alaska

Lake Henshaw, Southern California

Big Bear Lake, Southern California

Silverwood Lake, Southern California

Railroad Canyon Lake, Southern California

Lake Berryessa, Northern California

Lake Sherwood, Southern California

June Lake, Central California – Eastern High Sierra Mountains

Silver Lake, Central California – Eastern High Sierra Mountains

South Lake, Bishop, California – Eastern High Sierra Mountains

Lake Sabrina, Bishop, California – Eastern High Sierra Mountains

Green Valley Lake, Southern California

Mexico, Rillagigedos Islands (Long range)

Coronado Islands, offshore San Diego, California

Bamfield, Vancouver Island (west coast), British Columbia, Canada

Blackfish Sound, Mainland, British Columbia, Canada

Rivers Inlet, Mainland, British Columbia, Canada

North Pacific Springs, Mainland, British Columbia, Canada

Cook's Inlet River, opposite Kenai Peninsula, Alaska

Gulf of Alaska, Homer, Alaska

Englefeld Lodge, Queen Charlotte Islands, British Columbia, Canada

I have enjoyed some of my best days on the water while fishing at Englefeld Lodge with one of my best fishing buddies, Ron Simons. We met at Cal Poly University back in the 1960s and maintained our friendship throughout the years. We have had many superb fishing expeditions together but our two trips to this lodge have been tops. This area is absolutely pristine virgin timbered islands owned by the Haida Indians. On our first trip there two years ago, it had only been in operation for two years. A fisherman goes there for the solitude, camaraderie, superb accommodations, first class equipment and the total appeal to indulging fishermen. It can only accommodate forty-four fishermen at a time and each person must choose between a three or four day trip. There are thirty-three crewmen, or lodge workers, to attend to the fisherman's needs. The only way to arrive there is by sea-plane or helicopter. The object is to fish for several species of salmon with a focus on Kings and halibut. Bottom fishing is allowed for those who enjoy the depths for rockfish. Ron and I have never failed to catch more fish than we needed. This last year, 2003, was our most successful. We really loaded up on the fillets...more than 100 pounds for each of us!

This year (2003) was especially fun for me. Ron has such a great spirit about himself and fishing. On the second morning, I was having all the luck getting the hook-ups. The first five hook-ups were mine which meant that Ron was having to control the boat to keep me in proper position with the fish, get his own gear out of the water and into the boat each time I had a hook-up, retrieve both down riggers, and get the net ready so that when the fish was in position, it could be netted, and he could lock the fish. This action would take place in a matter of only three or four minutes, which meant Ron was jumping through hoops like a cat on a hot tin roof! Then the process started all over again. I had to bait my hook again, which gave him a little respite, he had a breather getting his own gear back in the water, and once I was back in the water, begin the troll. As I said, this went on for five hook-ups in a row after which I profusely thanked Ron for being the best lackey that I'd ever had on a trip!

I have fished other places. Sometimes we didn't have a great catch and occasionally we got skunked. But they were still fun days! I never had a bad day fishing. You may have seen the bumper sticker, "The worst day of fishing is better than the best day at work!" I think there is some truth in the statement.

---

[1]   White-water Adventure on Wild Rivers Of Idaho, *National Geographic*, Vol. 137, No. 2, February, 1970, pages 232-233.

CHAPTER NINETEEN
Roots of Success: My Foundational Beliefs

I have lived a good life, however, I am not a man who feels or believes that I have accomplished a lot in my life. To my way of thinking, I have certainly done better that I ever expected with God's graciousness and goodness to me. Yet, I have left nothing for humanity in the generations to come as a great literary, scientist who discovered a cure for a horrendous disease, or some great sports figure that fans adulated and adored. That is not me. I am glad of who I am, nevertheless. I am a peasant boy. The Great Creator made me. What I know is that God made me in His own image. I was sinful but now I am perfect in His sight through His grace. I will never be a perfect individual because of my sin. My life has been blessed in ways that I could never have imagined. God has been more than wonderful to me. I have a strong conviction that the benefits, which have come my way, are a result of many factors and people who have positively impacted my life.

As I look back at my heritage, I see ancestors who believed in God and practiced the Christian faith daily. Probably not all of my ancestors became believers. I know that many of them were faithful in their journey with Christ. I am both fortunate and thankful for the example many of them provided and handed down to me through family ties.

There was my great great grandfather, Thomas S. Moudy, who was born in Virginia and made his way to Arkansas, where he ministered and pastored in the Chickalah Baptist Church. Many of his children and grandchildren became converts because of him or his influence. Some of the Moudys were Methodists when I was a child in Belleville. Regardless of their denominational preference, they loved and believed in God. I did not know any of my distant ancestors personally so my reference points are far removed and detached but, nevertheless, they remain a part of my God given heritage.

The Roarks practiced Christianity as well. In this family a majority seemed to initially be Presbyterian and some later became Baptist. With this family, it was not so much a preference of one denomination over another as it was what church association was available to them on the frontier of America. John Roark speaks to this point in his book. What is most important is simply that they loved God and practiced their Christian beliefs day by day. These early frontier Christians had to rely upon a supernatural power to help them through the struggles that never seemed to end. I am once again blessed with the seeds of Christ planted in my family heritage.

At this time, I cannot speak for the Smith or Apple families. I do not know enough about their histories to identify with their spiritual convictions.

Information about the early Talley family has not been clarified sufficiently to enable me know the extent to which they may have believed in God and the salvation available to one and all believers in Christ. However, I do not have any doubts about my grandfather, Andrew Jackson Talley and his family. He certainly taught the 'Good Book' to his offspring. Some of his children took it to heart more than others, as it is in most any family.

I can personally attest to the fact that every night, as long as I was at grandpa Talley's home, he personally read the Bible aloud to family and guests alike who stayed late enough or were spending the night at his home. This was without fail. It did not end there either. Many times he would discuss or comment on his convictions about specific Bible verses and what they meant to him. Yes, it was his interpretation but he was well versed in the Bible. He was a great believer in the Book of Revelations. This prophetical book with its' symbolism relating to the ultimate destruction of the world order as we know it and the salvation of the souls of believers and their redemption from hell in the end times was of prime importance to him. This book in the Bible depicts the great second coming of Christ, which is a Biblical promise from God. There is also the great battle of Armageddon to be fought where, "blood will flow from the dying soldiers of the armies of the battle and it will be as deep as the horses bridles."

Grandpa Talley loved to interact with his visitors. He would sit on his large front porch and discuss the Bible with anyone. He had a zeal for God's Holy Word that was second to none. He talked it, lived it and believed it with all his heart. He purchased a family Bible in the late 1880's, which used to sit on top of a small table near a window or on the sewing machine in the newer half of the house. That Bible is now in my possession. I never open it because the pages are so fragile and the paper in such poor condition, I am afraid it would literally tear or even disintegrate if turned. It was one of the very few things that became a family heirloom. It is so big and cumbersome that Grandpa had another Bible, which he used for his daily reading.

Grandpa Talley attended church almost every Sunday as long as he was in good health. He walked or rode in the wagon to the Riley Creek Church. He was dedicated and believed with all his heart the teachings of Jesus, the One who ruled his life. I have already discussed how he realized that God was working in his life when he was making whiskey. That was a major turning point in how he lived his life from that day forward. In my opinion, if there ever was a 'man's man', Grandpa Talley was the man!

My mother was strongly devoted to her Christian beliefs as well. She tried to live her life so that it was pleasing to God. I'm not trying to say that she was perfect. She had her faults, as we all do. Yet in God's eyes she was cleansed and made whole. She knew it was important for me to learn the ways of Christ and taught me from my earliest recollections. In those early years, my mother and I went to church all the time, so it seemed. I am most certain that every time the doors opened, we went. I find it a depth of joy, even today, to still be able to sing the old hymns from years ago. They were sung over and over again at church and I eventually memorized many of them.

During my recent visit to Arkansas, Doyle and Melba had a singin' at there home during the county fair time. That's when the most visitors are in town. People are invited to come and sing songs, old gospel songs. These musicians are not professional by any means. The piano is played and everyone has a chance to select a song to sing at any time during the evening.

They had songbooks…old paperback hymnals. I found myself singing along with the words in my mouth without having to look down at the pages and it had been many years since I had heard some of those songs. I had a great time that evening with many of my cousins there to join in.

I have spoken of my Aunt Bessie (Moudy) Barrick. She had a significant role in teaching me about Jesus and His love for me as well. She was the pastor to the Assembly of God Church in Belleville where I first recall going to church. It was always just my mother and me going to church. My father wasn't to become a Christian for many years to come. Church meetings in those days could last for several hours. Preaching could go on and on. The believers felt the 'power of God come down and they would speak in other tongues' (to which the Bible refers). Only an 'interpreter' in the congregation could make the message in other tongues understandable through translation. The interpreter would make the translation after the message had been brought in tongues. This was a rather common occurrence. In fact, there would sometimes be multiple messages given in tongues. 'People would shout and dance in the spirit' as they praised God! It was a joyful time if you were a born again Christian. If not, it could be rather jarring to your psyche, feelings and confidence. In general 'outsiders', including non-Christians or even believers from other denominations where tongues were not spoken, could not understand what was happening.

I accepted Christ into my life at the age of twelve. It was in a church service at the Oxnard Assembly of God Church and my dear Aunt Bessie was preaching that Sunday. She had not gone to seminary but that didn't hinder her from proclaiming the truths of the gospel. She had learned the word of God through others. She understood what she read, and through the power of God working in her life, she was able to minister to many unbelievers. Her harvest for the Kingdom is unknown to us mortals but she has seen many conversions as the result of her commitment to Jesus Christ. From her viewpoint and religious convictions, getting saved was only the first step. To become a true believer meant that you had to have evidence of the Spirit of God in your life through the manifestation of speaking in tongues, the heavenly language. There was also the practiced belief that a person could backslide. That is, a person could fall away from

God's mercy and grace by not following His commandments. If you died in that condition, you were doomed to hell. So people were always rededicating their lives to God and gaining forgiveness of their sins once more. It was a trying kind of life in many respects with most believers seeking forgiveness of their wrongdoings almost as a given constant. When, how often, and for what did you ask forgiveness? When were you considered a backslider? These were important and profound issues for those desiring to walk the straight and narrow road.

On the other hand, the Baptist believed that 'once in grace always in grace.' In other words, once you became a believer, you could never lose your salvation. It was akin to saying that once you became a 'Child of God', you became a member of the Family of God. That was easily understood because in an earthly family, once you were born and became part of a family, in reality, you could never be disinherited. You were always a member of that family. This issue is merely one difference existing in Protestantism that affects people trying to live a life pleasing to God.

When Bev and I married, I made a new commitment to Christ in my life. I felt that was important as we started our life together. It never hurts a person and is a good thing to rededicate your life to Christ every once in a while. It helps you to remember your relationship to Him. It helps to renew your faith and invigorate your soul to know that you will have a life in the hereafter.

I praise God and give Him all the glory for what he has done in my life. He is my strength and my salvation, in Him will I trust forever. My favorite Bible verse is Isaiah 26:3. "Thou will keep him in perfect peace whose mind is stayed on Thee." I was never perfect and could never be in man's eyes. But through God's generous gift on the cross of crucifixion, "He gave His only begotten Son that whosoever believith in Him shall not perish but have ever lasting life." (John 3:16) Thank God for His love and mercy toward mankind. His peace abides in me that passeth all understanding. How true that is!

There is a song, the music and words were written by Bart Millard and copyrighted in 2001 by Simpleville Music/ASCAP, which is entitled *I Can Only Imagine*. I love the words of this song because it lets me know something about the hereafter when we meet Jesus face to face. I have copied the words below:

I Can Only Imagine

What it will be like
When I walk
By your side.
I can only imagine
What my eyes will see
When your face
Is before me.
I can only imagine.
I can only imagine.

Surrounded by Your glory,
What will my heart feel?
Will I dance for You, Jesus,
Or in awe of You be still?
Will I stand in Your presence,
Or to my knees will I fall?
Will I sing, "Hallelujah"?
Will I be able to speak at all?
I can only imagine.
I can only imagine

When that day comes
And I find myself
Standing in the Son.
I can only imagine
When all I do
Is forever,
Forever worship You.
I can only imagine.

This song strokes my heart's cords every time it is sung. It is incredible to think about when I pass through heaven's gates, shake hands with Saint Peter and have him tell me, in answer to my question, "Where is the throne of God, I want to see Jesus?" What a glorious day!! I truly love the Lord with all of my heart and all of my might. My mother taught me to do that from the time I was a child!

CHAPTER TWENTY

A New Generation: New Frontiers to Conquer

My daughters were wonderful gifts reflecting God's love for me and my wife. However, grandchildren are God's very special gifts! One wants to be with them and love them from the day they are born. Each is so very different and yet they all come from basically the same genes. Some of them have no worries, as they shouldn't at this early age, and see life as one world of fun and play. Some are quite reserved in almost everything they do. Often, they have to be gently 'pushed' to get them to even try something that they haven't done before whether it is taking a bite of food that they haven't tasted before or being convinced to try a ride at the fair or carnival. Some are very self-confident, there is not too much they think that they can't do! Some are head strung and have to be handled with more control and care. Others are very compliant and want to please. Then I see some that are very quiet. They are the listeners and don't want to speak out for fear that they will be embarrassed or perhaps they are just learning by listening. Right now, some of them are comfortable around adults; the others not as much. They are all active physically; some are dancers, play roller hockey, baseball, basketball, football, softball, soccer, water ski, snowboard, or snow ski, and golf. A couple of them even like to fish! They stay busy almost all of the time. I find this an amazing mixture in six beautiful young people whom I love so very much and so deeply. They are part me.

It is amazing to me that the entire human race is so closely aligned scientifically. This is in fact the truth regardless of your ethnic background. Recent discoveries by science indicate that each of us humans has about 40,000 genes. In addition, 99.9% of all humans have exactly the same genes; it's only 1/10 of 1% that makes the difference in each of us. That is amazing when you think of the differences that we see in each other from just the physical viewpoint! The example of gene comparison given was startling when I heard it on the radio news coming home from work one evening in 2002. The reporter talked about Wilt Chamberlain, the seven foot two inch black basketball star and compared him to Willie Shoemaker, the renowned Caucasian racehorse jockey who was only four foot two inches. They were 99.9% identical in terms of their respective genes!! So here we are with mothers, fathers, children and grand children all 99.9% alike yet so very different. I suppose we can say, 'It doesn't take much to make a big difference!' I like the differences in my kids and grand kids.

I am so fortunate to have an equal mix of three granddaughters and three grandsons. That in and of itself does not mean very much because I would love them regardless of their sex. I love to be with them and see them interact with their peers. I see them growing up far too rapidly. Just yesterday, they were all babies. I was visiting them in the hospitals when each of them was born. Already, in no time at all, they are all in school. Today, they are all in high school, junior high or elementary school. Next week, they will be in high school and then college and getting married. I want each one of them to be very successful in whatever he or she chooses to do. Most of all, I want them to love Jesus and let Him help them with their important choices in life. I have no preconceived ideas relating to what career or profession they should choose. I just want them to find happiness in what they decide to pursue. To be completely successful, they must choose to follow Christ individually.

Who are these incredible kids? In chronological order there is: Collin, Claire, Willy, Donovan, Kiley and Mackinsey. Their horizons are bright and virtually unlimited. Whatever their limits, that will be determined from within themselves.

I marvel at the age in which they live. The knowledge of our universe is expanding rapidly at an exponential rate. It's hard for me to imagine the inventions that will be realized in their lifetimes. I thought my world was such a major step forward in human history as compared to that of my ancestors. That was not obvious to me as I was growing up. I can only use twenty-twenty hindsight now and know the real truth of that point. It's an experienced point of view that comes with maturity.

Their future is mind boggling when one just lets our occluded and limited minds try to imagine their future and where their world is going. Will lifetimes become eternal here on earth? Will major disease, which we suffer today, be completely eradicated? Will humans routinely travel to other galaxies and universes? What will replace the automobile and fossil fuels? Will travel be in mass or individually? What will be done for entertainment? Will there be a world under one government? Will the idea of various cultures disappear and humanity dissolve into one world culture? Will man continue to depend upon God, the Great Creator and Savior of mankind? How will the world's warming trend impact us globally in this century? Will poverty become a thing of the past? Will a completely classless society exist? Can love ever completely replace hate in the human mind?

I am old fashioned I guess. I liked my world with all of its economic, social, political and religious discrepancies and faults. I liked the world of my ancestors. I'm not sure if I would like the new world that is coming in the next several decades. It is for the new generations. It is for my grandchildren and their children to live in, adapt to and find their way. Regardless of the conditions and circumstances that they encounter, I hope there is one foundational truth that they hold onto forever: there is only one true God. He is the giver of life and salvation who brings eternal life to everyone who accepts Him personally in faith believing. He has promised in the Bible that He will give each one of you eternal life. That is what I hold on to day by day. That is what your grandmother and I have tried to teach your mothers, Leslie and Jacquelyn. That is what my grandparents taught me.

Each of you, my grandchildren, will find that living your lives is not always easy although you will have both good times and other times. Your ultimate success will depend upon how well you cope with success and adversity. Adversity may come as an intransigent into your life, very unwelcomed and greatly disliked. Yet adversity is an important part of the crucible of life. Such trials should make you a stronger person not weaker. It should breed will, desire, unequalled energy, and a commitment to overcome through the love of Christ.

Each generation is mankind's hope for tomorrow and they are God's manifestation that we live in His world that He has master designed and made for us. Each generation has a responsibility to make the world a better place than it was when they were born in terms of social, economic, environmental conditions, and in recognition that there is only one true God in the universe. God gives us the ability and foresight to do that. There is great consequential behavior in what you do with your life knowing and believing that God has a plan for your entire lifespan. Each one of you, my precious grandchildren, will have the opportunity to contribute in large and small ways to these needy objectives. It will be up to each one of you to make a choice as to how you will make your effort.

It is my prayer for each of you that you will remember your God given heritage in terms of Christian principles and ethics. You have been given a very special inheritance from your earthly ancestors and your Heavenly Father. Accept His gift of eternal life early in your own life; make it your business to convey this message to your parents, relatives and others so that they too can learn about God and His gift of eternal life for them through His Son, Jesus Christ. Don't deprive your friends and associates of the love that Jesus has for them. Tell everyone about the love, goodness and mercy of the Lord. He reminds us in the Bible that if we are not ashamed of Him in this world, He will not be ashamed of us in Heaven.

My love for each of you reaches to the depth of my heart and is broader than the span of our galaxy. Each one of you is extra special to me. I wish I could live to experience each one of you reaching chronological maturity with your own families. Generally, that is not part of God's plan for our lives. He puts us here for three score and ten years. There's a reason! Grandpas and grandmas have the opportunity to pass onto their grandchildren the most important aspects of life during the most tender, formative and influential years of your lives. That is an important role that I have seen for grandparents in the lives of young ones. I pray that I do my best for you before I pass on.

CHAPTER TWENTY-ONE
Moving Towards
a Disappearing Sunset

Every time that I go to a funeral, I leave thinking how soon life is over. In my early years it seemed life here would never come to an end and later you realize how very quickly it flees. I suppose that is human nature to think that way. As a kid or young adult, your life is in essence ahead of you. Then, as the years slip away, you begin to understand the Biblical principal of 'three score and ten.'

In 2001, when I decided to make the trip to Arkansas, it was with the realization that I might never visit my birthplace again. That thought was disheartening to me. My life started in Arkansas. It is the place where I first began to remember and learn. It is the place of my heritage. It is the place where the standards for living my life began to develop.

The inevitable is sometimes very hard to accept because you want to go on living. At other times, it is easier to contemplate the end knowing that your pains and suffering will all be over. Finally you will be at complete total peace and in the presence of all of your loved ones, who chose Christ, for all eternity. So it is that Arkansas holds so much nostalgia, love, family history, and is such an integral part of who I am.

This last trip was very special. I had looked forward to the trip with great anticipation, yet I had not visited there in nearly twenty years. I was also hesitant. Would my cousins and distant relatives receive me with open arms? They did, and I was most pleased and gratified. It made the trip more worthwhile than I had expected. Every one of them seemed glad to see me and I enjoyed their company and the time we were able to spend together.

I did not get to see or do all that I would like to have done, but that would be the case regardless of what was accomplished or even how frequent my visits. I was able to see and visit with most of my cousins still living in the area; took time to see a local county fair; went to a school reunion; went a 'singing'. Also attended church; had dinner out with several cousins; picked up lots of information relating to my family; met relatives who I had not known before; and thoroughly enjoyed myself. Doyle and Melba Barrick, my cousins, insisted that we stay in their home and use it as our 'headquarters'. Hopefully, we did not take advantage of them. They certainly did not make us feel as if we did. Doyle was my ever present 'tour guide' which I appreciated more than he will ever know.

It was apparent from the beginning of my visit that Doyle was the leading authoritarian on local family history and knew everybody from whenever in time. He has a superb memory and loves to tell stories of the past and the many pranks he performed or heard about. He is a living library of information. He was really a special treat. Melba, his wife, is also a historian in her own right and has written several books about the families related to her life. I have copies of all of her publications. She is a storyteller *extraordinaire* as compared to being a detailed historian. That makes her a very special lady!

Doyle asked me if I would like to visit Riley Creek while I was there. That had been one of the items of prime importance on my agenda. I was most pleased that he was willing to take Bev and me through the back roads. As we rode over the dirt roads, he seemed to know any and everybody or family who had lived in a given location at one time or another for the last hundred years. That included places where barns or houses were still standing, or just some remnants of debris from buildings long since disappeared, or just nothing at all except for an old tree or some other landmark. It was in his head. He was an absolute kick and most enjoyable. I enjoyed the day immensely.

My Trip To Riley Creek

(Tour Guide – Doyle Barrick – My Cousin on September 19, 2001)
One of the days in Arkansas was spent making a trip to Riley Creek from Danville via Dutch Creek and Moss Creek. I had never been over those

roads before. Even so, they seemed somewhat familiar since I had heard my parents speak of these communities and areas many times during my childhood. My 'Tour Guide', however, knew every house and farm building that we passed or came upon. In addition, he could even tell about homes, houses, farms, churches and other places where people had lived that had completely disappeared from sight…many, many years ago! It was a fun and an interesting trip. On one curve in the road (dirt) Doyle pointed out that the side road on the left going up the hill in a slightly wooded area was the old road that led up to the Johnson family's home. It was my mother's aunt's home on Moss Creek. He remembered it as being about four miles back off the 'main dirt road. "Not much left of the old place nowadays", he stated with authority. I did not doubt him either since I am more than sure he had been up that road many times. The Johnson's he was referring to were my Grandmother's, Rebecca (Smith) Talley, sister. My mother referred her to as 'Aunt Sissy'. This was in the area of Moss Creek.

At this point, the car began to climb up a fairly good grade. Known as the 'Backbone' mountain. From the other side of the mountain, I had looked at it from the front porch of my Grandpa Talley's home many times. In fact, it was a major landmark you looked at many times a day. It became known as the 'Talley Backbone' in terms of a reference point geo-graphically. The Talley Backbone was sometimes called the 'Devil's Back-bone'. It had always made me feel proud as a kid to know that my grandpa owned the property all the way to the top of that mountain.

When we reached the top of the Backbone, there was another road (dirt) going left and right along the very ridge of the mountain. Doyle reminded me that this was the 'Talley Backbone Road'. Yes, I had heard of that, too, but never before had I traveled over it. Since I was driving, I started to go on the down side of the mountain towards my Grandfather Talley's old place. Doyle interrupted and asked if I would like to drive down the 'Backbone Road' a little ways? Of course I would! After all, there was no way of knowing if I'll ever return and have such a knowledgeable tour guide. So we backed up and turned left. Doyle said that if we went down the road a couple of miles, we could see the 'Talley Knob.' Oh, yes, I remembered that landmark. Any time there was a discussion about the home place (Talley Farm) by anyone, often there was a reference to the singularly uniform and rounded high point in the local mountains. It was the 'Talley Knob!' I had seen it many times as well as a kid at the farm. The weather was misty and threatening rain. We tried to peer through the heavy density of the trees and mist to see the 'Talley Knob'. It was difficult. We drove on trying to find a better place, which would provide us a vantage point. Finally, I settled on one. We stopped and I got out of the car with my faithful camera and took as good of a shot as I could. (It actually turned out pretty good!). From that point on, I was looking for a place in the road where I could turn around. You see the road is only one lane wide in this part of the country.

My venture on down the road was time not wasted as Cousin Doyle continued his dialogue of the past. He pointed out a place in the road where in days long past the stagecoaches were run. The old stagecoach road intersected now with the Talley Backbone Road. In fact, he remembered that the stagecoach's route ran along the branch (small stream) right in front of my granddad's home. That was enlightenment for me. I had never heard that story before!

We made the turn around and headed back to our starting place and on down the mountain. At the bottom was the branch that I previously referred to earlier. Without hesitation, Doyle says, "This is Little Riley Creek that we are crossing over." I knew it as merely the 'branch'. When Grandpa lived here, we had to travel along the side of it on a dirt road to get from the main road up to Grandpa's house. In the rainy season, the branch would often fill and overflow. As it crossed the main road, it was just an open streambed which cars and wagons had to cross. Now, the natural streambed was gone, cemented over to prevent erosion and deterioration of the road, I guess. But in doing so, the stream had lost much of its natural beauty of just a meandering country branch, I thought.

On the left, after passing the branch, was my granddad's former farmland now turned into a pasture. There wasn't any evidence remaining of the fields, barns or sharecropper's house that existed in the good days of my childhood. Granddad's old log cabin and sawn wood house combination was completely gone from view. It was as if the road that once traversed along the branch had never even existed. We stopped at a gate and Doyle asked if I would like to drive up through the pasture to the site of the old combination log cabin and sawn lumber home of 'Uncle Jack's' as Doyle and most everyone else referred to my grandfather. "Yes, yes, that would be great if we could!" I said. Then to my surprise, Doyle said, "Turn in here and I'll unlock the gate! Jim Mitchell (the present owner) has given me a key to the property." This was really great and a great surprise. Doyle informed me that Jim Mitchell had purchased a large portion of the property on Riley Creek, including the Haywood Haire, Andrew Jackson Talley, Reed and other properties, and now raised cattle on the property. He named his operation the 'Backbone Ranch.'

For a moment, as we drove into the pasture, I rolled the window down and I could smell the grass and fresh air; I could even hear the old 'dinner bell' ring when Grandmother would be calling everybody in the fields, barns or elsewhere on the property, that she had dinner ready and it was time to come and eat! There was Grandmother calling 'Jacent' to do something for her. I could hear Granddad calling out, "Gee!" and, "Haw!" to his mules trying to get them to line up properly in the field so he could till the soil and get ready to plant the corn. I remembered the sound of a freight train whistle that would ricochet and echo repeatedly off the mountains into our ears. In the quiet of the time, I recalled and heard the cows mooing or bull bellowing in the pastures; when close to the pigpen, there was the sound of grunting coming from a happy pig or the squealing of one in distress! All around were a number of chickens happily clucking as they scratched in the dirt and you could never forget the rooster standing tall on the fence in front of the house crowing to awaken us all early in the morning.

I listened and heard the dinner bell ring once more. Grandma was calling us to come and dine. If one was really quiet, you could hear the breeze rustling the leaves on the three big oak trees in front of Grandpa's house. There was the clean smell of the hay in the barn and the rotting manure pile near the milking stalls that gently wafted past my nose. This is where my mother and her sisters spent many days working the fields and learning about life. This is where they grew up. What a rush it was for me to momentarily feel, "I'm back home on hallowed ground where my life started." This is where I learned a lot of lessons at my grandfather's knee. This is where I heard him read the Bible out loud every night before bedtime. This is where I became keenly aware of his love for Jesus Christ! This was the cradle of my being.

The tall weeds scraped underneath the car as we drove through the pasture. I looked and looked at that knoll, from every angle where the old homestead once stood. The only thing I recognized was one old, old oak tree, which stood in the corral of the barn and above the dirt-covered cellar at the edge of the cornfield, which was down below. The sounds of years gone by are recorded and buried in its trunk no doubt. I wish I could hear them come to life once more. I took all the pictures I needed almost pretending that the old place was still intact as I looked through the camera lens.

As we returned to the gate, Doyle opened it to allow me to drive through. After re-locking the gate, he got into the front seat again. Remembering a story of the past, he recited a story about 'old Uncle John Trentham.' I had heard my mother refer to him in a kind way on many occasions but in essence saying that he wasn't all there mentally. It seems that a group of young people had been to Moss Creek to have a social outing. When they were returning they were crossing Little Riley Creek when they noticed Uncle John Trentham to the right in the middle of the stream with his pants legs rolled up but with his pants down. One of the young men, knowing that Uncle John didn't have a right mind, hollered out to him, "Uncle John, what are you doing?" Upon which Uncle John replied, "I'm fixing the water fence," referring to the fences used to keep debris from washing down stream during heavy rains. The young ladies in the group obviously expressed their dismay at his behavior since they were more modest in those days and Uncle John's actions exceeded their limits of tolerance!

Doyle was an absolute kick with all of his folkloric stories. Some left you feeling sad while others made you laugh with gusto! It was a mix of joy and excitement but some left you wondering about the tragedy and how dreadful the occasion must have been. You never knew what his next recital would be, but you knew it would be really good and worth your time.

We had made our way down the old dirt road for a mile or so when

Doyle said, "Stop here." To the right was another pasture; to the left, a sort of path cut through the yellow pine trees and brush. What remained of the cut plants, shrubs and weeds, was about ankle high. Without hesitating and with a statement as if I would know, Doyle says, pointing to the left, "Right over there is where the Reed house used to be." I remembered there was a Reed family house but I didn't remember it being there per se. In reality, I could not remember everything accurately and Doyle had spent a lot more time on Riley Creek.

Turning back to the right side of the car, he pointed to a couple of small bushes beyond the fence, about twenty-five yards away in the pasture, and related the story about the death of Mr. George Washington Woodall. He was my great grandfather Smith's brother-in-law. They had come to Arkansas together from North Carolina with their parents many years before. George Woodall was shot to death by 'bush whackers' within six feet of the spot where his six motherless young daughters buried him. Doyle says he is buried right there. On the other hand, there is contention from my Cousin Ann Moore that Mr. Woodall is buried in the Talley Cemetery back in the woods on the left. I do not know who is correct. One thing is for sure, Mr. Woodall was killed and is buried somewhere within one hundred yards of either place.

It was time to get out of the car and Doyle and I made our way to the Talley Family Cemetery on the left side of the road. It was not very far off the road, maybe thirty to forty yards. I saw for the first time what it looked like with a headstone in place. The last time that I had been here was almost twenty years before when my Uncle Lee showed me the graveyard and I learned that it existed for the very first time. At that time, there was nothing but a few stacked up flat rocks denoting a place of burial. Now the land had been cleared some and there were earth mounds identifying several graves. It was sort of hidden away in the shade and shadows of the nearby pine trees. It was restful in its appearance. During the last two years, I had Cousin Anne Moore secure the headstone and get it delivered and installed at the site. It was nicely made and had five names on it. I was pleased that it looked so nice and that I had done something special for my relatives that I had never known or seen in my life. Anne says there are more members of the family buried there. She is going to get their names and add them to the other side of the gravestone.

Time that day was passing quickly so we hurriedly got in the car and drove on towards Belleville. We passed the old Haywood Haire home, now owned by the Mitchell family. I remembered where some of the Johnson family had lived across Riley Creek just beyond the Haire place on the left.

Doyle told a story on himself as a kid when he was not more than six or seven years old. The Barrick family was living about half way between the Haire place and the old Riley Creek schoolhouse. Doyle's folks decided to move for some reason. It seems that he took sick about that time. However, the family was moving anyway and so he had to be moved on a hand carried makeshift stretcher. Four men had to carry him about two miles and, of course, they lamented the fact that he was so heavy. Throughout the journey, they huffed and puffed and reminded him about how heavy he was. You can imagine just how heavy he really was since he was just a tadpole of a kid. Even so, and as badly as he was feeling, the men made him feel better.

On another occasion, Doyle and his brother, Wayne, were out in the barn when a severe rainstorm came. They were caught in the barn and could not go to the house. They decided to keep warm by building a fire. Needless to say, the hay in the barn caught on fire and the whole barn burned down. They tried for a while to put it out but couldn't. The rain didn't come to their rescue either. Their dad, Chester, came home late that evening and asked if they knew what happened at the barn? They didn't tell the truth, but managed to relate the fact that there had been a rainstorm with thunder and lightening. They guessed that the storm had caused the barn to burn. Doyle said his dad did not ask any more questions about the incident and neither he nor his brother was going to fess up to it.

We passed the Riley Creek Cemetery but didn't stop on this day. The moisture was pretty heavy and the ground was starting to get wet and muddy. In Arkansas, the red clay soil sticks and builds up under your shoes with every step you take; and this was not the day to walk in the cemetery. I told Doyle that I had to visit the cemetery but that I would do it on another day, so we drove on. It was apparent that many people had lived on Riley Creek in the past many decades and that Doyle knew them...often times quite intimately. He knew everybody it seemed.

We crossed Dead Man's Creek. I pointed out to Doyle as we headed down the hill towards Petit Jean Creek that my Grandfather Talley owned and farmed a lot of the Petit Jean bottomland to the left of the road when I was a kid. When we were nearing the Wilson Community Church, Doyle pointed to the right and said that's where the old 'double log cabins' used to be. That struck a bell with me. I had heard my own father talk about the double log cabins. They were the seat of county government before it was moved to Danville. Doyle said that there were two cabins or buildings joined together with a cover. It was a busy area with people doing business and taking care of family and other matters.

Our destination took us through Belleville and on out the other side of town. We kept on moving and Doyle continued 'telling stories and remembering when' as we were on our way to the Piney Fork Cemetery. That was where my Moudy grandparents are buried. I also found out that there are many relatives from the Apple family buried there as well. I took a lot of pictures of the headstones in hopes of identifying them at some time in the future.

Our last objective was Spring Lake. It was being built, or modified, when I was a kid. I went to the lake with my parents for a big shindig of some kind. Could have been the dedication of the dam after it was built. There were many people gathered with plenty of food to eat. It was a potluck dinner. Like any youngster about four or five years old, I did my usual exploring that day. Much to my surprise, I found what I thought was a great big fish swimming in a very small channel. The water was crystal clear. To me the fish looked two feet long! I ran to tell my mother and convinced her to come and look at the fish. When we returned, guess what, the fish was gone! Dog gone! No, fish gone! I was really disappointed because up to that time, that was by far the biggest fish that I had ever seen. On this day, some sixty years later, the lake looked beautiful although it did need to have the rubbish cleaned up near the dam area. We took some pictures and headed for home and called it a day!

A term, which I had never heard before, was related to me by Melba Barrick. We were talking about the rather high quantity of pictures my mother took as she was growing up and, in particular, as a late teenager and in her early twenties. I always wondered why the people posing for the pictures were seemingly dressed in their finest clothes but were out in the country on the dirt roads and in places where it would be easy to get your clothes dirty. Melba said that the young ladies and friends would usually go out after church on Sunday since they were dressed in the best attire. They referred to the picture taking expeditions while they were out and about as *Kodaking*. Good term for such an activity! As you can see when looking at the pictures, the young men and ladies would sit on bridges, wade in streams, sit on plows, sit on the ground, or wherever. I guess they didn't worry about getting their clothes dirty after church.

It's My Turn to Tell A Story

The morning arrived when it was time to turn our thoughts to making the long drive back to California. I had almost finished packing my suitcase and clothes bag. All I had left to pack were my Levi jeans. I had hung two pair of Levis in the closet in the bedroom but I could only find one. I looked carefully at the clothes left hanging and could not find my other pair of Levis. I knew that this was Doyle's closet and in the evening before going to bed, he would retrieve his work clothes that he wanted to wear for the next day.

I looked at the sizes of Levis still left in the closet. As anybody knows who has worn Levis, there is a leather identification tab sown into the right hand backside of each pair. Imprinted on the label is the waist size and inseam length. None of the remaining pairs was my size. I inquired as to whether or not they inadvertently had been put in the wash. The answer was, 'No." It then dawned on me that just maybe, by mistake and chance, Doyle had picked out my Levis to wear to his work at the local high school. That seemed to be the most reasonable and plausible answer. But Doyle was at work already and he could not be asked about the missing pair of Levis.

I did not really care if Doyle had worn them. In fact, I had already decided to leave the pair of Levis if indeed he had them. As I thought a little bit more about it, I recalled seeing him in a pair of Levis one day and they looked just a little bit bigger than I had seen him wearing previously. Levis shrink a little after many washings so I just figured he bought them a little big so they would fit nicely later. But now it made sense. He had probably grabbed a pair of mine without realizing it!

Much to our surprise and unexpectedly, Doyle stopped by the house to tell us 'goodbye'. It was about nine o'clock. I had told Melba that my size was 38 X 30. So when Doyle came walking in, she checked out the label on the Levis he was wearing. She said to him, "You've got Roe's pants on." By that time, we were all huddled around him looking at the pants and the label. All of us started to laugh, thinking it was funny. Doyle could only gather up a sheepish smile trying to figure out how he got involved in this plot. He said he wore a size 36 waist. That seemed right based upon what I knew. Well, Doyle had trouble believing that he had my pants on. In fact, he thought we were joshing him and pulling his leg. He asked more than once, "Are you sure, I have Roe's pants on?" To put him at ease, I said, "Doyle, don't worry about it, I'm going to give you this pair of pants!" He still was not sure how this situation was stacking up and had a look of disbelief on his face. But I assured him that it was okay. We got into the car and left, the three of us still laughing about what had happened, and Doyle still believing that his leg was being pulled!

Three weeks passed and I got a package in the mail. To my surprise, Doyle had returned the Levis to me. Perhaps Melba had convinced him of what had happened. Melba had written and tucked a note in the package restating that Doyle thought all three of us were joking and pulling his leg. The fact was, the situation had bested him! I don't know if Doyle will tell this story on himself, but I know that I will have a lot of fun telling it over the next several years!

On another subject, I think as an individual grows older, their appreciation for life increases substantially. Little things become more meaningful. At least that is what I have found to be true. Thought processes change and the things around you change including your focus about what is important. Risk factors are minimized or eliminated as much as possible. I found a poem that identifies with the aging aspects of life. It had been reprinted from CASA, Energizing Seniors, Spring 2001 in the publication *Atherton Today*, Volume 29, page 2, and I copied it here.

Aging With Humor

The Advantage of Aging:

In a hostage situation you are likely to be released first. Kidnappers are not very interested in you.

People no longer view you as a hypochondriac.

There's nothing left to learn the hard way.

You can eat dinner at 4:00 p.m.

You consider coffee one of the most important things in life.

You constantly talk about the price of gasoline.

You enjoy hearing about other people's operations.

You get into a heated argument about pension plans.

You no longer think of speed limits as a challenge.

You quit trying to hold your stomach in, no matter who walks into the room.

You send money to PBS.

You sing along with the elevator music.

Your back goes out more than you do.

The signs of aging tend to creep up on us before we know it. Then the aches and pains become exaggerated because there is not much left to focus on with activities becoming reduced and limited. It is indeed an effort to try to maintain and stay healthy. It becomes easier to understand some of Shakespeare's writings relating to the loss of our senses, sans eyes, teeth, and hearing as we get older. We do not want it to come...but it makes its inevitable march against us.

Roark and Beverly Moudy
1999

Epilogue

There are countless more acts and events which I have not recorded which could extend this writing and leave more family history for posterity. However, I think the real essence of life as it was lived in the 1800s and 1900s has been described and identified adequately herein. There are numerous pictures of family members of later generations which could have been included in the body and were not. Some of them have been selected for publication and are included in this chapter. Obviously, pictures relating to my kinfolks of the early 1800s are nonexistent. Paintings were probably too expensive to have engaged a painter to do the work. Photographs did not arrive until approximately mid-century.

Referenced from pages of the 1850 census of the Southern Division of Davidson County, North Carolina recorded on the 14th day of October was done to establish these relatives' homes and point of origin. Looking closely at the top of the page, there is a note of reference in the title identifying 'free inhabitants', which is an interesting insight to the fact that slavery was an integral part of the life in that part of the country. As the record reflects, and the researcher has noted, Leonard Smith, age forty-eight at the time and Rebecca Smith, age forty-eight, were the parents of Obediah Smith. Leonard Smith is identified as a farmer who apparently owned one hundred thirty acres of land. Thomas E. Smith, age fourteen, who is listed below Rebecca, would have been their second son.

According to the Haire family Bible: Washington Woodall, (George Washington Woodall) was born 1/24/1818. He was the husband of Elizabeth E. (Evoline) Woodall, born 11/8/1822. She was the daughter of Leonard and Rebecca Smith. Evoline was Obediah's sister. George and Elizabeth had a son, Alfred F. (Franklin) Woodall (born 2/15/1849). At the 1850 census, he was only one year old. Alfred died before they left North Carolina for the wilds of Arkansas. Other family members were born after they arrived in Arkansas and included: Susan Angeline (4/15/1856), Martha (12/4/1857), and Merry Elendar 3/23/1859).

The Woodall linkage is important later as members of these westward settlers would occupy and live their lives in parts of Yell County, Arkansas. They would intermarry and become an integral part of the fabric of human life in the local community. All of these families would become the strands exhibiting the staying power that ultimately became the strength of the communities. Because of the solidarity of these people during these times, it is often difficult to tell where many families started and ended.

Washington Woodall's parents are thought to be recorded on the following page of this same 1850 census. They were John Woodall, age fifty-two and his wife, Elizabeth, age forty-seven. Their children (apparently still unmarried at this time) included David, age twenty-one, Margaret, age twenty-four, and Ellen, age twenty-seven. Interesting, the record indicates they owned 2,800 acres and were farmers as well. These family members did not make the trip and remained near Salisbury, North Carolina.

The third important listing here is the Rider family. John, age sixty-two, and Irene, age sixty. John Rider's occupation was a break foreman. Their children included Emily, Obediah, John, Cecil and Margaret, ages twenty-six, twenty-four, twenty, eighteen and sixteen, respectively. Margaret married Obediah Smith. They were to become my great grandparents. John and Irene Rider would then be my great great grandparents.

Ten years later, some of them are listed in the 1860 Arkansas census. They show in the records in similar fashion as they did in North Carolina. Leonard and Rebecca Smith now ages sixty-two and sixty respectively. Thomas E. Smith, age twenty-four, is believed to be the brother of Obediah Smith. Thomas married Elizabeth A. Ward, age twenty-five. At this time they had siblings including Noah W., age six, Rusberg C., age one.

A picture of the Will Apple homestead located on Mount Magazine. It was painted in 1994 by Mary. In the background on the property to the left is the storage barn where the corn crib was located and onions were stored. In the back center is the family's smokehouse. To the right is where canned fruit was stored. One of the buildings was the shop where repairs were made to farming implements or anything else needing repair. In the center front is the homestead house. This picture was provided by Helen (Apple) Hill.

Here is my grand uncle George William 'Will' Apple and his wife, Cordelia Carter, probably at their home place on Mount Magazine. Circa 1930. He was an excellent farmer and sold his produce mostly to merchants in Belleville and Havana, Arkansas.

Pictured above are several of the offspring of Lewis Apple and Mary Louisa Patterson (my great grandparents). Left to Right: Annie Drucilla (Apple) Moudy (my grand-mother), James Elisha 'Lish' Apple, George Willaim 'Will' Apple, Harvey Galeton Apple, and Bessie Apple. The two missing children are Maggie Belle Apple and Markus, who died as a baby. The brothers are my granduncles and her sister is my grandaunt.

Right: Standing together be-side the Liberty Church is my grandmother's sister, Maggie Belle (Apple) Payne with her husband John Wesley Payne. Maggie was said to be a very beautiful woman. circa 1925.

Group picture of the Apple Family at a gathering, circa 1945. The adults and older children are more easily identified. Back row L-R (maiden names given in parenthesis): (1) Alfred Lee, Helen Irene (Sharp), (2)Jimmie (Rodgers), Willie Boyd, Cordelia (Carter), George 'Will', (3) Louis Franklin, Phoebe (Hays), (4)Emery Valentine, Rosa (Apple).
2nd row kneeling (# identifies parent couple): Nancy (3), Rosa (4), Donald (2), Helen Dean (1), Maxine (2), Frankie (3). 3rd row sitting: Jimmy (2), Joe Charles (?), George Leslie 'GL' (1). Small children: Mary (1), Jerry (?), Ramona (2), Hanson (?).

Harley and Helen Dean (Apple) Hill family. Helen and Harley live in Drumright, Oklahoma at the present time. Helen is the daughter of Alfred Lee Apple and Helen Irene Sharp. Alfred was the son of George William Apple and Cordelia Carter. circa 1985. L-R: In the front row – Lowana, Harley, Helen, Reba, Edwina. In back – Jerry and Terry (missing is Harley Gene).

These are children of Alfred Lee Apple and Helen Irene Sharp. Included in this picture L-R: Joe Apple, Helen (Apple) Hill, Mary (Apple) Hixson, Charles Apple and George Apple. Circa 1985.

The Harvey Galeton Apple and Etta Mahala Ewing family. circa 1935. Harvey was the son of Lewis and Mary Louisa Patterson, my great grandparents. Harvey Galeton and George William 'Will' Apple are brothers and my grandmother, Annie Drucilla (Apple) Moudy was their sister. Harvey and Etta are in the middle left of the picture (the older couple) along with most of their children, sons-in-law, daughters-in-law and probably two grandchildren.

This is a picture apparently of only the children, six of eight present but unidentified, without their spouses of Harvey G. Apple and Etta M. Ewing. They had eight children, three boys and five girls. They were: Gertie, Patterson, Myrtle, Herbert Winston, Vera, Naomi, Charles Louis, and Wilma Marie. circa 1935.

Annie Drucilla (Apple) Moudy, my grandmother, with her sister, Maggie Belle (Apple) Payne taken at my grandmother's home in Belleville, Arkansas. Circa 1954. My uncle, Oscar Lee Moudy built the home for her to live in after her husband, Thomas W. Moudy had died in 1938.

John Quinton Moudy was my grandfather's, Thomas Waldron Moudy, brother. This picture of his family was taken circa 1915. Interestingly, the family appears to have been dressed up for the occasion. Standing in the back row L-R: Frankie, Odell I., Clyde Harriet, and Kate. In the front row L-R: Ferdinand, John Quinton, Cecil H., Lettie Jane (Bigelow) Moudy, Johnnie Mae.

Celebrating Fifty Years together – John Quinton and Lettie Jane (Bigelow) Moudy with some of their children at the event in South Gate, California. circa 1952. Seated: John and Lettie Jane. Standing L-R: Clyde Harriet (Moudy) Dickey, Odell, Frankie (Moudy) Fowler, Kate (Moudy) Payne, and Ferdinand. Ferdinand was the banker in Belleville for a period of time.

My Grandfather, Thomas Waldron Moudy, had four sisters and four brothers. Here is his oldest sister and her family. As was tradition in those days, offspring were named after members of their own family. No doubt Ailcy was named for her own mother. Although individual members aren't identified, this family included: four boys, John, Nick, Henry and Alfred and one daughter, probably standing in the back and married, Mrs. Fred Snelling. The gentleman is presumed to be Mr. Brown but not factual. Ailcy is sitting on the right holding her youngest son. Ailcy was married to Mr. Daley, Mr. Brown and Mr. Vick in that order. No information is available regarding her husbands.

The offspring of Thomas Waldron Moudy and Annie Drucilla Apple. L-R front row: Kate (Moudy) Tucker, Bessie Lou Ellen (Moudy) Barrick, Lennie Lou (Moudy) Walker, Jennie B. (Buckman) Moudy, Hestella (Talley) Moudy, Florence Christian (Wilkerson) Moudy. Back row: Jesse P. Tucker, Lillard Chester Barrick, Albert Wilson 'Jack' Moudy, Oscar Lee Moudy, Willaim Lewis Moudy, and Herbert Earl Moudy. Missing: Helen Eulerle (Riech) Moudy, wife of Albert Wilson Moudy, and Seth McKinley Walker. Circa November or December, 1958 (The event was the death of my grandmother Annie Drucilla (Apple) Moudy.

Uncle Albert Wilson 'Jack' Moudy was one of the first in the family to relocate permanently to California. This picture was taken in front of his home in Camarillo, CA, circa 1940. Pictured L-R: (1) Aunt Kate (Moudy) Tucker (my dad's sister), (2) Uncle Jesse P. Tucker, husband of Aunt Kate, (3) Eula Blanch Moudy (in front), daughter of Uncle Jack, (4) Ruby Faye Tucker (in back), (5) Laverne Moudy, daughter of Uncle Jack, Uncle Jack Moudy, and Wendell R. Tucker. Aunt Kate and Uncle Jesse lived in Oxnard, CA.

Oscar Lee Moudy family, circa 1945. L-R Seated: Aunt Jennie B. (Buckman) Moudy, Larry (baby), Elnora, and Uncle Lee. Standing: Robert Thomas 'Bobby Tom', Anna Belle, Opal Lee and Edna Dell. Uncle Lee was a long time merchant in Belleville, AR owning a general store, gas station, and ran a taxi service. Bobby Tom became a dentist, Anna Belle followed her father in business, and Edna Dell was a hairdresser.

This was a family gathering where all five children of Herbert Moudy and Florence (Wilkerson) Moudy were present in March, 1971. Pictured L-R: Morris Lavon Moudy (identical twin), Aunt Florence, Mason Laverne Moudy (identical twin), Lois Verdell (Moudy) Green, Wanada (Moudy) Havener, and Vernon Maurice Moudy.

Aunt Bessie (Moudy) Barrick and Lillard Chester Barrick had six children. They are all pictured here in the front yard of Uncle Lee Moudy's home in Belleville, AR. Circa 1965. L-R: Doyle Kenneth Barrick, Earl Eugene Barrick, LC Barrick, Velda Pauline (Barrick) Harris, Harold Wayne Barrick and Virginia Lamoyne (Barrick) Moudy. The two biggest teases when I was a kid in Oxnard were LC and his cohort sister, Lamoyne. They would scare me to death driving in the car and pretending they were going to crash. Doyle' stories are half of this publication, I think! Aunt Bessie was my favorite aunt on my dad's side of the family.

Aunt Linnie Lou Moudy married Seth McKinley Walker. The family lived near Centerville or Mt George, AR during my growing up years. This picture was taken in front of their home,circa 1950. L-R: Linnie Lou (Moudy) Walker, Anna Lou (Walker) Jones (in back), Sammy Don Jones (boy in front) and behind him is Jackie Lee, Seth McKinley Walker, Sam Jones holding Judy Ann Jones, and Nelda Sue (Walker) was later to marry Roy Allen Dennis.

My father, William Lewis Moudy. The picture was taken in his front yard in Oxnard, CA. He was short on formal education but more than made up for it with his hard work. During most of my childhood, he worked two jobs each day to make ends meet. He taught me the work ethic, which I cherish today. After his conversion to Christ, he was a real zealot for ministry to others he met. I loved him deeply. circa 1967.

Margaret Ellen (Talley) Chambers married Thomas Palmer Chambers in 1888. My grandfather, Andrew Jackson Talley lived with her (his sister) when he was dating Rebecca Adeline Smith. Margaret and Thomas lived initially in Logan County, Arkansas before moving to Chickalah, in Yell County. They may have also lived in Alabama.

Mary C. (Talley) Smith married William Meridia Smith on March 27, 1870. She was eighteen years old at the time. She is the daughter of Joel Talley and Sarah Elizabeth Roark. She and her husband assisted Andrew Jackson (my grandfather) and Benjamin, their brother, bury their father, Joel A. Talley and brother Joseph W. Talley in Yell County, Arkansas when they died of poisoning. Their deaths occurred about 1870. This could possibly indicate that Mary and William accompanied her father and brothers when they made the trek into Arkansas. There isn't any evidence to prove this as factual.

The Johnsons. Sarah Caroline Smith was my mother's aunt. She was the sister of Rebecca Adeline (Smith) Talley (my grandmother). This picture was taken in 1911. The house was located on Mount Nebo, Arkansas west of the creek that ran close by. This is the house where Levin was born. According to my mother's comments, David Levin was one of her favorite cousins and they corresponded until their deaths.

L-R: David Harrison Johnson, Sarah Caroline (Smith) Johnson (David's wife), Lee Horn, Jeanette 'Nettie' Savanah Johnson, David Levin Johnson, and Quinn Sutherline. The coon dog was named 'Drum'.

The Stanberry family was another branch of the Smith family. Rebecca Adeline (Smith) Talley's sister, Dolcinia, was the middle born of the three Smith girls. She married Solomon Stanberry and they lived in the Riley Creek community. Solomon and Dolcinia had seven children of which three were boys. Samuel Grant Solomon was the youngest boy. He married a woman who had a previous marriage, Anna (Halbert) Webb. Anna had at least two children in her prior marriage, Charlie and Paul. This picture of that family is circa 1927.

Back row: Samuel Grant Stanberry, Anna (Halbert) (Webb) Stanberry, Hugh Webb, Bessie (Unknown) Webb, Frank Webb. Both Hugh and Frank could possibly be Anna's brothers. Front row: Vera Elaine Stanberry (daughter), Charlie Webb and Paul Webb (Anna's sons) and Jack Stanberry. The latter may be a nickname since Sam is believed to have a son named Alfred Henry Stanberry.

This is another group of the Solomon Stanberry and Dolcinia (Smith) Stanberry family. In the picture are three people with the last name of Downey. How they may be related to the Stanberry family is not known at this time. It would appear that the lady in the back row, Vicie Downey is the mother of the two Downey children. The remaining people are all related to the Solomon family. The young lady in the back row and last on the right is Dulvania 'Dovie' Stanberry. She was retarded. Picture is circa 1915.

Cemetery records would tend to indicate that the Stanberry family in general relocated from the Riley Creek community in the latter years. They didn't seem to move great distances but work and opportunity may have been a factor. Several members of the family are buried at the Riley Creek Cemetery.

L-R Back row: Joe Byrne (husband of Caroline Stanberry, the daughter of Soloman and Dolcinia not in the picture), Claude Franklin (Son-in-law to the Solomon's and husband of Bessie Lee Stanberry), Solomon Stanberry (my grand uncle and my mother's uncle), Bessie Lee (Stanberry) Franklin (daughter of Solomon and Dolcinia), Vicie Downey, Dulvania 'Dovie' Stanberry.

L-R Front row: Lona Arizona Byrne (daughter of Joe and Caroline Stanberry), Thogel Denton Stanberry (son of Nathaniel Elmore Stanberry who is a son to Solomon), Tressie Byrne (daughter of Joe and Caroline), Loyd Downey, and Urra Downey.

Interestingly, these four Talley sisters dressed 'in style' for this picture (very similar to our children today). Note the dresses are all different but the style is the same. Here, from L-R: Ollie, Elizabeth, Alice and Hestella. circa 1924.

Pictured here is my great grandmother, Mary Louisa (Patterson) Apple with two of her grandchildren, both of whom are children of Cordelia (Carter) and George William Apple. On the left is Louis Franklin Apple and on the left is Bessie Ray (Apple) White. circa 1930.

This publication would be incomplete without this picture. These are my cousins, Jack Stirl Moore and Anne H. (Zdankiewicz) Moore near the time they were married in 1954. Anne has been an absolute bridge to needed information, extremely helpful with her research on many Arkansas relatives, continuous support and a source of encouragement for me while writing this book. I am deeply indebted to her.

Index

S